1985

Marketing Handbook

Volume I: Marketing Practices

Marketing Handbook

Volume I: Marketing Practices

Edited by
Edwin E. Bobrow
Mark David Bobrow

DOW JONES-IRWIN Homewood, Illinois 60430

© DOW JONES-IRWIN, 1985

This publication is designed to provide accurate and
authoritative information in regard to the subject matter
covered. It is sold with the understanding that the
publisher is not engaged in rendering legal, accounting, or
other professional service. If legal advice or other expert
assistance is required, the services of a competent
professional person should be sought.

*From a Declaration of Principles jointly adopted by a Committee
of the American Bar Association and a Committee of Publishers.*

ISBN 0-87094-523-8

Library of Congress Catalog Card No. 85–70439

Printed in the United States of America

1 2 3 4 5 6 7 8 9 0 K 2 1 0 9 8 7 6 5

Dedicated to the memory of
Abraham D. Bobrow.

PREFACE

This book is about marketing practices. If you are looking for guidance, information, and counsel from proven professionals, the *Marketing Handbook, Volume I: Marketing Practices* provides the state of the art in applied marketing. It is a companion book to the *Marketing Handbook, Volume II: Marketing Management*. Together they could prove to be the most inclusive set of references on applied marketing available today.

The strategies that one company uses to achieve its marketing goals will probably not be the same that another company would use, even under similar circumstances. In order to help you develop the strategies that are responsive to your company's particular needs and to the peculiarities and changes in the marketplace, fresh ideas, new concepts, and, most important, "how-to applications" to help develop your unique approach are provided in these books by proven practitioners. With the shifts that are going on in virtually every area of marketing in America today, it is vital for each company to develop strategies that will give it a differential advantage in the marketplace. Contributors to this practical, state-of-the-art marketing practices manual are all authorities in their areas. Each chapter sets forth their ideas, their views. You may agree with them—you may not agree with them. The important thing is that they will provoke your thinking and perhaps bring you new insights.

We have done our best to select topics that cover every aspect of marketing. We did not want to put together a tome that would serve only as a reference book. Rather, our aim was to offer a work in which you can selectively find practical, solid thinking on the subjects most vital today. We did not even want this book to be in one voice. Rather, we wanted each of the authors' writing styles and approaches to the subject to come through loud and clear, as their method of presenting the material is sometimes as important as the material itself. There are even cases where the same subject is covered in several chapters. Where this is done, you will find that the subject is being approached from different views, and therefore it gives you a fuller understanding of the subject matter.

Some profess marketing to be a science . . . others, an art. In our view, marketing is an art that uses the latest scientific tools for its successful practice. We hope this book will be a well-used tool for you as you practice the art of marketing.

Edwin E. Bobrow
Mark David Bobrow

Editorial Advisory Board

Dr. Robert F. Vizza
    Dean, School of Business
    Manhattan College

Bernard F. Whalen
    Managing Editor
    Marketing News

Larry Wizenberg
    Vice President, Consumer Marketing Group
    Yankelovich, Skelly, and White, Inc.

ACKNOWLEDGMENTS

Special thanks must be given to the outstanding group of individuals who contributed so much through their service on our Editorial Advisory Board. Not only did they present us with ideas and concepts, but they reviewed the works of the contributors and, in many instances, made suggestions that added dimension to these works. Some had the interest and took the time to contribute chapters of their own to the book.

The content of any written work is enhanced by good editing. We believe (and hope you will agree) that this book has been well-edited by our staff and that of Dow Jones-Irwin. For this reason, we particularly single out Gloria Bobrow and Maura Tobias for the help that they gave us in the compilation of the manuscripts.

We thank all the authors for their dedication, for meeting deadlines, and for giving us the kind of cooperation that made the compilation of this book a pleasure.

Edwin E. Bobrow
Mark David Bobrow

CONTENTS

Part 1
MARKETING PRINCIPLES

Product Costs. Advertising Costs. The Product Life Cycle. Selecting Your Strategy: *Push Strategy. Marketing Considerations. Promotional Mix. Pull Strategy.*

Part 2
RESEARCH

Part 3
DEVELOPING THE MARKETING PLAN

to Make the Goals for These Programs Specifically Measurable for the People Charged with Implementing the Plan. Theory as Practice—A Real Situation: *Fortune 500 Capital Equipment Manufacturer. First and Last, the Operating Management Must Direct and Control the Planning Effort.*

Part 1

MARKETING PRINCIPLES

1

MARKETING FOR THE 80s

by
Ed Flanagan

Sales Executives Club of New York

THE MAN WHO INSISTS ON SEEING WITH PERFECT CLEARNESS
BEFORE HE DECIDES—NEVER DECIDES

Henri Frederick

OVERVIEW

Nobody wants bean counters now. Corporations want marketers who
know about product life cycles and how to develop product strategies.
They want executives who understand that basic marketing means
moving goods and services from the producer to the consumer. Ones
who know which industries are growing and which are failing. How
consumer lifestyles and work habits affect product choices. Executives
who are wise enough to understand these changes and see new opportunities for their companies. And know how to get the job done!

Why are bean counters out of favor? As stated above, a single
event or a clear major change is not always necessary to pinpoint the
why. Some point to early 1979 when, for the first time since World War
II, the *average family with two wage earners experienced a decline in
its disposable income.* Economists say that, barring a major technological or energy breakthrough, it's estimated that it will take *10 to 15
years* for the average family to recover its lost buying power. They
conclude that total American buying power has been crippled for the
decade of the 80s. This reduction in purchasing power, combined with
what economists describe as the *ratchet effect,* will have a direct impact on the mix of goods and services purchased in this decade. The
ratchet effect refers to the fact that Americans tend to "live up to," or

"ratchet upward" toward increased income and, once having increased their living standards, cannot easily reduce them.

Still others claim that the figures from the 1980 census were the key point of change from emphasis on financial bean counting on a short-term basis to marketing. As we all know, the 80 Census told us that *only* 7 percent of the 82 million households that were surveyed fit the standard description of the "typical American household": a working dad, a homemaker wife, and two children! Other shocking data came forth. Fifty-four percent of the moms worked full- or part-time, and more than 50 percent of all households comprised only one or two persons. Twenty-four percent of all households are now headed by singles. And 20 percent of all households included persons 65 or older, and it's growing.

The impact of these events and data said to all: the so-called mass market has splintered. Companies couldn't sell their products the way they used to. It is a new ball game for corporations and for marketing executives in particular.

Excellence in marketing will be the competitive edge in the 80s. It will separate the winners from the losers. The era of the short-term-thinking bean counters is gone. The era of the astute, flexible marketer is here. He or she will be the driving force. They'll make the decisions, not always based on perfect understanding of the changes or events that affect their individual businesses, but they'll be the key decision makers.

CHALLENGES AND HOW TO MEET THEM

It's oft been said that marketing begins with information. So let's look at some of the more pertinent challenges we marketers face as we move into the second half of this decade. More important than recognizing their existence is planning to meet them head-on with practical strategies—ones that work.

A list of the key challenges that affect marketing:

I. ECONOMIC
Inflation
Materials Shortage

II. SOCIAL
Consumerism
Consumer Protection

III. LEGAL AND ETHICAL
Law and Regulations
Court Decisions
Trade Practices

IV. COMPETITION
   Benefits of Competition
   Dangers of Competition

V. ENVIRONMENTAL CONCERNS
   Air and Water Quality
   Supply of Raw Materials

VI. INTERNATIONAL
   Trade Barriers
   Cartels
   Events

Right now you're saying to yourself, "How can I control these challenges?" The answer is—you can't. Marketing managers, for example, are at the mercy of economic conditions and the prevailing legal environment. They have no say over international events, changes in consumers' tastes, and actions by their competitors. The point is that smart marketers have to recognize the factors which affect the way they market their goods and services. They plan. They gather data on a regular basis. They're responsive to change.

These disciplines were forgotten in the 60s and 70s because inflation kept sales moving upward. Marketing took a back seat. The mood of the times was more to corporate acquisitions, cash management, products for everyone—everywhere. Then along came the recession, which brought changes in lifestyles, work habits and households, intense international competition, maturing markets, rapid technological changes, and deregulation. It was enough to make the everyday garden variety marketer yearn for early retirement, or a full professorship at an obscure business school. But to those with no rich relatives, and poor luck in the state lotteries, all of this means a return to the sound fundamentals that were brushed aside in the late 60s and 70s. We must sharpen our skills. We must take advantage of these challenges. We must use the new technologies as marketing tools to aid us in meeting the challenges.

Perhaps those of us in marketing should restate the marketing concept which has been an effective managerial tool for over 30 years. It has stood the test of time and yet it has been adaptable, which again attests to its soundness. A restatement in these times might be: A philosophy of management that seeks to determine and satisfy long-range consumer and public welfare using integrated and targeted marketing programs to achieve organizational goals.

NEW PRINCIPLES THAT WILL APPLY IN THE 80s

Some of us are older and recall some of the popular theater and early TV programs that usually featured an act where a nimble individual spun many plates high atop thin bamboo sticks simultaneously. As a few plates started to wobble, the performer gave the appropriate stick a few turns to again make that plate stable. Yes, there's a lesson there for marketers of the 80s. It is one of balance, of discipline, of responsiveness to change, and of teamwork.

These are not, of course, new principles, but they are principles more necessary in the 80s than perhaps in the two preceding decades. Let's look at them in light of the changes and challenges facing marketers.

Balance

Marketers have to decide where they want their companies to go and when they want them to get there. They have to develop well-defined, realistic primary and secondary goals. They have to anticipate the many challenges and changes. All of this requires an individual who has good balance. He or she has to develop a good system of priorities, for example, which bamboo stick gets the first turn, which plate can be left alone for a little while—a solid generalist approach but one of balance.

Discipline

The discipline to stick to the stated objectives and strategies to get there is needed. No longer can marketers have an office and salespeople in every market. They have to practice target marketing. They have to deal with the well-defined segments identified by their research. The days of being all things to every consumer group are gone, perhaps never to return. They have to understand better the constraints of predetermined financial goals. The days of "Give me my budget number and let me get going" are also gone, never to return. It takes extreme discipline to stick to the goals, but it's a trait—or skill, if you will—that the marketer of the 80s must possess.

Responsiveness

Consider that the following is now happening and, in some industries, a bit faster than others:

- New competitors enter your field.
- Your competitors and suppliers change pricing.
- There are new and substitute products in the marketplace before you realize it.

- Consumer preferences are fickle, e.g., today's winner is tomorrow's loser.
- Your industry is being deregulated.

These points say merely that the marketer of the 80s has to be responsive—or perhaps the better synonym is flexible. It is a necessity. There are too many in Chapter 11, or in interesting copy under the heading "Where Are They Now?" to argue this point. It also says that perhaps marketing executives should also recognize that the "lean and mean" label of the early 80s is a must. If you can't be responsive to the marketplace, perhaps you have too many layers of management. Slow response time is the deadly enemy of the marketer of the 80s.

Teamwork

A hallmark of the 80s will be working together. And not just because Japan, Inc. is doing it. It's just another principle whose time is here again. As products and services become more complicated and more key decisions are being moved further back in the organizational structure, teamwork becomes a necessity. Marketing and sales functions cannot be at each other's throats. It's no longer a me, a they, or them— it's us! It's our team, our working together which will make or break a company. Marketing and the marketing executive is the natural leader of this team. He or she is the most logical one to be the driving force. And, to this end, the marketer of the 80s has to be—must be—the master communicator, steeped in the skills of organizing, motivating, and managing the core team of people charged with marketing the goods and services that their company produces.

Global Viewpoint

Marketers of the 80s must view the world as the potential marketplace for their goods and services. Our economy is part of a global structure, moving away from isolation and national self-sufficiency. As a result, we will no longer be the world's dominant force.

Marketers who still believe that once our steel mills and factories get rolling full-steam again we'll be number one are behind the times and changes. All the industrial countries, including Japan and Germany, are beginning the phase of deindustrialization. It's predicted that, by the year 2000, the Third World will be manufacturing as much as 30 percent of the world's goods. Simply stated, they've got the work force and can produce basic goods for less. Shared production will expand.

Marketers must constantly reevaluate the markets for their goods and services on a worldwide basis. For some industries the time is now as some markets mature and others shrink. But the lesson is clear—the others will soon follow.

EDUCATION

Most executives and their corporations have recognized the value of education. Some see the word *commencement* as meaning end. Their college commencement ceremony meant an end of their collegiate days. To the marketer and marketing company of the 80s it has to have its dictionary meaning—a beginning, not an end.

The Concept of Life-Long Learning

The marketer of the 80s must make a life-long commitment to continue keeping pace with the changes within his or her industry. Second, they must, on a planned path, continue to educate themselves. They can do this by attending higher-institutional programs at local universities. They can take advantage of the special training programs offered by their companies. And third, they can join industry and special professional associations. They must fully understand that all motivation is self-motivation and that their companies, the colleges and universities, and the professional societies will not do the job for them. It is they—the marketers—who have to embark on a career of life-long learning.

Further, they have to accept the fact that rapid technological change will be with them throughout their careers. New applications will make their jobs easier and provide numerous opportunities—provided that they view high-tech as tools, not ends in themselves.

And, last, they should cultivate the entrepreneurial drive within themselves and the marketing function they manage. It is this entrepreneurial spirit that brought into being the wondrous products and services that put real meaning into the label, *Made in the U.S.A.*

Each of the following chapters is a solid block of useful information written by an experienced, firing-line marketing executive. Each will show you the best practical methods and techniques upon which your marketing function should be built. Some information will be fast absorbed. Some not so fast. You'll be surprised at the end by the sheer knowledge and depth of understanding you've achieved. Be where the action is—in the 80s, in marketing—the real cutting edge for successful companies in this decade.

2

CHANGE: ITS IMPACT ON MARKETING

by
Belden Menkus

Management Consultant

Marketing may be defined as the process of planning and achieving change in the environment in which a product or a service must be sold, rented, or leased.

Marketing does not occur simply because, say, salespeople make more calls on prospects or ads/commercials are designed that will increase the number of impressions made upon prospects in some time period. Such things are important in themselves, but to focus on them confuses the means used with the ends sought. Marketing is a process, not an activity or the sum of various activities.

DEFINITIONS

Change, also, is a process; it is the function of altering something so as to make it significantly different. Its very occurrence assumes a departure from the status quo. Change is an internally powered process; once initiated, it tends to continue relentlessly to its conclusion. As a practical matter, change cannot be terminated; the marketer can only hope to alter the pace at which it occurs or the force of its impact.

STRATEGIC OPTIONS

A marketing executive can deal with change in one of three ways.

Inaction

Change can be ignored, on the assumption that the organization or the product/service involved can succeed in isolation from external events and influences. The illustrations of what can occur in this context are many. For instance, there were a number of buggy and whip makers who believed that the automobile posed no threat to their future—until it was too late for them to do anything about it. Again, in the 1930s and 40s there were hordes of "traditional" drug and grocery retailers who believed that the self-service operations posed no threat to their future. And, there were food processors who saw no future for convenience products or fast-food restaurants. They ignored the inroads that these made into their sales—until it was too late.

Reaction

The marketer simply can await the onset of forces and events that bring about change and, when they arise, try to respond to their impact. This approach does delay the investment of time and funds in response to change, but it restricts the time and opportunity available to the marketer in which to plan and make this response. Often there is only one chance to respond to these change agents; that one shot too often must be the best because it is the only shot available. That's risky at best!

Opting to react to change can be successful marketing strategy, but it is very likely to fail. The icebox makers and the companies that sold ice for residential and commercial use found this out in the mid-1930s. They tried to counter the successful introduction of electric motor-driven mechanical refrigeration devices by a marketing campaign that claimed that "natural cool is better." It didn't work; it was too late and lacked credibility. At times, however, reacting to change after it is recognized can prove successful. For example, in the mid-1950s many of the older moving and storage companies realized that their large number of poured-concrete, so-called fireproof warehouse structures were standing empty much of the year; people simply no longer stored furniture in connection with moves or during the off-season. Most of these companies were able to reposition themselves in the commercial warehousing market by storing goods on consignment from various retailers and manufacturer's representatives and leasing compartmented space within the building to various concerns on a turnkey basis.

Action

The desirable course in handling change in the marketplace is to anticipate the likely occurrence of change-generating events and to be prepared to control and counter their impact. The truly effective marketer is, to some degree, a *futurist*—an active student of the events, forces, and trends bringing about change. Here, again, many illustrations of this approach to handling change can be given. For instance, in the late 1930s RCA management foresaw the eventual appearance of commercially viable television technology and began to field test both transmission and receiving equipment, even though there was almost no feasible market for even a modest number of these devices at that time.

Again, in the late 1970s more than one U.S. publisher began to realize that even text-editing automation would not defer indefinitely the cost pressures generated by price rises in paper stock and other production expenses. And, these same people began to realize at about the same time that television and radio broadcast news coverage practices were changing the way in which the public in general understood and valued the news-reporting process and, especially, the form in which news material was presented. Some publishers began to put more background, feature, and other nonhard news material in their publications. Others began to diversify into other fields—including the ownership and operation of local cable television franchises. And, some even began to develop alternative news-reporting services that exploited the newer technologies. Obviously, no single optimum strategy exists for reacting successfully to the impact of change in the marketplace.

TACTICAL POSSIBILITIES

Once a marketer decides to respond to change there are only two approaches (apart from either abandoning an existing—or creating a new—product/service) that are feasible; at times, some combination of these two may be called for.

There is an element of risk taking in following either of these approaches. The nature and extent of the risk involved varies, of course, with the environment in which the marketer must act. Yet, the presence of risk exists—even in inaction. In fact, it must be assumed that the successful marketer will be a risk taker.

Reorientation

This calls for changing the form, structure, composition, and/or nature of the product/service and the way it is presented to the potential customer. Typically this involves such things as altering the design and function of the product, the way in which it is to be used, the way in which that use is presented to the prospective customer, and the scope and composition of the target prospect group.

Of course, in some instances a combination of these changes may be called for. And, in most instances the changes actually made should be substantive in nature rather than superficial or cosmetic. (More than one marketer has discovered that such things as changing packaging color or graphics really provides only a stop-gap response to change and that a more substantial action is required for a successful response to the change impact being dealt with.)

Sometimes all that is called for is a reassessment of the scope and composition of the potential market for a given product/service type— taking a broader view, if you like. Take, for example, the experience of IBM, which has long dominated the computer marketplace. However, IBM was a latecomer to this marketplace; Sperry Univac, as it is now called, was the leader in the field. At that time it was felt generally that this technology had only a limited potential market; primarily it would be used by a handful of research institutions or in specialized military or federal government agency environments. But IBM recognized that the technology could be applied to the more general business accounting and recordkeeping environment, where its electronic (so-called tab card) equipment already was well established. This was where the IBM success story really began.

However, this sort of insight may be lacking at critical times; this is true even for IBM. A dozen or so years ago, after the decision just discussed was made, another division of the corporation entered the microfilm field. A number of optical devices developed for military agencies under contract were adapted into a number of well-designed readers and related units. The trouble was, the people assigned to market the products couldn't!

An associate and I met at this time with several of the senior marketing executives responsible for this IBM product line to review microfilm marketing opportunities and to suggest realistic means for exploiting them. (At the time of this meeting the two of us had 20 years of experience in the microfilm field between us, both as users and as designers of various products. By contrast, the IBM marketers had only recently become involved with microfilm products; they had been working for some years in selling data processing products.)

The IBM executives responded to our presentation with scepticism: "We would have to change a number of our basic sales management practices. We can't do that; it would impact our commission structure and bring us out of step with the other divisions." Apparently these people were unable to change to meet a new marketing situation. They didn't change; two years later the IBM microfilm effort ended, and the product was sold to another corporation.

Innovation

This calls for the development of new products/services and the creation of new marketing approaches. (Here, it is interesting to note, the limiting factors are the vision and imagination of the marketer, the advertising specialists, and the salespeople involved—not the insights and understanding of the existing and prospective customers.) Customers and prospects are notoriously unaware of their real wants and needs. The successful marketer, in fact, is able to show them wants and needs that they had not previously envisioned or been able to articulate!

At this point, it is wise for the marketer to avoid trying to articulate or to exploit a previously unexpressed want or need that simply doesn't exist. There is a particular danger of doing this when one is trying to apply a new or complex technology such as holography or quadraphonic sound reproduction to the marketplace. The products developed in those areas worked well; the trouble was that almost no one bought them. It is possible for a marketer to be so impressed with the complexity, elegance, or efficiency of the technology supporting a particular product/service that the realities of the marketplace are ignored.

Some years ago I was asked by one of the major copying machine makers to evaluate the potential market for an about-to-be-introduced color copier. It was an exceptionally well-designed device; the copies produced were very good from a graphic standpoint. I was able to identify and define a market for the product. The trouble was, it wasn't as large as the one they were accustomed to working with. I suggested in my report that the product would not be profitable for them; it wasn't. The product, despite extensive remodeling of the advertising effort and cosmetic changes to the exterior of the device, has remained one of the rare marketing failures in the corporation's history.[1]

Clearly, change cannot be forced, no matter what marketing investment is made.

THE THRUST OF CHANGE

Yet, life during this entire century has been marked by continued far-reaching change in social values, cultural norms, individual knowledge and awareness, and general business practices. The rate of change and the willingness of society in general—and people in particular—to accept and assimilate change has grown progressively since the end of

---

[1] I learned later that several other consultants who advised on the same matter arrived at more optimistic conclusions regarding the sales potential of the product. My suspicion remains, however, that it was announced more for reasons of organizational politics than as a result of any reasoned assessment of market projections by corporate management.

World War II. Barring an unforeseen cataclysmic event such as a major military conflict or a general economic collapse, this growing rate of change will accelerate during the remainder of this century.

Change in this century has led to a number of profound alterations in many things that critically affect the assumptions which underlie most marketing efforts.

- Family structure is less stable; divorce and delayed marriage are more common.
- People are more mobile; job tenure is shorter.
- People have reached higher levels of education and are more socially aware; on the other hand, educated people appear less learned.
- Job tenure is shorter; people change jobs—and careers—more frequently.
- Corporate management practices and procedures based on assumed employee loyalty and lengthy job tenure have proven unworkable.
- Labor-intensive jobs have proven to be too expensive to sustain; automation has begun to replace them.

The remaining decades of this century should see increased use of automation—especially in terms of the employment of robotics, both in and out of the manufacturing environment and in the home and the school. (The reindustrialization of America, unfortunately, will reduce drastically the number of people in the work force.) Microelectronic technology, whose measures of power—expressed in terms of cost/performance relations—appear to be doubling about every three months, will make new ways of collecting, evaluating, and communicating information available on a truly worldwide basis. During this period, the developed societies will shift from an energy-intensive structure to one becoming information-intensive. The gap between the developed and nondeveloped countries will widen, not lessen.

These changes, in turn, will bring into being new norms for communication, economic transactions, and the like which will radically restructure the environment in which products/services are marketed. The marketing principles could remain unaltered; the way in which they are applied most surely will not.

BEING PREPARED

The marketer who seeks to deal successfully with change will undertake the following four-fold effort.

Study

Become a *futurist;* develop the habit of looking beyond the present considerations of marketing plans and reports. Try to keep up with general developments in the technologies that can have an impact on your marketplace and the nature of your product/service. Also, try to get at least an informed amateur's awareness of social, economic, cultural, and technological developments in the areas beyond your immediate work focus.

Review

Don't let marketing methods and plans become routines that repeat themselves from year to year. Challenge every assumption and practice periodically; try to step aside from your familiar viewpoint and take an outsider's look at both your marketplace and at the way in which you identify prospective customer wants and needs—and convert them into orders.

Rediscover Imagination

Try to find a regular time for exercising your inventiveness and ingenuity. Look for new ways of doing things and new things to do in every aspect of the marketing venture. Discard no idea just because it is out of the ordinary or because applying it violates some long-established marketing practice or industry custom. Try to establish what amounts to a regular regimen for exercising your creativity—just as you might systematically work at gaining proficiency in the use of any other valuable skill.

Plan

Anticipate the likely and the unlikely things that reasonably can be expected to have an impact on the environment in which you are active as a marketer. Be prepared for success beyond your expectations—say, when customer demand exceeds what was anticipated. And, be prepared for crisis situations—for example, when the supply of a raw material critical to your product/service is cut off.

Change is a key element in successful marketing. Anticipating and managing change can be the key element in a marketer's career success.

3

MARKETING VALUE VERSUS MARKETING PRODUCTS/SERVICES

by
Howard Berrian

It has long been stated that people buy benefits of a product or a service. They do not buy features. There is no argument with this truism. However, to extend this thinking and give it more marketing worth and direction is the intent in the following pages.

Buyers, whether end users, corporations, associations, special interest groups, or societies, are better educated and more informed. This prompts a more in-depth study of a product or service before buying. Envision your prospects, customers, and clients looking through your products and services and hoping to find a package of values, a family of values that will satisfy their logical and psychic needs better than your competitors.

The marketplace has become more value-oriented. Its value-seeking buyers are looking well beyond product features and benefits and asking what are the long-term, high-value worths in one supplier's offering versus another. The first graphic provides an overview of the arena in which value selling and marketing succeeds or fails.

In the current and future marketplace, the marketer will have to focus both on value selling and marketing versus product and service selling and marketing. This chapter is designed to contribute to that task and challenge.

Value-Seeking/Value-Providing Interface

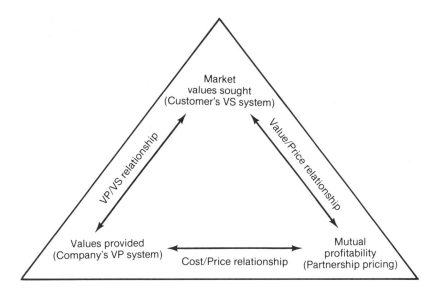

A five-component action system is suggested as the way to become a value marketer. The five components are:

1. Define and communicate the value strategy.
2. Balance the value-providing/value-seeking scale.
3. Price like a value provider.
4. Gain total company commitment.
5. Police performance and adjust.

DEFINE AND COMMUNICATE THE VALUE STRATEGY

A *strategy* is the direction a company takes in order for its business to grow and satisfy the needs of its customers. There are extensive listings of criteria for evaluating a defined strategy, some of which are: (1) has long-range duration, (2) capitalizes on company strengths, (3) is compatible with stated assumptions, (4) exploits competitive weaknesses, and (5) supports business definition. A value-oriented strategy contains a clear statement of the major high values provided by the company, so clearly stated and eventually demonstrated that the marketplace can't misread the company's value intent.

A *value* is the worth that buyers expect to receive from the utilization of a product or service when it is taken into their environment and life. Buyers examine products and services looking for in-use worths—worths that have lasting merit plus appeal to personal intrinsic needs. This value-seeking behavior is common to all buyers. The easier a company makes it for a buyer to see the in-use values in their products or services, the more likely the seeking buyer will become a customer.

Listed, by type of company, are examples of the values-provided element contained in their strategy statements.

Type of Company	Customers	Values Provided
Machinery manufacturer	Paper manufacturers	Reduced manufacturing costs Improved product quality Lower capital investment
Agricultural chemical manufacturer	Dealers	Lower inventory costs New users Lower application costs
Agricultural chemical distributor	Growers	Lower application costs Increased yield per acre Lower cost per acre
Carpet manufacturer	Retailer	Increased revenues Financing Incentives
Electronic information system	Corporate librarians	Lower information management costs Decision-making information In-House system compatability
Lead qualification	All companies	New revenues Lower sales/marketing costs Improved lead/closing ratio
Department store	Women	Personal image enhancement Balanced price/value Improved self worth

In the defined strategy statement, the values must shout out loud and clear their worth. What should be printed on the company T-shirt are the values provided. Usually found there is the company name and its products.

BALANCE THE VALUE-PROVIDING/VALUE-SEEKING SCALE

Successful marketers accept the reality that they must provide a high-value package if they are to seek successfully their own value-sought package. The better the company balances the value-providing/value-seeking scale, the more successful it will be. If the scale is tipped too greatly out of balance, the enterprise faces failure. If it attempts to provide too many values (cost generators) and seeks to price high to recoup such costs, the marketplace may well say, "You ask too much for what you give."

All business enterprises seek three major values, and if they can achieve them, growth may be assured. The values sought are:

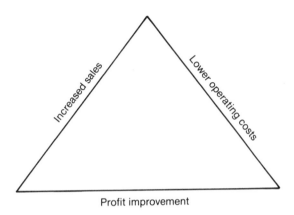

Profit improvement

A value-driven business strategy conveys to the marketplace your value package and the fairness in the price you ask for it. A value statement must convey, "This is a good deal for me, and I'll gladly pay the price asked." Getting your customers to say this helps you bring home the three big values sought. Remember, most business customers want the same major values you seek.

A starting place for examining your value providing is the old reliable feature/benefit matrix with an in-use value component added.

Features	Benefits	In-Use Values

Marketing-oriented companies have understood for quite awhile that their customers do not just buy a product or service. They buy an

The QLS Value-Providing System

In-Use Value Matrix *(by position)*

Salesperson	*Sales Manager*	*Marketing Manager*	*Advertising Manager*	*Product Manager*	*Marketing Research Manager*

Bottom-Line Values

"augmented product," as so clearly and accurately stated by Ted Levitt of Harvard. Value marketers call their offering package a value-providing system designed to produce high worth-in-use values.

A BAI client in the lead qualification business uses this graphic to visually show their marketplace value-providing system and its in-use worths.

They also go a step further, using this matrix to list the in-use values of the key users who are involved in their lead qualification system. When a marketer focuses this sharply, each customer sees clearly the in-use value to him or her. Such personalization permits sharper selling, advertising, promoting, and servicing. All value seekers say, "Hey! There is something of worth in this for me."

PRICE ACCORDING TO VALUE

Price is perceived differently by all types of buyers. Buyers are classified as prospects, customers, and clients, and all three types generally read your price differently. The price/reading matrix shows the differences in pricing perceptions.

Buyer	Definition	Price Readings
Prospect	A potential buyer of company's products or services and a source of potential revenue.	Price too high. Competitor's price is better. Price is negotiable. Price/value balance is poor. Lower your price.
Customer	A regular or periodic buyer of a company's products or services and a contributor of revenue.	Price is OK for now. Price shopping is ongoing. Price comparisons are daily Price is paramount. Price can be better.
Client	A buyer with which the company has an ongoing, mutually profitable relationship.	Price/value balance is excellent. Price is good. Price is not paramount. Price is expected to be fair. Value far offsets price.

It is obvious that, for clients, price is only a minor element in the supplier/buyer relationship. If value received is high, the price asked becomes a low price. The more perceived values a company provides, the less concern a purchaser has with the price asked. Mercedes Benz, Tiffany's, Sony, Bloomingdale's, and Disneyland have all premium-priced their products and successfully marketed at those prices because they have coupled a premium-value offering to their price. Buyers see high value in what these companies provide and also perceive a fair price being asked. Premium pricing is not pricing as high as you can get away with. It is pricing in relationship to the in-use values a buyer will realize from his or her purchase.

An objective of a value-driven strategy is that it helps create and sustain client relationships which, in turn, support premium pricing which, in turn, produces corporate profit which, in turn, sustains growth.

GAIN TOTAL COMPANY COMMITMENT

The entire work force of a company needs to make a total commitment to making the value strategy work. Each executive and employee must say, "We are/I am in the business of providing in-use values to our purchasers." To gain this commitment, each executive and employee has to be positioned in the external value-providing system and understand their internal value-providing relationships. If the value-providing system is not razor sharp in its performance and all components in synchronization, it won't make it in the marketplace.

Step one is to define the system and its components. A large number of components is not the answer. The larger the number of components, the more difficult it becomes to (1) organize, (2) manage, (3) build in premium worths, (4) adjust quickly to change, and (5) communicate values. Five to seven components, experience has shown, are manageable numbers.

Step two is to audit each system module for its customers' and clients' values. If the component cannot be related to a sufficient quantity of user values, you should question strongly its inclusion in the system. An example of such an audit is partially shown in the graphic below:

Component	Lead Qualification	Lead Tracking
In-Use Values	Improved lead to sales ratio	Focus on hot leads
	Lower sales training costs	Focuses marketing on hot leads
	Higher-quality hot leads	Profiling of hot leads
	Improved sales to expense ratio	Improved cost efficiency
	Eliminates nonviable prospects	Buying cycles developed
	Instant capturing of prospect data	Forcing of four hot lead calls
	Improved conversion rate leads to sales	Shorter closing time

Step three is the positioning of each executive and employee in the value-providing system and their internal value-providing/value-seeking relationship. By positioning each employee in his or her system component, which is easy to accomplish, you relate them directly (1) to your marketplace, (2) to your customers and clients, and (3) to their value-providing marketing role. In most organizations, only a small percentage of the employees are related directly to the company's product or service users. Once placed in this role, a higher self-worth is

---

Value-Providing/Value-Seeking Relationships

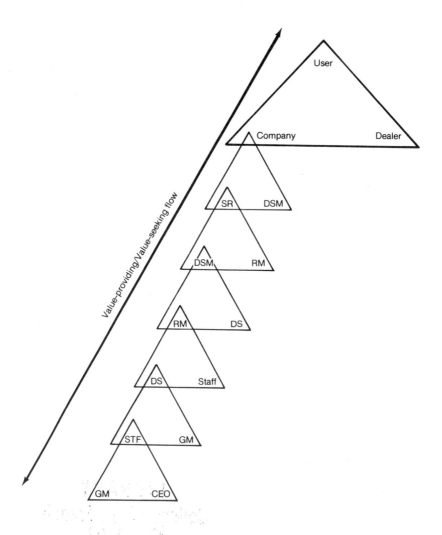

embodied in each employee. This value is sought by most people and achieved by few.

To improve the value-producing productivity of employees, a clarification of each value-providing/value-seeking relationship is required. When asked, most employees perceive themselves as providing their associates with a higher-value package than the ones their associates provide. In fact, both parties have a very clouded picture of what each seeks and each provides in the way of worths to each other. This value-provided/value-received gap between parties erodes the overall value behavior of the enterprise. The next graphic shows the value-providing/value-seeking relationship from the CEO to the end user in the marketplace. The defined value strategy is the thread tying all relationships together. The following worksheet is an example of a sales manager's 10 key VP/VS relationships.

Motivating all employers to support value-added marketing calls for bringing about the three Ps: participating, partnering, and profiting, as expressed in the following graphic:

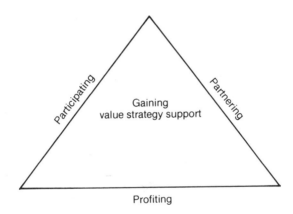

All three sides of the 3P triangle have to be clearly seen by all employees, and the company must take appropriate actions so that employees see the worth in total strategy commitment. Following are some commitment actions taken by some companies:

Participating
    Committee membership
    Off-the-job product testing
    Opinion questionnaire recipient
    Out-of-town seminar attendance
    Department representation
    Job rotation

Partnering
    Field trips to customers
    Involvement in decision making
    Product assessment assistance
    Special task force assignment
    Research panel membership
    Selling team membership
Profiting
    Incentive program
    Bonus reward
    Profit sharing
    Cost reduction sharing
    Suggestion implementation reward
    Salary increase

Sales Manager's Value-Providing/Value-Seeking Profile

Position	Values Provided by Me	Values Sought by Me
Chief executive officer		
Executive vice president		
Contract sales manager		
Field sales manager		
Merchandising manager		
Product line manager		
Style and design manager		
Advertising manager		
Marketing planning manager		
Sales representative		

AUDIT VALUE-PROVIDING PERFORMANCE

Profit and growth achievement performance is the key evaluation of your value-providing performance. Doing well in profit making and meeting your growth objectives says: (1) the marketplace sees a high value in your total marketing offering (not just product) and (2) your value-providing team (all your employees) are fulfilling their value-providing responsibilities.

Going to the marketplace on a regular and planned basis to determine your value image and performance is a must. Researching product performance and image is common, where value-providing performance is not. Sales and profit performance is high, assuming the company's value-providing performance is perceived as top draw.

Asking clients, customers, prospects, and end users what values they perceive in your company, what values they have received, and what values they'd like to receive is the only way to avoid the assumption bear trap. Once you misread the trap and are in it, you can bet a competitive or substitute value-providing system has dethroned you. Recovering is costly and often unachievable. Take your value-providing reading at least once every year. There are a variety of basic research techniques and methodologies to get at your validation task. Companies have tested their value positions in the eyes of their clients, customers, prospects, and users, and even in the eyes of their own employees. The winning methods have been:

- Telemarketing interviewing
- Mail questionnaires
- Personal face-to-face interviewing
- Group face-to-face interviewing

The keys to a productive value "reading" are your script/questionnaires, interviewers, and marketplace sample. All three components require top-draw quality.

A laundry list comparison of product selling/marketing versus value selling/marketing is a most convincing testimonial to "go for value."

Selling product creates these obstacles to your success:

- Prompts competitive comparison.
- Promotes numerical counting of your features versus competitors.
- Produces a downward price pressure from your customer.
- Causes the company to be product-driven.
- Tempts price lowering to get business.
- Inspires your customer to continue to shop for a better deal.
- Assumes your customer will translate to in-use value.
- Diverts your customer's mind away from bottom-line thinking.

Selling values helps to assure your success in these ways:

- Widens the gap between your competitors.
- Creates a longer-lasting relationship with customer.
- Encompasses total work force.
- Helps insure values sought will be realized.
- Relates all employees to customer.
- Improves employee's self-worth.
- Drives customers' thinking to bottom-line.
- Requires your company read your business backward, from market place inward.
- Prompts more frequent auditing of product line and supportive services.
- Supports your higher prices.

A high percentage of reputable enterprises produce quality products. A much, much lower percentage translate this competence into a value strategy targeted at the in-use benefits of their product. How is your company positioned?

DEFINITIONS

Buyers. Purchasers of products and services.

Users. Purchasers of products and services who focus on the utilization of the purchase in their lives.

Value. A worth that buyers expect to receive from the utilization of a product or service when it is taken into their environments and lives.

Worth. A quality that has lasting merit and appeals strongly to the intrinsic needs of a person.

Value-Providing System. A product or service surrounded by a family of high-value support services, each of which is perceived by the purchaser to have a worth.

Partnering. Relationship between: (1) supplier and buyer, (2) supplier employee and buyer employee, (3) employer and employee, and (4) boss and subordinate where both recognize the values produced from the responsibilities in such a relationship.

Profiting. Gaining a high degree of extrinsic and intrinsic "riches" from a purchase, a job, a task well done, a relationship, and/or an experience.

Participating. The feeling that you are being asked, being heard, and that evidence substantiates this.

4

CONSUMER GOODS MARKETING

by
Harvey Stein

The Hallmark Group

The marketing of consumer goods has changed dramatically in the last two decades. It became obvious to the marketer that there was more to satisfying the demands of the marketplace than just presenting product. It was recognized that strategies had to be developed based on the finite knowledge of what the consumer wanted. Marketing decisions had to be made based on what benefits consumers were looking for in the purchase of their products. This forced many companies to change from a sales orientation to a marketing point of view. With this change in thinking came new studies in consumer attitudes and consumer behavioral patterns. These studies gave the manufacturer the ability to identify new opportunities in the marketplace as well as evaluate existing products.

There was also a strong rise in consumerism. The marketer had to take into consideration how the product affected the consumer and also determine whether or not the product itself was compatible with the company's long-range goals.

It is unfortunate that many of them failed to look at the long-term nature of the marketplace. The criticism of American business during these last two decades was that it had a short-run focus rather than a long-term consideration for the customer that it was serving. Their marketing disciplines were criticized, often with considerable justification. Bruce Young, editor of *Business Week,* stated,

> Probably the most important management fundamental that is being ignored today is that of staying close to the customer, to satisfy his needs

29

and anticipate his wants. In too many companies the customers have become a bloody nuisance whose unpredictable behavior damages carefully made strategic plans and whose activities mess up computer operations and who stubbornly insist that the purchased product should work.

The consumer's reactions or needs for a product will change from season to season, by peer group pressure, and are affected by changes in styles and consumer attitudes. Whether or not the marketer will have success with this product depends on how the numerous factors which we will call the marketing mix are integrated. The marketing mix includes product planning, pricing, promotional strategies, and distribution. The marketer's objective is to develop a marketing mix that gives the end user satisfaction in the purchase that will be made.

In most cases, planning is a long-range procedure. Therefore, it takes into consideration what the future will hold and what steps are necessary to make sure that the marketer will have a successful program. This is referred to as *strategic planning*. It is the most comprehensive part of the marketing mix, as it must take into consideration all of the corporate goals, marketing goals, and any alternate strategies that are part of the corporate goal. In order to do this, there must be sufficient data base, as well as strong communications, between top management and the marketing department. Top management must understand the potential of the marketing program, as well as how it fits the corporate goals. The marketing goals must exist in a sense of harmony with the corporative goals. Once this understanding and harmony exists, the marketing mix can be developed.

ELEMENTS OF THE MARKETING MIX

Product Planning

When the strategic planning is completed, product planning takes over. Before we go any further, we should develop an understanding of product planning from the marketer's viewpoint. Product planning involves not only the physical product but also warranties, design, packaging, trademark, longevity of product, and so forth. In its final analysis, the product is no more than another means of monetary exchange through which both parties will receive a level of satisfaction for the goods or dollars they have received.

When we talk about product planning, we normally think about the development or introduction of a new physical product. There are, of course, varying degrees of newness. We can walk into the supermarket or drug store and see introductions of the new Kleenex, the new Tide, and the new Crest toothpaste. The degree to which the consumer views this newness and its acceptance by the buying public are key factors in product planning.

Pricing

Pricing is another part of the marketing mix. Obviously, product must be priced at a level where it will be profitable for the manufacturer. On the other hand, we must not forget that the price must be at a level at which the consumer can justify the purchase. The consumer will think not only of our product but also as to how it compares with similar products in the marketplace.

In developing the pricing strategy, remember that it is also possible to destroy the profitability of a product by pricing it too low. Consumers associate high quality with high price. It is possible to create marketing resistance by introducing a product at too low a price. Contrary to many opinions, there is a strong price-quality relationship. Other elements that must be taken into consideration when determining the pricing level are brand strategy, trademarks, and warranties.

Distribution

When we think of distribution, we think of the post-manufacturing process of getting the goods to the marketplace. In its purest form, distribution includes the manufacturing of the product, inclusive of the acquisition of raw materials for manufacturing.

The selection of channels of distribution very often is no more than a reflection of corporate philosophy. Is it in the best interests of the manufacturer to ship the goods directly to the dealer for availability to the consumer? Should the goods be placed through the traditional wholesale distributors? The selection of a channel of distribution will be affected by our choice of a push or pull marketing strategy.

The truth of the matter is that there is no one correct answer. It should be remembered, however, that the cheapest method of getting the product to the marketplace is sometimes the most costly when the loss of sales is considered. In the final analysis, it should be remembered that the channel of distribution is nothing more than the vehicle through which we must take the product so that we can place it in the hands of the ultimate consumer.

Promotional Strategy

Promotion is the function of influencing and persuading the end user's decision. It is highly dynamic and one of the more difficult areas for the marketing manager to develop and control.

An effective promotion relies on a proper mix of advertising, sales promotion, personal selling, and public relations. No single element is more important than another. Depending on the company and the product being promoted, there will generally be a variation as to the emphasis placed on each of these areas.

PROMOTIONAL MIX

Advertising

Advertising takes many forms. In most cases, it is referred to as non-personal selling. It is that selling which is directed at a large number of potential customers.

Depending on the strategy and the philosophy of the company, advertising will vary greatly. It may be directed in support of a specific product, i.e., sale of a car or home. It may be the advertising of a major retailer trying to attract customers into their stores. On the other hand, it may be nothing more than institutional advertising, such as a major brokerage house trying to create an image of reliability.

Sales Promotion

Sales promotions are those marketing activities other than personal selling. These include special in-store displays, trade shows, national expositions, in-store demonstrations, discount coupons, and other types of giveaways. They are all keyed to building traffic and creating additional sales.

Personal Selling

This is where we depend on the good old salesperson. This might be an independent representative, a direct factory person, a door-to-door salesperson, or a salesperson in a department store. These, of course, are just a few examples of the different types of selling. A new area of personal selling that has developed in the last few years is that of telemarketing. Regardless of the type of sales force that is selected, the marketer should always remember to introduce a proper management structure to control the sales force. Many outstanding products and marketing programs have failed because the sales force was not properly directed and managed.

Public Relations

This area of the promotional mix is least understood both by the marketer and by the public. Public relations is the communication used by the marketer solely for the purpose of improving the image of the product being brought to the market. Public relations is often thought of as the unpaid press received in newspapers, magazines, and trade journals. You will often find this type of material in new-product areas in trade publications.

The public relations department is often the unsung hero. While public relation type of promotions are often perceived to be inexpensive, this is certainly not the case. The PR department in most sales-driven companies is a major part of the marketing budget.

As in the case of the marketing mix, there must be a careful blending of the different elements of the promotional mix. Many expensive mistakes can be avoided merely by observing the marketplace and learning how competitive products are being presented. This will often allow you to prioritize the various areas in the promotional mix.

With a properly developed marketing and promotional mix, we can now begin to develop our overall marketing strategy. You will see that while there seems to be a trend toward a hybrid or integrated approach between the push and pull marketing strategies, we will deal with their development individually. In this manner you will be better able to isolate those areas that are most pertinent to your product and select your strategy accordingly.

PUSH VERSUS PULL MARKETING

Pull/Push—Push/Pull

Does it sound like an athletic contest? Well, it might be. We spoke earlier about the sense of harmony required between the marketing and corporate goals. The finance, sales, marketing, and manufacturing departments all must understand their individual roles. They must orient themselves to a team play. If not, it can be just a contest between them with no winners, only losers.

The spoils of victory do not always go to the company that expends the greatest amount of dollars and resources. The victory will, in fact, go to the company that understands all the nuances of the push and pull strategies and then makes a total commitment, well thought out, with a clear definition of its marketing goals and objectives.

Goals and Objectives

The importance of the interdepartmental working relationship cannot be over-stressed. Management should set the goals and objectives for the corporation. These should include an acceptable return on investment as well as expected sales volume. Before we deal with the various elements, we should have clear definitions of the push and pull strategies.

PULL STRATEGY

Pull strategy is the promotional effort that the seller uses to influence the final user demand. The target of all the sales advertising and promotional activity is directed at the ultimate consumer. Direct sales or sales promotions are either in a subordinate position or a second-level integrated position. The marketer, in this case, structures a program that will create demand beforehand. This demand will then exert pressures on the many distribution channels to fill the void.

In its simplest form, the use of a pull strategy by the manufacturer is used to create demands for the product so that the end user, or consumer, will ask their favorite store to carry the product. The retailer is then forced to purchase the product, either directly from the manufacturer or through the distributor. In this manner, the product is pulled through the marketplace.

PUSH STRATEGY

Push strategy relies heavily on the direct sales approach. Here is the case where personal selling comes to the forefront. It is the responsibility of the sales force to carry the message to the marketplace through the various channels. Integral parts of the push strategy are promotional activities including trade discounts, cooperative advertising allowances, customer rebates, sales staff's spiffs, and point-of-purchase displays, to name a few.

In its simplest form, the product or service is sold by the sales person to and through the various channels. The product ultimately will reach the end consumer. While these two definitions and strategies are often presented as alternatives, the majority of marketers depend on elements of both in order to accomplish their marketing goals. While the pull strategy relies most heavily on advertising, and the push strategy relies more on personal selling, the two actually have many elements in common.

EVALUATING THE INFLUENCES OF THE MARKETPLACE

In order to understand better the development of the push or pull strategy, we will first review the elements in the market that influence your choice of strategy. All of them will affect the consumer's motivations for making the purchasing decision.

Information

The strategy must provide information to the marketplace. This information should allow the intermediate channels of distribution, or the ultimate consumer, to have sufficient grasp of the product or services in order to make an intelligent and, most important, comfortable decision.

Increased Demand

The result of all the expenditures must be an increase in demand in proportion to the dollars being spent. In other words, will the increased demand be consistent with the company's goals and objectives for their return on investment?

Market Perception of Product Differentiation

There must be a distinct differentiation between the product being promoted and introduced and that of the competition. There must be no doubt in the buyer's mind as to the features and benefits of the product being bought.

Development of Product Worth

There must be an increase in the user's mind as to the worth of the product. The user must feel that the dollars were expended judiciously.

Maintenance of Sales Position

The marketer must seek to maintain or improve current sales position as it relates to the marketplace. A foundation should be built that will allow the marketer to develop a secondary or, for that matter, a long-range strategy after the initial product introduction.

Defense of Position

The positioning of the product should have a built-in defense strategy, taking into account the fact that the competitors will enter the marketplace as soon as the product proves successful. (And sometimes even if it is not successful.)

Other Influences

In order to avoid misinterpretation and incorrectly set goals, every company should develop some degree of marketing data. Though data may be different from company to company, generally a few categories of information will be consistently helpful for all types of research. These are:

1. *Sales figures.* This is information that deals not only with gross dollar sales but with units sold. The information should be interpreted by national territories, market segment, type of customer, and end user.
2. *Financial data.* While it generally deals with a company's profit and loss statement and the goals for return on investment, it should be inclusive of data that will affect the selection of the push or pull approach. These include discounts, credit, freight policies, and promotional expenses.
3. *Inventory data.* Proper planning of inventory significantly determines the amount of capital required. This information should include inventory requirements for seasonal variations.

COMPETITIVE CLIMATE

The first question that the marketer has to ask is whether or not to compete. Are there comparable products currently existing in the marketplace? How are these products perceived by the end user? At what price level are they being sold? It must be remembered that regardless of the situation, competition creates a constant change in the marketplace.

In developing your research and market data, you should first determine how a comparable product has been offered to the marketplace. Has it been placed there through a push or pull strategy? Did the competition give sufficient consideration to the cost of the product information?

The company wishing to develop a pull demand for its product might have to sell at a higher price. Therefore, it must make a distinct differentiation in the product in the end user's mind and increase the product worth as well. Remember, regardless of the strategy of your competition, the end user must ultimately pay for the dollars being spent to promote the product.

A classic example of the competitive climate and how rapidly it changes can be seen by the introduction of consumer purchasing of telephones after the government divestiture of AT&T. The initial introduction of telephones placed heavy emphasis on promotional one-piece phones. At initial market introduction, the promotional phones were selling in the area of $25. Manufacturers and retailers soon started to vie with each other on the basis of price. Each hoped that by reducing their price, they would increase their market share. Little did they realize the size of the marketplace was not sufficient to support their increase in inventory levels. Within a period of a few short months the market deteriorated both for the manufacturer and the retailer. The retailer was able to buy a product for $6 that a few months earlier was being purchased for $12. They then found themselves selling the same product for $7 or less, rather than $25. The end result was that both the manufacturer and retailer lost money on the promotion and sales of the inexpensive phones. This example clearly illustrated what can happen in a short term in a highly competitive product classification. Promotion of one-piece telephones went from approximately 50 percent of unit market share to less than 5 percent in a six-month period. The manufacturers overproduced, the retailers overstocked, and neither one was able to realize a profit. The product dissipated itself in the marketplace.

ECONOMIC CLIMATE

What is the nature of the economic climate? What is the status of disposable income? What is the outlook for employment? Are savings up or down? In themselves, no one of these elements can determine whether or not to use the push or the pull strategy. Combined with the other factors, though, they should help reach a proper conclusion.

It should be remembered when looking at the economy that its performance is not consistent in all regions of our country. You must also recognize that the economy is cylical in its nature, following a traditional recession/depression recovery pattern. Too many companies allow a downturn of the economy to make a decision for them on the overall question of whether or not to introduce a product.

A perfect example of an upbeat industry during the 1980–83 recession was that of woodburning stoves, kerosene heaters, and woodcutting tools. In the midst of one of the country's most serious recessions, sales in these categories reached an all-time high. The consumer faced with higher energy costs looked to alternative means for heating the home. The sales of these product categories escalated rapidly. Unfortunately, many of the companies entering the arena did not take into consideration the severe competitive climate. Overproduction took place, the economy started to rebound, energy prices dropped, and the product lines fell into disfavor with the consumer.

CONSUMER CLIMATE

What is the nature of the consumer climate? How does the consumer review the product category you are presenting to the market? Has anything occurred that will make the consumer disillusioned about your product as compared to that being offered by the competition?

There are numerous psychological factors to consider when discussing consumer climate. Much of this has to do with positioning of the product, or placement of the product, in the marketplace as it relates to that of your competition. A good example of this would be the automobile industry during the recession in the early 80s. Domestic manufacturers refused to consider the fact that the consumer wanted a smaller, more economical care. They also did not recognize the swing toward quality. As a result of that, domestic manufacturers lost position in the marketplace for small and mid-sized cars to the Japanese and other importers.

PRODUCT COSTS

What will it take to promote or support the introduction of your product? The economic climate might be right, but the competition might be such that your costs of product prohibit you from using a large advertising campaign or, in that case, a pull strategy. A perfect example of this would be the recent air fare war between airlines after deregulation. The cost of service was ignored by many of the major airlines when they continued a strong pull strategy to gain market share. As a result of this poor definition of market strategy and cost control, many of the airlines lost huge sums of money, and others like Braniff and Continental entered bankruptcy proceedings.

ADVERTISING COSTS

Advertising in the aggregate is the most expensive means of promotion. While there is a lack of good data on advertising costs for all related products, you can be sure that the costs are significant and, as a rule, difficult for the smaller companies to finance. Considerable dollars must be spent up front in order to create demand before the products start to be pulled through the marketplace.

Manufacturers must take into consideration the restricted use of advertising funds to be applied only to specific geographic areas. After the product begins to gain marketshare, additional funds can be made available. The end goal is the reduction of advertising per cost of unit.

The cost of the product has the same relationship and problems in the push strategy as it does in the pull strategy. As a rule, the direct sales contact can run anywhere from 5 percent to 20 percent. Many manufacturers have chosen to sell through independent representatives, where they can have a fixed cost of selling and eliminate the sales expense of recruiting and training. Whether you choose push or pull, the cost of the product will directly relate to the strategy you choose.

THE PRODUCT LIFE CYCLE

Products go through various life cycles. As with most human beings, they go through introduction (birth) to an early growth phase, reach a goal of maturation, and finally move into a period of decline and death.

The promotional strategies will vary depending on the stage of the life cycle. When introducing a new product or concept to the marketplace, the marketer must first make the consumer comfortable with the product classification itself. A consumer has to be comfortable with the fact that they are buying a garbage disposal, a personal computer, or laser beam recorder. The marketplace must be told that the product category exists. The marketer must provide information to help the consumer recognize the category's worth.

As the product moves through its various stages of growth, the marketer will consider the areas of competition, economic climate, cost of product, and advertising costs of product life cycle. A proper analysis of these influences will help to determine which strategy will be most effective.

SELECTING YOUR STRATEGY

Push Strategy

In order to effectively utilize the background material that we have developed thus far, we will use an actual product and relate it to the elements of the marketing and promotional mix in developing our push strategy. We will then take that same product and develop a pull strategy. For present purposes, we will choose a national manufacturer of faucets and plumbing-related products. You will see how the company and its strategy changes when presenting the product in a push strategy versus a pull strategy. We will call the company Samsco Faucet Manufacturing Company.

Samsco was already a major manufacturing producer of faucets for the traditional builder trade. Their product was being sold through plumbing wholesalers to the plumber. The product was very often listed as a specification on residential and commercial construction. Samsco recognized that there was a developing market for their product to the do-it-yourselfer. The cost of installation from a traditional plumber had escalated. An analysis of the market had indicated that the average consumer was not only capable of making the installation of the faucet but was also desirous of doing so.

How were they to attack this market? Would the sales of a new product hurt their old line and existing customer base? Top management and marketing were in agreement: if this new market could be tapped without hurting their existing customer base, then they should proceed. The first area that had to be dealt with was the development of their criteria.

Information. The consumer had to have enough information in order to make a comfortable decision. This was done through the development of an elaborate package. The package clearly showed the product and listed the features and benefits. It told the consumer that it was easy to install with a minimal number of tools. The product was given the Good Housekeeping seal of approval, and a detailed installation instruction booklet came with every faucet.

It was obvious that Samsco already had a major share of the market. There had to be a justification for all the dollars being spent. Could they, in fact, increase their market share by introducing the new do-it-yourself faucet?

Making the Product Differentiation. In this case, Samsco would be the major competitor for this new faucet. While there were any number of competitors in the marketplace, Samsco saw itself as its own competition. In order to avoid any confusion on the consumer's part and any animosity from its existing customer base, Samsco decided to give the product a new name. They called the new faucet line Paragon Faucets.

Development of the Product Worth. This new product would cost the consumer more. The new faucet had special packaging, installation instructions, and a built-in advertising allowance for the retailer. It would be necessary for Paragon to make the consumer feel that their dollars were well spent. Much of this was accomplished in the package itself. It was the first faucet to have the Good Housekeeping seal of approval. This along with an unlimited warranty for the consumer helped to launch the product.

Maintenance of Sales Position. As we stated earlier, Samsco wanted to make sure that its existing leadership position in the faucet industry would not be damaged by the introduction of a new faucet line. Thus, they made the decision to call the faucet Paragon. As part of the strategy, the initial SKU's product offer was a limited one. It was the intention of the marketing department to offer additional faucets from the existing Samsco line as the public accepted the Paragon line.

Marketing Considerations

Now that the basic corporate objectives were established, the marketing department had to review their areas of consideration.

Competitive Climate. The competitive climate at the time appeared favorable for the introduction of a new product. There was no product line being offered by the competition solely for the do-it-yourselfer. While traditional products were being offered by the competitors to retail hardware outlets and mass merchandisers, the packaging and presentation of these products detracted from their potential sales.

Economic Climate. The economic climate at the time was strong, personal income was up, and consumers were spending money on the improvement of their homes. The determination was also made that even in a down economy, the Paragon do-it-yourself faucet line would be a winner.

Consumer Climate. Fortunately, or unfortunately as one might view it, there had been no history of a similar product introduction. The only time that a consumer could have been disillusioned by the purchase of a faucet was with the difficulty of installation, not the quality. It was felt that proper packaging and product modification would overcome these objections.

Product Costs. In order to develop a product that the consumer could install, it was necessary to add installation fittings that would allow the consumer to make the installation easier. While Samsco, the parent company, had already developed maximum manufacturing efficiencies, they could not eliminate the additional cost for packaging the Good Housekeeping seal and the installation booklets. Considering the fact that there was no direct competition for a similar product, increases in the product cost were not considered a major obstacle.

Considering that there was no existing sales base, corporate decided not to develop a strong advertising campaign. The majority of advertising funds was allocated to trade journal publications, highly effective literature showing the product, and a specific advertising allowance for each faucet purchased.

Product Life Cycle. An analysis of the product life cycle indicated that there should not be any strong cyclical variations or, for that fact, the traditional cycle of introduction to decline. In fact, the contrary was very evident. Once consumers recognized the category worth of do-it-yourself faucets, they would, in fact, begin to replace other faucets in their house as the need arose.

With the objectives developed and the considerations fully analyzed, it was obvious to Paragon that a push marketing strategy would be in order. The task at hand now was to develop the proper marketing mix.

Product Planning. It was obvious that corporate management and the marketing departments were in complete harmony and the strategy was in place. Paragon was going to offer the first truly do-it-yourself faucet that would guarantee the consumer a trouble-free installation with a fully guaranteed product. The existing Samsco product was modified so that the exterior of the faucet did not resemble that of the Samsco division. Product development costs were kept to a minimum inasmuch as the interior mechanisms were only slightly changed from the Samsco product.

Pricing. It was determined that pricing of the faucet would, of course, be higher than the Samsco product because of the packaging, product change, and advertising.

Promotional Strategy. The first decision confronting Paragon was that of selecting a sales force. The initial strategy was to use the existing Samsco sales force, who were already familiar with the company's products and policies. This strategy quickly proved to be ineffective. There was an obvious conflict of interest on the part of the Samsco sales staff. They were concerned about injuring their relationship with their existing customer base. Consequently, they did not properly present the product. The decision was made to select and train a new sales staff who would be oriented toward consumer products.

The advertising portion of the promotional strategy was initially limited to a fixed dollar amount to be used on a cooperative basis with the customer.

There were to be two major sales promotions over the course of a year, where the consumer was offered free merchandise packed in with the faucet. Depending upon the free goods being offered, the promotions had varying degrees of success.

Distribution. The final factor for consideration was the development of channel distribution. The traditional Samsco customer base was the plumbing and heating contractor. The Samsco product that had found its way to the consumer was channeled there through the traditional hardware wholesaler.

The decision was made to sell the product directly to the retailer. After analyzing the cost of the product, it was determined that traditional two-step distribution would add considerably to the cost of the product and deter potential sales.

After reviewing the various elements of the marketing mix, Paragon was ready to put in place a strong push marketing program relying most heavily on their promotional strategy. In order to understand the unprecedented success of this program, we will now look at the promotional mix as it evolved.

Promotional Mix

Sales Department. Heavy emphasis was placed on the selection and training of independent representatives. The sales department conducted an extensive series of interviews and selected representative organizations that were already familiar with the potential customer base. These organizations were thoroughly trained in product knowledge and habits of the potential consumer. The initial commission structure given to these newly appointed representatives was considerably higher than the industry average, 5 percent.

Tremendous pressure was applied to these sales organizations for a significant commitment of time and energy. The sales department decided that an organization of highly trained and skilled independent representatives would allow them to make maximum market penetration at a fixed cost. The sister company, Samsco, had been successful with this approach, and they felt that they could repeat that success story. Each salesperson was supplied with sample kits and point-of-purchase display material. Strong support literature and audiovisual presentations were developed.

Promotions. Up to that point, there was no history of any competitor offering any type of promotions to the marketplace. The question was how to go to market without disturbing the pricing integrity of the product. As indicated earlier, major promotions were developed whereby the consumer was given free goods, which had a perceived value, packed in with each faucet. These promotions included everything from free aerators to fishing lures. There are, of course, many other potential promotions that could be developed for this type of product. The key here, of course, is to develop what we call *dealer loading*. This is a classical part of the push promotional strategy.

Cooperative Advertising. A sound co-op program is an integral part of every push marketing strategy. The retailer today is demanding significantly greater ad contributions from the manufacturer. At the time the Paragon faucet was introduced, there was really no comparable program. The program that was developed and the allocation of funds, while it was on a fixed amount per faucet, related to a variation of 2 to 3 percent. Heavy pressure was placed on the sales staff to make sure the customer advertised the product. Utilization of advertising funds was one of the methods in which the sales organization was measured.

Price Discounts. As was the case with Paragon, the manufacturer must always consider the level at which price discounts must be offered in order to give incentives to the customer to buy the product in maximum quantities. Paragon developed a three-tier pricing, allowing the retail dealer to buy maximum price for small quantities. The thought process here was to allow for direct shipment to the individual stores rather than penalizing those dealers that did not have central warehouse locations.

Packaging. As related earlier, Paragon developed the first package for the do-it-yourself faucet. Strong packaging is more vital in the push marketing strategy than it is in the pull. While most manufacturers have sophisticated packaging regardless of the method with which they go to market, it is truly essential in push marketing. The package must clearly identify the product for the consumer and list all of the features and benefits. The consumer must clearly understand the differences between the product and its competitors and have a sense of value about the purchase.

Point-of-Purchase Material. Point-of-purchase material has become more important than ever for retail sellers. With less help available on the sales floor, it is important for the consumer to make an intelligent and comfortable purchase. While the product packaging is important, strong point-of-purchase displays are an essential ingredient for a successful program.

Paragon introduced the first faucet displays in the do-it-yourself faucet industry. Basic product was shown on a plush, carpeted display. The product was clearly identified, with a feature and benefit listing on the front of the display unit. A major part of the success of the Paragon program was attributed to the early development of faucet displays.

Education. Push marketing strategy often requires a strong educational program for the sales personnel at the retail level. Paragon Faucet Company went to great expense to have the most thoroughly trained sales organization. This sales organization was supplied with complete audiovisual presentations to be shown at the store level to the store personnel. A reporting method was developed to evaluate each training session and its effectiveness. While a knowledgeable sales force is helpful in the pull strategy, it is certainly more important in the push strategy.

While the above elements of the promotional strategy were used by Paragon, others are equally effective in today's marketplace. There are:

Rebates. Consumer rebates have become a strong element in the push marketing strategy. Most manufacturers anticipate that they will have no more than a 10 percent rebate redemption, therefore giving them more bounce to the ounce in terms of the advertising that the retailer gives them when using the rebate program. Products offering rebates generally wind up in a high area of visibility in the store.

Coupons. Coupons have also proven to be effective in creating consumer demand for the product. Most often this gives the product an advantageous position in the store. Retailers will tend to put coupons at check-out registers or on endcap displays.

Sweepstakes. Sweepstakes have become another popular method of promoting goods. The sweepstakes offered generally have high individual values enticing the consumer to purchase that particular product or brand of product.

Dating. As indicated earlier, a strong element in the push strategy is dealer loading. This is often accomplished by deep discounts, tied in with dating programs. This gives the manufacturer the ability to ship products early, making sure the customer has ample products on the shelves for the end user. Consideration here has to be given to the significant cost of money in today's marketplace.

As you can see, the push marketing strategy relies most heavily on the sales promotion activities in order to get products into the end user's hands. All of the ingredients are essential to the successful implementation of a push marketing strategy. It should also be remembered that corporate management and marketing must have a strong definition of their marketing objectives if they are to succeed.

Pull Strategy

The development of the pull strategy, which places heavy emphasis on advertising, is certainly more glamorous than its sister, push strategy. While the same sequence of events must take place for the determination of the pull strategy, there is generally more emphasis placed on advertising as opposed to the direct sales contact.

The problem with many companies when developing the pull strategy is a tendency to de-emphasize the importance of the salesperson, rather than blending it into the advertising program.

To better understand some of these concepts, let's continue with Paragon Faucet Company and see what happens when a sales company starts to evolve into a marketing company. You will see a decisive change in the marketing strategy. Instead of all of the pressure being placed on the sales organization to push their product through the market, the emphasis is now changed to a strong national advertising program that will create demand for the product by the consumer, pulling it through the marketplace. Now the sales staff no longer has to introduce the concept of do-it-yourself faucets to the customer but rather must make sure that the channels are full of product in order to satisfy the demands of the consumer.

Objectives—Information. Inasmuch as the consumer is already aware of the Paragon product in the product category, the dissemination of information to the consumer is no longer top priority. The information that does pass through the channels of distribution is more in the form of public relations.

Increase Demands. The main thrust of the new strategy by Paragon Faucet is to increase demand for the product. Even with the significant increase in the advertising budget to be spent through the medium of TV, the increase in market share and units sold would justify the expense. The target is to have 50 percent of market share.

Product Differentiation. In the pull strategy, the Paragon Faucet Company has a new adversary. The Samsco product produced by its sister company is no longer the major consideration. Now that Paragon has evolved into the leader of the faucet business, there have been a number of other product entries. The Paragon Faucet Company must now make a distinct differentiation between its faucet and its competitors'. It then embarks on a new program called hands-free installation, telling the consumer that their faucet is easier to install.

Development of Product Worth. By means of this strong advertising program, Paragon creates in the mind of the consumer the idea that the product is worth more than that offered by its competitors. In this way it also conditions buyers for the retail outlets to think positively about the product.

Maintenance of Sales Position. Through the new pull strategy a foundation is now being built that will allow Paragon to develop their long-range strategy. This strategy includes introducing related plumbing products to tie in with the sale of Paragon faucets.

Competitive Climate. One of the main factors that led Paragon to decide on a pull marketing strategy was the increase in competition. It was necessary to reach the ultimate consumer influence. The competition was going directly to the buyers, offering strong incentive deals, cutting prices, and giving other incentives in order to have that buyer replace the Paragon faucet line. To insure their position, Paragon went to the consumer to create demand for the product. In this case, the increased competition was a stimulus for developing the pull strategy.

Economic Climate. At the time the pull strategy was introduced, the economy was in a serious recession. Residential and commercial construction was off significantly. Management saw this as an opportunity to increase the sale of their faucets to the do-it-yourselfer, hopefully making up any short fall in sales and production through their more traditional Samsco line.

Consumer Climate. The consumer was obviously receptive to cost savings. The fact that they could buy a faucet and install it themselves, saving anywhere from $50 to $100 for the plumber's charge, was incentive enough. Paragon reached the consumer and told them the story.

Product Cost. Paragon did not have any significant changes in product costs. Minor improvements in the product were not reflected in increased costs. As a matter of fact, increased production of efficiency allowed them to hold the price line, putting profit pressure on the competition.

Advertising Costs. It was determined that advertising was going to be the most expensive part of the promotional program. An analysis of the projected sales increase determined that there would be a sufficient increase in product to absorb the increased advertising cost.

The Marketing Mix—Product Planning. Paragon felt that one of the ways to expand its customer base was to expand its product offering. Its initial product line would be its middle pricing point. It then developed an introductory pricing point of promotional faucets and a more expensive series of designer faucets. It was felt that with these new lines of product available, there would be a faucet for every consumer's need.

In developing this product plan in the market mix, Paragon was able to concentrate its pull strategy on presenting the Paragon easy-to-install faucet as opposed to a specific product within its line.

Pricing. Consistent with the development of their new product lines, Paragon had the ability to establish a new pricing strategy. By developing the concept of a good, better, best, and deluxe line, they were able to maintain the pricing integrity of their product. While they certainly could not ignore the competition, the pull strategy removed some of the price sensitivity at the point of retail. Price cutting was not the word: quality and reliability were.

Distribution. The initial channels of distribution remained unchanged. The majority of the product continued to be sold directly to the retailer. While a two-step distribution did become a factor, it did not replace the initial strategy of the direct sale.

Promotional Strategy. The role of the direct salesperson significantly changed in the pull strategy. By this time the Paragon faucet was well established in the marketplace. The salesperson was no longer the educator. The role became one of maintaining the company's position in the marketplace and introducing new additions to the product lines. Along with this, it was the sales force's responsibility to make sure that the buyers at the retail level clearly understood Paragon's commitment to their advertising program, which would create demand for their product at the consumer level.

As we noted before, the pull strategy cannot rely solely on the advertising campaign. Many of the same promotional elements used in the push strategy are utilized for the pull strategy. They will vary, however. Let's take a look at Paragon's strategy.

Price Discounts. Paragon again maintained the same sales posture. There were volume discounts offered to the retailer. In addition to the traditional retail discounts, there were volume incentive rebates offered for two levels of volume purchases. The new increase in demand enabled many of the previous customers to enjoy these larger discounts. Paragon, therefore, realized cost efficiencies in shipping and production.

Dating. Dating did not seem to be a major consideration. The turn of the product as related to the volume requirements for max discounts were good enough so that there was not heavy pressure placed on the factory to offer dating programs. Many companies do utilize dating programs, however, to insure that there is sufficient product in the marketplace as the consumer demand develops.

Rebates. A strong rebate program was developed to tie in with the heavy TV advertising and magazine promotions. Two major promotions were offered during the year, giving consumers significant rebates on their purchases. The manufacturer must be extremely careful in the development of a rebate program, as it can adversely affect the profit picture. In this particular case, Paragon incorrectly measured the impact of the rebate program on the market. The redemption was considerably higher than the industry average.

Cooperative Advertising. Paragon continues to maintain a strong cooperative advertising program, even with their pull strategy. This is a case where success feeds success. The more faucets the retailer sold, the more advertising funds they accumulated, and the more they tended to advertise their product. This was a by-product of the pull strategy which is generally ignored by many manufacturers. There is a tendency to believe that you can take the dollars out of the cooperative advertising program and put them into your TV program. The truth is that a successful pull program should also have a strong cooperative advertising program.

Point-of-Purchase Materials. The expansion of product required a change in the point-of-purchase displays. As the product line expanded, Paragon found it necessary to develop a flexible display program. The product mix was virtually different for every customer purchasing the product line. The point-of-purchase program was so successful that it was actually enlarged to support the pull strategy.

As you can see, the Paragon Faucet Company evolved from a sales-oriented company using a push strategy (with a heavy emphasis on the sales force) to a marketing company emphasizing a pull strategy (using advertising and support by the sales organization).

The key to successful use of either push or pull strategies lies in the clear definition of company objectives. If the corporate mission has been properly communicated and its parameters clearly defined, you're guaranteed to have a better return on your dollars expended.

5

INDUSTRIAL MARKETING

by
Thomas C. Jones CMC

Tom Jones and Company, Inc.

DEFINING INDUSTRIAL DISTRIBUTION: ITS IMPORTANCE AND COMPONENTS

Why Are both Choosing and Managing the Channels Critical?

Effective performance of your distribution channel builds strong customer loyalty and repeat business, your economic life's blood. As Theodore Levitt, Edward W. Carter Professor of Business Administration at the Harvard Business School, says,

> The relationship between a seller and a buyer seldom ends when a sale is made. Increasingly, the relationship intensifies after the sale and helps determine the buyer's choice the next time around. Such dynamics are found particularly with services and products dealt in a stream of transactions between seller and buyer—financial services, consulting, general contracting, military and space equipment, and capital goods.[1]

Corporate direction and strategy are implemented by the sales, marketing, and physical operations. Industrial distribution systems take years to establish or change and, as a result, such changes are difficult and costly to implement.

Take a quick, self-administered test. The key factors to consider when choosing your type of distribution are presented in Figure 5–1. Simply place an asterisk (*) in the column which most closely matches

---

[1] Theodore Levitt, "After the Sale Is over . . . ," *Harvard Business Review*, September–October 1983, p. 87.

FIGURE 5–1 Which Distribution System Is Right for You?

Rank your business unit on a scale of 1 to 5. The correct choice will become graphically clear.

	Direct 1	2	Mixed 3	4	Indirect 5	
	100–0 percent	75–25 percent	50 percent	25–75 percent	0–100 percent	
Technical product						Standard product
Long lead time						Next-day delivery
National service						Local service
Few large customers						Many small customers
Negotiated bid						Routine rebuy
Complex buying process						Simple buying process
High dollar volume/ sales call						Low dollar volume/ sales call
High dollar potential/territory						Low dollar potential/territory
Poor brand recognition						Strong brand recognition
Financially strong						Financially weak
High/low market share						Medium market market share
Direct industry practices						Indirect industry practice
Weak middlemen available						Strong middlemen available

your operation/product line's place on the ranking for each of the opposite pairs.

If most of the asterisks are under the *direct* column, then *direct* should be the appropriate choice. Most companies have *mixed* distribution: *direct* salespersons or company branches in areas with a high concentration of potential market and *indirect* elsewhere. Very strong management is required to set and enforce the policies necessary to obtain optimum results from the mixed channel. We advise choosing either direct or indirect whenever possible.

Do you have the distribution system that's right for you? Is it yielding the results you expect?

The Small Company with the Right Distribution Channel and the Wrong Market Share

After 10 years of dedicated effort, this company with a premium-priced restaurant equipment line had less than 5 percent of market share. A detailed study of the successful versus the unsuccessful sales representatives established the following critical factors:

- There was predatory pricing by the market leader: low on directly competitive models and 20–30 percent higher on other sizes.
- Unsuccessful salespeople were selling on price rather than benefits.
- Successful salespeople were highly motivated and *were* selling benefits.
- There were few first-rate distributors; however, most had the potential for improvement.

Now management had a series of subproblems which could be addressed in order of importance. In this case, improvement in market share resulted from sales training, sales motivation with monetary incentives, and selective price changes. *Analysis = Commitment of resources = Dramatic results.*

What Is the Industrial Buyer's Problem, and What Complicates the Buying Process?

The industrial buyer—your customer—has a large problem. Even in relatively mature industries, the buyer is faced with rapidly changing technology or design, a wide variety of choices, and poor end user–seller communications. Industrial products are frequently conceived on an engineer's drawing board with limited customer input. Salespeople are given their bags and pushed out the door. Customer service is often based on the squeaky wheel principle. There is often a damaging lack of clear, concise communication.

When your product claims are greeted with skepticism by the marketplace, selling and distributing costs become inflated. Industrial buyers must spend valuable hours searching for a product and frequently settle for something which only partially satisfies actual needs and wants.

The solution? The much advocated, rarely practiced (for industrial products) marketing concept. According to Hill, Alexander, and Cross,

> *Begin with the needs of the ultimate end user.* This means that the properties with which industrial products and services are endowed, *together with their distribution* and promotion, should be *derived from the businesses, government bodies, and institutions to be served rather than be conceived for them.*[2]

Excellent companies are close to their customers, and yet this is one of the management fundamentals being ignored today. As Thomas J. Peters and Robert H. Waterman, Jr. stated in *In Search of Excellence,*

> That a business ought to be close to its customers seems a benign enough message. So the question arises, why does a chapter like this [Close to the Customer] need to be written at all? The answer is that, despite all the lip service given to the market orientation these days, . . . the customer is either ignored or considered a bloody nuisance.[3]

Complexity of the industrial buying process reflects these factors:

- Formal organization.
- Number of persons involved.
- Technical and economic factors to be considered.
- Environment in which the firm operates.
- Large sums of money involved.

The Sheth model of industrial buyer behavior, Figure 5–2, summarizes the decision processes of industrial buyers. It focuses on the buyers' expectations, perceptions, and perceived risk.

Many individuals other than the purchasing agent influence the industrial buying decision. Backgrounds, information sources, and satisfaction with past purchases influence the decision; and "different

[2] Richard M. Hill, Ralph S. Alexander, and James S. Cross, *Industrial Marketing,* 4th ed. (Homewood, Ill.: Richard D. Irwin, 1975), p. 16.

[3] Thomas J. Peters and Robert A. Waterman, Jr., In Search of Excellence (New York: 1982), p. 156.

FIGURE 5–2 Sheth Model of Industrial Buyer Behavior

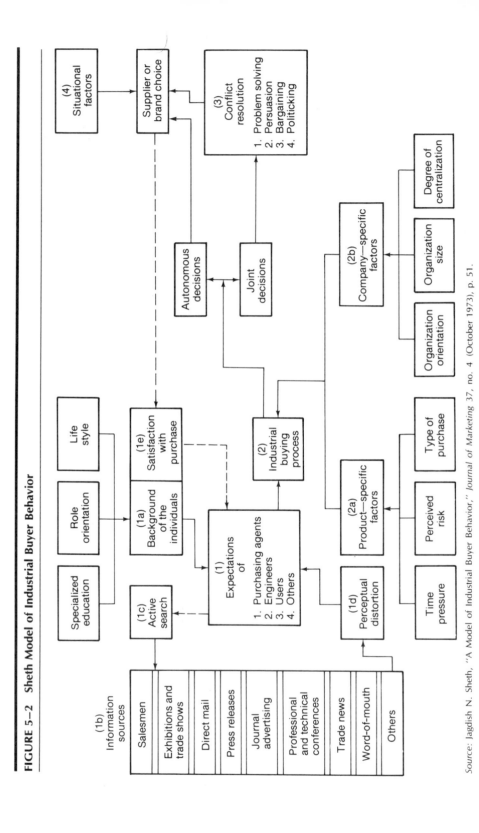

Source: Jagdish N. Sheth, "A Model of Industrial Buyer Behavior," *Journal of Marketing* 37, no. 4 (October 1973), p. 51.

participants use different buying criteria and rate alternative vendors differently. *For example, production personnel are likely to emphasize delivery time and reliability. Engineering personnel are likely to focus on product quality variables, and purchasing personnel are likely to emphasize reliability and price.*"[4]

What influences the level at which a purchasing decision is made?

- Its importance to the customer's organization (summarized in Figure 5–3).
- The class of product.
- Its application.
- Its relative price.

FIGURE 5–3
Who Makes Industrial Buying Decisions? Many Influencers, Few Decision Makers

Decision-Making Level	Importance of Purchase to Corporation		
	High	Medium	Low
President/general manager	Decide	Influence	—
Chief engineer/plant manager	Influence	Decide	—
Project engineer	Influence	Influence	Decide initial purchase
Maintenance manager	Influence	Influence	Decide
Material manager	Influence	Influence	Influence
Purchasing agent	Implement	Implement	Decide routine purchase

Construction of a new plant will usually have board of director's approval for the overall project and the commitment of funds. The major production equipment vendor may be selected by the senior managers and the CEO. However, routine items such as raw materials and maintenance supplies are frequently chosen by a purchasing agent assigned to a particular commodity. Detailed performance criterion and financial analyses affect this decision. Finally, the purchasing de-

---

[4] Frederick E. Webster, Jr., *Industrial Marketing Strategy* (New York: John Wiley & Sons, 1979), pp. 30–31.

partment administers the paperwork and handles the buying process for most of the items purchased.

The Buyer and the Seller—Who's Leading the Dance?

If you are an aware industrial marketer, you know that customers (end users) can be more than sales. They can be quasipartners (or antagonists) in many areas of the industrial manufacturing and distribution picture.

When are buyers dependent on suppliers? When they need assured supplies of raw materials, components, and subassemblies. When they require continued supplies of repair parts and skilled repair service for capital equipment. When they want efficient order handling, delivery, and credit.

How can the sellers doubly profit from their buyers? When they are aided in end user demand by advertising, such as the Sea Island Cotton Growers advertising the ''rediscovery of cotton'' or Du Pont advertising synthetic fibers. When they are given annual contracts, guaranteeing certain sales for certain discounts. Gould Pumps, for example, has utilized the annual contract as an effective competitive weapon in their drive for market leadership.

When can conflict enter into the relationship? At any one of these points, plus others.

Recognize that industrial marketing is, in this way, very different from consumer marketing. It can prod you into building that knowledge into your industrial distribution system so that both you and your buyers benefit.

If Sellers Are Doing the Proper Job, They Are Leading the Dance. As Theodore Levitt writes, ''The sale merely consummates the courtship, at which point the marriage begins. How good the marriage is depends on how well the seller manages the relationship.''[5]

What Are Today's Trends?

Individual Wholesaler Distributors Now Have Strong Incentives to Grow. Why? Larger operations have higher productivity and lower costs when managed to take advantage of marketplace changes. Failure to innovate has led to poor results and acquisition by strong operators seeking new territories.

---

[5] Levitt, ''After the Sale,'' p. 87.

Consolidation of industrial distribution was well established by 1976. Thirteen publically traded chains were identified then by *Management Practice,* a publication of Management Practice Consulting Partners. Among them were Associated Spring Corporation, with 14 warehouses in the United States and Canada; Bearings, Inc., with 130 distribution centers; and W. W. Granger, Inc., with 131 branches.

There Is Pressure to Reduce the Cost of Selling and Distributing. It is continuing and intensifying. The average cost to close a sale, according to Edward Flanagan of the Sales Executives' Club of New York, is over $900 and varies widely depending on the number of calls per day and calls to close. As a result, indirect channels are now growing faster than the overall economy, and this trend is expected to continue into the next decade.

Technology Is Creating Opportunities to Improve Service and Reduce Costs. Microcomputer-based systems are among the latest innovations and include telemarketing, teleconferencing, and on-line ordering systems.

New Value-Added Services Are also Providing Growth Opportunities for Wholesaler Distributors. New types of industrial selling and distributing organizations are being formed to sell systems rather than components. In the power transmission industry increased sophistication in electronic control systems has created a void. Medium-sized manufacturers of durable goods may need advanced control system engineering. To be competitive they need the latest and the best, but they can't afford the technical talent. The manufacturers of sensors which detect motion, heat, and light are generally small operations and are not able to provide detailed customer engineering assistance. The solution is the specialist sales organization, distributor, or representative which engineers and selects the components that will best meet the OEM customer's requirements.

WHAT IS INDUSTRIAL DISTRIBUTION?

Industrial distribution includes both physical distribution and the marketing channel. Physical distribution involves the physical flow and inventory of your product. The marketing channel includes the individuals, organizations, and middlemen who buy, sell, and service the product as it moves from you to the ultimate end user. Note our use of *ultimate end user—industrial marketers often mistakenly consider the distributor or OEM to be the customer.* Actually, they are only intermediaries in the channel. The successful marketer satisfies the needs and wants of the ultimate end users and takes the time and effort necessary to know them.

WHAT ARE THE 10 FUNCTIONS PERFORMED IN THE DISTRIBUTION CHANNEL?

These functions, which must be performed regardless of the type of channel, are presented in Figure 5–4. The efficiency with which distributors or selling organizations implement these functions determines their viability in the marketplace and the profitability of distributorships/organizations.

FIGURE 5–4
10 Functions Performed in Distribution

Selling

Transporting

Market intelligence gathering

Assorting

Financing

Storing/inventorying

Risk taking

Installing

Servicing

Buying

The channel itself is summarized in Figure 5–5. The product physically moves from manufacturer to end user through warehouses, distribution points or distributors, and OEM manufacturers. Depending upon frequency of purchase, size of the market, local stock, and service requirements, the product moves either directly from manufacturer to end user or through one or more independently owned intermediaries. Let's take a look at some of the major functions in the channel.

Buying and Selling

Buying is done at all levels of the channel including: distributor/wholesaler, dealer/installer, OEM manufacturer, and end user. Selling is done at most of these levels plus at the sales rep or agent level. Large companies frequently employ direct field salespeople who work with the distributors, dealers, OEM manufacturers, and ultimate end users.

FIGURE 5–5
The Marketing and Physical Distribution Channels

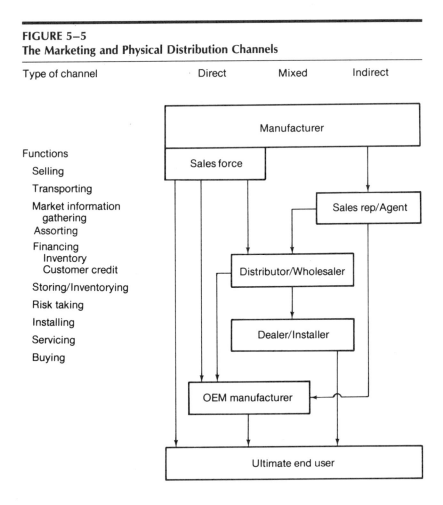

Type of channel   · Direct   Mixed   Indirect

Functions
- Selling
- Transporting
- Market information gathering
- Assorting
- Financing
  Inventory
  Customer credit
- Storing/Inventorying
- Risk taking
- Installing
- Servicing
- Buying

Manufacturer
Sales force
Sales rep/Agent
Distributor/Wholesaler
Dealer/Installer
OEM manufacturer
Ultimate end user

In smaller organizations, the sales manager and the assistant sales manager work closely with the sales representatives, who in turn work with these customers. *Good results require hands-on channel management by the manufacturer.*

Market Information Gathering

This is a difficult and sensitive issue. The direct organization has the ability to require salespeople to fill out call reports and provide timely market insights. Indirect organizations such as sales representatives are interested in activities with near-term payoff. Well-managed marketing companies utilize their staffs to assess the market.

Assorting

This is the assembly of a full line of merchandise to be sold to a particular class of customers. Capital equipment manufacturers may sell all the component parts for the installation of a compressor station. In other cases, the customer plus an architect and an engineering firm select the machinery and equipment from a variety of suppliers. In the welding equipment industry a distributor carries a wide range of Linde or Airco bottled gas, torches, welding guns, power supplies, and accessories provided by a primary supplier, plus Lincoln arc welding machines, TWECO torches, and other items manufactured by established specialty manufacturers.

Financing

Manufacturers may provide floor plan programs or own the finished goods inventories. Some wholesalers and dealers provide trade credit financing. The final sale to the end user is financed through third-party leasing arrangements as in the computer field, or by credit provided by the manufacturer's financial subsidiary organization.

Financing is an area of intense wheeling and dealing, and each industry has its own practices. In the hand tool industry, the distributors give customers only terms which are financed by the manufacturers. In the heating equipment and building supplies industries, distributors finance credit to contractors and dealers.

Installation and Servicing

The performance of after-sale work is critical to the reputation of the manufacturer and often determines who gets the next order. Modern marketing organizations like Pitney-Bowes are exploring a variety of new ways to utilize the service and installation functions available in their distribution channel. Among the alternatives explored are:

- Contracts with third parties.
- Utilizing service personnel to obtain leads for the sales organization.
- Computerized scheduling and dispatching programs.
- Modular products which can be easily serviced by the end user or quickly serviced by the technician.

One recently developed service concept in welding is the throwaway TIG torch. Parts replicators were copying the replacement parts in the torches of one manufacturer. The answer was to build a torch that required few or no spare parts and that could be inexpensively replaced. Detailed surveys of end users (welders) showed that they welcomed that idea. Parts replicators are a particularly thorny and expensive channel issue, and there are no easy answers. Efficient parts service at competitive prices is a difficult goal for many manufacturers to achieve.

The organization in the channel assigned to perform each service is shown in Figure 5–5. Such assignments will depend on the 10 factors presented in Figure 5–4.

Well-Designed Marketing Channels Make the Trade-Offs Necessary to Get Each of the Functions Performed Efficiently

In a direct-to-the-end-user channel, the manufacturer assumes most of the responsibility. Some functions, such as financing and assorting, may be left to the customer. The manufacturer may leave the performance of all the functions to the end user (e.g., platform pick-up) when the product is picked up at the factory by the customer who pays cash upon receipt.

In the indirect industrial channel, the middlemen perform many or all of the functions. They are cost effective because they spread the selling and administrative costs over two or more manufacturers. Where significant technical expertise is required and the unit of sale is relatively large, the manufacturer's representative or agent may perform customer communications functions similar to those performed by the company's direct salespeople.

WHAT ARE THE FIELD SALES OPTIONS?

You, the industrial marketer, have three sales organization choices:

- Direct salespeople.
- Sales representatives or agents.
- Stocking distributors.

Direct salespeople are employed by the manufacturers. They normally do not represent any products not manufactured or distributed by their employers.

Sales representatives or agents are independent businesspeople or sales organizations. They may represent two or more noncompeting manufacturers with products sold to the same group of customers. They do not take title to the product and are generally utilized for product lines which need sophisticated technical information and engineering in order to compete.

Stocking distributors are independent businesspeople. They take title to the product, stock it, and sell through their local sales force and/or dealers. Sales representatives in industrial supplies (and in other industries which require local availability for products, repair parts, and service) will sign up and manage a group of stocking distributors in their geographical territories.

Seven factors, summarized in Figures 5–6 and 5–7, govern which type of distribution to choose. Many factors affect this judgment. Technical products tend to be sold directly, and standard products indirectly. Most products are in between, and the channel choice question is, "Are we closer to a technical product or a standard product?" Mixed systems, *both* direct and indirect, should be avoided if possible.

**FIGURE 5–6
Direct or Indirect? Which
Organization Does the Job?**

Seven key factors

End user/customer requirements

Nature of the product

Size of the market

Competitive practices

Company's competitive position
in the industry

Size of business unit

Middleman availability

**FIGURE 5–7
Which Organization in the Channel Performs the Channel Functions?**

	Selection Criteria	Direct Sales	Sales Reps/Agents	Distributors/ Dealers
1.	End user/customer requirements			
	Customized and engineered features	Direct	Use as "bird dog"	n.a.
	Off-shelf, standard product		Indirect	Indirect
	Customer service	Critical and highly technical		Local rapid · response

FIGURE 5–7 (concluded)

Selection Criteria	Direct Sales	Sales Reps/Agents	Distributors/Dealers
2. Nature of product			
Capital equipment	Large and infrequent purchase		Small and frequent purchase
Component parts and supplies	Large customers		Small customers
Frequency of purchase	Medium/low	Medium/low	High
Type of purchase	Negotiated bid		Routine rebuy
Complexity of selling process	High (e.g., custom product and negotiated bid)		Low (catalog item)
3. Size of market	Large	Small	Large/small
Number of customers	Few		Many
$ volume and profits/call	Large	Large/medium	Small
$ potential/territory	High	Medium	Low/medium
4. Competitive practices		Strong reasons required to violate industry norms	
5. Company's competitive position			
Market share	Large	Small	Large/small
Pricing strategy	High prices	Competitive	Competitive
Features/quality/ reputation/promotion/brand recognition	Push/Pull strategy	Pull strategy more likely to succeed	
Capital required/available	High cost	Lower channel costs	
Control and feedback required	Good	Poor	Poor
6. Size (dollars) of business unit	Large	Small	Small/large
7. Middleman availability		Mature industries have long-term relationships. New industries (e.g., personal computers) have volatile situation.	

SWITCHING CHANNELS—WHEN SHOULD YOU CONSIDER IT?

Major changes in your company's distribution channels should be considered in the following situations:

— A new company, venture, or division is formed.
— A new product or line is developed or acquired.
— The market has changed:
  • Demand is increasing or decreasing, shifting geographically or among new/old customer groups.
  • Buying habits are changing.
  • The competition is changing the way they or the market does things.
— Distributors have changed or developed new channels or methods for handling the company's products. (An example is the emergence of the industrial distributor chain.)
— The present channel has failed to meet sales, profit, and productivity objectives.
— Analysis reveals the possible advantages of a change.

Channel Decisions Are Major Ones for Industrial Products. Industrial marketing is a general management responsibility. Changes in marketing strategy frequently involve capital commitments for new equipment, changes in research and engineering activities, and departures from traditional engineering and manufacturing approaches.

Since, as we've said, industrial distribution systems take years to establish and are difficult and costly, these decisions have company-wide implications. Marketing identifies these needs. General management decides on the course that the company will take. It must provide the resources and follow-up to ensure that the course is pursued in every functional area.

Lessons from consumer marketing must be applied with seasoned judgment. Marketing in the consumer products field is a middle-management function. Major changes in marketing strategy can be made and carried out within the marketing department through changes in advertising emphasis or weight, promotion emphasis or type, and package design.

DIRECT, INDIRECT, OR A MIXTURE—WHAT ARE THE "WHYS" AND "HOWS" OF DISTRIBUTORS AND SALES REPRESENTATIVES?

"Direct or Indirect" Is the First Decision. Companies base this decision on a variety of internal and external factors summarized in Figure 5–6.

The Most Important Factor is Serving the End Users and Customers with the Products and Services They Need and Desire. ''A loose rule of thumb is possible: the broader the line, the higher the unit price; the more concentrated the customers and the higher the profit per call, the more economically feasible is direct selling.[6]

Indirect Channels Are Generally Poor Choices for Highly Technical or New Products. When complex products are sold through indirect channels, strong technical support organizations are needed. Budget is a critical limitation and may force you to compromise.

Existing Channel Arrangements Are Important. Your desired coverage must be compared with the available sales representatives and distributors located in each territory. First-rate middlemen are needed to achieve first-rate market penetration. Analyze potential wholesaler or rep contacts, their competence, policies, services, cooperativeness, creditworthiness, buying habits, and reliability.

Consider your company's organization, its traditional structure and the background, and experience of its sales and marketing staff. Several clients with historical biases toward direct selling are having difficulties with their distributor organizations. They lack the instincts to treat distributors as partners, to listen to and follow their advice, and to provide incentives to get them to perform adequately.

There Are Many Advantages to Selling Directly to the End Users or OEM Manufacturers. Harry Novick, president of Permutit Co. and author of ''The Case for 'Reps' versus Direct Selling: Can Reps Do It Better?''[7] provided information for the following paragraphs. He states that with direct selling you can:

- Enlist the dedication of each salesperson to the company's interests.
- Achieve technical training of sales personnel.
- Direct the salesperson's time to tasks which do not have an immediate return, (e.g., market research, new-product introduction, and customer service).
- More readily obtain reports of sales calls and customer intelligence.
- Readily transfer personnel from one area to another.

---

[6] John M. Brion, *Corporate Marketing Planning* (New York: John Wiley & Sons, 1967), p. 119.

[7] Harold J. Novick, ''The Case for 'Reps' versus Direct Selling: Can Reps Do It Better?'' *Industrial Marketing,* March 1982, pp. 90–98.

When Should You Maintain or Develop Your Own Direct Sales Organization? Direct selling is appropriate for companies or product lines which have:

- A successful direct sales program.
- Sales costs under control.
- Primary customers who expect to deal directly with the company.
- Recruiting and training programs which attract, develop, and maintain top salespeople.
- A geographically concentrated group of customers which permits efficient travel schedules.
- High dollar values per sales call.
- Technical products which require significant expertise in the selling situation.

What Are the Primary Advantages of a Sales Representative Organization? When rep organizations are selected to suit the needs of the company and are properly supported and monitored, the advantages can include:

- A high level of professionalism in the sales force beyond that of most direct employees.
- Long-term customer relationships which can yield great selling success. (In many established firms, the partners and senior salespeople average 10 years of customer continuity.)
- The business acumen of the reps which can give significant input to short- and long-range planning.
- An improved cash outflow. (A rep's commission is usually paid only when the manufacturer is paid.)
- A predictable sales/expense ratio regardless of sales volume fluctuations.
- Expanded sales coverage—more sales personnel in the field for the same cost as a percent of sales.

Situations that suggest that a rep organization be maintained or developed include those where:

- Income and cash flow are insufficient to support direct personnel.
- Compensation and benefits are inadequate to prevent turnover of good salespeople.
- The market is too small to support direct salespeople.
- You have a successful rep network.
- Long-term relationships between sales personnel and customers are a key to success.

It's a Fact of Life: Companies Frequently Operate with both Direct and Indirect Channels. The successful companies have very clear and strict policies governing when and where the direct salesperson is used. Conflicts over commissions, territory, and who does what are inevitable and must be dealt with in a fair, consistent way. This isn't easy. Reps and distributors understandably lose their enthusiasm when they fear that their livelihoods will be taken away if they become too successful! However, you, the manufacturer, may be forced by customers to make changes. Many large customers expect to deal directly with *you*.

The company-owned distributor is one variation found in the industrial distribution channel. In the welding products field, one major company buys local distribution companies when they no longer have effective ownership on retirement of the founders. These company-owned distributors carry competing lines when it is necessary to fill out the line. Also, when a suitable distributor is not available, you may need to start up your own operation.

Exploring the Company–Rep–Distributor Relationship. Before beginning business the manufacturer and the sales rep/distributor will want to know that mutual expectations are clear. They should thoroughly interview each other and come to clearly defined agreements on all operating and financial points.[8] Ask the prospective distributor, agent, or sales rep to describe their method of operation. Ask for information about:

- History: founding, key people, and their principles.
- Future plans: explicitly written, for existing lines, new lines, personnel.
- Territory covered: geographical areas, depth of coverage, deviations, and primary and secondary markets.
- Physical facilities: locations, warehouse size, TWX and WATS line communications, computer systems.
- Personnel: management backgrounds, key people involvement, and number of inside and outside salespeople.
- Product lines: principals, fit with new lines, and conflict with other principals.
- Selling methods: quotations, systems proposals, telemarketing, lead generation, and sales calls.

---

[8] Good examples of interview forms and agreements are found in the *1982/83 Electronic Industry Manufacturers Locator,* published by Electronic Representatives Association, 20 E. Huron Street, Chicago, Ill.

• Marketing: sales forecasts, market surveys for manufacturers, sales performance monitoring, and monthly reports to manufacturers.

How to Get Good Results from Reps/Distributors

Effective Management of a Distributor or Rep Organization Requires Time, Effort, Understanding, and Communication. You are selling through independent businesspeople who are risking their own capital, time, and energy. They can't be successful without strong support from you. Figure 5–8 summarizes the principles of good channel management.

FIGURE 5–8

How to Obtain Good Results When You Sell through Reps and Distributors

Consider them part of your company

Tell them about products, new products, engineering changes, policies, problems, future plans (without revealing competitive secrets), and your expectations of their performance.

Listen to their advice and suggestions.

Treat them the way you want to be treated.

Work to win their loyalty and support

Construct fair policies.

Employ even-handed implementation.

Make it easy to do business with you.

Help them to become more successful

Train their salespeople.

Inform their (your) customers with literature and seminars.

Help them to set up and use modern management systems and techniques for accounting, inventory, order entry, and planning.

Provide incentives

Companies that Market through Distributors or Reps Need to Be Aware of the Way Their Reps Think. Each manufacturer must compete for the time and resources of their distributors and reps. Indirect salespeople push hardest for the products with the greatest volume and profit possibilities. Some companies lack control over their marketing programs. Because of rep attitudes which include:

• When their sales volume with one manufacturer gets too high, reps fear replacement by direct field salespeople.

- Prosperous reps and distributors may develop "fat cat" attitudes and slacken their efforts.
- Commissions paid too far in the future are weak motivators. This is especially true when they involve speculative missionary work or marginal commissions for effort.
- Reps resist providing useful feedback because it doesn't produce immediate financial rewards.

Channel management requires a support organization. A large company such as Linde (division of Union Carbide) has a large marketing and sales staff in the field which supports their distributors. Small companies employ as many field sales and support personnel as they can afford. Coldelite Corporation of America, a $-million-plus food service equipment manufacturer, employs a sales manager, a marketing manager, 20 sales reps, and selected distributors.

Provide Your Distributors with the Know-How and/or the Financial Resources to Take Advantage of Microcomputer Management Systems and Modern Management Practices. It's good business. Lagging efficiency can jeopardize your sales and profits.

Recognize that You Are Partners on the Team. The manufacturer and the distributor or rep should know that *both* must profit. Many successful companies which sell through distributors or reps view them as their top sales management. They establish close working relations with them, work to understand the distributors or rep's problems, and join with them to look for solutions.

Distributor advisory councils are used by many companies to bridge the communications gap. These councils bring together key members of the manufacturer's sales team and selected top management of its major distributor organizations. The distributors have the opportunity to discuss their points of view, and the company can give the distributors insights into future plans. Steps can be taken to prepare for anticipated events and to solve the inevitable problems. The time to talk is when policies are being formed.

Some manufacturers have used direct assistance programs to supplement the modest resources of independent selling organizations. They provide marketing tools such as cooperative advertising, selling aids, promotional materials, market research information, and control information.

Training distributor or rep sales personnel is another form of direct assistance, stressing product knowledge and product applications. Seminars are also given to inform the distributor's customers and end users.

Do You Provide Managerial Guidance? A few companies have worked to improve the competence of the management at their distributor organizations. These manufacturers provide practical help in coping with the everyday problems of the distributor's business. These include:

- Selecting and installing microprocessor/minicomputer-based management systems.
- Inventory management.
- Order processing.
- Cost control.
- Merchandising.
- Handling of parts and service.
- Financing and purchasing.

Telemarketing is a current topic. With it your distributor can eliminate the need for customer contact in many routine sales situations. *Productivity improvement is one of the major managerial assistance benefits to the rep or distributor.*

BIBLIOGRAPHY

Brion, John M. *Corporate Marketing Planning.* New York: John Wiley & Sons, 1967.

Corey, E. Raymond. *Industrial Marketing: Cases and Concepts,* 2d ed. Englewood Cliffs, N.J.: Prentice-Hall, 1976.

Hill, Richard M.; Ralph S. Alexander; and James S. Cross. *Industrial Marketing,* 4th ed. Homewood, Ill.: Richard D. Irwin, 1975.

Morrison, Robert S. *Handbook for Manufacturing Entrepreneurs.* Cleveland: Western Reserve Press, 1973.

Novick, Harold J. "The Case for 'Reps' versus Direct Selling: Can Reps Do It Better?" *Industrial Marketing,* March 1982, pp. 90–98.

Porter, Michael E. *Competitive Strategy, Techniques for Analyzing Industries and Competitors.* New York: Free Press, 1980.

Webster, Frederick E., Jr. *Industrial Marketing Strategy.* New York: John Wiley & Sons, 1979.

6

MARKETING TO THE PUBLIC SECTOR

by
Steven E. Permut, Jr.

*Yale University
School of Management*

Lloyd B. Chaisson

McKinsey & Company

INTRODUCTION

In 1984, federal, state, and local government purchasing expenditures will surpass the $300 billion mark. These funds will be used to buy nearly every conceivable type of good and service sold within the United States: cars, computers, office supplies, furniture, food, light-bulbs, consulting services, and more will make up the mix of products needed to sustain all levels of government. Spending at a rate of over $1 billion of taxpayers' money every working day, government is both price-conscious and value-oriented (although occasional deviations from these goals do occur). Key success factors for marketing to the public sector are similar in many respects to those in commercial and industrial markets, but they also differ in many important ways. Firms pursuing sales to the public sector must therefore first understand how this unique marketplace is organized and how it functions.

Like corporations, governmental entities must continually decide if it is more sensible to buy a product or service in question or attempt to make or provide it directly.[1] To do the latter necessarily entails the

---

[1] For a good capsule summary of the "make or buy" decision-making process, see Stephen Gordon and Joseph Kelley, "The Private Delivery of Public Services: A Public Service Option," *Resources in Review,* Municipal Finance Officers Association, November 1981.

commitment of scarce capital resources which might have been better employed elsewhere. By contracting with a private sector concern, the unit of government can draw effectively upon the institutional capabilities of the corporation which otherwise would be very expensive to duplicate. Arthur Young and Company has identified a number of advantages and disadvantages to public sector entities that relate to the decision to "contract out" (see Table 6–1). It is through this contracting-out process that most private sector organizations come to do business with the public sector.

TABLE 6–1
Advantages and Disadvantages Experienced by State and Local Governments through Contracting out

What are the potential advantages of contracting out?
If it is done well, contracting can:
Contain costs by targeting resources in a more efficient and effective manner.
Lower costs due to increased competition.
Cost less per unit or allow for economies of scale (the more you buy, the less you pay).
Compensate for the lack of specialized equipment, available capital, qualified personnel.
Provide quick responses to constituent needs by avoiding the excessive bureaucracy of public agencies.
Free managers to focus on planning and exceptions rather than day-to-day supervising.
Provide a yardstick for measuring government efficiency and effectiveness when government retains a part of the service delivery.
Provide a means to amortize infrastructure upgrades or new equipment without incurring debt.

What can go wrong?
Opportunity for conflict-of-interest and cronyism charges.
Constituent complaints if service requirements are not well defined in the first place or if the contractor does not perform.
Reduced control over service delivery.
Higher total costs for contract administration and performance evaluation.
Higher costs when not enough suppliers compete.
Personnel morale and labor relations problems.
Rumors and citizens' concerns at the mere mention of starting the contracting-out analysis.
Excessive price increases at contract renewal time.

Source: Arthur Young and Company, *Contracting out: A Buck for Business, an Option for Government,* 1981.

MARKET STRUCTURE OF THE PUBLIC SECTOR

Every five years, the federal government's Bureau of the Census conducts a census of governments to catalog a variety of important characteristics of state and local government. This census is used by the federal government to determine eligibility for many federal grant-in-aid programs and to help target many federal agency programs. This same information has an ancillary benefit in that it also provides companies seeking government business with a detailed picture of public sector market segments and characteristics.

With over 79,000 state and general-purpose local governments in the United States, a firm seeking a business relationship in the public sector is faced with the task of identifying and grouping public entities into some appropriate segmentation scheme. Table 6–2 shows a rudimentary approach based strictly on form of government.

TABLE 6–2
Number of State and Local
Governments in the United States

Type of Government	1977	1972
Total	79,912	78,268
State government	50	50
Local government	79,862	78,218
Counties	3,042	3,044
Cities	18,862	18,517
Townships	16,822	16,991
School districts	15,174	15,781
Special districts	25,962	23,885

Source: U.S. Department of Commerce, "Government Organization," 1977 Census of Governments, Vol. 1, no. 1.

While this approach provides a framework for defining the scope of the market, it requires further refinement based on variables of particular relevance to the firm's own product/service mix. Variables that have proven useful to some firms include: geographical location, patterns of product use (including amount, type, and timing of usage), budget cycles, and other demographic-based characteristics often found in traditional private sector marketing. Although segmentation schemes based on psychographic characteristics of public sector entities—using variables such as "innovativeness," "risk perception," or "style of conflict resolution"—appear to be particularly relevant in this sector, published studies are unfortunately rarely found in the literature of marketing. Marketing managers are urged to explore the potential of these nondemographic segmentation schemes in addition to more traditional approaches.

While the structure of state government as a marketplace appears relatively homogeneous on rather simple segmentation variables, the local government market is less so. In addition to cities and counties, local government also includes school systems and special districts (e.g., transit authorities, sewer districts, etc.). In many cases these local governments actually have their own taxing authority granted by the state and have purchasing processes distinct from other local governments. In other cases these entities, as well as cities and counties, will purchase goods and services under *political body follow-ons, joint administrative (consolidated) purchasing,* or *joint bid intergovernmental cooperative purchasing.* Political body follow-ons generally take the form of a local government appointing the state as its agent for purchases routinely made by political subdivision within the state. Consolidated purchasing is an arrangement where purchases of two or more local governments are made by a shared administrative agency created for that purpose. Intergovernmental cooperative purchasing is an arrangement where two or more governmental agencies opt to buy a good or service from a single supplier under a single request for proposal (RFP) or invitation for bid (IFB). Each of these arrangements enables local governments to enjoy lower prices and reduced duplicate administrative efforts. The increased buying power also tends to insure a higher level of vendor performance.

School systems and special districts outnumber cities and counties by an almost 5 to 1 margin. While the bulk of government purchases (dollarwise) is made by cities and counties, special districts represent the fastest growing market segment of the public sector. As a percent of total public sector expenditures, these cities, counties, schools, and districts control 40 percent of every dollar spent by the public sector. Cities alone purchase nearly $100 billion per year. Counties spend over $50 billion per year.

Like businesses, these governments have their own professional and trade organizations at the state and national levels. In addition to legislative activities, these organizations share information of mutual benefit through meetings and publications and develop the capabilities of their respective elected and appointed members. In a sense these organizations, such as the National League of Cities (NLC) and the National Association of Counties (NACo), have self-structured the market and allow corporations seeking to do business with their respective memberships an opportunity to participate in their organized marketplaces.

THE SIX Ps OF PUBLIC SECTOR MARKETING

As in classic consumer and industrial marketing approaches, the four Ps (product, price, promotion, and place of distribution) play a major role in structuring a successful public sector marketing and sales operation. However, the public sector environment requires the inclusion of two more Ps—procedure and public accountability. While private sector marketing embraces the last two Ps in the form of corporate procurement rules and shareholder accountability, the public sector perspective is more properly viewed in terms of legislative/regulatory requirements and public notification. Both are held as supremely important to the state or local government involved in competitive procurement activity, and both must be explicitly considered by the marketer.

Recognition, attention, and patience with procedure and public accountability prior to establishing a vendor relationship with a political body will make the subsequent marketing effort considerably more effective. We turn to the six Ps of public sector industry marketing in more detail, starting with the two most important—procedure and public accountability.

Procedure

No doubt everyone has heard of a situation where a vendor has invested thousands of dollars and hours in developing a responsive proposal to a government RFP, only to find out that the procurement is delayed or suspended. In fact many potential vendors wonder if all the upfront investment of labor and dollars is really worth the effort when a price-based award is viewed as likely to squeeze profits. These and other situations are examples of poorly designed public sector procurements and are the exception rather than the rule. Generally, the legal and regulatory environment of the public sector precludes a shopping-around approach to purchasing. Enabling legislation (including statutes, charters, and ordinances) spells out exactly which rules must be followed in the expenditure of public funds. Regulations and procedures, governed by commercial, antitrust, and foreign trade and exchange laws, set out the specific processes to be followed in procurement. Additionally, certain federal, state, and local laws provide for preferential policies in awarding contracts. These may include minority participation or preference given to local/regional vendors.

The American Bar Association, in cooperation with various professional and trade organizations, has published *A Model Procurement Code for State and Local Governments,* which is designed to provide public purchasing agencies with:

- Policy guidance and statutory language for managing and controlling procurement.
- Guidance for resolutions of controversies relating to public contracts.
- A set of ethical standards governing public and private participants in public procurement.

This model code is rapidly finding its way into many state and local purchasing agencies and should provide vendors with a certain degree of uniformity that does not exist today.

Because procedures are not uniform among local or state governments, the potential vendor must become familiar with the various practices of the different market segments, as well as variations within those segments. For example, doing business with a government unit would typically involve one or more of the following requirements or activities:

1. Provision of general information regarding vendor products or services (allows different bidders lists to be created).
2. Execution and provision of a nondiscrimination certification (insures that the vendor is in compliance with all relevant federal, state, and local antidiscrimination statutes and ordinances).
3. Purchasing and contracting lobbying registration (insures that all lobbying activities are documented and controlled).
4. Government/industries conferences (a cooperative effort between vendors and the governmental body to better define a complex procurement).
5. Pre-bid conferences (enables potential vendors to understand a procurement and its requirements fully prior to bid submission).

The procurement itself might take one or more of the following four forms:

1. Open market purchases
This method is used when a firm quantity of items at firm prices with a specific delivery schedule is desired (most common method).
2. Supply agreements
This method is used when firm prices are desired for a given period of time on an "as needed" basis.

3. *Confirmation purchase orders*
   Issued by departments to the supplier after receipt of material, these purchase orders are generally used when immediate delivery is required.
4. *Petty cash purchases*
   Incidental purchases not exceeding a set dollar amount are made under this method, usually from readily accessible vendors with a stocked inventory.

Public Accountability

Any corporate purchasing activity is ultimately subject to the scrutiny of stockholders; however, most go unnoticed unless a situation arises where a key indicator—such as ROE (return on equity)—suffers as a result of poorly managed or wasteful purchases. Generally, shareholders do not examine each and every purchase that exceeds some set amount, such as $10,000. As long as critical economic and accounting performance indicators are met or exceeded, purchases are assumed to be consistent with corporate goals.

The public sector, too, has its shareholders, more commonly known as the voting public, that are typically represented by special interest groups that monitor City Hall activities. These "shareholders," through their local and state elected officials, have devised a series of laws, regulations, and codes which spell out how business is to be conducted. In general, public notice of any significant purchase in excess of $10,000 (and often less than this amount) is required for any intended purchase of goods or services. In addition, proposals submitted by competing vendors become part of the public record (unless proprietary information covenants are invoked) and are thus open to scrutiny by the general public to insure fairness and consistency in final awards. Key indicators in the public sector, unlike the corporate sector, are more qualitative in nature and do not lend themselves to uniform quantitative analysis.

Product

A product offered for sale to a public entity is, broadly speaking, examined more closely than one offered to a commercial or individual customer. Brand names often carry less direct influence in the actual purchase decision since buyer behavior, by law, is restricted to a prescribed set of guidelines to insure an absolutely competitive and non-prejudicial purchase. This is not to say that only one brand will emerge as the preferred supply for a given product group. Requirements and weights attached to product attributes may differ among purchasing units, resulting in some brands being more competitive in some jurisdictions and less competitive in others.

An example of competitive versus noncompetitive product offerings is found where two jurisdictions requiring the procurement of personal computers give different weight to after-market service, financing arrangements, and technical assistance. Other jurisdictions might not see these specific product/vendor attributes as important (perhaps due to in-house capabilities or, simply, different needs). Vendors with good service and financing arrangements would be very competitive in the first market segment but less so in the second due to large allocated costs in support of their service and financing arrangements. Likewise a vendor with few costs to allocate other than direct product costs would appear very competitive in the second market segment.

Price

Many public sector entities are moving away from price as the exclusive determinant of contract awards. Under a price-driven procurement (generally involving a good or service classified as a "commodity" where brands are not differentiated), the contract award is always made to the lowest-priced bidder. However, what is emerging today is a value-oriented, life-cycle costing approach to governmental purchasing in which all costs involved with purchase, usage, and disposal are considered—not just the initial purchase price. In effect, a spreadsheet is developed for the useful, or intended, life of the product or service (including all associated governmental costs) and a present-value calculation is made. The purchasing agency specifies in advance what criteria will be used to develop the spreadsheet and how each will be weighted (and thus evaluated) in awarding the winning contract. This bid evaluation formula is relied on exclusively to select the successful vendor from among all vendors.

Often governmental units incorporate items known as value incentive clauses in their RFPs to encourage vendors to make specific commitments, such as that relating to noise reduction or energy savings. The commitment can offer a vendor an important competitive advantage if the product is quieter than other vendors' or uses less energy. Such a commitment can be given added weight in arriving at an evaluated bid price (EBP), which we review briefly below.

Four models of an EBP formula approach to purchasing capital equipment outright, under lease, and through a lease-purchase arrangement, are illustrated in Table 6–3, followed by an EBP approach to a service purchased with an energy-efficiency incentive (Table 6–4). In

---

TABLE 6–3
Evaluated Bid Pricing under a Variety of
Procurement Schemes

Capital

1. Purchase: EBP = FIC + OC + MC + IC − SV

   where

   > EPB = Evaluated bid price
   > FIC = Front-end investment costs
   > OC = Operating costs
   > MC = Maintenance costs
   > IC = Insurance costs
   > SV = Salvage value

2. Lease: EBP = MLP + OC + MC + IC

   where

   > EPB = Evaluated bid price
   > MLP = Monthly lease payments
   > OC = Operating costs
   > MC = Maintenance costs
   > IC = Insurance costs

3. Lease–Purchase: EBP = MLP + OC + MC = IC + FLS − SV

   where

   > EPB = Evaluated bid price
   > MLP = Monthly lease payments
   > OC = Operating costs
   > MC = Maintenance costs
   > IC = Insurance costs
   > FLS = Final lump sum
   > SV = Salvage value

4. Services purchase: EPB = PBD + BDY = TNY

   where

   > EPB = Evaluated bid price
   > PBD = Price per unit delivered
   > BDY = Units delivered per year
   > TNY = Total number of years

---

these examples, more than a simple purchase price or monthly lease price is used to arrive at the final cost of procurement. This multifactor approach insures that the public sector entity can determine its true cost of the good or service in question. Thus, price should be viewed in its broadest sense when selling to the public sector, since the initial

---

TABLE 6-4

Illustration of How Evaluated Bid Pricing (EPB)
Works with an Energy-Value Incentive Clause

Energy-consuming equipment purchase
Evaluated bid price (EPB) = FIC + OC

where

FIC = Front-end investment costs (price)
OC = Operating costs (consumption of fuel at
$1.50/gallon)
O and M costs assumed to be equal

Raw bids (price only)

Bidder	Price (low to high)	Yearly Fuel Consumption (gallons)
A	$10,000	30,000
B	11,000	28,000
C	12,000	28,000
D	13,000	25,000

Revised bids (using EBP formula)

Bidder	Price	(+) Cost of Energy (high to low)	EPB
A	$10,000	$45,000	$55,000
B	11,000	42,000	53,000
C	12,000	42,000	54,000
D	13,000	37,500	50,500

Bidder A was the apparent low bidder, but an EPB demonstrated that Bidder D was the low-cost vendor despite having the highest upfront equipment price.

---

purchase price is often treated as only one component of the total costs of ownership. (Parenthetically, this same orientation is commonly observed in the private sector as well, although it is rarely *mandated*, as is true in many public sector buying situations.)

Promotion

Some say that product promotion to the public sector is money wasted because brand recognition, buyer behavior preferences, and the purchase decision process itself are regulated by law (and, therefore, blind to outside influences). Still others see promotion as a *key* element in the public sector marketing mix since it provides a powerful mechanism to further differentiate and position their product in the minds of local elected and appointed decision makers. The real value of promotion, it would seem, lies more in the intended objectives of a public sector promotional program and in how well promotional elements (including advertising, public relations, and sales promotion) can be linked to the overall marketing strategy. Awareness of a product and its performance characteristics and benefits is critical if a marketer intends to develop a perceived preference for its product or service among state and local decision makers.

Demonstrating successful experiences of other public sector purchasers with your product or service is one approach employed by many successful public sector marketing strategists. The influence of opinion leaders can be stimulated by portraying successful users/situations in appropriate publications, allowing decision makers to obtain a firsthand account of your product's performance from a trusted peer group member. Personal influence of this type appears to carry more weight than any other single element in a vendor's marketing program. If appropriately orchestrated, your current clients (mayors, city managers, county commissioners, etc.) can be your most effective sales force.

Place of Distribution

As a general rule, a vendor's product distribution network is less important than its service distribution network when dealing with public sector clients. Most RFPs will call for the prospective vendor to quote a price inclusive of delivery. If transportation costs are a key factor in pricing a proposal, the vendor with closer proximity has an advantage. The most important factor, however, is after-market servicing. A value-added approach to public sector sales entails close client-vendor relations which can only come about if service access is timely and *guaranteed.* If a distributor sales and servicing arrangement is proposed, the vendor must be able to guarantee performance beyond the point of sale. Too often products are delivered to public sector buyers with little or no follow-through. Those who sell to governmental entities must demonstrate their intention to develop and maintain a total client relationship well beyond the initial sales event itself.

TARGETING YOUR STRATEGY

The goal of any corporation entering the public sector purchasing realm should be to sustain a competitive advantage in all six Ps. Randomly responding to RFPs and hoping for a good hit rate on awards by being the low-cost producer are simply not sufficient. A successful vendor needs to carefully consider the nature of the company's participation in the public sector market. Will the activity be limited to bidding in cities and counties with populations in excess of 50,000? Will creation of a special distributor network be necessary? Can the firm make an honest commitment to "add value" to the sales relationship with the full support of the organization's managerial and technical resources? Viewing public sector procurements as an unwanted stepchild will quickly demonstrate itself to be an unsuccessful marketing strategy.

With the company's role and strategic orientation defined, it is necessary to identify the firm's particular strengths and weaknesses relative to your public sector clients, competitors, and your own internal organization. Do you have separate public and private sector sales forces? (Most successful public sector marketers do.) Do your competitors have public sector strengths that you lack, such as speed of delivery, large inventory of spare parts, or a high level of technical field support?

And finally, the potential vendor must determine how its own strengths should be blended together into a successful sales effort. Questions to be considered include the following: How can we conclusively demonstrate that our product/service adds more value to our public sector customer's business? Are we geared up for getting the sale while also fully supporting after-sale service? Have we analyzed our past government contracts to see how and why we were the successful bidder? Have we learned all we can from those situations in which a customer switched to a competing vendor? These and other questions must be asked and answered before a targeted marketing strategy can be shaped.

Corporations which seek to conduct business with state and local governments must remember two things:

1. Price is not the absolute determinant in successful bidding. More and more units of state and local government are employing value analysis and life-cycle costing techniques. This approach to pricing necessitates a full understanding of "consultative selling."

2. State and local governments are scrutinizing expenditures more closely than ever before. If a decision is made to buy, the successful bidder will be the one who shows a thorough understanding of customer needs, as well as a *commitment* to follow through before, during, and after the sale. Government contracts and purchase orders should no longer be viewed as markets where poor vendor performance is tolerated. Networks of information exchange on commercial vendors are rapidly becoming more prevalent throughout state and local government associations. Market information of public purchasing agents is becoming more comprehensive and timely each and every day.

Many potential suppliers of goods and services fail to recognize and understand the concerns facing local decision makers. Public sector market forecasting must take into consideration macroeconomic factors on national, regional, and state levels. Intergovernmental factors such as transfer payments, block grants, state and federal regulations, categorical grants, and statutory mandates define the shape and nature of the public sector market—and, therefore, must be considered in building an effective marketing strategy. In sum, the smart vendor will recognize opportunities within the state and local government structure by becoming intimately familiar with policy and program trends and how they are apt to influence future buyer behavior.

SOURCES OF STATE AND LOCAL GOVERNMENT MARKETING INFORMATION

All effective marketing programs depend on marketing intelligence and customer research. Unlike sources of private sector marketing data, state and local information is more scattered and, in many ways, less sophisticated. Nevertheless, the secondary data which do exist are sufficient to provide the astute manager with enough information to structure and plan the marketing effort.

Unlike corporate America, state and local governments do not have limitless volumes of statistical data describing outside procurement of goods and services. Nor do state and local governments have a centralized listing of goods and services, as is the case with the federal government (by means of *Commerce Business Daily*). However, one major industry research organization, McGraw-Hill, is beginning to fill this gap by compiling data on state and local government major product and service purchases. Called the Product Information Network (PIN), this service allows the exchange of information among cities regarding past and future procurements. For example, a city interested in purchasing a sophisticated data processing system could contact McGraw-Hill to see if the network has posted experiences of other cities that may have purchased a similar system. In cases where a sufficient amount of purchasing information and experience exists, PIN puts together a complete guide for local government on how to evaluate and structure a procurement. Although McGraw-Hill's PIN network is in its early development stage, it will undoubtedly forge new ground for vendors as well as purchasing agents while giving a deserved advantage to those vendors whose products and services continue to meet or exceed customer needs.

Another excellent starting point is a review of the International City Management Association (ICMA) Profiles of Individual Cities (PIC). This particular data set provides statistical information on all cities in the United States with populations greater than 10,000. PIC profiles provide an excellent overview of the individual government, its fiscal status, its political framework, and more.

Tables 6–5 and 6–6 (which are reprinted from ICMA's Municipal Yearbook Series) show the extent of information readily available on most major U.S. communities. Note that the profile also contains areawide economic and demographic trends useful in forecasting future government programs and priorities. Of particular importance is the Government Structure section which details the decision-making infrastructure of the municipality. Because there are currently five formally recognized forms of government (mayor-council, council manager, commission, town meeting, and representative town meeting), the astute marketing manager will recognize that the purchasing function and process will take a generically different form in each.

TABLE 6–5
Profiles of Individual Cities (PICs) Data Sets by Year

Item	1976	1977	1978	1980	1981	1982
Demography						
Age						
Percent population under 18	X					
Percent population 25 and over		X				
Percent population 65 and over	X					
Education						
Median years		X				
Housing						
Number of year-round units		X				X
Percent structures one-unit		X				
Percent units occupied		X				
Percent units owner-occupied		X				
Percent change in number of						
units 1970–80						X
Income						
Per capita	X		X	X	X	
Percent change 1969–75				X		
Percent change 1969–77					X	
Percent of population under						
poverty level		X				
Land area	X					
Metro status	X			X	X	X
Nonworker-worker ratio		X				
Population density		X				
Population totals						
1960					X	
1970	X				X	

TABLE 6–5   (concluded)

Item	1976	1977	1978	1980	1981	1982
1973	X	X				
1975			X	X	X	
1980						X
Percent change 1960–70	X				X	
Percent change 1970–73	X					
Percent change 1970–75			X	X	X	
Percent change 1970–80						X
Race and ethnic background						
Percent black						X
Percent Hispanic						X
Percent nonwhite	X					
Percent white						X
Economics						
Manufacturing						
Number of employees			X		X	
Percent change in number of						
employees 1972–77					X	
Number of establishments			X		X	
Percent change in number of						
establishments 1972–77					X	
Retail						
Number of employees			X		X	
Percent change in number of						
employees 1972–77					X	
Number of establishments			X		X	
Percent change in number of						
establishments 1972–77					X	
Amount of sales			X		X	
Percent change in retail sales						
1972–77					X	
Service						
Number of employees					X	
Percent change in number of						
employees 1972–77					X	
Number of establishments			X		X	
Percent change in number of						
establishments 1972–77					X	
Amount of sales			X		X	
Percent change in service sales						
1972–77					X	

Source: Municipal Yearbook, International City Management Association, 1982.

TABLE 6–6
Profiles of Individual Cities (PICs) Data Sets by Year

Item	1976	1977	1978	1980	1981	1982
Employment and payroll						
Number of municipal employees	X		X	X		
Number for administration				X		
Payroll						
October total				X		
Average October earnings				X		
Finance						
Expenditure						
Bond rating	X	X	X	X	X	X
Total debt			X	X		
Percent of debt that is full-faith and credit				X		
Percent of debt nonguaranteed			X			
Total expenditure less capital outlay	X					
Percent of expenditure other than capital outlay			X	X		
Revenue						
General revenue			X	X		
Revenue from own sources	X					
City personal income tax		X				
Property tax rate		X			X	
Estimated assessed property valuation		X			X	
Percent of revenue from property tax				X		
Sales tax receipts		X				
Governmental structure						
Ballot type	X		X			
Council						
Council member compensation						X
Number of members	X		X			X
Number of members elected at large			X			X
Number of members elected by ward or district			X			X
Term of council members			X			X
Overlapping terms			X			
Provisions for direct democracy						X
Election-type	X		X			X
Form of government	X	X	X	X	X	X
Year form adopted			X			
Mayor						
Membership on council		X				X
Method of election	X		X			X

TABLE 6–6 *(concluded)*

Item	1976	1977	1978	1980	1981	1982
Salary						X
Term			X			X
Voting power			X			
Manager/CAO employed			X			
Other areas						
Municipally operated utilities	X					
Fire rating	X					

Source: Municipal Yearbook, International City Management Association, 1982.

Federal Sources of State and Local Government Marketing Data and Information

The Bureau of the Census performs a quinquennial census of state and local governments in the United States. Data on the number and characteristics of state and local governments include information on organization, political structure, employment, finance, transfer payments, as well as historical statistics in each area. In addition to the five-year census, the bureau also publishes special censuses conducted at the request of state and local governments. Most of the bureau's data are available through printed reports, computer tape, and special tabulations. Indexes are also available to assist the potential user in locating information on specific subjects. Further information can be obtained by contacting:

> Public Information Office
> Bureau of the Census
> Department of Commerce
> Washington, D.C. 20233
> Tel: (301) 763–7273

An annotated bibliography follows which details only relevant sources of information on state and local government census information particularly useful to understanding the state and local government market.

A. *1977 Census of Governments*

- *Volume 1: Governmental Organization*
  Number 1: Governmental Organization

State and local governments are detailed according to size, type of government, locations (including county and SMSA breakdowns), and governmental structures.

Number 2: Popularly Elected Officials

A breakdown of elected officials on a state-by-state basis by form of government and office. Also includes information on election districts and compensation laws.

- *Volume 3: Public Employment*
  Number 1: Employment of Major Local Governments

Contains information on employment and payrolls of county and major city governments and special districts.

Number 2: Compendium of Public Employment

Employment and payrolls by type of government and function are included. Of particular usefulness is the summary of local government employment by SMSA.

- *Volume 4: Government Finances*
  Number 1: Finances of School Districts
  Number 2: Finances of Special Districts
  Number 3: Finances of County Governments
  Number 4: Finances of Municipalities and Township Governments

These four volumes contain information on revenues, expenditures, debt, and relative financial assets.

Number 5: Compendium of Government Finances

This volume is a summary of the census findings on governmental finances. Breakdowns by type of government, state, and county are included.

- *Volume 5: Local Government in Metropolitan Areas*

Derived from the previous census reports, this volume contains breakdowns by SMSA of local governments according to type, size, employment, and finance.

- *Volume 6: Topical Studies*
  Number 4: Historical Statistics on Governmental Statistics on Governmental Finances and Employment

Contains data on revenue, expenditures, and indebtedness of state and local governments from 1956.

Number 5: Graphic Summary of the 1977 Census of Governments

This volume is a compilation of all tables and maps appearing in volumes throughout the *1977 Census of Government.*

● *Volume 7: Guide to the 1977 Census of Governments*

This volume is the official index and directory for users of the *1977 Census of Governments*. It provides capsule summaries of each volume and includes representative samples of relevant data.

B.   *Other Bureau of the Census Data Sources on State and Local Government*

● *County and City Data Book, 1977*
● *Directory of Federal Statistics for Local Areas, 1976*
● *Guide to Recurrent and Special Government Statistics* (continuous)
● *State and Local Government Special Studies* (continuous)

Periodicals and Publications of Note

1. *American City and County Government* (monthly)
   Buttenheim Publishing Corporation
   Berkshire Common
   Pittsfield, Massachusetts 01201
   A private monthly magazine which addresses many day-to-day issues of local practical concern such as solid waste management.

2. *Index to Current Urban Documents* (quarterly)
   Greenwood Press
   88 Post Road West
   Westport, Connecticut 06881
   Provides an index to official publications of largest city and county governments.

3. *The Model Procurement Code for State and Local Governments*
   American Bar Association (ABA)
   Sections: Urban, State, and Local Government Law;
             Public Contract Law
   1800 M Street N.W.
   Washington, D.C. 20036
   Provides a model statute and regulations for all public purchasing including a variety of competitive sealed bid methods.

4. *Book of the States* (biennial)
   Council of State Governments
   Iron Works PIFF
   P.O. Box 11910
   Lexington, Kentucky 40578
   Provides information on structure and function of state governments and their respective agencies.

Associations Serving State and Local Government

While there are over 100 associations serving state and local government, only a handful are truly considered sources of useful marketing data. The following seven associations generally maintain comprehensive data sets, mailing lists, and other statistical information for sale to the general public. Each recognizes the importance of effective public/ private relationships, and each is committed to strengthen state and local government including the quality of purchasing.

Listed in each association profile is relevant information on membership, publications, and a comment by the author on the associations' unique character. The "Purpose" statements were reproduced directly from literature of the respective organizations.

It is important to note that, almost without exception, each city in the United States is directly or indirectly associated with one or more of these groups. Entry into the distribution channels of these organizations (either through tabloids or annual conventions) will allow direct access to state and local decision makers in an extremely credible fashion.

International City Management Association (ICMA)

1120 G Street, N.W.
Washington, D.C. 20005
Tel: (202) 626–4600

Purpose

"To strengthen the quality of urban government through professional management; to strengthen the competence of appointed urban managers and ensure qualified talent to meet urban government needs; to provide information and analysis of data, management ideas, and methods for urban government management; and to participate in the development and translation of new concepts for urban government management."

Membership

6,810 city managers, county administrators, and chief administrative officers, with 44 state chapters.

Publications
  Public Management Magazine
  ICMA Newsletter
  Municipal Management Series
  Municipal Yearbook
  Urban Data Service Reports
  Management Information Service Reports
  Product Information Network (PIN)
  Newsletter and Product Purchasing Guides (in conjunction with Mc-
  Graw-Hill)

Comment
ICMA is the best source for statistical data on cities and counties in the United States (more current than census data). Each year an anual convention and product exposition is convened, the only time during which major local government management decision makers are assembled in one location. Mailing lists, directories, and indexes are available from ICMA for a fee. The Product Information Network (PIN) is the first attempt at organizing local government procurement practices and procedures on a national basis. Guides are produced which detail purchasing considerations on a variety of goods and services. Contact ICMA for further information on PIN.

National Association of Counties (NACO)
1735 New York Avenue, N.W.
Washington, D.C. 20006
Tel: (202) 783–5113

Purpose
"To serve as the voice of county government at the national level; to promote county government's heritage and its future; to serve as a liaison between county government and other levels of government; to achieve public understanding of the role of counties in the federal system; to provide information and analysis of data."

Membership
Elected county officials representing 2,090 counties.

Publication
County News (weekly)

Comment
NACO is the only body in the United States representing counties. Although policy decisions are made by elected county officials, appointed officials are very active in the organization. NACO has perhaps the strongest membership network of all the associations. *County News* is the major communication vehicle with members. A very large products and services exhibition is conducted during an annual meeting. State Association of Counties also convene annual meetings and generally provide a scope of services which rivals NACO.

National Governor's Association (NGA)
Hall of the States
444 North Capitol Street
Washington, D.C. 20001
Tel: (202) 624–5300

Purpose

"To act as a liaison with the federal government and to serve as a clearinghouse for information and ideas on how state and national issues can be solved."

Membership

The governors of the 50 states.

Publication

Governor's Bulletin

Comment

NGA is a relatively small organization representing a small but politically powerful constituency. Participation of appointed state government officials is extensive. As an association, NGA is primarily concerned with lobbying in Washington and is not as strong as the local government interest groups in the areas of data collection, information, and assistance.

National League of Cities
1301 Pennsylvania Avenue, N.W.
Washington, D.C. 20004

Purpose

"To strengthen the role and capacity of state municipal leagues and municipal governments through research programs, information exchange, legislative representation, and federal liaison activities."

Membership

Elected officials of over 1,000 cities and 49 state municipal leagues.

Publications

Nation's Cities Weekly
Directory of Local Officials
Regular surveys of city officials on a variety of topics

Comment

The National League of Cities is perhaps the most comprehensive of all local government associations. While considerable activity is focused on federal relations, NLC's primary mission is to enhance the capacity of cities as effective, responsible organizations. Unlike ICMA, NLC's membership is composed of local decision makers who ultimately decide on most major procurement activities. An annual Congress of Cities and Exhibition is held each year, attracting a wide range of participants from city managers to mayors and council members. Through a network of 48 state municipal leagues, NLC is in direct contact with virtually every city within the United States. State municipal leagues convene annual meetings and product exhibitions and maintain limited data sets on their membership.

U.S. Conference of Mayors (USCM)
1620 Eye Street, N.W.
Washington, D.C. 20006

Purpose
"To promote cooperation between cities and the federal government; to promote responsible and responsive local government and effective municipal administration; and to promote exchanges of information and experiences among elected city officials."

Membership
Mayors of 750 American cities.

Publication
The Mayor

Comment
The U.S. Conference of Mayors, like the National Governors Association, is a smaller organization that wields considerable decision-making power at the local level. Although not a marketplace like NLC and NACO conventions, USCM annual meetings are important gatherings of the nation's top local government decision makers, where word-of-mouth communication is at least equal to the more formalized marketing activities found at other governmental trade meetings.

Municipal Finance Officers Association (MFOA)
180 North Michigan Avenue, Suite 800
Chicago, Illinois 60601
Tel: (312) 977–9700

Purpose
"To establish professional policies and practices of governmental finance by: researching and establishing technical practices and policies of governmental finance management for state and local government; expanding the opportunities for professional recognition and career development of all persons who serve the financial and related areas of government; identifying and researching major issues of intergovernmental fiscal policy and informing those interested in such issues; and extending cooperation and assistance to other associations and professional organizations concerned with government finance management."

Membership
8,100 municipal finance officers, with 55 state associations.

Publications
MFOA Newsletter
Auditing and Financial Reporting
Governmental Operating Budget Manual

Comment

Many cities with a population of 30,000 and below have a single individual who serves as finance and purchasing director. As more sophisticated purchasing arrangements necessitate complex financing arrangements (e.g., lease-purchase), MFOA's interest in public purchasing decisions is becoming more evident. National and statewide annual meetings are held.

National Institute of Governmental Purchasing, Inc.
1735 Jefferson Davis Highway, Suite 101
Arlington, Virginia 22202
Tel: (703) 920–4020

Purpose

"To raise the standards of the public purchasing profession through the interchange of information and ideas."

Membership

143 individual members as well as 920 agency members representing most major cities, counties, and states.

Publications

NIGP Letter Service Bulletin
Value Analysis Program Guide
Public Purchasing and Materials Management Series
Competitive Sealed Proposals
Basic Purchasing Guides for Local Governments

Comment

NIGP is the professional organization of state and local public purchasing agents. The association certifies its members through testing and examination with the title, Certified Public Purchasing Official (CPPO). Annual meetings are held each year with an extensive product exhibition area. While computerized data sets are not available, the organization staff does generate an informal information exchange network through its *NIGP Letter Service Bulletin Series.* As with McGraw-Hill's PIN network, NIGP is steadily compiling purchasing guides on a variety of commonly purchased goods and services from lawn mowers to sophisticated building energy management systems.

7

SERVICES MARKETING

by
Gregory D. Upah

Wunderman, Ricotta and Kline

Thinking and writing about the unique aspects of services marketing has grown dramatically, particularly over the past five years. Accompanying this growth in thought is a consensus that the differences between goods and services produce differences in marketing. Perhaps the most vivid expression of the contrast between goods marketing and services marketing was made by Lynn Shostack, senior vice president, Banker's Trust. In an address to the Second American Marketing Association Services Marketing Conference, she held up a can of Campbell's soup, contrasted it to services, and asserted that "marketing soup was just not the same as marketing a service." The uniform chorus of agreement was not confined to the attendees of that meeting.

Many of those in services industries—particularly executives experienced in packaged goods marketing—recognize the unique challenges in the marketing opportunities they face and the marketing strategies used to capitalize on these opportunities. These differences may vary in terminology but the underlying premise is clear: services marketing is different.

What are the key differences between goods and services? What impact do they have on the strategies/approaches needed for successful marketing management in service industries? The remainder of this chapter will focus on these two topics. The principal focus will not be on identifying and providing a rationale for goods-services differences. The reader can look to several other sources for a more detailed discussion (e.g., see references for Berry, 1980; Shostack, 1977; Uhl & Upah, 1983) of these issues. This chapter will focus on emerging views as to how to foster successful service marketing both strategically and tactically.

GOODS–SERVICES DIFFERENCES THAT MAKE A DIFFERENCE IN MARKETING

Academic and industry people cite a variety of differences between goods and services. Within this diverse set of differences, however, are fundamental differences to which many of the others are related. The first of these is intangibility. Most all services are intangible, noncorporeal; they cannot be touched, seen, or smelled. Services are not goods on a shelf—they involve the performance of activities or the provision of equipment or facilities for another's use. Some services can be *represented* by tangible objects—an accountant's, consultant's, or physician's report, for example. However, the service itself—the thought processes and the conclusions drawn by these professionals— form the essence of what is being purchased.

The second key difference is perishability. Lacking tangible properties, services cannot be stored and saved for future use. Unused hotel rooms, airline seats, or an attorney's unspent time cannot be recalled for use at a later date when demand for the service outstrips supply. Most goods, in contrast, can be inventoried and retain their ability to be sold.

A third key difference—related to intangibility—is the lack of transportability of most services. Few services can be produced, transported, and consumed elsewhere (services conveyed by electronic media are an exception). Most services require the physical presence of the recipient of the service or property owned by that person. As such, most services need to be produced in the customer's locale.

Many services—haircuts, lodging, entertainment—are produced and consumed simultaneously. For example, most medical services cannot be transported. Car rentals and airline flights cannot be mass produced in one location and then transported to be sold to customers in other locations. Ticket or rental counters and equipment and people needed to facilitate transactions must be present when the service is provided.

A fourth difference—perhaps more one of degree than kind—is that in providing a service there is more personal interaction between buyer and seller than in the marketing of products. Consider the number of people involved in rental car and airline transactions: reservationists, sales/counter people, pilots or courtesy bus drivers, and flight attendants or garage personnel. The same holds true for many financial and health care services. The personnel who interact with customers play a pivotal role in influencing the perceived/actual quality of these services.

There is, of course, a growing use of electronic and other impersonal means of delivering and acquiring services. Automated teller machines and in-home banking and shopping are services that do not rely on the involvement of human service providers and, as noted above, may allow for some degree of "transportation" of service. Thus far, however, the tasks performed by these automated devices have been fairly routine service transactions. The major services provided by banks (priority and private client banking, etc.) have begun to be even more people-intensive as banks upgrade their service mix to attract customers and more effectively compete with other financial institutions. Thus, while technology does offer opportunities to make services less people-intensive many nonroutine or complex services appear to be getting more people-intensive as service organizations shift resources to better serve their better customers.

Furthermore, it still is not clear that the great majority of consumers in the United States will welcome electronic and/other non-personal means of service delivery. Nevertheless, some growth projections for videotex—an electronic home information/shopping/entertainment system—call for use by 10 percent of households by 1990 and 40 percent by the year 2000. One major issue is whether or not consumers will be attracted to these systems for services that have typically required a great deal of personal interaction (e.g., legal, medical, financial/tax planning) as well as for such routine types of services as bill paying, information retrieval for weather, or stock market information.

DEALING WITH INTANGIBILITY: THE NEED FOR EFFECTIVE IMPRESSION MANAGEMENT

While services are intangible, consumers seeking to evaluate a service are often able to draw inferences as to the nature and quality of a service from the tangible or visible elements surrounding that service. Our discussion of impression management will focus on five areas: communications; people; the interaction process; physical/environmental cues; and atmospherics and design (see Figure 7–1). It is because services are intangible that service firms may find it beneficial to ensure that all forms of tangible evidence of the quality of their services work to produce a consistent impression—one which is consistent with the firm's marketing objectives and strategies. In sum, it is important for service marketers to remember that customers often evaluate what they can't see by what they can see.

Communications

Advertising brochures, letters, or direct-mail materials are tangible cues about the nature and quality of the service being offered. As such, the impact (positive or negative) of these cues on customer perceptions should be considered when designing them. Advertising itself can be

FIGURE 7–1
Tangible Cues of the Nature and Quality of Service

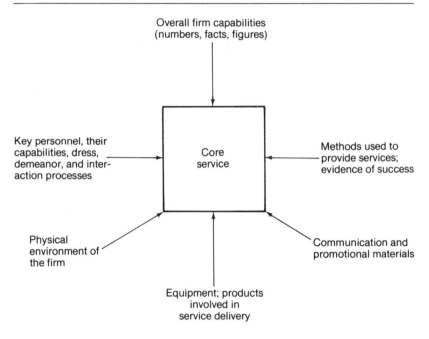

characterized in terms of a tangible-intangible continuum. Should advertising, for instance, be too intangible, it may further cloud the reality of the service and inhibit customers' understanding of the nature and benefits of that service (Shostack, 1978).

Several authors have emphasized the need to "tangibilize" advertising for services (Berry, 1980; George & Berry, 1981; Shostack, 1977; Uhl & Upah, 1982). A variety of more concrete aspects of services and service capabilities can be addressed in services advertising. These include: unique equipment or facilities, people and their particular background and expertise, facts and figures pertaining to the firm, years of service, area of specialization, customers served, and evidence of past successes in service to clients. In addition, many service organizations, particularly in the financial services area, have used symbols of their capabilities: Prudential's rock, Travelers' umbrella, and, of course, the Merrill Lynch bull.

People

Impression management in services marketing goes far beyond advertising. An executive of a large advertising agency put it this way: "In service businesses, people deal with people—these people influence their expectations as to what will happen when they use that service" (*Advertising Age*, 1979). The demeanor, dress, and personality of employees—particularly those in public contact positions—can have a marked impact on perceptions of an organization. This point is, of course, no revelation to any capable marketer. What may be less obvious, however, is the opportunity and need for a systematic effort to manage the impression made by employees. Employees should provide cues that enhance perceptions of the service firm's strengths or, at the least, not undermine them. Several firms have made highly successful use of internal marketing efforts designed to promote desired employee-customer interaction. Two highly successful service organizations—McDonald's and Disney World—have done and continue to do this with formalized codes of dress and demeanor.

Delta Airlines found that customer-directed advertising which highlighted and applauded its employees' efforts resulted in improved employee attitudes and better customer relations (George & Berry, 1981). A similar result was obtained by an employee-centered advertising campaign used by a major bank.

The physical appearance of public contact personnel can be a major element in service design/marketing. Many airlines expend a considerable effort in the design of clothing for flight attendants and counter personnel. A number of major corporations—from Hertz, IBM, and Disney World to Century 21—have formal and informal dress codes. For instance, Century 21 real estate agents reinforce the organization's promise to provide a consistent level of service quality by wearing the distinctive gold jackets with the Century 21 label.

The Interaction Process

The interaction process between personnel and their customers is also a key element in service design and customers' evaluation processes. Midas Mufflers is one organization that recognizes "process" as an intangible cue to the quality of service received. Midas uses a simple interaction device that enhances customer satisfaction with its services. Prior to installing or repairing an automobile exhaust system, the mechanic escorts the customer into the shop area, shows the actual part requiring repair or replacement, and discusses the recommended repair procedure and the cost. This guided visual inspection informs the customer of the nature and severity of the problems and gives reassurance that the solution recommended is appropriate. Customers are also provided with a spacious waiting area with complimentary coffee and donuts, television, and current magazines. Midas is focusing on process design to contribute to customer satisfaction with the core service (i.e., the maintenance and repair of exhaust systems).

Service firms may find it useful to carefully manage each aspect of this interaction process. One management tool that can be used for this purpose is scripting. *Scripting* involves carefully specifying how the service encounter should be managed (e.g., specifying the dialogue to be followed) and ensuring that employees follow the script (Smith & Houston, 1982). A broader notion of this form of process control is the basis for what Shostack calls blueprinting (1981). *Blueprinting* involves mapping in explicit detail all the essential functions required to deliver the service in the desired manner.

Banker's Trust has used this blueprinting approach in the design of its new discount brokerage service. Every element in the process—from the customer's first contact to follow-up mailings and confirmations of the transaction—has been mapped to ensure standard performance. The correspondence materials have been carefully designed, as have the particular choice of words used by the telephone account representatives when conducting a transaction. The choice of these process design elements was based in large part on extensive pretesting of each aspect of the blueprinted system.

Atmospherics or Design

The final element of impression management that we will discuss is atmospherics or design. Impressive facilities, office environments, public areas, and prestigious locations can all be an important determinant in promoting positive customer experience with and successful marketing of services. Artwork, certificates, diplomas, and equipment may also influence the customer's perceptions of the service. The same physician, stockbroker, accountant, or attorney may inspire far less customer confidence and engender far less customer satisfaction if the office decor and location create a negative or uncertain impression of the service provider.

Offices need not have the finest wood paneling or the most finely crafted furniture. The decor should flow from the firm's concept of what it wants to be and from the image the firm wishes to convey. The use of color, fabrics, flooring, cabinet materials—even the location of the receptionist's window or desk—can have a marked impact on these impressions. A dentist's office designed to provide a light, airy, cheerful setting with high-quality furnishings, as opposed to one appointed in a darker, more serious way with chairs and tables of barbershop quality, is likely to elicit more positive feelings from patients—particularly those who have negative expectations about dentists. The former approach has been used successfully by many of the new, franchised dental clinics throughout the United States.

Many aspects of design that should seem obvious are often taken for granted. Many of the most successful service organizations—from

McDonald's to major banks to brokerage offices—have recognized the importance of atmosphere and are now managing the use of design elements in a highly systematic fashion.

One photofinishing services firm encountered an atmospherics impediment to their efforts to expand the range of goods and services sold in its retail outlets. The firm had an extensive network of photo huts located primarily in shopping center parking lots. The parking lot location and the customer's uncertainty as to how safely their treasured film would be transported and processed contributed to a lack of confidence by some segments in the quality of these services. When this firm added a key-duplicating machine/service, an additional segment of photofinishing customers was distressed. They simply did not like the idea that metal shavings from the key-duplicating service were in the same tight space with their film and finished photographs. Thus both the interior and exterior environment of this firm's outlets worked to diminish the appeal of this service to a large group of customers. The firm dropped the key-duplicating service shortly after it was introduced.

The previous example illustrates the need to consider *what to exclude as well as what to include* in designing a service environment. The Rouse Company's efforts with the Quincy Market and South Street Seaport developments in Boston and New York, respectively, have drawn considerable acclaim. One of the major guiding principles in the design of these shopping environments is to seek only those tenants whose services/goods are consistent with the concept behind the development and are likely to produce excitement, enjoyment, and a positive buying atmosphere. Banks and travel agencies do not appear to work as well in this regard and have, for the most part, not been included.

IMPLICATIONS OF THE IMMEDIATE PERISHABILITY OF SERVICES

Because services cannot be produced and then stored for later sale, unused service capacity is lost forever. Therefore, service firms require far more synchronization of service capacity and demand for that capacity. Kotler (1980) has used the term *synchromarketing* to describe the effort to match capacity or inventory with demand.

H & R Block provides a vivid example of a service organization with an acute need to manage capacity. H & R Block cannot produce tax preparation service in advance of demand and sell it as people demand it during tax time. Customers must be dealt with during tax season. In addition, however, H & R Block seeks even utilization of its service capacity throughout the year.

Because tax preparation services cannot be inventoried, managing demand on a day-to-day basis during tax time is of critical importance. H & R Block can, through its mix of hours of operation and personnel on hand, help synchronize demand and capacity. Appointment mechanisms would seem to be another key strategy to achieve a steady flow of demand. However, H & R Block discovered that many of their customers did not like the appointment mechanism: they preferred to walk in for service whenever *they* were ready, even if they had to wait to meet with a preparer (Bloch, 1982).

H & R Block has used other methods to help maximize utilization of service capacity in off-peak nontax preparation periods. At times other than tax season, many leased or rented offices remain almost idle. One solution developed by the company was to offer tax preparation courses in these offices during the off-season. In addition, the company often subleases these offices to other organizations.

A substantial need exists to manage service supply and demand to compensate for the immediate perishability of services. The tools to accomplish synchromarketing are many and varied. For adjusting service supply, several options exist. Firms can add *temporary* capacity in peak periods (e.g., rent additional facilities and equipment); share capacity with other firms (e.g., airlines sharing gates, baggage handling and ticketing at airports), and postpone less urgent tasks until after peak-period needs are satisfied. There are several other methods, including speeding flow-through rates and offering self-service options when the service can be delivered in that way and when a substantial portion of customers are willing to make use of those options. (These methods are outlined in Table 7–1.)

TABLE 7–1
Altering Supply to Meet Demand

Some principal methods
1. *Adjusting flow-through rates*—e.g., decreasing the time taken to serve individual customers.
2. *Temporary capacity extensions*—e.g., the use of part-time employees or rental of additional equipment or facilities on a short-term basis.
3. *Postponement of selected less urgent service needs*—in the public accounting field, nonessential, nontax-related matters are postponed until after tax season.
4. *Sharing service capacity with other organizations*—e.g., airlines sharing ticket counters, baggage-handling facilities.
5. *Expanding skills of service providers*—as employees' skills expand so does their ability to perform multiple service tasks.
6. *Expanding customer's role in service delivery*—e.g., through greater use of self-service such as self-service customer checkout systems at major hotels and rental car companies.
7. *Substituting equipment for human labor*—ATMs remain the prime example; home computers for home banking, bill paying, etc., provide another.

Demand adjustments can also help to maximize efficiency. Some, such as peak-load pricing, are well known. Promotional devices such as giveaways and discounts may bolster demand during slack time. The provision of alternate services such as summer sports activities at ski resorts or, as mentioned, tax courses offered before tax season, can all help to stimulate demand for use of idle or underutilized facilities. (A set of these methods is discussed in Table 7–2.)

TABLE 7–2
Adjusting Demand to Meet Supply

Principal methods
1. *Peak-load pricing*—used in a variety of industries from air travel to telecommunications to public transportation.
2. *Peak-load promotions*—promotions (premiums, contests, "early bird" programs) can be used in some fashion to more closely match demand to supply.
3. *Advertising*—e.g., Postal Service mail-early campaign, snow/ski reports from ski resorts.
4. *In-house alternative services*—may help to spread out demand for most popular services, lead to greater customer satisfaction for those waiting for these services (e.g., horseback riding as an alternative to tennis).
5. *Service expansion*—e.g., McDonald's breakfast service, H & R Block's income tax courses prior to tax season, summer sports activities offered by ski resorts.
6. *Appointment/Reservations systems*

DEALING WITH LACK OF TRANSPORTABILITY

For many of the same reasons discussed above, there are substantial limits on the ability to transport a service. Service capacity (facilities or people) can be transported, but (with few exceptions relating to electronic delivery systems) the service itself cannot. The services of physicians, attorneys, hair stylists, and auto repair cannot be mass produced and then shipped to desired locations for later sale. Disney World's services must be experienced in Disney World. Films and brochures describing the experience are highly inadequate substitutes.

Often the production facilities and marketing/sales facilities must be combined and placed in multiple local outlets—e.g., one-hour photofinishing centers, one-hour dry cleaning services, real estate, and some banking/financial services. The potential problem that ensues is the reduced economies and efficiencies that result from the lack of centralized production. In the photofinishing business, for example, before the one-hour facilities were inaugurated, pick-up points at drug stores, camera stores, photo huts, etc., could all be devoted to providing customer contact. Actual processing was done at large, centralized processing facilities.

The challenge is to retain economical and efficient service production and delivery without losing important customer contact points or failing to provide the service levels customers demand. Some service organizations which don't require the physical interaction of customers and facilities/personnel can achieve some advantages through the use of mail, telephone, and computer hook-up. Banks, particularly via nationwide ATM networks, can service their customers even when these customers are far from the bank's main facilities.

There are, however, other ways in which service organizations can achieve economies (see Table 7–3). First, they can, via some corollary

---

TABLE 7–3
Achieving Economies in Production When Multiple Service Outlets Are Employed

Major methods include:
1. *Greater centralization of service facilities/tasks*—requires promotional efforts to draw customers from greater distances to fewer outlets.
2. *Separation of customer-contact facilities from production facilities.* Lower-cost contact facilities—e.g., pick-up points may be separated from higher-cost production facilities (e.g., processing plants).
3. *Reducing range of customer needs served by particular facilities/personnel*— certain customers/customer problems would be referred to specialized, central facilities/personnel (e.g., limited-service bank branches, legal service outlets).
4. *Combining complementary services into central facilities*—e.g., H & R Block and its partner—Hyatt Legal Services—share some locations and facilities.
5. Mechanizing via scripting or blueprinting to achieve more efficient service delivery.

---

efforts, utilize fewer facilities. This involves employing a variety of means to draw customers to the central production facility. One way to accomplish this is to locate the service facility near complementary facilities. For instance, dental organizations, law store franchises, and real estate and brokerage services are located in some Sears stores. Sears clearly has benefited from walk-in business in the dental clinics and financial centers it has placed in selected stores. Another is the development of a multifaceted service facility—e.g., comprehensive health clubs with tennis, racquetball, swimming, exercise rooms, and hairstyling salons. Medical/professional complexes with physicians' and dentists' offices, pharmacists, opticians, and related medical service firms provide another example. The combined attraction of all services may create an increased willingness on the part of tenants and customers to utilize and travel to their facilities.

As mentioned above, many service firms have benefited from separating production facilities from customer contact facilities (e.g., photofinishing services and dry cleaning). Satellite facilities handle basic transactions, while actual production takes place at central locations. The Law Store, a legal service franchise organization, has set up special phone booths in department stores to connect clients with its staff. Many legal problems are handled strictly by telephone.

There also is the well-known means of achieving economies in marketing by tying local outlets together through franchise arrangements or ownership and promoting these outlets under a common corporate name. The critical requirement for the most productive use of this approach in services marketing is a guarantee of consistent quality throughout the facilities utilized. These control methods are the glue that holds any successful franchise together (see Table 7–4).

TABLE 7–4
Key Means of Promoting Standardizing, Desired Service Quality

People-oriented approaches
  Careful hiring of employees, setting proper criteria—assuring that the employee is likely to fit the job.
  Training of employees.
  Shaping reward system to promote desired performance among key service personnel.
  Internal marketing efforts designed to encourage desired performance.
Operations-oriented approaches
  Development of service procedures/standards for performance.
  Using equipment or software to substitute for or augment efforts of human service providers.
Control procedures
  To ensure that standardization efforts are working.

Advertising economies are achieved because the multiple outlets band together to advertise. In addition, the advertising is likely to have greater impact because the credibility of the advertising promise is enhanced by the standards set by the franchise organization. Business economies are achieved because satisfied customers learn to expect the same quality of service as they move from city to city or outlet to outlet.

Finally, the use of process design mechanisms, such as scripting or blueprinting, may help to eliminate employee uncertainty or deviation from desired procedures and ultimately lead to more efficient service delivery.

DEGREE OF PERSONAL INTERACTION

The final key difference we will cite is the degree of personal interaction in the marketing of a service. This carries with it several implications—many of which have been alluded to before.

The Need for Quality Control and Standards of Performance for Key Employees

Because of the increased likelihood for variation in quality in a labor-intensive setting (Upah, 1980), these standards are even more important. Furthermore, as noted above, the quality of experience/service in one area will have an impact on perceptions of the organization and its outlets in other areas. The blueprinting/scripting procedures discussed earlier clearly play a role here.

Communication of the Existence of These Quality Assurance Systems to Customers

As mentioned above, services, because they are intangible and not the result of the stamping of identical units on a production line, are difficult to judge before purchase and use. Communications relating to quality assurance procedures, extensive employee training, or institutional arrangements can help to alleviate or minimize any customer uncertainty or anxiety that may result.

The use of equipment (e.g., diagnostic machines used by physicians, financial planning models for brokers and bankers) also may foster consistent levels of service quality in the interaction process and increase economies in service delivery. In addition, this equipment may actually enhance the ability of key service producers or public contact people to provide the service.

How does the importance of personal interaction in services businesses and the benefits of formal procedures to manage this interaction relate to the growing use of nonhuman delivery systems in many service industries? Automated banking (via ATMs or in-home systems) and in-home shopping and information services are, with certain exceptions, exhibiting substantial growth in use. The convenience, time-saving benefits, and high-tech appeal of these systems have drawn certain segments of customers to organizations that offer them. One major reason for the dramatic growth of Citibank over the past decade is their extensive ATM network—and the early and substantial commitment they made to creating it.

Self-service systems may serve not only to reduce costs to the service organization but also to increase the attractiveness of the service organization, as in the case of Citibank's ATM network. The situations and the relative benefits and drawbacks of substituting machines for employees will be different for each service firm. However, one key requirement may typify all successful self-service arrangements; i.e., the provision of a real and clear-cut customer benefit that results from the use of the self-service system (or any new technology).

There are trade-offs between customer acceptance and the degree of self-service provided. Citibank encountered a substantial backlash from customers and the general public when it announced its policy (later rescinded) to allow access to human tellers only to customers who met a minimum balance requirement. Others were required to use ATMs.

For customers of People Express, carrying one's luggage to the gate (along with other labor-saving devices) means clearly lower airfares. For investors who do their own research and develop their own investment plans and goals, discount brokers provide substantial savings in brokerage fees.

In contrast, self-service coffee and salad bars at a top restaurant, the lack of valet and bellhop service at a major hotel, or the lack of personal assistance for major financial services will, even with some cost savings, obviously fail to provide a clear customer benefit and may lead to substantial dissatisfaction with the service organization.

The issue of relative customer benefits has been a major one in the growing electronic information services industry. Information, editorials, and advertising conveyed via newspapers can be delivered electronically. The question is whether or not consumers prefer, even at minimal cost, electronic display to receiving a newspaper on their doorsteps and reading that newspaper at their convenience while sitting in their favorite chair.

It is important for service organizations to ascertain the existence and magnitude of a perceived customer benefit for self-service before developing and offering the self-service system. Once this is done, the self-service or nonpersonal delivery system may take on the dual role of being a cost-savings device for firms and an attractive means of drawing customers to the service organization. The assumption that new technology is better technology is itself a form of marketing myopia. The real question is whether or not the new technology provides a better way than existing approaches to satisfy customer needs.

CONCLUSIONS

This chapter outlined some of the major differences between goods and services and some of the marketing implications of these differences. In addition, this chapter provided an overview of issues and a discussion of possible services-marketing strategies and tactical options. The reader is encouraged to look to the growing body of knowledge about each of the service-marketing ideas discussed.

Clearly, there is considerable room for the refinement of existing principles regarding services marketing and for the development of new ideas regarding the unique requirements for effective services marketing.

Perhaps the most important managerial implication of this chapter is for managers to consider the ideas discussed and assess whether or not these ideas apply to, or merit further thinking for, their particular service business. This kind of critical evaluation and testing will help to produce an even more detailed and productive body of information for the management of service businesses.

Finally, large numbers of executives at major service organizations do find that services (as opposed to goods) marketing has its own unique challenges. A small number has found appropriate and highly useful solutions to these challenges. Many of these kinds of solutions were discussed in the chapter. Service marketing and service marketers need this kind of in-practice assessment. All those interested in and/or working in services industries stand to gain a great deal by sharing thoughts and experiences on this subject.

REFERENCES

Berry, Leonard L. "Services Marketing Is Different." *Business*, May–June, 1980, pp. 25–26.

Bloch, Thomas M. "Innovations in Service Marketing." In *Emerging Perspectives on Services Marketing*, ed. Leonard L. Berry, G. Lynn Shostack, and Gregory D. Upah. Chicago: American Marketing Association, 1982, pp. 22–24.

George, William R., and Leonard L. Berry. "Guidelines for Advertising Services." *Business Horizons*, July–August, 1981, pp. 52–56.

Kotler, Philip. *Marketing Management*. Englewood Cliffs, N.J.: Prentice-Hall, 1980.

"Service Business Is People Dealing with Other People." *Advertising Age*, 1979.

Shostack, G. Lynn. "Breaking Free from Product Marketing." *Journal of Marketing*, April, 1977, pp. 73–80.

———. "How to Design a Service." In *Marketing of Services*, ed. James H. Donnelly and William R. George. Chicago: American Marketing Association, 1981, pp. 221–29.

Smith, Ruth A., and Michael J. Houston. "Script-Based Evaluations of Satisfaction with Services." In *Emerging Perspectives in Services Marketing*, ed. Leonard L. Berry, G. Lynn Shostack, and Gregory D. Upah. Chicago: American Marketing Association, 1982, pp. 54–58.

Uhl, Kenneth P., and Gregory P. Upah. "The Marketing of Services: Why and How Is It Different." *Research in Marketing*, 1983, pp. 231–57.

Upah, Gregory D. "Mass Marketing in Service Retailing: A Review and Synthesis of Major Methods." *Journal of Retailing*, Fall, 1980, pp. 59–76.

8

INTERNATIONAL MARKETING

by
Robert C. Vereen

National Retail Hardware Association

AMERICA'S NEED TO EXPORT

Why should any company want to export when the American market is so big that the average company is not getting a substantial market share already and would be happy to earn a 25 percent market share of this vast U.S. consumer/industrial marketplace?

There are many sound reasons why American companies should look abroad for sales while still aggressively courting the domestic market. First, there is the opportunity to develop incremental sales, with the benefits this added volume offers in terms of lower production costs and greater operational efficiency. The second reason might best be described as the opportunity to even out the peaks and valleys of domestic sales. Many manufacturers find that world markets lag behind those in the United States. Thus one has the opportunity to fill in the valleys and round off the peaks with overseas sales.

There is, in addition, a national need to export. For many smaller companies, the idea of responding to a national need may seem like a peculiar reason to export, but all one has to do is look around the U.S. market today to realize that countries and companies all around the world are setting their sights on the U.S. consumer/industrial market. American companies must respond by becoming exporters themselves.

No one's company is safe from the threat of imports. Self-preservation dictates that all companies must expand their horizons and consider, as overseas competitors now do, that the world, not merely their native country, is their market. America must achieve a balance of payments. If more small U.S. companies become aggressive exporters, both they and the country will benefit.

WHAT ARE THE OPPORTUNITIES?

Worldwide, consumers have growing expectations of what the "good life" can and should be for them. This is brought about both by television, which spreads the story and style of other lifestyles, and other improved communications methods. With better communications, people everywhere learn that others enjoy air conditioning, telephones, radios, television, automobiles, vacations, indoor plumbing, etc. The list of consumer wants and needs is indeed endless, once a people learn what others have and enjoy.

Of special importance is the fact that there is a rapidly enlarging middle class developing in many nations. In many countries, consumer markets formerly consisted either of the very well-to-do or the very poor. Now middle classes are emerging, and their numbers are increasing—opening new markets for many U.S. products.

The growing trend toward urbanization, noticeable in many countries, also stimulates interest in—and demand for—consumer products. When people lived in rural areas, they expected to have a lower lifestyle than those living in the cities. Now, as more move to urban areas, they seek the accoutrements of "the better life." Indicative of the growing interest of overseas buyers in U.S. products is the ever-expanding number of foreign visitors who are attending U.S. trade shows.

Despite the economic recession that has troubled so many countries over the last few years, incomes generally are growing; and, as they grow, lifestyle expectations grow. (They often grow faster than incomes, as a matter of fact.) Thus, in developing nations where people previously sought only to obtain the basic necessities of food, shelter, and clothing, one today sees an almost revolutionary transformation.

A good example is transportation. Once people were satisfied to walk or ride horses, mules, or cattle. Then they graduated to bicycles, then to motorcycles, and, as their incomes increased, they quickly began buying cars. Traffic jams are now commonplace in Taiwan, Hong Kong, Manila, and many other cities and countries not long removed from near poverty. Now auto care is a market with potential in most countries, and American automotive after-market manufacturers find world markets attractive and valuable.

The automobile is just one striking example. Every element of life sees this insatiable demand for upgrading—clothing, food, shelter, appliances, etc.

These improving lifestyles afford American manufacturers an opportunity to export products which have become commonplace in the United States but which might almost be considered luxuries—or at least, new and exciting—in many other parts of the world. A case in point is an American manufacturer of a portable cooler which operates off a 12-volt car battery instead of requiring ice. Advertising it to the world market as an export product, the manufacturer was inundated with inquiries, and not necessarily only for its use in the United States. Rather, many people overseas—from a number of different countries—saw the product as an affordable small refrigerator for the masses who could afford only a small amount of money for refrigeration and who had neither the money nor housing space to accommodate larger and vastly more expensive refrigerators. A market was there but not solely in the form that the U.S. manufacturer had expected.

Many American products are world-renowned for their quality and for their extra features and consumer benefits. Thus the very elements that build a domestic market are, properly evaluated and exploited, exportable.

Perhaps the most amazing opportunity that exists for American manufacturers is the exporting of a bit of American lifestyle over the last decade—the do-it-yourself movement. What began in the United States as a hobby and then developed into an ongoing marketing phenomenon is now a valid part of lifestyles in many developed nations. The rate of adoption of DIY (and those three initials identify the do-it-yourself movement around the world, even in Japan) varies by country, but it is spreading inexorably. Because American manufacturers have been developing products, packaging, and promotions for the DIY movement domestically, they are light years ahead of foreign manufacturers in catering to the special needs of DIYers—explicit instructions; affordable products; the changing of commercial-oriented products into ones that can be installed by amateurs.

The growth of DIY has directly stimulated the sales of hardware, tools, paint and accessories, and lawn and garden merchandise. Even in plumbing and electrical categories, where overseas consumers resisted DIY the longest, there is now pronounced activity among typical consumers.

Because the United States has lead in the development of DIY through product and packaging innovation, there is a considerable opportunity for American manufacturers, especially in the area of building materials that can be consumer-installed. In some other basic categories such as paints and accessories, U.S. leadership and specialization in developing easy-to-use and unique products means that these products offer great potential overseas.

Often there is insufficient demand in any one country to develop highly specialized products at the right price. Therefore, an overseas market becomes an extension of a sales effort already successful in the United States, where the vast domestic market has provided the necessary volume-price foundation.

Still other opportunities exist because of improving technology. America's development of personal computers, for example, brings some of this high-tech marketing to other nations.

IF IT'S SO EASY, WHY ISN'T EVERYBODY DOING IT?

There are problems, of course. It isn't a sure thing nor as easy as expanding into another state. But if one looks at the problems to see how they can be overcome, one sees that with some adjustments and modifications, the same marketing strengths and efforts that work in the United States can be applied overseas.

First of all, if a company has never exported before, it is probably fearful of the strength of the dollar. Currently, there's no doubt that this is the most difficult handicap facing a domestic factory that wants to ship its goods overseas. But this is a temporary drawback. Just a few years ago the dollar was very weak on world markets and American products were the world's best bargain. Somewhere between those currency valuations and today's high dollar is the norm.

So, aside from the temporary difficulty of an artificially high dollar, what are some of the problems inhibiting someone from exporting?

Too many manufacturers are too impatient. They realize that domestic sales take time to build, but they seldom are as willing to allocate the same time and resources to developing international sales. One cannot walk into a new market overseas and dominate it in a few weeks or months. Sometimes it will take years. Japanese companies, for example, have been working for years to carve out chunks of U.S. markets. It didn't happen overnight for them, but as long-time traders, they have been more patient than most American firms would have been.

Unfortunately, some U.S. companies look at the overseas markets as an opportunity only when domestic sales slack off. Then they court overseas buyers aggressively. However, in the past they often have dumped the new buyer rather unceremoniously when domestic sales picked up. As a result, if production was oversold, it was the overseas buyer who suffered. This has happened too often and has incurred a degree of caution on the part of foreign buyers when dealing with new-to-export U.S. companies. Now they wait a bit longer to see just how serious and committed a company is. At major international trade shows, for example, it is often necessary for U.S. firms to exhibit two or three years before making substantial headway. People look them over, check them out, and see how committed they are before embracing the line and source wholeheartedly.

Another drawback, one that can be resolved, is the lack of marketing information on foreign markets. It is not always as absent as one might think, but it is not found quite as easily as is domestic information. The International Trade Administration, Department of Commerce, overseas American Chambers of Commerce, and some domestic market research firms—together with the consulates of the targeted foreign markets—can supply much information that will give a domestic factory at least rudimentary marketing knowledge to put together a starting plan.

The availability of information keeps growing at a steady pace. For example, the U.S. Chamber of Commerce recently announced the availability of a new series of slide and cassette programs on international trade which are available to businesses, organizations, and individuals in the form of a package entitled: "Meeting the World Trade Challenge." These illustrate the benefits, opportunities, and obstacles in the international marketplace today. One title in the series instructs would-be traders on how to get started. The complete series contains more than 200 color slides, audio cassette narratives, and script booklets with convenient listings of further sources of assistance on exporting.[1]

One sometimes also lacks information on ways in which products are distributed. These can vary widely by country, so cookie-cutter copies of American distribution networks will not necessarily apply. However, like the marketing resource material, these are solvable problems. In most industries there are export-boosting organizations at work—committees, marketing councils, subassociations, etc.—together and sometimes with the U.S. Department of Commerce to solve these problems for American factories.

HOW CAN THE PROBLEMS BE SOLVED?

The first place a company should turn when looking for export opportunities is to the International Trade Administration within the Department of Commerce. There is a wealth of valuable information available, and the local Department of Commerce offices can supply books, pamphlets, personal advice, etc. These range from a basic *How to Export* booklet to publications like *Business America,* an interesting and fact-filled magazine current on trade and business outlooks around

---

[1] The series is available from the U.S. Chamber of Commerce as a complete set or as individual slide programs. Titles in the series include: "The Case for Two-Way Trade," "The Real World of Exporting: Opportunities and Realities," and "Export for Profit." Ordering information may be obtained from the Special Projects Division, U.S. Chamber of Commerce, 1615 H St. N.W., Washington, D.C. 20062 or by calling (202) 463–5755.

the world. (At the end of this chapter is a listing of some of the government publications that are available free or at modest cost.)

In addition to the Department of Commerce, one can turn to state commerce departments in many states for help. These organizations often develop trade missions to boost the sale of products manufactured in their own state. Beyond these, in many cities there are World Trade Clubs whose members range from experienced to neophyte world traders. Regular programs enable members to keep current on world opportunities and trading problems as well as to meet local exporters who can assist them in their efforts to grow.

One of the prime sources of help can be the multitude of seminars on exporting which are conducted on a regular basis by a wide variety of individuals and organizations. These are conducted by the regional offices of the Department of Commerce, by state organizations, World Trade Clubs, industry associations and councils, banks, colleges and universities, the American Management Association, etc. A call to the DOC in one's local area, to state commerce officials, or to the business department of a local college or university can lead to sources that will be most convenient from a geographic standpoint.

Most industries also are attempting to boost export activities through their respective trade associations. Typical of what is being done in other fields, the hardware/housewares industry has launched numerous programs. The American Hardware Manufacturers Association now has an active Export Committee. The National Housewares Manufacturers Association has sponsored a group exhibit of U.S. firms at the International Housewares Show in Cologne, Germany, for more than a dozen years. Last year the American Hardware Manufacturers Association did the same thing at the International Hardware Fair in Cologne, and they will be sponsoring a similar group exhibit during 1985.

The Worldwide DIY Council coordinated a group exhibit of American manufacturers in November 1983 at the Asian International Hardware Exposition, a show held in Singapore and sponsored by an American firm, Cahners Exposition Group of Des Plaines, Illinois.

The Automotive Parts and Accessories Association, which sponsors its own show, likewise has an active Export Committee and urges U.S. firms to participate in international shows. Still another group that helps U.S. firms develop export business is the Worldwide DIY Council, a marketing-based group of some 80 active exporting companies. Any manufacturer not presently exporting should certainly check with his or her industry associations to see what self-help programs already are being offered.

Another broad-based group is Sell Overseas America, a private group that describes itself as an association for American exporters. Membership in this group includes banks, export agents, and manufacturers from widely diverse fields.

IF YOU WANT TO SELL, WHAT ARE YOUR CHOICES?

A manufacturer has many ways to go to market internationally. One way, of course, is to do it yourself. This requires the greatest commitment of time, money, personnel, and effort but can yield very substantial returns. This necessitates establishing networks of agents, distributors, wholesalers, etc. overseas. As mentioned earlier, it can take considerable time. In some instances, depending upon product, one might wish to engage in a joint venture or to license an overseas company to produce an American product.

A less expensive and faster way to enter the international marketplace is by engaging the services of an export management company. These firms take title to one's product and handle all shipments, claims, and credits. In effect, they become one's overseas sales and collection agency. An American manufacturer used to dealing with manufacturers' agents domestically has learned that the quality and service of representative agencies varies widely. The same is true for export management companies. Some are very solid, substantial, and reputable. Others almost operate out of their homes. Care should be taken in evaluating them. Talk to principals of other companies they represent. Are they familiar with your kinds of products? Seek one that specializes in handling lines of merchandise that would be complementary to your products. This means that they already have contacts with potential buyers overseas; they have a network of established distribution; the start-up time on your line would be greatly reduced. Do they exhibit in major overseas fairs for their companies? Investigate before you commit.

Much newer in America, since it has only now become legally possible, is the export trading company, similar to trading companies already in existence in countries like Japan. These are being formed by banks and large companies like General Electric, Sears, and National Intergroup (formerly National Steel), etc. These companies can offer broader services than export management companies, including financing, barter, and countertrade. Since this is such a new concept, any interested manufacturer should contact the local Department of Commerce office or trade association to determine if an export trading company already exists to work with manufacturers in his or her field.

Another source of help can be found in existing U.S.-based export publications. There are several, including *Export*[2], *Worldwide Hardware*[3], and *Showcase USA*[4]. Each of these magazines can be a source of much valuable information—overall market statistics, trends, and indications of product interest for various product categories by country, distribution peculiarities of countries, etc. In most instances, they have market/media factfiles that can be a starting point in evaluating international opportunities and which will help neophyte exporters in establishing the right priorities as to which countries might best be served.

Worldwide Hardware, for example, lists the top 20 U.S. markets by department, for a number of basic DIY products. Excerpts from that data are included in this chapter as an illustration of the kinds of material that export publications can provide American firms.

No serious effort at exporting should be undertaken without attending some of the major international trade shows in one's specific field. These trips should be made before one decides to exhibit. In effect, they become important fact-finding missions. What kind of competition does one face from other countries exhibiting at the show or trade fair? What kinds of design, packaging, merchandising, and promotions are currently being used, and do you have a differential advantage? Will it be necessary to get one's product approved by government agencies—similar to Underwriter's Laboratories, for example? What can one learn about distribution channels? Attending an international trade fair also gives one an opportunity to visit with local trade/business publication executives who can generally provide a quick briefing on trends in their own country.

Visits to fairs like Macef in Milan, Italy; Frankfurt, Hanover, and Cologne in Germany; Birmingham in England—plus many others—are inexpensive investments in future sales development. One can learn what international fairs might be of interest by checking with the International Trade Administration within the Department of Commerce, manufacturer trade associations, or the export magazines named ear-

---

[2] Published by Johnston International Publishing Corp., 386 Park Ave. S., New York, NY 10016. Johnston publishes several international editions covering a variety of product categories.

[3] Published by the National Retail Hardware Association, 770 N. High School Rd., Indianapolis, In. 46224. This is a semiannual publication designed to help manufacturers of consumer hardlines expand their export sales. It was founded in April 1980 and is published in April and October of each year.

[4] The export publication of Sell OverSeas America, it is published at 5950 Canoga Ave., Woodland Hills, CA. 91367. It comes out six times a year, as does *Export* magazine.

lier. Another source is the consulate in any particular country in which one might be interested.

One of the interesting low-cost market development programs of the Department of Commerce is a so-called catalog show. These are run periodically by the DOC in various countries to allow U.S. firms to ship over catalog material on their lines and, for as little as $200 to $300, get an idea of market potential. An American generally is on hand to work with overseas visitors to the catalog show. Often a trade publication representative or trade association executive from the field is the resident expert on hand. The Department of Commerce, in Washington, publishes lists of these shows, and local DOC offices can provide information about them.

Another very inexpensive but valuable way to determine overseas interest in a product line is via publicity in *Commercial News,* another DOC publication issued from Washington, D.C. This is essentially a new-product publication that goes to the various embassies and consulates around the world. There, overseas personnel scan the items in each issue, decide if a product might have potential in that particular country, and then translate and reproduce the material for their own bulletins that go to distributors, wholesalers, import agents, etc. in each country. DOC officials claim that as many as 200,000 possible buyer/agent exposures can be obtained in this way.[5] The costs are very low. All products publicized must be American-made. Periodically, complete issues are devoted to a single field for maximum impact—e.g., sporting goods, computers, etc.

There is no way that one chapter can teach anyone how to export, but the body of helpful information is growing daily. Foreign departments of banks can help answer the credit/collection problems and explain letters of credit and other documentation required. Freight forwarders take the mystery out of shipping. Overseas sales insurance requirements can be explained by competent insurance agencies. Too many U.S. firms imagine difficulties that don't exist or fail to realize how many sources of help already exist.

Any company that has not seriously explored the export market may very well be missing tremendous sales potential. Not all U.S. products are exportable, of course, but a world market that is as large or larger than the U.S. market certainly should not be ignored. The time and effort to determine if your product can be sold in some of the 167 nations in the free world could be the best investment you can make in your company's future growth.

---

[5] Information on how to submit a product to *Commercial News* can be obtained through the local DOC office or by writing the editor, Ann Watts, in care of *Commercial News,* Department of Commerce, Washington, D.C.

SOURCES OF INFORMATION

— International Trade Administration, Department of Commerce, Washington, D.C., or any of the 48 regional offices. See local telephone directories.

— U.S. Chamber of Commerce, 1615 H St. N.W., Washington, D.C. 20062.

— Departments of commerce of many state governments.

— International departments of major banks in major cities.

— Freight forwarders (see Yellow Pages in telephone directories).

— American Management Association, 135 W. 50th St., New York, N.Y. 10020.

— Business departments of many colleges and universities, especially those with international courses or strong marketing departments.

— Business and trade associations within one's special field.

— Consulates and embassies of targeted potential markets can be found in telephone directories of most major cities, especially New York, Chicago, Los Angeles, and San Francisco.

— Export Publications: Johnston International Publishing Corp., 386 Park Ave. S., New York, N.Y. 10016; *Worldwide Hardware*, 770 N. High School Rd., Indianapolis, IN. 46224; *Showcase USA*, 5950 Canoga Ave., Woodland Hills, CA. 91367

— Chase Trade Information Corp., One World Trade Center, Suite 7800, New York, N.Y. 10048—a source of credit information.

— National Association of Export Management Companies, 200 Madison Ave., New York, N.Y. 10016—a source of firms that serve as export management companies which can be supplied based on their specialization.

PROGRAMS AND SERVICES

Export Counseling

The International Trade Administration District Office offers individual counseling services to advise businesses on (1) marketing goods and services, (2) identifying foreign markets, (3) locating agents or distributors, (4) sources of credit information, (5) financing, (6) payment methods, (7) insurance, (8) export documentation, and (9) export control regulations and other special export assistance.

In addition, the district office can provide counseling and information on other export support organizations: FCIA (Foreign Credit Insurance Association) which offers a program covering commercial/

political risks abroad on export receivables; Export-Import Bank of the United States, an international financial institution of the U.S. government which extends loans and loan guarantees to foreign buyers; and OPIC (Overseas Private Investment Corporation), a U.S. government agency which provides guarantees on U.S. investment in developing countries.

Trade Opportunities Program (TOP)

This computerized program furnishes export sales leads from U.S. commercial offices overseas, available in two forms: The TOP Notice provides, to an individual subscriber, specific leads in his/her line of products; The TOP Bulletin is a weekly computer printout of all TOP Notices worldwide for that period.

Export Mailing List Service (EMLS)

This computer service provides lists of potential foreign importers or manufacturers of products or services selected according to country, products/services, and activities.

Trade Lists

These listings—either by country or products—identify prospective agents, distributors, importers, etc. arranged by Standard Industrial Classification. They may be purchased for a nominal fee.

Agent/Distributor Service

This is a custom service designed to locate an appropriate representative in targeted countries for a U.S. manufacturer's specific product line. It provides the opportunity for the foreign prospect to actually review and render a judgment on handling the line in that country. A nominal fee is charged to conduct the survey.

World Traders Data Report (WTDR)

While not a credit report, these reports will provide background information on any foreign firm in evaluating them.

Product Marketing Service (PMS)

"An office away from the office," for those U.S. companies intending to visit a city in which a U.S. export development office is located. The office can be used as a base of sales promotion in that country of visitation.

New Products USA Program (NPIS)

For a nominal charge, new products can receive publicity in various commercial newsletters that are sent out by the U.S. Foreign Commercial Service Offices around the world. It is available to U.S. products new to the domestic market in the past two years which have not been sold in more than three countries and which are genuinely new and with unique features.

International Market Search

This program will help you reach an estimated 200,000 key executives in business and government abroad for a nominal fee. If your products are identified among several preselected industries and have not been sold in more than 15 foreign country markets, you can qualify for this program. Inquire at the district office for current product themes being featured.

Joint-Venture/Foreign Licensee Program

U.S. firms seeking overseas joint-venture partners, licensing, and investment proposals can receive publicity in various commercial newsletters that are sent out by U.S. Foreign Commercial Services Offices around the world.

Catalog Exhibitions

These are special displays featuring American product catalogs, sales brochures, and other graphic sales materials at U.S. Foreign Service Posts or in conjunction with trade shows. This is an inexpensive marketing tool in identifying foreign market receptivity to your product or service.

Trade Missions

The department sponsors two types: (1) Specialized trade mission which is planned and led by the department after determining the product theme and itinerary on the basis of research to identify strong market opportunities; (2) Industry Organized Government Approved (IOGA) which may be organized and led by state development agencies, trade associations, or similar business organizations.

Trade Shows Abroad

The district office provides advice and other assistance for those who wish to participate in various trade fairs around the world.

Commercial Exhibitions

The Commerce Department participates in U.S. pavilions at major international exhibitions. Commerce also sponsors solo exhibitions of American products when there are no suitable trade fairs available. Such exhibitions are scheduled only when in-depth research reveals excellent sales opportunities for these products.

Technical Sales Seminars

The department sponsors or assists in sending four to six technically qualified U.S. businesspeople to overseas markets to participate in a formal program for the presentation of technical know-how and state-of-the-art information. Sales and direct business negotiations are part of the program.

Trade Complaints and Inquiry Service

The service is designed to help U.S. and foreign traders settle trade disputes informally and amicably.

Major Export Projects Program

The department helps qualified U.S. firms compete for contracts for major projects—those $5 million or more—enables U.S. firms to obtain a bigger share of major construction, engineering, and development projects around the world.

Export Control Service

The department assists U.S. firms with export control regulations, Commodity Schedule B classifications, and export documentation.

Export Seminars, Conferences, and Workshops

Indianapolis staff is available for speaking engagements and conducting seminars on various subjects involving international trade.

U.S. Trade with Selected Countries ($ millions)

Area and Country	U.S. Exports				U.S. Imports			
	1980	1981	1982	Jan.–June 1983	1980	1981	1982	Jan.–June 1983
Western Hemisphere								
Barbados	136	149	155	85	96	81	106	68
Belize	58	69	64	20	60	43	36	14
Bermuda	136	150	172	88	13	18	12	8
Bolivia	172	189	99	34	182	177	109	94
Guyana	96	106	56	15	120	104	71	30
Leeward, Windward Islands	152	282	174	73	36	32	27	16
Suriname	137	138	128	59	109	179	60	30
Western Europe								
Gibralter	4	53	47	25	2	1	1	1
Iceland	79	71	77	34	200	198	184	106
Ireland	836	1,025	983	546	417	498	556	251
Malta	26	33	48	51	9	10	14	14
Near East—North Africa								
Bahrain	197	296	220	70	16	35	30	1
Iran	23	300	122	97	456	64	585	276
Jordan	407	726	620	280	2	2	7	2
Lebanon	303	296	294	215	33	18	19	10
Libya	509	813	301	105	8,595	5,301	512	1
Qatar	129	157	153	63	235	115	106	10
Syria	239	143	138	48	26	83	10	6
Yemen (Sana)	77	44	38	43	1	(*)	1	(*)

Far East–South Asia								
Bangladesh	292	158	227	101	85	85	70	41
Brunei	70	45	79	30	280	329	211	8
Burma	29	34	34	8	9	15	17	5
Macao	2	1	14	(*)	114	154	201	95
Pacific Islands, Trust Terr	49	58	62	32	7	16	6	5
Papua New Guinea	38	55	66	33	53	50	18	10
Sri Lanka	62	90	198	40	125	154	175	88
Sub-Sahara Africa								
Angola	111	268	158	38	742	904	697	390
Burundi	3	4	4	1	40	28	41	20
Congo	22	25	69	8	143	286	652	301
Ethiopia	72	62	43	22	87	83	102	54
Ghana	127	154	116	89	207	246	362	94
Guinea	34	53	28	9	94	96	121	57
Kenya	141	150	98	29	54	52	71	36
Malagasy Republic	7	16	24	14	91	70	63	42
Malawi	4	5	3	1	25	62	31	7
Mauritania	20	27	26	20	(*)	(*)	1	(*)
Mozambique	69	35	26	11	105	83	51	19
Rwanda	5	6	6	2	68	40	33	12
Senegal	41	42	30	14	9	1	1	1
Sierra Leone	21	26	15	7	77	45	35	4
Sudan	142	208	270	72	17	58	16	11
Swaziland	6	7	2	3	58	66	28	6
Tanzania	62	48	41	11	32	19	29	9
Uganda	12	7	9	3	126	101	156	51
Zambia	99	68	69	21	200	114	30	34

Note: The selected countries are those for which U.S. exports or imports were valued at $25 million or more in 1982 and are not otherwise covered in the country articles in this issue. Exports are valued f.a.s. (free alongside ship); imports, customs values.

* Less than $500,000.

Source: *Business America*, August 22, 1983.

Contact Facilitation Service—Export Trading Companies

The department has established a clearinghouse for both U.S. suppliers and export trading companies (ETC). This service assists U.S. producers identify and contact newly formed ETCs. Similarly, ETCs may want to use this program to identify possible clients for their services. Registration is free, but a nominal fee is charged to conduct a search.

For more information on any of the programs and publications contact:

> ITA District Office
> U.S. Department of Commerce
> 357 U.S. Courthouse Bldg.
> 46 E. Ohio Street
> Indianapolis, IN. 46204
> Tel.: (317) 269–6214

COMMERCIAL PUBLISHERS

The Foreign Trade Marketplace, ed. George J. Schultz. Detroit: Gale Research Co., 1977, 662 pg., $48. Contains a listing of more than 700 export management companies with sections covering export opportunities, trade shows, financing, insurance, and transportation.

Exporters Directory, U.S. Buying Guide, The Journal of Commerce, 445 Marshall Street, Phillipsburg, New Jersey 08865. Lists more than 40,000 export firms including manufacturers, export managers and export merchants, as well as products exported and trade associations. 1979/1980 ed., $150.

DEPARTMENT OF COMMERCE DISTRICT OFFICES

Albuquerque, 87102, 505 Marquette Ave. N.W., Rm. 1015, (505) 766–2386.

Anchorage, 99513, P.O. Box 32, 701 C St., (907) 271–5041.

Atlanta, 30309, Suite 600, 1365 Peachtree St., N.E., (404) 881–7000.

Baltimore, 21202, 415 U.S. Customhouse, Gay and Lombard Sts., (301) 962–3560.

Birmingham, 35205, Suite 200–201, 908 S. 20th St., (205) 254–1331.

Boston, 02116, 10th Floor, 441 Stuart St., (617) 223–2312.

Buffalo, 14202, 1312 Federal Bldg., 111 W. Huron St., (716) 846–4191.

Charleston, W. Va., 25301, 3000 New Federal Office Bldg., 500 Quarrier St., (304) 343–6181, Ext. 375.

Cheyenne, 82001 6022 O'Mahoney Federal Center, 2120 Capitol Ave., (307) 778–2220, Ext. 2151.

Chicago, 60603, Room 1406, Mid-Continental Plaza Bldg., 55 E. Monroe St., (312) 353–4450.

Cincinnati, 45202, 10504 Fed. Bldg., 550 Main St., (513) 684–2944.

Cleveland, 44114, Room 600, 666 Euclid Ave., (216) 522–4750.

Columbia, S.C., 29201, Fed. Bldg., 1835 Assembly St., (803) 765–5345.

Dallas, 75242, Room 7A5, 1100 Commerce St., (214) 767–0542.

Denver, 80202, Room 165, New Custom House, 19th and Stout Sts., (303) 837–3246.

Des Moines, 50309, 817 Federal Bldg., 210 Walnut St., (515) 284–4222.

Detroit, 48226, 445 Federal Bldg., 231 W. Lafayette, (313) 226–3650.

Greensboro, N.C., 27402, 203 Federal Bldg., W. Market St., P.O. Box 1950, (919) 378–5345.

Hartford, 06103, Room 610-B, Fed. Bldg., 450 Main St., (203) 244–3530.

Honolulu, 96850, 4106 Federal Bldg., 300 Ala Moana Blvd., P.O. Box 50026, (808) 546–8694.

Houston, 77002, 2625 Federal Bldg., 515 Rusk Ave., (713) 226–4231.

Indianapolis, 46204, 357 U.S. Court-House & Federal Office Bldg., 46 E. Ohio St., (317) 269–6214.

Jackson, Miss., 39201, Suite 500, Providence Capitol, 200 Pascagoula, (601) 969–4388.

Kansas City, 64106, Rm. 1840, 601 E. 12th St., (816) 374–3142.

Little Rock, 72201, Rm. 635, 320 W. Capitol, (501) 378–5794.

Los Angeles, 90049, Rm. 800, 11777 San Vicente Blvd., (213) 824–7591.

Louisville, 40202, Rm. 636, U.S. Post Office and Courthouse Bldg., (502) 582–5066.

Memphis, 38103, Room 710, 147 Jefferson Ave., (901) 521–3213.

Miami, 33130, Rm. 821, City National Bank Bldg., 25 W. Flagler St., (305) 350–5267.

Milwaukee, 53202, 605 Federal Office Bldg., 517 E. Wisconsin Ave., (414) 291–3473.

Minneapolis, 55401, 218 Federal Bldg., 110 S. 4th St., (612) 725–2133.

New Orleans, 70130, Room 432, International Trade Mart, 2 Canal St., (504) 589–6546.

New York, 10278, 37th Floor, Federal Office Bldg., 26 Federal Plaza, Foley Sq., (212) 264–0634.

Newark, 07102, Gateway Bldg. (4th Floor), Market St. & Penn Plaza, (201) 645–6214.

Omaha, 68102, 1815 Capitol Ave., Suite 703A, (402) 221–3665.

Philadelphia, 19106, 9448 Federal Bldg., 600 Arch St., (215) 597–2866.

Phoenix, 85073, 2950 Valley Bank Center, 201 N. Central Ave., (602) 261–3285.

Pittsburgh, 15222, 2002 Fed. Bldg., 1000 Liberty Ave, (412) 644–2850.

Portland, Ore., 97204, Room 618, 1220 S.W. 3rd Ave., (503) 221–3001.

Reno, Nev., 89503, 777 W. 2nd St., Room 120, (702) 784–5203.
Richmond, 23240, 8010 Federal Bldg., 400 N. 8th St. (804) 771–2246.
St. Louis, 63105, 120 S. Central Ave., (314) 425–3302.
Salt Lake City, 84010, Rm. 340, U.S. Post Office and Courthouse Bldg., 350 Main St., (801) 524–5116.
San Francisco, 94102, Federal Bldg., Box 36013, 450 Golden Gate Ave., (415) 556–5860.
San Juan, P.R., 00918, Room 659, Federal Bldg., Chardon Ave., (809) 753–4555, Ext. 555.
Savannah, 31412, 222 U.S. Courthouse, P.O. Box 9746, 125–29 Bull St., (912) 232–4321, Ext. 204.
Seattle, 98109, 706 Lake Union Bldg., 1700 Westlake Ave., North, (206) 442–5616.

INFORMATION SOURCES FOR EXHIBITING INTERNATIONALLY

This brief list of information sources is not considered to be complete or definitive; it merely represents those publications most frequently consulted.

Overseas Export Promotion Calendar
Industry Participation Division
Office of Export Promotion & Room 4102
U.S. Department of Commerce
Washington, D.C. 20230

Fast Facts European Hotel Locator
Denhamwood, Inc.
4069 Hayvenhurst Avenue
Encino, CA 91436

What Every Exhibitor Ought to Know
Andry Montgomery Group
11 Manchester Square
London WIM 5AB
England

Export Information Services for U.S. Business Firms Hot to Get the Most from Overseas Exhibitors
Focus on Trade
All of the above publications are available from any Department of Commerce District Office

World Trade Activities
Glahe International Inc.
1700 "K" Street, N.W.
Washington, D.C. 20006

Internal Show News & World Calendar of High-Technology Events
TWI
1150 Karlstad Drive
Sunnyvale, CA 94086

Getting around Overseas
Personal International Directory
The Well-Informed Executives Handy Guide to International Communications
All of the above publications are available from:
AT&T Long Lines
Room 3A1040
Bedminister, NJ 07921

Creative Selling Through Trade Shows
By Al Hanlon
Hanlon Associates
56 Summer Street
Shrewsbury, MA 01545

Trade Show Week International
Editorial Department
8687 Milrose Avenue
Los Angeles, CA 90069
Circulation Department: P.O. Box 716
Back Bay Annex
Boston, MA 02117

World Convention Dates
The Hendrickson Publishing Company
79 Washington Street
Hempstead, NY 11550

Gavel-Annual International Directory
Meetings & Conventions
Ziff-Dafis Publishing Company
1 Park Avenue
New York, NY

Exhibits Schedule
633 Third Avenue
New York, NY 10017
(212) 986–4800

Canadian Industry Shows and Exhibitions
MacLean-Hunter Ltd.
481 University Avenue
Toronto, Ontario M5W 1A7

Successful Meetings Annual International Convention Facilities Directory
Bill Communications Inc.
1422 Chestnut Street
Philadelphia, PA 19102

Guide to Efficient Show Planning
By Harold E. Bartlett
Andrews Bartlett & Associates
1849 West 24th Street
Cleveland, OH 44113

Bringing World Market Closer to Home
A Guide to International Trade Procedures and Documentation
Unz & Co., 190 Baldwin Avenue,
Jersey City, N.J. 07306. $12.50

Here Today and Gone Tomorrow
By Suzanne Hilton
Published by:
The Westminster Press
Philadelphia, PA

How to Participate Profitably in Trade Shows
By Robert B. Konikow
Dartnell
4660 N. Ravenswood Avenue
Chicago, IL 60640

Traveller
Lunn Poly Ltd.
Taylor Gardner Associates Ltd.
1 Russell Street
Leamington Spa CV32 5QA
England

The Travelore Report
The International Letter for People Who Travel
222 S. Fifteenth Street
Philadelphia, PA 19102

Budget Guide
Display Rules and Regulations
Exhibit Industry Guide
International Exhibitors Guide
Exhibitors Workbook
All of the above publications are available from:
NTSEA
4300-L Lincoln Avenue

Rolling Meadows, IL 60008
(312) 359–8160

The Exhibit Medium
By David Maxwell
Published by: Successful Meetings Magazine
1422 Chestnut Street
Philadelphia, PA 19102

Exhibitions: Universal Marketing Tools
By Alfred Alles
Published by: Halsted Press
John Wiley & Sons
New York, NY

Trade Shows: Where Prospects Call on You
Reprint from:
Sales and Marketing Management Magazine
633 Third Avenue
New York, NY 10017
August, 1979

Source Book—The "How to" Guide for Importers and Exporters
Unz & Co., 190 Baldwin Avenue,
Jersey City, N.J. 07306. Free

Selling Overseas: An Exporter's Guide to Information Sources
1st Ed. 10/80. The National Trade Show Exhibitors Association,
1027 Connecticut Ave., N.W., Washington, D.C. 20036.
Members: $2.50, Nonmembers: $3.50.

The International Exhibitor's Handbook
1st Ed. 10/80. The National Trade Show Exhibitors Association,
4300-L Lincoln Ave., Rolling Meadows, Ill. 60008.
Members: $15, Nonmembers: $45

Sources of Aid and Information for U.S. Exporters
1st Ed. The Washington Researchers, 918 16th St., N.W.,
Washington, D.C. 20006. $30 per copy.

9

THE MODULAR
MARKETING PROCESS

by
Charles W. Stryker

Trinet, Inc.
A Control Data Subsidiary

INTRODUCTION

Take a minute to add up the costs to your company of making a marketing contact. There are salary, benefits, travel expenses, advertising expenses, support staff, etc. If you really could obtain the true cost information, the results would shock you. Some of these cost factors have been tracked over the previous 10 years. For example, the cost of a single industrial sales call has increased over 300 percent. That is an increase from approximately $60 in 1973 to over $225 in 1983, and that cost is for a *single* industrial call. For some industries (e.g., office products) the number of sales calls required to obtain a new industrial order has increased from 10 calls in 1973 to over 20 calls in 1983. The compounding of these two effects—cost of a call and number of calls required to obtain an order—has created a six- to tenfold increase in the cost of obtaining a new industrial order. Put simply, many firms can no longer afford to market through traditional methods. This reality has caused many marketers to search for new approaches to productively implement the marketing function. The days are gone forever when you could simply hire a bright young person, equip the new rep with a sales presentation, and send the rep through as many doors as possible, hoping to find new orders.

The questions, therefore, are:

- How will marketing executives implement the new marketing function in the 80s?
- What are the basic ingredients of an effective marketing system?
- How can the new system be implemented to be flexible and adaptable to future changes?
- How does one begin implementation of such a system?

These questions will be addressed in this chapter. To begin, let's call this new approach *modular marketing.*

MODULAR MARKETING—OVERVIEW

The concept behind modular marketing is to separate the marketing process into its fundamental components or modules. Once this has been done, each module of the process can be analyzed individually to identify those methods that can improve marketing efficiency. The concept of modular marketing parallels what was done in the manufacturing process 75 years ago. Managers realized that the most efficient way to assemble a car, for example, was not to have one man build the total car. The production process was broken down into its fundamental parts, and efficient methods were found to perform each unique part of the process. Today, the salesperson is operating under the same principles that production workers did before the time of Henry Ford. The salesperson is told to perform the total sales job: find the prospect, qualify the prospect, communicate the sales message, evaluate the prospect's response to the communication, establish product awareness, develop proposals, close contracts, and manage and control the territory from both revenue and cost viewpoints. Not only are sales representatives asked to perform all these jobs, each requiring very different skills, but they are asked to do this with no technology and minimal training and support. It is clear that in the mid-80s, this procedure must change. To begin this process of change, let us first examine the basic modules of the marketing process.

As displayed in the figure, the marketing process has three fundamental components. These are:

- Front-end analysis
- Back-end processing
- Measurement

The Front-End Analysis

The *front-end analysis* consists of those modules which communicate the basic product benefits message to the marketplace. Based on this

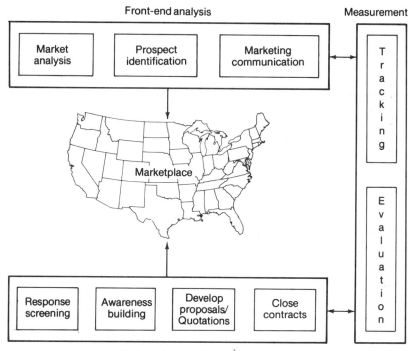

Front-end analysis   Measurement

Back-end processing

communication to the marketplace, prospects are identified who have indicated an interest in the product. To perform front-end analysis effectively, three distinct modules must be implemented. These modules are market analysis, prospect identification, and marketing communication.

1. The *market analysis* module identifies the characteristics of high-potential prospects. These characteristics could be such factors as the industry of the business prospect, the size of the business, the title of the decision-making executive, the age and income level of the executive, etc.

2. Once the market analysis module identifies the factors that describe the high-potential prospect, the *prospect identification* module identifies specifically those businesses and/or individuals who meet the high-potential criteria. The output of the prospect identification module could take the form of a prospect list of names and addresses or a target market specified by geodemographic communities, as well as many other possible formats.

3. Once the high-potential prospects are identified in a specific manner, the *marketing communication* module takes over. It is the function of the marketing communication module to communicate to the identified prospects the product benefits message. This module should select not only the most effective communication content but also the most effective communication medium (e.g., mail, telephone, TV, radio, print, etc.).

The result of implementing these three front-end modules is communication of the benefits message to all high-potential prospects. This activity will result in a subset of the high-potential prospects declaring an initial interest in your product. This interest inquiry may take a variety of forms, including telephone calls, mail inquiries, walk-ins to retail stores, etc.

Back-End Processing

The interest inquiries from high-potential prospects are the result of the front-end analysis. These inquiries (or responses from the marketplace) now enter the *back-end processing.* The back-end processing consists of those modules that allow the interest inquiries to be converted into closed sales orders in a cost-effective manner. The last three words of the previous sentence, *cost-effective manner,* are often overlooked by marketing and salespeople when responding to interest inquiries. The days are gone when a company can afford to respond equally to all inquiries. Only those inquiries that justify sales expense must be processed.

To perform the back-end analysis effectively, four modules are required. These are response screening, awareness building, proposals/quotations, and closing contracts.

1. The purpose of the *response-screening* module is to ensure that sales resources are allocated only to those accounts that justify the anticipated sales expenses. There are three primary methods used to screen prospects. The most common is the use of a telephone-screening system where questions are asked of respondents to determine their sales potential. The second method uses secondary research tools, for example, the use of credit report information. The third method is to make a face-to-face sales call. This is, of course, the most effective but, unfortunately, the most costly method.

2. For those respondents who pass the screening criteria, the *awareness-building* module begins the initial phase of the contact selling process. The purpose of this module is to communicate effectively to the prospect information about your company and its products. The communication should concentrate on product benefits. To be effective, this module should communicate enough information to allow high-potential prospects to understand how your company and its products can benefit their business. The contact method of communication typically involves sales calls to decision makers, but mail, telephone, and retail methods are also used. The result of a successful awareness-building process is prospects who request a proposal or quotation.

3. Once the awareness-building process is complete, the next module processes the requests for *proposals and quotations*. The purpose of this process is to ensure that accurate and timely proposals and quotations are delivered to the prospect. By the time a prospect requests a proposal or quotation, your company has invested a significant number of sales dollars in developing the account. It is critical to ensure that the machinery is in place to deliver proposals and quotations in an accurate and timely manner.

4. Once proposals or quotations are delivered to qualified prospects, the next phase of back-end processing is the module to *close contracts*. The purpose of this process is to ensure that the proper resources and skills are brought to bear so that as many proposals as possible are converted to orders. This process ensures that the proper skills to deal effectively with objections and the proper resources to combat competitive forces are available at the proper time.

The result of effectively implementing the four modules of back-end processing is signed contracts. Equally important is that this process ensures that the signed contracts are obtained at an acceptable level of sales cost.

Measurement

Measurement is the third component of an effective marketing system. The purpose of measurement is to monitor constantly and report on the performance of the seven modules in the front-end analysis and back-end process. To monitor the performance of the modules, the measurement process has two modules of its own. These are the tracking module and the evaluation module.

1. The purpose of the *tracking module* is to collect and report the performance statistics associated with each module. For example, the tracking system might report how many successfully screened prospects subsequently requested proposals. This measure would be appropriate to monitor the performance of the awareness-building module.

2. The second module of the measurement process is the *evaluation module*. Its purpose is to understand why the performance of each module is as observed. The evaluation module examines why performance is as good as it is and what barriers limit the effectiveness of each module. For example, those prospects who were successfully screened who did not request proposals could be interviewed to determine why they had no further interest. Was the problem the price of the product? Competition?

The measurement process acts as the quality assurance manager. The process constantly monitors, reports, and explains where the overall sales system is operating effectively and where improvements are needed.

The following sections describe in more detail the methods used to implement each of the nine modules overviewed above. As you read through them, keep in mind how you currently perform the functions contained in the modules.

METHODS OF MODULAR MARKETING

Obviously, the modular marketing methods appropriate for your specific marketing situation cannot be described here, as each specific case requires a unique combination of methods. However, the following discussion should provide some new ideas appropriate for your marketing situation.

Module 1—Market Analysis

The objective of the market analysis module is to identify the characteristics of high-potential prospects. The characteristics to be obtained on your high-potential accounts should be those factors that relate closely to the need for your product. At the same time, the factors used for classification of potential should be readily available on many, if not all, of your prospect accounts. For example, if you were an industrial marketing firm selling word processing equipment, one of the factors you may use for classification might be the number of secretaries in a target account. If the number of secretaries is greater than 10, you classify the prospect as high-potential; less than 10, as low-potential.

When thinking about what factors to use for classification, it is often productive to think not only in static terms (e.g., how many secretaries in the prospect firm) but to think in dynamic terms (e.g., how many new secretaries have been added in the last year). Some of the best opportunities for sale result from changes taking place in prospect accounts.

The key questions in the market analysis process are what factors to use for classification (e.g., number of secretaries) and, second, what value to establish for each factor to separate high-potential from low-potential accounts (e.g., 5 secretaries versus 10 secretaries). Four basic methods can obtain the information required for the market analysis module.

1. The first method is simply to ask your salespeople what factors they feel represent a high-potential prospect. A good way to phrase the question to your sales reps is, "If I could put you face-to-face with the ideal buyer, what characteristics do you feel that buyer should have?"

2. The second method to use in the development of your high-potential profile is to analyze the characteristics of your recent customer acquisitions. There is no better indication as to the type of prospect to target than to find a prospect with the same characteristics as your recently acquired customers.

3. The third method of building your marketing success profile is to identify the characteristics of your competitors' customers. An apparent difficulty with this method is that you must be able to identify recent buyers of your competitors' products. This difficulty tends to be quite easy to overcome. For example, you could ask your salespeople to identify prospects who have recently bought from your competition. Another method might involve capturing information on financial liens. If your competitors' products are typically leased (e.g., computers), the leasing company will often file a lien on that property (UCC1) with the state. You could examine these financial records to identify what specific prospects have recently obtained your competitors' products.

4. The fourth method of building your market analysis profile involves market research. You initially specify a high-potential market based on your judgment and experience. Then you sample this market in a manner that is statistically sound. You then conduct interviews (mail, telephone, face-to-face) with potential buyers within the target market. These interviews ask the identified decision makers to define what buying actions they would take as you describe different product features and benefits. Some decision makers will disclose preference for a combination of features and benefits that you offer (or plan to offer). The characteristics of these respondents form the basis of your market analysis profile.

To summarize, there are four basic methods used to build the market analysis profile. These are:

- Ask the salesperson
- Analyze recent customer acquisitions

- Analyze competitive placements
- Research

It is quite typical for all four of these methods to be used in concert to form a consolidated market analysis profile.

Module 2—Prospect Identification

The objective of the prospect identification module is to identify specifically those businesses and/or individuals who meet the high-potential criteria developed in the market analysis module. The output of the prospect identification module is either a list, by name, of high-potential prospects or a more aggregate identification such as Zip codes derived from census data. Regardless of the form, the result is the same. The prospect identification module allows the marketing process to identify specifically high-potential prospects. When performing the prospect identification function, the key question to answer is where to obtain information on prospect accounts. In the United States there are basically five sources of information about prospect accounts. These are:

Government Data. The government (federal, state, and local) requires certain businesses and individuals to submit many facts for government examination. This is particularly true for regulated businesses (hospitals, physicians, lawyers) and public companies. This information is then placed, by the government, in the public domain.

Trade Association Data. Many trade associations collect a variety of information about their membership. Trade associations then make this information public to better serve the interests of their membership.

Telephone Company Records. When a business or individual wants a telephone book listing, they make information available for publication in the telephone directories. This information therefore becomes part of the public record.

Response Lists. When people make inquiries or place orders for products and services, their identity and information about themselves may become public. There are currently over 20,000 response list data bases available in the marketplace.

Credit Reports. When a company or individual wants to purchase an item on credit, typically the supplier requires a statement of credit history. To meet this requirement, the buyer applying for credit will make public a credit report.

For typical implementation of the prospect identification module, selected sources are chosen from the above five categories. These sources are then organized and combined to form an integrated prospect identification list.

Module 3—Marketing Communication Module

The function of the marketing communication module is to communicate to the prospect list the product benefits message. The questions, of course, are how to communicate the message and what message to communicate. The *how* question is answered through TV, radio, print, mail, telephone, and face-to-face contact. The mix of the above vehicles depends on the characteristics of the high-potential prospect list: how many prospects, whether they are clustered by city, by industry, by size of firm, etc. *What* message to communicate is the next consideration. There is an interesting trade-off to consider when constructing your marketing communication program. This is the relationshp between response rate and interest level. *Response rate* is the relationship between the number of high-potential prospects that declare interest and the size of the target audience. For example, if the target audience had 100 prospects and 10 declared interest as a result of your offer, you would have achieved a 10 percent response rate. *Interest level* relates to the quality of the responses. If in one program targeted to an audience of 100 prospects you achieved a response rate of 10 percent, and 7 of the 10 respondents purchased your product after one sales call, you would have a conversion rate of 70 percent.

Typically, in the design of your marketing communication programs, you can increase response rate but sacrifice conversion rate and vice versa. For example, in one case you may choose to send a letter to each high-potential prospect to describe your product and ask for the prospect to call you if he or she wants to buy the product. This communication would yield a very low response rate. However, anyone who responded to such an offer would be very interested in your product. On the other hand, you could send a letter to the same prospect describing the benefits of your product and ask the prospect, if interested, to attend a demonstration of the product's capabilities. The response rate to such an offer will be much higher. However, the interest level will be lower, on the average, as more people will want to see the demo even if they are not sure about their buying intentions.

This trade-off between response rate and interest level is critical in the management of sales resources. Of course, in a real situation you would want to test a number of marketing communications to determine the optimal relationship between response rate and interest levels.

Module 4—Response Screening

The purpose of this module is to ensure that sales resources are allocated only to those accounts that justify the anticipated sales expenses. When a prospect, even a high-potential prospect, makes an inquiry, to a large degree that act is at the discretion of the prospect. Remember that from that point on, how your company responds to that prospect inquiry is largely at your discretion. This is one area where salespeople must begin to fight their instincts and historical training. Due to the ever escalating cost of sale, salespeople can no longer respond to every inquiry in the same manner. Some inquiries require immediate and complete attention, some require lower-priority follow-up, and some inquiries you simply can't afford to follow up. To handle all inquiries as hot, high-potential leads simply means you are spending too much time and money on too many prospects. Once you decide to allocate high-cost resources to an inquiry, the sales cost will add up fast. The time to be careful is when the inquiry is made, before large cost of sales dollars are gone.

The first step in screening the account is to verify that it is on the high-potential list. If it is, this may be sufficient justification for passing the response screening. If the inquiry is not on the high-potential list, the next step might be to call the prospect and conduct a telephone screening. This screening could ask questions with respect to interest level, level of potential, available budget, where the prospect is in the buying cycle, what competitive forces are at work, whether the inquirer is the decision maker, etc. Based on the responses to the telephone screening, the prospect is placed either in the high-potential category or is rejected.

An interesting strategy to be developed is what to do with the inquiries that do not pass the response screening. Although they may not have sufficient potential to justify sales activity now, they may represent good opportunities in the future. You simply cannot ignore the inquiry. On the other hand, you cannot afford to follow up with the same activities that high-potential accounts require. The answer lies in a strategy that groups together low potentials in a manner that allows follow-up. For example, you might telephone a group of low-potential respondents and invite them to your office to see a demonstration of your product. In essence, the prospect pays for the travel cost and time, and you can use your scarce resources to present product capabilities to many prospects at once. At the same time, you are offering a fair alternative to those prospects who are not part of the market to which you can sell in a cost-effective manner. Remember, you can't afford to sell to everybody, and you can lose a lot of sales expense dollars trying.

Module 5—Awareness Building

Once a prospect passes the response screening, you have made an investment decision: you have now decided to invest significant sales expense to sell your product to the identified interested prospect. The first phase of this selling process is awareness building. The purpose of this module is to communicate, in depth, the specific benefits of your product to the interested decision makers and related decision influencers. The key questions to address are:

• How much time and money to invest?
• Where to invest your resources (which decision makers, what frequency of contact, etc.)?

It is important to examine these questions at the beginning of the awareness process. Many salespeople have made many sales calls to a specific account. When asked after the call what was the purpose of the call, and what was accomplished by it, it is often hard to elicit from them what return is expected on that $200 sales call investment. There are many salespeople who have made 10, 20, even 100 sales calls on a prospect account and still can't be sure how close they are to an order.

This awareness-building process is very hard to manage. The key to effective management of this process is the *account plan*. As soon as the decision is made to begin the awareness-building process, the development of an account plan for that account should be required. In the account plan, the representative should identify:

• The decision makers and influencers who will be called on.
• When they will be called on.
• What the objective of the call is.
• What the expected results of the call are.
• What potential is in the account.
• What the planned total sales cost is.

Whenever account plans are discussed for the first time with sales representatives, the idea seems impractical. How can a sales representative plan when to call on a particular executive? Typically, the problem with implementing the account plan is not the *plan* but the *schedule*. You may not be able to accomplish what you want, when you want. However, the plan is the important ingredient, much more important than the schedule. It is interesting to observe the sales management process with respect to account plans. Typically, managers pay close attention to the schedule ("Will you have $500,000 of revenue by the end of June?") and do not pay attention to the plan ("Has the legal department approved our proposal?").

Module 6—Develop Proposals/Quotations

Once the awareness-building module is implemented to its positive conclusion, the prospect will request a proposal or quotation. This is a significant milestone in the selling process, as this is a strong, measurable indication of interest. It implies that the prospect does understand the benefits of your product and is willing to consider an investment decision. The key ingredient of an efficient proposal and/or quotation module is to take full advantage of the fact that, most likely, other similar proposals have been developed. It is interesting to observe sales rep after sales rep developing proposals and quotations as if none had ever been written before.

The first area in which to improve efficiency is to standardize the contents of proposals and quotations. Once the contents are standardized, they can be reviewed by sales, financial, and legal departments. Standardizing by no means implies that every proposal must be identical. Each standard clause would have many options that customize it to the particular account situation. Today, the technology available in the word processing environment facilitates this process. The second area of efficiency is in the pricing function. Over and over sales reps are observed wrestling with price books, guides, tear sheets, and home office letters attempting to bring some sense to the pricing information. This tends to be a function attractive to automation. The concept of maintaining one centralized pricing file, on computer, available via telephone to all sales offices and/or representatives, often is an attractive alternative to manual records.

Module 7—Close Contract

At this point in the selling process, you have completed six modules and have accomplished a great deal:

- You have found a prospect and have stimulated the prospect's initial interest.
- You have verified that the prospect is worth the time, energy, and dollars involved in implementing a costly sales process.
- You have identified the key decision makers and influencers and have communicated to these individuals the benefits of your product.
- You have gone through the often tedious process of developing a comprehensive proposal/quotation.

To this point you have spent time, energy, intelligence, and money on this prospect. Don't lose discipline now! It is time to close the deal. This process is fundamentally a task that only an experienced sales representative can perform. The process of identifying and overcoming objections is as much an art as a science. However, discipline, knowledge, skill, and planning still apply. The key, again, is the *account plan*. What sales contact must be made, to what decision makers, for what purpose, etc.? With the successful implementation of the account plan, this module, of course, is the most rewarding—signed contracts.

Module 8—Tracking

Just as important as the effective implementation of the seven modules described above is the effective implementation of the two measurement modules—tracking and evaluation. If you cannot measure results, you cannot improve the process. As the old saying goes, "If you can't measure it, it doesn't count."

The tracking module monitors the performance of each of the seven modules described above. This system tracks the identified prospects, the prospects who received the marketing communication, the prospects who responded, the prospects who requested proposals, the prospects who received proposals, and the closed contracts. By monitoring information on each of these prospects, the system can identify modules that are not performing adequately. For example, this system might indicate that the marketing communication was directed to a large number of businesses of a particular type, and that few responses occurred for businesses of this type. This system may also indicate, for example, that many proposals are developed for a certain type of prospect, but rarely do these proposals result in a signed contract.

Periodically (e.g., weekly), as sales programs proceed, tracking reports are produced that display module performance by week, territory, type of prospect, etc. The objective behind this analysis is to identify the performance level of each module and to understand the nature of the observed performance. In addition to displaying actual module performance, these reports should also display anticipated performance so that a comparison can be made.

It is also important for the tracking process to display the trends of module performance. You must identify not only what the module performance is but whether it is improving or deteriorating over time.

In summary, the tracking process monitors the performance of each module. In addition, the system compares actual performance to anticipated performance and displays performance trends.

Module 9—Evaluation

The second key module of the measurement process is evaluation. The purpose of the evaluation module is to understand the prospect decision-making process. The primary question to be answered follows.

WHY AREN'T ALL HIGH-POTENTIAL PROSPECTS CONVERTED TO ORDERS?

The most successful approach in performing the evaluation process is based on telephone interviews. The methodology is based on direct telephone contact with decision makers who were exposed to various modules of the sales process. Questions are asked of the decision-making executives to understand their resultant behavior. This process begins by identifying the segments to be analyzed. There are many possible ways to select the segments of interest for your situation. The following example is a typical segment structure.

The first segment contains those individuals who were targeted with the marketing communication program but did not respond. The second segment contains those individuals who were targeted with the communication program, responded to it, but did not sign a contract. The third segment contains those individuals who were targeted with the communication program, responded with interest to the program, and did sign a contract. The following diagram summarizes this segmentation.

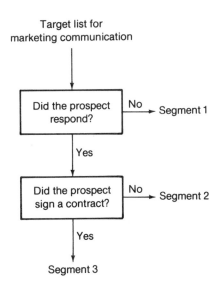

Segment 1: Nonrespondents to Direct Marketing Program

These individuals are in decision-making positions within companies that have been assessed to have a need for your product. The objective of this telephone interview is to understand accurately why this lack of interest in your marketing communication exists. Of course, the interview need not be conducted with all individuals who fall into this segment. A representative sample of these individuals is appropriate. The questions to be asked, as part of this interview, address the following interest barriers:

- Does the account truly have sales potential?
- Was the correct individual targeted?
- Was the creative content of the marketing communication effective?
- Are the perceptions that the individual has about your company a barrier to interest?
- Are the perceptions that the individual has about your product a barrier to interest?
- Is the individual committed to a competitive product?

If the above evaluation indicates, for example, that the major barrier to interest is that targeted individuals feel that the product is too expensive, your marketing communication should be modified to address the cost effectiveness of the product. If, however, the research indicates a commitment to a particular competitor, the marketing communication should be modified to highlight the advantages of your product over the competition.

Not only does the above research effort identify key barriers to improve marketing performance, this approach also provides a method to continually monitor the effects of competition.

Segment 2: Respondents/Nonbuyers

These individuals are in decision-making positions in companies that have been assessed to have potential. When probed for interest via the marketing communication, this segment of individuals responded with interest. However, when sales reps implemented the sales process, no order resulted.

The objective of the telephone interview process with this segment is to understand accurately why individuals who apparently have potential, and have indicated their interest, do not buy. Again, the interview need not be conducted with all individuals who fall into this segment. A representative sample of these individuals is appropriate. The questions to be asked as part of this interview cover the same barriers as in Segment 1 (level of potential, correct individual target, quality of creative material, etc.). However, additional questions should be asked to determine the effectiveness of the sales representative module. These questions include:

- Did the sales representative follow up?
- Did the sales representative have adequate product knowledge?
- Did the sales representative have adequate application knowledge?
- Did the sales representative have adequate sales skill?

If the above evaluation indicates, for example, that the major barrier to closing sales was lack of product knowledge by sales representatives, then a sales training course may be called for.

Again, not only does the above research effort identify key barriers, this approach also provides a method of evaluating the effect of sales training programs.

Segment 3: Buyers

The third group of individuals to interview are those who were interested in the marketing communication and did buy your product. This segment forms the class of individuals for whom the module worked. The objective of this telephone interview is to understand accurately the decision-making process of buyers so that this behavior can be amplified within the nonbuyer segments. Again, the interviews need only be given to a sample of individuals who fall into this segment. The questions to be asked as part of this interview process include the following:

- What is the application for the product?
- What was the appeal of the creative material?
- What perceptions does the individual have about the company?
- What perceptions does the individual have about the product?
- What competitors were examined?

To summarize the evaluation process, the objective is to gain an accurate understanding of the decision-making process. The most effective method of collecting the required information is through telephone interviews. The information is collected in such a manner that future sales programs can be modified to overcome identified sales barriers and capitalize on sales program strengths.

Integrating the results of both the tracking module and the evaluation module provides feedback information so that the sales program can be managed for maximum effectiveness and future programs can continually be improved.

HOW TO BEGIN—THE WORKSHOP

Once you have read this chapter and considered how the modular marketing concepts can be applied to your organization, your work has just begun. The question is how to begin integrating these concepts into your existing workflows. A good way to begin is to conduct a workshop. In this workshop you should call together those executives within your firm who have responsibilities that are affected by the modular marketing concept. Typically, marketing planners, sales planners, sales managers, and salespeople should be involved.

The first task of the workshop is to guide the group in specifying the modules of your marketing process. Then, for each of these modules, you should guide the group in a discussion to describe how the modules are performed today, including an evaluation of the associated costs. Following this review of current activities, you should describe the appropriate methods of modular marketing presented in this chapter. Then you should guide the group in a discussion of how each module could be made more efficient through the use of these methods. The next topic for the workshop is to examine each of these ideas and prioritize them in terms of which ideas will create the largest savings or improvement in productivity. The last topic of the workshop is to identify what tasks must be performed (and who will perform them) to ensure that the improvements are introduced.

To summarize, the topics for the workshop are:

- Specify modules appropriate for your organization.
- Understand how the modules are performed today (including the associated costs).
- Describe new methods for modular marketing.
- Identify appropriate methods to improve your module efficiency.
- Prioritize methods based on return on investment.
- Identify and assign implementation tasks.

Not only does the workshop begin the implementation process for the modular marketing concept, it also creates an atmosphere of participation and ownership by those executives who must be the avenue of implementation for the concept to be a success.

SUMMARY

As we proceed through the 80s there is a degree of uncertainty about the future in many aspects of our business life. When it relates to the marketing function, one thing is certain: the cost of marketing will continue to increase. This escalating cost is causing us to change our methods and seek new levels of efficiency, and that is positive. Many firms are beginning to consider the efficiency of their marketing program as their biggest competitive advantage. As the 80s continue, the successful companies will be those which recognize that the efficiencies to be gained in marketing represent dollars that go directly to the bottom line. As you consider your firm's situation and future, the question won't be *will* you need to implement the modular marketing concept. Rather, the question is *when* do you implement the concept to begin benefiting from the resulting efficiency.

10

PURCHASE BEHAVIOR

by
Dick Berry

University of Wisconsin

INTRODUCTION

The act of purchasing is but one of a multitude of behaviors unique to the human species. As humans developed the ability to communicate and to socialize, it became natural to exchange and barter possessions. Some of these possessions—much like blue jeans to today's young people—developed a greater value and were in demand by others. Forms of monetary exchange evolved, and the barter economy became a monetary economy, including the acts—behaviors—involved in buying and selling.

As money became the keystone of modern life, the suppliers of commodities and services hit upon the ideas now represented by modern business establishments—stocking, displaying, merchandising, promoting, and selling. Marketing evolved, and soon the merchant became a sophisticated marketer, with deep interests in the purchase behaviors of customers. Marketers became interested in consumers and also in the aggregation of persons representing the organizational purchasing process.

It would be nice to simplify this discussion by saying that people buy—exhibit purchase behaviors—because they need or want something. In reality, this is true, but the processes are more complicated than that, involving unique actions and formalities.

Central to an understanding of purchase behavior is the need to understand human behavior and the theories that explain why people act as they do. This chapter will attempt to advance and understand the behavioral processes, then center on purchase behavior and its unique characteristics, and finally will review a modern theory to explain the manifestations of behavior within the framework of individual and group purchasing.

IN SEARCH OF A BEHAVIORAL THEORY

A variety of behaviors may be indicated for any one purchase situation. The variety becomes almost endless if we analyze the actions of a typical American family as they go through a day of their lives.

Mr. Jones arises early and drives to the office for a special meeting with his purchasing department. Before turning onto the freeway, he notices that the gas gauge is on empty, so he quickly pulls into a self-service station and pumps in $5 of gasoline. On the way to the meeting, he stops at a vending machine and gets a cup of coffee. The meeting was called to review requirements for a new product being introduced by his company. The design engineer argues that she wants a specific vendor to be selected for the microprocessors required for the new product. This is her first involvement as a project leader. She wants the product to be a success—her professional career is on the line, and she has really worked hard in bringing the new product to completion.

As the drama unfolds, we realize that the buyer assigned to electronic component purchases doesn't favor the recommended vendor because of difficulties experienced in a prior situation. Rather, he'd prefer to select from several vendors on the approved vendor list. Mr. Jones finds himself in the middle of a heated debate that doesn't seem to be reaching a satisfactory outcome. He concludes the meeting by asking the engineer to review the suitability of alternate microprocessor selections from an approved vendor, if for no other reason than to be sure of an alternate source of supply for the component. He schedules continuation of the meeting for the next week.

Meanwhile, back at the Jones residence, Mrs. Jones has finished preparing her shopping list and has compared the list with the newspaper ads and her collection of cents-off coupons. Before leaving for the warehouse supermarket that she visits every Thursday morning, she calls her hairdresser and asks if she can make an appointment with Jessica for that afternoon. She has been making plans for starting up the bridge club and wants to be sure to have a new permanent before the first meeting.

Billy Jones is out in the garage, working on his bike. He will be leaving in a few minutes with a gang of friends, to ride out into the country for a swim at the lake. Billy and his folks shopped for a new 10-speed and made a deposit at Motorless Motion for a bike they'll assemble for him next Monday. He wishes he had it for the ride that day—frankly, he's a bit embarrassed to ride his old BMX model with his friends, who all have 10-speeds. Billy is using money saved from his paper route to buy the new bike. Dad wanted to buy it for him, but Billy insisted on using his own money for this, his first major purchase.

As these scenarios unfold, we realize that a number of behaviors—purchase behaviors—have been demonstrated:

- Mr. Jones makes impulse purchases of gasoline and coffee.
- Design engineer recommends a specific vendor for purchase of microprocessors.
- Buyer objects to recommended vendor, suggests selection of vendor from approved vendor list.
- Purchasing agent (Mr. Jones) recommends that the design engineer consider an approved vendor as an alternate source of supply.
- Mrs. Jones prepares to shop at warehouse supermarket, compares wants with newspaper advertisements, prepares to use cents-off coupons for purchases.
- Mrs. Jones calls hairdresser, makes appointment with specific person.
- Billy Jones and family shop for bike. Billy makes deposit on new 10-speed bike that he will pay for himself.

The marketing or sales executive searching for a behavioral theory to explain this smorgasbord of behaviors will be hard pressed to find one or two that will suffice. As a matter of fact, a search of the literature would easily yield a dozen suitable explanations posing as theories of purchase behavior. Kotler suggested five models that offer a frame of reference for analyzing buyer behavior.

Marshallian Model. The so-called modern utility or economic theory holds that purchasing decisions are the result of rational and conscious economic calculations. One might construe that Mr. Jones or the buyer were operating under this premise.

Pavlovian Model. Most persons are familiar with the experiment of the Russian psychologist, Pavlov, leading to the premise that behavior is learned. Pavlov experimented with dogs, ringing a bell each time they were fed. This led to the dogs salivating each time the bell was rung. Modern psychologists have advanced these concepts to suggest the stimulus-response models of behavior. Noteworthy to this school is the work of B. F. Skinner, designated *behaviorism*. Perhaps one could construe that Mrs. Jones' behavior—her response—is a direct result of the stimulus derived from the newspaper ads and redemption coupons.

Freudian Model. The psychoanalytic models derive from the work of Sigmund Freud. The thesis is that we all enter the world driven by instinctual needs, leading to a complex set of behaviors arising from our efforts to achieve gratification of our needs. The psyche of a person—comprising the id, ego, and superego—is central to this approach. The substance of behavior is suggested to be the efforts of our ego trying to maintain a balance between the oppressive power of the superego and the impulsive power of the id. A scenario could be developed involving the boy, Billy Jones, explaining his gratification resulting from purchase of the 10-speed bike, with his id winning out over his superego.

Veblenian Model. This is the social-psychological model suggesting that humans are social animals, conforming and responding to the forms and norms of our cultural existence. The model suggests that our behaviors are shaped by our group memberships, causing us to fit in or stand out in our relationships with others. Much could be said about the bicycle purchase and each of the Jones family members in their role relationships with one another, explained by the Veblenian model.

Hobbesian Model. Offered as the organizational factors-based explanation of our behaviors, this model suggests that man is instinctively oriented toward both preserving and enhancing his own well-being. Mr. Jones, in his purchasing agent role, as well as the buyer, can be construed to be embroiled in this kind of justification.[1]

As an experiment, we might ask each of the persons involved in the Jones scenarios, "Why did you act like you did in the circumstances we've just described?"

The answers would most likely be one of the following: "It seemed like the best thing to do," "I guess I don't know," or perhaps, "I always do it that way."

Task-Oriented Models

In analyzing the purchasing tasks in organizational buying, Webster and Wind have identified several models of industrial purchase behavior.[2] These models are easily applied to consumer purchase situations.

Minimum-Price Model. This model assumes that a firm will attempt to minimize the price paid for goods and services; in the case of organizational buying, to minimize cost and to maximize profits.

---

[1] Philip Kotler, "Behavioral Models for Analyzing Buyers," *Journal of Marketing,* October 1965, pp. 37–45.

[2] Frederick E. Webster, Jr. and Yoram Wind, *Organizational Buying Behavior* (Englewood Cliffs, N.J.: Prentice-Hall, 1972).

Lowest Total-Cost Model. An extension of the minimum-price model, the assumption is that an attempt will be made to include all of the opportunity costs for quality, delivery, reliability, and other non-price variables to achieve the lowest total cost.

Rational-Buyer Model. Simply stated, the model assumes that a purchaser will rationally assess all alternatives and payoffs, making the purchase decision that maximizes expected gain.

Source-Loyalty Model. This model assumes that many purchase decisions are routinely made by busy people. With this premise in mind, it is most logical to assume that purchase activities will favor familiar sources.

Buyclass Models. Researchers have devised a number of variations on the original buyclass model proposed by Robinson, and Faris, and Wind.[3] The original model theorized a matrix relationship with three buying situations (new task, modified rebuy, and straight rebuy), with three dimensions of difference in the buying situation (newness of problem, information requirements, and consideration of new alternatives). Figure 10–1 illustrates the buyclass concept.

FIGURE 10–1
Buying Situation Matrix for the Buyclass Model

Buying Situation	Newness of the Problem	Information Requirement	Consideration of Alternatives
New task	High	Medium	Important
Modified rebuy	Medium	Moderate	Limited
Straight rebuy	Low	Minimal	None

Source: Adapted from P. J. Robinson, C. W. Faris, and J. Wind, *Industrial Buying and Creative Marketing* (Boston: Allyn & Bacon, 1967).

The buyclass model suggests important tactical considerations for vendors. Upon analyzing a buying situation, a vendor realizes the characteristics of an anticipated customer purchase and adjusts tactics to suit. For example, an established supplier would logically want to maintain the status quo for the purchase of an item, whereas a new

---

[3] P. J. Robinson, C. W. Faris, and Y. Wind, *Industrial Buying and Creative Marketing* (Boston: Allyn & Bacon, 1967).

supplier would want to stress the need for modification or change of the buying situation and for consideration of new alternatives. This oversimplified example explains much of the pushing and shoving that takes place in the traditional selling/purchasing activities of the organizational purchasing process.

THE PURCHASING PROCESS

The next logical area to be explored is that of the buying process itself. This may range from a spontaneous, impulsive consumer purchase to a complex series of steps for an organizational purchasing situation. The industrial adoption process suggested by Ozanne and Churchill offers a five-step process: awareness, interest, evaluation, trial, and adoption.[4] The behavioral activity of an organizational group or a consumer is implied for each phase of the process. One must recognize that the process could span all phases in a moment of time or extend to a day, a month, or a year. The key to initiation of the process is information—in the way of personal or impersonal messages that are derived from firsthand involvement or media sources. Such information may be thought of as cues, in each case stimulating a behavioral response—a component of the purchasing process. Immediately, one must recognize that this perspective suggests an array of stimulus-response sequences in the purchasing process.

Berry depicts an interaction model—purchasing interaction model—in Figure 10–2 for the various participants in an industrial purchasing situation.[5] Although somewhat simplistic, the diagram illustrates the complexity and involvement of the purchasing process for industrial and organizational situations. Many of the linkings also are applicable to consumer purchase situations.

Motivated Behavior

Each of us is a bundle of interests, attitudes, and values instilled through a lifetime of learning. We respond to situations that provide satisfaction and rewards. We continuously go through a mental sorting process, directing ourselves to select courses of action that lead to desirable outcomes. The courses of action are behavioral patterns. The outcomes are our expectations. Following are some of the constructs

---

[4] U. G. Ozanne and G. A. Churchill, "Adoption Research: Information Sources in the Industrial Purchase Decision," in *Marketing and the New Science of Planning*, ed. R. L. King (Chicago: American Marketing Association, 1968).

[5] Dick Berry, *Industrial Marketing for Results* (Reading, Mass.: Addison-Wesley Publishing, 1981). Used with permission of Addison-Wesley Publishing Company.

FIGURE 10–2
Purchasing Interaction Model

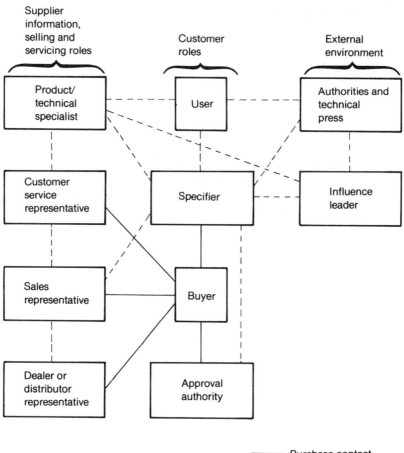

Illustrates relationships of the industrial customer to a selling organization.

Source: From D. Berry, *Industrial Marketing for Results* © 1981, Addison-Wesley, Reading, Massachusetts. Pg. 12, Fig. 2.1. Reprinted with permission.

useful in understanding purchase behavior from the vantage point of motivational theory.

Motivation can best be understood in terms of our psychological needs and the different means in which these needs can be satisfied. Our needs are ever-present until satisfied or replaced with a stronger need. When needs are aroused, an individual develops a drive toward a goal or reward that is perceived to satisfy the need, or at least to remove the deprivation. This process by which behavior is energized is called *motivation.*

Our striving to satisfy needs is the principal driving force of human behavior and is the basis for the need satisfaction theory of motivation. One variation of this theory—Maslow's Hierarchy of Needs—is widely accepted throughout business and industry as the preferential theory of motivation.

Maslow's theory suggests that we have an aggregation of needs at various levels in a hierarchy. From the lowest to highest levels, we have needs for physiological survival, safety-security, love-belonging, self-esteem, and self-actualization. Maslow contended that a person's needs transcend—as lower-order needs are satisfied, higher-order needs emerge. Thus, as our more basic needs for nourishment, security, and love are eventually satisfied, we strive for power, achievement, recognition, and creative expression. This conceptualization is summarized in Figure 10–3.[6]

We can extend this line of thinking one step further—to begin operationalizing motivational theory—by using the test instrument, Motiquiz II, illustrated in Figure 10–4. To try the instrument, think of a purchase, or plans for a purchase, or acquisition of a product or service, and respond to the instrument. After you've made your selections, use the analysis format at the bottom of the instrument to summarize your motivational inclination relative to your intended purchase behavior.

The Expectancy Theory of Motivation is a second important conceptualization. It suggests that we are motivated to perform in a particular way because a specific goal or reward is perceived to be the outcome of the behavior. The theory suggests that we attach a valence to, or preference for certain outcomes, thus causing us to direct our efforts—behavior—to the high-valence outcomes. Conversely, a negative valence outcome would suggest a demotivating influence.

The thread that holds these two theories together is the supposition that we continually strive toward need satisfaction, goals, and rewards. A psychological need, for example, for a love-belonging relationship,

---

[6] Dick Berry, *Understanding and Motivating the Manufacturer's Agent* (Boston: CBI Publishing, 1981). Used by permission of CBI Publishing Company.

FIGURE 10–3
Maslow's Hierarchy of Needs

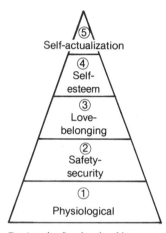

⑤ Self-actualization	Intense job challenge, full potential, full expression, creative expression.
④ Self-esteem	Achievement, respect, recognition, responsibility, prestige, independence, attention, importance, appreciation.
③ Love-belonging	Belonging, acceptance, love, affection, family & group acceptance, friendships.
② Safety-security	Security, stability, dependency, protection, need for structure, order, law, tenure, pension, insurance.
① Physiological	Hunger, thirst, reproduction, shelter, clothing, air, rest.

Depicts the five levels of human need as theorized by Abraham Maslow. Most individuals will exhibit needs from the higher levels of the hierarchy. This assumes that the basic needs—physiological and safety–security—have been satisfied. Maslow contended that a person's needs transcend—as lower-order needs are satisfied, higher-order needs develop.

Source: From Dick Berry, *Understanding and Motivating the Manufacturer's Agent* (Boston: CBI Publishing, 1981). Used by permission of CBI Publishing Company.

can be synonymous with a valenced outcome—goal or reward—such as the desire for a friendly or loving relationship with a person or group of persons.

To complicate matters, each of us has a multitude of needs and outcomes that influence us at any one time. No matter which theory you wish to accept, it remains that you must think of yourself and others as being influenced by a bundle of needs and/or valenced outcomes that are continually changing. The following definitions are useful in understanding these conceptualizations:

- *Drives* refer to strong internal stimuli that impel action. Drives are also called *motives* or *needs*. Bundles or groupings of attitudes suggest a drive, as illustrated by the Motiquiz II instrument.
- *Cues* are weaker stimuli in the environment or individual that influence when, where, and how we respond. Cues stimulate our need system and help us to focus on specific outcomes.
- *Response* is an individual's reaction—behavior—to a particular configuration of needs and cues.

FIGURE 10–4
MOTIQUIZ II *(An Exercise to Determine Consumer Purchase Motivation)*

To perform the exercise, identify an investment, product, service, or consumable item which you have acquired or plan to acquire. Next, read the statements on this page . . . *mark those which explain why you have made or plan to make the acquisition.* Review the selected statements . . . encircle numbers of those which most honestly represent your feelings.

237	To achieve a future economic or social benefit	361	To gain acceptance by a social group
386	To gain acceptance by other persons	543	To contribute in your self-expression
455	To achieve a feeling of importance	116	To provide bodily warmth or cooling for yourself
229	To achieve a desired arrangement or relationship	215	To achieve a measure of protection
551	To contribute in creative expression by yourself	538	To take advantage of an opportunity which offers personal reward
585	To afford an opportunity for personal growth	129	To provide protection from the elements for yourself
184	To satisfy a thirst for liquid refreshment within yourself	335	To achieve a sense of belonging in a social group
423	To attain recognition by others	283	To satisfy a custom or procedure
572	To contribute in attaining your full potential in a personal endeavor	347	To enhance the opportunity to be with others
131	To provide personal comfort	461	To satisfy a sense of responsibility
329	To assist in displaying your love for another person	527	To satisfy a strong desire, leading to personal satisfaction
519	To contribute in fully expressing yourself	374	To gain the love of another person
313	To enhance your acceptance by another person	197	To satisfy your hunger for food
497	To gain the admiration of others	439	To gain the appreciation of others
278	To provide a measure of security	172	To provide a pleasant feeling for yourself
398	To enhance friendly relations with another person	478	To satisfy a sense of independence
414	To gain attention of others	352	To assist in expressing affection for another person
143	To provide sexual satisfaction for yourself	292	To offer protection from danger or hazard
246	To achieve a stabilizing effect	168	To improve your personal health or well-being
564	To satisfy a strong urge, resulting in personal satisfaction	596	To provide a challenge
155	To satisfy a craving within you	261	To achieve a saving of time or money
486	To gain respect from others	442	To satisfy a need for achievement
		254	To satisfy an external influence

Explanation of results: The statements are divided into five categories intended to represent the five levels of Maslow's hierarchy of needs. The first digit in each statement number indicates the category. These categories are: 1—physiological; 2—safety-security; 3—love-belonging; 4—self-esteem; 5—self-actualization. Your purchase motivations are suggested by the statement categories.

Source: From Dick Berry, *Understanding and Motivating the Manufacturer's Agent* (Boston: CBI Publishing, 1981).

The Expectancy Theory of Motivation is compatible with the Need Satisfaction Theory and offers a way to understand motivated behavior, as distinguished from instinctive behavior. The combined theories suggest that people are goal-directed and strive to attain outcomes to which they attach a positive valence, based on their needs.

A DRIVE-EXPECTANCY THEORY OF PURCHASE BEHAVIOR

We now explore a composite schema to describe purchase behavior, based on the need satisfaction and expectancy theories. This conceptualization is offered as a single, useful explanation that can be applied in most attempts to analyze purchase behavior. We employ the persons and purchase situations described in the beginning of this chapter as a basis to develop the Drive-Expectancy Theory of human behavior.

Figure 10–5 summarizes the purchase situations for Mr. Jones, the design engineer, the buyer, Mrs. Jones, and Billy Jones. Included in the figure are responses to the Motiquiz II instrument, the indicated need (drive) in each situation, and the anticipated goal or reward expected by the person. For example, we find that the buyer's motivations were principally in the safety-security category of Maslow's hierarchy, with the expectation being to achieve a satisfactory outcome and to reduce problem situations. Obviously, the buyer is functioning within the context of his position description, fulfilling responsibilities expected by his supervisor, Mr. Jones, and the company. But, principally, he is a person responding to the situation at hand, exhibiting his personal needs and expectations.

This rationale leads us to conclude that our psychological needs are predictive of behavior. Analysis of any variety of situations also supports the notion that a person's behavior exhibits their needs. A secondary premise is that need arousal leads to the visualization of goals and rewards. In the foregoing example, Billy Jones had the need to self-actualize with the new bike—to "do his thing"—meanwhile building his esteem in the minds of his peers. Pehaps the goal expectation was a combination of attractions—a vision of his friends admiring him as he raced along on a 10-speed bike. Certainly, these ends could not be achieved with the old BMX model bike.

Two other premises are important to this rationale. The first is the realization that our needs are continually changing as a result of learning. To illustrate, as Billy Jones experiences the purchase and use of the new bike, his needs and expectations will change, leading to need arousal and setting of other goals. This process is affected by our attitudes, interests, values, desires, and life experiences, particularly

FIGURE 10–5
Motivational Drives and Goals of Participants in Purchase Situations

Person	Purchase Situation	Motiquiz II* Selections	Motivational Drive/Need	Goal or Reward
Mr. Jones	Gasoline for car	229, 131, 278, 246, 215, 283, 463, 292, 261	Safety-security and concern for self-esteem	Get to work safely and without hassle
Mr. Jones	Vended coffee	184, 131, 155, 197	Physiological	Personal satisfaction and need for a "pickup"
Mr Jones	Microprocessor purchase	455, 229, 398, 246, 361, 543, 283, 461, 261, 254	Safety-security with love-belonging and self-esteem	Satisfactory situational outcome, resolve conflict
Design engineer	Microprocessor purchase	455, 551, 585, 572, 519, 497, 543, 478, 442	Self-actualization and self-esteem	Personal satisfaction from success of new product/project
Buyer	Microprocessor purchase	386, 229, 246, 283, 461, 261, 254	Safety-security with some esteem and social concerns	To achieve satisfactory outcome and reduce problem situations
Mrs. Jones	Supermarket shopping	237, 386, 455, 423, 497, 414, 486, 361, 335, 461, 439, 261	Self-esteem with some love-belonging and safety-security concerns	To provide best buys for family well-being and financial stability
Mrs. Jones	Hairdresser appointment	386, 551, 329, 519, 398, 143, 564, 486, 283, 374, 439, 172, 352	Heavily driven by love-belonging, supported by all other needs	To look attractive and enhance relationships with friends and husband
Billy Jones	Bike purchase	386, 455, 551, 585, 423, 519, 497, 414, 564, 486, 361, 543, 527, 439, 442	Self-actualization and self-esteem are the principle drives	Peer pressure and the desire for features of a 10-speed bike

* The first digit of each selected number indicates the need category described in Figure 10–3.

FIGURE 10–6
Drive-Expectancy Model of Human Behavior

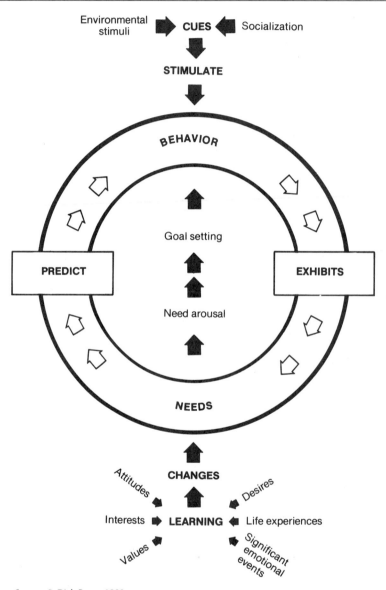

Source: © Dick Berry, 1983.

by significant emotional events (SEEs) that have an impact on our lives.

Second, the effect of cues is important to the behavioral process. Cues are stimuli that arise from environmental exposure and socialization. No doubt Billy Jones was stimulated by a variety of cues—contact with his friends, seeing other boys and girls with their bikes, television and print advertising, or perhaps seeing the new bike and being influenced by the salesperson in the bike shop.

These conceptualizations are summarized in Figure 10–6, illustrating the Drive-Expectancy Model of Human Behavior. We conclude that purchase behavior is but one form of human behavior, a subset involving the process of exchange, as persons strive to satisfy their needs and achieve their goals or strive for rewards.

SUMMARY

We have discussed behaviors of individuals and groups of persons representing the consumer and industrial purchasing processes. Theories of purchase behavior and motivation have been advanced to provide a conceptual basis for understanding purchase behavior.

Behavioral models which have been reviewed include the following, some designated as purchase behavior models, some as motivational models, and several more broadly construed to be behavior models.

Marshallian Model. A rational, economic theory of behavior.

Pavlovian Model. A stimulus-response theory extensively supported by research with animals.

Freudian Model. A psychoanalytical representation, assuming that instinctual needs and their gratification explain behavior.

Veblenian Model. A theory based on the premise that behaviors are based on our cultural existence and desires to conform to the norms of group membership.

Hobbesian Model. An organizational factors explanation suggesting that we are instinctively oriented toward preserving and enhancing our well-being.

Minimum-Price Model. The premise that organizational buyers will attempt to minimize price, in order to minimize costs and maximize profits.

Lowest Total-Cost Model. An approach used in organizational buying, to achieve lowest total cost by including all opportunity costs in developing a purchase price.

Rational-Buyer Model. The theory that purchasers will assess all alternatives and payoffs to maximize gain in a purchase transaction.

Source-Loyalty Model. The supposition that routine purchases are made from familiar sources.

Buyclass Models. A series of representations for analyzing purchase situations based on matrices that relate buying tasks to degrees of difference in the information requirements.

Industrial Adoption Process. A conceptualization in organizational purchasing that suggests a five-step buying process: awareness, interest, evaluation, trial, and adoption.

Purchasing Interaction Model. A representation that portrays relationships of role participants in the transactions between industrial customers and selling organizations in industrial purchasing (see Figure 10–2).

Need Satisfaction Theory. A motivational theory that suggests need satisfaction as the principal driving force of human behavior.

Expectancy Theory of Motivation. The notion that we are motivated to perform in a specific way because a specific goal or reward is perceived to be the outcome of the behavior.

Drive-Expectancy Theory of Human Behavior. A conceptualization that portrays human behavior to be the result of our psychological needs and expectations for goal or reward attainment, resulting from need arousal (see Figure 10–6).

The Drive-Expectancy Model of Human Behavior is offered as a preferential treatment for those desiring a singular representation to specifically delineate purchase behaviors or to more broadly understand and explain behavioral processes.

Those desiring to interject stimulus-response phenomenon into the behavioral process, particularly to explain effects of promotional effort, are offered the suggestion of cueing as an element within the drive-expectancy model. Similarly, those who perceive that learning causes adaptations of the purchasing process are offered this variation of behavioral change as an element of the drive-expectancy model.

Purchase behavior is not a singular, easily explained phenomenon. Much like human behavior itself, purchase behavior is complex and difficult to understand. The explanations offered here should be useful to plan and organize marketing effort—with a high degree of confidence in the expectations for a successful outcome.

11

PRODUCT LIFE CYCLE

by
John A. Murray

Geocel Corporation

This chapter will explore how the product life cycle works in theory and how it can be applied effectively in marketing. The theory has enough merit to provide some structure to the marketing of a product. However, since a slavish adherence to it can easily cause a company to self-destruct, there is also a section on when and how to ignore the theory.

The theory of product life cycles is that products have the following discrete periods:

1. Launch.
2. Early growth.
3. Maturity.
4. Relaunch/Flankers.
5. Decline and discontinuance.

The time periods can and will vary, but all products will go through this process. The positive benefits of applying this theory to the product life cycle primarily focus around the scientific management of the resources devoted to the product.

A curve can be drawn for any product which shows an early (hopefully steep) upward growth curve which is followed by a leveling off and then a decline.

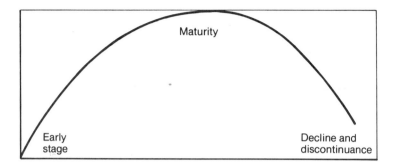

Later thinking evolved the corollary that active promotion could rekindle life into a product for a period of time and thereby forestall the inevitable decline. The curve could be adapted as follows:

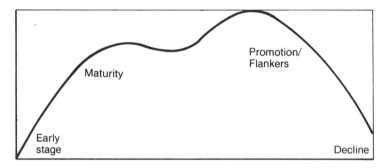

CHARACTERISTICS OF THE PRODUCT LAUNCH

The product launch period is characterized by high hopes and a commensurately high investment. Market share is usually the basic determinant of success. The entire resources of the corporation and/or division are solidly behind the product. The product launch is constantly reviewed, with a formal review occurring whenever some meaningful market measure, such as Neilsen, is available. Investment spending is adhered to. Sales force enthusiasm is high. The initial sell-in of the product to the trade usually reflects very healthy sales figures.

The major danger facing the success of a product in its launch cycle is a premature evaluation. This often will occur as soon as market share objectives are not met. Suddenly, a greater investment is called for, explanations are demanded, and often support is cut back at the most critical stage of the product launch. Management then avoids the blame for maintaining a losing investment but can never really answer the question as to whether the product would have been successful or not.

The following characteristics emerge as the major factors in a launch period:

1. Optimistic share targets.
2. High investment.
3. Heavy sell-in period.
4. Enthusiastic commitment of top management.
5. Premature evaluation.

The significant winners—the obvious stars—survive the premature evaluation. However, many long-term winners are consigned to the scrap heap because support is withdrawn too early. It is worth noting here, however, that companies who have been most successful in launching new products—like Procter & Gamble and 3M—often spend years in test marketing or even concept development. They commit heavily to ensuring that the product launch is done effectively and completely.

CHARACTERISTICS OF EARLY GROWTH

Once the product has survived the rigors of early launch, its period of early growth begins. It is safe to say that unless early share objectives are met, the product will never reach its full objectives. Consequently, careful monitoring of all the elements in the plan is essential. This is a time for continued investment as well as continued research. The entire plan should now be subjected to the very rigorous test of "Is it working?" The consumer should be researched to ensure that the original target group is still valid, that the advertising approach is working, and that the initial media assumptions were correct. If any of these elements are not working as originally planned, then realism demands that the plan must also be changed to reflect these changes.

Sales force enthusiasm must be kept at a high level during this period, and an effective feedback system for upper management must also be employed so that the enthusiasm is maintained. Financially, this is a critical time in the product life cycle. Profits and payback seem to be a long way off. Media and promotion pressure must be kept at a high level, and there may be some voices saying that the product is bleeding red ink.

Competitive retaliation can now become a factor. Often, competitors will not react early in the product launch period but will counterattack vigorously after all the initial launch resources have been used up.

The early growth period is characterized, then, by the following:

1. Rapid share growth.
2. Continued investment.

3. Research and revision of the initial plan.
4. Ongoing promotion.
5. Uncertainty concerning payback.
6. Competitive retaliation.

CHARACTERISTICS OF MATURITY

After successfully achieving a viable market share, the product will enter into a period in which further investment in increased market share will show increasingly diminishing returns. Conversely, the market share the product has achieved allows for a certain amount of security. The product has achieved a niche from which it will not be easily dislodged. High market share allows for high advertising expenditures and promotion expenses, even though as a percent of sales these dollars are less than competition has to spend to maintain its market share. They are significantly less than the percent or even absolute dollars a new competitor would have to spend in order to mount a significant, if high-risk, challenge to the product.

At this point, the market will also have matured, thereby slowing growth opportunities and making the market itself considerably less attractive to competition. Share gains will be very slow, market saturation will result in fewer new users, and brand switching will become generally less prominent or, at least, less enduring.

At last, too, these circumstances will result in high profitability for the brand. Research will become more of the dipstick variety, merely checking to see that brand awareness and preference remain high. Promotion and advertising will be relatively predictable; sales growth will be steady and slow.

A SECOND CYCLE

As seen on the second curve above, the product can, however, now enter into a second growth cycle. This cycle will have a very rapid growth rate similar to the launch period. The growth period will, however, be quite short relative to its earlier growth.

A review of the opportunities inherent in this approach is always in order before accepting that a product is beginning its decline phase.

These characteristics are usually prevalent in a second growth cycle:

1. Breakthrough new advertising which exploits a new positioning for the brand.
2. Consumer saturation point is still far from being attained, and

acceptance for the new positioning focuses on a tangible unful-
filled need.
3. The brand is a leader in its market and has had a consistently
high profile through advertising and promotion.
4. The brand is quite profitable and can support a large increase in
advertising and promotion.
5. Competition is either cutting back support or is otherwise not in
a position to exploit the new position being opened up.

Flankers

As a product nears the end of its maturity, another significant way in
which to prolong its life is to begin developing flankers. The strategy
here is to take the product's root name and launch additional products
with the suffix "II" or "Plus." Aspirin manufacturers are doing this to
launch their nonaspirin pain-killers like Anacin III. Similarly, Miles
Laboratories successfully launched a cold remedy called Alka Seltzer
Plus. General Electric, in the caulking field, has recently exploited this
approach in its launch of Silicone II. This approach has enabled them
to launch an entirely new brand on top of their already successful
silicone product, as opposed to merely launching a "new, improved"
product, which most likely would have shown only a marginal sales
improvement.

Successful flanker strategy depends on:

— High brand awareness for the parent.
— Ability of the company to divert sufficient advertising funds to
create a meaningful degree of awareness for the flanker.
— The flanker's ability to deliver a significant differentiable
benefit.
— The "deluxe" aspect of the flanker.

The greatest risk is that the flanker will not be perceived any differently than the parent. In such a case the flanker will not be successful.
In addition, it will tend to confuse consumers as to what the parent
actually does. It could, therefore, result in sales losses for the parent.
Hence, there is a need for strongly differentiable characteristics and a
separate budget large enough to communicate these characteristics to
the consumer.

Cannibalization of the parent by the flanker will occur to some
degree or another. However, as long as the flanker delivers more gross
profit per unit sold and the two brands together do not lose sales,
cannibalization should not be considered a problem. Allowing a flanker
to be less profitable is a mistake.

PRODUCT DECLINE

After maturity comes decline. The product and/or its market, after several years of declining rate of growth, gradually enter into a cycle in which sales actually decline. This is the period in which products should be milked. Advertising support is withdrawn gradually. Promotion support may actually increase for a while, but later that is also reduced significantly. No more money is spent on market research, packaging, or any other activity which calls for new money to be put behind the brand. All the emphasis is on profitability. In the early period of decline profits will shoot up, as the previous years' marketing momentum maintains the product. Loyal consumers still buy it. Its market share still justifies good distribution. Buyers still stock the product at its pristine levels until it is obvious that the downturn in turnover is a trend. Events then snowball. Purchases are cut back. Distribution and retail facings are lost, and all these events work together to accelerate the decline until the product is ready for discontinuance.

The chief characteristics of the decline phase of the product life cycle are:

1. Steady decline in sales due either to market decline or market share loss.
2. Withdrawal of advertising support.
3. Withdrawal of promotion.
4. Withdrawal of other direct product expenses, such as market research.
5. Sharp, but short, increase in profitability.
6. Decline in facings and distribution.
7. Decline in warehouse purchases.
8. Discontinuance.

Since these events almost always occur in that order, a company can, with a fine-tuned marketing effort, orchestrate the eventual discontinuance much to its own advantage. Aggressive promotion after all advertising is withdrawn would be one way of achieving this and could for a time actually increase market share, while still allowing quite high profits.

IS THE THEORY WORKABLE?

There are several advantages to accepting the product life-cycle theory:

1. The acceptance of the inevitable decline of a company's star product should allow for more development of new products.

2. Plotting the life cycle should ensure that optimum amounts of promotion are put behind the brand during its various phases, allowing management to gradually withdraw support from the brand as it enters its peiod of decline. This advantage is expected to allow for a planned transition period of methodically switching dollars from products which have become cash cows to the rising stars in the company's product mix.

Nonetheless, these advantages, while theoretically sound, depend on some premises that are emphatically not sound. In practice, the theory of product life cycles can be extremely harmful to a company. When weighed against a far more practical marketing orientation, the theory is found wanting; in many ways, it is a major contributor to the marketing myopia which seemed to paralyze American corporations in the 70s—which is still with us to a great degree today.

Let us turn first to the areas in which the product life cycle can be harmful.

1. By definition the product life cycle limits the life span of a product. A slavish commitment to this approach therefore structures the corporate definition of its product as something very finite. If it's a buggy whip, then that is all it will ever be. It cannot be conceived as an instrument to regulate the speed of a vehicle. The practice of marketing products, however, goes beyond defining products as something manufactured and rather defines products in terms of the needs they fill. One definition is static; the other is capable of evolution. One is myopic; the other is capable at least of some vision. Careful attention to the need one is filling allows plenty of scope for adapting to changing needs. Commitment to a theory that dooms the product to its current shape or form also dooms it to no longer fulfilling changing needs. It is a classic self-fulfilling prophecy.

2. A second problem is that the theory assumes the company embracing the product life-cycle concept is going to be able to develop strong new products that will replace the dying star, now the cash cow. It seems highly unlikely that a company which cannot adapt its major product to a changing environment will somehow display the marketing and research expertise to develop wholly new products. Indeed, this often can become a blueprint for misspending funds for the sake of showing action, without any real progress.

3. Few people have the ability to accurately judge that a product has entered into a period of irreversible decline. In fact, if it can be tracked quantitatively, then it is already too late to take action. The person responsible for the prediction often will err on the safe side and predict a decline well before the product has actually entered that stage. Accordingly, actions are taken to milk the brand. Promotion support is withdrawn. Research and development funds are no longer available for improvement. Market research funds are withdrawn, except perhaps to maintain quantitative studies to prove with morbid satisfaction that the prognosticator was correct.

Product Improvement

Another problem that the life-cycle theory creates is that product improvement becomes a waste of time and money. U.S. companies spend far less money improving their current products than do foreign competitors. That is one reason for our lack of competitiveness in so-called mature areas. Refining products and finding ways to make them better and cheaper somehow is looked down upon in most companies. Mature products often have years—even decades—of healthy profit delivery ahead of them if properly nurtured. The long list of markets which we have simply abandoned to the Japanese attests to this. There are no technological breakthroughs in black-and-white TVs, radios, and cameras. However, product evolution has been practiced on these markets to the nth degree by the Japanese and left alone by American industry, thus depriving ourselves of very large, lucrative markets. A proper appreciation of the product life-cycle theory does not necessarily have to lead to product neglect and premature death.

The Product Improvement Team

The most effective way to ensure long-term viability of any product is to assume that it will go on forever. This implies continued investment in the product along several lines. Investment, as used here, should not be confused with deficits—there is no reason for an established product to be unprofitable. Investment simply means support—support in advertising, promotion, and customer and product research.

Product research on an established product seems to be one of the more forgotten practices in current management techniques. Once the quality assurance department has established a satisfactory testing system, it seems there is a built-in prejudice against change. Evolution gives way to revaluation, the doctrine of product obsolescence prevails over a commonsense approach to product improvement. However, there are few more fertile fields for improving market share, without major cost, than constant attention to improving the product's quality as the years go on.

A product improvement team has a tough time in today's organizations. It is not glamorous, it requires open, honest communications between departments, and it flies in the face of the wisdom of product life cycles and cash cows. The product improvement team, however, can be a vital link in terms of product longevity. It should consist of marketing, production, research and development, and purchasing. Its goals should be limitless and not explicit. It should be allowed complete rein to review any aspect of the product—from formulation to packaging to customer service. Customer feedback should be solicited as actively as if it were of the same status as a breakthrough formulation change.

Consumer Research

The final major recommendation for maintaining product vibrancy is to focus research on the consumer and the need the product is filling.

Once a product is considered "established," research in most companies changes its focus to determining how the product measures up against certain predetermined yardsticks, such as awareness of product features, market share, etc. The orientation is now on measuring progress. Focusing narrowly on numerical evaluation, however, often contributes to early decline. The research is no longer identifying the consumer, his or her need, and how the product fulfills that need. The only really certain thing in marketing is that the consumer and the consumer's needs will change. Emphasis must be placed in research on this ever-changing need hierarchy in order to ensure that the product is still satisfying something important. A product can continue to score well in consumer awareness of its attributes, but this is meaningless if the consumer no longer feels that these attributes are important.

The U.S. automotive industry's blind insistence in the 70s that consumers did not want really small cars had all kinds of research to back it up. Detroit's behemoths scored well on product attributes on scales more relevant to the 50s than to the 80s. Relevance of the research was the problem. Detroit was not looking at consumer needs; the Japanese were.

Product longevity depends upon the product fulfilling relevant needs. These needs must be researched constantly and the product adapted to them as they change.

CONCLUSION

In summary, the product life cycle can be a useful marketing tool as long as it is used to maintain the product. The following points should be kept in mind in utilizing this theory successfully.

1. The product launch should pursue major market share and not be cut short too early in the launch cycle.
2. The product growth period should maintain growth as its primary objective.

3. The product maturity period is the time in which to maximize profitability while maintaining enough promotional and advertising support to keep competitive cost of entry high.
4. A relaunch period can greatly increase market share and product longevity as long as the product has maintained a relevant benefit for a major consumer need.
5. A flanker strategy can deliver additional sales profitably and open up new markets—as long as it is a differentiable product with a meaningful advertising and promotion budget.
6. The decline and discontinuance period for a product simply should not be accepted. Products should be viewed as ongoing entities which can continually be adapted to ever-changing consumer needs, as long as the company is alert to what these needs are. Product longevity should be the centerpiece of any marketing strategy.
7. A product improvement committee should be set up for every major brand to ensure that it is kept up to date and responsive to its marketing environment.
8. Consumer research on the product should anticipate needs and identify changes in the marketplace rather than merely focus on where the product is relative to yesterday.

With these points in mind, the product life-cycle theory can help ensure the long-term viability of a product rather than doom it to premature discontinuance.

Part 2

RESEARCH

12

FINDING THE RIGHT RESEARCH RESOURCES

by
James Lazarus

Burst-Lazarus Associates, Inc.

This chapter is a nuts-and-bolts approach to selecting the right market research choices and provides an overview of what decisions must be made for a productive research project. It is aimed at the needs of an operating manager who, at one time or another, is called on to be a market researcher.

This chapter will describe the different types of market research and their strengths and weaknesses. It will also explore ways that the manager-turned-researcher can evaluate the agents and field resources he or she might require.

The first step of any research project is to separate the "need to know" from the "nice to know." If you draw too wide a circle at first, you will dilute the important results and perhaps will not select the research methodology that provides a clear-cut analysis of the primary problem. This is not to say that you may not end up with new insights into secondary issues; but at the beginning ask yourself what is the information that you absolutely must have to make an informed decision.

For example, the marketing manager of the towel division of a large textile company was considering changing the fiber content of his towels from a blend of polyester and cotton to 100 percent cotton. He felt that there were a number of consumers who would only purchase 100 percent cotton towels. Yet he had lower costs making towels using a blend of polyester and cotton. His need-to-know information was what percentage of his target consumers would not even consider buying his blended-fiber product.

As this market manager started to think about his market research project, he began to add nice-to-know information concerning styling and distribution issues. These add-on issues raised the cost of his research project to the point that the president of the division requested that he change the methodology of the project to bring down the cost. Instead, the marketing manager rightly chose to eliminate the secondary issues and focused the project on the primary question of fiber blend.

Once you have isolated the critical issues, you are in a better position to give the problem some financial parameters. This leads to step number two: ask yourself how much it will cost your organization to make the wrong decision and how much your organization might profit by the correct decision. If the potential loss or gain is small, you may want the marketplace to be your market research and save your market research money and energy for the more costly decisions. This occurred in the case of a hosiery mill that had developed a new soccer sock with the assistance of a well-known athlete. Since the cost of producing the product and marketing it to soccer clubs was minimal, the product manager decided to bypass any market research and test the product in the marketplace.

If either the potential loss or potential reward is large, and if the results of the market research can help minimize risk and maximize profits, these are good indications that research would be a good investment. In looking at the whole risk-reward situation, you may want to add other ''soft'' losses or profit to the risk-reward formula. These might be such things as reputation, company momentum, customer goodwill, credibility, employee morale, etc. In some cases these less tangible factors are as significant as the hard dollars and cents.

In the case of the hosiery mill's soccer sock, a significant soft cost might have been letting its competition know about the new product before it was fully tested. This added factor may have tipped the balance away from bringing the new sock directly to market and back to some kind of controlled market research approach.

When you have identified the need-to-know information and the risks and rewards attached to it, you are in a position to select the research methods or series of methods that have the best chance to answer your critical questions.

SECONDARY RESEARCH

Secondary research uses existing data sources, whereas primary research uses data generated for the first time. Secondary research is usually underrated and does not have the glamour associated with conducting one's own primary research; but, if a manager clearly understands the limits of secondary research, it can be extremely useful in understanding the marketing environment and in making marketing decisions.

. Secondary research can also provide some helpful ideas for methodology and context of primary research and can provide a useful first step in any research project. Secondary research can be especially valuable to seasoned managers who can manipulate and sift the data into a useful form, whereas a market researcher new to an industry may have difficulty shaping the same data into useful information.

A good example of this type of situation is information from trade organizations. This information is often based on statistics from member companies. Since all companies involved in the industry may not be members of the trade organization, statistics from the omitted companies must be approximated to have useable industrywide information. A market researcher might have more difficulty manipulating the data than would an industry insider.

One of the major strengths of secondary research is that it is very cost effective. This is because someone else has conducted and paid for the data.

However, secondary research has a related disadvantage. The new user has no control over the quality of research and has limited means of evaluating how well the research was conducted. Furthermore, the analysis of data may not be precisely what the new user requires, and the raw data is rarely available. A common problem with census data, for example, is that categories are so large that a user in a specialized area may not find the information useful.

Other problems with secondary research are that it might be out of date or some chronological information may not be available to establish useful trend lines. Finally, useful secondary research data may be difficult to locate and often requires a lot of perseverance and creativity to uncover.

Although you will undoubtedly have to rely on many of your own ideas for uncovering sources of secondary research information, these are some starting places appropriate to almost any information search.

A good place to begin secondary research is a complete business library like the Harvard Business School Library in Boston or the Conference Board Library in New York. Most of these libraries can do a computer search by subject for most general and business publications that they carry. Although these general publications may not have the detailed information that you will ultimately require, they may provide you with clues as to what more detailed reports are available, what organizations compile data on your particular area of interest, and which individuals might be knowledgeable about the subject.

It is likely that governmental reports on the federal, state, and local levels will be listed. Although the statistics may not give you the information you require to answer directly your research problem, they can provide excellent background information to frame the question.

It is hoped that in this literature search you will begin to turn up studies by private groups, such as white papers by business school professors, reports by special interest or public interest groups, reports commissioned by corporations or other organizations, and annual or periodic reports by trade groups.

Some reports will be in the public domain, and some will be proprietary information. If you are not a direct competitor of the company or individual that holds proprietary information, you may be able to gain access to the information as a courtesy.

Once you have uncovered the useful secondary research from a literature search, you might want to start using personal contacts in the trade and "networking" to gain new contacts. If you are a manufacturer, talk to your contacts in the distribution channels or among retailers to get names of knowledgeable people in your area of concern as well as trade organizations. Often large retailers conduct their own consumer research, and you can gain access to their research as a valued vendor.

If you are a manufacturer, also explore contacts with your suppliers, for they often compile statistics from the raw material perspective. If you are a retailer, talk to your suppliers or people in the distribution channels for contacts in trade organizations or access to other experts.

If this is a new area of business for you, talk to your contacts from an organization that also does business in that area and ask for names of people in the organization who might be helpful. Editors of trade magazines, newspapers, and newsletters can be particularly helpful as their business is to know people in a particular field.

As you discuss your area of interest with the knowledgeable contacts, you will not only develop a broad-based perspective and hear many different opinions but you should also discover other written reports or research not identified through library research.

In summary, secondary research can be cost effective and timely. However, you have no control over its quality, its form, and its timeframe. It is also somewhat like a treasure hunt: you may uncover some gems, but then again you may come up empty-handed.

PRIMARY RESEARCH

Primary research is original research. It can be divided into three categories: qualitative (soft research), quantitative (hard research), and audits.

The advantage of primary research is that you are able to focus directly on the problem at hand while maintaining control over quality, methodology, and timeframe. Disadvantages of primary research are that it is usually costly and you will probably have to evaluate and select outside suppliers for some phases.

Often the first type of research used to address a set of issues is qualitative research. The advantage is that you are able to determine in depth what consumers feel about a given topic. You can find out what they might do, why they will do it, and the strength of their feelings. Another advantage of qualitative research is that it is usually less expensive than quantitative and can sometimes be used before quantitative to narrow the options and make the quantitative research more valuable.

An example of this type of approach is a computer software company that wanted to target new products at the most marketable segment of its customer base—small businessmen. The company had decided to conduct a phone survey to find out how small businesses were using their microcomputers and what needs were not being satisfied. However, before conducting this expensive survey, the president of the company wanted to make sure that all possible uses were being covered in the survey and that the terminology would be understood by these consumers. Therefore, the computer software company did some relatively inexpensive qualitative research to find out some of this information and to make the survey more reliable.

The most common forms of qualitative research are focus groups and open-ended interviews. Focus groups generally consist of 6 to 12 people, usually consumers from the target population. The participants gather in an informal setting, such as a conference room, with a group leader who leads the discussion in a nondirective manner. Usually this session is tape recorded or videotaped for later review, and the people who commission the research can sit behind a one-way mirror. Focus groups are most often done in sets of two or four sessions to get input from different groups of people and, on occasion, multiple sites.

An open-ended interview is usually conducted one on one. The interviewer asks an open-ended question where the appropriate response is like the answer to an essay question on a test. In this type of research, as with a focus group, you are seeking not only what the consumer will do but why they do it and how strongly they feel about it. However, one-on-one interviews eliminate the group interaction that is present in focus groups.

The great disadvantage of qualitative research is that it is not statistically reliable or even projectable to the population at large. This is why qualitative research is often called ''soft research.'' To get answers to such questions as, ''How many women between the ages of 24 and 44 will buy product A versus product B," or "How many women will vote for candidate A versus candidate B," you require quantitative research.

Surveys, which can be conducted by phone or mail, are the most common form of quantitative research. The well-known national opinion polls such as Gallop or Lou Harris use surveys. However, surveys can be conducted on a much smaller scale and still be statistically projectable. Obviously, the larger the sample size is, the less error factor there will be in the results. A professional market researcher will be able to help you choose a sample size that reflects the degree of certainty you need balanced against the expense of increasing the number of respondents.

Besides the high cost of survey work, the biggest problem with survey data is that managers are unable to convert the results into meaningful decision making. The results from quantitative research are merely lists of numbers. You should know what percentage numbers are going to dictate action A and what percentage numbers are going to dictate action B before the research is conducted. This requires hard thinking before the survey is constructed to decide on what theories and hypotheses are being tested, and what different approaches can be taken to test these theories with consumers. Usually this planning should be conducted with the help of a professional researcher.

The great strength of quantitative research is that it is hard research. In other words, you get a fairly accurate range of numbers that are projectable. This assumes of course that the questionnaire and methodology are well designed to avoid prejudicing the results or creating unintentional bias.

Another type of widely used quantitative research is the consumer diary panel in which a large number of consumers are given incentives to mark in a diary all their purchases. Companies can buy panel results in the form of computerized reports for any consumer product area in which they are interested. They also receive demographics for the responding consumers.

Since a number of companies receive parts of the same piece of research, it is less costly than custom research. However, there are some disadvantages. If you wish to change something in the report, a number of the other participating companies must agree to the change. There is also a significant built-in bias to this type of research because the type of consumer willing to keep a diary for incentives may exclude certain types of consumers, such as those with higher incomes. Also, products such as automobiles that are purchased infrequently are inappropriate for this type of research, due to the fact that the results will fluctuate widely based on a small annual purchase base in the survey.

The third major type of primary research is auditing. Audits are a form of market research in which actions or transactions are monitored, categorized, and summarized. Audits do not deal with opinions, ideas, or concepts but rather with actions.

One of the better-known audit companies is A. C. Nielsen, which conducts ongoing audits of the movement of certain packaged products off the shelves of major grocery stores across the country. However, anything that can be counted can be audited, from the number of inches of advertising devoted to towels in women's magazines to the number of shopping centers in a county or state. The strength of auditing is that it will tell you what is happening at a given time; but, the overriding weakness is that it does not tell you why it is happening.

In summary, there are three general categories of primary research: qualitative, quantitative, and audits. Qualitative or soft research is usually used to gain insights into consumers' feelings and the strength of those feelings. Quantitative or hard research is usually employed to get a statistically reliable answer to a question and to predict behavior. Audits are samplings of what is actually happening in the marketplace.

SELECTING AGENTS AND FIELD RESEARCH RESOURCES

There are usually two functions to be filled in most primary market research projects: choosing an agent and choosing a field research house. In qualitative research, the agent will usually help you select the correct type of research, develop a screening guide for selecting consumers, develop a questionnaire guide, moderate focus groups, and write the research report. The field research house completes some of the more mechanical aspects of qualitative research, such as providing the conference room, taping focus group sessions or the one-on-one interviews, and screening and selecting the actual participants.

In quantitative research, the agent will help you select the research methodology and the sample size as well as help writing the questionnaire, managing the field research house, selecting the cross tabulations, and writing the report. In quantitative research some of the responsibilities of the field research house are: printing the questionnaire, conducting the survey, editing the questionnaires, and putting the results into a computer for cross-tabulations.

Word of mouth is probably the best way initially to find the names of agents and field research organizations. A good place to start is the market research professional in a major corporation in your field. You can also talk to one of the principals of a major research house like Lou Harris, Gallop, Stanford Research Institute, or A. C. Nielsen for recommendations. Some other ideas are talking to business school professors who teach market research, advertising agencies, or perhaps consultants you have used on other projects.

The next step is to interview the most promising agents. In general, an agent with some direct marketing experience will be better suited to qualitative research; and an agent with a statistical market research background will be better suited to quantitative research.

When talking with agents who conduct qualitative research, it is best to talk with the person who will moderate. Usually focus groups are conducted in a series, and you should know the moderator's suggestions for selecting the participants. Does the moderator use an interview guide? What's the moderator's philosophy on stimuli? Ask the moderator about methodology for relistening to the sessions and if the moderator will be directly involved in writing the report.

In the case of quantitative research, you will want an agent who has a market research, statistical background. You should know if this person will be communicating with the field research house and who will write the questionnaires. You should find out who is responsible for the cross-tabulations (question the agent on the value of simple cross-tabulations versus multivariant tabulations) and for establishing the criteria for evaluating the survey data. You also need to know who will be writing the report. Finally, you need the agent's recommendations on sample size, methodology, and questionnaire design, so that you can evaluate these recommendations on the basis of common sense and what you have learned in talking with other researchers.

Finally, for both qualitative and quantitative research, you should select an agent who has shown an understanding of your problem and seems to have a good rapport with the people with whom he or she will be working.

Usually, the agent will make some recommendations of field research houses; however, if you are in a position where you must evaluate field research houses as well as agents, here are some ideas for narrowing the choices.

First, check to see if the field suppliers are accredited in the "green book" or the *International Directory of Market Research Houses and Services.* In the case of qualitative research, talk to the houses and discuss recruitment policies as well as location and a description of the physical characteristics of the facility. You may want to have a representative of your company check the facility, and you may narrow down the selection of two relatively equal sites by a review of *Sales and Marketing Management's Survey of Buying Power* to check on the suitability of the general marketing environment. The selection of the field research supplier may be finally decided on convenience and cost.

In selecting a field research house for quantitative research, you should know who instructs the interviewers, what standard materials are used, and what mechanism exists for quality control. Standard materials set standards for such things as sampling procedure, proportion of refused interviews to actual interviews, length of interviews, and so forth. If there are no standards or the standards seem lax, the field research house is suspect. Quality control procedures include such things as editing procedures for questionnaires and percentage of interviews validated by a second interview (which usually should be no less than 15 percent).

In summary, selecting an agent and field research house is much like selecting a professional in law, accounting, or medicine. You rely on recommendations, organizational rapport, professional accreditation, and personal interviews to establish who does the important work and how professionally it is accomplished.

CONCLUSIONS

Any modern business uses market research, whether or not it is formalized or even thought of as market research. The sales manager who calls the 10 biggest customers or the president of a consumer product company who decides to stand behind the sales counter of a retail store for one day are market researchers.

Too many managers abdicate the responsibility of market research to the researchers and are then dissatisfied with the final results. The real learning in market research is not just in the final report but in the process of making the many decisions that create a useful market research project. Only the manager who knows the limitations of any particular research will have the confidence to use the research results to greatest advantage.

13

MARKET SURVEYS: PRACTICES AND PROCEDURES

by
Edward Epstein

Edward Epstein and Associates, Inc.

If intelligent marketing decisions are to be made, it is important to know what customers want and believe. Many years ago, those in business had frequent contact with their customers, often the people in their area. As businesses grew and the number of steps in the channels of distribution between manufacturers and the ultimate consumers increased, producers had less and less direct contact with consumers and thus less knowledge of what those consumers wanted, how they felt about various products, etc. Today, most of the feedback from consumers comes from market surveys.

TYPES OF SURVEYS

In terms of objectives, there are two broad types of surveys: developmental surveys, which are designed to learn the consumer's desires and behavior so as to develop better marketing strategies and tactics; and evaluative surveys, to learn which of the various tactics conceived by the marketer have the best potential, and why.

Developmental Surveys

Most professional marketing researchers lament the fact that not enough marketing research money is spent for developmental surveys as an aid in developing intelligent long-range plans, successful products and promotional devices, and other parts of the marketing mix. More

184

money is not spent on developmental research because this type of research does not answer a very specific question (as is the case with evaluative research), and thus it lacks an obvious payoff. However, with developmental research, *all* marketing decisions hopefully will be made more intelligently because of the knowledge gained about the ultimate target consumer. Developmental research is often designed to learn some of the following:

— Is the consumer aware of my brand? Is it the one thought of first?
— Which brands have ever been used (i.e., trial)? Which brands has the consumer used in the past year (recent trial)? Which brand did the consumer use last time (the best measure through surveys of each brand's share of consumers)?
— What do consumers like and dislike about our brand and our leading competitors' brands?
— What factors are most important when selecting between alternative brands?
— What is the image of our brand on these factors versus those of other brands? What are the strengths that can be exploited? What weaknesses must be overcome?
— What knowledge, experience, attitudes, or beliefs differentiate a person who is aware of our product but has never tried it from one who has tried it? What differentiates a person who has tried it and rejected it from a person who is a repeat customer?
— Are other related product categories competing with our product category? (For example, Do I sell an aluminum foil or do I sell a food wrap?)
— What are the usage patterns in this product category?
— Who uses our brand and competitive brands ("who" can be defined demographically or in terms of lifestyle, personality, frequency of use, etc.)? Why do some types of people choose one brand and other types choose another brand?
— Who are the heavy (large-volume) users, and how can we appeal to them?
— What media are our customers or our best potential customers exposed to so that we can most efficiently reach them?

Developmental research often uses both qualitative and quantitative research. Qualitative involves studying in depth a relatively small number of consumers; quantitative involves studying in somewhat less depth (because of cost constraints) a larger, more representative sample of consumers. Often, when time and costs permit, the marketing researcher may recommend a two-phase plan in which the first phase will involve qualitative research to help understand the consumer, generate hypotheses or tentative conclusions, and learn the types of follow-up information needed from a repesentative sample of consumers. This is then followed by a quantitative research phase to pinpoint how many and which people act or think a particular way and to learn which hypotheses are correct.

There are two basic types of qualitative research—in-depth interviews and focus groups. During the 50s and early 60s, in-depth interviewing was the more popular qualitative technique. From the mid-60s through the 70s, this technique lost favor in the industry while focus groups had an explosive growth. In the more recent years, focus groups have still been much more popular than in-depth interviews, but the latter have started a comeback.

What are the differences in these two techniques, and what are their relative advantages and disadvantages? *Focus groups* normally involve a trained moderator sitting with 8 to 12 consumers who are recruited based on criteria selected by the researcher. The moderator sits with these consumers for about two hours to learn what they know and think. A moderator's guide, which is an outline of the subject matter to be covered in the group, will normally have been prepared in advance. Like a good teacher with a lesson plan, a good moderator covers the material in the guide but lets the flow of conversation and activity in the group determine the order in which it is covered.

These focus group sessions are normally conducted in a facility which offers equipment that enables the research sponsors to listen to the consumers' responses. In addition, there is usually a one-way mirror to enable the sponsors to watch the respondents. These sessions are almost invariably audiotaped and sometimes videotaped.

A good moderator plans how the necessary information will be elicited from the respondents. The moderator should be and usually is knowledgeable about marketing or advertising, aware of the objectives of the research, sometimes trained in psychology or other social sciences, and hopefully skilled in the ability to elicit unbiased comments from the group.

The primary advantage of a focus group is that it allows people to interact not only with the moderator but with each other. As a result, more ideas are often generated by the people in the group; and since others have expressed their feelings, they are sometimes more willing to say how they really feel. A talented moderator knows how to generate this interaction and to create a mood in which people are encouraged to express ideas and their true feelings.

Another advantage to a focus group session is the opportunity that the session affords the marketing and advertising people in the viewing room. Sometimes this represents the only exposure they get to their consumers; and when several decision makers interested in the same marketing issue simultaneously concentrate on what is happening in the group session, ideas are often generated by the interplay of their individual reactions.

Focus groups can usually be done quickly. In many instances, the people can be recruited and the sessions set up within a week, and a trained moderator can tell the client what was learned almost immediately after the group. However, there is the danger of drawing conclusions too quickly based on the moderator's initial reactions to the group session. Final recommendations should be prepared only after a careful listening to the tapes.

In-depth interviews, or one-on-one interviews as they are sometimes called, have similarities to the group sessions but also have some important differences. As with group sessions, there is a trained interviewer—perhaps the same person who would moderate a focus group—conducting the interviews. This interviewer would have a guide similar to the moderator's guide; however, in this case one respondent is interviewed at a time. Sometimes these interviews are conducted in an environment which allows the client to listen in a back room, but these are usually the exception; in most cases these in-depth interviews are conducted without an audience.

It was noted that the major advantage of a focus group is the chance for people in the group to interact with each other. That is also the greatest disadvantage of a focus group and the major relative advantage of the in-depth interview. Because people are interacting with each other in a focus group, each person's real feelings often are not expressed. All it takes is one or two people who feel strongly about an issue and other people in the group are afraid to express a contrary opinion. Or, if one person gives a fact about a brand, everyone in the group then knows that fact. In the in-depth interview, of course, the respondent does not know what other people have said and thus each person's individual feelings are obtained.

Another advantage to the in-depth interview is that much more information can be gathered from each respondent. A focus session runs up to 120 minutes, and if there are 10 respondents in the room, the average person's opinion would be expressed for only 12 minutes; in an in-depth interview, which might run anywhere from 20 minutes to 2 hours, each respondent's opinions are discussed for that length of time. Still another advantage of an in-depth interview is the ability to have a more heterogeneous sample. Group sessions usually cannot be conducted with too wide a variety of age groups—for example, when discussing a food product, it is a rare 20-year-old homemaker who would contradict a 45-year-old homemaker in the same group. If, for example, four focus groups are done, then there might be different age ranges for each group to try to eliminate that problem; but people with different economic, educational, and ethnic backgrounds could also have difficulty communicating with each other.

The primary problem with all qualitative research is that too many nonresearchers have too much faith in it. It is an excellent technique for eliciting ideas from consumers, for getting some initial understanding about how people think and what the critical issues are, and to develop hypotheses for further testing. However, to draw conclusions about the total market from either one of these qualitative techniques is a very dangerous practice. First of all, the number of interviews conducted or people present at the group sessions is very limited. Second, and possibly even more important, is the fact that by nature these interviews or sessions do not follow a standardized procedure because the moderator or interviewer is flexible about how and in what order the material is covered. Conducting hundreds of individual in-depth interviews or dozens of focus group sessions (if one can afford it) will result in a meaningful sample size, but it would never qualify as a substitute for quantitative research because the information is not gathered in a standardized manner. (In addition, in focus groups the interaction between people in the groups prevents individual opinions from being elicited from each person.) Some people may commission qualitative research in anticipation of a follow-up quantitative survey but then not do that second phase, either because of time or money constraints or because they believe they have such a clear answer from the groups or in-depth interviews that the quantitative phase is not necessary. That is a very dangerous practice. If the marketer clearly states the objectives and the time and budget constraints to a marketing researcher who does both qualitative and quantitative research, then money and time can be allocated so that some quantitative research could be conducted in addition to the qualitative research.

As noted earlier, *quantitative developmental surveys* involve interviews with a larger, representative sample of consumers. This technique uses a standardized stimulus (a structured questionnaire) which is presented in the same way to individual subjects (respondents). Because of the larger number of interviews and the environment in which these quantitative surveys are often conducted, there is a limit to the length of these interviews and thus a limit to their depth.

Quantitative surveys for developmental research are often called either attitude and usage studies (A&U studies), strategy research, or segmentation studies. The latter is a type of quantitative developmental research which became popular in the mid-60s and is still being used. It is an attempt to take advantage of the contribution of psychologists and other social scientists in the context of a quantitative survey. A need developed for segmentation studies as marketers learned that they could not sell to everyone and should therefore concentrate on selling their product or service to specific targeted segments. Before these studies became popular, markets were targeted based on demographics or on behavioral measures such as users of a particular type of product or frequent users of a product. Segmentation studies are an attempt to segment or divide the total market by psychological characteristics, lifestyles, needs, or attitudes—what is known as psychographic segmentation. Psychological or attitudinal scales are given to a large number of respondents. Modern computers using a mathematical multivariate technique—either factor analysis or cluster analysis—enable the researcher to learn which groups of people are similar to each other, not in terms of whether they are young or old, rich or poor, but whether they have similar psychological traits, needs, lifestyles, or attitudes. The computer literally takes everybody's answers to the various questions and then clusters together those people who gave similar answers. This technique has proven invaluable to some marketers as it has enabled them to find meaningful segments at which to aim their marketing efforts. However, these studies can be very expensive and time-consuming; many marketers commission them without any clear-cut objective in mind other than some vague hope that in finding psychographic segments they will find the magic road to increased profitability.

Evaluative Research

The bulk of survey dollars is spent to evaluate alternative stimuli. These stimuli might be the product or service of the research sponsor or the different parts of the marketing mix used to influence people to buy the product or service (advertising, packaging, etc.)

More money is probably spent on *product tests* than on any other type of market survey. Marketers want to know whether consumers perceive their product to be as good or better than competition and if so, why, and if not, why not. In addition, product tests are conducted because someone in the laboratory or elsewhere in the company has developed what is believed to be an improved or a less expensive product. Before the brand's franchise is risked by a product change, the marketer will often commission a product test to have consumers determine whether they prefer the improved product or accept the less expensive one; or, alternative formulations are developed for a new product, and the decision must be made as to which formulation to sell. Other times, competitive products are tested, especially when a potentially strong new competitor enters the market. Sometimes product tests are done to offer legal substantiation for an advertising claim of product superiority.

In most cases, "blind" product tests are conducted. If the marketer wishes to learn how the product compares to competition, then it is important to eliminate any identification of all the products in a test; otherwise, feelings toward the products could influence the respondents' reactions to them. When possible, the alternative products are placed in plain containers with code letters so that the respondent does not know what is being tested.

It is hoped that the product test will ascertain not only which of the alternative products is best but also the strengths and weaknesses of the different products. Those involved in the development of the products should be asked what differences they anticipate between the alternative products, so that the researcher can probe for these expected differences.

Sensory features such as taste, smell, or appearance often can be judged immediately in interviewing situations. However, if one is to understand fully how the consumer feels about various products, nothing can replace a home-use test. A food product might taste different when it is prepared by a housewife and not by a researcher or a home economist (as often occurs in an immediate taste test); a perfume might create different reactions when it is applied in the privacy of one's home rather than with a stranger (the interviewer) standing nearby. A floor wax might look beautiful when applied to a new piece of vinyl but might not work as well when applied to a scuffed floor. For most products, the consumers should do the testing where those products will eventually be prepared and used.

In some instances a description of the product is given before the respondent is asked to try it. This is often done when the product is unusual and it is necessary for the consumer to understand something about it before trying it. For example, if the product has an unusual appearance, the consumer might be very negative unless told why it looks that way. This research obviously does not allow for a pure rating of the product's performance since people will be influenced by what they are told in the opening statement; but, in certain situations, it can be the only really fair test for a product. The hope is that if several products are tested, the opening statements will be equally positive so as not to create an unfair advantage for one product over another.

Much money is also spent doing *advertising copy research*. While not every product category involves substantial expenditures for media advertising, those industries that spend the bulk of the money in marketing research are the same ones that usually spend a high proportion of their marketing dollars on advertising. Such basic questions as "Is the advertising any good?", "Will it be noticed?", or "How can the advertising be improved?" should be asked by anyone who spends a high proportion of the marketing budget on advertising.

Advertising research can involve pretesting or posttesting. Pretesting is testing the advertisement or commercial prior to ever spending any major media or production money on it while posttesting involves evaluating advertising that has already been run.

There are two fundamental disagreements among researchers and advertisers as to how copy testing should be done:

1. Should the advertising be tested in a natural viewing or reading situation or in a laboratory setting? In a natural situation, it is aired in a limited number of cities or is placed in limited editions of a magazine (or sometimes inside a dummy magazine where the respondent believes the purpose of the test is to study the editorial matter of the magazine, not the advertising). The most popular method of testing television commercials in a natural situation is what is known as on-air recall. The commercial is aired in a few cities in a normal slot for the commercial, and people are called either immediately after the program is over or, more commonly, the next day. Viewers of the program are located and then asked what they remember about the commercial. If a company has done its developmental research and knows what it wishes to communicate for each of its brands, it can then use this technique to determine which commercial most efficiently communicates the points it wishes to make.

Other people argue that while a natural situation does offer the advantage of seeing which commercials or advertisements can attract and hold viewers' and readers' attention in the natural environment of watching a program or reading a magazine (after all, people do not watch a television show to see the commercials), it has some serious disadvantages. First of all, it is not a controlled situation. As a result, the performance of the commercial or advertisement can be affected by the program material or reading matter surrounding it. Second, the respondent can be exposed to other advertising by the advertiser or its competitors between exposure to the commercial or advertisement under study and the time the interview is conducted. Another problem mentioned by many in regard to a natural situation is the fact that one natural exposure does not afford the researcher any way to measure changes in attitudes or buying interest.

Those who favor artificial (forced) exposure situations use a variety of techniques. Some believe in putting a group of people in one place while commercials are shown either alone or surrounded by program material. Others will show people the commercials on a one-to-one basis. Test print ads are shown by themselves—not surrounded by editorial matter. In all these situations, the interview immediately follows the respondent's exposure to the advertising, thus eliminating any intervening stimuli. Also, the environment in which the commercial or advertisement is shown is carefully controlled and standardized from one execution to the next.

2. The other major debate in advertising research concerns the criteria used to evaluate the advertising. Obviously, the ultimate goal of most advertising is to get more people to buy the product. However, advertising by itself usually does not sell or unsell a product. There are many other variables in the marketing mix interacting with the advertising, such as the product itself, its price, packaging, special promotions, etc. Some argue that it is unfair to evaluate advertising in terms of sales or even buying intentions, but rather one should settle for measuring whether communications goals are being achieved. Communications goals include such things as: whether more people know the name of a product, whether they learned some additional facts about the product, or possibly if they have changed their opinion toward the product. Those in favor of measuring sales or buying intentions argue that while measuring communications goals is easier, it is not appropriate if that is not the objective of the advertising. These people, while they might not expect to measure actual sales performance as a result of exposure to a single commercial, at least want to measure a shift in purchase intention—they seek what is usually called a measure of "persuasion."

Regardless of whether forced or natural exposure is used, regardless of the measure or measures used to determine which commercial or advertisement is best, most researchers also include some diagnostic information. Nothing is more frustrating to a copywriter than to hear that none of the commercials is good without hearing any guidance as to how to develop a better one. While a single measure of evaluation of the advertising (or a number of measures combined in some mathematical formula which results in the best one) may be necessary to decide which vehicles deserve the support of the advertising budget, the diagnostic questions are important if better advertising is to be developed in the future.

Other special methods of advertising research have been developed—for example, an eye camera which takes readings of the consumers' eye movements as an advertisement is shown to learn what they look at in the ad and in what order. Other methods have been developed to measure physiological responses to the advertisement such as pupil dilation or the amount of perspiration, in the belief that certain physiological responses occur with certain emotional responses.

Another type of testing research is *concept research*. This involves testing something in the early concept or idea stage before it is fully executed. The concept might be either a new product or a new positioning, campaign, or strategy for an existing product. Sometimes marketing and/or R&D people have developed a wide array of product ideas and want to know which ones are worthy of further developmental time and money. In this case, the concept research is done to screen the various alternatives and select the ones with the most promise. Other times the concepts for just one or two new products have been developed and the marketer wants to learn if there is potential for these products, and, if so, what can be learned to help develop them further.

Concept research could also involve testing different consumer claims prior to development of alternative advertising strategies or positionings for a product. Will our resealable metal can for carbonated beverages sell better if it is promoted as an unbreakable bottle or will it sell better if promoted as a resealable can? Should our new breakfast candy bar be sold as an opportunity for those who do not have time to eat a nutritional breakfast or should it be promoted for those who now eat a nutritional breakfast but can get the same nutrition more quickly?

Sometimes the concept (either product or advertising) is presented with one or more sentences typed on a card, while other times the concept is tested with a fuller execution, such as a rough ad. Those who argue for the former say they do not want the execution to influence the reaction to the concept, while those who argue for the latter say that eventually the concept will have to have an execution, and the only fair way to evaluate it is to test it with an execution.

Packaging research is also a common type of market survey. In this world of self-service, there are many product categories in which the package often has to replace the salesperson. The package is frequently evaluated in terms of its physical characteristics such as whether it is easy to open, to reseal, to carry, to pour from, etc. However, more often it is researched for its contribution to the marketing mix. For example, will it get the customer's attention on the shelf, and will it communicate the image and positioning for the brand? The shape of the package, the colors, and the graphics can all affect the imagery of the brand and the visibility of the package.

The *name* of the product is sometimes researched. Those people who have limited budgets will often make a decision about a name without any research, as it is usually considered a less critical element of the marketing mix. But sometimes name research is important, because the name is important. For example, sometimes there is a question as to whether the name communicates a negative feature to the product. Other times the name plays an important role in communicating the image desired for the brand.

The *price* of a product is sometimes researched. However, price research is not often done via surveys because:

1. Price can often be tested in an in-store situation by controlling the prices in a limited number of stores and then reading the relative sales figures.

2. Researching price via interviewing people often leads to unreliable data because of the implications of being seen as the type of person to select either a higher- or lower-priced product. Special research designs try to avoid this bias and thus allow for reliable pricing research by consumer survey, but these are beyond the scope of this book.

Another type of testing research is called a *tracking study*. This is often similar to the attitude and usage study described in the developmental surveys section. However, tracking studies are conducted periodically in order to measure changes in the marketplace over time. People's attitudes, behavior, usage patterns, etc. are obtained periodically to see the total effect of the marketing effort.

Sometimes tracking studies are done on a national basis, and other times they are done only in a test market where the reactions of consumers are ascertained over time in a small area of the country where either a new product is launched or a new marketing strategy (such as a new advertising campaign or a new price) is tested. These studies act as a "report card" to indicate how well the new product or strategy is doing; optimally, they are also designed to show how to do things better in the future.

Test market simulation has grown dramatically in the past decade. All elements of a new product or a new marketing approach are tested as a unit and presented to people in a controlled environment. Trial and repurchase intentions are ascertained. These data, plus the client's expected level of awareness and store distribution, are all input for a special computer simulation program which then estimates future brand share. It is usually conducted either just before actual test marketing or in place of it.

There are other kinds of studies, but those described represent the most common types.

STEPS IN CONDUCTING A SURVEY

This section covers the various steps in conducting a research survey. Some of these steps involve both the sponsor of the study and the research firm conducting it, while others are done only by the research firm. However, it is important for the buyer of research to understand all the steps in the research process and the alternative ways they can be conducted.

Determining the Problem or Need

No step is more important than this. Unless the problem or the reason for the study is clearly stated and understood by both the sponsor of the research and the company responsible for it, there cannot be any assurance that the research will solve the problem or fulfill its objectives. The more specific the objectives, the better the research will be. For example, a problem stated as, "Why are sales declining?" is of little aid in selecting a research design, while a problem stated as, "Why are we losing customers as fast as we acquire them?" suggests a specific research design and some very specific questions.

Study Design

One of the goals of marketing research is to attempt to apply the scientific method to gather data that helps solve problems and make marketing decisions. Unfortunately, unlike scientific laboratory research or even psychological testing, it is very difficult in the real marketing world to control all the conditions and variables. However, the researcher should always select a design which comes as close as possible to meeting the criteria of good research: reliability (consistency), sensitivity (discrimination), and validity (measures what it claims to measure).

Research design is more important for evaluating alternative stimuli than it is for quantitative developmental research (where questionnaire design and analysis are critical). Three basic research designs are generally employed in evaluating stimuli, each of which has its appropriate use. For purposes of illustration, this section describes how the various designs could be applied to product tests. The same design could be used for evaluating alternative advertisements or packages or any other marketing tools.

Monadic Testing. Each person is exposed to only one of the products. Matched groups of samples are established, each of which is given one of the products and asked for reactions to it. The advantage of this design is that it is closest to the real world in the sense that when people are exposed to a new product, they compare it to what is in the marketplace and to their own experience; in the real world, they rarely compare two new products or two new packages against each other. The major disadvantage of monadic testing is that it involves many interviews, because each product is presented to a different group of respondents. It is also considered less sensitive than a paired comparison.

Paired Comparison. Each respondent is exposed to both of the products: half the respondents are exposed to Product A first, then it is either removed from their sight or consumed, and they are then given Product B; the other half of the respondents is given the products in reverse order. After using both products, the respondents are interviewed to determine which one they prefer. The advantages of the paired comparison are that it entails a smaller number of interviews (since both products are presented to the same group of respondents), and it tends to exaggerate differences between the two products as it is much easier to see differences when the same people are comparing the two directly. However, this exaggeration of differences is also one of the negatives of paired comparison since at times it is important to know not which product is preferred, but whether it is preferred enough to be noticed by the consumer (e.g., when one product is going to cost more to produce than the other, and thus it is important to know whether people notice the better product). Another disadvantage of paired comparison is that it is not comparable to the real world (the corollary of the major advantage of monadic testing)—that is, people in the real world do not normally compare two new products against each other but rather compare one new product at a time against their past experience. "Me-too" products often win over unique new products with paired comparison, while in the marketplace few want a me-too product.

Protomonadic Testing. In their search to gain the advantages of both monadic and paired comparison testing, researchers developed the protomonadic technique. Each group of respondents is given one of two products to use. They are asked to evaluate this product on a monadic basis. They are then given the second product to use and are asked paired comparison questions. The major advantage of this technique is that it provides monadic readings for both products to determine what happens when the respondent tries just one product, and then it affords the opportunity to see any small differences which might be exaggerated in the paired comparison. The disadvantage of this technique is that it requires three interviews with each respondent (including the placement interview), thus adding to the cost per respondent.

Other special research designs are used at times. For example, a technique often called the *triangle test* determines whether people really can differentiate between two products. For instance, if a paired comparison of two products is done and half the respondents say A is better and the other half says B, does that mean that half the people really preferred A and the other half preferred B? Or does it mean that they really had no preference and that half of them, when encouraged to give an answer, randomly chose A and the other half randomly chose B? One way to answer this question is to do a triangle test in which there are two of one product and one of the other—for example, A, A, B (but, of course, no two will have the same code letter). The respondent is told that one of these products is different from the other two. By chance they should be able to guess one third of the time that B is the different product. If the respondent cannot do better than chance, then the researcher would conclude that people really cannot tell the difference.

A competing technique is called the *double paired comparison.* Respondents are given Products A and B to test and asked which one they prefer. They are then given A and B again, with different code letters, and asked which one they prefer. The researcher can then tell whether people are consistent in preferring the same product twice in a row or whether they randomly choose A in the first pair and B in the second pair, thus showing they really cannot tell the difference.

Another survey design that can be very efficient is called the *factorial design.* This is used when two or more variables are being tested simultaneously. Consider this example of a factorial design showing four cells (A, B, C, and D), each testing a formulation for a new drink:

	Level of Sweetness		
Color	*Sweet*	*Dry*	*Total*
Pink	Cell A	Cell B	Pink (A + B)
Amber	Cell C	Cell D	Amber (C + D)
Total	Sweet (A + C)	Dry (B + D)	

Reading the chart, Cell A was given a pink, sweet liquid, Cell B a pink dry (unsweet) liquid, etc. To see if pink or amber is preferred, Cells A + B combined is compared to Cells C + D. To compare sweetness levels, A + C is compared to B + D. Thus each cell is used for two different tests—color and level of sweetness. In addition, any interaction of color and sweetness level can be seen (and statistically tested) by looking at the four individual cells. For example, a pink sweet formulation might be perceived as too sweet, or an amber sweet formulation might give conflicting cues to the respondent (amber drinks are usually expected not to be as sweet as pink ones).

How does the researcher select which design to use? This requires thorough knowledge of the nature of the real problem—for example, is this a product test between two equal products? Is one a cost-reduction product? Is one supposed to be an improved product? How many variables need to be tested? Also, the researcher should ask the marketer which is more important: to conclude something is better when it is not or to conclude something is not better when it really is? Of course, time and cost limitations can also determine the design.

One component of research design is determining whom to survey. Should anyone who uses the product category be interviewed; and, if so, what is meant by the product category (e.g., all those who fly, or business flyers, or anyone who travels long distances)? Also, should a large percentage of the respondents be current users of the test brand? This is particularly important if one is thinking about changing the product formulation or the current advertising or package; it is usually critical to be sure that the current franchise will not be upset. If it is very expensive to find a particular respondent, then it is more practical to obtain as much information as possible from that respondent; therefore, one is discouraged from using the monadic design and encouraged to choose the protomonadic design.

Questionnaire Design

A questionnaire usually consists of closed-end questions (there are a limited number of prelisted answers), open-end questions (respondents are asked to tell in their own words what they have seen, what they like, etc.), and scale questions (people evaluate something on the basis of a scale—usually standardized—which could be either verbal, pictorial, or numerical). Open-end questions are harder to administer, harder to interpret when the interviews are completed, and less structured and thus less objective. However, the open-ends do offer the advantage of giving respondents the opportunity to tell in their own words what they feel. Omitting open-end questions assumes that the researcher can anticipate all of the respondents' possible answers and all the relevant factors in a decision. In addition, the major advantage of the open-end question is that it gives the researcher a chance to learn what is on the respondents' minds, without the researcher influencing their thinking. For example, one of the ways to find out what is really important in selecting a brand is to see what people volunteer as reasons for either selecting or switching to their current brands.

The closed-ends have some major advantages over open-ends. In scientific research, the measuring instrument (i.e., the questionnaire) should be presented to the subject in a standardized manner: every respondent or subject ideally is interviewed in the same way. There is no way to control the fact that different respondents are interviewed by interviewers with different training and under different conditions. But with closed-ends, at least there is assurance that the questionnaire will probably be administered in a consistent manner. With open-end questions, most researchers want interviewers to probe. That is, if a respondent gives a vague answer such as, "It is convenient," an interviewer is usually asked to probe by asking something such as, "In what ways is it convenient?" However, once interviewers are allowed to probe, they are being given permission to ask additional questions as they see fit, with the hope that they will all ask those questions in basically the same way and without leading the respondent. With closed-ends, this problem does not exist. Another advantage of closed-ends is that the researcher learns exactly how many people feel a particular way about a subject. The fact that 23 percent of the respondents mention "mildness" as a reason for liking their current brand means only that *at least* 23 percent think their brand is particularly mild. Many other respondents might also feel that way but decide there are reasons to mention factors other than mildness, or they just forget to talk about the mildness of the product. If they are asked specifically to consider if their brand is exceptionally mild, then an exact count can be obtained of how many feel that way.

When developing a questionnaire, there are some basic rules which should be followed:

1. Ask a question for which the respondent is not given any cue (called an unaided question) before asking a question for which the respondent is given a cue or help (an aided question). For example, respondents should be asked to name whatever brands they can think of in a product category before they are asked specifically whether they have ever heard of Brand X.

2. In most cases, the particular brand or subject under study should not be identified or revealed to the respondent before it is necessary. Some people like to say only nice things; if the respondent can be prevented from learning what we are really after, we can minimize this potential bias.

3. Whenever multiple products, advertisements, concepts, or other stimuli are exposed to each respondent, rotate their order of exposure from one interview to the next to avoid possible position biases. Communications researchers have found through experimentation that being in the first or last position is usually better than being in a middle position. Rotating the order avoids any potential bias.

4. Any possibly embarrassing or personal questions are, when it is feasible, placed at the end of the questionnaire because they could cause the respondent to terminate the interview. In addition, asking these questions at the end avoids changing the environment of the interview.

5. When surveys are done in various parts of the country, it is important to make sure that the same words mean the same thing in different areas. For example, what people in New York City call *soda,* people in New England call *tonic.* In New York tonic is quinine water.

There is a real art to designing a questionnaire that flows properly through the interview and elicits the necessary responses in a valid and unbiased manner. Many people feel that they are capable of writing questionnaires without any experience, but anyone who has had experience with questionnaires and has seen the results obtained from them knows that there is definitely an art involved. Therefore, it is strongly recommended that a professional, competent researcher always be used to design a questionnaire.

One of the major problems in marketing research today is a tendency to make questionnaires too long. There is always a hungry computer at the end of the research process waiting to absorb all the possible data a researcher can gather from the respondent. However, respondent fatigue or boredom does come into play, and one must doubt the results of the later questions in a long questionnaire. There is a saying in the marketing research business that if you ask a question, you will get an answer. However, is that answer always something you can trust?

Sampling

Except for the U.S. Government Census, all surveys use sampling. No one could afford or have any reason to interview everybody. To those of you who wonder whether you can trust sampling, it should be pointed out that sampling is widely accepted in everyday life. For example, when you go to the doctor, would you rather a small sample of your blood be taken or would you rather all of it be taken? When you are flipping the channels looking for a television program to watch, you are willing to decide after watching one for a minute or so whether or not it is a program that you would enjoy. It is possible—and statistical theory tells us just how possible—for a relatively small proportion of all the people you are interested in to give an accurate reading of that entire population.

Two factors make for a good sample: an adequate size and good quality (in the sense that you select people who are representative of all those you wish to study). Researchers from academia often disagree with researchers in the business world as to the relative importance of a very precise sample. Academemicians tend to want a perfect or close-to-perfect sample because only then can the researcher be sure there is no bias; also, the rules of statistics apply only to probability samples, and no other sample should use those rules. Practicing researchers, on the other hand, know that there are errors in the research process that can be much greater than sampling errors. Although those other errors are not measurable (as are sampling errors), the researchers are willing to spend less on drawing the perfect sample and use more of the budgeted money to do a better job among those whom they have selected for their sample. Even courts and the quasi-judicial bodies of the government are accepting nonprobability samples, if that is the generally accepted practice in the marketing research field for that type of study.

What is a probability sample? It is a sample in which every person in the universe or population being studied has an equal or at least a known chance of being selected. The universe or population is the group you wish to interview; it could be users or buyers of your product category or users or buyers of your brand, it could be households, or it could be individual people.

It is very difficult to get a perfect probability sample. That requires selecting people or households in an unbiased way and then interviewing all or nearly all those selected. For example, if you want to do a telephone survey of listed households in a county, you could take the directory for that county and call every thousandth name in that book; that would be a probability sample. However, there are a great many problems with even such a simple probability sample because it requires that everyone selected to be interviewed will be interviewed; and many people refuse to cooperate.

This does not mean to imply that probability samples are not recommended. They certainly represent the best form of sampling, and they assure lack of bias in selecting a sample. They are particularly important when it is critical to have optimum accuracy in the responses.

Probability samples are rarely, if ever, used for certain types of research such as product or copy tests. It would be too expensive to attempt a product test in which the product is placed on a probability basis. The amount of additional accuracy would not warrant a probability sample in most cases. However, even when a strict probability sample is not used, it is possible to utilize some of the principles and benefits of such a sample by using some of its procedures. For example, if a product test is being conducted by sending interviewers to people's homes, and the interviewers are told to go anywhere to do their interviews, they will tend to select neighborhoods where they feel comfortable. Therefore, the researcher will not get a good distribution of households but rather will get a sample composed mainly of income and ethnic groups that are probably similar to those of the interviewers. Instead, locations could be assigned and interviewers told that they must work in a particular area with a particular pattern of going from house to house. While this is not a strict probability sample of the market or of the country—since the areas selected may not have been chosen by the rules required to meet the criteria of a probability sample—it does mean at least that the researcher has taken away the interviewers' discretion as to whom to interview, forced greater heterogeneity in the sample, and thus greater representation of the total market or markets.

An example was given previously of telephone interviewing using a probability sample which involved selecting one out of every thousand names in a telephone directory. If that formula were followed strictly and people who were not home or who refused at first to be interviewed were called back until most of them accepted the interview, and those who ultimately refused to be interviewed or who could not be reached were properly replaced, then that would be a good probability sample. However, it would be a probability sample of *listed* telephone households. Therefore, those with unlisted numbers would not be represented, and those with two telephone numbers would have twice the chance of being selected as those with one telephone listing. To avoid this problem, a system called *random digit dialing* has been developed for telephone probability samples. The area codes and exchanges are selected based on those in working order in the market, and the last four digits of the number are chosen randomly by computer. Business numbers can be eliminated; there are services that remove any numbers that appear in the Yellow Pages. Other obvious business numbers can also be removed.

Surveys through the mail allow for probability sampling at least in terms of the mailing. However, mail surveys have the problem of lack of response by a large proportion of the sample. Therefore, while the researcher might have started with a probability sample, the end result may not be representative because of what is called *nonresponse bias*; that is, people who respond may be different from those who do not respond. For example, in a mail survey those people who feel strongly about the subject are more likely to respond than are people who have no strong opinions one way or the other.

Data Collection

There are four common methods of collecting data for a market survey. Each offers some advantages and disadvantages.

Door-to-Door Personal Interview. In the 40s through the early 60s, this was the dominant method of collecting data. However, it is no longer as important. Door-to-door interviews work particularly well when there is a long or intimate interview involved: sitting in the respondent's home uninterrupted generally is conducive to such an interview. In addition, because the survey is done in person, the respondent can be shown visuals (e.g., concept statements, ads). However, if the people to be interviewed are difficult to find (what is known in the field as *low incidence*) or if they are geographically scattered, then the costs of door-to-door interviewing can become prohibitive. In addition, it is difficult to get interviewers to work in dangerous neighborhoods, and there can be problems in convincing people to open the door—both of which contaminate any possible probability sample.

Personal Interviewing at Central Locations. A major method of collecting data today is personal interviewing at central locations, usually permanent interviewing facilities at suburban shopping centers. With the growing expense of completing interviews door-to-door and the growth of suburban malls which offer a convenient place to find many people together, the central location interviewing facilities have had a meteoric rise. As it is conducted in person, the central location interview allows the showing of visual aids. In fact, at such locations it is easier to show commercials on a videotape machine than at home; and if there are limited prototypes of a new product or package for the interviewers to use, all the interviewers at one location can share these prototypes. Because the interviews are done at a central location, there is tighter control of the interviewers and a closer check on the validity of their work. However, most people in a mall are middle-class suburbanites.

Telephone. This is the other method of data collection that has taken up the slack left by the decline of personal door-to-door interviewing. It is less expensive to screen and find people to interview by telephone than in person, especially compared to door-to-door personal interviews. The problems with telephone interviewing are that there is a limit to the length of the interview conducted through this medium and there is no opportunity to show anything to the respondent. Ownership of telephones in the United States is so high that inability to interview nonowners is no longer a serious bias.

There are three ways to do telephone interviewing. The first—and lowest in quality—is to have the interviewers call the respondents from their own homes. The next best method is to have the interviews done from a bank of local central telephones that can be found in most cities. The highest-quality telephone interviewing—which affords the tightest control and the best geographic distribution—is to have all the interviews done at one central location. These central locations use WATS lines and communications satellite systems such as MCI, Sprint, and Western Union. Telephone interviews can be done at a fairly reasonable cost, quickly, and with tight control possible by having all the interviewers working out of one location. However, this interviewing is more expensive than using central telephone locations in each market.

Mail. While the least expensive, mail is also considered the least sophisticated marketing research tool for the following reasons:

- There is no control over who completes the questionnaire.
- It was previously noted that this instrument is prepared in a way so that certain information is gathered before other questions are asked (e.g., unaided before aided questions). With a mail questionnaire, there is no way to control whether the respondent will go back after reading some of the later questions.
- It is difficult to get complete responses to open-end questions as there are no interviewers who can probe.
- Unless they are very interesting, mail questionnaires must be kept brief.
- There is a problem with those who do not respond to the questionnaire. While people also may refuse to participate in personal and telephone interviews, they refuse because of unwillingness to cooperate in an interview, not because they can read the questionnaire and decide whether they have an interest in the subject. There is much more bias when people do not respond because of a particular attitude toward the questions to be covered.

The great majority of marketing research firms, when they have interviews done throughout the country, do not have their own interviewers nor do they recruit interviewers just for a study. There is a network of independent local field services throughout the nation, each of which has many trained interviewers available to work for them. All local supervision and briefing traditionally is done by these local field supervisors. The field services work either on a cost-plus basis or quote a flat rate based on the given specifications.

Data Processing

When the interviews are completed, the marketing research firm edits the data to prepare them for tabulation. Any open-end questions require coding—that is, grouping the answers into logical categories so that the frequency with which various points are mentioned can be determined. Then the data are ready for tabulation.

Occasionally studies are tabulated manually. However, if the questionnaires are long or if there are more than 100 interviews, they are traditionally tabulated by computers. The output of these computers is usually in the form of annotated tables showing the number of people giving various answers, the percent of the sample that those answers represent, and any special summary statistics such as the mean or the median.

Software programs developed for marketing research allow the results to be shown not only for all the respondents who answered a question but also for various segments. The printout shows tables with up to 20 columns of data, each column representing a particular segment of the market that is of interest.

Analysis and Presentation

Sometimes marketing research firms are asked to produce only the final tabulations, and the analysis is then done by the marketer, a consultant, or the advertising agency. Other times, the marketing research firm is asked to do the analysis. Obviously, in the latter situation the buyer must be assured of the competency of the person at the marketing research firm who will actually do the analysis. When outside researchers do the work, they can utilize their experience across many different product categories and marketing techniques. Also, their conclusions and recommendations are less likely to be influenced by internal politics. However, they are less likely to know the product in as much detail as employees of the sponsoring company.

The analysis of the data is, of course, critical. It is from this analysis that answers to the original questions and the fulfilling of the original objectives will occur. Sometimes the analysis will involve statistical techniques; other times statistics are of little importance. The analysis can be presented orally or in writing, or both. Very often it is first presented orally so that everyone involved can discuss the results and their implications; that is then followed by a written report.

When an outside firm does the analysis, it will usually draw final conclusions and make recommendations, hopefully recommendations that can be acted upon and that fit the capabilities of the study sponsor. Most marketers do want these recommendations, not because they feel they must follow them, but because of the advantage of an outside opinion as to how the data should be used. Of course, executive judgment, which takes into account not only the results of the study but everything else the executive knows about the business situation, might result in the rejection of all or most of the recommendations; but if the recommendations do make sense, hopefully they will be followed.

14

RESEARCH ALTERNATIVES FOR INDUSTRIAL MANUFACTURERS

by
Ronald N. Paul

Technomic Consultants

INTRODUCTION

In this chapter the term *industrial* is used to describe marketing research activities for a business or organization that is interested in obtaining information business to business (i.e., about or from *other* than individual consumers). For example, a business selling a service to other businesses is in the same situation as a manufacturer of an industrial product when it comes to applying marketing research techniques. Likewise, a hospital interested in determining its image with health-care professionals in its local environment would use the approaches described in this chapter. Although common usage supports the term *industrial marketing research,* the techniques, approaches, and applications described here apply to virtually any nonconsumer situation. Thus, this chapter has five purposes:

1. To identify briefly the differences and similarities between consumer and industrial marketing research.
2. To review the various types of research and their respective applications.
3. To outline the appropriate steps for organizing a study and to discuss who should conduct the research.

4. To describe alternative approaches and methodologies available to the industrial researcher.
5. To share some thoughts about analyzing the data that result from a study.

DIFFERENCES AND SIMILARITIES BETWEEN CONSUMER AND INDUSTRIAL MARKETING RESEARCH

Differences

First, in industrial marketing research typically there are *fewer purchasing units,* and the markets being surveyed are concentrated. As an example, a supplier of automotive components has relatively few potential purchasers compared to the consumer manufacturer of soap, which would have literally millions of potential buyers; and, in the industrial case there is a concentration of purchasing power: for our hypothetical supplier of automotive components the large automotive manufacturers (Ford, General Motors, Chrysler) dominate the total marketing potential, even though there may be another 50 to 100 potential accounts.

Second, in the industrial or nonconsumer situation, *purchasing influences are diffused;* it is not always obvious to the marketer who makes the purchase decision, and very often multiple individuals contribute to the final decision. In the case of an industrial product, purchasing, engineering, and perhaps the manufacturing staff of the buying organization will all contribute to the purchase decision. In selling advertising agency or consulting services, again multiple individuals within the purchasing firm will contribute to the ultimate selection of the agency or consultant.

Third, for a variety of reasons, *data bases describing industrial marketing are not as readily available* as those for consumer products and services. In the consumer situation there are diary panels and other forms of syndicated research that provide the consumer marketer with considerable information about the potential market. Fewer data are available from published sources for industrial and service marketers, and there are very few syndicated services available to aid nonconsumer organizations.

Fourth, closely related to the absence of data bases are the *difficulty and the cost of obtaining data* from desired respondents when the respondent is a business or professional person as opposed to an ordinary consumer. Consumers can be recruited for panels at relatively small costs—even a $5.00 gift is sufficient incentive to obtain their active and enthusiastic participation. On the other hand, cooperation fees offered to physicians, airline pilots, and other professionals would have to be substantially large before they would be attractive. This statement does not imply that cooperation fees are frequently paid or have to be paid to obtain interviews because they are usually not. In order to gain cooperation, special techniques are required; these are discussed later in this chapter. Nevertheless, there is a higher level of difficulty attached to securing interviews and information in the nonconsumer situation than in the consumer situation.

Similarities

First, *marketing research is equally important.* The motivations, rationale, and logic for employing effective marketing research approaches are equally valid in the industrial situation as they are in the consumer case.

Second, *the value of the research is related to the importance of the decision* in both consumer and industrial marketing research. There is no difference in the thought processes and evaluations required to determine the level and nature of marketing research approaches between the consumer situation and the nonconsumer one. Ultimately, the cost of the research has to be weighed against the potential risks associated with not conducting the research. If a $10,000 expenditure for research can potentially save a manufacturer a needless $50,000 expenditure in developing a prototype that will not be acceptable in the market, then, of course, the $10,000 expenditure is justified. In most situations, the cost of the research will be quite small, compared to the monetary consequences of making a wrong decision.

Third, virtually *all techniques available to the consumer marketing researcher are available to the industrial marketing researcher.* Although there are some differences in frequency of use, costs of execution, and implementation, nearly all techniques are available both to consumer and industrial marketing researchers.

With these differences and similarities recognized, let us discuss the various applications—the decision situations—in which a marketing research approach can prove valuable.

TYPES AND MAJOR CATEGORIES OF RESEARCH

Marketing research activities can be categorized in several ways. One broad way is to review the results of a survey conducted by the American Marketing Association a few years ago (see Table 14–1). The figures show that the usage of various kinds of marketing research studies by nonconsumer companies has increased to the point that most of the

TABLE 14–1
Selected Marketing Research Activities of 200
Industrial Companies

Type of Research	Percentage Doing
Business economics and corporate research	
Short-range forecasting (up to one year)	98%
Long-range forecasting (over one year)	96
Studies of business trends	97
Pricing studies	93
Plant and warehouse location studies	84
Acquisition studies	47
Export and international studies	76
Internal company employees studies (attitudes, communications, etc.)	75
Product research	
New-product acceptance and potential	93
Competitive product studies	95
Testing of existing products	84
Packaging research (design or physical characteristics)	65
Sales and marketing research	
Measurement of market potentials	97
Market share analysis	97
Determination of market characteristics	97
Sales analyses	97
Establishment of sales quotas, territories	95
Distribution channel studies	87
Sales compensation studies	79

Source: American Marketing Association Survey of Marketing Research, 1978.

kinds of studies are conducted, to a greater or lesser extent, by virtually all firms.

This listing demonstrates that marketing research activities can be utilized to develop data for a wide variety of corporate needs. Because the American Marketing Association has not updated this study, we can only speculate that the percentage of companies conducting research approaches 100 percent in most categories. Note that the lowest-percentage response is related to acquisition studies. This result is surprising because the difficulties of making successful acquisitions have been so well publicized that companies would be expected to be more cautious before entering into such agreements. Given the experience of the past few years, it seems reasonable to expect that nearly all firms will recognize the validity of using marketing research techniques in this risky area.

Another—and perhaps a more useful—way to explain the diversity of applications is to consider some of the specific kinds of decisions that companies are frequently considering when they employ marketing research. Some of these primary use areas follow:

Image Assessment

Such studies are frequently conducted to provide an overall assessment of how a company is viewed by its customers, noncustomers, suppliers, and competitors. Although image and fact are not the same, these kinds of data can often provide useful input in selecting advertising and other strategies and also may help a company understand its competitive ranking on factors that are viewed as important.

Present Product Research

A variety of valuable issues can be dealt with in researching a company's present products. For example, data can be derived on what the company's market share is and what trends are developing. Frequently, it is worthwhile to research whether the channels of distribution being utilized are the most appropriate and whether channel alternatives, either additions or replacements, should be considered.

Present Market Research

The issues in a present market research study relate to the emphasis that the market should receive in such activities as new-product planning. A review of total market data frequently leads to a better understanding of the emphasis the company should place on its existing markets versus alternative new markets. For example, by examining data on growth rate of the market, the company's relative position in the market, and long-term attractiveness of the market, a firm will obtain useful input in assessing the importance of the existing markets in which a firm is active.

New-Product Studies

Research on identifying and evaluating new products is one of the most frequently employed applications. Normally, different kinds of techniques will be used during each stage of the new-product development process. At the outset, research may be used to generate users' problems or complaints about existing products which can give clues to the kinds of features or benefits that a new product should offer. Later in the process, large-scale research may test the specific product concepts under consideration by the company prior to committing to major investments.

New-Market Research

If the results of reviewing the company's existing market indicate that the firm's growth and profit objectives cannot be met without entry into a new market, a company should utilize market research techniques to evaluate potential new markets. For example, a company can determine through research the likely growth of the new market, the competitive structure, the appropriate channels of distribution, relative profitability, and the critical skills and other factors required for success in the market. This and other information is extremely helpful to have before capital and human resources are committed.

Competitive Analysis

As companies have found the growth of their base markets slowing, they recognize that a legitimate way for a company to grow is by increasing market share, i.e., taking business from a competitor. The development of strategies, programs, and tactics to do so can be best executed after gaining a thorough understanding of competition. In addition to developing data on each competitor's size and image, an analysis of product lines should be provided. Further, marketing research techniques can also aid a firm in developing an understanding of competitive strategies and likely future actions. With such an understanding, it is possible to anticipate how competition will respond to different kinds of situations. For example, are they likely to meet our price reductions? If a new product is introduced, are they likely to follow? A key question that this kind of marketing research should address is, "What weaknesses does the competition possess that can give rise to programs or actions on our part that can increase our share without decreasing margins?"

Pricing Research

Data gathering in the marketplace can provide information on prevailing price levels and answer such questions as, "What is the likelihood of obtaining premium pricing?"

Acquisition Identification and/or Evaluation Studies

As mentioned earlier, the techniques that aid a company interested in making an acquisition to enter new markets are well developed. Marketing research can play a major role in identifying companies that should be of interest and in developing data on each of these so that intelligent screening can take place. After a firm has been approached to determine whether acquisition is possible, successful acquisition-oriented firms have learned that there is significant value in conducting a detailed study of the potential acquisition candidate prior to acquisition. This kind of study is similar to a marketing audit and is usually done parallel to the accounting audit that often precedes completion of an acquisition transaction.

International Studies

Before embarking on an international expansion program, many companies have found it worthwhile to utilize marketing research techniques to identify what countries would be most receptive to their products, what the critical success factors are, and what method of entry (i.e., acquisition or joint venture) would be most appropriate.

Two additional ways to demonstrate the diversity of uses for marketing research activities are illustrated in Figures 14–1 and 14–2. The first shows how the various applications relate to a firm's (or its product's) position on the life-cycle curve. The second illustrates the ways in which marketing research can have an input in a firm's strategic planning process.

This represents just a partial listing of the kinds of decisions that generate marketing research activities in companies that recognize the benefits to be gained in making more informed decisions. Since most of these have a market or marketing relationship, it should be pointed out that there are nonmarketing applications as well.

Nonmarketing Applications

In considering the nonmarketing-type application areas, it may be best to stimulate the reader's imagination since the areas of application are ultimately limited only by the sources that a well-executed marketing research program can tap. As shown in Figure 14–3, the possible respondent groups are sufficiently broad that even when the decision or issue is outside the marketing arena, the application of marketing research techniques may provide useful and valid data.

Two examples are *compensation* and *plant location*. In the case of the former, marketing research techniques could be utilized to obtain very specific data on present pay and fringe benefit programs of specific competitors and/or firms in an industry that a company is planning to enter.

In the case of a plant location decision, published information is

FIGURE 14–1
Usage of Market Research by Life-Cycle Position

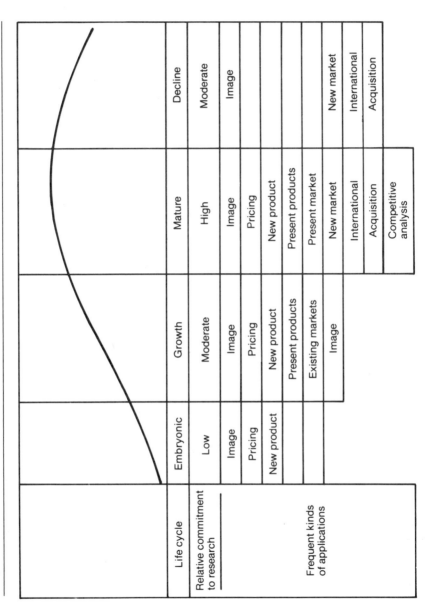

Life cycle	Embryonic	Growth	Mature	Decline
Relative commitment to research	Low	Moderate	High	Moderate
Frequent kinds of applications	Image	Image	Image	Image
	Pricing	Pricing	Pricing	
	New product	New product	New product	
		Present products	Present products	
		Existing markets	Present market	
		Image	New market	New market
			International	International
			Acquisition	Acquisition
			Competitive analysis	

FIGURE 14–2
Relationship of Marketing Research's Potential Contributions to the Strategic Planning Process

Process steps	1. Situation analysis Where are we?	2. Setting objectives Where do we want to go?	3. Developing the plan How are we going to get there?
Examples of marketing research data that can be developed	Data on: Environment Present products and markets — Competitive data — Industry trends — Technological threats/ Opportunities — Perceived strengths and limitations	Analysis and data on alternative opportunities — Diversification New products International Integration— forward/backward	Identification/evaluation of competitive strengths/ limitations—likely strategies. Identifications of suitable acquisition candidates or joint venture partners.

FIGURE 14-3
Potential Sources of Data

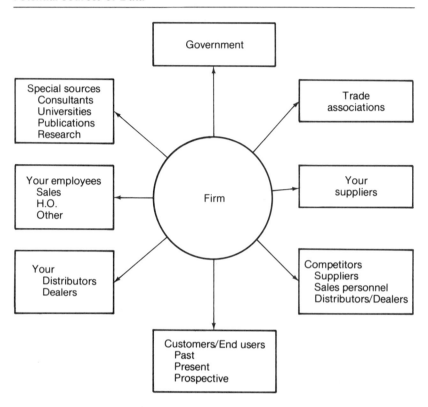

almost invariably insufficient to portray completely the reality of the proposed location. As a result, in addition to collecting basic secondary data about alternative locations, a field marketing research approach within the highly likely alternative communities will often reveal information and insight that could be useful to a company prior to making a commitment. For example, the attitudes and influence of community leaders may be important, as is the general ease or difficulty of obtaining employees with the skills needed by the company entering the community. Without such information, a company may encounter surprises when it actually locates a plant within a community that has not been adequately researched.

Thus, regardless of the functional area of the business, and to the extent that management and managers are concerned about issues that are affected by the attitudes or practices of individuals or organizations outside the company, marketing research techniques can and should be employed to implement the decision-making process more effectively. The next section of this chapter deals with the specifics of organizing and conducting industrial marketing research programs.

ORGANIZATION AND CONDUCT OF RESEARCH PROGRAMS

In discussing how a typical research study is conducted, the overall industrial marketing research process and each of the steps that constitute that process must be considered. These steps are listed in Table 14–2 and discussed in some detail below.

TABLE 14–2
Steps in the Industrial Marketing Research Process

1. Establish goals or objectives of the study (What are the questions to be answered?).
2. Plan the overall conduct of the study, including time and estimated costs.
3. Identify the sources and specific kinds of data to be obtained.
4. Determine and plan how to collect the data.
5. Obtain the data and interpret the results.
6. Prepare a comprehensive report and an executive summary.

Establishing Goals and Objectives

As indicated, the payoff from most research studies or activities results from answering important questions. Therefore, at the outset attention should be focused on establishing the priority questions that the research should address. Such objectives and/or questions should be committed to writing.

Planning the Study

As expected, the costs associated with the study often reflect both internal and external costs. Later in this section we will deal with how the decision to utilize outside research assistance is made. In general, the major costs of conducting a study are related to the time and expenses associated with obtaining the data.

Identifying Sources and Data Needed

As discussed earlier (Figure 14–3), the following sources should be considered in obtaining research input:

Secondary (published sources)
   Government reports
   Trade magazine studies

Company data
Other published materials
Primary sources (potential interview's sources)
Government agencies
Private consulting firms
Industrial experts
Trade publications
Customers/noncustomers
Distributors/middlemen
Brokers/salespersons
Competitors/producers
Raw material/component suppliers

Depending upon the data that are to be obtained, some or all of these sources may be appropriate.

Rarely will secondary sources yield the information being sought in an industrial marketing research study. Even if the data were available, experience suggests that there is validity in confirming its accuracy. All too frequently, secondary source estimates are found to be significantly in error when a thorough primary research effort is utilized.

To oversimplify, the primary data can only be obtained by one of four methods:

1. Mail surveys
2. Telephone surveys/interviews
3. Individual or group personal interviews
4. Observations

Space does not permit an evaluation of each of these methods but, for most industrial situations and for most of the applications discussed earlier, mail surveys have, at best, only limited application. Personal and telephone interviewing is thus the primary method required to obtain the data, even though the costs of such techniques are the highest per interview contact.

Collecting the Data

How the data are collected is frequently related to the size of the marketing research staff and the sensitivity of the information to be obtained. Given the small size of most industrial marketing research staffs, the actual interviewing is frequently contracted to a research or consulting organization. The interviewing, whether telephone or personal, is either structured or unstructured. In structured interviewing, which usually can be conducted by any marketing research organization, the questions are put into a formal questionnaire that can be administered by someone who does not have a working knowledge of the product or industry. This kind of research technique is often limited in industrial cases to obtaining data from customers and noncustomers. On the other hand, when scheduling the interview, gaining cooperation in discussing the subject matter, and getting to the right people become crucial, the structured technique does not work, and an unstructured interview is mandatory. This kind of interview is most often conducted by consulting firms knowledgeable in the product areas and in the industry under consideration. An interview guide rather than a questionnaire is employed, and the consultant/interviewer must establish rapport with the interviewee/subject in order to gain cooperation and the desired information.

Use of the Company Sales Force. A frequently considered alternative is use of the company's sales force to conduct the interviews. Some of the claimed advantages for using the sales force are as follows:

- The sales force has regular access to customers.
- Salespeople are bright and intelligent.
- Salespeople benefit by being involved in product planning.

On the other hand, there are several major disadvantages, as listed below:

- Sources are usually limited to existing customers.
- Valuable time of the salesforce is taken, and the loss of sales may result.
- There is the strong possibility of bias in the response of customers.
- The salespeople often lack expertise in framing questions and/or pursuing qualitative suggestions.
- The research may not be of interest to salespeople and may discourage them.

Experience has shown that the disadvantages considerably outweigh the advantages, and, if the sales force is used at all, it may be only to obtain some basic factual data about present customers, i.e., the number of pieces of equipment and their age or other such simple facts that the salespeople can record as a by-product of their normal call procedures.

Use of Outside Assistance. Outside marketing research consultants are frequently employed because they represent a source of specialized skills, including experience in conducting difficult interviews. They are able to obtain interviewee cooperation by sharing information they have gained earlier in the market research process. Businesspeople are usually not motivated by a cooperation fee. Rather, their strongest motivation in agreeing to be interviewed results from the consultant convincing them that they will also gain from the information exchange. Obviously, the consultant is careful not to give away too much and compromise his/her responsibilities to the client. Furthermore, the consultant brings a degree of objectivity to the study and frequently aids in getting management's acceptance of the conclusion by keeping the company from being directly identified with the research. Consultants are also able to interview effectively such sources as competitors—although that would be difficult for the firm itself.

Overall, in some situations outside consultants may also be a more cost-efficient way of obtaining the data and answers to the questions than any other method.

In order to use outside consultants effectively, the following six steps are recommended:

1. Have a clear understanding of the issues or questions to be researched and how the results will be used.
2. Involve consultants at an early stage.
3. Know what research procedures will be used and why.
4. Check references and evaluate prior experience.
5. Give emphasis to the consultant's expertise and relevant experience.
6. Obtain written proposals and provide for an interim review.

This fourth step then in the industrial marketing research process represents the most important component because if it is not done effectively, the entire value of a study and its conclusions will be in jeopardy.

Interpreting the Results and Communicating the Findings

To complete the process, the marketing research professional must present the materials to management in a concise and understandable format. An oral presentation of the findings is frequently made to supplement the written report. The typical outline for both the written report and the oral presentation is as follows:

1. Background and statement of objectives.
2. Brief description of methodology.
3. Summary of findings.
4. Detail on findings.
5. Appendix and supplemental materials.

Management frequently criticizes research reports because they are too long and contain too much extraneous material. As a guideline, the executive summary of a research report should typically be one to five pages long; a total research report should be less than 30 typewritten pages. Similarly, most good presentations should be less than one hour in length; any greater time allocation should be made only in response to questions and/or to provide time for group discussion.

IMPROVING THE USEFULNESS AND CONTRIBUTION OF MARKETING RESEARCH

In summary, management should use the following five rules in planning and using industrial marketing research:

1. Good research should be decision-oriented.
2. The number of marketing research techniques is limited; don't let them confuse you.
3. Who does the research can be more important than how the research is done.
4. Keeping the users of marketing research results involved is a key to the execution of a successful study.
5. Good marketing research can be justified on the basis of lowering the risks on important decisions.

In conclusion, marketing research can be effectively used to improve the decision-making process in virtually any company. Nonconsumer companies are no exception.

REFERENCES

Cox, William, E., Jr. *Industrial Marketing Research.* New York: John Wiley & Sons, 1979.

Lee, Donald D. *Industrial Marketing Research.* Westport, Conn.: Technomic Publishing, 1978.

Myers, James H., and Richard R. Mead. *The Management of Marketing Research.* Scranton: International Textbook, 1969.

15

SERVICES MARKETING RESEARCH

by
Shelley Wilensky

THE NEED FOR MARKET INTELLIGENCE

All businesses have a need for market intelligence. By *market intelligence* we mean specific feedback to the manufacturer or service provider about the product or service that has been purchased by the consumer. The manufacturer needs to understand why the consumer tries the product, how he or she responds to it, and whether the consumer will buy it again. The manufacturer also needs to know how the product compares to competitive entries. Answers to these questions will guide the manufacturer in future product development, manufacturing, marketing, and sales efforts.

THE ROLE OF MARKETING RESEARCH

Marketing research is one of the tools available to the manufacturer to satisfy the need for market intelligence. It is a study of consumer behavior that uses survey research techniques to obtain information. For many years, techniques of traditional consumer research have been applied by various packaged goods manufacturers. They have been able to develop sophisticated methods to track consumer attitudes, satisfaction, and predictive purchase behavior in a wide variety of product categories. And, in fact, a recent study completed by Market Facts, Inc. reported that "grocery and drug product companies spend 250 percent as much on marketing research as comparably sized durable goods and services companies"![1]

Why the disparity in spending in such an important area? Because the use of market intelligence in service industries, using survey research techniques, is a relatively recent phenomenon.

According to Langeard, Bateson, Lovelock and Eiglier, for the past quarter century or more marketing has been a dominant management function in consumer goods firms, offering strategic direction as well as tactical expertise.[2] Professional marketing management is still relatively new to the service sector. However, the increasingly competitive nature of many service industries, deregulation, technological advances, and a more demanding consumer have created a strong need for traditional sales-driven industries to begin to develop a marketing orientation in order to maintain profitability objectives. Marketing research is an integral participant in the marketing process.

HOW SERVICES AND PACKAGED GOODS MARKETING DIFFER

Historically, packaged goods manufacturers depended heavily on marketing research because of the tremendous capital investments needed for building manufacturing plants (i.e., bricks and mortar). Upfront research could determine whether the capital outlay was warranted. Additionally, new packaged goods products have required long developmental lead times, from testing the initial product concepts, the research and development (R&D phase), testing alternative product formulations, positionings, means of distribution, and communications and media strategies. Many products are put into test markets which determine whether or not the product will succeed on a national or selected roll-out basis. Careful testing can take several years before a product is fully launched.

In contrast, a service product such as a new money market fund may require less than six months to develop. Once the product features are proposed and approved by the regulatory authorities, a product may be up and running in a relatively short timeframe. Appropriate research should be conducted prior to development of the product's features; however, often it is done concurrently with the manufacturing process.

---

[1] Market Facts, Inc., *Consumer Market Research Techniques, Usage Patterns, and Attitudes in 1983*, April 28, 1983.

[2] Eric Langeard, John Bateson, Christopher Lovelock, and Pierre Eiglier, *Testing a Conceptual Framework for Consumer Service Marketing* (Marketing Science Institute, 1978).

While this sounds like a much easier way to manufacture and sell an item, many factors differentiate the sales and marketing processes of services and packaged goods companies. These result in a marketing research process for services that can actually become more difficult than that for consumer goods. This is due to the qualities of the service being sold. For example, M. Ven Venkatesar explains that, "Unlike products, services have problems inherent in their intangibility, perishability, simultaneous production and consumption, and lack of quality control. A goods is an object, thing, or device. Service is a deed, a performance, an effort; it's experiential."[3] And often, this service is delivered by someone not in your direct employ—for example, a waitress at one of your franchises.

Therefore, the consumer may be judging the service on multiple dimensions. For example, the service received in a bank may be the composite of the customer's experience at a branch (length of time to wait in line, efficiency and courtesy of teller or bank officer, working condition of ATM) *plus* accuracy of his/her monthly statement *and* current rates charged for specific products. The bank needs to be able to supply knowledgeable customer service personnel, a physical environment appropriate for the customer base, efficient ATMs, statements that meet the needs of the clientele, and charge prices that enable it to meet its profit goals, while being competitive. In addition, it needs to understand the relative importance of all of these factors in the consumer's decision-making process, from when he or she opens an account to determining where to purchase additional services.

In contrast, a consumer buying a blouse will judge it on fit, style, and durability. If the customer is unsatisfied, it can be returned to the retail outlet at which it was purchased or taken directly to the manufacturer. But it is relatively easy to question the consumer about the blouse, and reactions to specific features can be measured fairly simply. And, if the product was not performing adequately, there would be a huge number of consumer complaints, returns, and a noticeable lack of reorders. The manufacturer might get feedback from the wholesalers as to what the problem is, as the consumer complaint is fed back.

Not so the services provider. The bank, for example, may not totally lose the consumer. A customer may continue his or her checking account because of the physical location of the branch and the branch network. However, if any one of many experiential factors displeases the consumer, he or she will not add any additional money to the account or take advantage of other services. In fact, the bank has

---

[3] M. Ven Venkatesar, in a speech delivered to the Dayton Chapter of the American Marketing Association, April 1983.

lost opportunity to expand its relationship with a client and increase firm loyalty.

Another factor that differentiates services providers from consumer products manufacturers is the level of risk associated with the delivery of the service. For example, after a consumer opens a bar of soap, feedback about the product is immediate. He or she can judge it on the degree of lather, how well it cleans, its fragrance, shape, color, texture, etc. With a financial services product, a consumer may not be able to judge the performance of a money market fund for several months or years. Satisfaction with the product and the consumer's intention to add assets to the fund will be a function of his or her internal investment objectives (e.g., long-term growth or capital appreciation), the fund's performance versus competitive funds, the performance of the market as a whole, interest rates, etc. But only time will allow the consumer to be able to judge this investment experience, and this experience will also be colored by a financial commitment that is much larger than buying a bar of soap! So the risk is substantial, and the marketing and sales process needs to persuade him or her that the risk is worthwhile.

Another level of risk for the services provider is in having distribution mechanisms that are not under direct control. The claims made by an air freight express-mail company for overnight delivery may be accomplished more successfully if they own their own fleet; however, reliance on second and third parties may make on-time deliveries more difficult. Similarly, companies that use independent agents to sell their services may not like the way the services are described or sold to customers but may lack the control that a large packaged goods manufacturer has with a retail store chain.

Yet another difference is inertia. *Inertia* is defined as the time between when a prospective customer is exposed to a product or service and the final sale. Unlike a packaged good, which is available immediately, a service may consist of components that will become available with the customer's signature, such as a credit card or an insurance policy, and often with the assistance of a middle man such as the agent, broker, bank teller, etc. There can be a sizable amount of inertia, or time elapsed, between when all of the elements of this sales process are initially exposed to the prospect and the prospect's decision to try the service. Unlike the packaged goods manufacturer, feedback is rarely immediate due to these factors.

One further difference between service and product marketing relates to the ways in which the product positionings are communicated. Often, with packaged goods, a product mystique has to be built in order to make the product more interesting to consumers. In service marketing, particularly with financial products, the attempt is to simplify or demystify the process.

KNOWING YOUR COMPANY AND PRODUCTS/SERVICES

Before you can really plan a research program, you need to understand the products and services that you are selling. How does your product or service get to the consumer? Is it taken off the shelf? What about direct mail? Maybe the only product the consumer ever receives is a package mailed from your company to a home or business address.

Investigate the sales process. Understand who makes the consumer aware of the product initially and who then provides the reinforcement. Who makes the transaction that the consumer wants—is it a clerk, an agent, a computer programmer? Who does the consumer call when he or she wishes to make another purchase? How does the consumer get charged, and what are the means and terms of payment?

If there is a company training program, try to sit in on some of the classes or take the training yourself. In this way, you'll be able to experience firsthand the marketing and sales processes.

DEVELOPING YOUR RESEARCH OBJECTIVES

As you begin to learn about the company, you will undoubtedly have picked up some of the myths about the company that are held by co-workers. For example, you may hear that this product or service is used only by men, or is for older people, or is used exclusively by upper-income people. Many company myths are true in the beginning of the sales process but change over time. Therefore, you should plan on developing a list of hypotheses about the consumer and confirm or reject them as part of your research program.

Second, you need to determine what kind of future actions are being planned by marketing and sales for the next several months or calendar year: Will they be launching any new products or services? Will they be doing any advertising? If so, through what media, in what markets, and during what timeframe? How do they know if the current advertising campaign is successful in communicating the benefits of the product? Will any sales promotion be done? You need this information before you can put your research plan together.

TARGETING YOUR AUDIENCE

When any product or service is developed, it is theoretically produced in response to one person's idea or need. The success of the product in the marketplace will be determined by how many other people have this need and are willing to buy this proposed solution. This will be a function of several factors: (1) the size of the consumer population who have this same need, (2) the extent to which this need is felt, (3) the price of manufacturing and distributing the product, (4) the buying power of the target audience, and (5) the right message (advertising, sales/communication), distribution mechanism (sales force/direct response), service personnel, and media (mix and levels) to sell the product. Needless to say, the first step in the research process is to identify your target audience.

Many service companies have dual audiences. While the consumer or ultimate purchaser is important, the selling agent (known as a salesperson, account executive, broker, etc.) is a critical element in the sales process. It is usually the salesperson who speaks directly to the consumer, determines his or her needs, and recommends a service to accommodate those needs. It is usually the salesperson who the consumer sees as representing the entire company. And the salesperson knows what *will* and *will not* sell. Therefore, the marketing research approach should be targeted to two groups of consumers—the purchaser *and* the sales agent.

In addition, you may have to do some digging to identify who your primary purchaser is. In selecting an air shipping carrier, some companies may choose only one carrier, or have lists of approved carriers, or have no guidelines at all. The consumers can be as diverse as the company president, the controller, the head of the shipping department, the secretaries, or the managers themselves. It is your job to determine which population is the right one from which to gain information about your service.

While it is difficult to scientifically measure the consumer's experience in a services environment, there is one advantage that many service companies do have over packaged goods companies. That is, they have access to knowing who their customers are, from applications, records of transactions, etc. Most companies today keep these records on file as a data base from which much valuable information can be retrieved. For example, a data base allows you to identify who are your most frequent customers in terms of transactions and who are your most valuable customers, with respect to profitability. Where do your customers live? What kinds of products or services do they purchase? Which accounts are active or relatively inactive?

Answers to these types of questions can form the basics of a marketing and sales effort. The data base can be used to identify consumers with certain common characteristics and provide market-sizing information (for example, 200,000 clients or 15 percent of the customers represent 80 percent of the heavy users). You will then know the extent of a specific universe or sampling group in which to carry out further consumer research.

The information that is retrieved directly from the customer file is only as valid as the goodness of the input. If the input questions aren't worded properly or codified correctly and the information isn't updated fairly regularly, it is unwise to utilize this information. It is far better to attempt to undertake a customer census, perhaps in the form of a mail questionnaire or a billing insert, or to complete a consumer survey that could be used as the basis of a predictive model for the entire customer base. With any of these approaches it is important to target a special follow-up effort to nonresponders. It is imperative that you know in what ways nonresponders differ psychologically and/or demographically from responders in their usage of your service.

DEVELOPING A RESEARCH PROGRAM

A research program should be developed as a function of the company's plans and sales objectives. In a service marketing milieu, that may include:

Identifying the Customer
- Demographically, psychographically, and behaviorally understanding the customer's wants and needs.
- What does he/she want from the service?
- How does he/she perceive your company and the service provided on delivering the desired benefit?

Understanding the Sales Process
- Identifying the branch officers/agents by geographics, demographics, and contribution to sales.
- What tools are needed by the sales force to aid in client sales?

Understanding the Competitive Framework
- Who is the competition? How are they perceived in delivering the desired benefit?

Measuring the Company Image
- How is the company seen versus a specific product? versus competitive companies?

Measuring Customer Satisfaction
- How does the service perform? What aspect of the service could be improved?

Measuring Price Value
- How is the pricing perceived relative to the service delivered? Relative to competition?

Reaction to New Products and Services
- What is the likelihood of trial? What are perceived barriers to trial?

Tracking Customer and Prospect Attitudes
- How do attitudes change over time?
- What is the role of advertising versus service performance within these changes?

RESEARCH TECHNIQUES

As mentioned previously, the tools of the marketing researcher are typically survey-oriented. They may include interviewing target consumers or prospects individually or in groups, by mail, telephone, in person, and any combination of the above. They are selected based on the type and amount of information required, the level of sensitivity, etc. Most often, while you may formulate your own research objectives, you will purchase the services of an independent marketing research company (often referred to as suppliers or vendors) to implement the research.

CONCEPT TESTING

Before choosing an appropriate marketing research vendor it is important to address concept testing, because the product concept testing stage of research is perhaps the most important step of the marketing research process. Here decisions are made which are pivotal to the success of the entire endeavor. In many instances services providers are testing ideas that are so revolutionary that they represent a whole new way of life. Consumers may reject these concepts due to a fear of the unknown or a fear of trying something new, rather than actually rejecting the service. It is critical to look below the surface when analyzing the responses in order to ensure that the service features can fulfill consumers' needs despite the reservations that may occur due to the newness of the ideas.

Recent examples are seen in the financial services industry. When major banks tested Automatic Teller Machines (ATMs), initial response by consumers was exceedingly negative due to a number of factors—the impersonality of dealing with a machine as opposed to a human being, fear of losing money in a machine, anxiety about security, etc. However, ATMs also solved a major consumer problem, which was lack of cash availability after traditional banking hours, in the evenings, on weekends, etc. Research analysts had to be very sensitive to read beneath the negative responses and understand the enormity of the consumer need for cash. This enabled the banks to decide to invest an enormous amount of money in the ATM networks. Similarly, two other recent financial services products have been introduced that have essentially ignored the lack of consumer need. The debit card, a plastic card that instantly debits the consumer's bank account at point of sale, actually provides a negative benefit in cutting off his or her float. Pay by phone, a service initiated by many banks, provides a service that most consumers find easy to do for themselves. These services have not gained wide consumer acceptance due to the lack of need. Proper interpretation of concept testing should have alerted the banks to these factors.

With respect to product concept testing itself, many services companies use the same techniques as developed by packaged goods manufacturers, with some modifications. Since many of the service ideas are so unique, it is best to describe the product or service as thoroughly as possible. The less left to the consumer's imagination the better. A recent example of concretizing an abstract concept was seen in a concept test done by a major travel and entertainment (T&E) charge card company. The company wished to introduce a replacement point-of-sale authorization terminal to the restaurants and retail stores that accepted their card. The terminal would provide faster authorization time, be easier to operate than the existing models, and take up less counter space. Three alternative terminals were available, each with varying combinations of features that would provide this improved service.

The original plan was to do personal interviews with a sample of restaurants and retailers, show them a written description of one of the terminals, and compare their reactions to their existing terminal. Each concept would be seen by one third of each group. However, in pretesting this method, it became clear that the size of the terminal was an extremely important feature in the merchant's decision, and a written description was unable to communicate this benefit well enough. The solution? Lightweight cardboard models of each terminal were built to actual scale. These models could be easily put together by the interviewers and the merchants could take them, place them near their existing terminals, and make a meaningful size comparison. After that, they were able to concentrate on rating the other features of the terminals.

This research was extremely effective in determining how this T&E company could best service its important accounts. It targeted the right consumers, asked the right questions, and examined all responses in depth. It went beneath the surface.

It is also important, in many cases, to include the company name of the services provider in the concept description. Unlike packaged goods, where the success of Jell-O may not necessarily be related to its association with General Foods, the success of a service like the Cash Management Account was very much linked to its introduction by Merrill Lynch. In the services business, images of the provider and the service provided must be consonant with each other in the consumer's mind in order for the service to be deemed acceptable.

Finally, in testing consumer interest in a new service, it is important to use purchase or trial interest questions that provide a wide variety of choices. For many of the reasons already cited, the decision-

TABLE 15–1
Issues to Be Considered in Requesting a Research Proposal

Specifications	Types of Questions to Be answered	Example
1. Define your population	Who is the respondent from whom you want feedback?	New customer. Customer between 30–50 years of age. Sales agent.
2. Incidence of respondent in population	How many of these respondents are there: In the United States. In a geographic area.	10 percent of U.S. population. All residents of Des Moines or Northeast Sales Territory.
3. How will vendor find these respondents?	Will you supply names and addresses or will telephone books, maps, or special samples be used?	Responders to brochures or coupons.
4. What method of data collection should be used?	How sensitive is the level of questioning? Does the respondent need to see exhibits/ads/brochures?	Mail questionnaires. Personal home interviews. Personal intercept interviews. Telephone interviews. Monthly statement inserts. CRTs.

5.	What size sample is needed?	How detailed is the required level of data analysis? How projectable do the results have to be?	Typically varies from a low of 100 to thousands in quantitative surveys.
6.	What is the interview length?	How many questions will be asked?	Typically ranges from 5 to 90 minutes.
7.	Is a respondent incentive required? If so, what should it be?	Is the respondent someone very hard to reach?	Can be cash, product coupon/sample, etc.
8.	How many open-ended questions will be included?	What do you need to hear in the respondent's own words?	Varies. Has heavy impact on final cost estimate.
9.	What are the data processing requirements—regular and special analysis?	Are there a certain number of data cards to be processed? Are there any special statistical analyses?	Can include factor analysis, trade-off analysis, etc. ASK!
10.	What is the required output?	Do you need a memo, a thorough written analysis, an oral presentation?	Check with your supervisor or product managers beforehand.
11.	What is the estimated time from approval to finish?	When do you need some information? All information?	Can obtain some quick, top-line data and several weeks later get final results.
12.	What is the validation procedure?	How does the vendor know that the field work is accurate? What are the checks?	Vendor should do validation as soon as possible and share results with you upon request.

making process is an extremely complex one, often involving a high-risk, deep emotional commitment which does not lend itself to an immediate response. For example, instead of asking whether a person would try the product (yes or no), a scale ranging anywhere from 4 to 11 points should be utilized. With four options, verbal anchor points can be used; with 10 or 11 points, a numeric continuum with verbal endpoints can be used.

Example: After seeing *(concept description for service A),* how likely would you be to try *(service)?* Would you be:

4-point scale	Definitely likely to try it	2 positives
	Somewhat likely	
	Somewhat unlikely	2 negatives
	Definitely not likely	
5-point scale	Definitely likely	2 positives
	Somewhat likely	
	Neither likely nor unlikely	1 neutral
	Somewhat unlikely	2 negatives
	Definitely not likely	
6-point scale	Extremely likely	3 positives
	Very likely	at varying
	Somewhat likely	levels
	Extremely unlikely	3 negatives
	Somewhat unlikely	at varying
	Very unlikely	levels
11-point scale	From 0 to 10, where 0 means the lowest possibility of trying it and 10 means the highest (or strongest) possibility of trying it. This latter scale is recommended for use when the respondent needs to be given the greatest flexibility in choosing a point which is most suited to his or her mind set.	

When you have finally selected a scale that seems to work in your surveys, you should continue to use it in order to build a set of comparative norms.

CHOOSING A RESEARCH VENDOR

The selection of a qualified vendor is a critical component of the success of the marketing research process. The more familiar the vendor is with your company's type of products and sales procedures, the less time it will take for you to familiarize the vendor with your objectives and the more thorough thinking will be reflected in the proposals you receive.

Most companies expect that you will obtain competitive bids from two or three vendors. This will provide you with different outlooks on the project objectives and some variance in the proposed method of obtaining and analyzing the information. Your selection of the vendor will be a combination of your perception of their understanding of the project, their innovativeness, their prior experience with your type of product or service, their cost and timing estimates, and, finally and importantly, your level of comfort with the person servicing you and his/her support personnel.

Ideally, you should look for vendors that already have some form of experience in doing research in your product/service category. Reputable vendors will inform you if they are currently or expecting to do business with one of your competitors. However, if they have prior knowledge in your category, it is to your advantage to use them since they will add some of their perspective to your specific project. If you are dealing with a unique new product that has no analog, you'll do best with a research company that has at least some history of doing research in a related field.

Finding a vendor can be done in several ways. You can go to published sources such as *The Green Book,* published annually by the New York chapter of the American Marketing Association, and the telephone book; you can also get information by word of mouth or from your local American Marketing Association chapter.

When obtaining a proposal for a project, the following specifications must be discussed with the vendor. All of them must be given the exact same information—so that you really do obtain competitive bids. (See Table 15–1.)

SUMMARY

The focus of this chapter has been to educate the reader about the many different facets of the marketing and sales process for services providers versus traditional packaged goods approaches. Services marketing—because of its lack of tangible products or services delivered, the complexity of the definition of the service, the high levels of uncertainty in product delivery and in consumer acceptance, and the amount of time between product exposure, sale, and ultimate delivery or performance—is fraught with risk. The research conducted for management in service industries must be able to identify potential problems and opportunities in light of the aspects of the sales and marketing efforts that are peculiar to these industries. This chapter is not as much a how-to-do-it approach as it is a how-to-think-about-it one.

ACKNOWLEDGEMENTS

The author acknowledges, with grateful thanks, the contribution of ideas for this article from the following persons:

Dr. Kevin J. Clancy
Vice President and Director of Research
Clancy-Shulman & Associates, Inc.
13 Riverside Ave.
Westport, CT 06880

Paula Drillman
Executive Vice President
McCann Erickson, Inc.
485 Lexington Avenue
New York, NY 10017

Leslie Moran
Executive Vice President
CLT Research Associates
600 Third Avenue
New York, NY 10016

Jinny Henenberg
Principal
Jinny Henenberg Qualitative Research
155 East 84 St.
New York, NY 10028

Ellen Sills-Levy
Executive Vice President
Engelhard & Associates
136 East 57th Street
New York, NY 10022

Judy Dimon
Vice President
Consumer Credit Marketing
Shearson/American Express
2 World Trade Center
New York, NY 10048

16

RESEARCH NEEDS OF RETAILERS

by
J. Leonard Schatz

J. L. Schatz Research, Inc.

HOW RETAIL RESEARCH DIFFERS FROM RESEARCH BY CONSUMER GOODS PRODUCERS

This chapter is aimed at retail marketing managers and also at industrial or consumer goods marketing managers who are faced with having to acquire retail know-how in a hurry, due to their corporate moves to share the business of America and the world.

I have done marketing research for industrial product makers, for consumer product makers, and for retailers. I can report to you that retail research is the *same* as research for the other two in the way we use sources of information and the way we assess information to guide decision on investment. Retail research *differs* in emphasis from the others on the *subjects* of its research because the work of retailing differs from the work of manufacturing.

Presently there is some merging of the producing and distributing tasks. Larger organizations who come from one of these fields tend to be reaching more and more into the other. The motivation for this is apt to be survival. The everchanging environment and growing size of organizations demand a way to pull together varying functions to achieve efficiency.

The trend is more toward retailing than manufacturing. We have become more expert in manufacturing technology; fewer people produce more goods. But look at employment statistics. Retailing is a growth part of the economy, and it is also labor-intensive. The public can afford a greater variety of services. So this is where businesses turn to preserve their share in the economy.

Look at General Mills, for example. From being primarily a flour miller, this giant moved into processed and packaged foods, breakfast cereals, cake mixes, and so on. Today General Mills owns a number of leisure goods manufacturers and retailers such as Eddie Bauer as well as the Red Lobster Inn restaurant chain.

Or, take a look at the Pillsbury Company. This food firm has added to its traditional worldwide flour milling by diversifying also into package goods and extensively into restaurants. In 1983 restaurants produced 41 percent of Pillsbury sales and 46 percent of operating profit. Pillsbury owns Burger King, Steak & Ale, and Bennigans and recently bought the Häagen-Dazs ice cream chain.

IBM and Digital Equipment Corporation operate chains of retail stores to distribute their own and related equipment and supplies. W. R. Grace is the largest operator of home improvement stores.

Large chain retailers in turn have expanded their manufacturing capabilities, thus integrating backwards. Private-label goods may form a fifth or more of large food retailer packaged goods sales. Some items they manufacture directly, and others are contracted out. But packaging design and quality control are done by the retailer, whether it be Safeway, Jewel Companies, Sears, or CVS.

Clearly, consumer goods manufacturers place their research emphasis on product development and marketing. They spend a large part of their marketing budgets on television advertising. Product marketing research historically has employed many talented hands. This has been augmented—because of the dominance by television advertising—by many researchers in advertising agencies and specialists in private research companies who try to forecast what to show and tell, how to do it, and where to do it.

Retailers, in contrast, particularly the chain stores, emphasize store location research. Their corporate investment is largely allocated to store fixtures and leasehold improvements, to cash and merchandise inventories, and to the physical stores dotted about the city, region, or nations where they operate, and for which they have signed leases for periods of 20 or more years. While use of television by retailers has grown, newspapers and circulars remain the dominant media.

Forty years ago consumer goods manufacturers were the major employers of researchers. Formal retail research was done at Safeway and Kroger, and not by many others. Today there are marketing research departments at most large chain store companies with 50 or more stores. Firms with 30 or 40 stores or less engage outside retail research specialists to satisfy their needs.

Retailing in the context of this chapter includes both product and service retailers. It includes restaurants, banks, dental offices, and shopping center developers, plus urban downtowns. It includes food and drug stores, clothing stores, hardware stores, and auto supply stores, just to name a few types.

We should note also that the same techniques that retailers use to locate stores are used by builders of and investors in apartment complexes, condominiums, office buildings, and industrial parks. Medical facilities are required by many states to supply a study of the need for their proposed expansions.

Another characteristic of retailing that directs its research needs is the impact of diversity. The nature of retailing demands learning how to acquire, handle, and sell vast numbers of differing categories of goods as well as brands and sizes. For supermarkets, assortments number over 10,000 items. Department stores may handle 60,000 to 100,000 stockkeeping units. Retailers have to develop skills to deal quickly and correctly with masses of products.

Each of these products, in turn, has had to be carefully designed, crafted, packaged, and marketed. The producer deals with specialization and knowledge of materials and production.

A final aspect of the need for formal research by retailers is growth of competition. When Rayco was the only chain of auto seat cover installers, they found it easy to forecast sales for new sites. When others entered the business, new conditions had to be given consideration.

In summary, retailing research continues to grow due to retail growth and greater competition. A wide variety of research tasks may be needed because of the diversity of products carried and different activities included in retail operations. At the same time, a large part of retail research continues to concentrate on forecasting sales for new stores since stores require the bulk of a retailer's investment.

GENERAL CONDITIONS THAT REQUIRE FORMAL RETAIL MARKETING RESEARCH

One can distinguish between research normally done by each retail employee and that done by research specialists inside or outside a company.

Retail company offices are staffed by a host of highly specialized and highly skilled experts. Each buyer, merchandiser, advertising manager, or accountant knows his or her own subject and necessarily spends a good deal of time learning about that field. Such people know more about the ins and outs of their own specialty than anyone else in the organization, including market researchers.

There are, however, specialized information-gathering, assembly, and analysis techniques employed by researchers that most other staff members are not trained to use. Among these skills are use of statistics and statistical analysis, design of surveys and information-gathering devices such as questionnaires, knowledge of library and reference sources, how to draw conclusions from data, and how to communicate effectively with the organization.

Formal research will be done and will prove productive when certain universal conditions apply. These conditions are: (1) Intention to make a major investment; (2) Alternative investments are available, and a choice must be made, but the best choice is not self-evident; (3) Obtainability of valid information (where *valid* means information that answers the question). If all three conditions do not apply, then retailers should make small-scale, quick tests and not depend on researchers for help.

Now that you know the general conditions that call for specialized marketing research in retail companies, you are ready to look at specific tasks that researchers perform. This is best approached by looking at two dimensions.

The first dimension concerns specific problem situations that managers typically have to solve. See Table 16–1. The second dimension is the kit of tools or techniques for gathering information that researchers use to get answers to these problems.

Many of these techniques are used to deal with a number of different problems. Table 16–2 is a cross reference that shows which techniques are used in combination to deal with each problem. It also shows that a given technique often provides information useful for a number of problems.

DEPARTMENTS WHERE RETAIL RESEARCH ASSIGNMENTS ORIGINATE

Requests for formal research are most likely to come from four of a retailer's leading departments: executive office, real estate, marketing, and store operations. These parts of retail organizations are most likely to deal with problems of large investment and choice that are the conditions for use of formal research.

Table 16–1 lists situations that each department has to deal with. (A brief sketch of each situation follows.) While these are the main project-originating departments and their frequent problems, we have observed that other divisions also have needs. A human resources department may need a survey of employee attitudes. Accounting may need help in making long-range sales forecasts for the firm. Warehousing may need information about labor markets or highways for plant location purposes. Research managers who know how to stay in touch with other people will be looked to for help in appropriate situations.

TABLE 16–1
Types of Retail Research
Assignments, Grouped by Company
Division Likely to Originate Them

Executive office
  Store expansion to new markets
  Store expansion within present markets
  Acquisition analysis
  Diversification evaluation

Real estate department
  New site sales forecast
  Size of present store trade areas
  Size criteria
  Shopping center market feasibility

Marketing department
  Competition evaluation
    Pricing
    Store image
    Assortment
  Consumer survey
    Shopping habits
    Media use
    Demographics
    Attitudes
    Consumer shopping pattern
  Problem store analysis
  Promotion evaluation
  Inventory management

Store operations department
  Remodel potential
  Department profitability
  Payroll management

TYPES OF RETAIL RESEARCH ASSIGNMENTS

This is what retail executives are likely to say to the research manager.

Company President

Store Expansion to New Markets. We operate stores profitably in two states. We have the staff and finances to grow. Which of the eight adjoining states should we seek to establish ourselves in next?

Store Expansion within Present Markets. We lack coverage in a number of cities where we now have stores. How many units should there be, where should they be located, and what sales should we expect at each area?

Acquisition Analysis. We have been approached to consider purchasing a 10-store chain that operates in our area. Are the locations good ones? What market share do they have? Can we do better than the present owners? What will the Federal Trade Commission think?

Diversification Evaluation. We are good food merchants. Should we open pharmacies? (Or toy stores, or tobacco shops, or clothing stores?)

Director of Real Estate

New Site Sales Forecast. I have been offered this site for a new store. How much volume can we expect? How will this affect our existing stores?

Size of Present Store Trade Areas. When we look for store sites, how close can we go to present stores without taking away too many of their customers? Is there any common pattern that our trade areas have, of shape, or distance from the store?

Site Criteria. We want to do greater volume at future sites. What characteristics of a site and of the customers in the area do we need to have to achieve profitable volume?

Shopping Center Market Feasibility. We want to build a shopping center at a specific site that we have assembled. We need to attract tenants, particularly anchors. Are we likely to attract tenants? How much sales will the main types do, including the department stores or supermarkets? How big should the center be?

Marketing Manager

Competition Evaluation. What do our customers think of certain of our main competitors compared to what they think of us, as to overall image, variety, pricing, quality, service, and advertising? What are marketing practices of competitors? What market share do they achieve?

Customer Evaluation. Is there any special customer group that we serve more than others? What do they think of us? What advertising do they see and hear? What are their shopping habits? Whom should we serve that we are missing? How do customers move about our store?

Promotion Evaluation. We have a big campaign coming up. Can you track how many people will have heard our story and what they understand of it, as successive weeks pass? Or, we got a big sales gain with our recent promotion, but did we make any profit?

Problem Store (or City, or Part of Country). We have this store (or area) that is just not making it. Can you tell us what is wrong?

Inventory Management. Can you work out a system to tell our buyers which items to consider dropping from the line? The warehouse is bulging, and store shelves are groaning. Yet we suffer from out-of-stocks. Or, we have too much money tied up in inventory. Can we reduce the investment and still maintain a reasonable in-stock level?

Store Operations Manager

Remodel Potential. We have 10 stores that have worn out physically. But we can afford to work on only five this year. Which ones should we do first?

Department Profitability. I suspect that some of the departments in our stores are not profitable, while others are. Our accounts do not give us useful figures. Can you?

Payroll Management. Help!

TECHNIQUES USED FOR RESEARCH

Your research manager should be able to respond to the wide range of questions described above. The manager will use a group of tools, techniques, or sources with which he or she has experience and competence and will decide whether to do the work in his or her own department, or whether to farm out all or parts.

The manager will mix the various techniques in the most efficient proportions for speed, accuracy, and lowest cost. He or she will mix science with art.

Ten areas of investigation and their usual sources follow. Printed material is important, but nothing matches talking to many people— and to the right people.

Internal Company Sources

1. Sales Analysis. Researchers in retail establishments have to become experts in understanding sales trends over the years, variation from store to store, seasonal trends, department mix, daily and hourly patterns. Store sales results provide an ongoing laboratory for understanding. Visual charting is invaluable. Sales records, when understood, are the basis for forecasting new store sales. The effect of price inflation has to be factored out to properly reflect impact on sales of numerous internal programs and external factors.

2. Manager and Supervisor Interviews. Your own people on the spot are often pretty bright and well informed. Their information should be tapped. They know companies, customers, competitors, vendors, officials, and the events that have occurred over time. The dynamics of operation over time tell more than the current snapshot.

3. Distribution Cost Analysis. This is a combination of accounting, statistics, and observation aimed at understanding comparative profit of parts of your business not revealed by the usual accounting system. How do small-town stores compare with city stores? How do merchandise departments profit on a bottom-line basis, not just on a gross margin basis? Which vendors' goods pay you the best return?

Customers

4. Demographic and Population Analysis. Who are your customers, and who are not? What kinds of people live around your store? Which ones does your store catch as a filter does, and which ones get away, walk out without buying, or never come in? Remember residents, visitors, tourists, and those who work nearby. You will observe, use customer surveys, government censuses, newspaper surveys, commercial information sources. The latter assemble data by computer. However, you have to tell them what trade area to include.

5. Customer Origins. What trade area do customers come from? How far will they travel, or how long? You will mainly interview shoppers in your stores but alternatively use sales slips, credit accounts, or license plates. Every forecast of a new store requires skilled culling of existing store behavior in comparable location types. From customer origin analysis you learn the impact of barriers, competitors, share of market obtained, sister store overlap, and media impact.

6. Customer Attitudes. What do consumers think of your overall operation, or your prices, quality, service, assortment, advertising? How do you compare to what they think of competitors? You deal here with perceptions in people's minds and vagaries of questionnaire design and interpretation. Sampling is necessary to keep cost down by talking to a small but representative number of persons. Your researcher will choose to interview in stores, in shopping centers, by telephone, in homes, or by mail. Or, your researcher may use small groups called *panels* or *focus groups* to get ideas and language but not to reflect the true picture of your total customer group.

Competition

7. Competition Inventory. Locate, count, measure, map, observe, and evaluate direct and indirect competitors who sell what you sell. Don't forget government stores for military personnel or veterans. Sometimes newspapers or industry directories have this information. To be up to date you will have to do the legwork. And don't forget to ask the local people what is coming up. See the newspaper, Chamber of Commerce, city planner, local industrial development agency, and perhaps realtors and developers.

Researchers should learn how to estimate the sales of competitive stores. One of the most reliable indicators of sales is the size of the store staff since this is a major expense item and normally held under close supervision and control. With experience, your researcher will learn to measure the total dollar market available for sales of your kind and to determine what other units as well as your own do the sales to make up this total.

Access and Visibility

8. Access Observation. This requires personnel to drive and observe how roads lead to a site and how the retail store and sign will be seen by the public. Public transportation is a factor as well. A current map should be obtained, as well as information on planned changes in streets and potential barriers. Sources are local and state highway offices.

External Sources

9. Local Sources. Site researchers have to gain a true picture of the store site and its vicinity. What are special problems, strengths, weak-

TABLE 16–2
Typical Retail Research Assignments and Techniques Used to Perform Them

Techniques Used

Assignments	Sales analysis	Manager interviews	Distribution cost analysis	Demographic and population analysis	Customer origin (trade area)	Customer attitude survey	Competition inventory	Access	observation	Local sources	Trade sources
Expand new markets	•			•	•	•	•			•	•
Expand old markets	•	•		•	•	•	•			•	•
Acquisition				•			•	•		•	•
Diversification				•			•				•
New site sales forecast	•			•	•		•	•		•	•
Trade area size	•			•	•		•			•	•
Site criteria	•		•	•	•	•	•	•			
Shopping center feasibility				•	•		•	•		•	•
Competition survey		•	•			•	•				•
Consumer survey				•	•	•					
Problem store	•	•		•	•	•	•	•		•	•
Promotion evaluation	•		•								•
Inventory management	•						•				
Remodel potential	•	•		•	•	•	•	•		•	•
Department profit	•		•								
Payroll management	•	•	•								

nesses, growth, or decline outlook? The researcher will talk to the local newspaper and broadcast stations, trade groups, government and utility planning agencies, redevelopment and transit authorities, and school officials.

10. Trade Sources. Researchers should know where to find information and the best way to get it. Information is gotten from people and published material. There are trade associations, journals, directories, and the vast resources of the *U.S. Censuses of Population, Hous-*

ing, and Retail Trade. Retail research departments will buy reference materials for their libraries or borrow from public or school libraries. Trade associations can be joined and meetings attended. Contacts are made by personal visit and by telephone.

DIMENSIONS OF SITE SELECTION

Although retail research encompasses all subjects that marketing research deals with, the attention to site selection is a central activity. This is because only retailing has so much of its investment tied to sites.

This chapter can only touch on a broad outline of the art and science of site selection, area research, or location research, which are different terms for the same thing. There are full volumes by competent practitioners on this single subject.

There are four related aspects of site selection work for retail or service companies who conduct business with the public at a physical location. These are: (1) site strategy planning, (2) elements of site analysis, (3) different approaches to site analysis, (4) use of computers.

Site Strategy

Site strategy results from the plans drawn to achieve the survival and objectives of an enterprise. Site strategy defines the rate of development in number and dollar investment allocated to building or buying stores. It further defines the kind of business to be conducted, the kind of store and its location, and geographic area priorities.

A site strategy plan means that an organization is taking the initiative to design its own future, as opposed to being at the mercy of outside brokers and developers.

Such a plan arises from earning ability of an enterprise. If you run a profitable business, you have the cash and confidence of lenders to finance expansion. This plan is necessary to allocate discretionary investment of earnings and borrowing proceeds to inventory, offices, warehouses, and to stores. This plan becomes the blueprint for the work of the real estate department, as well as the guide to other departments who deal with the securing and training of qualified personnel.

The location strategy will define the proportion of activity to develop new areas, fill in old areas, rehabilitate existing property, or acquire someone else's stores.

Site strategy considers the needs and resources of the firm and of the public, and the level of competition, as well as the economic and political climate. Good site strategy is a prerequisite for good site selection and analysis.

Site Analysis Elements

Site analysis evaluates specific store locations that fit into your overall site strategy. The locations are actual and available land or buildings, either existing or to be built. They come from offerings by owners, developers, or real estate brokers. The firm may advertise its needs in real estate journals or attend industry meetings where buyer and seller meet. Examples are annual conventions of the International Council of Shopping Centers and the National Association of Corporate Real Estate Executives.

The real estate department receives written descriptions of properties available for sale or lease. They then make an initial screening of submissions to eliminate those that do not fit the plan. The remaining possible sites then get a preliminary evaluation.

Some sites are on their face desirable and feasible. Others are questionable and need finer screening. The organization large enough to have a research department will then request site analysis by researchers.

The product of site analysis is a sales forecast for a store at the given location and overlap, if any, with sister stores.

The sales forecast is generated by examining three subjects in depth: demand, supply, and physical appropriateness.

Demand. What is the amount of business of your kind generated in the likely trade area of the site? This is the total market. It comes from numbers and type of purchasers for your offering. It depends on how your business is geared to serve that public, how you build, run the store, and promote yourself.

Supply. What are the present stores of competitors? What is their number, character, and mode of operation with respect to the market and relative to your operation? Have you a new kind of store with little or no direct competition? Do you run a store very similar to existing stores? What plans do the competitors have?

Physical Appropriateness. What are the degrees of access, visibility, and type of location, whether free-standing, shopping center, or downtown? The relative importance of these elements for a sales forecast will vary for the unique, dominating, and wanted merchant as opposed to the somewhat differentiated operation, or to the copy of the programs already offered to the public.

After study and manipulation of data, a forecast of sales will result. The forecast is often stated as first year, third year, and fifth year, depending on the needs and practices of the organization. The forecast is fit into pro forma (proposed) financial analysis along with full real estate analyses and recommendations.

The real estate committee will meet periodically to assess offerings and agree on action.

Different Approaches to Site Analysis

After forecasting store sales at new sites for 25 years, I am convinced that the best forecasts are made by the judgment of skilled and experienced retail people, supported by appropriate figures.

Many approaches to the figure methods have been developed by different analysts and are in use at this time. All these approaches use the basic building blocks of supply, demand, and physical appropriateness.

Retailing by its nature is affected by innumerable physical and human forces. We do not yet know how to quantify most of these forces. The mind absorbs information and can assign priorities and relative value to multiple influences. What this means is that you and others involved in site decisions will have, and should have, your own estimates of volumes and your own conclusion about accepting or rejecting specific sites.

Four formal methods of forecasting in use at this time are described in *Site Selection,* by John S. Thompson.

The *analog system* uses existing stores that are comparable, or analogous, to the proposed new site in order to guide the forecast. Analysts interview customers of existing stores to learn where they come from to shop. The number of customers in each area is used to estimate the amount of sales that your store draws from that area. The resident population of areas around the store are determined from population censuses. The store sales per person for the geographic segment is then computed by simple division.

All areas in the contiguous primary trade area (PTA)—that by general agreement accounts for about three quarters of the total store sales—are thus rated for generating sales for the store. These dollars are added together to give the figure expected to come from the primary trade area. All sales coming from more distant points are considered sales from beyond the primary trade area. Sales rates naturally are higher close to the store, where travel is easiest, and they taper off as distance from the store increases. Estimated sales from beyond the primary trade area are added to sales within the area to arrive at the total sales forecast.

This system works well for supermarkets and many kinds of specialty stores that sell mostly to nearby residents in suburban communities. But it does not work for restaurants surrounded by offices, industrial parks, or tourist attractions. Where multiple sources like these generate customers, the forecast is more complex and may be more error-prone.

Shopping center sites serve the population drawn by the center. That traffic is a function of the mix of major tenants, the mix of minor tenants, the cumulative mix, and cumulative effect of individual and joint promotion.

Shopping center sites need forecasting that considers multiple forces. Adaptations of analog systems have been made to weight elements such as total center footage, competition from other centers, demographics of the area population, and location of the site within the center. I call this the *score card* method. It is an offshoot of the analog system that works well for do-it-yourself, nonresearchers and for operations that specialize in shopping center sites.

The *normal formula* method used by Safeway Stores is described in *Site Selection*. There are similarities to the analog system, and a few more steps.

Customers are surveyed in existing stores. They are located on maps as living in one or another of concentric mile rings around the site. The total sales generated by all people living in these areas for your kind of business is estimated. Your customers' origins reveal how much your existing stores get of the total available. This permits calculation of market share percentages for successive distances away from stores. The greater the distance, the lower the share. These percentages are averaged for stores in areas with similar population densities.

These patterns of share of generated sales are the company's own experience. They can then be applied to areas around new potential sites, with judgment based on special local circumstances. Sales beyond the primary trade area again have to be added to the sales from within the primary trade area figure to arrive at the total forecast.

Analyst judgment is needed to modify the normal formula for unusual site anomalies within the PTA and to decide the amount of sales from beyond the PTA. Analyst judgment is, therefore, an important element in this forecast, as it is in the analog system.

Modeling is the term used to describe a set of numerical relationships between sales of existing stores and 8 or 10 measurable external factors that affect a particular kind of store. The statistical name of the mathematics involved is *multiple regression*. This simply means calculating the relationship of one figure—sales—to other figures that cause sales.

The number of existing stores of similar type and market has to be 30 or more to get reliable averages for the constant weights that are calculated and plugged into the regression equation. Mile rings are not used. But more external variables can be used, such as population number, population character, and competitive store size, type, and site character. The mathematics can be done manually, but this is complicated. Mathematicians are needed to work up these equations, which are done more easily by computer assistance.

Generally, the regression model requires the user to have many existing units, to assemble many statistics relating to sales for these units, and to have consulting help to handle the data. Also, the process has to be repeated in entirety every few years as merchandising, competition, and the economy change. For example, one chain stopped giving trading stamps and reduced prices during a test that we were making of a model. A whole new set of higher sales figures that resulted from the promotion made the research work up to that point obsolete.

Regression is good where all the proper conditions apply. It will not work for situations where the new site to be analyzed has features different from those of the existing stores used to build the model.

Another forecasting system used by some is called a *gravity model.* This derives from efforts to demonstrate that shopping at different available stores compares with magnetic attraction between masses in space. Bigger stores and bigger markets have more attraction than smaller ones, and smaller distance to travel is more attractive than greater distance. Merchant strength or image has to be quantified and factored into gravity model calculations.

There can be as many forecasting methods as there are kinds of stores. Each analyst or retailer may have personal methods that work. Industry standards are not yet developed. Each organization that makes forecasts has to tune its own scheme by checking forecasts with actual results after stores have opened and by making changes in methods as needed.

Using Computers

Computers so far do not make forecasts. People make forecasts. Computers can help by assembling data for people to use with discretion.

One use for computers is tabulating results of customer surveys; a second is presenting population and housing statistics for trade areas that analysts define in each particular location case. Other uses include developing mathematical regression equations; filing information about stores in data banks; and creating multiple calculations of combinations of file data for analysts to use and to select from for forecast elements.

The computer tool is being applied to store sales forecasting problems. But we still are dealing with social science not physical science. Marketing managers can be assured that they are not being replaced by machines, and machines so far do not replace the retail researchers.

ORGANIZING FOR RESEARCH

Researchers should have training in marketing, statistics, and their employer's business. It is all right to select someone inside the business and train that person in research methods. Consultants and trade associations provide such training; or researchers with training and experience can be hired from outside.

The researcher should report to the same management office to which real estate and marketing managers report. That way the research work serves company needs rather than departmental convenience.

Research assignments have to be selected with an eye to guiding realistic investment decisions. Priorities should follow company planning needs.

To get longer-range projects done, such as new market entry analysis, it is likely that this work will have to be assigned to researchers not tied down to day-to-day site study. The immediate problem will always bump the long-range problem, unless separated. Outside sources can solve this for smaller organizations. Some retail organizations expand research departments when expansion is underway and contract them when sales declines call for cost reduction.

Researchers can make full-scale forecasts, or medium-task forecasts, or short preliminary evaluations. Not all site submissions require the full treatment that takes a week or more to perform. The time, in any case, varies with the store size and type and with amount of distant travel needed.

Good research is done by good researchers. Creativity and initiative should be encouraged. Researchers should join and participate in the work of professional organizations. Good researchers merit skilled supervision to achieve high productivity.

REFERENCES

Applebaum, William, et al. *Guide to Store Location Research, with Emphasis on Supermarkets.* Reading, Mass.: Addison-Wesley Publishing, 1968. See particularly Chapter 13, which is a concise outline for a store location strategy study.

Eilenberg, Howard. *Research Techniques for Retailers.* Dobbs Ferry, N.Y.: Oceana Publications, 1968. Emphasizes department store research.

Schatz, J. Leonard. *Retail Issues,* vol. V, no. 2, August 1979 and no. 3, September 1979. Lexington, Mass.: J. L. Schatz Research. Lists typical research assignments and techniques used to perform them.

Thompson, John S. *Site Selection.* New York: Chain Store Publishing, 1982. Practical guide to store sales forecasting.

ACKNOWLEDGEMENTS

Thanks are due to the following research professionals who described their activities to the author:

Morton J. Kubar, Director of Marketing Research, Zayre Corp.

Vincent E. Osborne, Director of Market Research, Ames Department Stores, Inc.

17

MARKET RESEARCH IN THE NONPROFIT SECTOR

by
Ardis Burst

Burst-Lazarus Associates, Inc.

Marketing, like many other aspects of management, continues to be as much an art as a science. But because of marketing's tremendous uncertainties and its large financial risks, managers have developed techniques for making marketing more scientific. One of the most widely used methods is market research.

Market research can be as simple as showing a group of your own employees an idea for a new product and asking their opinions of it; or it can involve thousands of interviews, extensive computer analysis of results, and lengthy interpretations of implications. At the forefront of market research are some large consumer products companies, with market research budgets of over $50 million and large in-house staffs.

Traditionally, market research has been used less frequently in the not-for-profit sector than in such large companies. In part this is because nonprofit organizations have not been marketing-oriented. In larger part, however, it reflects the fact that management of many not-for-profit corporations and organizations has not had an opportunity to become familiar with techniques of market research and the advantages each can offer to their organization. The objective of this chapter is to present enough general information on market research so that the nonprofit manager can consider using these tools on a regular basis.

With this in mind, the following topics will be covered:

1. Why do market research?
2. How can one justify research from the financial point of view?

3. What types of market research can be done?
4. Who should conduct the research?
5. How does one find and evaluate outside suppliers?

WHY DO MARKET RESEARCH?

The question of whether a not-for-profit organization should have a "marketing orientation" and exactly what it means to have such an orientation is beyond the scope of this chapter. Instead we will start with the assumption that the organization or corporation has some familiarity with marketing and is somewhat user-oriented. If this is the case, why should the organization then do market research? Isn't it sufficient to think in marketing terms?

The best way to demonstrate why a nonprofit organization should do market research is to describe some issues that might be addressed through research and provide examples of how such research has proven helpful to other organizations.

First, market research can help an organization identify more clearly its users and potential users. This, in turn, can help the organization develop marketing plans, predict demand, and anticipate user needs.

One city hospital found that demand for certain tests ordered by staff physicians was increasing faster than the increase in the patient population warranted. The hospital administrator had to determine if this was a temporary or permanent change. He hypothesized that a shift toward older patients was responsible for the alteration. He conducted an in-house research project comparing admitted patient age for the same week in the last five years. He found that patients aged 50 and over had gone from 10 percent to 25 percent of the population. He was then able to use the results of the study to demonstrate changing usage patterns and to project future user needs.

Second, market research can help managers learn exactly what their users want and why they want it. Lack of this information can lead to a long-term decrease in the level of user satisfaction and ultimately to a reduction in the viability of the organization.

For example, a community theater in a suburb of a large city wanted to increase season ticket sales to bring in funds early in the season and to guarantee income. They conducted a mail survey among nonrenewing season ticket holders asking them for their likes and dislikes regarding the theater as well as the reason they had not renewed their season tickets. The survey indicated that people did not like to be locked into using the same number of tickets for each of six performances. Consequently, the theater restructured their program so season ticket holders could use any number of tickets for any one show and still get a season ticket discount. The theater was able to raise substantially more money early in the season by identifying a need they did not know existed until they asked their users.

Third, market research can be used effectively to develop feedback on how both users and nonusers perceive an organization: its pluses, minuses, and how it differs from other organizations that provide the same services. This information can, in turn, be used by an organization to improve its standing in the community and to become more competitive with other organizations that users see meeting essentially similar needs.

To return to the example of the community theater, when the theater surveyed prior subscribers regarding their likes and dislikes, the results indicated that one thing subscribers liked most was the offering of family-oriented plays because so few opportunities existed for families to do things together. The next year, the theater not only included two more family entertainments in their repertoire but also sent advertisements to schools in the community to let teachers know of their offerings. This boosted attendance substantially and helped the theater differentiate itself from those in the city with which they were competing.

The fourth way in which market research can be helpful to not-for-profit organizations is by providing an opportunity for them to test out new ideas or to evaluate several available alternatives without spending the money to put those ideas or alternatives into practice.

A small national organization that focused on promoting the role of women in management was interested in offering some sort of membership program to individual women managers in order to increase visibility and get feedback from women managers. Using a list of individuals put together though personal contacts, the organization conducted a phone survey to ask each woman which of four types of programs she would be most interested in joining (e.g., one with a newsletter, one which offered regular local meetings, etc.). The survey results indicated that the women favored a program that did not require that they attend meetings. The organization then developed a program which focused on newsletter subscriptions rather than membership in an organization per se. This program required much less investment of management time yet appealed to a larger number of the women the organization wished to reach. Furthermore, the organization was spared the time and expense of putting together several programs, only one of which would have ultimately been offered by the organization.

Finally, and sometimes most important, market research can be used to supprt strategic decision making.

One community hospital in a large metropolitan area was approached by a teaching hospital in the same community with a proposal that they merge their organizations and together build a new hospital that would serve both their patient groups. Neither the hospital administration nor the staff of the community hospital wanted to accept this offer, but they were afraid that if they simply turned down the offer, they would jeopardize their future relationship with the teaching hospital.

The hospital trustees commissioned an outside market research company to conduct a survey of their former patients and ask them if they would use the hospital more, less, or the same if it moved, if it merged with the other hospital, and if it made no changes. The survey clearly indicated that the patients would be much less likely to use the community hospital if it moved to the proposed site. The community hospital's trustees were then able to meet with those of the teaching hospital and show them that they would not be serving the needs of their constituency by moving. This took the edge off the rejection and allowed both hospitals to save face and continue to have a friendly relationship.

As the above examples illustrate, there are definitely instances when market research can be very helpful to a not-for-profit organization. But the next question that must be answered is whether the expenditures required to conduct the research can be justified in an organization that probably is constantly facing economic pressures and must often account to funding organizations or individuals for every dollar spent.

HOW DO WE JUSTIFY RESEARCH FROM THE FINANCIAL POINT OF VIEW?

In thinking of the economic justifications for conducting market research, managers of a not-for-profit organization must first be prepared to think in terms of fully allocated costs. It is easy to identify the direct outlays that must be made for research, especially if an outside supplier is used. But it is harder to go through the exercise of seeing all the costs the organization incurs in trying out options. Not only must the salary of those involved in developing programs be included but overhead and supervisory costs also must be taken into account. Then there is the "opportunity loss" involved: what would this staff member have been doing instead? Could he or she have been doing fund raising? public relations? development of some other program? Has the organization in fact incurred losses by not doing these things?

If management takes these hidden costs into account, it becomes clear that experimentation can cost more than research. So the first economic justification for conducting market research is that overall it may actually be less expensive than simply trying things out.

The second economic justification is easier to recognize. This is the cost of making a mistake that could have been avoided through research. For example, the community hospital described earlier could have merged with the teaching hospital, with a resultant loss of patients but an increase in operating costs to support a new plant. This costly mistake was avoided because the hospital conducted research and acted on its results.

A third cost, and another that might be easy to overlook, is the indirect cost to an organization of making wrong choices. The indirect costs are in management time and in organizational morale. Management time is often the scarcest resource in a not-for-profit organization, yet management time is the resource used most in making the kinds of choices described above. In addition, a plan or program which doesn't work out can demoralize an organization at all levels, from the director down to the newest volunteer, ultimately costing the organization money, talent, and momentum.

A more positive economic justification for market research is that it is sometimes able to turn up opportunities in unexpected places. These opportunities might be to save money, to generate funds from unexpected sources, or to find new efficiencies by combining marketing or presentation of products or services.

For example, an organization that promoted good health habits for individuals had written a large number of position papers on varied aspects of personal health such as smoking, sodium in the diet, and wearing seatbelts. The organization wanted to increase readership of these papers, which originally were published individually with hard covers.

Working with an outside consultant familiar with advertising and media, the director developed three ads and ran them in three comparable publications. One ad offered the papers singly in the hard bindings for a higher cost. One offered them singly as inexpensive throwaways. A third offered papers packaged together by theme, such as all those related to diet. By comparing the orders the organization received from each ad, the director was able to determine that he would appeal to the maximum number of people by offering the papers singly in the less expensive form. Thus he was able to reduce printing costs while increasing distribution. If he had not conducted his market research, he might have been able to increase readership, but he probably would not have felt confident with the decision to offer the papers in the less expensive form.

One final point should be made regarding justifying market research from the financial point of view. The not-for-profit organization should be careful in looking at the for-profit organizations for examples of when and how to conduct research. A large consumer goods company, for example, may be willing to commission a very large and very expensive market research project in order to be sure that they obtain information that is as close to perfect as possible. They may survey thousands of people, for example, to increase the statistical reliability of their sample to 90 or 95 percent. This is appropriate when millions of dollars are at stake and when differences that are almost unnoticeable to the average consumer can make or break a product.

But for a smaller organization, the cost of perfect information may be prohibitive and the value of obtaining such information may be questionable. For example, the director of the organization interested in improving public health only ran one set of ads in his research program. A product manager at a big company might run a year-long campaign in a similar situation to make sure that results are accurate and could be duplicated over and over. He might spend more on his test than the organization's director would spend on all his advertising for five years. Yet the director can be reasonably sure that he made the correct choice. Even if he did not totally maximize the response to his ads, he succeeded in reaching many more people than the organization had ever reached before.

In other words, in planning market research nonprofit managers should be aware that their information is not perfect and usually does not need to be. At the same time, they should always be willing to administer a strong dose of common sense and experienced judgment to the findings they do obtain. This should save the experienced manager from falling into the bottomless pit of imperfect information that the manager in the large corporation is able to avoid with a big research budget.

WHAT TYPES OF RESEARCH CAN WE DO?

There are two general types of market research: primary research and secondary research. Secondary research uses existing sources of information, and in primary research data is generated for the first time.

Secondary Research

General Published Sources. The broadest and most easily assessable secondary research resources are general publications, including books and periodicals. A local library can often provide a starting point for gathering background data or for obtaining a general perspective on a topic in which you are interested. The *New York Times* is indexed in most libraries, as are general and business periodicals. Local libraries often tie in with one another and with some specialized libraries in a union catalog system for books, enabling the researcher to consult a special card catalogue and order books from outside the library itself. General periodicals, newspapers, and books can be useful in providing ideas for other sources of published data such as special government reports, which are often issued with press releases that are picked up by the general press or excerpted in general topic books.

Specialized libraries such as those at universities, at large corporations, or those established by foundations or special interest groups can often provide specialized periodicals and books on a given topic. Sometimes these libraries are open to the general public and/or are a part of a cooperative library system. Other libraries such as that maintained by the Conference Board in New York City or the Harvard Business School Library in Boston are only open to organizations that have paid a membership or subscription fee.

Even in a general library the reference librarians can often offer suggestions about special guidebooks available that can lead to other data sources. For example, many libraries have a book which lists all associations in the United States. This book can be very helpful in providing names of trade associations which can then be contacted for further information as detailed below.

Government Data. Federal, state, and local governments publish an enormous amount of data on a wide range of topics. Often this data is collected in repository libraries around the country (e.g., complete census reports are usually available in each county). Also government offices at various levels often have published data available, both for use in their libraries and for purchase.

The problem generally is in determining what information is available rather than in getting copies of what you want. There are several ways to narrow the scope of your search. First, the offices of elected officials are often willing to answer requests that government offices are unequipped to address. Your congressman, senator, state elected officials, and county and city representatives all have local offices with staff who are often knowledgeable and helpful. Second, the librarians referred to previously can also help identify published information, especially if they specialize in a narrow field, such as a reference librarian at the Foundation Center Library in New York City. Third, as described above, major reports on special topics are often referred to or covered in the general press, so a literature search can turn up names and descriptions of useful publications that you might not find otherwise.

Studies Done by Private Groups. Besides government studies, many studies conducted by private groups may provide important secondary research information. The names and descriptions of many of these reports will turn up through librarians and published sources. Consulting experts in the field in which you are interested—e.g., professors at universities and practitioners in the field who write papers and give speeches—can also result in leads to valuable secondary resources.

These studies may be easily available (e.g., those put out by special interest or public services groups). Often the cost of obtaining copies of the studies is minimal. On the other hand, there are studies that are commissioned by corporations or other organizations for their own use, often at substantial expense. These may be unavailable at any price, particularly if the organization sees the study as providing them with a competitive edge.

Sometimes, the organization or corporation will be willing to provide such information to a not-for-profit group as an act of generosity. In this case, however, the decision to share the study would have to be made by a fairly high manager in the organization, so it might be best to begin by writing a letter to the president or chair of the corporation or organization stating your request and credentials. Such a letter should usually be followed by a phone call to make sure the letter was received by the proper person and to move along the decision-making process.

A third type of study is that to which a number of organizations subscribe and for which they pay the costs. One such study that is consistently covered in the general press is the *Monitor* study by Yankelovich, Skelly and White, a large market research company. Subscribing organizations pay thousands of dollars for the details of this study, which focuses on changing attitudes and values in the United States. While an overview of the study is released as a publicity piece, specific data such as that which might form part of a secondary research base is only available to those who pay for it.

Trade Organizations and Special Interest Groups. Trade organizations and special interest groups can serve as sources of specific publications and reports or studies and also can provide another form of secondary data. Often these organizations have a full-time staff whose job it is to know what is going on among the people they serve or represent and to know the whole field in which they operate. These staff members can provide information directly to a researcher. They can also be useful in helping the person engaged in secondary research test out ideas and hypotheses he or she has developed in the course of reading other information and taking to other people.

Usually, the easiest way to find out about such organizations and groups is through the guidebooks available at most libraries (referred to above) and through reading articles in the general and special press about the topic being researched. These articles will often quote people from the groups or associations or will refer to the work of these groups.

Primary Research

Primary research is ordinarily thought of as market research—research conducted in the field, often among ordinary consumers.

Surveys. This is the most well-known form of market research. The researchers design a questionnaire that elicits information from the respondent and then asks his or her opinions, preferences, attitudes, behavior patterns, and so on. The national public opinion poll conducted by phone is one of the best-known types of surveys. But this form of research can also be conducted on a much smaller scale, in person or by mail as well as by phone.

Surveys are useful in getting a wide range of general information from a large group of people, ranging from perhaps 25 people (if the researcher wants general ideas about answers to the question) to thousands of people (if the researcher wants to establish a high degree of statistical certainty about a large number of issues).

Focus Groups. At the other end of the research spectrum is the focus group. Focus groups consist of 6 to 12 people gathered in an informal setting such as a conference room. A group leader discusses issues with the participants in a nondirective manner. The group's progress is usually tape-recorded, and often the clients (i.e., the persons who commissioned the research) are in an adjourning room behind a one-way mirror.

The findings of a focus group are not statistically reliable nor are they even projectable to the population at large. However, the informal, nondirective setting provides an opportunity for researchers to find out consumers' thoughts on a topic that they might be reluctant or unable to talk about in other settings. Also, a focus group can provide insights into problems that the researcher can then validate with broader forms of research such as a survey.

Usually focus groups are conducted in pairs so that the researchers can get a clearer picture of consumers' opinions. If only one group is conducted on a given topic, it is possible for the people using the research to be overly influenced by one or two people in the group who have strong opinions or personalities.

We can return to the case of the community hospital with the "unwelcome suitor" for an example of how these two forms of primary research might be used. After the trustees finalized the decision not to merge with the other hospital, they decided to conduct other research to determine if it would be possible to increase utilization of the hospital at its present site. First, the hospital sponsored a series of focus groups among different segments of the community. One pair of groups consisted of couples with young families. In the group discussions, several families said that they chose a hospital on the basis of whether or not it was family-oriented: could husbands be present at childbirth, could parents room-in with sick children, and so on.

In order to confirm that this was how such families made their choices, the hospital then surveyed 200 similar families. The survey showed that family orientation was a key decision point and that families would be willing to change hospitals and even doctors to get these policies. Furthermore, the survey indicated that respondents felt no other hospitals in the area met those needs.

These findings led the hospital to develop a plan to increase utilization through changing obstetric and pediatric policies. Ultimately, utilization of the hospital increased without the hospital having to make additional capital or operating investments. The hospital was successful in identifying unmet needs and then confirming them through the combination of soft research (focus groups) and hard research (survey).

Audits. Audits are a form of market research in which actions or transactions are monitored, categorized, and summarized. This instrument does not deal with opinions, ideas, or concepts but rather with actions.

There are a number of well-known market audit services available in the for-profit sector. For example, the A. C. Nielsen company conducts an ongoing audit of the movement of certain packaged grocery products off the shelves of major grocery stores across the country. A cereal manufacturer might purchase this audit to provide an indication of how a product was moving in comparison to other cereals in each of 20 major metropolitan areas on a biweekly basis.

What is the applicability of such an approach in the not-for-profit area? To return to the previous example, the community hospital conducted an audit of hospital admissions before and after they changed their OB and pediatric policies. By comparing admissions, they were able to prove that hospital admissions in these groups had risen. This, in turn, assured them that their changes in policy were producing the intended effects.

Concept Tests. A concept test is the test of an idea. It is one of the simpliest types of research to describe in terms of objectives, but it is one of the most difficult types of research designs actually to develop and implement because the test must take a form that does not affect the result. Concepts may be tested in focus groups, through surveys, or through individual interviews. For example, the group described above which was interested in reaching management women conducted a concept test via phone interviews.

Like focus groups, concept tests may be more valuable in giving direction and in refining broad ideas than in providing perfect data which can be acted on with certainty. Still, the attraction of testing ideas rather than sending an organization off in one direction after another when ideas prove unattractive or unworkable makes concept tests a valuable tool to keep in mind.

Other Types of Market Research. A number of other types of market research are frequently used in the for-profit sector. Most of these tests are oriented toward some specific marketing variable. For example, there are special comparison tests of packaging, advertising messages, advertising levels, promotional devices, and so on. If your organization has several specific and concrete alternatives to test against one another, this is the type of market research that would be appropriate.

SHOULD WE CONDUCT THE RESEARCH OURSELVES?

The preceding sections of this chapter have addressed the whys and hows of market research in general. We will now turn to two questions related to actually performing specific research. The first is whether you should conduct the research yourself or hire an outside firm or consultant. The second question is how to find an outside resource to conduct the research should you decide that this is the way to go.

First, we will examine the advantages and disadvantages of conducting research in-house. The key advantages are as follows:

1. It is frequently less expensive, even in terms of fully allocated costs, to conduct research in-house. This reflects the fact that the outside supplier not only has direct costs such as the salaries of interviewers and phone expenses but also marks up these costs to make a profit, while there is no mark-up on work done in-house.

2. There is little start-up time for conducting a research project if an organization uses its own staff, providing the staff or at least the person in charge of the project has some knowledge of the fundamentals of conducting research. An outside supplier will have to take time to get to know the organization before formulating the research problem, developing a design that fits the organization's desires, and interpreting the results in a way that is meaningful to that organization. The insider will already have this knowledge.

3. A completed study that has been conducted in-house may have more applicability long-term than one provided by an outside supplier. The insider who supervises the study and thus best understands the subtleties and details of the results continues to be available to the organization whereas an outside supplier usually provides all the data, makes a report, and then essentially terminates the organization's relationship with the client (your organization).

On the other side there are some major disadvantages to conducting research in-house. These must be evaluated against the advantages described above.

1. An in-house study may not have the objectivity of an outside study, no matter how good the intentions of the person in charge of the study are. Even if he or she uses outsiders to conduct research, the final interpretation will be made by someone who already has some opinions and interest in the results of the study.

Even if the supervisor of the research is extremely objective, there is always a possibility that the person and the organization will be accused of bias. In a case such as the community hospital with the unwelcome suitor who desired a merger, it was important that there not be even an opportunity to imply bias if the suitor was to accept the results of the survey. Therefore, before undertaking a research project in-house, the organization should always ask itself first whether it can be objective, and second, whether it is important to enhance the appearance of objectivity through the use of an outside supplier.

2. Rarely does an organization have on staff a widely experienced, well-trained market researcher, unless the organization already does extensive market research. Therefore, when a staff member is appointed to do a research project, there may be a significant amount of start-up time involved in learning how to do a project. Furthermore, the person supervising the research and those conducting it will not have a history of experience to draw from, nor will there be the economies of scale that an organization that does nothing but market research has available, such as special telephone systems for doing surveys and computer software for analyzing survey results.

Then, too, there is the possibility that an inexperienced person may make errors in designing or analyzing the results of the research. These errors may not be identified, and the organization may consequently make decisions based on erroneous assumptions and findings. Perhaps the best reason for using an outside researcher is to avoid mistakes.

3. Finally, a not-for-profit organization often suffers from a shortage of management talent. It may be difficult to make up for the time a staff member takes away from his or her regular duties to conduct a research project. This may create the temptation to relegate the research project to a lower-level staff member. Given the need for reliable results and a sophisticated level of data interpretation, this is often a less than ideal choice. It would be better in such a case to decide whether or not to do the research based on the cost of using an outside supplier who would provide the quality of research necessary to make the project reliable and useful.

Two guidelines can help an organization balance out the advantages and disadvantages of using in-house staff to do market research.

1. Evaluate each project on an individual basis. Your organization might have the perfect person to conduct a series of focus groups, and this might put very little strain on your organization while providing benefits in cost savings and ownership of the results. But your organization might be overwhelmed by the attempt to conduct even a modest phone survey which could involve hundreds of phone calls over days, or weeks.

2. Do not hesitate to use an outsider who has skills in market research to discuss each project and the advantages and disadvantages of conducting the project in-house. This person might be a marketing consultant or a specialist in market research with whom you establish an ongoing relationship. The expense of these meetings in terms of the consultant's time will be more than offset by the savings you can make on even a small project by doing it well the first time and getting the information you really need.

HOW DO WE FIND AND EVALUATE AN OUTSIDE RESEARCH SUPPLIER?

We now come to the final question your organization is likely to face. You have decided to conduct research and to use an outside supplier. How can you find a person or a firm that is reliable, professional, and economical?

There are several sources for obtaining the names of market research suppliers. First, there is the literature search. In marketing literature or in reports on major studies in the general press, market research companies are often mentioned. It is useful to begin keeping a list of such companies, noting what areas they appear to work in, where they are located, and what kind of organizations they appear to serve. Some of these companies only do a certain type of research, while others have a custom research division. Some only handle very large projects but may refer you to another company that handles smaller projects. In conducting your literature search, do not hesitate to note names of local or regional companies since these companies often handle projects of all sizes.

Second, there is word of mouth. Often you can obtain names and recommendations from nonprofit managers you know professionally. This is a useful way of identifying research suppliers who have worked in your field before. Also, you should take advantage of any contacts you or your organization have at for-profit companies with large research budgets. Often these large companies have very stringent requirements for outside suppliers, and so their recommendations are valuable as their suppliers are prescreened.

Third, there is a "green book" published by the New York chapter of the American Marketing Association that lists suppliers by geographic area, describes their principals and staff, and the kind of work they do. Entitled *The International Directory of Market Research Houses and Services,* it is available from the AMA at 420 Lexington Avenue, New York, New York 10017. The cost of the book is quite high ($45.00 in 1983); however, many libraries, especially those with good business sections, carry the book.

Now that you have a list of names, there are several ways of choosing between suppliers. First, phone several organizations that you think might offer the services you want, describe briefly your needs, and make sure that they do projects of the size and type in which you are interested. If you identify several, you can return to the word-of-mouth network for informal evaluations of their work.

Next, set up a meeting with the companies who sound most promising. It is quite acceptable to discuss a possible research project with more than one company, asking for bids on the specific project and for references for similar projects. However, it is very important that you inform each company in advance that you are asking more than one company to bid on the job and that you explain the criteria on which you will evaluate the bids. Some small companies may not have the labor force to bid on your project. Other companies may operate on the philosophy that although they have the personnel, it is too expensive to go out and talk to every possible client.

If you have trouble getting companies to provide competitive bids, you may have to use recommendations and word of mouth to make a choice of a company in advance. Of course, you always have the option of choosing not to do a project at all or to do a project in-house if the estimate you obtain from the chosen company is way beyond your budget. Usually, however, it is possible to get at least a ballpark number for the cost of your type of project without having a supplier go through a formal bid process. Also, you might be able to ask your informal network for the prices they paid for similar projects.

When the possible suppliers do make their presentations, you should evaluate their proposals not only on the basis of price but also based on how well they understand your project, who will be assigned to supervise the project, and how right their approach seems to you. As the manager commissioning the project, you ultimately have the best understanding of your needs. If the supplier seems insensitive to your organization before the project even begins, it is unlikely that the project will be a success from your point of view, no matter now economical or elegant it appears on paper.

SUMMARY AND CONCLUSIONS

Market research has proven its value in the for-profit sector and is becoming used more widely in the not-for-profit sector. The main deterrent to more extensive use in the latter area is not absolute cost, lack of applicability, or lack of need. Rather, it is, for many organizations, lack of information about the options they have available.

With the above rationales and descriptions in mind, the not-for-profit manager can begin thinking in terms of doing research either in-house or using outside suppliers. To begin thinking about research is often the key to seeing its usefulness. Reading, thinking, and talking to peers in similar organizations can give the nonprofit manager the confidence to go further and the expertise to make good choices that in the long run will benefit his or her organization.

Part 3

DEVELOPING THE MARKETING PLAN

18

DEVELOPING MARKETING GOALS AND STRATEGY

by
John C. Faulkner

Management Consultant

The marketing organization that knows its long-term goals and its strategy for achieving them is much more likely to be successful than the one in which management and salespeople strike off in many uncoordinated directions.

ESTABLISHMENT OF GOALS

Marketing goals should define the longer-term broad targets that the marketing function wants to achieve—perhaps three to five years out, and sometimes longer. They must be practical and realistic, or they will lose credibility and the interest of those who should be working to achieve them. Examples of goals might be:

— Achieving a 20 percent annual growth rate.
— Broadening the line to appeal to more customers.
— Achieving a leading market share (overall or within certain channels).
— Becoming known as the best-styled line in the industry.
— Shifting the product mix toward higher-priced, higher-styled products.
— Increasing profit margins to specific higher levels.
— Becoming the leader in pricing.
— Maintaining the best price/value relationships in one segment of the price/volume pyramid.

— Achieving worldwide market penetration.
— Becoming a well-known name to consumers.
— Becoming known as an innovator that customers turn to for new ideas.

Relationship to Corporate Goals

Before establishing marketing goals, a full understanding of corporate goals is desirable. Then marketing can develop and detail its functional goals in a manner that will ensure its coordination with and furtherance of the corporate objectives.

Occasionally, marketing will find that corporate objectives cannot be realistically attained—e.g., rate of growth in sales or earnings. If such unrealistic objectives are used, under corporate pressure, to set marketing goals and to make sales and earnings projections, the results can be disastrous. Corporate financing and expansion plans based on such projections have led to bankruptcies. Therefore, if corporate goals are considered unattainable by marketing after study, discussions should be held with top management on either revising the goals or seeking their attainment through external growth such as acquisition or merger.

Background for Goal Setting

The establishment of sound goals and the following development of effective strategies should be preceded by a careful analysis and assessment of market opportunities within the present and anticipated marketing environments. This includes obtaining the best available information on the following:

— Present market sizes and projected growth rates by geographic area, market channel, and customer group.
— Present market shares and trends.
— The niche that the company now has in the marketplace, its current reputation, and any patent-protected position.
— The type, character, and intensity of competition in each market segment.
— Anticipated goals of competitors and their apparent strategies for reaching them.
— Present and anticipated profit margins and return on investment in the various market segments and in the several pricing brackets.
— The present assets and anticipated future ones that the corporation might employ to hold or improve its position in each market segment.

— The risk/reward ratio in each market segment, taking into account such factors as:
- Seasonal and cyclical fluctuations in sales and profitability.
- Rates of obsolescence in the industry.
- The probable reaction of competitors to company success in invading their markets, including larger companies that might have long staying power in subsidizing losses to retain their market positions.
- Risks of product liability suits or government actions against any environmental damage caused by products (agricultural chemicals, children's toys, asbestos products, etc.).
- The requirements for success in each market segment and the estimated level of resources that will be required to hold, increase, or milk a profitable sales volume.

Participation in Goal Setting

While goal setting for marketing is ultimately the responsibility of the vice president of marketing, he or she should encourage key line and staff personnel to participate in the process. They will thus have a better understanding of what the goals are and a greater enthusiasm for striving toward the goals that they have helped to establish.

When the goals are established, they should be submitted for review and approval by general management so that it can know the specific goals sought and discuss and modify them if found advisable. Once approved, the written goals should be disseminated broadly within the marketing organization so that everyone can work toward common objectives—unless there are serious concerns that any confidential objectives and thinking might be compromised if revealed to employees and/or the trade. For example, advance knowledge by competitors that the company is targeting a new distribution channel for market penetration could cause them to plan strong actions to counteract the company's efforts.

Periodic Reviews

Goals may not remain constant over a period of years. They are affected by the growth of the company, changes in the marketplace, and changes in competition. Therefore, marketing goals should be reviewed annually to see whether they should be added to or modified.

DEVELOPMENT OF MARKETING STRATEGY

Marketing strategy defines *how* the goals are to be achieved. *Strategy* normally involves a course of action that will be pursued for a year or more (as opposed to *tactics,* the often more opportunistic actions taken in the short term to deal with a particular problem or opportunity).

Need for Multiple Strategies

A single marketing strategy may suffice for a company with a narrow product line sold through a single distribution channel. As companies grow more complex, however, they are likely to require multiple strategies—one for each segment of the business. As examples, a different strategy may be needed for differing:

Product Lines. Large, specially engineered speed reducers may be sold direct to users; smaller, standardized ones may be sold through stocking distributors.

Distribution Channels. Commodity-type consumer products may be sold in large quantities at low prices to mass merchandisers; department stores may be offered a higher-styled, more varied product line and distinctive brand, accompanied with sales training for floor personnel, at lower order quantities and higher prices.

Customer Types and Sizes. Larger stores purchasing substantial quantities may be sold direct, whereas telemarketing and trade show contacts may be employed to obtain orders from individual specialty stores and other smaller customers.

Geographic Areas. New York City may need a direct salesperson, the Rocky Mountains a manufacturers' representative, and Venezuela an export agent.

Background for Strategy Development

As mentioned in the goal-setting section, the development of sound strategy requires careful factfinding and analysis in advance. This homework includes a vigorous review of the company's present niches in the marketplace, its capabilities, customer needs and purchasing practices, strengths and weaknesses of competitors, market trends, and opportunities and requirements for success. Warning: changing market conditions of today or tomorrow may destroy the company's solid niche of yesterday, and thus require a change of strategy.

Considerations in Selecting Strategies

It will be evident from analysis of competition that there are a variety of successful strategies. Like fingerprints, however, each company has unique differences—in its internal capabilities, market position, and opportunities—that require strategies customized to its own particular needs. These strategies should be viewed from the perspective of, "How do they encourage customers to prefer *our* company as a supplier and also provide us with an adequate level of profitability?".

The broad marketing strategy for each business segment is in reality a combination of coordinated substrategies developed for each facet of the marketing function. Each facet is important. Like an America's Cup race, the winner is not likely to be one who does one or two things right but one who fine-tunes all phases of the operation to mesh together smoothly and effectively.

Following are some of the considerations (undoubtedly each company can add more) that may be helpful in developing and testing the merit of particular substrategies. These considerations are clearly not all of equal importance, and the careful weighting and blending of these will create the overall strategy. While there is a need for adequate performance in each area, priority attention should obviously be given to seeing that the key factors are especially well executed.

Uniqueness of Product or Service. A patented, or proprietary, hard-to-duplicate product or service or one where the cost of business entry is high can help to maintain or increase market share—but marketing should beware of any smugness resulting in insensitivity to customer service needs. Obsolescence rates are increasing, and style cycles are shortening. Therefore, even with proprietary-protected leadership, it behooves the company to seek out fresh products, designs, and ideas that will maintain that leadership and to provide the supporting services that keep customers satisfied. (Horrible example: a chemical company with a near monopoly on a major agricultural chemical kept its prices so high and its services so unsatisfactory that its discontented major customers offered long-term commitments to encourage several competitors to enter the field.)

Competitors' Strategies and Their Possible Reactions to Moves by the Company. Should we chip away gradually at areas of competitors' weaknesses, or should we challenge the market leaders head-on for large and rapid changes in market share? Any changes in the company's strategy that clearly threaten the success of competitive marketing efforts and market shares may bring strong reactions. It is important, then, to understand the strategies and reactions of competitors. Sophisticated companies keep book on the temperaments, personalities, experience, and operating methods of key competitive management personnel so that their probable reactions to any changes in strategy can be anticipated. (Example: if we offer temporary price incentives to gain a foothold for a new product, will competitors react by striving to hold their margins or might they panic, cut their prices generally, and keep them low until we—or they—find it uneconomic to continue, thus destroying profit potentials for all participants?)

Sometimes major changes in an industry can be anticipated, such as might result from too broad installation of new machinery to produce products in high cyclical demand (such as polyester knits a few years ago). It may be wise to develop scenarios of probable future competitive conditions and, from those, to determine whether the best strategy calls for pulling in horns, pushing hard for market share, or just waiting out competitors. (For one company differing offensive and defensive strategies were prepared that could be utilized during the expected chaos and post-chaos recovery periods.) While marketing should take the lead in assessing present and anticipated market trends, the impact of conditions such as those described above can be so serious that strategy of the whole company, not just the marketing function, may well be involved.

Business Cycle. A strategy formulated with only one half of the business cycle in mind may cause a long-term deterioration of the company's reputation in the marketplace. For example, a too substantial increase in the sales force to broaden the customer base during the expansion phase of the cycle, followed by an accordionlike contraction during the recession phase that severely reduces sales coverage and services, could lead to unhappy customers. Conversely, the constriction of sales coverage when goods are tight only to larger, good customers in times of prosperity, and expanded coverage to smaller ones only when demand is low, could also lead to an unhealthy ''love 'em and leave 'em'' reputation. Moreover, in the former example, the periodic contraction of the sales force might well encourage better salespeople to seek steadier employment elsewhere.

Product Line Positioning and Related Costs. What is our niche in the marketplace? Do we want to stay there, broaden it, or change it? Are we a low-priced supplier of commodities? Or do we want to depend upon style, design, technical service, or superior delivery and the like to de-emphasize price and raise our position on the price/volume pyramid? Possibly we want to cover more than one niche and may offer one brand with appropriate services and support in the department store field, and reduced service, lower-priced, differing styles under another brand for the discount channel. When significantly changed product positioning is being planned, particular attention should be given to whether the traditional costing system actually reflects the real (and often subtle) changes in cost that can radically affect projected profitability. Different requirements for success in the new positioning that may not be fully recognized by the cost system might include longer or shorter production runs, differing packaging requirements, changes in inventories and speed of delivery support needed, different frequency and time of sales coverage, changes in advertising support, styling, and design costs, and technical and maintenance service.

Pricing. Pricing, often related to product positioning, clearly has a great impact on sales volume and the financial success of the strategy. Many new businesses, in particular, tend to underestimate selling, service, promotional, and continuing development costs and thus much too optimistically shorten the time period at which breakeven is forecast. Loss of credibility with top management can exhaust the patience which might be needed to make a good strategy successful. Questions such as the following may be important in determining the viability of the pricing strategy:

— Can we set our prices as the leader? Will we be followers under the umbrella of another leader? Should we expect varying and narrow margins as a result of broad competition? Or, should we plan life-cycle pricing to obtain greatest margins when demand is rising?

— Is our strategy and its forecast financial results based on pricing during the prosperous half of the business cycle or does it also reflect possible reduced margins during recession?

— Does the anticipated price level and projected margin adequately cover tool and die, developmental, market introduction, warranty, and product liability costs? Or, will a rapid obsolescence rate and changes in competitive pricing have an impact on our recovery of initial and contingent costs (particularly important in fast-changing, styled apparel businesses and high-tech industries such as computers)?

— Should we give away the razor (equipment) to get the razor blade (supplies) business?

— Do we need to buy our way into the marketplace to obtain some "flagship" installations where we can show off our products and services to other prospects?

— Should we keep initial capital goods prices lower by charging separately, at higher margins, for costs of manuals, technical services, installation, maintenance, and parts?

— Will we vary our margins greatly in response to negotiated or competitive bids to get wanted business—and, if we vary prices, do we risk punishable law violations unless we provide for the costs of careful monitoring and control the sales staff's activities?

— Should we offer terms or seasonal discounts to level out our production cycle?

Product Line Design, Styling, and Breadth. The breadth of product line needed is greatly influenced by the market channel chosen and price bracket positioning. Hardware and department stores, boutiques, and specialty dealers may prefer a broad variety of sizes, styles, designs, or colors, whereas mass merchandisers may have room for only the top one to three styles. The latter also have reduced the numbers of their suppliers, preferring to spend buyers' energies only with those having enough selection to supply a substantial portion of the chain's needs for that product category. Some of the other considerations in setting the product line strategy include:

— How will an increase (or decrease) in product line breadth affect inventory costs and turnover, risks of obsolescence, and the rate of product returns from customers?

— How critical is it that a styled line have one (or more) of the most popular designer or character licenses?

— Will more styles and sizes add additional dealer shelf space and tend to freeze out competition, or will buyers refuse to stock more products in enough volume to justify their styling and packaging costs?

— Will the addition of related products be welcomed? Are we strong enough to force them on dealers? Or, will dealers be unwilling to displace well-regarded existing lines on which we impinge?

— Should we stock replacement parts for your mother's ancient car, or fill-ins for tableware patterns, or can we cut off production of old patterns quickly and still retain trade and consumer support?

— Should we change models and specifications frequently to discourage other manufacturers from tooling up to copy our products?

— Should we offer limited-life products that must be replaced frequently or higher-priced, low-maintenance products that must be sold on a lifetime-cost basis?

— Should considerations of product liability influence the materials, design, breadth of line, and even the distribution channels used and customer groups sold? (You might sell portable electric tools to professionals, but not do-it-yourselfers more likely to injure themselves.)

— Are related machinery and equipment products and supplies needed so that the customer can have all his or her needs produced or assembled by one responsible source, thus eliminating buck-passing on operating and maintenance problems?

Sales Force and Distribution. There are a wide variety of alternative methods for selling and distributing products. The distribution of automotive parts and services is particularly complex because it seems that every company unable to obtain good distribution through traditional channels invented a new pipeline to the huge market. Thus selling and distribution strategy must be based on a sound understanding of both the sales and service support required by the ultimate customer and on the probable effectiveness of various combinations of sales representation and distribution channels. One should take into account the positions of competitors in the trade channels and the probable receptivity, enthusiasm and support needed for selling the company's products. Some of the questions to be considered in determining sales and distribution strategy are:

— Does the ultimate customer—and perhaps the dealer—buy in sufficient quantities to justify the costs of direct sales coverage or is a rep or distributor salesperson required who can divide costs of sales coverage among many lines?

— How much product and technical knowledge and service are needed to sell the line, and can these be obtained if a direct sales force is not used?

— Are margins sufficient to permit a three-tier distribution system (producer–distributor–dealer) rather than a two-tier (producer–dealer) or a single-tier system (producer–user)?

— How fast delivery will be required for regular orders, fill-in orders, and parts? (A product line shutdown or delay while the car is on the garage lift can be costly, and replacement parts should often be available rapidly.)

— Should the producer maintain national, regional, or local stocks, or ship to distributors or chain warehouses, or deliver direct to dealers or to user customers?

— Should distribution be broad, through many channels and competing dealers, or should it be carefully controlled and confined—perhaps to authorized or franchised dealers—to stimulate better stocking, sales attention, and possibly superior installation, repair, and maintenance services?

— Is it practical to broaden distribution by using both national and private brands so that comparison shopping will be difficult between different types of stores?

— Can a sales force be effectively supplemented or replaced by sales made at trade shows, by telemarketing, or by direct mail (perhaps covering the smaller accounts only by telephone and catalog)?

— If direct salespeople or reps are used, should they be expected to "cream" their territories for large accounts only or to turn over every stone to sell the small accounts also?

— If a distributor–dealer network is utilized, will supportive training in product knowledge, technical service, and selling techniques be needed (and, perhaps, missionary calls on their customers by the company's own sales staff)?

— What kinds of support and supervision will be needed by the sales force to see that it is carrying out the strategy?

— If overseas sales are undertaken, how differently should the selling and distribution system be developed from region to region and country to country?

— If two or more product lines are being sold together, or if a new one is introduced through the existing sales force and distribution channels, will each line receive appropriate attention and service? Many companies have stubbed their toes on false synergies—where the purchasing influences and needs were subtly different. (Example: chain grocers and department stores have many buyers, and a salesperson calling on one specialized group may lack the knowledge, skills, and interest in spending time in an unfamiliar department, even of the same customer.)

Advertising, Promotion, and Packaging. A key part of the marketing strategy research will be to determine what influences the customer (and perhaps the dealer) to buy the first time and each time after that. Can a sales force do it alone or, as in most instances, should a portion of the marketing dollar be allocated to the advertising, promotion, and packaging segments? These are some of the considerations:

— Will the product be *pulled* through the distribution channels as a result of direct appeal to consumers via consumer advertising, point-of-purchase displays, and appealing packaging? Or, will the product be *pushed* through the distribution channels by trade advertising, dealer training, incentives for the trade, and the efforts of the sales force?

— Which demographics of customer and potential customer groups should be targeted?

— What should be the balance between consumer and trade advertising, and to what particular consumer and trade channel purchasing decision makers and influencers should they be directed?

— What is the purpose of the advertising—to open doors, create brand recognition, introduce new products, provide assurance of reliability, overcome past negative images, stimulate immediate purchase, etc.?

— Should packaging be protective only or should it be eye-catching?

— How important are good catalogs and technical data sheets for consumers and the trade (on engineered products, is it vital to earn a position as the engineers' bible in order to obtain specifications)?

— If point-of-purchase displays are wanted by marketing, can they be effectively placed and serviced?

— Can mailing pieces stimulate direct buying or the desire to visit dealers to obtain the products pitched?

— Are the benefits derived from trade shows and regional showrooms worth the substantial cost?

— How necessary are product warranties, how much should they cover, and what will they cost?

Technical Assistance and Repair and Maintenance. No factor can generate more critical discussion among consumers and the trade than an unsatisfactory record on providing needed technical advice and repair and maintenance services. When some or all of these are needed—and particularly if competitors are not doing them well—a market niche may be obtained by stressing the company's strong service orientation. Careful consideration must be given as to whether its distributors and dealers (or others) should have the training, inventories, and incentives needed to provide satisfactory services.

Other Considerations in the Development and Implementation of Strategy

As can be seen from the foregoing discussion, strategy development is complex and requires substantial, thoughtful attention. If strategy is considered only a theoretical plan, given lip service and ignored, the exercise will accomplish little. To make it work, the following thoughts and experience should be utilized in the implementation process:

Participation in Strategy Development. The depth of experience, knowledge, and research required for strategy development should be drawn broadly from marketing and sales management, including the product, marketing, and regional managers particularly close to trade, customer, and competitive conditions in their areas of concentration. As with goal setting, this broad participation will build a common understanding of the overall strategy among the participants, and enthusiasm and finesse in implementing it.

"We Tried It and It Didn't Work." Sometimes a previously unsuccessful strategy leaves such a sour taste in corporate mouths that no one will touch it with a three-meter pole. Nevertheless, it may have present merit that the group should consider with an open mind or at least it may provide useful guidance by understanding why it failed:

— Was the concept or strategy sound or were parts of it faulty?
— Was it poorly executed?
— Was it ahead of its time (or too late)?
— Did the competitive situation change?

Choosing the Battleground. Success with the strategy is more likely when emphasis is placed on developing business where the company has relatively great strengths, where competitors are presumably weak, and where it will be difficult for competitors to build defenses or recoup against the company's inroads. Usually, unless the company already has a dominant market share, a frontal attack on competition is inadvisable; it tends to upset competitors and galvanize them to stronger reactions. Often more subtle infiltration, at a somewhat more gradual rate, raises less alarm and may provide time for other companies to accept the stronger competition. Perhaps the company can first strip away fringe businesses from a competitor before tackling the basic business in which the competitor has a niche and probably performs best. Exceptions to this approach may be when the style cycle is very short and it's necessary to get in and out quickly—where a last-in, last-out, follow-the-leader strategy can be disastrous. Companies with patent or other proprietary product and service protection can also be more aggressive.

Timeframe for Strategy Implementation. A strategy usually needs up to several years to obtain expected results, but there are occasions when the timeframe may be radically shortened. Examples might be exploitation of a significant short-term technical advantage or a fad product (such as hula hoops) that, like an astronomical nova, suddenly rises to a high peak and then rapidly subsides; or a newly popular ethnic food chain concept that should be developed nationally before others jump in.

When these short-term opportunities arise, there may be little time for the planning and fine-tuning of all the niceties of a thoroughly developed marketing strategy and operation. Nevertheless, when a short-term opportunity promises large profits—and perhaps large losses—there are strategic considerations that should receive attention before plunging ahead. Among them are:

— Can the business stand (or fall) on its own or is the reputation of the sponsoring company and its other products and services also at stake?

— If the latter case, would it be better to proceed more slowly and soundly in market development in order to build a better product and supporting organization—at the risk of others gaining a foothold—than to risk angering the trade and customers currently served as a result of technical bugs, delayed deliveries, or poor technical service support?

— Can sales and forecasting controls be installed to prevent the acceptance of orders that cannot be delivered on time and to keep inventories lean enough so that if the market turns down rapidly, markdown losses will be minimized?

— If the company decides on franchising as a means to rapidly obtain additional capital, dedicated personnel, and market share, it should also ask:

• Will the company have the skilled personnel to select, guide, and support the franchisees or might angry franchisees and their often frequent business failures blacken the company's reputation?

• Will the company later be willing to pay the price needed to buy back franchises or might it be better to keep ownership and control by expanding only at the rate at which the company can generate its own capital internally?

Strategy and the Annual Marketing Plan. The marketing goals and strategy should be incorporated into the background section of each annual marketing plan. They then form the basic framework on which the detailed plans for the year are developed.

The annual marketing plan should also contain a review of the past year's results and of how successfully the strategy was carried out. Past problems in implementing the strategy should be noted. Either the new year's plan should be adjusted to deal with them or perhaps the marketing strategy should be modified if market conditions and opportunities have changed. If the company has a management by objectives system, these objectives for annual attainment should be well coordinated with the basic goals and strategy.

Incentive Compensation. Incentives—particularly for the field sales force—should be reviewed to see that they do motivate employees to carry out the strategies and marketing plan and do not to work in tangential or opposed directions. (Example: a company's strategy may call for de-emphasizing commodity products and building higher-quality, higher-margin products where design and sales services are more important. This may entail, in part, a shift to new categories of customers who need different types of sales attention. The sales staff, however, are paid on commission—a straight percentage of sales. They can earn more per hour selling low-priced commodity products in volume than they can selling significantly smaller quantities of higher-priced products to buyers with whom they are less familiar. The obvious answer: as part of the strategy, redesign the sales compensation plan.)

Management incentives that heavily emphasize short-term performance may also be inadvisable. They may cause management to adopt strategies that milk the business to gain larger profits in the present year, rather than investing in building a stronger marketing organization and product line that can generate greater sales and profits in future years. Companies like McGraw-Hill that reward their management for long-term, continuing growth have performed very well.

Testing out the Strategy. The elements of surprise and rapid implementation are often of critical importance in introducing a new strategy. Under these circumstances, the testing out may consist of the judgments of those who formulate the strategy by acting as devil's advocates to seek flaws in it. Any other management personnel closely related to the marketplace, the measurement and control of costs and investment, and the manufacturing and service functions may also offer useful critiques. Also, a few key customers or a consultant might be involved on a confidential basis. Often a computer program can be used, with "what-if" questions, to assess the risks and rate of return under varying assumptions of product mix, sales volume, margins, marketing costs, and the like.

When surprise and timing are less critical, it is advisable to test out the strategy in the field, much as a new product is test marketed. Testing may well enable a company to correct bothersome glitches that could destroy the effectiveness of the strategy—and perhaps the company's reputation—if it were implemented nationally without modification. Examples of strategies that may need testing in the field include:

— Shifting from distributor to direct sales.
— Evaluating the impact on dealer and customer goodwill of a shift to company-owned repair and maintenance centers.
— Testing the efficacy of telemarketing as a replacement for direct sales calls on certain sizes and classes of customers.
— Combining the sales of two or three product lines under one sales force.
— Substantially broadening distribution to make the product available to customers at more locations; or narrowing distribution to stimulate trade interest in promoting sales more aggressively.

Strategy Review Sessions. If there is no formal marketing plan with its development period that becomes a time for strategy review, there should be an annual review established to see that the strategy is satisfactorily moving the company toward sales, profit, and other goals. Stagnated strategies are likely to become obsolete.

More frequent reviews of strategy may be needed if important and sudden changes occur in the industry that have an impact on the competitive situation and opportunities. Unanticipated bankruptcy of a major competitor, its acquisition by another company, or a merger that strengthens two related competitive product lines may materially change the competitive situation and the best strategy for dealing with it.

Alternative Strategies. Sometimes a change in government law or policy can have a substantial impact on the industry (e.g., changes in tariffs or franchising law). Or the introduction of a new technology (such as more powerful personal computers) could greatly change the competitive situation in the industry. When these changes can be anticipated, it may be wise to prepare alternative strategies—one for use at the present and another for quick application if foreseen events actually occur. Management incentives to encourage use of this predictive management approach can help to bring problems to attention in advance and prepare needed actions. They can also help avoid the tendency to sweep possible upsetting occurrences under the rug in the hope that they will disappear.

SUMMARY

Long-range marketing goals should reflect the corporate goals. They should be realistic, based on research and an understanding of the marketplace. Participation in both goal and strategy development should be broad. Strategy defines *how* the goals will be attained. Usually multiple strategies are needed—one for each segment of the business (product line, distribution channel, etc.). Substrategies need to be considered for each facet of the marketing effort, taking into account the company's marketing niche, customer needs, present and future competitive climates, and the requirements for success. The company should carefully choose the battlegrounds where it has great relative strength. Annual marketing plans should be well coordinated with the strategy, as should short- and long-term incentive compensation. Strategy is not stagnant and should be reviewed annually—more often when trade conditions and opportunities change.

19

DISTRIBUTION CONSIDERATIONS

by
Sol Goldin

Marketing Affiliates Corporation

Dorothy E. Demmy

Demmy & Associates Inc.

PARAMETERS FOR DISTRIBUTION DECISIONS

Seldom can any manufacturer, in any industry, design and build its own distribution system from scratch. Physical distribution facilities alone—wholesaling and/or retailing—usually require greater investment in bricks and mortar, inventories, and other capital assets than the manufacturer's plant and equipment. Therefore, most distribution decisions start with review of existing channels, systems, and services available and appropriate for the products to be merchandised. Wholesale and retail choices are made in consideration of one or more of the following:

1. Marketing services needed to support product characteristics.
2. Dollar volume objectives for profitability (or unit volume for share of market).
3. Geographic coverage needed or anticipated.
4. Cost efficiencies relative to values added in distribution.

As illustrated by the following wide-ranging examples, product characteristics in themselves may dictate direction.

Consider canned soup or another shelf-stable food which requires brand assortment and distribution in limited store classifications (primarily supermarkets). Fast turnover makes local storage and frequent deliveries to stores important, although warehousing and transportation are simple. There is little if any use education beyond advertising, and no after-sale consumer services are required.

Think of automobile gasoline. Logistic services are complex, expensive to dealer level, and nearby supply is critical. Retailers (service stations) may be labor-intensive if repairs and related products are featured; conversely, self-service is becoming more common. In the automotive after-market, manufacturers generally supply training, promotion, even financing—and sell supplies, from uniforms to equipment, to franchisees.

High-fashion goods may be sold to retailers by manufacturers/designers without any wholesale step. Stores order (sometimes pay for) a broad assortment well in advance of the selling season. This calls for tall margins, with prices subject to markdowns. Stores absorb many consumer services including high-level personal selling and alterations, although the latter frequently are outboarded.

Appliance–TV distribution is far more complex at all levels of trade—with more pre-selling and after-sale services shared by manufacturer, wholesaler and retailer (several store classifications). Overnight delivery of size or model variations is required, with the accompanying expensive logistics. In-depth product knowledge and merchandising skills are essential.

Our experience, heavily oriented toward household durables marketing, indicates that appliance–TV distribution is more complex than other consumer goods industries. Our examples of appliance–TV distribution problems, decisions, and efficiencies should provide definition and direction for other fields, as well as approaches and applications for other situations. Thus, this chapter concentrates on:

- The complexities of appliance–TV distribution.
- Influence of retailing patterns, practices, and trends.
- Constructive roles of wholesale distributors.

The purpose is to help answer, by examples, many planning questions: What values can be added to the product by distribution channels? At what level can these values be added most economically? Which services, if any, can be deleted or cost-reduced without risk of volume? What controls can be and/or should be established by the manufacturer or brand marketer? What selling incentives can be and/or should be offered to independent distributors and dealers for increasing volume, market share, and profitability?

THE COMPLEXITIES OF
APPLIANCE-TV DISTRIBUTION

In the past 25 years, distribution of all consumer goods has become infinitely more sophisticated. One reason is volume—the ma-and-pa stores, which dominated retailing since the beginning of commerce, seldom can compete effectively with mass merchandisers. Another factor is pre-selling—mass advertising has made consumer purchasers far more knowledgeable, needing fewer advisory services. Important, too, are technological advances—logistics has become a science, and computerization has made wholesalers and retailers basically more efficient in functional areas.

Since the early 50s, when television receivers became a volume industry, white goods (major appliances) and brown goods (home entertainment, electronics) have marched hand-in-hand to the marketplace. A few companies, like GE, manufacture both white and brown goods. Most distributors wholesale both broad merchandise classifications with noncompeting brands—e.g., Whirlpool appliances and RCA consumer electronics have many common distributors. Most retailers are multiple-brand merchandisers, offering a choice of two to four or more labels in most product categories. And consumers are accustomed to shopping for white and brown goods at the same retail establishments which offer similar services for the several big-ticket household durables.

Currently, there is tendency to split the departments at retail. This is because each classification is large enough to be an independent profit center and because some newer products require special merchandising sklls. As shown in Figure 19–1, consumer electronics is expanding beyond audio, radio, and television and now encompasses new generations of video recorders and home computers.

In a general sense, the market for all these products is universal— every U.S. household. Most families own at least six of these products and need or want most of the rest. Although most of these products are relatively long-lived (5 to 15 years), they are replaced whenever they wear out or become obsolete due to new features or change of family size or lifestyle. This means that virtually every household is ready to buy one or more of the products listed in Figure 19–1 every single year.

In another sense, each of these products has separate markets. Each is in a separate stage of its life cycle—introduction, growth, maturity, or market-declining period. Some, like microwave ovens, still may be considered luxury items—still are being introduced, are low in saturation, and are bought primarily by first purchasers. Several are in the maturity phase—millions of families are now choosing their second or third refrigerators, ranges, and washers.

FIGURE 19–1
Appliance-TV Market Size and Composition
(1983 U.S. Factory Shipments, Unit Millions)

Major Appliances		Consumer Electronics	
Category	Millions of Units	Category	Millions of Units
Washers	4.5	B&W TV	5.4
Dryers (gas and electric)	3.3	Color TV	12.7
Refrigerators	5.4	Radios	28.8
Freezers	1.4	Audio components	9.3
Room air conditioners	2.3	Compact stereo	2.7
Ranges (gas and electric)	4.1	Audio recorders	28.7
Microwave ovens	5.6	Video recorders	3.6
Dishwashers	2.7	*Sometimes Included*	
Trash compactors	0.2	Videodisc players	0.4
Sometimes Included		Video cameras	0.4
Dehumidifiers	0.5	Video games	6.7
Water heaters (gas and electric)	6.4	Personal computers	5.0
		Telephones	14.2
Furnaces (gas and electric)	1.8	Calculators	28.7
Heat pumps	0.5	Autosound	21.0

Sources: Association of Home Appliance Manufacturers, Gas Appliance Manufacturers Association, Electronic Industries Association, adjusted by Marketing Affiliates Corporation.

Selecting the Channel of Distribution

The critical distribution decision for any product is to determine *where* the manufacturer places the product in position for consumers to see it, shop it, and buy it conveniently.

In major appliances, these places are easy to define. The consumer may:

- Buy appliances direct from the manufacturer or merchandiser via mail or phone from advertising, or cataloging, or door-to-door selling. Although this is unlikely, due to product weight and bulk, some appliances with little feature differentiation (e.g., freezers) are sold in these ways. This channel will grow with telemarketing and computer-to-computer shopping.
- Buy (or rent) appliances as parts of the home or apartment purchase or lease. Most new residences have ranges and dishwashers built in; all have heating and/or cooling equipment and

water heaters; many include refrigerators and some other appliances.

- Buy from one of 90,000 or so retailing firms in 20 or more store classifications. These include mass merchandisers (like Sears), appliance–TV specialists, traditional department stores, discount chains, furniture stores, utilities, and even tire, battery, accessory outlet chains like Western Auto.

Because no one can dictate where the consumer wants to shop, the manufacturer chooses the channels which will provide optimum exposure. As indicated in Figure 19–2, key decisions are whether to market through both builder and retailer and whether to go national brand and/or private label.

FIGURE 19–2
Major Appliance Distribution by Channels

Every year, some 23 to 28 percent of major appliances are sold through builder/government channels (first pie)—60 percent or more in some categories like dishwashers. At retail, some 25 to 30 percent of units are private labels like Kenmore sold by Sears (second pie). About 57 percent of national brand retail business goes through appliance-TV specialists—most of them offering all nine major appliances with a wide choice of models in two or three brands.

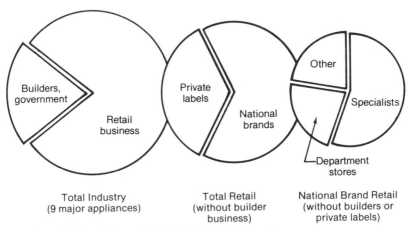

| Total Industry (9 major appliances) | Total Retail (without builder business) | National Brand Retail (without builders or private labels) |

Source: Whirlpool Corporation, Retail Marketing Department.

Developing Product Services, Adding Values

Few products are sold as physical entities. Most are sold with some services or "values added."[1] The customs of the trade in appliance

---

[1] Theodore N. Beckmann, "The Value-Added Concept as Applied to Marketing and Its Implications," in *Frontiers in Marketing Thought*, ed. Stewart H. Rewald (Bloomington: Indiana University, Bureau of Business Research, 1955), p 61.

marketing have developed a long list of services offered at various levels—ranging from broad assortment to product service, as indicated in Figure 19–3.

FIGURE 19–3
Services Frequently Offered with Major Appliances

	Manufacturer to			Distributor to Dealer	Retailer to Consumer
	Distributor	*Dealer*	*Consumer*	*Dealer*	*Consumer*
Product services					
In-warranty repairs		X	X		
Parts inventory	X	X		X	
Service training	X	X		X	
use instruction			X		X
Supply services					
Model assortment	X			X	X
Choice of color	X			X	X
Free delivery	X			X	X
Flat-rate installation					X
Purchase incentives	X	X		X	X
Exchange privileges				X	
Promotion services					
Advertising allowances	X			X	
Selling incentives	X	X		X	
Packaged promotions	X	X		X	
Display materials	X	X		X	
Sales training	X	X		X	
Literature	X	X	X	X	X
Financial services					
Floor planning	X	X		X	
Installment pay	X	X		X	X
Price protection	X	X		X	

Source: Marketing Affiliates Corporation analysis of Whirlpool brand offerings.

Good distribution planning requires that manufacturer, distributor, and retailer affirm (1) which of these several services are essential by whom and to whom, (2) how they can be made available at what cost/benefit, and (3) the extent to which they contribute to purchase decisions and satisfaction.

Competitive offerings are the overriding factor in whether any given value is added and within which margin. To illustrate, when industry custom is free in-warranty service to the consumer, few manufacturers would dare to change the offer from first year to 90 days or to charge for service calls. As another example, when cooperative advertising allowances are provided to retailers as percent of purchase price, few distributors would change these terms.

Most of the services/values listed in Figure 19–3 were retailer costs of doing business until the 1950s. Most retailers were servicing dealers, expected to provide installation and in-warranty repairs, carry parts inventories, and train their own technicians. Dealers were responsible for all merchandising services including sales training and incentives—except for cooperative advertising and some promotion materials. Dealers did their own inventory financing and asked for no special logistical services.

At that time retail gross margins on major appliances averaged 40 percent. Today margins generally run 20 to 25 percent, with manufacturers and distributors absorbing many former retail burdens. In the same time period, products also have become infinitely more complex. Today's more sophisticated appliances require a higher level of sales skills, more training for sales and servicing, and more user education.

Analyzing Physical Distribution Services

Distribution requirements also are more complex. Today a good refrigerator line includes 20 to 30 differet models in four to six color finishes, with 10- to 25-cubic-foot capacities, one- or two- or three-door configurations, special services like automatic defrosting and automatic ice making, and wide variations in shelving, fittings, and features.

A simple good-better-best display of 9 major appliances calls for at least 27 large products in a full-line brand. Multiply this by two to four brands, and one can visualize selling space and backup warehousing needs for a single outlet. Then consider the chain phenomenon—4 to 11 stores in a given merchandising area—for an estimate of one retailer's appliance floor space requirements.

Next, consider the transportation and storage services performed throughout the distribution process. The typical appliance is sold by manufacturer to a distributor—who resells it to a retailer—who resells it to the consumer—and often the "paper" is resold by the retailer to a financing unit. It is not unusual for the product to change title four times.

The most efficient physical distribution process is quantity sale (full truck or full carload) shipped direct to the retailer's central warehouse—two storage points, one shipment. Then display units move from retailer's warehouse to multiple store floors. As appliances are sold to consumers, most economic deliveries usually are from the retailer's central warehouse to consumer address.

Conversely, most appliances are sold LTL (less than truckload) or LCL (less than carload) with several shorter trips and stopovers. It is not unusual for the product to move from plant warehousing to manufacturer distribution center—STOP—to distributor warehouse—

STOP—to retailer warehouse—STOP—to store space—STOP—to consumer home—STOP. Product handling includes transportation and warehousing labor at each of these stops, uncrating and placement upon consumer delivery, and service technician's work for installation and any subsequent service calls.

The process is inefficient, cumbersome, and obviously expensive. Every effort is being made by more sophisticated producers for increased proportion of manufacturer–retailer direct-ships. Still bulk-breaking must be performed at two stops, at least—at distributor's or retailer's central warehouse for drop-ships of display quantities to stores and at store or retailer's central warehouse for single-unit deliveries to homes. Further complications occur when shipments are made from distributor's warehouse to new residential construction sites. These deliveries are time-critical in that appliances must be scheduled for installation upon completion of kitchens and utility rooms.

Development of the Wholesaling Channel

Throughout this discussion, we have mentioned *distributors* as the wholesaling resource. But wholesalers also may vary in format. The key alternatives are:

Independent Merchant-Distributors. These wholesalers generally buy from noncompeting manufacturers and resell merchandise to retailers and builders in geographically defined merchandising areas.

Factory Branches. These are manufacturer-owned wholesaling establishments that sell factory-owned merchandise to retailers and builders in given merchandising areas—usually with operations similar to those of independent distributors.

Independent Manufacturer Representatives. These are agents who generally sell manufacturer-owned merchandise to retailers and builders on a commission basis, usually without maintaining physical facilities and with less involvement in merchandising services.

Manufacturer Sales Force. "Reps" are on the producer's payroll (salary with or without commission added) and sell directly to retailers and builders without absorbing other wholesaling functions.

Among other forms of wholesaling which might be considered for some industries are the following: voluntary group wholesalers like IGA Foods; converters who may perform product assembly or processing functions; importers and exporters; drop-shippers or desk jobbers; cash-and-carry wholesalers; retailer cooperatives or buying groups; wagon (truck) distributors; rack jobbers; and industrial goods distributors. Some of these are used in major appliances in specialty and subsidiary functions. For example:

- Importers act as distributors for compact appliances produced offshore and still sold in small quantities in the United States.
- Wagon distributors may be typified by LPG marketers, who sell small quantities of gas dryers, ranges, and water heaters adapted for bottled gas usage—direct to consumers, usually in rural areas.
- Buying groups are becoming increasingly important in appliance–TV retailing.

The most recently published *Census of the Wholesale Trade: 1977* shows some 289,000 wholesale firms in the United States operating 383,000 establishments, doing $1,258.4 billion in annual sales, and with about 4.4 million paid employees.[2] More than 307,000 of these establishments were merchant wholesalers, 40,500 were manufacturers' sales branches or offices, and 35,000 were merchandise agents or brokers—the three primary wholesaling systems for appliance–TV distribution. The census reports 24,900 establishents were in electrical goods, doing almost $70 billion in sales with 277,000 employees.

Granted, electrical goods takes in many products beyond major appliances and consumer electronics. Still, we are discussing a huge business at the wholesale level. So it is important to know how and why the merchant wholesaler is essential.

WHOLESALING FUNCTIONS IN DURABLES DISTRIBUTION

The founder of one of the nation's largest appliance–TV distributors liked to tell the story about the manufacturer, distributor, and dealer sharing a common bed, with a common blanket. Whenever the manufacturer rolled over, the dealer was uncovered. When the dealer turned over, he pulled the blanket off the manufacturer. "But that guy in the middle always was covered!"

For the past 15 years, the role of the man in the middle—the merchant wholesaler—has become increasingly controversial in several industries. Resistance has come from a growing number of burgeoning retail chains where buyers believe their own companies or buying groups have the capabilities for performing most wholesaling functions.

---

[2] U.S. Department of Commerce, Bureau of the Census, "Wholesale Trade Summary: 1948–1977," *Statistical Abstract of the United States, 1981,* 102d ed. (Washington, D.C.: Bureau of the Census, 1981), p. 820.

Some of them do. Sears, the nation's largest merchandiser, has elaborate facilities—including highly automated regional distribution centers—to serve its 800-plus stores efficiently. Sears also has enough volume, with each of its several hundred suppliers, to consolidate shipments in optimum quantities for maximum physical distribution economies.

Other national and regional chains are developing comparable facilities—mass merchants like J. C. Penney and Montgomery Ward, discount chains like K mart, certain specialty chains like Western Auto and Lowe's Companies.

Further study reveals that most retailers—including many giant traditional department stores—can absorb only fractions of wholesaling services for only a few merchandise categories.

A long-ago declaration by the National Association of Electrical Distributors lists nine legitimate functions.[3] We have updated and generalized this list to cover wholesaling for most household durables in the early 80s as follows:

1. Maintain and warehouse adequate stock for the trade.
2. Maintain a merchandise display showroom to accommodate dealers.
3. Maintain delivery service and facilities for pickup service.
4. Maintain a selling organization trained to help retailers in merchandising functions.
5. Provide product and retailing advisory and training services.
6. Assist retailers in advertising and merchandising—with incentive plans and funds—to assure brand competitiveness in the marketplace.
7. Provide catalogs, other literature, and promotion material describing manufacturer and distributor offerings.
8. Extend or arrange for credit to the buyer on reasonable terms.
9. Maintain or arrange for repair services and replacement parts to supplement the facilities of the manufacturer and retailer.

It stands to reason that the most successful distributor is one who provides all such services most economically, thereby enabling the retailer to resell most profitably. But there are qualitative considerations, such as:

- The quality of the manufacturer's product line.
- The market coverage of the product line.
- The value of the brand in existing market share or growth potential.

---

[3] John Cameron Aspley and John Cousty Harkness, "Distributing through Wholesalers," *The Sales Manager's Handbook,* 10th ed. (Chicago: Dartnell Corporation, 1965), p. 138.

- The merchandising genius of the distributor's management and/or its sales force.
- The reputation of the distributor and/or historic success in assisting retailers.
- The depth of marketing support services available from the manufacturer and/or other distributor affiliates (e.g., distributor's advertising agency).
- The strength of competitive wholesale distribution systems with similar product and service offerings.

Logic suggests that the good marketing manager with a good product line could simply set out to locate and franchise the best established distributorship for the given merchandising area. But top distributors are not easily switched to other brands. Most have long-term relationships with their suppliers as well as with their dealers. Most have firm franchises with brand exclusivity for the area. In addition, they have made similar huge investments in their existing brands, products, and merchandising services as in their physical facilities.

Most good distributors have made major investments in their dealer structures in many ways over many years. Historically, a key strength of the independent distributor has been his or her independence. Typically, the family has invested its own money to build its own small business in its own way. Typically, business success is heavily dependent on personal merchandising judgment: the ability to buy the right merchandise in the right mix at the right time for resale to retailers and builders in its own market. Creatively and constructively, this business develops and provides services that increase the value of the products and puts them in the right retail environment for convenient and profitable consumer purchases.

Typically, wholesaling is a series of low-cost, low-margin services. Lowest product cost is dependent upon quantity purchasing. Highest selling price, therefore, top margin, is established by retailer interest based on consumer demand.

In recent years, costs of doing business have increased rapidly, while resale ceilings have been held steady by intense competition. So margins have been squeezed at all levels of trade. From the large retailer viewpoint, the wholesaler margin is most squeezable. Many major chains now clamor to buy direct—to skip the middleman and his or her 13 to 18 percent margin. They argue that the chain is self-sufficient in distribution. It no longer needs, and feels it should not pay for, a number of services developed for the small dealer with limited financial, physical, and management resources.

Thoughtful distributors agree to some extent. So they have been scrambling to adjust their service/cost structure to size and type of account. For illustration, they are encouraging direct-ships to retailer warehouse, although this results in excess capacity and higher costs in their owned warehousing space. Distributors are also allocating greater proportion of sales time to accounts with higher volume potential, although this may result in reduced volume with outlying accounts, rural markets, and certain store classifications.

My Market Is Different

Key advantage of the independent distributor is flexibility—independence in investment decisions. Given the common and continuing problem of increasing volume in a variety of market situations, here are a few of the ways independent wholesalers, in a single distribution system, have developed new business.

Two distributors in formative years needed not only volume but also stores and dealers. They financed, first, the immigration of relatives and friends from Europe. Then they financed stores from building to inventory to working capital and developed the retailers. Most became legitimate, successful, intensely loyal dealerships.

Two white goods distributors added brown goods, thereby discovering the "record" business. They developed separate national rack jobbing in subsidiary firms.

Another found a software business to go along with laundry appliances. After offering detergent as a washer premium, this firm started selling it through conventional detergent channels. Then they bought the formula and facilities, and now they are the nation's largest processor of private-label detergents for national and regional supermarket chains.

Several appliance distributors have added portable appliances, hard and soft surface floor coverings, furniture, and other household durables—diversification held within a most familiar dealer structure.

One western distributor developed the format for an ideal appliance-TV store, built it, named it, and used it for a retail lab. It became so successful that good retailers asked for the pattern. The distributor also helped in building and financing copies which now carry that distributor's brands exclusively.

Three different distributors developed three different responses to the buying group movement. Most innovative was the one that started its own local group, organized a store format, gave it a name, and licensed retailers to use the name and merchandising system throughout the state.

At wholesale (as at retailer and manufacturer levels), the race is on for volume to achieve per-unit cost reductions. Three avenues are apparent. The distributor or factory branch may expand geographically—reaching for larger markets with existing products, brands, and facilities. It may diversify—to achieve greater volume with existing customers and the same resources. Or it may strive for greater efficiency via automation, telemarketing, or redesign of physical distribution systems.

There is evidence of success. A recent study commissioned by the Distribution Research and Education Foundation predicted that total wholesale sales will grow in real terms by 4.2 percent annually through 1985, then step up to an annual growth rate of 4.9 percent by 1990.[4] By 1990, total wholesale sales should top $3 trillion in inflated dollars. And merchant wholesaler–distributor shares should climb to 58 percent of total wholesale in 1990, compared with 51 percent in 1972.

Case histories are many and varied (samples in box), but the overall guidepoint is productivity, usually measured by sales per employee. One oft-quoted example is Eastco, a Westwood, Massachusetts, distributor of major appliances, consumer electronics, and floor coverings with broad coverage in New England.[5] In 1970, Eastco's 365 employees moved about $40 million at wholesale prices. In 1983, the company reached about $100 million in sales with 158 people. And the ratio of nonselling to sales people in the same period dropped from 4.2 to 1 down to 1.8 to 1.

Eastco is a classic example of a small, family-held independent wholesale merchant becoming a huge and superautomated distributorship via three moves: territorial expansion, diversification, and logistics sophistication. Some 30 years ago, Eastco business was concentrated in the Boston area. It has since absorbed territory from contiguous distributors in three states. Its initial business was music-related. After phonographs came radio and television; then along came major appliances sold through the same or similar dealers. Floor coverings became a logical addition. And now Eastco merchandises computers through its strong household durables dealer structure. As the business grew, physical facilities were modernized and consolidated. Now one 230,000-square-foot warehouse, one inventory, one office, and a model data processing system serve a vast territory and several hundred dealers and builders, with smooth transportation flow and integrated marketing plans.

During the 1981–83 recession, most durables distributors became stronger, not weaker, primarily because retailer expansion was halted. Both small and large dealers leaned more heavily on distributor inventories. Distributor and manufacturer financial and management services were the literal salvation of many undercapitalized dealerships.

Every recession delivers a shakeout of sorts. In the late 1981–83

---

[4] Data are from a study commissioned by the Distribution Research and Education Foundation, as cited in Michael Alexander, "Dramatic Changes ahead in Distribution," *Dealerscope,* December 1983, p. 16.

[5] Ibid.

period, there were many dropouts in household durables distribution at manufacturer, distributor, and retailer levels. Some were by design (mergers, acquisitions, retirements, restructuring), others by default (bankruptcy).

In the 1983 turnaround, it is apparent that survivors in appliance–TV distribution are leaner, stronger, more stable, more efficient, and capable of faster and more profitable growth. Obvious, too, are vast improvements in distribution relationships, affecting both performance incentives and management controls.

Complex and Flexible Compensation and Incentive Plans

Both distributors and dealers, traditionally and logically, design their own primary compensation via pricing—profits within the margins. Margins may be increased insofar as these merchants can buy lower and sell higher.

Most manufacturers concentrate on buy-lower incentives on quantity discount structure, the rationalization being savings in freight, storage, and inventory financing. These discounts are supplemented frequently by seasonal and inventory adjustment allowances. Among common examples: preseason specials on room air conditioners; SPAs (sales promotion allowances) in which an extra $10 or so per unit is discounted or awarded on slow-moving models, close-out stocks, or in introductory periods when the marketing mission is to win new-model exposure on retail sales floors; and travel or merchandise bonuses that move given quantities within a critical time period.

Sell-higher incentives may include cash or awards on certain models to achieve step-up—to focus dealer or consumer attention on high-end, higher-margin models.

Other distributor and dealer purchase incentives might be more properly labeled *costs of doing business*. Cooperative advertising allowances are common in appliance–TV distribution. This is usually handled as a discount on the total purchases which is expected to be matched by the distributor and again by the retailer and expected to be used for brand advertising in traceable media at the local level.

Also frequently used at the distributor level is some incentive for increasing share of market. Some manufacturers cumulate special funds for market penetration achievements—for annual cash awards due to share-of-marketing gains for individual products or the full line. These funds generally are used at distributor discretion for advertising or for any program that increases brand dominance in the distribution area.

These many incentives may seem complex when one considers that several of, say, 1500 manufacturer SKUs may have an added incentive for purchase or sale at any given time. They are expensive, too; incentive plans aside from margins may reach 4 percent or more of manufacturer net sales. But remember, incentive programming also contributes to sales management controls.

Controlling the "Independent" Distribution System

Obviously, the manufacturer exerts optimum control over a factory-owned distribution system, particularly at the wholesale level (through the use of factory branches or direct sales force). In these situations, manufacturers can dictate merchandise mix and greatly influence product and service offerings. Conversely, independent distributors make independent decisions about what products or models to purchase, stock, and feature, about which factory-offered promotions or programs will work best in their area, and about how much to spend (and how to spend it) for local market development.

Maximum control is exerted at time of franchise of independent distributors.[6] Franchise negotiations usually cover degree of brand exclusivity; in appliance-TV marketing distributors may handle only one brand in a given product category. Primary merchandising areas usually are specified, normally by counties. Performance criteria may be specific or generalized—e.g., to increase or maintain share of market, to maintain product service facilities, to merchandise all product categories, or to provide retail sales training.

One critical factor in any franchise agreement should be the detail and time requirements of sales and inventory reporting. One manufacturer insists upon daily reporting of sales to dealers, by model number. This achieves, in turn, a highly sophisticated retail marketing intelligence system.

Depending upon the industry, there may be legal considerations (a topic too large to be covered in this chapter). Certainly there are cautions against local pricing influence, even price reporting. Special care must be taken not to collude, horizontally or vertically, on matters of pricing. There may be constraints against constraints—about whom or where the distributor should sell, about exclusion of competition, about cancelation of franchises. Antitrust laws have major impact on

---

[6] *Franchises* as discussed in this chapter should not be confused with the formal franchising systems of firms like Holiday Inn, Kentucky Fried Chicken, or Computerland. Such franchises are growing rapidly in many industries, often go far beyond the branded merchandise and on into business systems and supplies, and call for start-up investments and continuing license or royalty fees. This form of franchising has barely penetrated appliance–TV business, although it may be anticipated.

distribution agreements both in the way distributors sell to others and on those who sell to distributors.

In appliance-TV marketing distributors may or may not develop franchised retailer relationships. Current trends suggest informal selling agreements in that most dealers sell multiple brands, few dealers would be willing to report sales and inventories by brands, and no dealer is likely to agree to territorial restrictions.

Although there are few formal agreements in distributor-dealer relationships, there may be rules or guidelines on certain mutual merchandising activities. Cooperative advertising is one example. Distributors may detail several conditions, from choice of media through handling of trademarks, under which advertising allowances can be claimed.

CHOOSING THE RIGHT COMBINATION IN DISTRIBUTION

It is unlikely that any manufacturer's distribution system will be pure. A common arrangement at wholesale is dominance by independent distributors plus a few factory branches. And sometimes special products or special markets add a need for direct salespeople or manufacturer's reps.

Answers as to the best wholesale distribution system are found by a combination of economic analyses, market simulation, previous experience, availability of independents, and willingness to invest in field facilities. No rules can be established for a given industry, certainly not for a given company.

Guidepoints are even harder to come by at the retail level. In major-appliance retailing many long-time standbys are dropping out, and new formats are coming along fast. No ideal dealer structure exists. One complicating factor is that giant retailing corporations have been changing rapidly in recent years, due to mergers, acquisitions, new-store openings, management restructuring, and experimentation with new formats. With any major restructuring buying policies and practices may change. As diagrammed in Figure 19–4, a single retailing entity may buy a single merchandise classification by four or more distribution patterns. Further, this firm may pay several different prices for exactly the same product, depending upon its accompanying services.

Given today's and tomorrow's intense competition plus the race for volume in every industry by every company, these many patterns are likely to continue in combination, often with overlap.

FIGURE 19–4
Sample Variations in Retailing Buying Situations

This large retailing firm owns a number of traditional department store chains that are headquartered in several different markets, an appliance–TV regional specialty chain, and retailing specialists in other industries such as jewelry and books. This diagram shows how four different properties buy major appliances from more than 20 sources, including (1) direct from the factory, (2) several different distributors and factory branches, (3) its own resident buying offices (imports), and (4) as a member of a buying group.

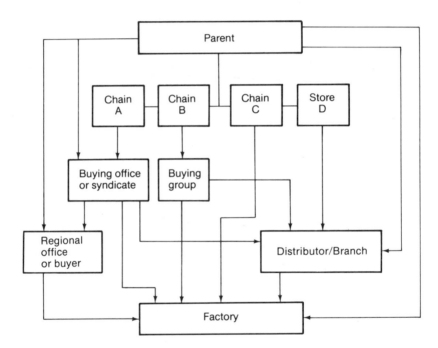

DISTRIBUTION PRESSURES IN OTHER INDUSTRIES

We have dealt primarily with appliance–TV distribution, industries garnering $25 to $30 billion in annual retail sales—variance dependent upon the product categories included. These are the largest departments of the nation's largest retailer, Sears, which merchandises a comparatively simple line (one brand, private label) through its own simplified distribution system. Most Sears competitors, however, merchandise multiple brands and buy through multiple distribution systems with many different values and services added, with complex methods, and with differing prices and terms. Thousands of retailers do less than $1 million in sales per year.

It may be important to stress that any given distribution system constantly undergoes change based upon developments in other systems and industries. Durables distribution, for example, has changed radically with the emergence of supermarkets, the most frequent form of U.S. shopping. Over the years food shopping has taught consumers self-service (wait on yourself and save money), to read advertising (know what you want before you shop), to depend on labels (for everything from brand name to annual energy usage), to watch for specials (there's always a sale somewhere), that bigness is goodness (you save money because we buy in quantity), and take it with you (no need to order and wait).

A strong independent distributor, as described on these pages, may move about $100 million a year in three or four household durables merchandise classifications. Wholesaling may be either much bigger or far smaller in other industries. Foremost-McKesson, for example, does more than $4.5 billion a year in pharmaceuticals distribution; it has computer-to-computer links with 200 manufacturers. An average outdoor power equipment distributor, on the other hand, may cover a full state with about $10 million annual sales. This, in turn, requires 30 percent gross to reach any respectable return on investment.

Packaged goods distributors may follow the broker format: wholesaling many brands, thousands of SKUs, but with very few, extremely simple services for supermarkets and drug stores. But thanks to universal product coding (UPC), electronic point of sale (EPOS) wanding, and modern data processing, the packaged goods broker gets comprehensive feedback plus automatic inventory control at the retail level.

Hardware distribution is developing a more useful and scientific stance with electronic input from packaged goods and merchandising lessons from appliance-TV marketing. This retail segment also is gaining from the formal franchise movement. Organizations like True Value and Ace are making the small, every-town hardware dealer significantly more productive and profitable.

No industry is an island in modern distribution. Each is gaining sophistication from distribution advances in many fields.

LOOKING AHEAD AND LIVING WITH DISTRIBUTION TRENDS

This chapter defies conclusions, with all distribution systems subject to radical and constant change. Several trends are worth watching, however, in the belief that distribution can and will be simplified and that someday decisions will be easier to reach. These trends include:

1. The big will continue to grow bigger and more efficient at all three distribution levels.
2. Distribution is becoming far more sophisticated with sciences stemming from logistics and computerization.
3. New distribution formats will keep on emerging, with greatest impact yet to be felt from telemarketing and nonstore retailing.
4. Formal franchising will keep on gaining as new technologies develop controls and media for retailing.

To reiterate, most distribution decisions start with review of existing channels, systems, and services available and appropriate for the products to be merchandised. The best system for any industry, any company, will come from combinations of formats and methods. Productivity and profitability will depend on values added and services needed beyond the merchandise entity.

20

INDUSTRIAL DISTRIBUTION

by
Sonja Muller Haggert
Keystone Filter Division/Met Pro Corporation

DIRECT SELLING

Industrial distribution can be divided into three basic channels:

1. Direct sales force.
2. Jobbers.
3. Manufacturer's reps.

The best way to begin is by looking at a diagram of the direct sales channel and how it operates (see Figure 20–1).

Direct selling can occur in one of the four ways shown in Figure 20–1.[1] Part A shows the direct sales force calling on sales agents who in turn sell to the industrial user. Often these agents have warehouse facilities. This is especially prevalent in industries where the industrial user may be small or only need a limited amount of the product. This method of distribution would also be very effective in instances where the industrial users are concentrated and it is possible for the rep to cover all customers with your product and a limited number of other manufacturers.

Part B provides for the possibility of sales being handled through agents or distributors to get to the final industrial user.

In some instances (Part C) the sales force operates from a source of supply in either a regional warehouse or at the company office and thus can supply the industrial user directly.

---

[1] Cochrane Chase and Kenneth L. Barasch, *Marketing Problem Solver*, ed. Edmund Van Deusen (Radnor, Pa.: Chilton, 1977). All figures in this chapter are taken from this source.

FIGURE 20-1

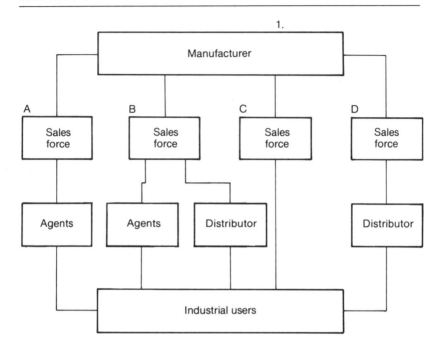

Last, Part D shows the sales force using only distributors to get their products in the hands of the industrial user. This is advantageous in situations where the distributor works closely with industrial customers, stocking merchandise in ample quantity to provide good service. Distributors become a disadvantage when they stock only as an order taker.

In order for a company to seriously consider using a direct sales force, it must have the sales and capital to support that sales force. This is especially important if the salespeople sell directly to the end user rather than using another subsidiary channel. In this instance, the company must provide not only the sales information but also all the other functions that a middleman would provide. These functions would include transportation, materials handling, finance, etc.

A direct sales force can be considered important, if not mandatory, in the following instances:

1. The product requires a great deal of technical expertise.
2. The product requires someone who is skilled in installation, maintenance, and/or handling.
3. The market you sell is made up of customers who are either

close together in location or few in number, or they encompass a particular market which is small in size.

4. Your customers need information upon application of product.

5. There is a need for lengthy and involved negotiations before the actual sale is made.

6. The company is expected to provide promotional assistance.

7. Your competition provides a direct sales force.

SELLING TO JOBBERS

In Figure 20–2 distribution method A shows the product going from the manufacturer to the distributor to the industrial user. If the distributor is a strong link, aggressive in dealing with an industrial customer, this is an ideal channel. It will also work if the product has a following and is asked for by name. At the other extreme, a product that is a commodity will work in this channel of distribution. Hopefully, however, the wholesaler carries only one brand of the commodity.

An agent, such as in method B, provides a push or added link to move the product. The agent is almost always useful, with the added advantage of his or her cost being a commission (there must be sales

FIGURE 20–2

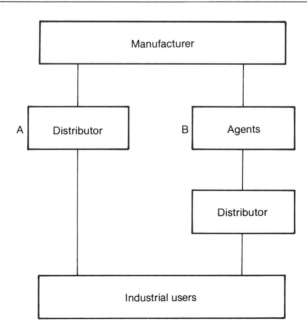

generated before the agent is paid). The rep is a generalist and therefore should be used only with products that require *some* sales push and *some* knowledge on his or her part.

Jobbers are distinguished by the type of service they provide. They may belong to one of the following four categories.

1. Full-line distributors, also called general line or mill supply houses, can be used to reach wide horizontal markets (e.g., maintenance supplies, general machinery, cutting tools, fasteners) or narrower vertical markets (e.g., oil wells, foundries, construction). They can stock as many as several hundred product lines; some stock over 10,000 industrial items, some of which may be competing brands. They cannot give intensive sales promotion to products of all manufacturers represented. They offer a limited amount of technical service; but most do offer credit. Full-line distributors make it possible for a customer to place a single order for all needs. Also, they make it possible for the customer to get all items on a single delivery.[2]

2. Specialized distributors limit their expertise, as the name implies. They specialize in a particular type of product or related products. This is because the items they carry require them to provide their customers with product information, technical service, or engineering help in applications. They can be found in industries such as electronics, scientific and/or medical equipment, air and hydraulic equipment, and power tools.

3. Limited distributors limit their expertise to a small group of products. These products are often unrelated. They do, however, provide prompt delivery, some sales ability and know-how, and merchandising. These distributors tend to be geared toward machinery and equipment of various types and industrial supplies.

4. Last, the departmentalized distributor carries a full line of products that are divided into departments. He or she has a good knowledge of key products carried and their applications. This method of distribution is recommended in any or all of the following instances:

a. The product is standard and requires only minimal technical and/or engineering guidance.

b. A new product falls in the above category or has a small profit margin and/or low cost.

c. Availability is an important consideration for the customer.

d. The product requires some installation and repair work.

e. Customers of the product area are scattered in a wide geographic area.

f. Orders are small in size and profit.

---

[2] Ibid.

g. Promotional efforts are required but not essential since often the distributor handles only one competitive line.

h. The wholesaler's customers insist on buying through this channel.

i. The competition sells this way.

Distributors are, in essence, a generalized sales force. Their biggest advantages are that they:

1. Buy in bulk.
2. Are accessible to buyers.
3. Have credit information on middlemen that could be a burden for the manufacturer to get due to the size of certain markets.

Naturally, distributors have disadvantages for the manufacturer. Probably the biggest disadvantage to the manufacturer is the lack of loyalty the distributor has for him or her. If the distributor disagrees with the manufacturer's policies or finds a preference for a competitors' item, often little can be done to keep the distributor from switching. The manufacturer can send influential people and certainly can add some spice. But there is no guarantee that these steps will sway the distributor's mind. In a distributor/manufacturer relationship the solidity of the rep relationship is missing. The manufacturer who makes only limited calls on the distributor is in an even less concrete position when the distributor looks at a competitor.

Last, the distributor, because he or she usually sells a large number of products, provides little market information except what becomes self-evident in sales.

USING MANUFACTURER'S REPRESENTATIVES

The manufacturer's rep can be an important part of the manufacturer/industrial user relationship. There are two important considerations for the manufacturer when appointing a rep:

1. Does the rep have a limited number of customers so he or she can manage the territory? (One person cannot handle three states no matter how small they are in terms of accounts.)
2. Does the rep carry only a certain number of profitable lines to which he or she can give attention?

The manufacturer's rep is an independent businessperson who carries more than one manufacturer's line. The rep acts as a kind of substitute direct sales person.

Reps sell noncompeting lines of various manufacturers, most often in an exclusive territory. They are paid on a commission basis which varies according to the type of product and its cost.

FIGURE 20–3

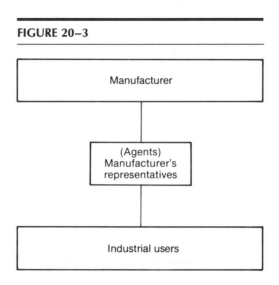

A rep is bound to the manufacturer's pricing, terms, territory, and other policies by a written contract.

The rep may or may not carry a stock of the manufacturer's product. This usually depends on the territory itself and whether the rep has the ability to perform a warehousing operation along with making calls.

Advantages of Using a Rep

1. A rep is an excellent way to introduce a new product. The rep is already familiar with the marketplace and provides a limited initial cost to the manufacturer.
2. The rep is an advantage to a company not well known because of the relationship he or she already has with potential customers. It would take a new direct salesperson a considerable amount of time to develop this same rapport.
3. The rep is advantageous to a company with a product that is used infrequently and requires year-round customer contact, but the company's sales would not support a year-round sales force.
4. Reps are advantageous to a company that does not have the finances or personnel to support a sales organization.
5. A company's sales force may be too busy to handle another product.
6. Reps are valuable if the market is large and spread out geographically.
7. A rep is an advantage if the competition has reps and/or the market is used to dealing with reps.

Disadvantages of Using a Rep

1. Because reps are generalists, it is hard to get specific feedback from them. They hate paperwork. It will probably be entirely up to the manufacturer to get the necessary market information.
2. The rep has a number of lines on which he or she concentrates, so yours will get priority only occasionally.
3. The manufacturer has little control over the rep. Independence is important to the rep, who will therefore handle the territory the way he or she deems appropriate.

MEETING DISTRIBUTION GOALS

Whether you are an established company or a new one looking at new markets, begin by looking at all the possibilities of where your product could be handled. Then, narrow down this selection process to avoid duplication. Analyze the channels used by your competition. Use this as a point of comparison.

Overall Market

In order to determine how best to cover all your potential markets, consider the following:

1. Look at the various markets and break them down according to the number of customers and the potential sales of each of these customers.
2. Determine the importance of each market in terms of the market share that your company can achieve.
3. Learn about other channels of distribution from executives in your own company, people in that industry who would not be competitors, and/or potential customers.
4. Use research sources available on other markets.
5. Look at the areas your competition has gone into, and evaluate how well they have done.

Percentage of Market

Begin your move into other markets by determining what percentage of each market you want to obtain. Evaluate the potential sales and profitability of the channels. You may wish to avoid some segments due to high initial costs or limited profitability.

Working with Channels of Distribution

Begin by determining how you intend to work with your new markets. First, will you be selling through distributors, on a direct basis, through manufacturers reps, or a combination? If you decide to work through reps, consider using the data form in Figure 20–4 to help you identify characteristics of organizations that would fit in with your goals.

Now develop a plan on how you will work with your channels. Keep the following points in mind:

1. Talk to them. Make up a schedule for yourself that requires you to phone or visit your channel on a regular basis. Some insignificant items turn into major problems when left to contemplate.
2. Get feedback from your channel on everything from advertising to pricing. This feedback should help you gain better insight into the market as a whole.
3. Evaluate and analyze performance.
4. Help them with customer contact.
5. Handle orders promptly.
6. Give dependable delivery information and make that information readily available.
7. Be free with recognition.
8. Be willing to offer periodic promotions and specials.
9. Provide technical assistance.

DISTRIBUTION COSTS

The following 10-step process should outline what your costs will be in the channels of distribution. Use these for each channel.

1. List all customers and prospects in each territory. Review this list with salespeople and sales managers for completeness. Determine the average number of buying influences per plant requiring regular calls.
2. Rank each customer and prospect by profit contribution potential. Group them by classes according to ranges of profit contribution (e.g., $5,000 to $9,999, $10,000 to $14,999).
3. Determine the number of customers and prospects in each range of profit potential.
4. Estimate the number of calls required for each group. This is based on past year's activity adjusted for next year's expectations.
5. Determine the total number of calls needed to adequately cover identified market potential.
6. Determine the average number of calls that can be made by one salesperson in one year.
7. Divide the average number of calls that one salesperson can make into the number of calls required to adequately cover the

FIGURE 20–4

REPRESENTATIVES' DATA FORM

Name of Organization:_____ Date:_____

Principals: 1_____ 2_____

Address:_____
  Street *City* *State* *Zip*

Telephone No.:_____(_____)_____
  Area *Number*

1. No. of years in business:_____

2. Territory covered:_____

3. Branch locations:_____

4. No. of salespeople:_____

5. How many sales calls per month can your organization commit to our line?_____

6. Gross sales volume last year: $_____

7. Do you have your own advertising/promotion program?   ☐ Yes ☐ No

8. Do you have stocking facilities?   ☐ Yes   ☐ No

9. Do you have a service staff?   ☐ Yes   ☐ No

10. Please list bank references:_____
_____

11.

Manufacturers currently represented (include addresses)	Products	Territory	No. of years representing

12.

Principal customers	Approximate $ volume sold to each last year

Note: This basic form can be used for obtaining data from agents and distributors. Of course, you can add other questions to obtain data relevant to your company's situation.

FIGURE 20–5
Call Requirements

Territory: California

(1) Customer and Prospect Profit Contribution Potential	Actual		Call Frequency		Planned		
	(2) Number of Customers	(3) Number of Prospects	(4) Customers	(5) Prospects	Calls Required for Year		
					(6) On Customers (Columns 2 × 4)	(7) On Prospects (Columns 3 × 5)	(8) Total (Columns 6 + 7)
Over $100,000	6	12	40	10	240	120	360
$75,000–$100,000	13	24	25	7	325	168	493
$50,000–$74,999	22	35	12	5	264	175	439
$25,000–$49,999	37	78	10	4	370	312	682
$10,000–$24,999	58	100	8	3	464	300	764
$ 5,000–$ 9,999	70	125	6	2	420	250	670
Less than $5,000	85	140	4	1	340	140	480
Total	291	514	—	—	2,423	1,465	3,888

market. This tells how many people are ideally needed to cover the market.

8. Determine the current number of salespeople employed.

9. Subtract the number currently employed from the number needed to determine how many new sales personnel are required.

10. Continue to add people until the present value of profits falls below the company's cost of capital (i.e., until it costs more to put the person in the field than profits generated).[3]

The information you have obtained could show up in a chart of a particular territory such as the one in Figure 20–5.

Now that all your data is in place, you can begin to implement what seem to be your best choices. Ultimately, all of the facts plus your own judgments will lead to securing new and stronger channels of distribution.

---

[3] Ibid.

21

THE MARKETING COMMUNICATIONS MIX

by
Robert F. LaRue

LaRue Marketing Consultants, Inc.

An early step in planning the communications mix is to identify the specific communications tasks. There may be dozens of them, ranging from the general (create awareness) to the specific (persuade an adult male prospect to visit a retail store in the month of September).

After listing the tasks, priorities, and messages to be communicated, the marketer is ready to deal with the matter of the mix. In order to do so, the marketer must have enough knowledge of each potential element to judge how much of each is required for effective impact. In the case of publicity, there is the opportunity to ask, "How much can I get?" Publicity professionals know that the answer to that question ranges from "Nothing" to "As much as you want—so long as it appeals to the audiences of the chosen media."

Good texts exist on advertising, publicity, and other elements of the mix, so there is little point in providing a recap of the basics or in trying to deal with the sophisticated advancements. Instead, let us deal with actual and recent cases. In many assignments the go-to-market portion of the project requires specific recommendations for the communications job. Figure 21–1 presents 12 different products and services as examples of how 13 alternatives to conventional media advertising can be utilized to help accomplish communications objectives. Clarification of why each of these alternatives is used in the particular situation follows.

FIGURE 21–1

Marketing Communications Alternatives

Product or Service	Clinics/Demonstrations	Direct Mail	Phone Book Covers	Display	Fact Book	Installation Instructions	Outdoor Signs	Package	Phone Pitch	Product Fact Tag	Publicity	Trade Shows	Yellow Pages Advertising
Decorative wood moulding				X						X	X		
Deluxe mail box				X						X			
Dutch flower bulbs							X				X		
Fast-food restaurant			X										
Home carpet cleaning service									X				X
Home smoke detector						X		X					
Garden sprayer												X	
Industrial oven					X								
Kit for assembling yard storage buildings	X										X		
Component for machinery		X											
Temporary help for office											X		
Snack cakes, pies								X					

PRODUCT: DECORATIVE WOOD MOULDING

Situation

Retailers of moulding tended to treat it as a commodity, regardless of whether its application was utilitarian or decorative. These particular machine-carved, hardwood mouldings were only for decorative purposes, commanded a much higher price, and were in fact a specialty deserving special attention.

Communications Alternatives

Instead of simply carrying the name of the manufacturer, the product was branded "Accent" to emphasize its decorative functions. A descriptive fact tag was affixed to each piece of moulding. The tags were then hung from peg board hooks below a header that illustrated the many applications for the product. The display configuration, four feet in width, made it possible for the marketer to get a specific space commitment from the retailer. Until these actions had been taken there was little point in communication to the consumer about multiapplications and the benefits of this particular line. During the introductory phase no consumer advertising was used. Editors of shelter magazines and home and women's service publications were eager to utilize material prepared for them that showed the many in-home applications. Reprints of these articles, one comprising 16 full pages, had great value to the marketer as the field force approached retailers to sell-in the deal.

PRODUCT: DELUXE MAIL BOX (for installation at roadside to replace the utilitarian covered wagon)

Situation

Even though the product's shipping carton was a highly functional display with effective graphics, it was certain that the retailer would remove the product from its carton for shelf display. During the early stages of product development, no provision had been made for a way to affix a fact tag.

Communications Alternatives

Because the product was a departure from what was available in the marketplace, publicity in consumer magazines and newspapers was planned and accomplished. Ad slicks and radio commercial scripts were made available to retailers for local use. A fact tag was designed and affixed to the mailbox prior to shipment from the factory. That was accomplished by providing a hole for the fact tag string. As insignificant as it may seem, the fact tag became a critical element in the total communications program.

PRODUCT: DUTCH FLOWER BULBS

Situation

Spring flowering bulbs—tulip, daffodil, hyacinth, crocus, etc.—must be planted in the fall. Consumers need to be reminded of this fact, and retailers need to tell the consumer that the product is in stock.

Communications Alternatives

Through the years a substantial portion of the total marketing communications budget was utilized to generate consumer publicity. To take advantage of consumer awareness, a vital part of the total communications program was a weatherproof outdoor banner carrying a silhouette of a tulip and a simple, straightforward message, "Holland bulbs are here."

PRODUCT: RESTAURANT SERVING FAST FOOD

Situation

A restaurant specializing in carryout orders knew that it was advantageous to have its name and phone number readily accessible to those who would telephone their orders.

Communications Alternatives

To supplement more conventional directory and reminder advertising, the restaurant contracted for space on the vinyl covers for telephone books that were distributed in its area by the cover producer. There was evidence that a significant percentage of households did in fact wrap their telephone directories in these covers. The program was particularly beneficial to this marketer since only one advertiser per business category appeared on the cover.

PRODUCT: HOME CARPET CLEANING SERVICE

Situation

A new concept in home carpet cleaning was being marketed. The system had significant differences and benefits when compared to conventional methods. It was determined that a substantial percentage of consumers, when in need of carpet cleaning, reach for the Yellow Pages in order to contact one or more services, usually for pricing information.

Communications Alternatives

A study of a sampling of Yellow Pages directories across the country showed that there was an opportunity for this franchisor to distinguish itself from all others by presenting the service benefits story with compelling graphics and much briefer copy. Another study showed that when franchisees of competitors were called, there was great inconsistency in their responses to inquiries about their cleaning service, prices, etc. Since a franchisee literally lives off inquiries of this sort, telephone inquiry handling became a vital part of the franchisor's training programs.

PRODUCT: HOME SMOKE DETECTOR

Situation

The product was being introduced at a time when most smoke detectors were being marketed by firms usually thought of as manufacturers of small electrical appliances. Consumer attitude studies showed that this new marketer was regarded as an instrument company which produced instruments that were trouble-free.

Communications Alternatives

The marketing communications program was quite complete, with all of the appropriate components required to take this product to market through retail outlets. It was desirable to separate it from all other offerings. The packages, therefore, were deliberately designed to have an instrument look. Further, installation instructions on the reverse side of the package included diagrams of dwellings, with suggested multiple locations for smoke detectors indicated. The purpose, of course, was to sell more than one instrument per household. The consumer guidance information proved such an effective selling device that many retailers deliberately displayed every other package reverse side out.

PRODUCT: GARDEN SPRAYER

Situation

A new product with outstanding new features and benefits required significantly greater trade penetration than earlier designs had been able to obtain.

Communications Alternatives

The challenge became how to use trade show exhibit space effectively to make a significant impression upon thousands of attending key retailers. In booth space 10 feet by 20 feet, the product was displayed along with all of the merchandising aids. The notable element that got attention and got the message across was the presentation every half hour of a five-minute skit. It was performed by two professionals who would close each show by introducing the aisle-clogging audience to the sales representative in the booth.

PRODUCT: INDUSTRIAL OVEN

Situation

This was not one of the major manufacturers of industrial ovens used for a wide variety of finishing operations such as the drying of paints and other coatings. The company had no real stature or position in the marketplace. It was seldom the recipient of inquiries about its products. As a consequence, salespeople spent most of their time making cold calls.

Communications Alternatives

It was found that prospective purchasers of industrial ovens needed to work with a variety of formulas, tables, charts, and other reference data. This information was scattered through a wide variety of texts and manuals. No one had put the data together in one place for easy reference. A 20-page, digest-size fact book was prepared. In order to get inquiries, the fact book was offered free in a variety of industrial magazines. The inquiry response was substantial, and there was literally no resistance to having the fact book hand-delivered by a field salesperson. Suddenly the field force was able to make meaningful sales contacts. Not surprisingly, the company came to be regarded as an authority in the industry since it was knowledgeable enough to compile relevant data and was able to explain its use on field sales calls. The sales personnel found themselves playing a counselor role as opposed to being in an adversary environment. Customer service personnel reported that they began receiving a substantial number of phone calls from companies who had concluded that this marketer was the authority for any kind of data related to industrial heating or finishing.

PRODUCT: KIT FOR ASSEMBLING YARD STORAGE BUILDINGS

Situation

This was a new concept in DIY kits that permitted the consumer to purchase pre-cut and numbered frame components for the basic structure of the buildings. To these were added siding, shingles, and hardware.

Communications Alternatives

Many consumers doubted that they could erect a storage building eight feet high, eight feet wide, and eight feet long in a single weekend. To obtain believability, actual demonstrations of the simple steps involved were presented in publications reaching the handy homeowner. One major publication covered each critical step in a four-page presentation. Seeing was believing at the point of sale as well. Retailers were offered the opportunity to have barn-raising clinics or demonstrations in their parking lot. Consumers were shown how easy the detailed instructions were to follow and were even encouraged to participate in the assembly.

PRODUCT: MACHINERY COMPONENT

Situation

This manufacturer's product was used as a component in a wide variety of machinery and equipment as diverse as printing presses, steel-rolling machinery, bridges, and ferris wheels. Larger manufacturers enjoyed greater market shares. This product actually had advantages over those competitors, but none was so significant that it could be the backbone of a communications program.

Communications Alternatives

In reality the marketer was splitting hairs about the eight advantages that it enjoyed over what was offered by other marketers. A direct-mail program of eight different mailing pieces was prepared that featured a cartoon character, "The Hair Splitter." Each piece covered only one of the advantages and touched on it only briefly. The piece contained a return postcard on which the recipient was given the opportunity to invite the marketer's sales representative to "come and split a hair with me." As the recipients received their fourth, fifth, and sixth pieces in the program, the postcard response climbed significantly. Out of this effort came substantial numbers of responses that were converted to sales.

PRODUCT: TEMPORARY HELP FOR OFFICES

Situation

This franchisor was a pioneer in introducing the concept of temporary help services. While the concept was still new, there was substantial interest on the part of women who could consider rejoining the work force and on the part of firms in the innovative service.

Communications Alternatives

As a pioneer, the marketer benefited from any editorial coverage on the subject. A press bureau operation was set up, and, through effective press relations, much of the initial communications objections were realized without the need to utilize advertising. As soon as offices were opened it became necessary to buy advertising space to list their locations. As the concept caught on and new competitors entered the field there was a need to identify competitive advantages that could not be presented through publicity. Again, advertising was enlisted to undertake these tasks, as was direct mail.

PRODUCT: SNACK CAKES AND PIES

Situation

This regional baker had product offerings and price points not unlike those of three national competitors.

Communications Alternatives

Television, radio, and newspapers were being used to reach the target segments. However, since the product offerings were much like those of competition, it was difficult to stimulate consumer preference and to get and retain the desired retail shelf space. To accomplish differentiation, packaging was enlisted, but not just in terms of different graphics or configuration. Instead, a new program was built around a package of six pies. This gave rise to the theme, "Pick a Pack of Picnic Pies," along with similar themes that provoked both consumer and retailer response.

The elements of the mix will vary according to the nature of the product, characteristics of the prospect, conditions in the marketplace, channel partners required (or chosen), the product's stage in the life cycle, etc. As an indication of the kinds of consideration that affect mix decisions, consider the 10 questions that must be addressed by a marketer of a do-it-yourself (DIY) product. As you read each of them, reflect on the impact these have on what constitutes an effective mix. Remember, too, that the considerations will be just as special when going to market with almost any product or service.

1. *What are the instructional requirements both in-store and at time of use?* Critical to communications for do-it-yourself products is the matter of instructional requirements. The package, the display, the fact tag, and the instruction sheet are all vital. It is imperative that the directions be presented in such a way that they appear easy to follow. This is accomplished by grouping the subactions so that there seem to be only three or four steps to completion. It is almost always possible to communicate a significant part of the instructions graphically, thus appreciably reducing the wording.

2. *The communications mix—do we have a real breakthrough that's going to grab attention or is this really rather mundane?* As a go-to-market plan is developed, it is time for a realistic assessment of the impact upon the marketplace of the arrival of this new product. Having an unbiased evaluation will dictate the extent of communications necessary and, to a very considerable degree, what the mix must be.

3. *Can publicity carry a significant part of the load of educating and stimulating users? Dealers? Other channel partners?* In the early stages of planning the communications program, it is important to identify various communications tasks. Once that has been accomplished, professionals are in a position to assign specific roles to advertising, publicity, literature, trade shows, etc. A marketer is very fortunate if a substantial portion of the communications job can be assigned to publicity. Cost per thousand impressions can be relatively low. When major consumer media give the product meaningful exposure there can be significant impact at all stages of the distribution chain. Usually it is possible to mount a separate publicity program directed exclusively to the distribution channels. Obviously, the marketer must acknowledge the restrictions of publicity, not the least of which is the inability to fully control what is said and when and where it is said.

4. *Same question for the in-store product presentation components—packaging, displays, take-one literature, etc.* In the retail store environment the package must often stand alone and do the entire selling job. The package must work hard to gain attention and to provide all relative information in a way that promotes understanding and generates confidence. In many retail situations it is possible to present the product as part of a display, or with display components such as a header or shelf talker. In the most fortunate situation nothing more is needed. That is not always the case. Sometimes a piece of take-one literature is helpful, even necessary, to assure the consumer that the product is right and that he or she can handle the project. In still other situations the take-one piece is, in reality, a take-home piece, helping another person contribute to the making of a purchasing decision. Wherever possible, it behooves the marketer to provide what it takes to get the message through.

5. *Clinics. Demonstrations. Useful? Necessary? Don't know?* There are those situations where product demonstrations or clinics, showing how to use a product, evoke enough interest and subsequent sales to pay for their costs. A secondary function can be increasing interest or comprehension on the part of retailers or their personnel. If one is not experienced in this sort of in-store activity, it is often difficult to determine how cost effective it would be. For a marketer in a quandary, it is reassuring to know that testing the effectiveness of such activities need not be costly. Fortunately, there are several highly knowledgeable specialists in this field who can provide excellent counsel regarding feasibility as well as the specific techniques that can be used.

6. *Will we get high-traffic locations in the store?* Everyone seeks prime locations for the presentation of their product. That is not always possible. On the other hand, if high-traffic, high-visibility locations are essential to product success, the marketer must build the overall program around this requirement and structure the offering accordingly. This may include size and mix of the assortment or deal.

7. *Trade shows. Will they help?* As in the case of all components in the marketing communications mix, the matter of trade shows must be addressed, utilizing the task and objective method. No different than any other medium, a trade show may be very effective in accomplishing certain communications objectives.

8. *At the order-writing shows, will we write enough?* More often than not, sales are not made on the floor of the show. Fortunately, there are shows in which orders are written. It is imperative that the marketer understand buying procedures, buyers' needs, and buyers' expectations—and then communicate effectively with those buyers.

9. *What do we want/need to know about acceptance once the product is out?* Once the product is in the pipeline it is important to track not only its performance but also the attitudes of users. What we learn from such studies can help refine the communications program—in terms of message, mix, media, and techniques.

10. *Have we considered special techniques that provide a high degree of exposure—contests, sweepstakes, mall shows, etc.?* The conventional components available for a marketing communications program are usually more than adequate to get the job done. Sometimes there are opportunities to get a high degree of exposure for the product through advertising, promotion, and publicity undertaken by others who elect to feature the marketer's new product as a key prize in a heavily promoted contest or sweepstakes. It is possible that the total cost of participation is no more than the factory cost of the products contributed to the promotion. Sometimes, at modest cost, shopping mall shows or other exhibitions can be important to the total program.

A review, such as this, of the many available elements in the communications mix, tends to imply that media advertising has limited value.

In many situations nothing could be further from the truth. Some messages, or images, cannot be communicated faster or more economically than through paid advertising. The point is: seldom should advertising be asked to do the total communications job. Look to publicity, packages, displays, and the other elements to complete a really effective mix.

And for the marketer who cannot afford to do enough advertising—so that it alone gets the communications job done—well, he has no choice but to sort out the many alternatives so that an effective mix can be put together.

22

DISPLAY NEEDS

by
John Murray

Geocel Corporation

This chapter will cover three major areas:

1. What types of displays to consider, with a brief critique of the advantages and disadvantages of each.
2. Means of objectively determining how to identify the best possible display.
3. The importance of fitting the display to the strategy, and how to go about it.

For present purposes, a *display* can be defined as any vehicle other than a standard shipper by which a manufacturer's products are shown to the consumer at the ultimate point of purchase. Displays, then, include almost any point-of-purchase piece developed by a manufacturer for use in a retail establishment and intended to obtain preferential visual position vis-à-vis the competition.

DISPLAY TYPES

Before determining needs it is helpful to review the basic display options.

Counter Display

This is typically a self-contained shipping and display unit, although it may often be contained with several other displays in a master shipping carton. It both organizes and displays the manufacturer's products. It usually has a small header card, giving it extra impact on the shelf, while still being as simple to stock as an open-stock item. Retailers like this approach since there is no need to devote extra space to the item, and the display/shipper is easy to handle from warehouse to shelf.

Unfortunately, there have been occasions when the retailer has insisted that the display item become the stock item, and the manufacturer becomes locked into providing a relatively expensive display for an open-stock item. This is particularly likely when the counter unit is offered as an introductory unit with a new product. The problem is greatly intensified when the retailer uses computerized stock numbers since there will be a reluctance to change stock numbers on a new product.

One of the most effective displays is a counter unit offered by an elastic stocking manufacturer. This unit is eye-catching, holds literature, offers a special sale, and contains only three pairs of stockings.

The unit takes only inches of space and yet, because of the high unit sale, it offers a very high return to the retailer. Elements such as high relative cost for the unit, high total retail value, consumer information, and consumer value would seem to be necessary elements in a good counter display. Without these, there is a high risk of failure.

Shelf Talker/Organizer

This display both organizes and displays products and at the same time provides useful information to the consumer. Considered a semipermanent unit, the shelf talker keeps the products in one neat area on the shelf, providing a very useful service to the retailer. This organization of the product also protects the manufacturer from encroachment by other products. The organizer usually has a wide lip in which is inserted product information such as name, price, and product uses—all of which tend to help the consumer in his or her purchase decision. The very fact that the shelf talker is there draws the consumer's attention to the product itself, and thereby increases its turnover. In this era of ever-increasing self-service, poor training of floor personnel, and very costly floor space, shelf talkers are one of the most desirable of all display techniques.

A major caulking products manufacturer has exploited these very well. Caulks are notoriously confusing due to the wide range of prices, product types, and manufacturers. This manufacturer has set up two-foot sections of shelf talkers for each of its products and displays pricing, formulation, life expectancy, and a minimum of worthwhile technical information for each of its products. Consumer information, ability to organize, and a means of attracting attention to the product are the ingredients to a successful shelf-talker program.

Shelf Spotter

Unlike the shelf talker, the shelf spotter serves merely to call attention to the product or to some special feature of the product. It generally is clipped onto the shelf in such a way as to be visible as the consumer walks down the aisle. It does not organize the product on the shelf. It can get in the way when consumers reach for product. It is the most temporary of all displays and is seldom used, unless put up by the manufacturer's own sales personnel.

We are not aware of any major successes attributable to shelf spotters. Indeed, they seem a waste of money.

Shelf Extender

This is a small shelf unit which usually holds pre-packed product, attaches to the shelf in some way, and extends out from the shelf. It is usually placed in front of the same product's normal shelf position. It can attract attention by increasing the product's visibility and doubling its facings. However, an extender is highly vulnerable to being knocked off the shelf. Even when secure, once a few items are removed, the remaining product tends to fall over or get knocked out of the extender as consumers inevitably reach over or brush against them.

Although many types of extenders are used and there may have been a time when they were successful, we are not aware of any recent successful campaigns using extenders. Passing over the aforementioned disadvantages, retailers simply do not like them.

Prepack Display

This is easily the most commonly used of all displays. It is a temporary, free-standing floor unit delivered with the product packed inside it in a tray and ready to be displayed.

It usually has three elements: a base to hold the display tray which has a header card behind it that explains the product or its special offer. This type of unit usually sets up very easily, is relatively inexpensive, and can usually be depended on to attract attention. It usually conveys some kind of offer to the consumer, such as a rebate, self-liquidator, pack, premium, or other attention-getting device. Unquestionably, these displays increase turnover, force additional distribution, and provide the consumer with an added reason to buy the product on display.

The major disadvantage of this type of unit is that it is a pre-pack. These displays are notoriously over-sold, and often a goodly number of them are left in warehouses where they chronically distort turnover figures while waiting to be broken up at great expense to the distributor or chain warehouse.

The most successful units are those used by analgesic manufacturers. These are automatically packed into trays as they come off the production line, thereby actually saving the manufacturer production and packer costs.

Simplicity, low cost, easy setup, and an eye-catching header card (with or without a consumer offer) are the key ingredients to a successful pre-pack display.

Display Unit with Packers

This approach is a variant of the pre-pack unit. The merchandise, however, is packed in its regular shelf containers along with an empty display made up of the standard tray, base, and header card.

We have used this approach with considerable success with distributors and chains which are reluctant to repack unsold pre-packs. With the merchandise in shelf packers, it is no real problem to break down surplus units after the promotion is over. When the choice is between strong distributor cooperation and the slight extra cost of putting the merchandise in shelf packers, the answer should be fairly obvious.

Semipermanent Free-Standing Display

The semipermanent unit usually emphasizes creativity in its approach. The display usually takes up minimal floor space, is highly visible, and displays a relatively large amount of product. Seasonality is usually a factor in the suitability of this type of display since it is designed to last only three to six months.

In recent years two caulk and sealant manufacturers were able to satisfy differing objectives through the intelligent use of semipermanent units. The first manufacturer is one of the leaders in the market. They opted for a well-designed circular unit which supplemented shelf sales. The other manufacturer, a regional company with very little shelf exposure, used a wire basket which held far more product than it could gain on the shelf. The display used up very little floor space and played a large part in significant share gains for this manufacturer.

A semipermanent unit can substantially increase sales when it is creative, takes up little space, holds a relatively large amount of product, and, perhaps most important, is in a seasonal market.

Permanent Free-Standing Display

The permanent display usually eschews shelf position among its competitors and strikes out on its own, attempting to become its own department. This is a highly risky strategy. Most manufacturers tend to develop this type of display out of frustration at being unable to develop shelf position through more conventional means. Unable to solve the fundamental marketing problems which are keeping them off the shelf, they fall victim to the delusion that a display will become a panacea.

The only time permanent free-standing displays seem to work is when the manufacturer has a unique, well-advertised position. This allows them to draw people to their display. In fact, they will come into the store looking for it. A well-known wood stain manufacturer has exploited this technique with great success in the do-it-yourself field. However, this example is the exception that proves the rule. In addition, one might question whether this manufacturer could, in fact, do even better if the funds devoted to this very expensive display were put into advertising.

DISPLAY EVALUATION

Having reviewed the various options available in terms of displays, it is appropriate now to evaluate how these displays will work for the individual company.

It is important to develop two objective analytical techniques for display selection. The first technique involves developing a simple mathematical tool which defines how important the display is both to the manufacturer and to the retailer. It is an attempt to provide some common frame of reference to relate to in discussing product display. The second technique involves testing and retesting display techniques.

Mathematical Evaluation

The manufacturer must be ready to "prove" that their display can provide some meaningful benefit to the retailer. The latter usually perceives the value of products in terms of sales and increasing margins. However, what the product really contributes to a store is its sales velocity times its gross margin, as expressed in terms of the square feet it takes up in a store.

One of the most successful home center chains in the United States has annual sales per square feet of approximately $375. (These figures are available for supermarket, drug, and discount chains through industry data, annual reports, or by simply asking.) It is safe to assume that this chain considers 40 percent a good gross margin. Working through the math, if a display can yield over $12.50 in gross margin, if it is set up for a month and does not measure over 12 feet by 12 feet then it is theoretically a good deal for the chain:

$375 sales × 40 percent gross margin × 0.0833 for
1/12 of a year × 1 foot

What we have now is a workable number. The formula must be adapted for actual square feet of selling space and individualized for the chain, but it makes a beginning point.

The following steps should then be taken to evaluate the manufacturer's product line and the display:

1. Determine actual sales of the product line per square feet per store.
2. Determine gross margin from average cost deducted from average selling price. (Be sure to figure in special costs during promotional periods and reduced retail price during advertised specials.)
3. Determine whether or not the product is an above-average profit contributor to the chain. If it is below average, then a display strategy probably is not going to improve this. A below-average figure indicates such things as: the product is not suitable for promotion; the product is being "footballed"; or the product needs a marketing overhaul.

In any case, a below-average figure should be seen as a potential problem not amenable to solution through display.

Assuming an above-average performer, the display program should incorporate: square feet of the display; total retail sales of display and sales per square feet; total gross margin and margin per square feet; multiplied by percent sales rate improvement because of display; multiplied by percent sales rate improvement because of sales message of display. This should result in a reasonably objective base to work with for both the manufacturer and the retailer.

Testing

Any company which routinely uses displays and has no formal testing program for them is inviting long-term disaster. A major display program which fails is very costly. The most visible expense is the displays that must be written off. The greatest cost, however, lies in the consumer movement lost, the contraction of the line sales, and the lost enthusiasm of the trade and the sales force. These are major cost factors made all the more unacceptable because timing in display evaluation is so slow. It can take an entire selling season to receive sufficient feedback on a display. It simply makes no sense to risk so much on such a subjective area as display selection. An ongoing comprehensive testing program is suggested for any manufacturer—large or small—who routinely invests 10 percent or more of the promotional budget (excluding advertising) on displays and/or the promotional motif carried by the display.

Testing should be continuous. Manufacturers may want to test different displays or other variables using the same displays. They can test rebates versus pack-on premiums. They can evaluate large versus small displays and off-shelf promotion versus shelf talkers. Whatever manufacturers intend to commit to, they should first test it as well as they can.

For the large manufacturer a formal research program is recommended, including turnover data, matched store tests, and geographic variances. The smaller manufacturer, on the other hand, can produce a small quantity of prototypes of displays and put them into various stores that can be visited personally and evaluated. Nothing will reduce the risk of failure in display selection as much as real-life testing. If there is concern about tipping one's hand to the competition, remember that marketing success does not necessarily go to the company that is first—it goes to the company that first does it right.

STRATEGY

One of the greatest reasons that display programs fail is that they are often conceived in a vacuum.

The sudden flash of inspiration, the creativity, the enthusiasm engendered by a display carries with it an individual commitment that simply does not exist in other areas of marketing. It is very difficult to reject a truly unique display presented by a product manager or advertising agency. Displays seem to have a life and personality all their own, and evaluating displays is, at best, a highly subjective exercise.

All the more reason, then, to rigorously subject the display idea to the question: "Is it on our strategy?" Displays are not strategies. They simply implement in one facet—at point of purchase—a product strategy which hopefully has been well articulated and well thought out in the marketing plan. The display must first and foremost fit this strategy. One does not use two-color rubber plate to promote an expensive line of colognes. If the strategy is to reduce the retail price, the display should convey a rebate or cents-off program, not an inflatable toy, as a liquidator.

Too often, creativity in the area of display selection can be used as a device to hide lack of thinking about product strategy. A willy-nilly display approach will ultimately blur a product's image; this kind of tinkering can kill a product.

Matching the Display with the Company

It is imperative that the display program be attuned to the company. A company which has basically been a conservative promoter, dealing from strength because it has excellent facings, should not suddenly put major emphasis on an off-shelf sweepstakes promotion and neglect its shelf strength. Neither should a company with a highly specialized product which is struggling to stay on the shelf attempt promotions which demand shelf space it has not yet earned. The first company could very well lose some shelf facings while pursuing a program for which it is not suited, while the other could jeopardize whatever strength and representation it has. Both companies would run the risk of an unsuccessful promotion because the trade is simply not going to accept a company's radical departure in strategy at first blush.

This does not argue that companies should not change strategies. It simply says that they must remain compatible with their image. They can change their image if they wish. Promotional strategies can be geared to that effort, but displays themselves cannot be expected to carry the load in what amounts to strategy changes. Displays can implement strategies, but they should never be confused with the strategies themselves.

23

THE IMPORTANCE OF PACKAGING

by
Dennis W. Shafer

Packaging has been an important marketing consideration in the United States since the first shipment of tea to the colonies, but the truly great advances in packaging as a marketing strategy have taken place in the 20th century. Some of the breakthroughs that come to mind are the bold graphics of Tide detergent, which has stood out on the shelves of supermarkets for over 50 years; the major technical breakthroughs which created a whole new form of consumer convenience such as fresh-frozen packaging, freeze-dried packaging, aerosol packaging, and lightweight, flip-top aluminum beverage cans; and a more recent example of using innovation and creativity to market an old product in a new way, the L'Eggs® packaging and distribution concept for pantyhose.

Product packaging has two basic roles in life: protection of the contents and communication about the contents. Protection is an important concern and a highly technical field of its own. It is the primary interest of manufacturers of industrial goods and large consumer durables. Many major advances have been made in this field in the past decade, and numerous articles and books are available on the subject. In addition, most packaging material vendors have highly trained support personnel capable of assisting with technical packaging issues. The major focus of this chapter will be on the communication aspect of packaging and, specifically, how it relates to durable and nondurable consumer packaged goods.

When packaging is viewed as a marketing communication tool, it begins to involve many complex marketing issues. The package becomes an integral part of the product itself and can have a significant effect on consumer perceptions of function, quality, value, and attitudes toward the brand.

INCREASING IMPORTANCE IN THE 1980s

Several prevalent trends in the 80s will force packaging into an even more important role in marketing. The decreasing level of new-product innovation in many consumer goods categories is creating an intensified level of competition. Packaging will become a critical consideration in fighting for limited shelf space. Consumers continue to place increasing value on their time, and shopping time will become more of a premium. Packaging which delivers the quickest and most informative message and makes shopping easier will rapidly win favor with the consumer. Retailer competition, sophistication, and focus on return on investment increasingly will concentrate attention on the cubic-foot investment in stores as the most important equity, and retailers will insist on packaging that delivers a high return on that investment. Product and communication clutter and the resulting assault on the mind will force packaging to communicate with more precision and clarity. Jack Trout and Al Ries, in their classic work, *Positioning: The Battle for Your Mind,* graphically describe the nature of the problem:

> The odds are overwhelming. Take advertising, for example. With only 6 percent of the world's population, America consumes 57 percent of the world's advertising. The average person consumes 94 pounds of newsprint a year (roughly the same as their annual consumption of beef). The average American family watches television over seven hours a day. An eight-ounce package of Total breakfast cereal contains 1,268 words of copy on the box plus an offer for a free booklet on nutrition (which contains another 3,200 words). The average supermarket in the United States has some 10,000 individual products or brands on display, and this is for a market where the typical new high school graduate has a working vocabulary of about 18,000 words.
>
> The clutter will only get worse. The universal product code allows 10 digits (your social security number has only 9 and that system is designed to handle more than 200 million people). There are some 450,000 active trademarks registered at the U.S. Patent Office, and 20,000 new ones get added every year.[1]

In this over-communicated society, nothing is more important than communication, and packaging must play a key role in delivering the right communication at the right time and under the right circumstances.

---

[1] Al Ries and Jack Trout, *Positioning: The Battle for Your Mind* (New York: Warner Books, 1981), pp. 11–20.

BASIC CONSIDERATIONS

In fulfilling its role of protection and communication, package design generally involves the following basic considerations:

Construction

The size, shape, and material utilized in the package design can have a significant effect on consumer perceptions of quality and value, as well as functional use of the product. Technical advances occur every day in this field, and specialists should be consulted as much as possible.

Cost

The package cost is generally considered a component of the total product cost and is oftentimes viewed as an opportunity for cost reduction. In many situations, however, an improved package which enhances the total value of the product as perceived by the consumer can create major breakthroughs in market penetration or market share. The result is that a more costly package actually reduces the total product cost through economies of scale.

I experienced a dramatic example of this effect. Approximately 75 cents was added to the package cost on a product with a total cost of about $35 in order to better communicate the product concept and its benefits, and to add some positive quality images which the product itself could not do because of some severe design limitations. This change, along with a total marketing program and a consistent communication strategy, increased market penetration and annual volume by a factor of five times over two years, with the end result that manufacturing efficiencies generated a total product cost reduction of well over $5 per unit.

The key issue is to avoid looking at package cost in a vacuum. Consider it an integral part of the product and look for ways of enhancing its value as well as reducing its cost.

Visual Impact

Color, graphics, and shape are utilized to create visual impact and offer great opportunities for creativity. Industrial designers and graphics specialists continuously track trends in colors and shapes, and they can help insure that your packaging is in tune with contemporary preferences and communicates the appropriate signals.

Consumers can distinguish between colors better than anything else in the world of sensory perception in the marketplace. Following are some examples of the communication role of color and visual impact.

Wonder Bread. White package because it is white bread; red and yellow polka dots on package are primary colors, used for attracting children. The red logo communicates warm, fresh-baked image for the company.

Canada Dry Sugar-Free Ginger Ale. Incorporates use of white in design to suggest lightness in color as well as low calories. Red and green are traditional, worldwide-known colors for ginger ale.

Oroweat Cereals. Earth tones of tan, browns, beiges, oranges are natural colors to connote natural foods.

Protein 21 Shampoo. Pink is used because it is a feminine product. Combined with white, it is supposed to separate the product from other shampoos on the market shelf.

Scope Mouthwash. The bright green depicts a distinctive mint color- and flavor-oriented overtone; the name, a medical overtone; and the bottle shape, a laboratory flask.

Ivory Soap. It is blue and white for freshness, cleanliness, and smoothness. The white soap bar represents purity, security, and a clean water connotation.[2]

Copy

The copy on the package should be considered the same as advertising copy and must focus on selling the concept, the product, and the brand. It must communicate to the consumer.

Value Perception

This is the consumer's perception of the quality and benefits of the product and is influenced by several items including construction, visual impact, and copy. The package is the primary tool for creating value in the store since the consumer generally has no ability to test the product itself or compare its function with competitive products. Value perception must be a primary consideration in any package design, and it should be thoroughly explored and tested.

---

[2] Carole Yurdain, *Connecticut Newspapers, Inc.,* May 30, 1982, p. E–1.

Retail Display Maintenance

Retailers are always trying to reduce labor costs in their stores, and packaging can play an important role in helping or hindering this effort. Considerations include shelf dimensions and logistics, warehousing and shelf-stocking procedures, and the ability of the package to maintain its appearance over its shelf life. Anything can happen in the store, and it usually does. We developed a package design for a large item generally stocked on the floor and were considering a white background on the outer package label. We discovered that the white background would quickly become black from janitors mopping the floors at night. Another example was a design that incorporated unique and dramatic graphics on four sides of a package, but unfortunately, the size and shape made it most practical for store personnel to stock the box on the shelf with the bottom panel facing out, clearly showing the shipping label and nothing else. The obvious caution is to check the stores, involve the retailers, and test concepts in the store before finalizing your designs. And be sure to include at least your brand name on every side of the package likely to be displayed.

Retail Security

Shoplifting seems to be increasing at a rate much faster than the gross national product. Retailers are desperately trying to reduce the cost of this problem, with some taking the extreme of locking their merchandise up in cages and behind glass doors. Most retailers realize, however, that locking up products runs against the grain of consumer shopping habits and is not exactly innovative merchandising. Package design can assist in addressing the security problem, although it will never totally solve it. Techniques such as packaging small products on a card or sealing the inner contents to prevent removal of parts may help, but the only thing that will stop the professionals is good store security and employee training.

Another sad statement on an unfortunate trend in store security is the need to provide adequate protection against product tampering. The Tylenol poisoning case brought this issue to national attention, and it is now a critical packaging concern with any food or drug product.

Manufacturing

The actual methods and procedures of placing the product into the package can range anywhere from a minor issue to the single most important element of the product cost. If important, manufacturing engineering personnel should be involved early in package design to look for opportunities for automation and efficiencies.

Warehousing and Shipping

Opportunities for efficiency should be explored with all components of the physical distribution channel, including warehousing and shipping procedures, freight carriers, distributor handling, and retailer handling. The cubic size and shape of the package should be designed to optimize handling efficiencies. If a single unit is impractical to handle, a component package or master pack should be designed for ease of handling and with a quantity of product appropriate for customer ordering convenience. If the product is shipped in single units direct to end users, Parcel Post and UPS have specific dimensional requirements and limitations.

Governmental and Legal

A variety of government agencies may have an interest in your packaging, depending on the contents and distribution. The Food and Drug Administration and the U.S. Department of Agriculture may be concerned with food and drug products, the Consumer Product Safety Commission is concerned with package safety (plastic bags, for example), and the Federal Trade Commission may be interested in the advertising messages contained in the copy. Some local governments also have regulations. Los Angeles, for example, requires that a city approval label be placed on many product categories. Legal counsel and a good advertising agency can provide proper guidance through the legal obstacle course.

Package design for international marketing involves all of these basic considerations but adds a totally new dimension to the task. Specialists should be consulted on issues such as shipping procedures, retail environment, and legal and cultural differences in each country.

The optimum marketing solution is to design a unique package for each country that focuses on individual cultural and target market characteristics. Manufacturing logistics or economies of scale often require a common design, however. Many companies attempt to treat the European Common Market as a true mass market. Even though trade restrictions are minimal, packages still need copy written in six languages, with the result that visual impact and communication clarity is usually destroyed.

The best approach to an international marketplace may be to focus on distinctive visual and graphic communication techniques on the package and use literature or other communication vehicles for detailed copy. The Coca-Cola® trademark and distinct graphic logo is recognized in every country of the world today and represents a common product and brand image, regardless of culture and language.

METHOD OF APPROACH

A package design plan should be integrated with a total marketing and business plan. Sometimes dramatic package design results from luck or unusual creative brilliance, but most companies are not blessed with either and need to approach package design on a more scientific and managed basis.

Good package design includes a focus on real consumer needs and wants, is based on a sound marketing strategy, is backed by careful research, and helps sell the product. Package design should follow a sequential plan beginning with careful definition of general marketing goals, comprehensive business and product situation review, clear definition of packaging objectives, and detailed action steps with responsibilities and timetables.

Marketing Goals

Packaging strategy and design should be developed as a subset of the marketing strategy. Marketing goals can be very comprehensive and specific but generally include one or more of the following basic thrusts:

1. Introduce a new product.
2. Gain market share.
3. Increase distribution (or build a new distribution channel).
4. Increase brand and product awareness.
5. Improve product profit margins (price, cost, and perceived-value relationships).
6. Improve total brand image and quality perception.

Make sure you identify and understand your key marketing and business thrust before embarking on a package design project. A brilliantly designed package directed against the wrong goals will die as quickly as a brilliant technical innovation with no consumer need.

Situation Analysis

A comprehensive fact-gathering process should begin with information probably already available right inside the company. Look for inconsistencies and problem areas in past direct research with consumers and distribution channels, trade magazine articles and surveys, correspondence from customers, competitive analysis and data, and a direct personal review of all existing packaging in the product line.

Primary market research may be necessary to fill in missing facts and could include quick or comprehensive surveys of consumers and distribution channels utilizing telephone, mail, or personal interview techniques. Even a quick 50- or 100-person telephone survey check can provide useful and important information in identifying problems and opportunities. Key retail customers occasionally have firsthand surveys of customer shopping habits and characteristics as they relate to your products, and they may be willing to share that information.

Probably the most important input to good package design is a careful analysis of the role of the package in the store rather than in your office. This can include a detailed photo audit around the country (various service companies are available to perform this function) to identify how your products and competitive products are currently being displayed in a variety of different distribution channels. You can also spend some time personally observing shoppers in the store and their reaction to your products and competitive products.

The key objective of this portion of the analysis is to identify the current perception of the products, their packaging, and the brand name as viewed from a consumer and distribution channel point of view. Try to identify how your customers perceive the value of the product and its capabilities in both absolute terms and relative to the competition. Review and examine your basic product positioning and creative strategy before leaping into a new package design. Is the appropriate product benefit aimed at the appropriate target market? Involve your advertising agency in continuously reexamining your basic assumptions on positioning. Check it out first, or you may do a brilliant job of redesigning a package to communicate the wrong thing.

Collect and reexamine all of the key product features, benefits, technical capabilities, and test data. Involve your R&D department in careful documentation and reexamination of these areas. Collect or generate current product and package cost data or design parameters for a new product in order to establish a framework for size, shape, and material decisions.

Formulating Packaging Objectives

The first step in formulating clear, strategically targeted packaging objectives is to carefully analyze all of the facts and data you have collected, looking for major problems and opportunities. Look at your consumer and distribution channel data and analyze the roll packaging plays in the marketing of your product. Analyze the competitive products, their strategic positioning, and packaging executions. Analyze your consumer perception of value as viewed in the store. Analyze the consistency of your graphics, colors, and brand usage across the line. Analyze retailer problems and point-of-sale deficiencies.

The purpose of a detailed analysis is to carefully define the problems and opportunities. Many times great packaging evolves from clear identification of what's wrong with the current package. Some of the most common packaging problems include:

1. A new product in a package that doesn't look new.
2. An expensive product in a cheap package.
3. A good product that consumers can't understand because of confusing packaging.
4. Colors, shapes, and names that deliver signals to the consumer which are not compatible with the product or brand image.[3]

An old business adage follows the logic that identifying the problem is the difficult part, and, once that is done, the solution is obvious. This is probably true in many packaging situations, but the next critical step is to focus and list in order of priority your objectives in a specific, measurable fashion. Package design can take extended periods of time and involve many trade-offs and compromises during the design process. A clear and concise statement of key objectives can help the process stay on strategic target even over a long period of development.

Typical packaging objectives may focus on one or more of the following:

1. Achieve greater awareness and recognition in the store—store impact (attempt to state the objective in measurable terms and develop methods of testing before and after results).

2. Achieve faster and better communication of the product concept and benefits—stronger "self-sell." There are many attractive or pretty packages on the market, but they are not necessarily effective at selling. Good communication of the product concept can make it easier for the consumer to understand and buy the product, and that is the primary measurement of a successful package. (If the product itself doesn't have a consumer reason for being and a distinct competitive advantage, don't bother designing a package for it!)

3. Achieve consistency with other advertising—consistent color, graphics, and product benefit copy so that all work together and reinforce the brand image and product concept. The clutter and confusion in the marketplace is severe enough without your own company creating more confusion within your product line.

4. Enhance perceived value of the product—add quality signals through creative use of color, graphics, copy, materials, and construc-

---

[3] "Common Mistakes in Home Products Design," excerpt from industrial design literature of King-Casey, Inc., 199 Elm Street, New Canaan, CT, 1983.

tion; velvet lining goes a long way toward justifying a $5,000 price on a diamond ring.

5. Specify cost targets—general cost guidelines are a necessary parameter for successful package design. The guidelines should, however, be related to the other packaging objectives and the overall marketing objective rather than past history or common experience.

6. Achieve better differentiation of models or items in a product line—this can be to accommodate easier customer selection of the appropriate item, encourage upgrading to premium items in the line, or encourage selection of useful accessories or complementary products.

Key Action Steps

Once packaging objectives have been established, a sequential design process has proven to be very effective in developing creative packaging that sells product. This process involves four key steps in the creative process—design generation, consumer test, refine design, and retest.[4]

If the package design effort is important (and if not, why do it?), greater success usually will be achieved by using outside expertise. Unless your company is involved in the continuous, everyday process of package design, you should consider using an industrial design firm with a reputation for packaging results. These firms are capable of providing far greater variety and quality of creative talent and expertise to your project than you would generally be able to recruit or maintain full-time on staff. In addition, they can bring an outside, unbiased viewpoint to the process.

Design. The design generation process should begin with a comprehensive review and education of the outside firm on your business, your products, and your marketing and packaging objectives and strategies. Even the most brilliant designers do not magically gravitate to the right design solutions. The best are artisans in the true sense of the word who use tools and skills to solve your business problems. After carefully indoctrinating your creative team on the project, step aside and give them the time and freedom to explore a broad range of design alternatives. Narrow restrictions at this point in design generation can prevent the truly great creative breakthroughs from occurring.

The design process usually focuses on the primary exposure of the product on the shelf (face panel, facing label, etc.). As many as 50 or 100 design alternatives may be generated during the process, hopefully

---

[4] Ibid.

with a wide range of creative concepts including perhaps even a few seemingly absurd or ridiculous ideas to stretch the imagination. The alternatives should then be narrowed down to a manageable range (three to six alternatives) based on management and creative judgment regarding the ability of the designs to meet the packaging objectives. The alternatives should, however, provide a range of distinct differences in order to generate meaningful test results and lead toward development of an optimum design.

Test. The second key action step is a consumer test of design alternatives. This is an extremely important step and should not be bypassed. If your design firm doesn't believe in consumer testing, find a new design firm. And if your company doesn't believe in consumer research, find a new company! At least try to do some structured research, even if it involves a semiquantitative study using a group of employees; but, ideally, use an outside research supplier in order to structure and conduct a valid test and select a research sample from your target market.

The objective of the research is to define which of several alternatives best communicates the product concept, benefits, and characteristics and has the highest perception of value and impact. A description of a specific example will illustrate research techniques designed to answer these questions.

A new package was under development for a line of products used in a specific home maintenance task. The package design objectives were to increase the perceived value of the product, deliver a stronger point-of-sale impact, maintain a strong and consistent brand identification, and do a better job of communicating product benefits and model differentiation. Four different face panel rough concepts were developed against those objectives and with the following different thrusts:

Package design "H." Product information concept—emphasis was on communicating several key attributes and benefits of the product. The graphic theme used a montage of product illustrations. (See Figure 23–1.)

Package design "N." Complete kit/promotion concept—emphasis was on a combination product approach with promotional aspects. The graphic theme exploited promotional concept with strong typestyle and straightforward component piece illustration. (See Figure 23–2.)

Package design "L." Benefits concept—emphasis was on key product benefits and end results, with graphic focus on illustration of the product in use. (See Figure 23–3.)

Package design "J." Product design concept—emphasis was on the product itself, with the graphic theme using tight, life-sized photography. (See Figure 23–4.)

FIGURE 23–1

FIGURE 23–2

The objective of the research was to determine which package design concept or combination would best meet the packaging objectives, and it was used as a diagnostic tool (packaging research should not be a beauty contest).

In addition to some basic concept questions, consumers were

FIGURE 23-3

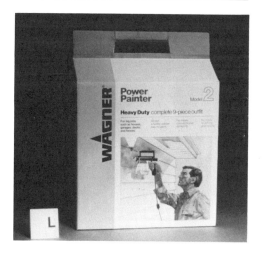

FIGURE 23-4

asked to evaluate the four alternatives in ways designed to determine the effectiveness of each in communicating the product concept, product attributes, and maximum value perception. Figure 23–5 shows a sample of the questions and the ratings for each concept. Package design "L" clearly scored highest on many attributes, but one other

FIGURE 23–5
Consumer Design Inquiry

Package which Best Fits Concept

Design	Percent
H	17
J	6
L	43
N	34

Attribute	Design Ratings			
	H	J	L	N
Easiest to use	36%	18%	58%	11%
Give the most professional results	24	11	51	23
Would be best for my needs	31	6	48	23
Would work the best	27	13	48	29
Most expensive	9	12	5	79
Least expensive	29	43	21	7
Save the most time	28	11	67	10
Best value for the money	19	9	30	47
Has the most power for the job	19	18	32	40
Make buying easiest	31	8	38	39
Easiest to understand	33	17	33	31
Would look at first in a store	18	7	27	56
Make buying hardest	19	38	17	27
Best looking	14	13	19	61
Most informative	25	6	43	36
Explains it is a complete kit	23	5	21	60

concept (design "N") scored highest on the key value question, "Best value for the money," as well as the general graphic impression, "Would look at first in a store."

Refine Design. This illustrates that the value of good market research is to provide management with a diagnostic tool to aid in good judgment; research is not a substitute for management judgment. In this situation, judgment indicated that design concept "L" best communicated the packaging objectives but needed to be refined with stronger graphics, typestyle, and photography to give a greater impact and higher perceived value. A decision was also made to continue through the process of retesting the refined design in order to insure that improvement was achieved, to use as a final check against objectives, and to use for additional information necessary to finalize all other panels of the package.

Retest. Figure 23–6 shows key results of the retest procedure using the current packaging as a control and evaluating the degree of improvement the new design achieved. The retest clearly shows achieve-

---

FIGURE 23–6
Design Refinement

Package design which best fits concept
   Current   18%
   New   82
Impressions of product attributes

Product Attribute	Impression	
	Current	*New*
Would be easiest to use	51%	89%
Would give the most professional results	44	89
Give the most for the money	23	89
Would be best for my needs	23	83
Includes everything to complete the job	11	92
Would work the best	41	88
Is most expensive	29	82
Would save the most time	34	91
Is least expensive	66	43
Has the most power for the job	45	88
Would be the best value for the money	27	89
Would make buying easiest	37	86
Is easiest to understand	23	84
Would look at first in the store	22	78
Would make buying hardest	67	40
Is best looking	31	82
Is most informative	8	92

Current versus new

Price Value Rating	Current @$89	New @$99
Excellent value	2%	14%
Good value	13	38
Just a fair value	21	28
Not too good a value	37	12
Not a good value at all	27	8

ment of each major packaging objective, including a dramatic increase in perceived value, even at a $10-higher price point.

This research technique is just one of many that could be used depending on the magnitude and importance of the project. Other degrees of research sophistication could include store "test lab" techniques, visual impact and eye recognition tests using advanced physiological measurement techniques, as well as live test markets. Regardless of the research technique utilized, keep in mind that research is a tool whose constructive use depends on the skill of the manager.

Design Specifications. The next step is to finalize the design specifications. A complete appearance prototype of the package should be executed and available to ensure that the design integrity is maintained through the execution and start-up manufacturing stages. Areas to watch and evaluate against the design prototype include color matching, photography and illustrations, graphic design, quality of printing and typestyles, size and shape, copy blocking and layout, and material. Detailed specifications should be documented and, in many cases, actual engineering drawings and bills of material developed. Also obtain final legal approvals at this stage.

Durability Check. Another useful check at this point is a durability test on a prototype to ensure that the package maintains the desired appearance in the store. A test could be developed to actually ship a sample unit through the distribution channel into cooperating retailers (the ultimate test, of course, would be to have the U.S. postal system handle the product!). If possible, a test in the manufacturing environment should be developed to head off any potential problems. A typical surprise is to discover that your primary brand identification or product illustration becomes an attractive target for factory workers stamping shipping labels and date stamps on cartons.

Finished Art. Producing finished art and final photography is the next step in package design. This is a field requiring graphics and production expertise, and a number of technical publications are available for further information.

Production Planning. Production planning can become a very critical step in package design since even a minor change in a package generally results in a new part number, with the resulting effect on many established systems and procedures in manufacturing and engineering. The critical marketing input here is to do a complete selling job throughout the organization. Make sure that the various functions

FIGURE 23–7
Typical Timetable

Activity	Week																				
	Start	1	2	3	4	5	6	7	8	9	10	11	12	13	14	15	16	17	18	19	20
Organize materials	----	----																				
Marketing objectives and definition			----	----																		
Retail audit store selection			----	----																		
Retail audit photography					----	----																
Product concept strategy check				----	----																	
Brand name consistency check				----	----																	
Package design concepts						----	----	----														
Test format									----	----												
Package design comprehensives for test										----												
Package design test												----	----									
Test evaluation													----	----								
Package design recommendations and prototypes														----	----							
Design specifications																----						
Internal selling and production planning																----	----	----	----	----	----	----
Finished art/photography																	----	----				
External selling																		----	----	----	----	----
Production start																						X

involved with implementing the change fully understand and are committed to the change and the reasons for it.

Introduction. Introducing the program to the outside world and merchandising it is the next critical step. Your sales force and your distribution channels must be sold on the new packaging. No matter how good it is, it is still a change; and any change is disruptive to established organizations and habits (not to mention the problems with disposition of old field inventory, sales samples, etc.). A careful plan must be generated for phasing in the new packaging, complete with supporting public relations activity and sales aids.

Follow-up. The final action step is to follow up and track results against your objectives. Track and evaluate if desired distribution expansion has occurred, if desired shelf exposure is achieved, if consumer awarenesss and perception of value has improved, and ultimately, if desired sales and profit growth has occurred.

This total action timetable may take as long as four to five months to the point of final design recommendations and prototypes, followed by as much as another two to four months' production lead time. Figure 23–7 shows a sample timetable with typical leadtimes for each step in the process.

SUMMARY

This has been a comprehensive discussion of a large-scale packaging effort. Many projects may be smaller in scope, but they should always include the following key marketing practices:

1. Do the necessary homework—analyze the situation, carefully define the marketing problem.
2. Check to ensure that you have clearly defined your marketing and business objectives—if you are unsure of your goals, any package will get you there.
3. Check your marketing strategy and the product positioning—if the product is wrong, packaging won't fix it.
4. Clearly define what the package design should accomplish.
5. Hire the best creative resource possible and give them clear guidance and a healthy dose of freedom.
6. Test with consumers—against objectives, not a beauty contest; combine good management judgment with consumer research.
7. Sell the change to the organization that has to implement it.
8. Sell the change to your distribution channel.

Throughout every step of the process, remember that the consumer is the key to successful design. Your product and company are what the consumer perceives them to be. Your package must make sure that consumers perceive what you want; and only consumers can tell you if you're successful. Design your package to treat them with intelligence, respect, clarity, and creativity, and they'll buy.

REFERENCES

Gage, Theodore J. "1980s: It's the Do-It-Yourself Package." *Advertising Age,* August 9, 1982, p. M12.

Kelsey, Robert J. *Packaging in Today's Society.* New York: St. Regis Paper, 1978.

Kesler, Lori. "Shopping around for a Design." *Advertising Age,* December 28, 1981, section 2.

Miller, Bryan. "Successes in Food Packaging." *New York Times,* April 14, 1982, p. C–1.

————, eds. *Packaging Design.* Locust Valley, New York: PBC International, 1982.

Reis, Al, and Jack Trout. *Positioning: The Battle for Your Mind.* New York: Warner Books, 1981.

24

PLANNING FOR COOPERATIVE ADVERTISING

by
Robert F. Young

Northeastern University

INTRODUCTION

This chapter will review some of the problems and opportunities presented by cooperative advertising. Following a few definitions, the text will discuss who should use co-op and will provide a few guidelines to determine to what extent a firm should emphasize its usage. Following, there is a brief outline of what objectives a firm should set for its own co-op program. For firms anticipating establishing co-op programs, the chapter will then talk about potential problems that might be encountered. Last, recommendations for management planning and guidelines which should prove useful for the operating manager will be offered.

OVERVIEW

Categories of Cooperative Advertising

Cooperative advertising is advertising communications whose sponsorship and cost is shared by more than one party. There are three principal categories of cooperative advertising: horizontal, ingredient-producer, and vertical.

Horizontal cooperative advertising refers to advertising sponsored in common by a group of retailers. Normally, the participating retailers are franchised or quasi-franchised dealers for a branded durable good. Advertising by a group of local dealers for a particular brand of automobile and advertising by local jewelers selling a specific brand of watch are examples of horizontal cooperative advertising. This particular form of cooperative advertising is not broadly employed for several reasons. Often retailers in a particular trading area are reluctant to cooperate with one another for competitive reasons. Additionally, most retail stores do not normally feature just one product or one brand in their advertising but rather prefer to run advertisements with a broader appeal.

Ingredient-producer cooperative advertising is supported by raw materials manufacturers. The objective of such programs is to help establish a branded end product incorporating a (different) branded ingredient produced by the material manufacturer. Its co-op funds are used to support advertising for both the consumer final goods manufacturer and the retailers of the product. An example is the cooperative advertising Du Pont used to develop the Du Pont 501 nylon brand for household carpeting.

Vertical cooperative advertising is initiated and implemented by retailers and partially paid for by a single or several manufacturers. This form of cooperative advertising is normally part of an overall program of promotional support that an individual manufacturer offers to retailers. Such programs often include suggested advertisement formats, materials for producing advertisements (mats), schedules of the manufacturer's national advertising to facilitate retailer tie-ins to the national program, and schedules of dollar allowances available; they may also include other related promotional materials (for example, point-of-purchase displays).

Vertical cooperative advertising is the most prevalent of the three types and is used by the widest number of manufacturers. It is the primary focus of this chapter.

Mechanics of Vertical Cooperative Advertising Programs

In vertical cooperative advertising arrangements, the retailer typically designs the advertisement (since it is the retailer's advertisement) and places it in the local media. Sometimes the advertisement will feature the store and a single manufacturer's products; often it will feature the store and the products of a number of manufacturers. After the advertisement has run, the retailer then requests reimbursement from the manufacturer in accordance with some preestablished schedule.

The amount of sharing often is determined on the basis of a percentage of media cost. A common arrangement is for a manufacturer to reimburse the retailer for 50 percent of the media expense. However, it should be pointed out that rates higher than 50 percent are found frequently, and lower ones occasionally. In addition, the manufacturer usually establishes an upper-dollar limit for reimbursement, most commonly based upon a percentage of annual (or monthly) merchandise purchases. Thus a manufacturer's hypothetical co-op allowance policy might be, "Our company will reimburse your store for 50 percent of media cost, up to 3 percent of last year's purchases of our merchandise."

Co-op programs used by most manufacturers include detailed restrictions, covenants, and requirements. Among these is often a specific request that the store buy and/or display certain quantities of merchandise. There are usually requirements that advertisements be of a certain size, that the manufacturer's brand name or logo be displayed, or that certain product features be included in the advertising copy. Normally, detailed verification procedures are required for reimbursement. In the case of newspaper advertisements, this usually calls for submitting a tear sheet of the ad. For the broadcast media the requirements often call for an affidavit from the station regarding costs and time of broadcast.

Classification of Cooperative Advertising

In many respects, cooperative advertising may be viewed as both sales promotion and advertising. As a sales promotion device, co-op is used to stimulate immediate buying response. It activates the consumer to actual purchases. It likewise takes on some of the characteristics of national advertising. It can contribute to brand awareness and help to develop an overall image for the brand name.

Figure 24–1 shows co-op's position relative to brand-sponsored advertising and sales promotion.

Distinctive Aspects of Cooperative Advertising

While co-op does resemble the above-mentioned communications tools, it also has some distinctive characteristics of its own:

1. Manufacturers partially pay for advertising over which they do not have direct control. On the other hand, retailers partially pay for advertisements that must adhere to certain guidelines that are drawn up by another business firm. This can create tension between the two organizations which may affect other facets of their business relationship. Specifically, the sharing of costs and messages between two organizations often results in conflict regarding message content. There is also occasional dispute regarding reimbursement arrangements from the manufacturer to the retailer.

2. In cooperative advertising arrangements, the flow of money is from supplier to customer, the reverse of what is normally true. This means that the supplier (manufacturer) is in a difficult position because

FIGURE 24–1

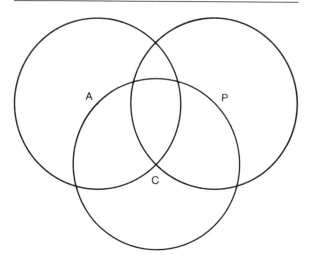

A = Brand-sponsored advertising
P = Sales promotion
C = Cooperative advertising

the goodwill of the customer (retailer) must be maintained for the manufacturer's larger purposes of overall retail marketing.

3. Cooperative advertising is both a consumer promotion tool and a trade promotion tool. While money flows to the retailer to influence merchandising support decisions, it is also intended ultimately to influence consumers through the running of advertising messages.

4. In the advertisements that result from cooperative advertising agreements, both of the sponsoring businesses present a marketing message. There is normally a brand message for the manufacturer's product plus a message from the sponsoring retailer. This fact results in a more complicated information-processing challenge for the recipient. We know very little about how people differentially respond to such a dual-signature advertisement.

5. There are very few formal evaluation methods for assessing co-op's effectiveness. The usual advertising tracking and evaluation services offer no systematic way of helping managers evaluate co-op's effectiveness.

Relative Importance of Co-op

While firms of every size and description use co-op, it is, in fact, relatively more productive for some firms than others. In trying to decide co-op's importance relative to other available marketing tools, the marketing manager can look at both the firm's market and the nature of the product being advertised. Figure 24–2 depicts consumer behavior, product characteristic, and market structure dimensions that

---

FIGURE 24–2
Conditions Defining the Relative Importance of Cooperative Advertising

---

Retailer-dependent marketing Cooperative advertising plays significant role in the marketing mix	*Manufacturer-dominated marketing* Cooperative advertising plays a lesser role in the marketing mix
Shopping goods	Convenience goods
Infrequently purchased goods	Frequently purchased goods
Relatively expensive	Relatively inexpensive
Considered purchase	Impulse purchase
Purchase for ego enhancement	Utilitarian purchase
Brand loyalty low	Brand loyalty high
Personal-service retailing	Self-service retailing
Selective distribution	Broad distribution

---

may prove useful as the manager is trying to decide the proportional weight to place upon co-op. The further a company or a brand is to the left on each of these scales, the more cooperative advertising will tend to be a relatively significant part of the communications mix. For firms that fall to the right, other promotional tools will probably overshadow the value of cooperative advertising.

Another way to view the generalization implied above is that marketing communications programs should coincide roughly with consumers' information needs. If the potential customer is strongly brand loyal and knows precisely where to buy a particular product (e.g., Heinz ketchup at Safeway), there is less need for information. A cooperatively sponsored ad will certainly stimulate some sales, but co-op is not one of the brand's major strategic weapons. On the other hand, in the uncertainty surrounding the purchase of a product such as bed sheets for the master bedroom, potential customers look for local promotional information in a very focused information search. They purchase such products infrequently, have substantial ego involvement in the choice decision, and anticipate a certain degree of expert help at the store level. In those cases co-op would most likely play a very significant role in selling the consumer. Conceivably it should be the *most* heavily weighted item in the marketing budget.

Objectives for Cooperative Advertising

To understand further why co-op is used so extensively by some companies, it is useful to explore the tasks that companies seek to accomplish with this marketing tool.

As would be expected, the most often mentioned purposes of cooperative advertising are to create demand for a company's product and to stimulate sales at both the trade and the consumer levels. However, other strategic objectives are often pursued. These goals or objectives can be arranged in the matrix shown in Figure 24–3. Intended audience (consumer and trade) and time horizon (short-term and long-term) are the two dimensions of the matrix.

FIGURE 24–3
Objectives for Cooperative Advertising

		Intended Audience	
		Consumer	*Trade*
TIME HORIZON	*Short-Term*	Immediate purchase Establish price and location	Sell in General influence Competitive parity
	Long-Term	Brand message reminder and reinforcement Image	Trade relationships Position in merchandising mix

---

Short-Term Objectives. The reason for using cooperative advertising that is most frequently mentioned by marketing executives is to motivate immediate sales at the retail level. The reason that co-op is effective for this purpose is that it results in retail advertisements that are specific with respect to a product and brand, the place where it is offered for sale, and its retail price. As such, a cooperative advertisement is highly informational; and, like retail advertisements in general, it tends to project a sense of immediacy to the consumer. The copy in store advertisements often contains limited-time price reductions. The realization that retail discounts are time-bound adds to consumers' perceptions of the need for immediacy. They know the store, they may even be used to shopping there, and they understand that a purchase today can mean savings.

To further understand manufacturers' objectives it is useful to explore how co-op works at the consumer level. Hierarchical models of consumer behavior, borrowed from the behavioral sciences, add some rigor and insight to intuitive concepts of this process. Several such schemes are in use today, with the most familiar being the following five-step model. This scheme posits that consumers move sequentially through several different stages on their path to a purchase:

Awareness → Knowledge → Liking → Preference → Action

In this stage model, each step depends upon the previous one and is a necessary condition for the next. Presumably, the potential customer moves through this process as a result of marketing activities and/or informal communication. Eventually, if the product being promoted satisfies the consumer's necessary conditions and compares satisfactorily with the competitor's product, a purchase results.

An application of this model to cooperative advertising could look like the following:

Awareness Knowledge	Desire Action
Liking	
National advertising	Local advertising (co-op)

Passage of time →

Here the steps in the sequence have been divided into two information-related clusters; one is related to national advertising, the other to local or cooperative advertising. The idea is that national media advertising, sponsored solely by manufacturers, is the primary influence in moving consumers to consider the brand and helps develop brand knowledge and brand preference. Later, when consumers decide that they will actually make a purchase, they undertake a short-term and local information search. At this juncture, local retailer advertising (co-op) supplies the consumer with the information they seek. Brands being offered, specific prices, and store location are all shown in those communications, thus helping to motivate the actual purchase.

This model helps clarify why many manufacturers prefer co-op when seeking short-term sales results. Specific buying information for the consumer, accompanied by a trigger for immediate action (for example, time-bound prices), nearly always constitutes the key copy points in co-op advertisements. Retailer advertisements meet the information needs of consumers as they move through the final steps of a purchase decision, and they achieve a congruence of information and information needs that would not be possible if manufacturers concentrated solely on national advertising. For example, a GE-sponsored television commercial for refrigerators may effectively focus on particular brand features, but only rarely would it be seen by consumers as a call to action for immediate purchase. In contrast, the expected result of retail advertising is a relatively short-term sales response from consumers at the store level. People in need of a new refrigerator would be much more likely to make a shopping trip as a result of a store-sponsored newspaper advertisement for a particular GE model.

Trade-Directed Short-Term Objectives. An obvious short-term objective of a manufacturer's cooperative advertising program is to persuade retailers to advertise the manufacturer's brands. Local retailer advertising is believed by manufacturers (and retailers) to be effective at generating immediate consumer sales. Knowing this, retailers ask manufacturers for partial reimbursement of their advertising expense.

Co-op funds are often part of a manufacturer's overall promotional program to reimburse retailers for a variety of retailer-initiated marketing tasks. From such promotion and advertising allowance programs, manufacturers expect two general responses from the trade. First, they expect that such allowances will stimulate the specific activity indicated (for example, advertising, display, price reduction). Second, they normally use such programs to sell in merchandise at or above the normal inventory levels. This loading of the trade not only achieves higher wholesale sales but also creates inventory pressure on the particular retailer. With higher-than-normal stocking levels of a particular item, the retail store will tend to put added selling effort behind that item.

Cooperative advertising works as a trade promotion tool because it makes retailers' buying less risky. When a large portion of a store's promotion costs for a particular product is reimbursed, the inventory and merchandising risks are lessened.

In practice, the amount of cooperative advertising reimbursement becomes fairly standardized for any one product category. Regular co-op programs, therefore, do not generally give any one firm a competitive advantage in trade selling. However, co-op does act to develop incremental trade buying volume when augmented co-op reimbursements are used.

Consumer-Directed Long-Term Objectives. Generally, national mass media advertising is employed to accomplish a company's long-term communication goals. For consumer goods such advertising is most often aimed at achieving objectives that precede action or actual purchase. In other words, advertisers may seek to develop awareness for a brand, to explain product benefits, and/or to establish preferences for a product or brand. They expect that national advertising will establish identity and preferences and that other marketing tools (display, sales promotion, retail advertising) will, at a later time, stimulate purchases.

However, in certain situations retailer-sponsored cooperative advertising can also play a role in the long-term communications strategy of the brand. It might be argued that constant repetition of brand and feature messages in local media can reinforce the basic brand image developed elsewhere. The effect of consumer exposure to these frequent product and brand communications can be rather similar to the effect of national advertising. This particular phenomenon is probably most effective with infrequently purchased goods, where local retailer credibility can add to the consumers evaluation of the brand.

Trade-Directed Long-Term Objectives. In many industries cooperative advertising programs are routine elements in the marketing programs of manufacturing firms—they have been offered by most firms for many years. Retailers have come to expect them as normal reimbursements for their merchandising and advertising efforts; and, the design and level of reimbursement of co-op programs have become relatively standardized in these businesses.

Any single manufacturer in such industries finds itself required to meet the industry standard, or something close to it, in order to be accepted as a supplier. Such merchandising supports are, to some extent, "the dues that must be paid." Since cooperative advertising is often viewed as routine, its inclusion in a marketing program may offer no distinctive advantage. Its absence, however, would be considered a serious detriment. A firm without such a program, in industries where they are the accepted norm, would find itself at a substantial strategic disadvantage.

Financial Objective of Cooperative Advertising

One objective of cooperative advertising that does not fit into the matrix shown above is that of cost sharing. Clearly, the manufacturer receives advertising exposure at less than full cost because it shares expenses with the particular store running the advertisement.

Another financial incentive is that co-op advertising space is often bought at the local rate. It has long been a common practice among newspapers to charge a lower rate to local retailers for advertising space than they do to national firms. Thus, by having retailers place the advertising, manufacturers receive advertising exposure at a lower cost than they would have paid on their own.

Summary—Objectives

Cooperative advertising may be used by manufacturing firms to stimulate consumer purchases, to communicate product attributes to reinforce a brand image, to link a brand with a store image, to tell consumers specifically where the brand is available, and to persuade store merchandising executives to stock and merchandise particular goods.

A hierarchy model of consumer decision making provides insight into how cooperative advertising works. In this conception, a two-phase process takes place in consumers' purchase of many products. The first step is a tentative decision regarding the product type and brands that are preferred. In this phase of the decision process, brand awareness and some preliminary brand/product preferences are determined, principally by tools other than cooperative advertising, such as national advertising. Then, in the second phase of the decision process, retailer-sponsored advertisements move the consumer the last step to actual purchase.

PROBLEMS WITH COOPERATIVE ADVERTISING

The rationale for cooperative advertising is that by sharing advertising expenses, both retailer and manufacturer can attain their respective objectives at lower net cost. Despite this seemingly reasonable arrangement, and in spite of evidence of broad general usage, many problems do exist with cooperative advertising. Some of these problems are legal and administrative. But there are vital strategic problems as well, namely, pressures for increased manufacturer budgets for advertising and issues of evaluating the effectiveness of co-op spending.

Legal and Administrative Problems

Much of the discussion found in books on cooperative advertising[1] and articles in the trade press[2] is focused on the legal and procedural prob-

---

[1] See Edward C. Crimmins, *A Management Guide to Cooperative Advertising* (New York: Association of National Advertisors, 1970); and Mosher S. Hutchins, *Cooperative Advertising* (New York: Roland Press, 1953).

[2] See George T. Donahue, "Basics of Co-op Advertising," *Marketing Communications*, March–April 1978; Martin Everett, "One Small Step for Co-op Advertising," *Sales Management*, April 3, 1972, p. 24; and Lois Panosh, "The Co-op Connection," *Merchandising*, May 1976, p. 15.

lems. These will be summarized only briefly here. We recommend the literature cited to any executive facing such problems and wanting a more thorough review of these important aspects of planning for cooperative advertising.

Legal Problems. Cooperative advertising allowances and the form they take are regulated by the Federal Trade Commission under provisions of the Robinson–Patman Act. The principal aim of these regulations is equal availability of cooperative advertising funds. Hence, they state that manufacturers must "treat their customers fairly and without discrimination and not use such allowances to disguise discriminatory price discounts."[3]

To comply with this particular regulation, companies are obligated to inform all competing retailers of any co-op offers and to ensure that alternatives are operationally available to all. For example, when a manufacturer offers a large department store a special cooperative allowance on a particular part of its line, this same offer must be made to all stores in the trading area that carry that line. Of course, there is no requirement that all retailers avail themselves of a particular co-op offer made by a manufacturer. And, in fact, some stores (usually smaller outlets) do not do so. Another provision of these regulations assigns manufacturers the responsibility of verifying that the intended services were rendered by the store and that the reimbursement is reflective of the retailer's true cost.

As a result of these several legal constraints, the programming of cooperative advertising has become highly procedural and legalistic. Complicated rules and definitions have been developed which tend to cause great misunderstanding and disagreements between the parties involved. Therefore, a substantial amount of the literature cited earlier is aimed at clarifying those issues and illustrating appropriate procedures to comply with the law.

Administrative Problems. A related set of problems concerns verification and reimbursements. To conform to the regulations, manufacturers' cooperative advertising plans typically include detailed procedures for retailers' submission of advertising claims.

Typically, when a retailer runs a cooperatively sponsored advertisement, it must send a tear sheet along with a form and transmittal letter to the manufacturer, requesting reimbursement. This flow of information and subsequent cash is the reverse of the relationship that

---

[3] Federal Trade Commission, *Guides for Advertising Allowances and Other Merchandising Payments and Services* (Washington, D.C.: U.S. Government Printing Office, 1972).

normally exists between the two parties (that is, regarding the product). These roles, awkward for both sides, contribute in part to the difficulty of reimbursement. Manufacturers are accustomed to receiving money, not sending it to retailers. Likewise, if a manufacturer has a disagreement with a retailer, the manufacturer may find it difficult to resolve the problem because of its interest in maintaining good relationships for the greater purpose of selling merchandise.

As was mentioned previously, the highly legalistic and complicated nature of most manufacturers' programs causes constant disagreements. In most instances the manufacturer must handle a large number of relatively small reimbursement requests on a regular basis. It is not unusual for a manufacturer to process reimbursements for several thousand retailers in a given week. Due to regulations by the government and the firm itself, on a typical day a company might find itself disputing several dozen payments, none of which involves more than $100. This administrative chore obviously creates operating headaches. The executive is committed to enforcing the provisions of the firm's program with some diligence. Yet the details of the thousands of transactions are overwhelming, and, through it all, good relationships must be maintained.

Partly to alleviate the legal and administrative problems, many firms use the services of the Advertising Checking Bureau. This company implements and administers many firms' verifications and reimbursement programs and thus introduces the objectivity of a third-party specialist. Nevertheless, it is still incumbent upon the sponsoring firm to structure the program properly and to set the legal and administrative policies.

Strategic Problems with Cooperative Advertising

Strategic problems with cooperative advertising can be categorized into three general areas. The first is the continuing trade and competitive pressures for increased manufacturer spending on co-op. The second is the resulting dilemma of trading off co-op increases against national advertising budgets. The third problem area concerns the effectiveness of cooperative advertising. Managers question whether co-op achieves the intended results and worry that there does not seem to be any known mechanism for assessing co-op's effectiveness.

Pressures for Increased Manufacturer Co-op Budgets. Co-op expenditures as a percentage of sales, total advertising, and promotion have generally been on the rise for the last 5 to 10 years. This trend is similar to that found in recent investigations into the pattern of spending for all sales promotion.[4] As Strang found with sales promotion, managers have learned that co-op can produce fairly immediate results. Thus they have tended to increase expenditures on co-op as a means to achieve short-term sales goals.

The increased pressure for more co-op spending comes both from the trade and from manufacturer's internal organizational responses to the trade. But trade pressure is not limited to any single manufacturer in a particular product category. Retailers' own cost pressures often lead them to urge other manufacturers to match special co-op programs offered by any single manufacturer. One consequence is a competitively driven escalation in co-op budgets, sometimes linked with only modest long-term increases in manufacturers' sales.

Cooperative Advertising versus National Advertising. A further consequence of higher co-op budgets is the trade-off problem many manufacturers see between co-op advertising and national advertising. Most executives think in terms of some overall level of spending for their firm's marketing activities. Therefore, when co-op expenditures increase substantially, it is often at the expense of national advertising. This is harmful when there is a clear need for sustained mass media advertising to support the brand's image or market position. Since this is often the case, a trade-off in favor of co-op can potentially prove detrimental.

Assessing the Effectiveness of Cooperative Advertising. Certainly concerns about the expense of cooperative advertising would be lessened if there were a sure-fire manner to assess its effectiveness. Unfortunately, such an evaluation scheme does not exist. Most executive opinions about co-op's value are based upon general field experience and day-to-day informal observations. Generally, managers in most firms which extensively use co-op agree that it is a very valuable part of the marketing mix. The problem is that it is often hard to see *how effective* it is, *how long* the effect lasts, and *how efficient* the expenditure is. Executives often do not know how to determine the answers to these questions.

These effectiveness concerns can further be divided as follows:

Sales effectiveness. Although a short-term sales increase is the single most important objective managers associate with co-op, there does not appear to be any accepted way of measuring or evaluating co-op's effectiveness as a sales-generating tool over the longer term. Companies sometimes try to analyze co-op's effectiveness by comparing

---

[4] Roger Strang, "Sales Promotion—Fast Growth, Faulty Management," *Harvard Business Review,* July–August 1976, pp. 115–24.

co-op expenditures with factory-level sales of a brand. Typically, this is done by looking at the statistical association between sales figures and co-op expenditures over several years. When the measures are positively correlated, the conclusion is drawn that co-op has been a cause of increasing sales levels. Similarly, when there is little or no statistical correlation, it is concluded that co-op was not a contributor to incremental sales. While such analysis certainly should be done, the conclusion can be accepted only with reservations. For the analysis to be valid one would have to assume that the historic figures used represent situations where other contributing factors to sales—such as national advertising, sales force effort, and consumer promotions—are held constant from year to year; that is, only in co-op do major changes occur. Moreover, competitive co-op activity would also have to remain constant. A clean, controlled experimental situation like this is, of course, highly unlikely. Thus the executive has to ask what other causes may have contributed to sales fluctuations (including competitive activity) and what the relative contribution of co-op was. Unfortunately, one firm's data on co-op spending and wholesale sales alone do not provide the answer.

A second caution must be entered regarding the application of this kind of numerical analysis, especially to cooperative advertising. This is the issue of the direction of causality. It is easy to conclude that when sales revenues go up simultaneously with co-op spending, then the increased advertising caused the sales. However, most co-op reimbursement plans contractually establish that co-op will increase (or decrease) commensurately with retailers' purchases. Thus, a valid argument can be made that sales volume may cause co-op expenditure levels rather than the other way around.

Attempts at statistical assessment of co-op's effects upon sales should not be abandoned. However, experience has shown that such analysis is of limited validity and is, at best, only a partial answer to the sales effectiveness assessment issue.

Effectiveness with respect to communications objectives. Beyond immediate sales effects, executives want cooperatively funded advertising to contribute to broader communications goals. They want to link retail advertising messages to national advertising themes in order to reinforce with consumers the brand image and manufacturer messages developed in national advertising.

The effectiveness of cooperative advertisements with respect to these communications goals is dependent on several factors—notably media choice and the specific content and look of the retail advertisements. The control, or lack of control, of these elements produces problems for executives in manufacturing firms. Since many co-op advertisements are largely designed by retailers, the manufacturer has limited ability to influence these communication factors. Also, of course, it is difficult to evaluate these effects.

Content and look of newspaper advertisements. Executives believe that copy points and layout are important determinants of retail advertising effectiveness. However, experience has shown that mass merchandisers often try to crowd many products into newspaper advertisements. This cluttered look, it is believed, detracts from the brand's selling message for some product categories. While this advertising policy is perfectly understandable, given the marketing strategy of many mass merchandisers, it does sometimes limit the effectiveness of brand messages.

The problem of conflicting objectives. Both retailers and manufacturers hold as an objective to sell the merchandise displayed in the advertisement. Despite this common goal there is a wide latitude for conflict. Stores want to develop foot traffic and to sell any merchandise currently on display. Only secondarily are they concerned about the particular item in the advertisement (although obviously they would like to sell that also). On the other hand, manufacturers want to sell their particular products and develop their brand image. They are only remotely interested in the welfare of the total retail enterprise.

These conflicts affect the manner in which advertisements are laid out, the amount and type of body copy, and the particular merchandise displayed. Such decisions are sometimes made in the merchant's best interests and may not be congruent with the manufacturer's.

WHAT MANAGERS CAN DO

Following are some guidelines for managers as they review their co-op programs. By addressing these issues within the context of a particular brand or product line, executives can begin an audit of their firm's co-op program.

1. *Controlling expenditures.* There are several strategies managers can consider in attempting to control accelerating co-op expenditures. These all involve placing limits on the availability of funds in terms of time, items, or media choice. Therefore, they may lessen the overall attractiveness to retailers of the manufacturer's program. However, this risk can be reduced if a manufacturer develops and implements these strategies cautiously and with consideration of the special roles the retailer plays in marketing the products.

First, a manufacturer can stipulate that co-op reimbursements are available *only during certain time periods.* This both limits the financial costs of the program and allows the manufacturer to coordinate the brand's marketing activities for maximum effectiveness. For example, if all of a brand's stores concentrate the brand's retail advertising during several short periods, the advertising could achieve substantially increased communications impact with consumers (compared to longer periods at somewhat lower per period spending levels). Further, the manufacturer's total annual co-op expenditure would probably be less, due to the fact that some retailers would not advertise as much in a limited time period as they would if given the opportunity to advertise throughout the year.

This *time limit* method of controlling co-op expenses has obvious drawbacks. Except during the stipulated periods, the retailer's advertising efforts for the manufacturer will probably be minimal under such a plan. For brands that call for continual advertising exposure in the local marketplace, such programs would weaken needed retailer advertising and merchandising support.

Second, manufacturers can specify that *only certain items* (for example, lines, models, styles) can be included in advertisements receiving co-op reimbursements. For instance, a firm can decide that only those products with higher than normal profit margins will be eligible for co-op reimbursement. Alternatively, a rule can be established that special promotional models (presumably with low profit margins) will not be eligible for co-op. Such a scheme obviously limits the opportunities for the retailer and holds down the amount of reimbursable advertising. It also gives the manufacturer the opportunity to direct the cooperating retailers' resources toward a preferred part of the product line.

In a sense, this *item limit* method of controlling co-op is another way of putting differential emphasis on specific elements of the marketing mix. In cases in which it may be advantageous to offer the lowest price possible on certain promotional items, the firm can decide to price these items below its standard profitability levels and allow no co-op reimbursements. This decision implies that for these offerings price is more important than promotion.

The obvious drawback of the item limit scheme is that some portions of the product line will receive little or no retailer advertising support. Such a decision is one of *basic marketing strategy*. It should be considered only when major parts of the product line will continue to be profitable with only minimal retail advertising support, or when there are other apparent motivations (for example, higher than average margins) for retailers to want to use their own funds for such activity. If such an item limit scheme is possible, total co-op expenditures will probably be reduced. Furthermore, the manufacturer receives retail support on those parts of the product line where support is most desirable.

Limiting media choice is a third way that manufacturers can curtail their increasing co-op expenditures. Historically, most cooperative advertising funding has been channeled into newspapers. However, many manufacturers also permit the use of other media for cooperative advertisements, and recently there has been an increase in the use of local television. Some media may work more effectively than others to achieve a manufacturer's objectives for its cooperative advertising program. For instance, in some product/market situations it is possible that advertising in suburban shoppers' guides will not contribute to a manufacturer's communications objectives. Similarly, the broadcast media may be inefficient in reaching the desired target markets for some other manufacturers. Thus, by disallowing particular media choices, a firm could increase its advertising efficiency while at the same time reducing its total co-op expenditure.

The *media limit* approach to containing co-op expenditures has the disadvantage of reducing retailers' flexibility. For obvious reasons they want as much latitude as possible. Often they understand the media efficiencies in their local markets better than would a geographically distant manufacturing firm. Thus, placing a constraint on the choice of media type should be done only after very careful consideration, including that of media complementarity to the manufacturer's national advertising program. Such limits potentially could inhibit an actual increase in efficiency or effectiveness.

One further way for manufacturers to effect cost savings in co-op is through *tighter administrative controls* over reimbursements. There are considerable differences in how stringently manufacturers enforce their own rules. It is apparent that in some situations manufacturers are very liberal in the standards with which they enforce their co-op policies and practices. A careful review by top executives of policy implementation could potentially yield cost-saving opportunities.

Some words of caution are in order with regard to this strategy. An overly legalistic enforcement of co-op regulations can easily lead to endless haggling and negotiating between manufacturers and retailers. Obviously, such disputes can be counterproductive to a desired positive working relationship between the two parties.

2. *Establish objectives for cooperative advertising as precisely as possible.* Decide what communications and trade objectives are being sought with the particular co-op advertising program. This review should include consideration of short-term and long-term aims. Likewise, it is important to establish the balance between trade-related goals and goals associated with the attitudes and behavior of ultimate consumers.

3. *For most effective results, use co-op in conjunction with strong national advertising.* In many situations it is difficult to develop product benefits or brand preference through the exclusive use of co-op. Many managers know that a co-op advertisement can frequently trigger a sale. However, co-op advertisements work best when the potential consumer has prior knowledge and/or preference for the advertised brand. This brand-franchise development is often most effectively accomplished by means of manufacturer-sponsored advertising.

4. *Do not consider budget decisions for cooperative advertising and (sole-sponsored) national advertising as direct trade-offs.* The objectives of each program, while related, are different. By treating the two decisions separately, manufacturers can make better judgments about how to achieve specific brand objectives with both consumers and the trade.

5. *Ask to what extent the product or brand is retailer dependent.* Executives should assess how important retailers' marketing or selling efforts are to the brand's success. Co-op is a relatively more important part of the marketing mix in situations where manufacturers are relatively more dependent upon retailers' selling or merchandising activities.

6. *Assess whether consumers seek product-choice information from retailers' communications or from manufacturers' communications.* For products where there is a strong consumer reliance on information from retailers, co-op will tend to be relatively more important.

7. *Emphasize cooperative advertising when a linkage with retailers' image in the local market is important.* When there is a need for image "rub-off" from the retailer to the manufacturer, the latter should attempt to accrue part of the retailer's goodwill in the local market. Cooperative advertising can be used to stimulate this linkage.

8. *Look at why retailers are not utilizing a firm's co-op program enough.* The reimbursement rate may be too low, the rules may be too rigid or complex, or company personnel may not be facilitating co-op usage. Alternatively, the collateral materials may not be attractive or may not be tied to the company's overall merchandising campaign. *Implementation and administrative details of co-op programs are important:*

- Guidelines and rules for retailers should be as simple as possible. They should be explained clearly and often.
- Whenever possible, co-op materials should incorporate themes or copy points from national advertising campaigns. As appropriate, other marketing themes (new-product introductions, seasonal promotions, display ideas, and so on) should be used in this material. Obviously, the co-op materials should make merchandising sense.

- Sales personnel should be well versed in both the merchandising advantages and the implementation details of the program. They must help merchandise the program.
- Managers should insure that reimbursement procedures are reasonably uncomplicated and that company office personnel are equipped to implement them expeditiously.

9. *Ask why cooperative advertising programs do not seem to be yielding results commensurate with expenditure levels.* Are the firm's funds being used:

- In ways that do not fit with the firm's *product strategy?*
- In *media* that are not considered effective?
- At disadvantageous *times of the year?*
- In *creative formats* (for example, advertisement size, content) that are inconsistent with the brand's communication objectives?

To remedy these perceived shortcomings, consider the limits such as those mentioned above:

- An *item limit* can focus both the manufacturer's and the retailer's resources on the most profitable, or salable, items in the product line.
- A *media limit* strategy might channel local promotion into those advertising vehicles most likely to achieve results.
- By establishing a *time limit* procedure both parties' efforts will become concentrated for potentially greater impact.
- To improve creative execution at the retail level, review the *variety, innovativeness, and attractiveness of supporting materials* such as mats and other artwork. Retailers should not be expected to work with material that might detract from their image in the local marketplace.

10. *Realize that to be most effective, cooperative advertising must indeed be cooperative.* Cooperative advertising represents a blending of the resources of two organizations, each with different goals but with certain shared aims as well. Appreciating what each party contributes to accomplishing these shared objectives and recognizing each party's ambitions will lead to the mutual benefits to be derived from a successful cooperative advertising program.

REFERENCES FOR FURTHER READING

Crimmins, Edward C. *A Management Guide to Cooperative Advertising.* New York: Association of National Advertisers, 1970.

Donahue, George T. "Basics of Co-op Advertising." *Marketing Communication,* March–April 1978.

Everett, Martin. "One Small Step for Co-op Advertising." *Sales Management,* April 3, 1972, p. 24.

Federal Trade Commission. *Guide for Advertising Allowances and Other Merchandising Payments and Services."* Washington, D.C.: U.S. Government Printing Office, 1972.

Hutchins, Mosher S. *Cooperative Advertising.* New York: Roland Press, 1953.

Panosh, Lois. "The Co-op Connection." *Merchandising,* May 1976, p. 15.

Strang, Roger A. "Sales Promotion—Fast Growth, Faulty Management." *Harvard Business Review,* July–August 1976, pp. 115–24.

Young, Robert F., and Stephen A. Greyser. *Managing Cooperative Advertising: A Strategic Approach.* Lexington, Mass.: Lexington Books, 1983.

25

PUBLIC RELATIONS AND PUBLICITY

by
Victor Gelb

Victor Gelb, Inc.

PUBLIC RELATIONS—RELATIONS OF AN ORGANIZATION WITH
THE GENERAL PUBLIC THROUGH PUBLICITY

Publicity is just one of the many tools to work with in marketing. How you can most effectively communicate with the public is all public relations, which incorporates publicity.

WITH WHOM DO YOU RELATE—AND WHICH RELATIONSHIPS ARE OF MOST IMPORTANCE TO YOU?

1. *Your customers.* Too often they are taken for granted. Whether your business is big or small, the relationship should be personalized.
2. *Your sales force.* Weekly or monthly newsletters and/or bulletins have great value. Don't have the newsletter written by the order entry people or sales administrator; personalize the newsletter by doing it yourself (or at least make sure it looks that way!)
3. *Trade publications.* Good relations with the trade press range from 5 to 10 on a 10-point scale of importance. In the hardware, housewares, and automotive after-market, it could and should rank in the 8-to-10 range.

4. *The consumer.* The ultimate decision maker as to the success or failure of your efforts is, of course, the consumer. Again, depending upon your product(s), your budget and your ability to relate to the ultimate consumer is of the greatest importance. A good press or good public relations must be worked on. It doesn't just happen. It requires an understanding of what it takes to make it happen. The results are not always measurable—but when they are, they are exciting. You can never have too much good press. You can never go wrong by over-communicating. You can, however, hurt yourself by inadequate or poor communications. Here are some paths to take in developing good communication.

First of all, you're in business to service your customers' needs. Your job is to be sensitive to these needs and to satisfy them better than anyone else. There are many large, successful companies who treat their customers as necessary evils. The only reason they can be aloof and stay successful is because they either have a proprietary product that their customer can't get from anyone else or they have created such a demand by their advertising that their customers can't live without it. *These people are missing the boat by not winning customers' affection as well as their business.*

Make your customer your partner by making him or her feel as though every sales marketing decision that you make has his or her needs as your prime focus. You want your customer to think of your company not as a corporate entity but as a live personality who really understands and appreciates their business. Too often, the only communications that a buyer gets from a factory is a price list, a price increase, and a catalog. People like to do business with people, not names and zip codes or 800 numbers. People contact is the key.

Direct mail is a major public relations tool. A monthly or quarterly newsletter individually addressed to all of the buying influence in each company can be a good investment. It should tell everything that's new in your company (i.e., products, promotions, people, trade show schedules, and new packaging). The best direct mail is personalized and, if possible, written by you in your style. No one knows or should know your customers better than you, so no one should be better equipped to make your customer realize that they are a part of your company—an important part at that, and privy to everything (well, almost everything) you do. To be sure the personal touch approach works, it is imperative that your mailing list is kept current.

In addition to frequent newsletters and special mailings, another approach that can bring you and your reps closer to the buyer is an honorary board of directors. Select those customers who represent 80 percent of your sales to serve on the honorary board. By personal letter appoint them as your honorary directors. You can design special plaques which can be presented by you or one of your sales managers to the buyer. The director's name should be engraved on the plaque as well as the name of his or her company. Each quarter, the director is sent a report, very similar to that which a C.E.O. would send to the directors of the board. Each director should also receive a quarterly dividend in the form of a specialty gift item that would be worth $2 to $6. We used this approach, and the bottom-line result was a unique, personalized relationship between seller and buyer.

The really extra-special company and the really extra-special sales management understand and appreciate good public relations with their customers. It doesn't take much money, and it doesn't always require a public relations agency, but it does require a commitment to the customer. Selling is a people business, and very often the only difference in determining which product or service to buy are the people who provide it. Good public relations can, and often does, make the difference.

DEVELOPING GOOD PR WITH YOUR SALES FORCE

It may not be at the top of the list, but something that should be on your list—particularly if you are working with manufacturer's reps—is a PR effort with your salespeople. Everything from your letterhead to your switchboard operator, from your shipping department to your own buyers, affects your business. Your sales force, in particular, must have pride and confidence in you, your company, and its products.

A weekly or biweekly communication to the sales force alerting them to all that's new in products, plans, and promotions is most important. They should be on the same mailing lists as the trade and consumer publications and receive news releases before they appear in print. The same holds true for copies and/or reprints of feature articles and print ads. Your sales force should be recipients as well as part of your public relations effort.

TRADE PUBLICATIONS—A GREAT OPPORTUNITY

Unless you have a substantial, seven-figure ad budget that can pull your product off the shelf (and most companies don't), your next-best bet is to convince your buyers and customers of your preeminence. The trade press presents an excellent vehicle for this as many industries are blessed with very good trade publications. Editors are often some of the most knowledgeable people in the industry, and many have superb industry contacts that can often help you.

Opportunities to get in print include:

- New appointments to your organization.
- New products.
- New promotions.
- New packaging.
- Revised packaging.
- New point-of-purchase displays.
- Plant expansions.
- Trade show specials.
- Annual forecasts.
- Year-end analysis.
- Annual or seasonal advertising plans.
- Creative marketers with good trade paper relationships can also develop special feature articles on their company.

TRADE SHOWS—ALWAYS A PR OPPORTUNITY

If you are working with a PR agency or any good ad agency, they'll make certain that you have a press kit ready for every trade show. Every trade show gets intensive press coverage, so having your press kit in the pressroom will make it that much easier for them to pick up news about your company. If you really have something exciting, staging your own press conference can pay plenty of dividends. Creating your own news event at a trade show is good PR, too. Some years ago, we decided to use a well-known chimpanzee named "Zippy" as an attraction to our booths at the National Hardware Show at the New York Coliseum. Unfortunately, only a week before at the Automobile Show, a model was mauled by a lion used by one of the exhibitors. As a result, the Coliseum put a ban on live animals of any kind. The chimp and I picketed the Coliseum with a sign claiming the Coliseum was unkind and unfair to chimps. We got good coverage in all media, including local TV.

Another sure-fire PR effort at shows is to use well-known personalities as booth guests. This approach is good for the mass media, the trade press, and for the customers who have their pictures taken with the personalities. During the late 60s and through the mid-70s, we selected an annual "Miss Body Beautiful" to promote our auto body repair materials. Many customers looked forward to each year's show in order to add to their collection of photos taken with the reigning Miss Body Beautiful. Good trade show PR, like anything else, requires advance planning. The boiler plate stuff comes easy if you just do your homework, but the big success comes from being creative.

GETTING TO THE CONSUMER

If you're going to invest in a PR agency, this is the area in which they can do you the most good and cost you the most money. More and more consumer magazines feature either new products or helpful hints as to how products currently on the market can help their readers. There are also syndicated columnists who specialize in featuring that which is new or the "how to" in their area of editorial expertise. The *New York Times, L.A. Times, Chicago Tribune,* and other major dailies have their own columnists on special subjects. A host of published free-lance writers also represent excellent opportunities for special stories. When introducing unusual new products, radio and TV news editors are good prospects, too. Good PR agencies know where to go and how to package the releases to get you maximum exposure.

MERCHANDISING YOUR "PRESS"

This is almost as important as getting into print or on the air. Reprints and publicizing the coverage that you get to your customers (distributors, retailers, etc.) is of vital importance. Most manufacturers have small ad budgets, so putting together an impressive roster of reprints from the magazines, newspapers, radio and TV stations, etc. that feature you and your product go a long way toward convincing one and all that you're a national advertiser and a company with which to be reckoned. We once impressed our customers (buyers) and reps with a 20-foot roll, 20 inches wide, filled with PR clips all printed within one year's time. Our ad/PR budget that year couldn't have been more than $50,000.

Good relations with various publics makes for better business. Develop the relationships wisely, with clear goals and strategies, so you can impart your message as well as your company's personality to your public.

26

SALES PROMOTION REQUIREMENTS

by
Kenneth B. Erdman

SALES PROMOTION

There are perhaps as many definitions for sales promotion as there are books on the subject. Each author or recognized authority on sales promotion includes different aspects of marketing under their sales promotion umbrella. Some, at one extreme, include all forms of advertising and personal selling as part of the sales promotion effort, while others narrow the sales promotion concept to those areas beyond traditional advertising mediums and personal sales. To avoid overcomplication of the subject and to facilitate market planning and budgeting, sales promotion could be considered those areas of selling persuasions other than mass media (i.e., radio, television, newspapers, magazines, direct marketing, or outdoor advertising). Even this approach requires some clarification.

Direct mail historically has been included in mass media ranking. In recent years, however, direct mail has been combined with radio, television, and telemarketing to form a new category, direct marketing. For present purposes direct mail can also be considered a facet of sales promotion. In contrast to separating direct mail from other components, specialty advertising is so related to premiums and business gifts that it is included in this consideration of sales promotion. A distinction also has to be made between outdoor advertising (primarily billboards), which is not considered in this chapter, and signs, which will be discussed.

The marketing manager has the following basic sales promotion tools to support the advertising and sales efforts:

- Business gifts
- Catalogs
- Contests
- Coupons
- Direct mail
- Incentives
- Point of purchase
- Premiums
- Public relations
- Sampling
- Seminars and meetings
- Signs
- Specialty advertising
- Technical publications
- Telemarketing
- Trade shows
- Trading stamps

Depending on product or service, some of the aforementioned categories may not be applicable to every company. All too frequently, however, and particularly among smaller companies, the marketing plan does not include enough of the available sales promotion tools. Accordingly, this chapter is designed to serve as a guide, checklist, and motivator for using sales promotion by those concerned with the advertising and sales of both products and services.

DIRECT MAIL

Marketers of the 80s have tended to include direct mail as a segment of the broad term *direct response* or the even broader term *direct marketing*. But there is a belief that a mailed piece(s) deserves to stand on its own, as opposed to the direct response/direct marketing concept that suggests a completed sale direct to the user (without benefit of other distributor functions) through mail and other means such as radio, TV, telemarketing, newspapers and magazines, inserts (stuffers), etc.[1]

---

[1] Direct Mail Advertising Association, a trade association, was formed in 1917. It changed its name in the 70s to Direct Mail/Marketing Association to reflect the expanded media. Again, in 1982, the name was changed to Direct Marketing Association—excluding any reference to "mail."

One of the advantages of direct mail is the many situations where it can be used. The Direct Marketing Association has compiled the following list of opportunities to use direct mail:

Situations Where Direct Mail Can Be Helpful

In an Organization

1. *Build morale of employees*—A bulletin or company magazine published regularly, carrying announcements of company policy, stimulating ambition, encouraging thrift, promoting safety and efficiency, will make for greater loyalty among employees.
2. *Securing data from employees*—Letters or questionnaires occasionally directed to employees help cement a common interest in the organization and bring back practical ideas and much useful data.
3. *Stimulating salesmen to greater efforts*—Interesting sales magazines, bulletins, or letters help in unifying a scattered selling organization, in speeding up sales, and in making better salesmen—by carrying success stories and sound ideas that have made sales.
4. *Paving the way for salesmen*—Forceful and intelligent direct mail, persistent and continuous, will create a field of prospective buyers who are live and ready to be sold.
5. *Securing inquiries for salesmen*—Direct mail can bring back actual inquiries from interested prospective customers . . . qualified prospects your men can call upon and sell.
6. *Teaching salesmen "how to sell"*—A sales manual, or a series of messages, will help educate and stimulate salesmen to close more and bigger sales.
7. *Selling stockholders and others interested in your company*—Enclo-

sures with dividend checks, in pay envelopes, and other direct messages will sell stockholders and employees on making a greater use of company products and services, and in suggesting their use to others.

8. *Keeping contact with customers between salesmen's calls*—Messages to customers between salesmen's visits will help secure the maximum amount of business for a firm from each customer.
9. *Further selling prospective customers after a demonstration or salesman's call*—Direct mail emphasizing the superiorities of a product or service will help clinch sales and make it difficult for competition to gain a foothold.
10. *Acknowledging orders or payments*—An interesting letter, folder, or mailing card is a simple gesture which will cement a closer friendship between the seller and his customers.
11. *Welcoming new customers*—A letter welcoming new customers can go a long way toward keeping them sold on a company, its products, and services.
12. *Collecting accounts*—A series of diplomatic collection letters will bring and keep accounts up-to-date, leave the recipients in a friendly frame of mind, and hold them as customers.

Building New Business

13. *Securing new dealers*—Direct mail offers many concerns unlimited

possibilities in lining up and selling new dealers.

14. *Securing direct orders*—Many organizations have built an extremely profitable business through orders secured only with the help of direct mail. Many concerns not presently selling directly by mail can and should do so.

15. *Building weak territories*—Direct mail will provide intensified local sales stimulation wherever you may wish to apply it.

16. *Winning back inactive customers*—A series of direct-mail messages to "lost" customers often revives a large number of them.

17. *Developing sales in territories not covered by salesmen*—Communities unapproachable because of distance, bad transportation schedules, or poor roads offer the alert organization vast possibilities to increase its sales by direct mail.

18. *Developing sales among specified groups*—Direct selling messages, specifically to prospects, in the language they will understand, and in a form that will stimulate action.

19. *Following inquiries received from direct advertising or other forms of advertising*—A series of messages outlining the "reasons why" a product or service should be bought, will help cash in on inquirers whose initial interest was aroused by other media—publications, radio, television, etc.

20. *Driving home sales arguments*—Several mailings, each planned to stress one or more selling points, will progressively educate the prospective customer on the many reasons why he should buy a product or service.

21. *Selling other items in the line*—Mailing pieces, package inserts, or "hand-out" folders will educate customers on products and services other than those they are buying.

22. *Getting products prescribed or specified*—Professional men, such as physicians and dentists, will prescribe a product for their patients if they are correctly educated on its merits and what it will accomplish. Likewise, consumers and dealers will ask for a product by name if they are thoroughly familiar with it.

23. *Selling new type of buyer*—Perhaps there are new outlets through which the product or service might be sold. Direct mail is a powerful tool in the development of new sales channels.

Assisting Present Dealers

24. *Bringing buyer to showroom*—Invitations through letters or printed announcements will bring prospective customers to the showroom or factory.

25. *Helping present dealer sell more*—Assisting the dealer with direct mail and "point-of-purchase" will sell a product or service faster, step up turnover. The right kind of dealer sales aids will win his hearty cooperation.

26. *Merchandising the plans to dealer*—Direct mail can forcefully present and explain merchandising plans to the dealer . . . and show him how to put promotion ideas and material to work as sales builders.

27. *Educating dealers on superiorities of product or service*—Memories are short when it comes to remembering the other fellow's product or service and its superiorities, especially when the manufacturer keeps telling his dealers the benefits and advantages of his product.

28. *Educating retail clerks in the selling of a product*—Clerks are the neck of the retail selling bottle. If they believe in a company and a product, their influence is a powerful aid to sales. If indifferent, they lose their sales-making effectiveness. Direct mail that is friendly, understanding, helpful, and stimulating will enlist their cooperation and raise the sales curve.

29. *Securing information from dealers or dealer's clerks*—Letters, printed messages, a bulletin or a company magazine will bring back helpful data from the individuals who actually sell the product or service . . . information that can be passed along to other dealers or sales clerks to help them sell more.

30. *Referring inquiries from consumer advertising to local dealers*—The manufacturer can use direct mail to refer an inquirer to his local dealer for prompt attention. At the same time, the dealer can be alerted with the details of the prospect's inquiry.

The Consumer

31. *Creating a need or a demand for a product*—Direct mail, consistently used, will stimulate the demand for the product or service and will remind the customer to ask for it by name.

32. *Increasing consumption of a product among present users*—Package inserts, booklets, etc., can be used to educate customers to the full use of the products they buy, especially new benefits and advantages.

33. *Bringing customers into a store to buy*—This applies to retailers. Personal, friendly, cordial, and interesting direct-mail messages, telling about the merchandise and creating the desire to own that merchandise, will bring back past customers, stimulate present patrons, and lure new people to the store.

34. *Opening new charge accounts*— This also applies to retailers. There are many people in every community who pay their bills promptly and do the bulk of their buying where they have accounts. A careful compilation of such a list and a well-planned direct-mail program inviting them to open charge accounts will bring new customers to a store.

35. *Capitalizing on special events*— Direct mail helps retailers capitalize on such events as marriages, births, graduations, promotions, etc. Likewise, letters can be sent to select lists featuring private sales. Other lists and formats can cover general sales.

36. *Building goodwill*—The possibilities of building goodwill and solidifying friendships through direct advertising are unlimited. It's the little handshake through the mail that cements business relationships and holds customers. Certain "reminder" forms also can help build goodwill.

37. *Capitalizing on other advertising*— Direct advertising is the salesmate of all other media. As the "workhorse" among advertising and promotion mediums, it helps the sponsor capitalize on his investment in all visual and audio advertising— especially when initial interest can be given a lift and converted into action and sales.

38. *As a "leader" or "hook" in other forms of advertising*—Publication space, as well as radio and television commercials, are often too limited to tell enough of the story about a product or service to make a sale. Direct mail provides the "leader" or "hook"—in the form of booklets, folders, catalogs, instruction manuals—that other mediums of advertising can only feature, to stimulate action as well as satisfy the inquirer with the full story of a product or service.

39. *Breaking down resistance to a product or a service*—Direct mail helps to overcome resistances in the minds of prospective customers.

40. *Stimulating interest in forthcoming*

events—A special "week" or "day" devoted to the greater use of a product, an anniversary, a new line launched by a dealer, special "openings", and scores of other happenings—can all be promoted by direct mail to produce sales.

41. *Distribution of samples*—There are thousands of logical prospects who could be converted into users of a product if its merits can be proved. Direct mail can help do this by letting prospects convince themselves by actual test . . . provided the product lends itself to sampling by mail.

42. *Announcing a new product, new policy, or new addition*—There is no quicker way to make announcements to specific individuals or groups, to create interest and stimulate sales, than through the personal, action-producing medium—direct mail.

43. *Announcing a new address or change in telephone number*—When these important changes are made, a letter or printed announcement sent through the mail has a personal appeal that will register the message better than any other form of advertising.

44. *Keeping a concern or product "in mind"*—Direct advertising includes many forms of "reminder" advertising—calendars, novelties, etc. Regular mailings help keep the company name in the minds of customers and prospects.

45. *Research for new ideas and suggestions*—Direct advertising research is a powerful force in building sales. Direct mail can be used to find market facts, cut sales fumbling, chart direct, profitable trails

to sales. It furnishes all the important tools for sales research, to discover what, where, how and to whom to sell . . . and at what price.

46. *Correcting present mailing lists*—Householders have an average annual change of 22 percent . . . merchants of 23 percent . . . agents of 29 percent . . . advertising men of 37 percent. Keeping a mailing list up to date is a most important detail. Direct mail can be employed to keep the list accurate, by occasionally asking the customer if his name and address are correct . . . or if there are others in his organization the message should be reaching.

47. *Securing names for lists*—Direct mail can help build mailing lists by securing names of customers and prospects from many sources—such as direct from distributors, salesmen, clerks, stockholders, employees; from people who have access to the names of individuals in specific groups; from recommendations of customers and friends; from special mail surveys, questionnaires, etc.

48. *Protecting patents or special processes*—Shouting forth the ownership of such patents or processes by direct advertising can leave no question in the minds of customers . . . present or prospective . . . as to who owns such a product or process. At the same time it gives greater protection from possible infringement.

49. *Raising funds*—Direct advertising affords an effective, economical method of raising funds for worthy causes.

Source: Reprinted with permission by the Direct Marketing Association, Inc., 6 East 43rd Street, New York, NY 10017.

In addition to the versatility of direct mail, the medium is both highly personal and direct. With the advent of computers and word processors, letters and envelopes can be personalized, even in the body of the letter, to reflect individual names, geography, lifestyle, addresses, incomes, etc. The recipients of your mail can be pinpointed to almost any variable of interest or demographics through the wide variety of mailing lists available for sale or rent or through house lists.

Direct mail can be inexpensive. Since you can select your particular market, you can evaluate waste readership. Through a creative approach and with attention to basic direct-mail guidelines, a relatively simple package—envelope with teaser copy, a letter, a brochure, or selling piece, and a business reply card or envelope—can be just as effective as a more elaborate four-color, multicomponent package.

Noted merchandiser John Wanamaker once said, "Half of the money I spend on advertising is wasted. The only trouble is that I don't know which half." That statement didn't include direct mail! Direct-mail results are measurable. Through the action (or inaction) of the recipient, measured with your reply vehicle, you can tell precisely how well your mailing performed. This opens up the area of testing—another unique advantage of direct mail. If one package didn't do as well as expected, you can use it as a control and alter all or segments of future mailings—a technique regularly used by mass mailers.

The flexibility of direct mail affords the creative people—designers, artists, and copywriters—almost unlimited reign. Variables can include paper stock; color of ink; die cuts; illustrations; photography; materials such as leather, plastic, wood, metal, tubes, boxes, or bags (instead of envelopes); enclosures such as advertising specialties, scents, sounds, and on and on.

Timing is often critical to a sales effort, and direct mail can be very time-sensitive. It can be designed and produced quickly and can, with careful planning, be scheduled to arrive within a two-day period (often delivered on a particular *day* but subject to the U.S. Postal Service).

The ultimate success of a mailing, assuming the product or service is viable, rests on the selection of mailing lists. Your options include:

- *House lists*—Those you develop from customers, old customers, inquiries, phone books, directories, referrals, etc.
- *Purchased or rented lists*—Available from list brokers who can be found in the Yellow Pages under the heading Mailing Lists.

A major concern of a mailing list is the rapidity with which they can become stale. *Mailing lists must be kept up to date to be cost- and results-effective.*

When considering postage your primary choices are between third-class (bulk) and first-class delivery. Bulk mail requires that you or a private contractor do much of the work (including Zip code sorting, etc.) but saves on actual postage cost. Its shortcoming is that this mail class does not receive priority handling. First-class mail moves much faster, saves time, and commands greater reader attention.

Addressing techniques are a consideration that varies with the quantity of pieces mailed and the purpose of the mailing, and includes plates—metal, fiber, paper, labels, hand addressing, or typewritten addresses. Computer-generated labels are now so common that they lose little impact on most advertising mail.

Unlike other media, direct mail can be produced in-house in even the smallest companies. This is not to suggest an amateur approach but rather to separate the effort from the need for artists, audio or visual personnel, and technicians associated with other media. The success of do-it-yourself mailings depends on basic knowledge readily acquired from the many excellent books available on the subject.

TRADE SHOWS

Trade shows vary in size and format ranging from the annual Philadelphia Flower Show, attracting tens of thousands of attendees, to a regional exhibit of a trade association with attendees numbering perhaps only in the hundreds. However, they all have common advantages. Frequently, the larger shows are open both to the public and the trade, with the public paying admission and the trade provided with special days when the public is not admitted. Typically, a major boat show is designed to attract wholesalers, dealers, and interested retail boat buyers. The exhibitors have an opportunity to display their products to a cross section of prospects.

Retail lines tend to be shown annually or semiannually at both national and regional shows or marts. Here, suppliers display their wares at exhibition halls, hotels, or industry buildings such as the major merchandising marts. Industrial products are typically shown at one or more of the many trade shows sponsored by trade associations, professional societies, or private promoters. In addition to products, a wide variety of services are also promoted through shows. The travel industry uses large and small, national and regional shows to sell hotels, airlines, car rentals, etc.

Although there are shows for every conceivable industry product or service, not all manufacturers or suppliers take advantage of this sales promotion technique. The common excuses include: space too expensive, too time-consuming, high cost of booth or display, lack of available personnel, or lack of results. Those who reap the success of show participation understand and benefit from these advantages of trade shows:

Low Cost/Exposure. By dividing the total expense of participation in a trade show by the number of people seen in your booth, you can establish a cost-per-exposure number. This figure is usually *substantially* lower than the cost of an in-person sales call figured on the same basis.

Active versus Passive Exposure. At a show, the customer comes to you rather than you going to the customer, providing a definite psychological advantage.

Opportunity for Hands-on Demonstration. Products that are too large, complicated, expensive, or fragile to be carried as sales samples or products that require demonstration are ideal for presentation at a trade show booth.

Target Audience. Because trade shows cover different industry and geographic segments you can pinpoint your exposure to perhaps a group as specific as instrument engineers in a three-county area of eastern Pennsylvania.

Buying Influence Penetration. While the salesperson has relatively easy access to a buyer, the real purchasing influence may be an executive, an engineer, a foreman, or even a stock clerk. Any or all of these influences could be attendees at shows because of their specific interest but be unknown or unavailable to salespersons.

Opportunity for Dialogue. Most sales calls are just that—a meeting between seller and prospective buyer to produce a sale. A trade show contact affords the opportunity for a relaxed personal meeting where many facets of business can and often are discussed, including the need for new products, competition, quality, new projects, pricing, etc.

Market Research. Trade shows provide an unusual opportunity to get the feelings of your customers in a concentrated period of time versus random comments or criticisms. Additionally, your personnel can and should be visiting the displays of others in your industry, including competitors, to keep up with the progress and products of your industry.

Some of the frequently mentioned disadvantages of trade shows are justified but can be overcome with careful planning. Consider these cost-cutting approaches:

- Relatively inexpensive regional shows can substitute for more costly national trade shows.

- Portable or tabletop displays are often as effective as more elaborate displays.
- Well-trained company personnel can be augmented by field sales people or manufacturer's representatives to staff your booth.
- Cost/exposure can be increased by pre-show traffic-building techniques to bring people into your booth.

Dollar for dollar, trade show participation may be sales promotion's biggest bargain (see Figure 26–1).

FIGURE 26–1
Trade Show Exhibit Cost Analysis

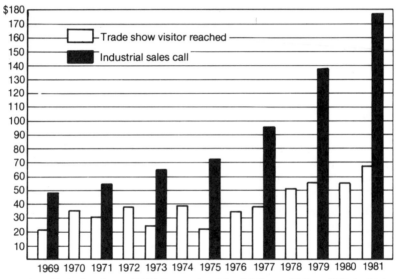

Note: Trade show figures: Exhibit Surveys, Inc. Sales Call Figures: McGraw-Hill Lab of Adv. Perf.

Source: Reprinted with permission by The Trade Show Bureau, 49 Locust Avenue, New Canaan, Connecticut, 06840.

SEMINARS

One of the newer sales promotion tools is the educational seminar. These seminars take different forms depending on the product or service. Some are designed to educate through product knowledge, and others serve just to whet the appetite of prospects for the product or service offered. Seminars can be sponsored directly by a manufacturer, cosponsored by a manufacturer on a co-op basis, or produced by a retailer.

Most seminars are designed to ultimately sell products and are free to attendees. Some, particularly those given following the purchase of a product, are offered for a small fee to cover costs. Typical examples of these seminar styles are:

1. Camera manufacturer's seminar on a co-op basis with both the distributor and retailer, open to the public, and designed to educate the prospective purchaser with the intricacies and techniques for using the camera and other accessories. Many seminars of this type provide models and free film to be used at the seminar.

2. Investment seminars sponsored by stockbrokers, banks, or estate planners that are free and designed to educate participants in investing and financial planning with the hope that enough confidence can be instilled in the attendees to make them prospects for future investments.

3. Electronic components manufacturers take advantage of seminars to provide technical information on their products to engineers and designers. These seminars are free and are often accompanied with a light meal or refreshments.

In addition to the soft sell of products, the seminar is an excellent method of generating leads for sales calls or other promotional efforts.

CATALOGS

Here again is another segment of marketing which can be considered in both the categories of advertising and promotion. The standard catalog falls into the category of advertising or sales, but several versions of the standard catalog might be included in sales promotion programs.

A registered catalog is a numbered and recorded version of a company's standard catalog. It is usually complete when distributed but is in a loose-leaf form so that it can be updated by the salesperson or by mail. When delivered, the recipient signs a card which is returned to the company and used as a mailing list entry for updating. The registered catalog is more often used by manufacturers of industrial and technical products. Its advantages are the flattering effects on the recipient because of the perceived value of the catalog and the opportunity to have a salesperson make more than just a routine call when the registered catalog is presented.

Other catalogs which might be considered in sales promotion are miniature catalogs which can be included with products, segmented catalogs which are portions of full catalogs reproduced for special or seasonal promotion, and catalogs produced in microfilm form.

All of these subforms of catalogs are particularly cost-effective because much of the production costs have been subsidized by the advertising budget.

TECHNICAL PUBLICATIONS

Closely akin to catalogs in the marketing plan are a diversity of technical publications ranging from instruction sheets or folders attached to or included with a product to technical books offered free or at a minimal charge. Basic technical literature can be included in the advertising program, but there are specific uses for technical information that serve a dual purpose as promotional pieces.

An example of a retail approach to technical literature might be the cookbook that's available from food suppliers or a photographic instruction book available either free or sold by camera manufacturers. Much less costly are items such as how-to booklets distributed with products like home workshop tools. The advantage of technical or how-to literature used in sales promotion is its ability to provide added value to your product at relatively low cost but with high perceived value.

SPECIALTY ADVERTISING

Among the most effective but frequently overlooked forms of promotion is specialty advertising, sometimes referred to as *remembrance advertising*. This medium includes the millions of items given away by businesses, civic groups, churches, and even professionals such as doctors, lawyers, and dentists.

Advertising specialties—the products—are defined as useful, freely given (no obligation—see premium section), usually inexpensive items which carry your company name, logo, and/or sales message. The tremendous value of specialties is the wide variety of items available in many price ranges. You can conveniently tailor a specialty to a particular theme, season, kind of business, product, etc. A radio station can use a ruler that is similar to the dial on a radio, a dentist can use a tooth-shaped magnet to hold appointment cards on a refrigerator door, and a soft drink manufacturer can have an inexpensive radio in a replica of its own can. And, would you believe, the health department of the city of Toronto is planning to use advertising specialties to augment its annual Birth Control Week? Other uses for advertising specialties are included in Figure 26–2.

Another advantage of advertising specialties is the available means of distribution: by mail, at trade shows, delivery by salespeople, with the products, and by an organization other than the original supplier.

FIGURE 26–2

---

100 Situations Where Advertising Specialties Can Be Used

Supplement other advertising efforts
Establish prestige
Reduce prejudices
Create corporate identity
Build broadcast audience
Spotlight favorable publicity
Make customer feel important
Obtain third-party endorsements
Imply third-party endorsements
Introduce new service

Introduce new management
Serve as souvenir in gift shop
Build customer loyalty
Round out marketing plan
Serve as dealer loader
Symbolize friendship
Promote meeting attendance
Collect from delinquent accounts
Reduce entertainment costs
Reward sales force

Raise funds
Commemorate special occasions
Encourage quality control
Symbolize safety effort to OSHA
Stimulate window displays
Symbolize new promotional campaign
Announce marketing plans
Symbolically apologize
Discourage brand substitution
Deliver institutional message

Tell success story
Publicize company policy
Increase catalog distribution
Stimulate word-of-mouth advertising
Serve as sample holder
Produce direct sales
Educate prospects about needs
Promote early buying
Enhance direct-mail response
Target message to influentials

Create new buying habits
Stimulate grand-opening traffic
Reduce required sales calls
Enhance employee pride in company
Impress present stockholders

Stimulate information requests
Enhance product distinctiveness
Improve community relations
Keep company's name in buyer's mind
Encourage trial usage

Reach altogether new target groups
Strengthen brand loyalty
Give sales reps something new to
  discuss
Increase psychological involvement
Enlist spouse's support
Extend peak sales season
Focus appeal to a specific segment
Produce sales leads
Stimulate sample ordering
Help organize sales presentations

Get users to recommend company
Increase product usage
Spotlight product or service features
Attract new users
Reach hard-to-see prospects
Test pulling power of an ad medium
Appeal to competitor's customers
Promote multiple-unit sales
Improve employee loyalty
Attract new stockholders

Discourage competing salespeople
Boost P-O-P sales
Welcome to community
Reduce vandalism
Promote demonstrations
Encourage use of P-O-P
Project ideas for new users
Offset competitive promotions
Offset seasonal slump
Give recognition for achievement

Encourage opening charge accounts
Reduce employee turnover
Recruitment
Promoting branch openings
Introducing new products/services
Motivating salesmen/sales department
  employees
Opening new accounts
Stimulating sales meetings

FIGURE 26–2 *(concluded)*

Developing trade show traffic	Moving products at dealer level
Balancing improper product mix	Improving client or customer relations
Activating inactive accounts	Building an image
Changing names or products	Motivating employees
Using sales aids for door openers	Promoting new facilities
Motivating consumers through premiums	Introducing new salesmen

Source: Reprinted with permission by Dan Bagley III, Bagley & Associates, 4404 South Florida Avenue, Lakeland, FL 33803; and Specialty Advertising Association International, 1404 Walnut Hill Lane, Irving, TX 75062.

The advertising specialty enjoys a longer life than most other mediums. The calendar, one of the most popular specialties, has a year's life. A T-shirt can last indefinitely.

A unique aspect of specialty advertising is its perceived value. People appreciate the gift aspect. Can you think of any other advertising that evokes a thank-you from the recipient?

There are literally thousands of advertising specialty manufacturers, each specializing in particular classifications. The pen manufacturer doesn't make mugs, and the ceramic manufacturer doesn't make T-shirts. To facilitate purchasing a network of specialty advertising counselors acts as distributors for most of the industry's manufacturers. Additionally, they often provide promotion counseling, art, copy, and distribution services.

To become a true believer in specialty advertising, just check your pockets, clothing, car, den, bathroom, kitchen, and office—you'll be surprised at how many inexpensive, imprinted, useful items have been *given* you which carry an advertising message.

PREMIUMS, INCENTIVES, AND BUSINESS GIFTS

A premium differs from an advertising specialty because it is not usually given freely but rather has an obligation of some sort as a condition of its distribution. Additionally, a premium is not always imprinted, and it is not generally of as low value as an advertising specialty.

Premiums may be best known for their use by banks and savings-and-loan institutions. Some customers complain that they don't know whether they are going to a bank or a hardware store. The inducements to open or increase accounts have ranged from blankets to television sets, with silverware and smaller appliances fitting in-between.

Other premium promotions are used by major manufacturers on a national basis to increase sales with the offer of some other glamorous or useful product at a reduced price with proof of purchase of their product. In this type of promotion, the product is probably sold at the price it cost the promoter and so is called a *self-liquidator*.

Premiums vary in quality, price, and diversity, from a ballpoint pen to a sail boat (used by a cigarette manufacturer). So varied are the available products sold on a premium basis (at less than retail based on volume) that a special show for marketing people, The Premium Incentive Show, is held each spring.[2]

Incentives are similar to prizes and premiums and are used to stimulate sales among distributors, retailers, salespeople, brokers, dealers, and manufacturer's representatives. Most frequently, the incentive takes the form of free travel for the winner rather than the traditional premium. Care must be taken in the selection of the destination and the timing of trips—both variables that have the potential to cause your program to fail.

Gifts have probably been given as part of business dealings since the beginning of trade. They can be used as a thank-you for past business or as an inducement for new or expanded business. Gifts are primarily given at holidays, with Christmas being the biggest gift-giving season.

The cost and appropriateness of gifts are the essence of any well-planned program. The wrong gift to the wrong person can spell doom for your entire effort. Similarly, the forgotten person—the one you overlooked—can counteract the positive effect of your program. Most advertising specialty distributors supply business gifts and can be found in the Yellow Pages under Advertising Specialties. In many major cities there are professional shopping services to help your company find just the right gifts. When gifts exceed a limit set by the IRS, they no longer qualify for tax deduction, so check with your accountant for the current ruling.

TRADING STAMPS

While some forms of promotion are gaining popularity, trading stamps have lost some of the glamour they enjoyed from the post-World War II years through the 60s. While trading stamps tend to build store loyalty, they have the disadvantage of a long-term commitment by the user.

Trading stamps, unlike other forms of sales promotion, require outside help from the producer and redeemer of the stamps. Fre-

---

[2] Produced by Thalheim Expositions, Inc., Great Neck, New York.

quently, the sponsor of a trading stamp program has to promote the program just as they promote their store or products. Although trading stamps are not applicable to all businesses, they may be particularly effective in communities where someone has already pioneered a stamp program.

COUPONING

Those little pieces of paper with the fancy borders, marked "valuable," can be just as valuable to your promotional program as they are to the millions of people who take advantage of them. The A. C. Nielsen Company's 1983 statistics showed an estimated 142.9 billion cents-off coupons offered to consumers. Although used most frequently by major manufacturers, smaller manufacturers, wholesalers, retailers, and service organizations can profit by using some form of couponing.

Coupons suggest special value and appeal both to those who need to watch their budget and to those who have a sense of thrift. Additionally, coupons offer a chance for involvement not unlike the yes/no token so popular in direct-mail packages. People tend to accept and treat the coupon as something of value.

Perhaps, however, the biggest advantage of couponing is to get someone initially to try a product. Coupons are also used to encourage the sale of additional products of the same company. New retailers can use coupons to attract their first customer as even established businesses use coupons to entice new buyers. The moving of seasonal goods is another appropriate use for coupons.

In addition to mailing coupons or including them in print ads, coupons may also be distributed in or on the product (matchbooks) through cooperating businesses, as part of paid coupon books frequently sold by fund raisers, at trade shows, or handed out at special events or on the street.

The rebate, another form of couponing, has recently become popular, especially among car and appliance manufacturers. The rebate offers the same advantages of the traditional coupon but is typically used for larger dollar refunds.[3]

If the couponing concept has a failing, it's that not enough companies consider it in their marketing program. Coupons can be used for the promotion of almost any product or service. A prime example is the use of coupons by the Claridge Hotel and Casino in Atlantic City, New Jersey, in a "Bring Home the Bacon" promotion to increase hotel and

---

[3] While rebates can exceed $100.00, A. C. Nielsen Company reports that the average face value for coupons was 24.1¢ during 1983.

casino traffic. The coupons were distributed on bacon packages in retail food stores.

SAMPLING

Sampling, like couponing, offers something of value to the prospect but differs from a coupon offer because the product promoted (usually in a smaller size or portion) is given free. Samples are particularly effective when the product is inexpensive and new. Cigarette, food, and cosmetic manufacturers have achieved notable success in new-product promotion through mass sampling.

Distribution techniques for sampling include direct mail, door-to-door delivery, in-store distribution, street distribution, trade shows or exhibits, seminars, conventions, sporting events, community events, and through civic and social groups.

If you need to be convinced of the effectiveness of sampling, try remembering the cheese, candy, beverage, or other food product samples offered in your local supermarket, or the pack of cigarettes that may have been at your place during a banquet, or the letter from the local health spa suggesting a free get-acquainted visit—all examples of sampling campaigns which actually were responsible for the successful introduction of new products.

A word of warning is certainly in order for those considering sampling: Carefully evaluate the product to be absolutely sure it is safe and properly packaged. Manufacturers have had legal problems when unsuitable, unrequested samples got into the hands of children.

CONTESTS

With any consideration of contests, the first thing that probably comes to mind is the multitude of sweepstakes which arrive in your mail every week (or so it seems). Actually, contests come in many forms, ranging from sweepstakes to a jelly bean guessing contest at a small retail store.

The common denominator for both the sweepstakes and other forms of contests is that someone wins something. There is a difference, however, between sweepstakes and other contests. A sweepstakes is based simply on chance and does not require skill on the part of the entrant. A sweepstakes differs from a lottery in that there is no consideration for entry, no money, no need to buy a product. Contests, on the other hand, require some degree of skill, no matter how little.

Why use contests? People enjoy participating! It's not only the desire for reward (the prize) but also the challenge and intrigue. There is also an element of ego satisfaction involved as the participant visualizes his or her publicity as a winner.[4]

Contests can be used to accomplish many marketing objectives, including but not limited to:

- Increasing sales.
- Building brand recognition.
- Introducing new products.
- Supporting a trade show.
- As part of "grand openings."
- Increasing seasonal business.
- Establishing new-product names.
- "Sparking up" meetings or seminars.
- Building circulation.
- Soliciting charitable contributions.
- Adding excitement to social, civic, or business events.

Contests and sweepstakes require careful planning and budgeting. To be successful, a contest should not be complicated. The rules have to be simple enough for *everybody* to understand. Though the rules are simple, they should be complete enough to cover all aspects of the contest.

Entering the contest must also be easy. Prizes should be appropriate to the target audience and of sufficient value to attract entrants. It's better to have multiple prizes than one big prize. The possibility of winning should be ·evident to all entrants. A tough contest narrows participation. If your contest covers an extended period of time, provide interim prizes.

A word of caution is appropriate to contests and particularly to sweepstakes. Both are vulnerable to local, state, and federal regulation. Local regulations are easy enough to check, but if you are planning national promotion, outside counsel is well advised. In addition to attorneys, companies that specialize in contest and sweepstakes design are familiar with existing regulations.

POINT-OF-PURCHASE PROMOTION

Popularly referred to as P-O-P, point-of-purchase promotions include in-store displays, special tags or labels on packages, counter cards, self-service dispensers, loose change mats, cash register magnets, shelf strips, extenders, wobblers, table tents, slide shows, and audio effects—almost anything designed to attract a prospect's attention at a

---

[4] Perhaps the biggest added benefit from contests is the opportunity to publicize winners while at the same time publicizing yourself.

place where they buy and at a time when the buying decision is being made. Because of the "last chance impression" (before a sale) of point-of-purchase promotions, it is most effective in self-service situations.

Considerations in selecting P-O-P items include design; production cost; shipping costs; size; appropriativeness to the marketplace; attention-getting features; ease of assembly by store personnel; need for movement, sound, light, and the risk factor of having the P-O-P item actually used.

Some P-O-P promotions are shipped to the customer to be displayed. The drawback here is that the customer might not get around to using your display (the basements and warehouses of retailers are filled with unused displays). A better—though more costly—approach is to have the display assembled and installed by sales or detailed people. Another risk factor in the drive to get your display used is the effect it has on the overall success of a store. The promotional effort may accomplish the manufacturer's goal of getting brand recognition and increasing market share—but it should also increase overall sales for the store.

There are times when the P-O-P piece can double as a premium, as was the case with the manufacturer who furnished suntan lotion in a picnic cooler for a seasonal promotion. The coolers attracted attention to the product, and the dealer got to keep the cooler (premium) when the lotion was sold. If your P-O-P display also serves as a product dispenser, its success depends on a refilling schedule which could be a consideration of the sales or detail person.

The P-O-P potential should be a major consideration when designing the package for new products.

TELEPROMOTING

Certainly a distinction has to be made between telemarketing and telepromoting. Telemarketing is all-encompassing and includes the use of the telephone to initiate a seller-to-buyer contact for the purpose of making a definite sale or to reinforce a direct-mail offer or solicitation. Telemarketing also includes lead follow-up.

The concept of telemarketing brings to mind people whose only job is sitting by a phone, continuously making calls with the help of a prepared script. In some cases these calls are even being made by sophisticated electronic equipment. This is not the role of the telephone in the original concept of telepromoting.

Telepromoting involves the use of the telephone on an occasional basis as a supporting element of another promotional effort. Typically, the telephone could be used to follow hot sales leads from a trade show. The telephone could play an important role in attracting attendees to seminars. It can be used to achieve quick penetration of the market and to introduce promotional programs such as contests and premium deals.

The successful use of the telephone in sales promotion depends on recognizing its importance and value and then *intentionally* including it in your plans rather than using it casually as you do in your daily routine work.

PUBLIC RELATIONS

A broad definition of public relations would tend to isolate the marketing function from sales promotion. There are, however, aspects of public relations that deserve to be at least emphasized in any review of sales promotion techniques. Publicity is one such area. Because publicity is a nonpaid insertion in newspapers, magazines, radio, or TV, it should be an integral part of most sales promotion programs. An important thing to remember about publicity is that editors really need publicity to fill pages and programs. The trick is to present your news release in the form most easily handled by editors. The format and guidelines for press releases can be found in a number of recent books on PR available at local libraries.

Specific opportunities where publicity can be used as a promotional aid include:

- New-product introduction.
- Advance publicity for trade shows.
- Introduction of a promotional program.
- Announcement of a premium offer.
- Results of a contest.
- Advising of availability of catalogs and technical publications.
- Information on special offers.

If press releases are included in your promotional planning, be sure to distribute copies of the release to your sales force so they will know what is being brought to the attention of their buying public before it's released rather than after.

SIGNS

For the purpose of sales promotion, there is a distinction between signs and outdoor advertising, which primarily includes billboards. Sales promotion signs could include storefront signs, rooftop signs, permanent in-store signs, sign directories, and sale signs. Too frequently, people forget about the visual impact of a well-designed, timely, or creative sign. Signs can excite, educate, intrigue, direct, and inform. In addition to their sales potential, signs can convey corporate image—good or bad. You are well advised to keep signs current, clean, and in good repair.

Though a professionally prepared sign would seem to be dictated, there are, for example, neighborhood gasoline stations that regularly use homemade signs to effectively create additional pump and repair sales.

Also included in a consideration of signs would be banners, flags, and awnings—all inexpensive but interesting attention-getters. An important consideration with sign use is the need to check local building and zoning codes which may define acceptable signs and requirements for a permit.

27

A NEW CORPORATE IDENTITY

by
Elinor Selame

Selame Design

WHAT IS A CORPORATE IDENTITY?

If we speak to those in public relations, they might say that a corporate image is established through annual reports, employee newsletters, news releases for the public, feature articles, the smiles on employees' faces, and community relations. They are right. Advertising agencies might define the corporate image primarily as the company message that comes across through printed and broadcasted advertisements, brochures, and billboards. They are right. Architects might vouch for the importance of the structural appearance, and competent corporate designers and planners will understand this. They are right. For some firms the corporate image might also be formed by packaging, traffic engineering, and landscaping. All these factors have positive or detrimental effects on how well a company is thought of. *The corporate image* is composed of all planned and unplanned verbal and visual elements that emanate from the corporate body and leave an impression on the observer.

The corporate identity, although it is one of the major influences on the corporate image, is all planned and all visual. A successful identity system visually separates and distinguishes a firm from its competitors. The corporate identity is the firm's visual statement to the world of who and what the company is—of how the company views itself—and therefore has a great deal to do with how the world views the company.

The major element of the corporate identity is the corporate symbol because it is the visible, easily recognizable face of a living, complex business machine. It allows the public to see who produces the goods or services they are buying and is therefore the foundation upon which corporate identity is built. The symbol becomes the focal rallying point of the corporation. It is the banner under which a president gathers his or her employees to meet the public.

WHY HAVE A CORPORATE IDENTITY?

One of the first identity goals of any commercial enterprise is to be seen and then remembered. In today's fast-paced, heavily populated society, to be seen and remembered is half the business battle. It is the faceless nature of many corporations that confuses and irritates the consumer. The public wants to know as much about you as you want to know about them. They want to know what it is that distinguishes your company from others. In what ways are you different?

A company's visual communication material is an expression of that corporation's philosophy, abilities, and culture. It can announce or mumble, inform, delight or depress, stimulate, and make or break a sale. It is therefore very important for every company to plan these materials carefully. Planned corporate identity has the potential to make tomorrow's business something more than chance.

Once the corporate identity is established through careful thought and with expertise and skill, it should be instituted as a long-range communication plan. As with any long-term business plan, it should allow for disciplined yet flexible changes and growth. When the overall corporate identity system is put into action, no more valuable time will be wasted on crash corporate-level communication decisions because guidelines for every detail will be available. The chief executive will be secure in knowing that the various representative materials carrying the company's banner are impressive, organized, professional, and truly representative of the firm's attitudes and objectives.

In the past, businesses usually have left the design of their products to engineers, the design of their factories and stores to several architects or contractors, their advertising to advertising firms, their letterhead and business cards to printers, their packaging and signs to suppliers, and so on. Each one, doing their best to get across the identity of the business as they saw it through the medium of their art, would develop a different corporate identification. When a top executive was not happy with one or all of these separate impressions, he or she would often waste valuable time with the printer or architect trying to get the ideas across. Because the supplier knew nothing about the company's corporate objectives, the solutions they arrived at could be short-range at best. A well-planned, well-executed corporate identity program would obviate these problems.

It is important to the contemporary business community and to the individual business to have its contributions and attitudes accurately reflected. A sampling of Illinois adults showed that they thought: (1) business makes too much profit, (2) most advertising is dishonest, (3) products have deteriorated in quality over the past 5 or 10 years, and (4) most large companies lack humanistic personal feelings toward their buying public.[1] Some of these feelings are not justified, as most business executives know. To counteract these feelings, the Illinois Chamber of Commerce launched a statewide program entitled, "Stand up for Business." Any company can launch its own program to counteract or prevent similar feelings: a corporate identity program that honestly communicates what, and at what price and with what services, it is offering for public consumption.

Research has shown that a company with a good corporate image has an ace in the hole with the consuming public. A study by Batten, Barton, Durstine and Osborn showed the following results:

1. When a company has a good image, the public is more likely to assume that it produces good products.
2. The public is more likely to pay more for a company's products and buy their new products if the company has a good image.
3. The public is more likely to take the company's side in disputes.
4. The public is more likely to consider the company's stock a good investment, and the stock is likely to suffer less in a general market decline than will the stock of a company that does not have as good an image.[2]

Implementing, administering, and supervising a new identity program is not a job for the fainthearted. The person responsible for this job must be both knowledgeable in the total scope of the company's communications and a good tactician. He or she must be capable of dealing with the human and complex needs of the various departments whose programs will be affected by the new visual identity. A new identity program will not only affect architecture, signage, interiors, packaging, advertising, internal and external graphic communications, and public relations, it will also affect such other departments as accounting (which will have to deal with implementation costs), the legal department (which will have to deal with trademark law), and so on.

A senior executive must be in command so that the program achieves the proper results in every department. This executive could

---

[1] According to the "Illinois State Chamber of Commerce Public Opinion Survey of Attitudes toward Business" (Chicago: Illinois State Chamber of Commerce, 1973). These facts are also published in a booklet entitled, *If Business Is Your Bag . . . Say So—Out Loud.*

[2] From the 1969 BBDO *Research Report,* Research Department of Batten, Barton, Durstine & Osborn, Inc., New York.

be called the Keeper of the Mark, as he or she will have to see that the program is adhered to at every level. In a large firm this is naturally a full-time job. In smaller companies it can be an added function for the director of corporate communications, advertising director, public relations director, or marketing director. These executives, of course, should be aided by a design consultant experienced in the development of corporate identity design systems. At the outset, they work together, and their plans are put into an identity manual, which then serves as their guide for the long-run program. Because the identity, once planned, will last, the manual must be as flexible as the program itself.

HOW TO SPOT IDENTITY PROBLEMS

If a company presents a dated or disorganized image, its best friends probably will not say so, and its competitors certainly will not. There are several danger signals that can be looked for, and if any of these signals apply, the company either has or will have an identity problem.

The first step in spotting a poorly defined identity is to appoint someone in the firm to collect all visual media being used by the corporation and its divisions; stationery, direct-mailing pieces, billing forms, checks, statements, photos of on-site and remote signage, photos of vehicle identity, advertisements, and packages. Mount all these materials on large, 20-inch by 30-inch boards and check the following danger signals against this composite of the company:

1. The company is growing fast and furiously internally and through mergers and acquisitions. Each change is represented by a different look, so the composite shows a group of unrelated materials. Each time a change takes place, the top executives are presented with design decisions concerning names, trademarks, letterheads, and so on; and the decisions have been made independently of previous decisions. Most outsiders and some insiders are therefore surprised when they are told about all the divisions of the company. They do not realize that it is large and diversified; they cannot tell from the communication materials.

2. If the collected communications materials vary depending upon which department or division they are from, the company probably looks disorganized to the outsider. We have already discussed the impact that a good image has on the public's opinion of the company's financial standing, its personnel, its products, and its reliability. Are the public relations director, the marketing, advertising, and sales managers, the purchasing agent, and the president speaking the same language and to a common end? Are the executives communicating with each other?

3. When viewed all together, does the visual output project a dynamic, organized company on the way up with all bases covered? Or, does it make the company look like a gangling adolescent, all arms and legs, each going in a different direction? Does the company look like it is having a hard time trying to form a cohesive family organization that works as a team? Does it look like the executives have confidence in their positions on the team?

4. Life is said to begin a 40. The company is about to celebrate its 40th year in business. Does it look it? If so, the firm will not attract as many new, young employees as it could and should. It will find it difficult to relate to the younger generation. With the buying power of this group, every company must relate to it. But, until the company's sales stopped growing, the executives did not seem to think they had to. Many established companies continue to grow (even if at a lesser rate with time) through sheer momentum. In the beginning it is innovation, flexibility, and daring that cause success and growth. Once established, many companies lose this dynamism and with time are preempted by younger, innovative organizations. Do the visual materials look old and tired? Inflexible?

5. The corporation has outstripped its one-store success story long ago. In fact, it has also outgrown its regional success story. It is now a national success. But success has not spoiled the company; it has not motivated it to change its image. It still looks the same as it did when it was a one-unit operation—like one person is running the store, greeting the customers, and knows every employee. This image could be a plus, but shouldn't the public also know how large the company is? Does the unchanged image meet all the different state sign and zoning codes and highway beautification programs? How can the firm meet all these different demands at prices it can afford? The building is the image. How can it be replaced, should it be replaced, and with what?

6. The company's various divisions are in different fields of business activities. They all do look alike, and they do adhere to one graphic design system as depicted in the *Graphic Manual for Corporate Identification,* which has acted as the corporate bible since the program's inception. However, is the graphic control system an exercise in rigidity? Is status quo thinking settling in over management? Is the firm promoting a look of corporate sterility or stagnation instead of corporate synergism and dynamism? Some corporations acquire other companies mainly for the top management of those companies. If the acquired entrepreneurs feel that their creativity or freedom is stifled within the framework of the identification program, there is danger that they will leave or revolt; the merger will have been for nothing.

7. In a group of related companies, there are often reasons for continuing the separate images of the constituents. It takes great experience and design skill to create a system for a corporation that develops an organizational corporate discipline that is valuable in the financial world while allowing diversity. Do the communication materials gathered reflect this expertise?

Studying the collected material provides more than a method of getting acquainted with the company's printed output. It often reveals costly and needless duplication. It can also reveal gaps in the material, which means the company has been making do with something other than what is proper or in good taste.

A new company might have little data to collect, but it will probably need all the materials a going enterprise uses in the course of doing business. It is better to plan ahead than make last-minute decisions. This would be the time for a new company to see what is needed and make sure the new identity design can work well in all possible media and for all possible needs in the near and far future.

The next step in a corporate identity program is designing the new materials and the overall look of the new identity. See Figures 27–1 and 27–2. If your company, like CBS or Olivetti, has an art staff noted for excellence of design quality, it is possible to achieve corporate identity on an internal basis. However, most firms do not have the need for such specialized design staff skills and must look to the outside for help.

How does a company go about finding a designer with the proper expertise and talents necessary to create totally unified and positive corporate identification programs?

An understanding of the design processes involved in corporate identification is a great aid in both choosing and working with the design firm. However, if the project director does not have any background in this field and does not have time to take a crash course, how can he or she, or any other executive in the company, distinguish between good and bad design, or between those designers that can and cannot execute their ideas? First, good design is original. It is also not just a matter of aesthetics, but one of filling a need. Every component of the system from signage down to menus should work both alone and as part of the whole program, and it should get the message across. Weak design, on the other hand, is a borrower. Tailfins belong on airplanes; the public did not take long to reject these useless appendages on automobiles.

FIGURE 27–1

Over the last 12 years the number of products and customers multiplied and the variety of designs and insignias was bound to confuse even the most sophisticated consumer. It was clearly time for a change—to create a unified, consistent identity, to build on the strong equity Kodak had already established with its corporate symbol, and to help communicate its identity more efficiently in an increasingly competitive national and international market.

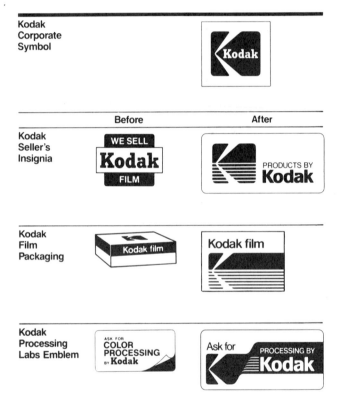

THE CORPORATE SYMBOL

The corporate symbol should be a positive visual statement of who the company is, or what the purpose of the company is, in a form that can be seen and recognized quickly, and then remembered easily.

Just as it is easier to remember a person's face than his name, so it

FIGURE 27–2

should be easier to remember a company's symbol than its name. The identity program ultimately relies on the symbol for its strength. If the symbol is weak, confusing, hard to remember or decipher, or badly proportioned, it can have an adverse effect on the entire program. The symbol must be, at the very least, functional: distinctive, simple, and

FIGURE 27–3

Management at Harlem Savings Bank of New York City felt the 120-year-old institution was handicapped by its name. Only 1 of its 16 branches was in Harlem, yet its name gave the impression of a local, small, and somewhat dated bank. To capture a new share of the changing bank market, Harlem Savings decided to polish up its image with a new name. Selame Design's research and analysis led to a revolutionary solution: borrow the nickname of its hometown, the Big Apple.

easy to remember. If, in addition, it is meaningful (tells a story) and is a delight to the eye, it will give the whole program a tremendous boost (see Figure 27–3).

A symbol, although developed by the designer, is chosen by the company's executives. The symbol can be expressed in as many ways as there are colors, typefaces, and shapes. What are the factors to consider in making such an important decision? What design considerations need to be taken into account?

Of course, underlying all symbol decisions will be the decision maker's personal likes, dislikes, and opinions concerning aesthetic considerations and image. Also influential in the final decision are the company's areas of visual exposure, the market segment to be reached, and the budget set aside for reproducing the symbol, as some are naturally more complicated and expensive to reproduce than others.

The ability and creativity the designer brings into its visualization will also affect the program's outcome. Again, when the designer is familiar with the various faces of the company and knows about the company, the better the chance that he or she will come up with the essence of the company in a simple yet meaningful symbol.

In general, the combination of mark and signature symbol can be most useful for unlimited applications. However, both businesspeople and designers have strong opinions about which symbol they prefer. Some do not like the combination symbol because it still involves words and pictures. There are good designers who argue that initials are quite valid and useful, and there are equally good designers who condemn "alphabet soup" symbols. Many people like the ambiguity of abstract marks. They feel that the designs do not pin down the business of the company and so can be used in the future when the company diversifies. However, some people also feel that abstract marks are meaningless graphic exercises. Instead of stimulating, they feel these abstractions are sterile. They also feel that the abstract mark has no meaning and is therefore forgotten as soon as it is out of the viewer's sight. The types of marks that allow instant recognition and are simple graphic illustrations, such as glyphs and alphaglyphs, are especially advantageous symbols for companies with little or no advertising budget that are now, or that are planning to go, international.

No matter which is chosen or why, well-conceived and well-designed symbols all have something in common. They manage to be distinctive but economical. They convey the name and/or the purpose of the company, or an image that the company wants to project, with the fewest possible graphic lines. See Figure 27–4 for some examples.

FIGURE 27–4

1. The Seal. A name or group of words rendered in a cohesive form. This might be the choice of a company that would find it difficult to depict their business in a pictorial mark.
Designers: New York Life, Lippincott & Margulies; Blue Seal, Selame Design Associates; Kodak, Kodak staff; Ford, Ford staff.

FIGURE 27–4 (concluded)

---

2. **The Monoseal.** A monogram or initial within a shape or seallike form. This has the same advantages as the monogram but also has the added benefits afforded by the seal's background.
Designers: Maytag, Dave Chapman, Goldsmith & Yamasaki; Westinghouse, Paul Rand; PPG, Lippincott & Margulies; General Electric, GE staff.

3. **The Monogram.** A letter or combination of letters rendered in a distinctive manner ideal for a company already widely known by its initials. It usually needs a large promotional budget and takes time to become memorable.
Designers: IBM, Paul Rand: AVX Aerovox and E–Z Shops, Selame Design Associates; RCA, Lippincott & Margulies.

4. **The Signature.** The company name rendered in a particular and consistent manner.
Designers: Eaton, Lippincott & Margulies; Hemingway Transport and Ludlow, Selame Design Associates.

5. **The Abstract.** A graphic device, geometric or otherwise. It has no visual connection with a company's products, services, or name, other than that relationship established through promotional effort.
Designers: Atlantic Richfield, Carol Lipper and Tomoko Miho; North American Rockwell, Saul Bass & Associates; Exolon, Selame Design Associates; Chrysler, Lippincott & Margulies.

6. **The Glyph.** Comprised of simple graphic lines and tells a visual story about the company's name, major product line, or area of business concern. Once learned, the glyph is easy to recall.
Designers: United Fund, Saul Bass & Associates; Woolmark, Francesco Saroglia; American Telephone and Telegraph, Saul Bass & Associates; CBS, William Golden.

7. **The Alphaglyph.** A mark whose initial provides a quick clue to the company's name, and the pictograph tells an immediate story.
Designers: Foreign Autopart, Selame Design Associates; International Paper, Lester Beall; General Cinema, Mutual Oil, and Goodwill Industries, Selame Design Associates.

Source: Copyright © 1983 by Elinor Selame.

ARCHITECTURE AND STORE PLANS

The aim of a successful store design is to attract, identify, and merchandise. No one of these areas can work without the others. If the unit attracts without identifying, it may lose the repeat business. If it identifies without merchandising, it loses potential current sales. One cannot merchandise without first getting attention and then identifying the ware. Each works with the other, or one can neutralize the effect of the other two. The physical plant for a retailer is therefore the principal means of communication. Often, the architecture and signs are the first selling points seen by the consumer. If they are not an inviting sight, no amount of in-store merchandising will lure the potential customer.

No matter what image the company seeks to establish, good design should not be sacrificed. Making the store attractive should not be thought of as a concession to environmentalists, but rather as the powerful merchandising tool it can be. An attractive, well-kept store tells the customer that the owners care about their customers and that they think enough of them to try to make them comfortable, honored guests.

A good design plan would aim for making the exterior signs enhance the environment, relate to advertisements, relate to the interiors, or help the interiors so that each would build on the other to strengthen the image. This facilitates customer recall and enhances communications.

Thinking and planning allows management to foresee long-range problems and solutions. Good design simplifies whenever possible. If making fixtures alike throughout the chain can allow mass production, which lowers costs and simplifies manufacture, the good designer and planner will do so. Simple, easy-to-care-for, long-lasting materials would also be a part of a good design scheme, as they would lower maintenance costs and simplify maintenance.

Once the benefits of good overall design plans are understood, the criteria for judging design effectiveness are obvious: if the design saves time, saves money, enhances communications, improves employee morale, and simplifies manufacture and maintenance, then the design is effective.

Of course, the store becomes the packaged product, and as such it is either salable or not. Just as careful planning goes into package design to attract, identify, and merchandise, so it should go into store design. The ultimate reason for good store design is that it helps sell the product.

Signage

In just a few years, if the establishment is not a visual asset to the environment, there will be very few welcome mats put out by the town fathers or by customers in other communities. An ugly sign or a court fight can ruin an otherwise good image. The signage must identify and attract—not identify and repel. With the use of the symbol, the signage can identify and create a positive image in the consumers' minds that will support and in turn be supported by the rest of the identity program (see Figure 27–5).

In essence, a sign, whether remote or on-site, says, "Here we are." If the passers-by react to that statement with "So what," or "Yes, but we wish you weren't," the signs are not serving their purpose. Signage should create a positive image that makes customers want to enter the store, or that interests and informs them enough to come back when they do want to shop that type of store. If a sign is not memorable, making it larger will not make it memorable. Flashy signs

FIGURE 27–5

Amoco coordinates its gas stations, product, and service lines
through a design system that includes a distinctive typestyle
and color plan for a unified, consistent look.

Amoco
Corporate
Symbol

	Before	After
Amoco
Companion
Mark	**AMOCO**	**Amoco**
Amoco
Repair
Service	**AMOCO
Auto
Repair**	**Certicare**
Amoco
Dealer
Program	**Red
Carpet
Service**	**All★**

might attract the viewer's attention but do not necessarily inform; in
fact, all the viewer might see is the flash. Simple, good design using the
identifying symbol will satisfy the viewer, the ordinances, and the
store, as it will identify, attract, and be attractive.

Packaging

A package must contain or hold merchandise, protect it, and communicate a message about its contents and the company marketing the
product. The package should also make a product easy to handle, ship,
and display. Product protection and communication are, or should be,
closely linked. Protection frequently takes the form of total enclosure,
thus hiding the contents which then must be identified. Of course,
communication should go well beyond product identification; it must
also sell the product, as it is often a company's only sales tool.

Colors can enhance and make objects more appealing. Trademarks serve as useful, functional ingredients in design and identification. Packaging decisions should not be relegated to the purchasing or manufacturing departments, where packaging would be purchased in much the same way as are nails, paper, and equipment. Purchasing and manufacturing departments buy to satisfy their company's cost and expense-control interests, but packages must also satisfy prospective customers and, thereby, the profit picture. Packaging is a marketing cost and usually a long-range one. The product visible only through or by its package is often the key element in advertising and certainly plays a major role in point-of-purchase displays.

In creating package designs for the mass market, it is important to keep the design as simple as possible, but informative. Find the one most important message, present it boldly with very few other competing graphic elements, and visualize the results of the design in a mass display. Does it have strong shelf impact? Will a busy consumer be able to spot the product quickly and easily understand its benefits?

In the need to attract the consumer, sandpaper, lawn tractors, and chocolates do have something in common. More and more, the package must tell its story simply with graphics. People readily understand and remember pictures. The proliferation of facts and details that must now go on packages places a new urgency on telling the main idea clearly and simply. The common thread of all good package design is finding the essence of the product's message, one that is an honest statement about the product, and setting it apart from other like products by presenting that message in a visually and psychologically appealing fashion.

Advertising might get the customers into the store, but good package design sells the products in the store. Good design that makes the identity of the product and manufacturer clear is as important as advertising, signage, and store design in attracting and keeping customers. For those retailers who are also manufacturers or who sell their own private label products, the symbol on the package will reinforce the identity, for good or bad. If the package *en masse* is a negative visual statement, the reinforcement will be bad, and the symbol seen anywhere else will take on a bad connotation. If the package and product are good, the symbol seen anywhere else will take on a positive connotation and promote sales. The importance of packaging for the marketplace cannot be overemphasized. See Figure 27–6 for an example.

Advertising

Advertising and promotion should have a basic verbal and visual message that effectively projects the company's identity, helps create the image, and sells the merchandise, centering on the corporate and/or

FIGURE 27–6

The previous packaging for General Sportcraft gave the impression that products the company manufactured and distributed were strictly for amateurs. A bold new symbol—a red-and-blue victory banner in the shape of an "S" applied to fresh, white packaging in both horizontal and vertical formats—now unifies the line and projects the strength of the company name. A simple graphic labeling system distinguishes one box from another, simplifying inventory.

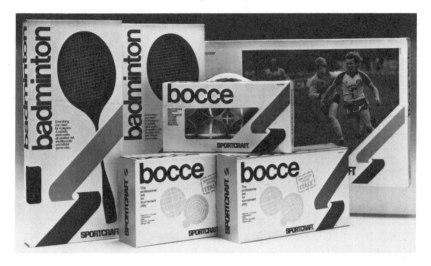

product identity. Advertising should not be a self-contained part of the business but rather an integral part of the total system and corporate identity program. This is because any time that a customer sees the symbols—on a truck, on a package, even on the employees' badges—the company's identity is being reinforced. And the key to advertising and recall is repetition (see Figure 27–7).

Advertising cannot fulfill its function to the highest degree if everything else the company is doing is not backing up that advertising. The company's basic message has been carefully translated into the components of the identity program, and this message should be repeated and kept constant. In a competitive market, the modern advertisement, like the modern package, must do more than attract attention to motivate a purchase. It must give the potential purchaser a reason to buy the product. With so many similar or identical products available, that difference will be the long-range, positive corporate identification. The ads must attract, identify, and then merchandise. Many sophisticated companies use their advertising to position the difference between

FIGURE 27–7

A name, symbol, and complete visual merchandising system
were created for Amoco's new automotive service program.
The constant and consistent use of the new design helps to
build equity in the total new identity system.

their company and products and those of others, not just to communicate advantages or features. If the company has clearly defined and projected its identity, this difference can be reinforced by all advertising using the symbol.

The most important part of such a program is constant and carefully controlled repetition, via all visual expressions put forth by the company. After a period of time, the potential customer will feel familiar with the firm. If someone needs a product for the first time, they will buy the name that is foremost in their memory, and that will be the result of the repetitive advertising that has recall. For those who are already customers, advertising can enhance the image.

The average consumer is exposed to a minimum of 560 advertising messages a day, 484 of which he or she completely blocks out. Bold symbols can help prevent the viewer from blocking out the ad in any advertising medium and, at the same time, will help identify the sponsor of the ad.

Because they are so often handicapped by small advertising budgets, many small companies need to review the efficiency of their advertising and to look for ways to stretch their precious advertising and

FIGURE 27-8
New England Gas and Electric Association Becomes
Commonwealth Energy System

Increasing governmental regulations and the growing needs
of customers caused New England Gas and Electric Association to consider how their system was organized and how it
operates. In effect, two divisions were formed—gas and electric. The gas division retained its legal name of Commonwealth Gas Company and adopted the COM/Gas logo. New
Bedford Gas and Edison Light Company became Commonwealth Electric Company, using the COM/Electric logo. The
other electric companies, Cambridge Electric Light Company
and Canal Electric Company, retained their legal names but
adopted the COM/Electric logo.

COMEnergy
COMGas
COMElectric

promotion dollars. An identifiable name and symbol that unifies every
division and product of the company can be the answer (see Figure
27-8).

There are visual media available to all where they can advertise
their companies and products at no extra cost. For example, the
trucks, company cars, and other rolling stock are not any more expensive to buy and run when they are attention-getters and corporate
communicators than are the tired, dated-looking vehicles that travel
along our highways. This is a great untapped source of free advertising
when fit with unique corporate identification.

Packaging, sales promotion, and signage all cost money for materials. If they do not help to actually advertise the company's products,
then they are not adding to sales and might just as well be plain to save
the printing expenses. Symbols that can become focal promotional
tools, whether on trucks, company uniforms, packages, or signs allow
the business to effectively communicate a sales message even within a
limited budget.

The importance of analyzing the market to be reached is essential
in advertising successfully at the best price, but that is true for any

company with or without a corporate identity program. Those with identity programs with strong symbols, however, have the advantage of ready-made repetition. If implemented properly, the corporate identity program allows the company to advertise at no extra cost in many areas—on trucks, signs, and packages.

A company's visual communication materials should not only communicate a product or service message to the consumer but should enhance the corporate image. A dynamic design system can act as a silent salesperson for the corporation and can be the single most cost-effective marketing expenditure a company can make. Each time a name, symbol, or package is recognized, marketing equity in the corporate identity increases. In effect, for a single expenditure, a corporation receives a continual return on its investment.

A good image can attract investors and consumers.

A bad image is simply bad business.

28

REVOLUTIONS IN RETAILING

by
Steve Feinstein

President, Eclipse Industries, Inc.

PAST HISTORY

The one constant in the history of retailing is the inevitability of change. Since the first cave dweller traded away a sharp-edged rock for one that looked better, the means of distribution of necessities and luxuries to consumers at all stages of the socioeconomic continuum have undergone constant change. The process continues at an accelerating pace as entrepreneurial spirits, ever alert to new technologies and to budding consumer needs and wants, keep refining and expanding the distribution channels.

This chapter will highlight some of the breakthroughs in retail distribution that are part of recent American marketing history and then move on to a discussion of contemporary trends.

The Department Store Phenomenon

Americans were buying most of their wares from specialty shops, general stores, or directly from producer/craftworkers when the mid-19th century wave of European immigrants introduced a new source of goods: the itinerant peddler who carried goods from town to town. Unaided by family wealth and unfettered by real estate, these wandering merchants served consumer needs where they found them. The mercantile experience they acquired in the process was, in astonishingly many cases, translated into a larger arena. Their knack for understanding profitable selling techniques underlay the retail revolution of the time: the development of department stores. In short order, scions of families that began doing business from pushcarts became, in the apt terminology of Leon Harris, the merchant princes of America.[1]

The immigrant families that established the department store concept bore names that remain familiar: the Filenes of Boston (Filene's Department Stores); the Strauss family which developed both Macy's and Abraham and Strauss in New York; the Gimbels of Philadelphia (Gimbel's Department Stores); the St. Louis Mays (the May Department Stores); Goldwater in Arizona; Marcus in Dallas (Neiman-Marcus); Loewenstein in Memphis; and the Lazarus family in Ohio. Along with native-born Americans like Marshall Field and John Wanamaker, they were the granddaddies of merchandising who broke through the existing frontiers of retailing.

The department store revolution was a phenomenon that introduced retailing innovations of enduring significance. Liberal customer credit was introduced by Rich's in Atlanta, while Macy and Strauss developed a strictly cash policy. Marshall Field inaugurated a liberal product return policy. Filene's made history with the basement store approach and a policy of automatic markdowns. Most important, the department store phenomenon made the offering of diverse products to meet basic and not-so-basic family and home needs—under one roof— a standard for operation of metropolitan marketplaces throughout the world.

The Mergers into Federated Groups. The establishment of popular and profitable department stores was quickly followed by expansion. Not content with the successes of their individual operations, most of the successful department store owners opted for merger into larger groups. The first of the national chains to develop from such a merger was the Federated Department Stores group, spearheaded by the Lazarus family from Columbus and Cincinnati.

Similar associations were formed by Allied Stores with Jordan Marsh in Boston, Bon Marché in Seattle, Joske's in Dallas, and with other stores throughout the country. The mergers served the useful functions of facilitating information exchange and strengthening buying potential through centralization. Not incidentally, the federated groups also provided opportunities for diversification of family holdings while creating more attractive equities to prospective shareholders.

The concept of conglomeration of department stores has grown to such an extent that there remain few independent department stores of national consequence. Some notable exceptions are Sears, Roebuck— which, by sheer size of sales volume, is larger than any of the depart-

---

[1] Leon Harris, *The Merchant Princes* (New York: Harper & Row, 1979).

ment store conglomerates—and the respectable multibillion-dollar chains developed by Penney's, Montgomery Ward, and Woolworth.

The Supermarket Revolution

The Revolutionary Concept. In a development related to the growth of department stores, supermarkets sprang up throughout the country to provide consumers with greater varieties of food items and related wares at lower prices. The operators of the new super-markets (the word is hyphenated here to remind the reader of its origin) sought to pass on to the buying public the cost benefits of utilizing larger stores with larger inventories but with less personal service than had previously been the norm.

In this area, as in all retailing areas, the successful innovators were the ones who accurately assessed the needs and opportunities in their markets. Piggly Wiggly did the original experimentation in Memphis in the 1930s, operating its first store like an automated cafeteria which permitted consumers to make automatic selections from dispensers. A&P expanded the supermarket concept, stripped of automatic service, to both coasts.

The supermarket revolution that started in the 30s spread rapidly throughout the country. The early leaders were followed by hundreds of other operators whose incremental innovations led to development of the supermarket that is now accepted as standard: a generously sized store featuring full display of products, self-service, and centralized check-outs.

That the philosophy and methodology is still undergoing change is attested to by the recent introduction of superstores that are distinguished by yet greater leaps in magnitude of physical facilities and of product diversification. In attempts to overcome the low gross margins available from food items, stores as large as 100,000 square feet offer multitudes of nonfood items including health and beauty aids, prescription drugs, housewares, basic apparel, hardware, flowers and nursery items, electronic products, and services such as cooking schools and restaurants. The newest supermarkets, in comprehensiveness as well as size, comprise fair-sized shopping centers of their own.

The effects of the ongoing supermarket revolution are widespread. Check-out retailing, no longer restricted to grocery items, has become the *modus operandi* for discount stores, hardware and lumber stores, and diverse other retail markets. It is no longer alien to department stores as the pressure to cut personnel costs increases for those outlets.

The Discount Store Cycle

In post-World War II America, a shortage of department stores to serve the burgeoning population facilitated the development of discount stores. Starting in the old mills of New England milltowns, discounters offered apparel in large inventories and styles at significantly reduced prices. The emphasis was primarily on first-quality goods although a few discount houses made their marks with closeout and irregular merchandise.

Other manufacturers, seeing the success of the discounters in the apparel field, made their goods available to similar outlets. Discount houses soon flourished with offerings of domestic linens, housewares, hardware, electronic items, sporting goods, and more. Competition between the discount stores and the department stores mounted as the range and diversity of products discounted grew to rival the merchandise retailed more conventionally. But conventions don't last long in the retailing business.

Retrospectively, it is easy to see that the department stores created the opening for the discount houses by working on gross margins of 42 to 43 percent (based on operating costs of 35 percent). The discounters were able to operate at 28 to 30 percent margins by keeping operating costs at roughly 25 percent through use of low-rent sites and supermarket techniques for sales of apparel and hard goods. As customers traded service for price discounts, personnel expenses were minimized.

By cutting expenses for rent, furnishings, payroll, and advertising, the discount innovators introduced a new era in retailing that would leave no facet of the industry untouched. As the discounting concept succeeded financially, its practitioners were able to adapt their styles and merchandise offerings upward to approach the selling strategems of the department stores. Discounters upgraded their sites and their store interiors and moved into advertising and credit sales.

But while the discounters moved toward the social and esthetic appeal of their prime competitors, the department stores veered toward the discount field by opening their own discount operations; and retailers, across the spectrum of markets, began discounting their prices.

The Rise and Fall of Korvette. The road to success traveled by the discounters is far from smooth. It is strewn with fatalities whose names were, in fact, once household words: Korvette, Arlan's, Topps, King's, Mammoth Mart, Food Fair, and Grant's. What made them fall by the wayside? No conclusive answers but some interesting insights are revealed by the story of E. J. Korvette.

Korvette was started in 1948 by a returning veteran who saw an opportunity in selling luggage at a discount in a small, second-floor location in Manhattan. Working on a very low margin with the hope of compensatory volume, he soon established a sound success at luggage sales. The demand of customers for other discounted merchandise led him to expand into other product lines, starting with appliances.

Further expansion led, in short order, to the establishment of full-fledged department stores on Long Island and, later, on Manhattan's Fifth Avenue. The discount operation spread throughout the eastern states and into the Middle West. Along with the geographic expansion the operation enlarged from hard goods to a full line of hard and soft goods. The future looked bright.

With corporate ambitions high, four separate and distinct mergers took place between Korvette and other companies. Each successive merger was accompanied by a change of direction that confused both the public and the internal organization itself. Korvette seemed to consumers not to know what it was about. The effect of that confusion was quickly revealed on the company's balance sheet. The stores were liquidated in 1980.

Rapid growth was a part of Korvette's climb to success. At its height, its shares brought $170 each on the New York Stock Exchange. Its sales approached a billion dollars a year. But as spectacular as the climb was, it could not prevent the corporate death and destruction. Mismanagement seems to have been at least partially responsible for the failure. Consumers cannot be expected to maintain loyalty to a business that zigzags, as Korvette did in one year, from sales of quality goods to low-end goods, then back again to high-end merchandise, and tops it by changing markups during the course of a year.

But that is pure speculation. Candidates for master's degrees at the most prestigious business schools may have other explanations for this company's demise. In any case the history of Korvette provides a most dramatic instance of a discount operation that failed after rapid growth and expansion to what appeared to be the pinnacle of success in retailing.

The Kresge Story. The most successful discounter to evolve out of the post-World War II phenomenon turned out to be a late entry into the field, the Kresge Company, whose thousands of units throughout the country now achieve sales of approximately $18 billion a year.

Kresge came into discounting slowly and carefully. Having established a solid national reputation through their highly profitable variety store chain, Kresge managers watched the early developments in discounting from the sidelines for a number of years. Convinced that their existing variety store strategy would fall short of achieving long-term corporate goals in a more competitive market, Kresge set out to learn from the successes and the mistakes of others.

The firm dispatched a team of senior executives—who were later to run the total company—to study the discount phenomenon. After cautious research and analysis, that team developed a prototype for a Kresge discount operation. The first K mart store met with almost instantaneous financial success. The enterprise flourished and for some years enjoyed meteoric growth. The success of the concept is evidenced by the change in the corporate name from Kresge to K mart Corporation in 1977. Under any name, and even with the slower growth rate that came with the maturation of the discount industry, the company's leadership role remains intact.

TODAY'S RETAIL REVOLUTION

What is turning retailing on its head at the moment is the retail revolution of the 1980s: off-price retailing. Dismissed by some as simply offering a new buzzword for discounting, the term describes nothing more and nothing less than the youngest generation of discounting. The new baby reveals enough family traits to be recognizable and yet displays enough new characteristics to show promise of challenge for all the old-timers. Retailers, as well as the manufacturers and distributors who provide them with goods, are well advised to heed the developments in off-price retailing while planning their own operations.

Warehouse Retailing. The origins of off-price retailing can be found in the experiments of supermarket chains with cut-carton retailing in the 1950s. They introduced discounts on case lots of merchandise and replaced attractive (and expensive) merchandise displays with high stacks of cartons, cut open to make products visible and accessible to consumers. Product prices were kept low by minimizing personnel costs for merchandise handling and eliminating entirely the cost of such fringes as fancy fixtures and displays. Carrying this approach further, contemporary warehouse food retailers often cut packaging costs by having customers bag their items in containers of their own or in shipping cartons.

Today there are warehouse food stores of all sizes. The German Aldi corporation started their warehouse operation in the United States in abandoned supermarket sites sized at approximately 20,000 square feet. Offering lower prices and fewer services than conventional food stores, Aldi was soon reaping American profits. At the other end of the spectrum, Heartland in Boston and General Grocers in St. Louis have made successes of similar operations based in stores that are five times as big—100,000 square feet and more. All these warehouse retailers emphasize low prices, stark store interiors, merchandise racking, and the barest minimum of services. Consumers seem to buy the concept; some of the stores achieve sales volumes that exceed $1 million a week. A good, traditional supermarket, by comparison, averages $100,000 to $150,000 in sales a week.

The Wholesale Warehouse Concept. A refinement of warehouse retailing, the wholesale warehouse concept has expanded the warehouse method to nonfood merchandise. This movement began in 1976 when the Price Company in southern California opened 100,000-square-foot stores offering food, beverages, and general merchandise to wholesale members and group members. For purposes of the Price Clubs, members of the public are eligible to become group members; wholesale memberships are available to those who have sales tax numbers.

Price Club stores maintain a limited number (roughly 4,500) of the stockkeeping items in their inventories. The mathematics of this business is drastically different from any other facet of retailing. The gross margins are a mere 11 to 12 percent. Operating costs are kept at 7 percent—there are no advertising costs to speak of. Very high volume is generated at each unit, with current average approximately $60 million each per year.

These numbers obviously require management to exercise great discipline and precise controls. Return on investment is high because inventory turnover runs at approximately 18 times a year, in contrast to a turnover factor of less than 4 for a traditional department store and a factor between 4 and 5 for a discount operation.

The wholesale warehouse concept has spread from California to Arizona, Colorado, Indiana, and Washington, D.C. Walmart, the very successful discounter (sales over $3 billion a year) whose geographical distribution has been limited to small towns, is currently expanding warehouse operations into Tulsa and will soon move into the Oklahoma City and Kansas City markets.

The Home Depot Story. An outstanding leader in warehouse retailing is the building supply/home center giant, Home Depot, whose dramatic progress in the last five years has earned it top sales records. Growth in sales has been paralleled by enlargement of individual store facilities (from the original 60,000 square feet to current sizes of 80,000 to 100,000 square feet) and by multiplication of merchandise offerings.

The fastest-growing company in the hardware, lumber, building supply business, Home Depot plans to add 4 stores at announced sites to its current operation of 10 units (each of which averages $18 million in sales per year). An index of its success is the fact that its stock has shown the highest increase in value of any publicly traded company. The firm has succeeded on the basis of these primary concepts:

— The terms *stores* and *warehouses* are synonymous; there are no central warehouses.
— The stores have no dedicated stock areas; overstocks are stored in warehouse racking above displays.
— Sales prices are lower than those offered by traditional hardware, lumber, and home center stores.

The viability of the warehouse retailing trend for the sale of building supplies/hardware/lumber is indicated by the apparent conversion of the largest retailer in the industry, W. R. Grace. Stores recently opened by the Grace firm in the New Orleans market—where they compete with Home Depot operations—exhibit some of the same characteristics. More warehouse stores, in the same industry, are doing business in St. Louis, southern California and southern Florida, Atlanta, and San Antonio.

Off-Price Apparel Retailing. Once the off-price apparel bandwagon started rolling, apparel sellers were natural riders, given the traits of their market. The prevalence of brand names familiar to consumers facilitates product identification. Consumers know what to expect in the way of quality and price when they see apparel labeled Arrow, Villager, Halston, Calvin Klein, Jonathan Logan, or Christian Dior. Brand-named apparel is easily identifiable; scaled-down prices are easily advertised and verified.

Furthermore, the success of Bloomingdale's has tempted most department store merchandisers to make a stab at upgrading their customers, increasing their margins, and moving ever higher on the price ladder—leaving a void down below. Discounters and off-price retailers are eagerly and industriously attempting to fill that gap, making apparel off-price retailing the fastest-growing facet of the contemporary retailing scene. Just about every major department store chain is actively entering the field. Consider the Marshall's division of the Melville Corporation, Dayton Hudson's Mervyn's and The Plum divisions, the T. J. Maxx division of the Zayre Corporation, and the new Designer Depots of K mart Corporation, to name just a few.

Through these and other operations, apparel off-price retailing now comprises 9 percent of the apparel business, according to Dr. Bert C. McCammon, Jr., Professor of Business Administration and Director of the Distribution Research Program of the University of Oklahoma's

Center for Economic Research. By 1990, McCammon estimates this segment to account for 25 percent of that industry.[2]

Factory Outlet Malls. One final noteworthy segment of the off-price retailing trend is taking the form of factory outlet shopping malls, scattered throughout suburban America. Entirely new in concept, these malls house only tenants that sell off-price merchandise of various kinds. Already on the scene are the Hammond (Indiana) Outlet Mall; the Halsted Outlet Mall, Chicago; the King's Point Factory Outlet Mall, Cincinnati; the Taussen Marketplace, Maryland; and the Pavilion Outlet Center, Seattle. Under construction in Missouri is a 30-acre outlet mall with 320,000 square feet of leasable space to house 60 outlet stores.

Computer Catalogs. What appears to be a wave of the future is hinted at by the appearance of at least one public company that is introducing merchandising of vast numbers of products through personal computers. With a data base accessible to over 200,000 individuals, the firm provides information on some 50,000 brand name consumer products, representing over 500 manufacturers. Consumers who plug into the data bank can elicit information regarding product features, availability, and pricing. Ordering directly through computer means is obviously the next logical and revolutionary step.

SOME ADVICE TO SELLERS

If the chronicle of events, past and present, that has filled these pages contains one truth, it is precisely what was stated at the outset: the selling business is always changing. Retailers and those who sell products to them must be alert and responsive to the trends that are growing, by ripple effect, from humble beginnings to tidal waves of change. No seller is immune to the effects of these changes.

To help manufacturers determine the impact on sales of their products, a lesson is drawn here from the hardware/building materials/home center industry. Consider, for example, a manufacturer of lighting fixtures who has been limiting distribution to department, discount, mail-order, and specialty stores. If taking advantage of the expanded market by selling to the entire home improvement industry is desired, the manufacturer must recognize and understand the different types of retailers within the industry as well as their differing modes of operation. The hardware stores, the lumberyards, the warehouse retailers,

---

[2] Bert C. McCammon, presentation to the Home Center Institute Seminar, Ft. Lauderdale, Florida, February 1983.

the hardware buying cooperatives, and the home centers must all be understood.

The light fixture manufacturer must examine his or her own pricing structure to see whether it rewards customers who require deliveries only to their central warehouses from which they service their entire retail operations. If that is the case, the manufacturer may be unwittingly overlooking the large and growing percentage of the market done by the warehouse retailers who depend on drop shipments since they maintain no distribution centers. If the manufacturer wants their business, adjustments to the price schedules may seem appropriate.

The light fixture manufacturer had better understand as well that to move into this area, different product packaging needs must be considered and accommodated. A plain brown box may do when it is out of sight until the sale is made, but warehouse stores—and even the more traditional home centers—are likely to stack the boxes right under the lighting display. If the product is to sell, the box had better show—on the outside—exactly what is inside, by way of a clear, precise description and, preferably, a color lithograph picture and an informative selling message.

What is true for this hypothetical light fixture manufacturer is true for all purveyors of goods. The changes in types of distribution and in types of stores cannot be ignored. Properly heeded, they offer big opportunities to alert marketers. They cannot depend on strategies developed in the 1960s or even the 70s to sell the savvy retailers of the 80s or 90s.

It is, then, a justifiable conclusion that the trends currently observable in off-price retailing comprise today's retail revolution, and this revolution is every bit as significant as was the development of the supermarket and the department store in earlier days. They will have long-term effects on consumer goods marketing. The sellers who will thrive on these changes and escape being counted among the casualties of this revolution will heed these cautions:

— Familiarize yourself with the selling stratagems used in your industry and in others and analyze their usefulness to your own operation.
— Realize that these developments are not necessarily restricted to the industries in which revolution has already surfaced, your industry could be the next one affected.
— Resolve never to make marketing policies, structures, or price schedules without understanding and accommodating the needs of each category of retailer with whom you do business.
— Keep your eye on the retail revolution of the moment if you want to be counted as a survivor!

29

FORMULATING EFFECTIVE DISTRIBUTION PLANS

by
Thomas C. Jones CMC

Tom Jones and Company, Inc.

Considerable fact finding and analysis should be part of your planning process. Ideally, the plan is developed at several levels within the organization.

1. At the highest executive levels, the overall strategy and goals for the corporation are determined. They also decide the nonroutine deployment of the company's resources.
2. At the operating or managerial levels, the detailed plans and budgets for achieving these goals are formulated.
3. At the managerial level, the marketing and distribution plan is developed.

It is essential that this plan selectively emphasize those crucial factors which are required for success. A good, brief plan can be updated as often as is necessary to keep it current. In some of our client companies within fast-moving industries, their one- to three-page executive summary business plans are updated *monthly*.

SETTING DISTRIBUTION GOALS

Distribution and marketing planning start with the goals of the organization. Ideally, these strategic goals for the business unit are set by the chairperson, president, and other senior executives. Middle managers must be given this essential guidance. *Don't leave them to figure out*

426

what's needed and then tell top management what they are going to do and why! (This is the case all too often.)

Distribution planning is part of the managerial process by which "managers assure that resources are obtained and used both effectively and efficiently in the accomplishment of the organization's objectives."[1] Distribution goals are an operating subset of the major goals and essential plans of the corporation (refer to Figure 29–1).

FIGURE 29–1
What Are Distribution Goals?

Distribution goals for manufacturing firms would selectively include the following:
Marketing system goals

Market share and revenues	Penetration by market, product industry, territory, branch, key account.
Profitability contribution and ROI	Profitability by product, product line, district, territory.
Expenses and expense ratios	Costs for selling, training, literature, quotations, installation, service, office and administration.
Productivity	Measures of effectiveness such as calls per order, calls per day, cost to close, etc.
Resources	Personnel, caliber and competence, facilities, equipment.
Management	Supervision, development, guidance, leadership.
Employee performance and attitude	Training, compensation, incentives, supervision.
Physical system goals Investment	Inventories, transportation equipment, data processing, warehouses, location.
Performance and productivity	Trends in cycle time, inventory turnover, order fulfillment costs, on-time shipments, back orders, order fill rates.

As an example, *overall goals for Vee Belts include 30 percent increase in sales*. Faced with this objective, Vee Belt distribution planners translate it into such action goals as:

- Establish five new distributors in Region Five by June 1.
- Increase the co-op advertising allowance by 20 percent by May 20.
- Conduct training sessions for all distributor salespeople in Region Five by March 1.

---

[1] Robert N. Anthony, *Planning and Control Systems: A Framework for Analysis* (Boston: Harvard University Graduate School of Business Administration, Division of Research, 1965), p. 27.

- Recruit five new salespeople. After training is completed, replace three of the most ineffective salespeople. Complete by September 1.
- Develop a new order fulfillment system which will improve service levels without increasing service stock; complete design by June 1, programming by December 1, and installation by the following December 1.

You cannot in one sitting effectively accomplish goal setting and the companion process of developing action programs. It *should* proceed as follows:

- Major goals are handed down by top management. These goals are within the context of the overall corporate strategy.
- First-cut distribution goals and operating plans are then defined by operating management.
- First-cut crucial factors for success are identified.
- Budget impact and results estimates are developed and analyzed by staff.
- Distribution goals are modified to meet the multiple objectives of market penetration, profit contribution, and customer service. Several revisions may be required.
- Crucial factors for success are refined and highlighted.
- Detailed action programs are written.

As the goals and programs are developed, we discard those which will have a poor long- or short-term return for the effort (dollars) expended.

Don't jump to conclusions and propose solutions before the goals and problems to be solved are accurately specified. A disciplined approach will produce better results. At the conclusion of the process, *each key manager should have no more than three to five crucial goals and related action programs.* If these are well managed, the organization will meet its overall goals in terms of distribution.

Follow-up and Control Are Essential

Specific checkpoints at specific times become part of the management process. For example, state that, "On January 15 the distribution goals and action programs will be finalized. On or before February 20, *X* will be accomplished by Mr. J.A.Z." Specific, quantified goals are the key to top managerial performance. Our thesis was succinctly stated by George R. Seiler in *Control: The Key to Successful Business Planning:*

> An ideal approach includes a simple, clear means of measuring activity in the critical success areas and communicating accomplishment of key

events, results, variances from the business plan, changes in the plan, and new aspects of the critical issues. Complexities only serve to obscure critical success factors.[2]

SETTING DISTRIBUTION POLICIES

These need to be reviewed periodically. Once set, distribution policies are seldom changed. Figure 29–2 summarizes the major distribution policies needed by the new organization.

ASSESSING CURRENT SUCCESS (or lack of it)

How well has your company been doing in meeting its distribution goals? Determining this is step 2. (In the case of the newly formed venture, company, or division, skip directly to step 4.) Review previous plans and budgets and compare them to actual performances. How many critical factors for success were well managed? Were the key action programs accomplished on time and within budget? What can you learn from the failures? Did you over-analyze and under-act?

Assessing action is critical. You can't know that it will work until you try it. As Peters and Waterman say in *In Search of Excellence:*

> Most of the institutions that we spend time with are ensnared in massive reports that have been massaged by various staffs and sometimes, quite literally, hundreds of staffers. All the life is pressed out of the ideas; only an iota of personal accountability remains.
>
> However, life in most of the excellent companies is dramatically different. One is more apt to see a swarm of task forces that last five days, have a few members, and result in line operators' doing something differently rather than the 35-person task force that lasts 18 months and produces a 500-page report.[3]

Many companies routinely track marketing and distribution performances. In those cases where information is not readily available, special studies must be made to correctly evaluate the situation. Examples of studies done for planning purposes are presented in Figures 29–3 and 29–4. Analysis of the size of account versus profitability confirmed the 80/20 rule in graphic detail.

Branch profitability analysis identifies offices to consolidate for cost reduction. Distribution maps are essential for planning. Market

---

[2] George R. Seiler, "Control: The Key to Successful Business Planning" (New York: American Management Association, 1981), p. 11.

[3] Peters and Waterman, *In Search of Excellence* (New York: Harper & Row, 1982), p. 120.

FIGURE 29–2
Outline for a Distribution Policy Statement

I. OBJECTIVES.
    A. Primary Objectives.
        1. Product availability.
        2. Assistance to sales reps and distributors.
        3. Share of the market.
        4. Fair return to company, sales reps, and distributors.

II. SALES AGREEMENT.
    The sales agreement defines the relationship with indirect channels and includes:
    A. Appointment and Territory.
    B. Warranty.
    C. Stocking Requirements.
    D. Return of Stock.
    E. Sales Promotion and Coverage.
        1. Company to provide:
            a. Sales literature.
            b. Cooperative advertising.
            c. Field sales assistance.
        2. Company reserves right to:
            a. Contact prospects directly to promote, advertise, and demonstrate products.
        3. Sales rep and distributor to provide:
            a. Qualified salespeople for proper market coverage.
            b. Stock and warehouse services where required.
            c. Sales promotion activity.
    F. Orders Subject to Acceptance by Company.
    G. Sales Rep and Distributor Agree to Follow Company Policies.
    H. Products.
    I. Type of Account in Territory.
    J. Type of Accounts Reserved for Direct Sales.
    K. Prices and Terms.
    L. Changes in Prices and Terms.
    M. Effective Date.
    N. Termination.

III. TERRITORIAL POLICIES.
    A. Selective or Broad Distribution.
    B. House Accounts.
    C. Resolution of Disputes.
    D. Handling of Inquiries and Orders.

IV. SUPPORT POLICIES.
    A. Sales Training.
    B. Field Sales Assistance.
    C. Inventory Management and Order Entry.
    D. Other Programs to Strengthen Operations.

V. CUSTOMER SERVICE.

VI. ADVISORY COUNCIL.

VII. MARKET FEEDBACK.

FIGURE 29-3
Resource Allocation Planning

Cumulative percent of total

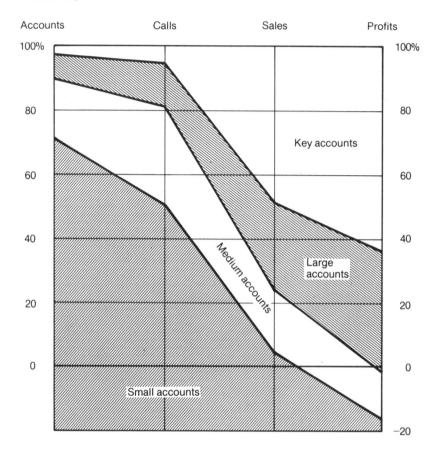

potential by city, county, marketing area, territory, and branch provide direction, as does identification of the locations of competitors' facilities, territories, and market shares.

IDENTIFYING PROBLEMS AND THEIR CAUSES

Step 3 is to clearly identify the problems that became obvious during the analytical phase of your program. Once they are pinpointed, the all-important job of identifying the possible causes can begin.

FIGURE 29–4
The Branch Fixed Costs Determine Shape of Margin Curve

Implications for performance payoff
   Look to larger branches for growth in income (dollars) but
      not necessarily for margin percent improvement.
   Look to small branches for margin percent gains through
      consolidation and by building moderate-size branches to
      large branches.

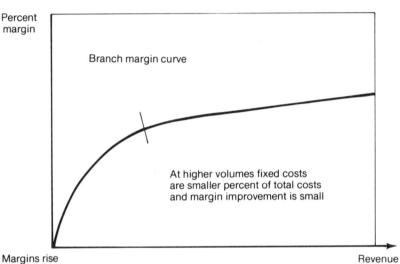

Percent margin

Branch margin curve

At higher volumes fixed costs
are smaller percent of total costs
and margin improvement is small

Margins rise
rapidly at low
volume because
fixed costs are
high percent of
(total, e.g. 75%)

Revenue

A problem, as Dr. Benjamin Tregoe defines it, is the deviation between what *should be* and what *is* actually happening. Typical distribution problems are:

- Sales of CB radios are off 20 percent from last year in the Toledo branch.
- Customers are receiving incomplete orders from the Atlanta warehouse.
- Joe Z. in Birmingham is having problems managing his distributorship.

Dr. Tregoe has a five-step process for problem solving. Disciplined thinking is required; therefore, it's more difficult to implement than it appears. His process is to:

1. Define the problems.
2. Select priority problems for analysis and solution.
3. Identify possible causes of each problem. "The cause is an event or combination of events, that, for all practical purposes, would exactly produce all of the facts in the specific description of the problem."
4. Select the most likely causes of the problems.
5. Agree upon specific corrective actions.[4]

New Operation or Venture

Are you in a new venture? If so, you are faced with such questions as, "Given the nature of my product, my market, and my financial resources, can I afford to sell directly, or is an indirect sales program more appropriate?" Figure 29–5 summarizes the key business planning decisions which need to be made by the executives of the new venture.

FIGURE 29–5
Distribution Planning for the New Venture

Decide on:
   The type of distribution system: direct, indirect, or mixed.
   Distribution policies.
   The geographical coverage desired now and in the near future.
   The makeup of sales management and support organizations.
   The sales pitch, training techniques, and how to overcome objections.
   Sales literature and promotional material.
   Order entry and paperwork systems.
   The physical distribution system.

SPECIFYING ISSUES CRITICAL TO SUCCESS

Step 4 is to pinpoint the critical issues which must be well managed in order to achieve the defined goals. Agreement on these requires a thorough understanding of:

- Your customers and their needs.
- The nature of your product and its uniqueness.
- Customer awareness and your product's position vis-à-vis the competition in terms of price, quality, delivery, and availability.

---

[4] Charles H. Kepner and Benjamin Tregoe, *The Rational Manager* (New York: McGraw-Hill, 1965), p. 18.

- Current problems and their most likely causes.
- Agreement as to the course of action required to solve those problems.
- Your company's financial position.
- Distribution channels appropriate for the product line at this point in its life cycle.

Figure 29–6 presents a more comprehensive list of issues designed as a checklist for executives in established businesses. More mature products require refined distribution planning methods in order to effectively meet and counteract competitors' strategies.

FIGURE 29–6
Checklist for Distribution Planning

SECTION I. OVERVIEW OF CRITICAL ISSUES.

This section, the last step in planning, is the manager's wrap-up of the distribution plan. It pulls together the distribution objectives, critical issues, supporting information, and major action plans. Additionally, it indicates direction and puts important issues into focus. This current plan should be compared to the previous plan, including comments on any major changes.

SECTION II. SITUATION REPORT.

A. Quantitative Record and Performance Goals.
  1. Refer to Figure 29–1 for a list.
  2. Marketing system.
    a. Revenues.
    b. Market share.
    c. Profit contribution.
    d. Expenses.
    e. Expense ratios.
    f. Productivity.
  3. Physical system.
    a. Investment.
    b. Performance and productivity.

B. Qualitative Description of Operations versus Competition and/or Industry Standards.
  1. Ten functions performed in the distribution channel.
    a. Selling.
    b. Transporting.
    c. Market information gathering.
    d. Assorting.
    e. Financing.
      i. Inventory.
      ii. Customer credit.
    f. Storing/Inventorying.
    g. Risk taking.
    h. Installing.
    i. Servicing.
    j. Buying.

FIGURE 29–6 (*concluded*)

2. Satisfying customer needs and wants.
   a. Product/System.
       i. Performance.
       ii. Reliability.
       iii. Features.
       iv. Quality.
   b. Pre-sale service.
       i. Literature.
       ii. Quotations.
       iii. Meetings.
       iv. Prospecting.
       v. Response time.
   c. Post-sale service.
       i. On-time delivery.
       ii. Installation.
       iii. Training.
       iv. Repair.
       v. Spare parts.
       vi. Manuals.
3. Organization.
   a. Structure.
   b. Process.
   c. People.
       i. Education.
       ii. Training.
       iii. Motivation.
       iv. Performance.

SECTION III. CRITICAL ISSUES.

A. Major Problems and Solutions.
B. Keys to Success of Plan.

SECTION IV. ACTION PLAN.

A. Refer to Figure 29–7.

DEVELOPING SPECIFIC PROGRAMS TO IMPROVE PERFORMANCE

You have now done the preliminary work necessary to outline your distribution plan. The plan will consist of four sections:

   I. OVERVIEW OF CRITICAL ISSUES.

   II. SITUATION REPORT.

   III. CRITICAL ISSUES.

   IV. ACTION PLAN (Figure 29–7).

FIGURE 29–7

| S824–E (671) **SINGER** Planning Program | Action Program | Group | Exhibit No. 17 |
| | | Division | Date |

Program Title:	Date:

Program Objective:

Major Steps in Action Program	Event Responsibility	Completion Date

First Prepare Section II, the Situation Report

This provides an opportunity to make quantitative and qualitative comparisons of the operating unit's performance both historically and versus the competition. The actual information recorded will depend upon the company's reporting and planning processes. For companies with formal planning programs, the detail is recorded elsewhere and doesn't need repeating. The level in the organization doing the planning is also of critical importance. The important factors for individual salespersons or distributors might include increased penetration of key accounts or analyses of the market potential in specific accounts or in certain geographic areas. Conversely, at the division or district level, the information would be combined. We stress again: *be selective.*

Section III Outlines Your Critical Issues

Select three to five of these factors from the overall analysis. *This is the major contribution of the planning process and should be limited to the most important issues which are within your control.* Examples of such specific goals could be:

- To upgrade the caliber of the sales force through selective recruiting and training by X date.
- To reorganize the sales information system to provide you with timely reports on performance problems that need attention.
- To expand distribution into a new territory by setting up new distributors.
- To improve the service response time in a specific district. All customer requests for service will be acknowledged within two hours.

Remember to Make the Goals for These Programs Specifically Measurable for the People Charged with Implementing the Plan

Include deadline dates and assign accountability. An action plan is based on these foundation steps.

Step 5 in developing the distribution plan is to summarize what is important and write Section I—Overview of Critical Issues. It should compare your current plan with the plan submitted the previous year. Include comments on any major changes in objectives or outlook and expected performance of the operating unit. In this section consider your overall goals, the critical factors you need to address in this planning period, and any changes in competition or ways of doing business in the channels.

You are now ready to implement your action plans. Don't forget: follow-up is critical.

THEORY AS PRACTICE—A REAL SITUATION

Fortune 500 Capital Equipment Manufacturer

This well-known manufacturer of capital equipment produces machinery for the oil, gas, and chemical industries. Changes in the competitive environment during the 1960s and 70s could be ignored by the old-line management because a highly loyal customer base preferred the quality of their engineered equipment. Inroads by foreign and domestic competitors in the late 70s and changes in customer preferences eroded the company's market position. Customer surveys in several important market segments led to *a decision to improve customer service.*

Improvements in customer service, in spare parts availability, and in serviceperson response times required major changes in the organization as well as commitments of capital funds. New distribution centers were constructed, and distribution managers were authorized to purchase spare parts from outside vendors in order to maintain a 98 to 99 percent order fulfillment ratio. A data processing system enabled branches to communicate rapidly in order to locate needed parts.

The solution to this problem required substantial investment and detailed plans by many people in the organization. *The key to successful planning is operating management involvement.* Unless your managers responsible for implementation "own the plan," it will gather dust.

The amount of detailed analysis necessary to make "fact-found" decisions presents a problem for an operating manager. There are just not enough nights and weekends to allow the hands-on manager to do a reflective and adequate job of data gathering and analysis.

Staff Assistance. Larger operations with continuing, year-round analytical needs should have on staff the appropriate planning personnel. Many lean organizations have found the services of outside business planning experts an efficient and cost-effective way to obtain an extra pair of hands plus the expertise necessary to quickly resolve the planning issues.

The planning staff provides you with specific assistance in the following areas.

1. *Focusing the distribution planning effort.* A carefully focused planning program eliminates excessive detail. It provides management with a limited number of usable recommendations and programs. To be successful, consulting firms and in-house planning staffs must *not* use the laundry-list approach to making recommendations. Good judgment is required to identify the crucial factors for success and *to convince executives that effective management of these factors will have a significant impact on business.* We have seen reports with over 100 recommendations! It's as true for business as for personal relationships: a long list of everything wrong with someone is rarely productive!

2. *Providing the expertise to guide line managers in the planning process.* In cooperation with management, the planning staff should (1) identify the information which is specifically required, and (2) develop action programs to obtain and analyze it.

3. *Conducting a distribution audit.* Well-managed companies *anticipate* problems. An effective way to do this is to have an outside consulting firm conduct a distribution audit. This can be done by experienced consultants in planned and focused interviews with the management and employees of the company. Lower-level employees often have excellent ideas for improvement of operations, but who hears them? An outsider can fill this communication gap. By comparing this operating situation with others in a wide experience, the effective consultant can quickly zero in on key areas for improvement.

First and Last, the Operating Management Must Direct and Control the Planning Effort

Planners are advisors. They can help think the situation through, but, to paraphrase Harry S. Truman, "It's on *your* desk that the buck stops."

REFERENCES

"Building a Sound Distributor Organization." *Experiences in Marketing Management,* no. 6, 2d printing. New York: National Industrial Conference Board, 1964.

Distribution Research and Education Foundation. "Future Trends in Wholesale Distribution: A Time of Opportunity." Washington, D.C.: National Association of Wholesaler–Distributors, 1983.

Kepner, Charles H., and Benjamin B. Tregoe. *The Rational Manager.* New York: McGraw-Hill, 1965.

Krause, William H. *How to Hire and Motivate Manufacturer's Representatives.* New York: AMACOM (Division of American Management Associations), 1976.

Locator (1982/83 Electronic Industry Manufacturer's Representatives). Chicago: Electronic Representatives Association, 1982.

30

SALES FORECASTING

by
Robert L. McLaughlin

Micrometrics, Inc.

The sales forecast: it *is* the grand premise. Practically everything we do in planning in corporations is based on some sales forecast. Indeed, it almost seems that we can't make a decision without one. And it is also the grand assumption: assuming that we can sell a million of them, what colors should we have?

Suppose for a moment that the sales forecast was correct—perfectly correct? The company could make no mistakes since it would have a perfect documentation of its future and would thereby know just what to do. We might almost say that the sales forecast *could* be the most important document published by the firm. But we don't. The reasons are many, but these are among the more important:

1. The sales forecast *must* be under the direction of the chief marketing officer, who would not be responsible for the total marketing effort if the sales forecast were not included. But this delineation of authority often does cause the sales forecast to be factional.

2. Sales forecasts often become political, particularly in larger, decentralized companies. The problem here is mainly in negotiating budgets: the top staff pushes the divisions to ever-higher heights, thereby causing a natural tendency to underestimate future sales. The problem is almost universal.

3. Forecasting of *any* kind is hard to do. In the early 1980s it was revealed by an extremely large international forecasting contest that mathematics and statistics do not necessarily improve accuracy! The contest also showed that complex models are not necessarily more accurate than simple ones—a discovery that has driven sales fore-casters back to basics: above all other things, know your business.

The now famous competition has caused a minor revolution in forecasting. The two number sciences (mathematics and statistics) reigned supreme from the dawn of the computer—giving us mechani-cal, automatic forecasting models that ran untouched by human hands. But now there are second thoughts everywhere, and sales forecasting is no exception. Make no mistake: math and statistics are indispensa-ble for organizing data, calculating, and measurement—the measure-ment of error, change, and patterns. But these are not forecasts; they are only helps to the forecaster.

Too much time and space have been given in the literature to the quantitative, to the long neglect of the qualitative. Quantitative models tend to be averaging processes, but much of the sales-forecasting prob-lem is not average; rather, it is the constant discovery of the excep-tional. The new (old) thing in sales forecasting is now the optimal blending of (1) the quantitative versus the qualitative, (2) the objective versus the subjective, (3) the mechanical versus the judgmental, (4) the theoretical versus the practical, (5) the average versus the exceptional, and (6) the common versus the unique.

GETTING STARTED

Sales forecasting generally means predicting the important time series, beginning with the business as a total and working down to at least the product line—in all, just a dozen or so time series. This chapter is about that kind of forecasting. The marketing research department in larger organizations is generally responsible for sales forecasting.

But it should be mentioned early that, especially in a manufactur-ing company, forecasting below the product line level is usually the responsibility of manufacturing and in larger firms is probably carried out by the operation research department. Here, the individual time series may not be as important as the summary time series at the top (that marketing is responsible for), but there can be hundreds of thou-sands of them! So, the net importance of the job is enormous: manage-ment science in a famous department store forecasts 350,000 items for store inventories; operations research in a replacement parts division of an auto company forecasts 750,000. The sheer immensity of the project *makes* the operation important, even though no single series may be important in itself.

In a multidivision corporation it is very possible that company policy will call for the divisions to *assume* a certain economic environ-ment (this is particularly so in the case of the coming budget year forecast). Here, the economic forecast is probably in the hands of the corporate planning department. Division forecasting can be simply summarized (see Figure 30–1). With the vastly different assignments of marketing research and operations research, the two become complementary, and every effort toward cooperation between the two should be encouraged. Their talents reinforce one another.

FIGURE 30–1

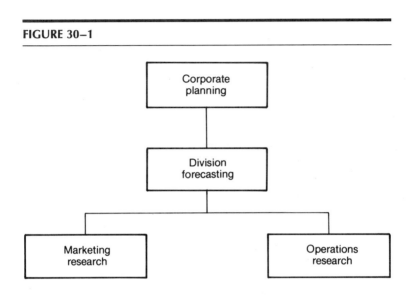

THE THREE-STEP SYSTEM

Sales forecasters have long used a popular three-step forecasting system that can be summarized as follows:

1. Build a Model. Anyone who forecasts a time series—monthly sales, quarterly GNP, and the like—has some kind of system. In other words there is a model. It may be an equation or some routine system that has worked reasonably well. Due to the enormous number of time series that operations researchers must deal with, they rarely get beyond just building an equation for each. This is not true of the market researchers who forecast only a few, highly visible time series. Because the few series are very important, management virtually X-rays any forecasts of them.

2. Go Eclectic. The word *eclectic* means to borrow from all schools of thought. And, since the sales forecaster deals with only a dozen or so high-visibility series, the rule is to be eclectic and test the model's forecasts against different ways of forecasting the same time series. In effect, then, the eclectic step is a testing step—checking and cross-checking different methods of forecasting the same series.

3. Judgment. The sales-forecasting process ends with the approval of management. No matter how well steps 1 and 2 are done, if management vetoes the forecast, it is back to square one. The final approval is always judgmental. We have meetings where we discuss the forecast, see it in the light of the whole operation, test it for balance among product lines, etc. Because the time series are few (but important), they are severely tested before being supported.

The three-step system of forecasting the important time series is widely used in industry and government. The system is highly recommended for sales forecasting.

GENERAL TECHNIQUES

The forecasting techniques of the market researcher are different from those of the operations researcher. The latter tend to be limited to quantitative methods, again because the number of series they control is so large. They use essentially mathematics and statistics and are heavily dependent on the computer for automatically forecasting the many items. Many OR techniques have also been used successfully in marketing research. However, the market researcher must maximize qualitative research, which means interviewing important people—both customers and in-house experts. In addition (because there are only a few time series), the market researcher is constantly pushed to verbalize the forecasts, make them visible with charts, and defend them!

In a classic survey of sales-forecasting methods by the Conference Board in the late 1940s, firms were asked how they forecast. The answers fit into seven distinct categories; and, despite the age of the survey, they are strikingly similar to what we do today.[1] All seven can easily be put together as a total forecasting system (Figure 30–2).

If (1) an *item* is made, someone or something (computer) must forecast it. It is the most basic forecast, and the methodology used by the production schedulers (operations researchers) is most likely to be (2) *extrapolation*. If the organization has a sales force, it is almost certain that the marketing management will survey them and ask what they expect to sell (particularly for budgets). The technique has long been known as the (3) *sales force composite*.

---

[1] Conference Board, New York, 1948.

FIGURE 30–2

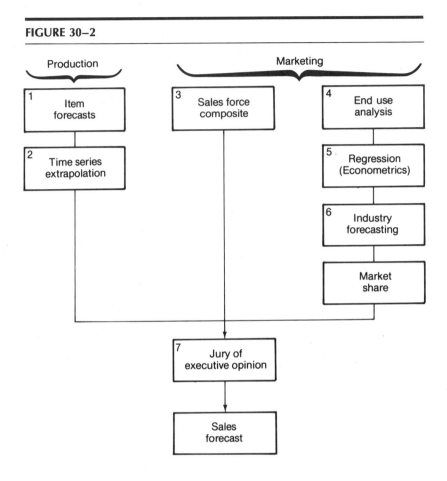

Whereas production forecasting concentrates mainly on extrapolating history over the next few months, marketing departments more often employ causal techniques—if the auto industry sells 10 million cars next year, how much steel can we sell?

Inevitably, market forecasts lead toward (4) *end use analysis:* who buys what I sell, how much, and why? This qualitative study then leads to a quantitative model through the use of (5) *regression.* Marketing research may build an econometric model of the (6) *industry.* This in turn leads to the need for predicting market share (not one of the seven, but a must if you start with an industry forecast).

Finally, as always, sales forecasts must run the rigor of approval by successfully winning the acceptance of the (7) *jury of executive opinion*—the people who ultimately take the responsibility for them. Having completed this all-important step, the forecast is formally issued.

THE SHORT, MEDIUM, AND LONG

Sales forecasting comes in three sizes: short, medium, and long. The *short-term* forecast covers the next few months and deals with the daily or weekly operations of the business. It is often called the operating forecast. It is dominated by statistics—not formal statistical analysis but graphs, seasonal patterns, and moving averages (Figure 30–3).

FIGURE 30–3

	Short	Medium	Long
Statistics	X		
Economics		X	
Demographics			X
Psychographics			X
Technographics			X

In the *medium-term* forecast we are interested in the annual budget, that principle upon which all organizations operate. It is called the *budget forecast* and is usually dominated by economics: What is the impact of the business cycle on next year's budget? What about government policy and, in turn, imports into our economy and exports out of it? What will interest rates do to investment, and what will the deficit do to those very same interest rates, and what will happen to the long-term plans? No matter how you see it, the overwhelming influence on next year's budget is the business cycle. Are we entering a recession? Are we to recover? Are we to get a second (and a third?) year of recovery? These are the critical questions in the most debated of all business forecasts.

The *long-term* forecast, perhaps the most underrated of the three, may very well be the most important. To give you an idea of just how important it is, the Edsel and Corfam were essentially long-term forecasting errors. Need we say more? The long-term forecast may be more difficult to be successful with than the others, if for no other reason than that it is so far away.

Many nebulous things enter the long-term picture. *Demographics,* the study of population, is among the most compelling: How many young adults will there be to buy my portable appliances in the year 2000? A crucial question. Don't forget *psychographics:* What will be tomorrow's lifestyles? And always, there is *technology:* Will the Japanese dominate the computer in the 90s? Which of our industries will replace people with robots?

The long, the medium, and the short are all different sales-forecasting problems. Don't try to solve them with the same technique. They don't lend themselves to such simplicity. A sales forecast of any kind is important. Stop there. Give it your full effort, because it *is* important. Extremely significant decisions will be made on the basis of the sales forecast you submit. Management *will* X-ray them; management *will* put them under the magnifying glass. Why not? What you've done will have a great influence on what your company does in the future. Treat your work to your best effort.

LOOKING OUT FOR NUMBER ONE: BUDGETS

Probably the number one forecasting problem in a corporation is the budget forecast, which sets what you are all going to be responsible for next year. It *is* number one. Whether it should be or not is another question. But the practical fact is that most corporations are highly geared to their budgets. If we can't get by next year's recession, why are we worried about 1995? Other things may be important but, in the middle 1980s, the budget rules the world.

It probably is a fact that the most important forecast you make will be the *budget forecast,* if for no other reason than that it is the forecast the CEO wants for running the company. We do not really know why all organizations in all countries are run by budgets, but they are, and they have one thing in common: all budgets encompass a year. It may be 12 months or 13, but it is a year. (Just about the only organization not run by a budget is the family, although we can presume many do have some nebulous system.)

When we talk of budgets, we talk of a *horizon* of many more months than is the case with short-term forecasting. For those who are on January 1 through December 31 (70 percent of the large companies), the process begins around July. It all comes down to "what will happen next year?" And *that* comes down to a forecast horizon of 18 months—the rest of the current year and the 12 months of next year's budget.

CYCLE ANALYSIS: THE ARRM MODEL

Cyclicality is at the heart of budget forecasting. As seen earlier, the medium-term budget forecast is dominated by *economics*. If we look ahead across a span of a year and a half, we inevitably begin to think of our budget being affected by recessions, recoveries, slowdowns, and all kinds of economic events, both good and bad. In this section we'll develop a judgmental model for forecasting out the next year or two, enough to get us through next year's budget. The ARRM model (average recession/recovery model) is a simple time series method in which only the time series we are forecasting plays a part. The model deals with cyclicality and requires only some history.

First, a word about history. The average *duration* of a business cycle is four years. It follows, then, that if we had 100 years of business cycles, we would have 25 cycles. But any statistician will tell us that a sample of 25 is dreadfully small (imagine a national political poll based on 25 people interviewed!). In the post-war period we have (as of 1985) only eight business cycles. With this as the sample, every bit of post-war history is crucial. Figure 30–4 shows a small company and how it

FIGURE 30–4

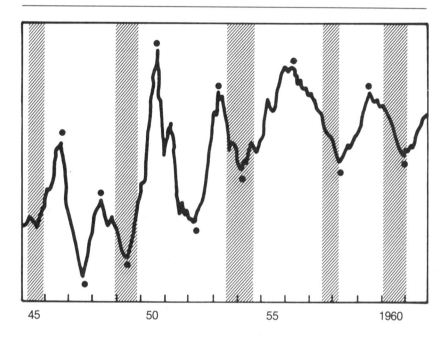

behaved in the 1950s—almost a cyclically pathological case. It is so cyclical that, in the first two post-war business cycles, this company got two cycles while the rest of us only got one! Needless to say, this ancient *cyclical* history is enormously valuable to a forecaster.

In order to prepare a sales forecast—that most crucial first premise for a budget—you should first thoroughly analyze the internal history of the time series you are forecasting. Then, forecast it using only its *own* cyclical history. Any history of the series is valuable. All post-war cycles (eight of them) would be optimal, but few companies have that much history. Nevertheless, even if you have only one business cycle (like the early 1980s), it is far better than none. In this section we use the ARRM model with monthly data to build a sales forecast.[2]

Indexing Declines

In Figure 30–5 you see eight post-war slowdowns (some became recessions). The eight lines declining from an index of 100 show how orders in one product line of a real company performed over several business cycles. In each, 100 equals the peak value. Every value thereafter is

---

FIGURE 30–5

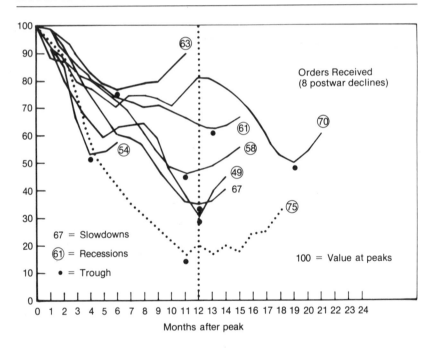

Orders Received
(8 postwar declines)

67 = Slowdowns
61 = Recessions
• = Trough

100 = Value at peaks

Months after peak

---

lower, until the revival begins. The dots show the troughs. The value of this type of graph is that, at the time of the 1975 recession, the circled line (which in the next recession becomes one more solid line) enabled management to monitor how this slowdown affected the specific prod-

---

[2] Special note: It must be said at this point that to build an ARRM model, your accounting data *must* be seasonally adjusted and then smoothed.

uct line relative to the way it behaved in seven former post-war slow-downs.

After two months the drop was about average; after four months—a rather short time span—the gravity was clear; finally, after just five months, it was a "worst case" example.

One of the great lessons in this graph is that management was able to *quickly* grasp the seriousness of the situation—not from an outside surgeon but from the internal history of the time series *as it developed month by month*. If you realize that these lines are all *seasonally adjusted* and then *smoothed,* you'll know why they are so sensitive to *change*—that all-important thing we try to forecast.

The plunge shown in the fan graph in Figure 30–5 really did happen in the 1975 recession. The product line kept going down, and orders finally struck bottom in the 11th month after the peak. At that moment the order level had dropped an astounding 85 percent; worse, it laid there for six months. The graph portrays a plunge far greater than you are likely to encounter. But, most important, the fan graph enabled the product manager to monitor the whole post-war experience. Look again: it is remarkable how quickly the 1963 decline stabilized and then improved. It is perhaps more remarkable how far the product line plunged in 1967, even though this cyclical experience was not ultimately classified as a recession. The fan graph shows how differently various industries and even product lines behave.

Indexing Revivals

Just as with declines, the fan graph can be equally useful in monitoring recoveries (see Figure 30–6). In this case you start the graph using 100 to equal the *trough* value for each past cyclical experience. But coming out of a plunge is a much more pleasant experience, and you can add a really useful new thing to it: growth. Note that in this fan graph, we have changed the scale to semi-log. Keep in mind that a straight line on semi-log paper means an equal *percentage* growth over time. In other words, 7 percent, 7 percent, 7 percent, etc.—the compound interest formula. (Arithmetic scales mean equal *amount* of change: $10, $10, $10, etc.—guaranteeing a declining rate of growth as the base gets larger and larger.) We live, not in an arithmetic world, but in a percentage world. It is all around us. The United States grows by a percentage. Companies are measured for their percentage growth. No president ever asks a company to grow $10 million per year. He or she is much more likely to expect 10 percent per year.

In this case the product line in the past generally came out of recessions at between 6 percent and 8 percent growth for about four

FIGURE 30–6

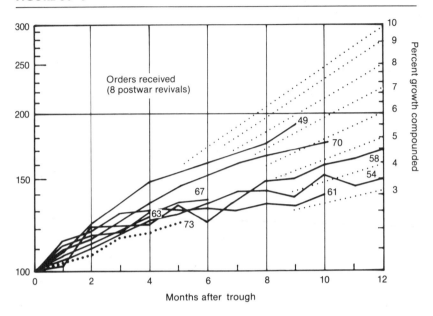

months. Then, growth slowed to something more like 3 to 4 percent— half. You can tell this by simply eyeballing the real slopes and comparing them to the dotted lines, which represent monthly percentage rates of growth. The graph says that, in order to double the volume from the recession low (100), you must grow at about 6 percent per month for the first 12 months after the recession. (Multiply 100 by 1.06 12 times, which equals 201.22.)

Once again, in the case of this product line, the product manager had a real problem. As you can see (circled line), the product never recovered as well as in previous recession revivals.

Look out for Orders

Most companies maintain net orders figures, meaning that they are new orders minus cancelations. This can be a double-whammy: not only do the orders go down in recessions, they are also canceled and later placed again, but at lower prices. It is a market cruelty one learns to live with. Also, do not necessarily expect sales billed to go as low as your orders received. Often companies can weather the storm by consuming their order backlog, while absolute new orders go down to much lower levels than the actual sales-billed volume.

THE SALES FORECAST: A CASE STUDY

Having made a thorough analysis of past behavior using fan graphs, the forecaster makes a sales forecast for next year's budget. To do this, we will build an ARRM model. This case study is from a real product line of a real multinational firm. In this real-world case, you first see the raw accounting data—*before* seasonal adjustment (Figure 30–7). The data

FIGURE 30–7
The ARRM Model: A Budget Forecast

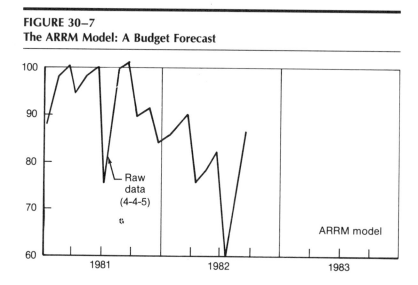

are plotted through September 1982—so we must be in October if we have September data. Note that the line portrays a 4–4–5 calendar: monthly data are collected in such a way that the first month of each quarter has 4 weeks, the second has 4 weeks, and the third month has 5 weeks, for a total of 13 weeks (multiply by four and you get a 52-week year). This is a popular accounting calendar. Note how this appears in the first two quarters of 1982: low, low, high; low, low, high. But then a two-week shutdown in July leaves only a two-week month, followed by a four-, then a five-week month (September). Since all these fluctuations in volume occur in the same month each year, they are seasonal; and a new time series can be developed after seasonally adjusting and smoothing the raw data, as has been done in Figure 30–8. This cyclical history superimposed on the raw data sets us up for forecasting.

Confrontation with a Turning Point

One look at Figures 30–7 and 30–8 suggests that we will confront a turning point sometime during the 15 months needed for the budget

FIGURE 30–8
The ARRM Model: A Budget Forecast

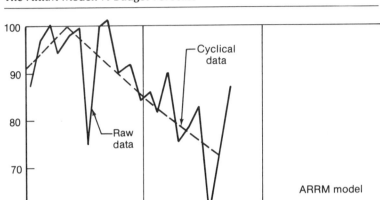

forecast. It seems inevitable when we see how long the line has already been declining. In turn this drives the forecaster into one of the most difficult challenges. Given the seemingly inevitable confrontation, we must make three decisions: (1) when will it happen (duration), (2) where will it be when it gets there (depth), and (3) how fast will we recover (slope).

1. Duration. The internal approach of the ARRM model—making use only of the historical data from the product line to be forecasted—greatly exploits averaging. Given that we have six recessions prior to 1980, simply count the months from peak to trough for each of the six declines in your fan graph. Add up these six durations, divide by six, and you get this product line's average post-war *duration* (Figure 30–9). This is the first step in building an average recession and is a forecast of *when* the turning point will occur: January 1983. The six small dots on the time axis show the durations from the product's cyclical peak in May 1981. The average duration is the circled dot.

2. Depth. If you think the cyclical line will continue straight, you don't have to worry about the *depth,* but this is quite an assumption. In Figure 30–9 we established the approximate month of the low. If you go for a separate analysis of the depth, then you have Figure 30–10. Simply divide the trough value by the peak value for each of your six recession declines. This gives you the severity of each recession. Then add them up and divide by six: in our example the average depth turns out to be 70 on the vertical scale. In other words the product line

FIGURE 30–9
The ARRM Model: A Budget Forecast

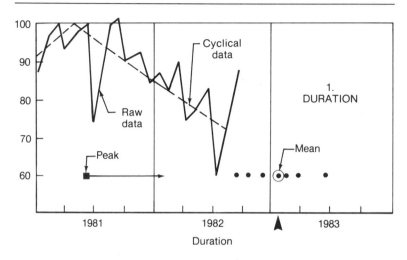

FIGURE 30–10
The ARRM Model: A Budget Forecast

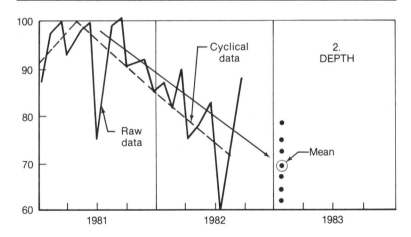

experiences a drop of approximately 30 percent in recessions. This is quite severe when we realize that the national Industrial Production Index drops an average of 10 percent.

You may not agree, but I highly recommend that both the duration (horizontal axis) and the depth (vertical axis) be carefully analyzed separately as above. If you chose simply to extend the dotted line to January by a roughly straight line, you will note that you would have gotten a lower depth than 70. This simply implies that the current experience (dotted line) is worse than average.

3. Slope. Given that we have decided that the turning point in this product line will be next January and that it will be at a depth of 70 when it gets there, we then must forecast how fast we will come out of this drop. Using the averaging approach, we calculate where the level of sales was 12 months after each of the past six troughs, relative to each trough value. The resulting ratio (say, 1.143) is multiplied times 70, yielding a forecast 12 months hence of 82. In Figure 30–11 you see

FIGURE 30–11
The ARRM Model: A Budget Forecast

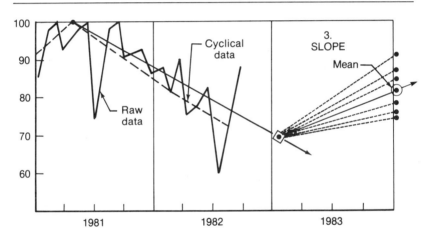

six small dots representing the level of sales 12 months after the lows of the past six recessions. These six levels are then averaged, which yields the mean *slope*.

Sales Forecast Values

Now that we have established the month of the turn (January), the depth at that point (70 percent), and the slope of an average revival bringing volume up to a point 12 months from the trough (82 percent), we calculate the actual sales figures. The first thing we do is get the cyclical figures (Figure 30–12), and then we put the seasonality back

FIGURE 30–12
The ARRM Model: A Budget Forecast

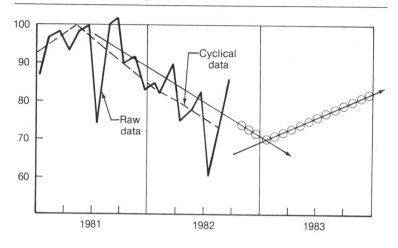

FIGURE 30–13
The ARRM Model: A Budget Forecast

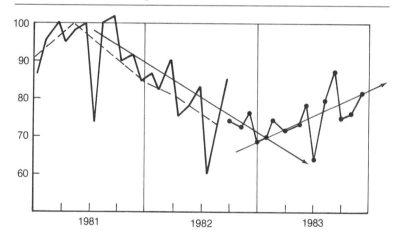

into the data before we give the final forecasts to management (Figure 30–13).

The process is as follows: estimate the values along the two straight lines. We will need figures for the fourth quarter, although they will not be a part of next year's budget. Then, beginning with January, you get the cyclical values for each of the 12 months of next year (Figure 30–12). Add up the 12, and you have next year's sales forecast.

But first the 12 individual monthly figures must be converted back to raw form. This is shown in Figure 30–13 (note the 4–4–5 calendar fluctuations).[3]

Caveats

Be careful not to get percentage growth mixed up with arithmetic growth. Throughout this exercise you should pay special attention to this. We *prefer* the percentage approach (as in the fan graph of the trough shown earlier), even though the example in the figures is shown using arithmetic scales. Another caveat of great importance is: don't confuse orders with sales. Although the two fan graphs used represent orders, they were chosen because of their violence. You, of course, would be forecasting your sales, not your orders. If you have both sets of figures, use both. Obviously, orders give you a lot of information about your sales, but they are *not* the same. Make your fan graphs using both orders and sales; but, for your ARRM model graphs, use sales and not orders. Each individual case will, of course, be special.

What Can Go Wrong?

Plenty. Besides the things already alluded to—such as percentage versus arithmetic change and the fact of the averaging process itself—there are many other things to look for in the way of dangers. Most important, the idea of an *average recession* does not have any reality. The eight post-war recessions have been so different from one another that not one of the eight conforms to what we get if we add them all together and divide by eight. Each had its own personality, which is really the same as saying that they were economically different from one another. But such is the case with using only data internal to the firm. Still, do it. It is an excellent exercise, but remember that you must also look outside the firm—your market share, your industry, the economy, the world. Finally, don't forget that there can be errors in the raw data, not to mention errors in the seasonally adjusted data that you (or your data processing department) must prepare. Finally, don't get discouraged. Reality is always a mess; we're just trying to organize it!

Calling the Turn Right. Here is a case where you call the turning point correctly as to timing, but still end up with a bad sales forecast. In Figure 30–14 you see the forecast as it was in Figure 30–13, but super-

---

[3] Be sure the *total* of the 12 cyclical figures is the same as the 12 raw figures. If these two numbers aren't close, the seasonal factors are not correctly calculated.

FIGURE 30–14
The ARRM Model: A Budget Forecast

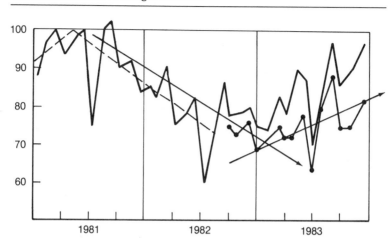

imposed over it is what *actually* happened after the year was finished. Imagine it is now February 1984, and our accountants have told us what finally transpired during the 1983 budget year. Notice right away that the *actual* data were always higher than our forecasts. In other words, we were too pessimistic. Note that we predicted the timing of the turning point to within a month—superb forecasting. But we were too pessimistic. Why?

Right Turn, Wrong Depth. The use of arithmetic paper might be a clue. When we extrapolated our straight-line cyclical index downward, we ran into a problem that is probably similar around all turning points. In other words, it doesn't stop on a dime. By the same token, it tends to accelerate after a turn. It doesn't suddenly leap up to maximum growth; on the contrary, it gradually speeds up.

The approach to the turn in this real case study (Figure 30–14) shows the product line slowing its rate of drop and not going all the way down on a straight line. Even though the timing of the turn was quite good, the level of the drop never reached the depth the forecaster expected.

But, the story is even worse *after* the turning point. A careful look at Figure 30–14 reveals that the post-recession slope was too pessimistic, in addition to the depth at the moment of the turn. The width of the gap is much greater at the end of 1983 than it was at the beginning of 1983, when the turn occurred. The long consistency of error as shown by the gap throughout the year on the same side of the forecast is enough to make you give up this approach. Don't. It is worth knowing all that can happen and why it is so difficult to be right. Gaps are bad in themselves because they represent consistent, systematic, repetitive error. And they tend to cumulate as well.

Wait! Read On. You may think it doesn't matter that we predicted the *timing* of the turn correctly. Absolutely wrong. If we had also had *that* decision wrong, we would have been in even worse trouble. In Figure 30–15 you see what would happen if the turn was forecasted to be six months later—let's say in July 1983, instead of in January. Needless to say, the gap in our sales performance would be even greater, as the huge asterisk indicates. We were better to predict January, even though it too produces a low forecast. Had we predicted July, the additional gap would be even *more* difficult to explain.

In this case study we changed only the dates. The actual case occurred a very long time ago—in the 1960 recession, to be exact. Not obvious is that the 1960 recession was the shallowest of the eight post-World War II recessions. Therefore, the choice of an average recession for this forecast was a bad one. Needless to say, an average recession was much worse than the shallowest one, and that is how it all came out. The forecast was simply too pessimistic for what ultimately happened. This was one of the several real-world experiences that led to the endorsement of the idea: Never forecast recession. You are usually better off working your way into recession and not forecasting the ultimate.

FIGURE 30–15
The ARRM Model: A Budget Forecast

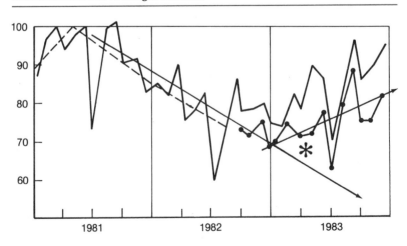

Be Brave. Who ever said forecasting was easy? It *is* one of the most difficult jobs, not to mention that it often comes with much negative recognition. The great thing about the ARRM model is that it covers the territory familiar to management—their own time series. It should always be one of the several inputs that management needs for developing next year's budget.

31

SALES FORECASTING WITH THE MICROCOMPUTER: A CASE STUDY

by
Dick Berry

University of Wisconsin

This chapter is the review of a forecasting case study for the national parts distribution center of a manufacturer of consumer products. The dialog relates to use of the microcomputer, employing a statistical program, to accomplish forecasting of parts sales on a month-by-month basis. Sales movement is to the variety of distributors and dealers who handle the company's products. The analysis and discussion are intended for an experienced sales or marketing executive. The use of statistical jargon is minimized, and references are suggested for the person desiring a more in-depth treatment of the subject and to source software and computer hardware.

The forecasting approach used in the case study is the causal method. This method assumes that a predictive relationship exists between the sales series to be forecasted and a reference economic data series. Once this relationship is quantified, the forecast is made by predicting or projecting the economic series—for example, for the next quarter or year—then, the sales series is forecasted based on the relationship. A linear regression equation is usually used to quantify the relationship between the two series.

THE FORECASTING PROCESS

In establishing linear regression relationships, a desirable methodology is to first plot the dependent data series and the independent economic reference series so that they may be visually compared—to determine if they are traveling together. If this process suggests a fit between the sales series and several reference economic series, a computer program is used to calculate a correlation matrix for the series being used. This process can be reversed, using the correlation matrix to select between variables. However, this approach is quite cumbersome if a number of lead–lag relationships are to be explored. It is important to shift the time relationship between data series, to lead or lag one another, thus to find better correlative relationships and enhance the forecasting process. If, for example, we can find an economic series with a strong correlation to a sales series—with the reference series lagging by several months or more—we have the ideal situation in forecasting. The linear regression equation is plugged with numbers from the reference series, and the forecast numbers are calculated.

In our discussion the sales series to be forecasted is termed the *dependent variable (DV)*. The reference series are termed *independent variables (IV)*. If the relationship between two variables is truly dependent, there is validity in using the method. It should be clearly understood that dependency should be well established before the forecasting method is considered reliable.

This process may sound complicated, but in reality it is as simple as the view of a mother and small child walking together, hand-in-hand. As the two walk along, the mother's path and direction are quite obvious and somewhat predetermined. Occasionally, she will change direction at a corner or intersection or perhaps strike off through a field along a winding path. The child, walking with the mother, covers pretty much the same course but may occasionally stray—stooping to pick up a leaf or to admire a flower, thus breaking step and maybe abruptly changing direction for a moment or two. The analogy with the causal forecasting method is that the principal economic series is the predictable one—the mother—whereas the sales series to be forecasted is the small child. Although the two may not lock step at every moment, one can expect that they will travel together, arriving at the same destination.

The ideal situation is to have a lagging independent variable (IV) to predict the course of the dependent variable (DV), then to use projected values of the IV in the forecasting calculations. For example, if we want to forecast the sale of appliance repair parts from a parts depot, we know that the task is difficult unless we have a good idea as to the future market demand factors. On the other hand it is not that difficult to read the numbers off a government report of economic activity for a lagging IV, or to make a reasonable prediction as to the course that the Business Week Index, Forbes Index, or Coincident Indicator Series 920 will take, then to plug the numbers from these series into a forecast equation—resulting in a forecast for the service parts series. At this point in our discussion, the effect of promotional activity is disregarded.

Preparing the Data for Forecasting

Consider it a rare occurrence if you have a sales series that can be used directly in a forecasting equation without some massaging. Chances are that your series needs to be adjusted for trading day variations, seasonal variations, unique irregular data points because of a strike, flood, or fire, or closing periods that don't coincide with available data on the IVs to be considered for forecasting use. Thus, the first step in forecasting is to put your data in usable form.

To illustrate the forecasting process, we will use the data for parts sales of a major consumer durable goods company. The available data start in January 1981, at which time a new centralized parts warehouse was put in operation. There are two dependent variables to be considered. One is total parts sales dollars, and the other is number of line items shipped. Data are available on a monthly basis, both for the DVs and the prospective IVs. Figure 31–1 illustrates the unadjusted data series for parts sales. The computer graphing program being used is not programmed to illustrate the dollar values, which range from a high of $874,452 in January 1981, to a low of $444,689 in May 1981. (The vertical line in a graph is designated the Y-axis, used to plot dependent variables. The horizontal line—designated the X-axis—is usually the time line or is used to plot independent variables.)

Normally, it is nice to have three to five years of data to determine seasonal index values for each month; but in this case we do not have that luxury. We should immediately be suspicious of irregular data in the first part of the data set, due to shipment interruptions and delays before the new parts center was put into operation. The high January and February figures in 1981 suggest an irregularity.

The parts sales data fulfil an important forecasting requirement by their very nature. Because parts sales are through the company's distribution channel to dealers and servicers of home kitchen appliances, the market is specifically segmented. It includes only those customers with much similarity in demographic characteristics. Forecasters should be wary of this consideration, as too much variability in the customer data sources will reflect in extreme purchase behavior differences, and the forecasting results may be erratic. As a guideline, it is

FIGURE 31-1
Sequence Plot of Parts Sales Data

This plot of the raw parts sales data illustrates the variability of shipping activity for the parts center. The plot covers the period 81.01 through 83.06, illustrating irregulars and seasonal components. The shipments range from a high of $874,452 in 81.01, to a low of $444,689 in 81.05. At this stage of analysis, a strong irregular appears to be evident in 81.01 and 81.02. The curve suggests a gradual upward trend beginning in the fifth month, 81.05.

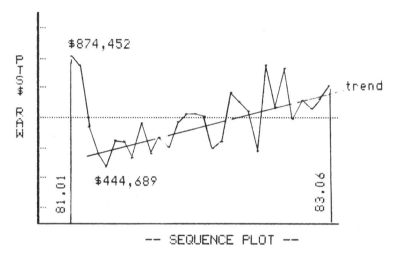

desirable if each data set being forecasted represents the market within a well-defined Standard Industrial Classification, preferably limited to a four-digit group.

Deseasonalize Data

Most sales data sets have a seasonal characteristic that must be considered in forecasting. For example, sales of soft drinks, foundry castings, machine tools, automobiles, and registrations in executive education programs are all seasonal to one degree or another. It is difficult to think of a product or service that is not seasonal. In the causal forecasting process, we compare a dependent data series with reference independent series, hoping to find an independent variable that is useful in predicting our data series. If either or both data sets are seasonalized in different ways, the likelihood of fit is reduced. Using our analogy of the mother and child, the child and mother may not recognize each other and thus not walk together in a predictable way.

The deseasonalization process is best explained with an example—
our parts sales data—illustrated in Table 31–1. The data should be
tabulated on a year–month basis, then perform the following steps:

1. Add month rows and calculate the mean (average) for each row,
   designate MM.
2. Add the new column (monthly means), record total, designate
   MT.
3. Divide MT by 12 to find the average value, designate YM.
4. Divide each value of MM by YM. This is the deseasonalization
   index, designate Monthly Index, MI.
5. If desired, calculate the percent of year for each month by dividing the 12 values of MI by 12. Multiply the numbers by 100 to
   express as a percentage.

As you review Table 31–1, you'll note that the index values range
from .78 for May to 1.22 for January. We can still be suspicious that the
January and February data and index values are distorted by an irregu-

TABLE 31–1
Calculate Deseasonalization Index

1 Month	2 1981	3 1982	4 1983	5 Monthly Mean (MM)	6 Monthly Index (MI)
January	$874452	$615187	$821355	$744820*	1.22
February	835508	647892	623716	741700	1.21
March	593810	647357	696839	620584	1.02
April	493062	635708	665625	564385	0.92
May	444689	512663	704339	478676	0.78
June	544450	539293	753781	541872	0.89
July	535426	727888	655105	631657	1.03
August	474585	692516		583551	0.96
September	609640	658802		634221	1.04
October	489290	501998		495644	0.81
November	554878	839068		696973	1.14
December	516930	670696		593813	0.97
Total	6966720	7689068		7327896	12.00
Average Monthly Value (YM)				610658	

* Note: Monthly Index (MI) is based on 1981 and 1982
only. It is desirable to use three to five years of
data to calculate the deseasonalization index. (Not
allowed because adequate data was not available for
example sales series.)

lar event—startup of the new parts center—but we'll not know for sure until following years when the index values are recalculated. Please note that data for the first seven months of 1983 were not used in calculating the index values. Another arithmetic step tells us that 10.2 percent of the parts sales activity occurs in January, and 6.5 percent in May—a 57 percent range in activity for the extreme months. We may not be able to forecast parts sales, but we have some ideas about vacation scheduling and the need for part-time help.

In the background, but not recorded here, was a comparable set of calculations to determine similar values for line items shipped. One of the forecasting questions was whether or not this activity had predictable characteristics of interest. This analysis determined that there is substantial difference between line item activity and parts sales in May, June, and November. The differences were not checked statistically for significance. This information gives us a hint that customers change their stocking patterns in these months. The company may decide to change its promotional practices to alter these patterns.

Smooth and Deseasonalize Data

Most data sets contain month-to-month irregularities that occur because of random happenings, both by customers and by those in the manufacturing and distribution network. If nothing else, seasonal mail delays and month-end manipulation of inventory and shipping patterns can cause distortions. To compensate for these irregularities, one will usually calculate a three-month moving average of the data set, then deseasonalize the data, before attempting to establish the causal forecasting relationships. An alternative approach is to use a curve-fitting process to smooth the data set, using a polynomial curve-fitting program in the computer. This technique is very useful for highly irregular data.

Table 31–2 illustrates the smoothed, deseasonalized data for parts sales. These data are going to be graphed and compared wih reference economic series—IVs—and processed through the computer to determine causal relationships and to establish the forecasting model, the process and equations for forecasting. A logical question at this time is whether or not the data have been massaged so much that "the mother won't recognize her child." To the contrary, we cleaned the kid up, taught it some manners, gave it a new suit of clothes; now we're ready to start out for Grandma's place. This is the time when the excitement builds, and many surprising bits of information jump out at you. In retrospect you'll comment, "I guess I'd have known that if I'd have taken the time to think about it!"

TABLE 31–2
Deseasonalize and Smooth Parts Sales Data

1	2	3	4	5
Month	Raw Data	Deseas. Index	Deseas. Data*	Smoothed Data**
81.01	$874452	1.22	$716764	$708010
81.02	835508	1.21	690502	663144
81.03	593810	1.02	582167	602868
81.04	493062	0.92	535937	562739
81.05	444689	0.78	570114	572598
81.06	544450	0.89	611742	567229
81.07	535426	1.03	519831	541977
81.08	474585	0.96	494359	533461
81.09	609640	1.04	586192	561538
81.10	489290	0.81	604062	558996
81.11	554878	1.14	486735	541238
81.12	516930	0.97	532917	507968
82.01	615187	1.22	504252	524206
82.02	647892	1.21	535448	558121
82.03	647357	1.02	634663	620336
82.04	635708	0.92	690987	660970
82.05	512663	0.78	657260	651398
82.06	539293	0.89	605947	656631
82.07	727888	1.03	706687	678002
82.08	692516	0.96	721371	687174
82.09	658802	1.04	633463	658195
82.10	501998	0.81	619751	663079
82.11	839068	1.14	736024	682405
82.12	670696	0.97	691439	700235
83.01	821355	1.22	673241	626716
83.02	623716	1.21	515468	623962
83.03	696839	1.02	683175	640716
83.04	665625	0.92	723505	769893
83.05	704339	0.78	902999	824483
83.06	735781	0.89	846945	795323
83.07	655105	1.03	636024	--

* Column 2 divided by column 3
** Three-month moving average of deseasonalized data.

Keys to Forecasting Success

There are several important keys to forecasting success. A forecaster must understand the mathematical and statistical concepts being employed. Even the experienced forecaster will have a friend to talk to about the validity of his or her work. The consequences of misapplying techniques can be severe (for example, to make an erroneous forecast because of a method error).

A forecast using the causal method will only be as good as the fit between the DV and the selected IV—or IVs, if multiple independent variables are used. This means that one must have access to appropriate reference data series to select from. Probably the best all-around source of these data is *Business Conditions Digest,* a publication of the Bureau of Economic Analysis, U.S. Department of Commerce. *BCD,* as it is called, is published monthly, containing a variety of charts and graphs of reference economic series. Some forecasters use a selection of trade association and industry data available from reputable sources. The *Business Week* and *Forbes* Indexes are useful, particularly because they are readily available and changes are graphically illustrated. It is important that publication of these series is timely, a comment that is not often made about publications of the Department of Commerce. *BCD* and a variety of statistical reference series are readily available from the reference section of most libraries.

Selecting a Computer and Software

For my forecasting work I use an Apple II+, with 64K of memory and two disk drives. The important thing is not the computer but the software used. Perhaps I was lucky to find a program called Statistics with Daisy, now with an advanced version designated Professional Daisy. Daisy does a variety of statistical tests, plots curves, has an internal spreadsheet for one's data, and is very user friendly. It has menu prompts and a simple, logical, mnemonic command structure. ENTE gets your data entered. DATA displays your data. REGR initiates the procedure to perform a regression. SEQU commands the plot of a data series. These amenities may not be important to the frequent user, or one with a good memory, but I find them very useful.

Having a software program that computes correlation matrixes for combinations of data series is imperative. A correlation matrix provides the initial encouragement that you have found a fit between your DV and one or more IVs. You'll make visual inspection for fit from plotted curves, next a correlation matrix suggests the best fit, and then a series of regression calculations tells you which IVs are most promising for your use. *Correlation* is a statistical term that means strength of relationship.

A variety of microcomputers, minicomputers, and mainframe systems are available, some with blazing color, beepers, and bells. But, if you can't find a software package that works properly, you're out of luck. A forecasting program should contain its own data spreadsheet; or, read another using the DIF industry standard data interchange format, plot curves, calculate correlation matrixes, and calculate two-variable linear regressions and multiple regressions. The software is the key to forecasting success—and some so-called forecasting packages do not have the desired capabilities.

Compare Data Series with Independent Variables

The next step in the forecasting process is to compare your data set with various economic series to determine which provide a likely fit. It is a useful practice to initially make comparisons with the basic leading, coincident, and lagging series published in *BCD*—for example, 910: index of 12 leading indicators; 920: index of 4 roughly coincident indicators; and 930: index of 6 lagging indicators. Figure 31–2 illustrates the parts sales series (deasonalized, three-month moving average), and the 910, 920, and 930 economic series. Inspection of these curves suggests a positive correlation with series 910 and a negative correlation with series 930.

Although none of the correlations appears to be particularly strong, the next step is to calculate the correlations for selected IVs. The reference series—potential IVs—that I normally use at this stage are the following, with designations I've assigned:

LD910	910. Composite index of 12 leading indicators.
COIN920	920. Composite index of four roughly coincident indicators.
LAG930	930. Composite index of six lagging indicators.
MON917	917. Composite index of money and financial flows.
PROF916	916. Composite index of profitability.
INV915	915. Composite index of inventory investment and purchasing.
WK CLMS5	5. Average weekly initial claims for unemployment insurance, state programs.
ORDERS 8	8. Value of manufacturers' new orders for consumer goods and materials in 1972 dollars.
MFGSL57	57. Manufacturing and trade sales in 1972 dollars.
STOCK 19	19. Index of stock prices, 500 common stocks, Standard & Poor's Corporation.
HLPAD 46	46. Index of help-wanted advertising in newspapers, Conference Board.
INDPRD47	47. Index of industrial production, Federal Reserve Board.
FORBES	*Forbes* Index, *Forbes* Economics Department, and *Forbes* magazine.
BUS WK	*Business Week* Index, *Business Week* Economics Department, and *Business Week* magazine.
CONS ATT	Index of Consumer Confidence, Survey Research Center, University of Michigan.
NAPM IND	National Association of Purchasing Managers' Purchasing Managers Index.[1]

---

[1] Numerically identified series are from *BCD*.

FIGURE 31–2
Sequence Plot of Parts Sales versus Economic Series

This composition of sequence plots for PTS$ 3AV and the three principal Department of Commerce economic series (LD910, COIN920, and LAG930) suggests a positive correlation between parts sales and the leading economic series. There is also a suggestion that parts sales is negatively correlated with the lagging series. The period is 81.01 through 83.06. The trough of the recent recession (November 1982), as declared by the Department of Commerce, is noted on the plots.

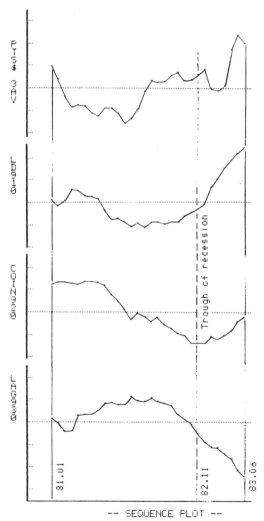

-- SEQUENCE PLOT --

The following designations are used throughout this work for the sales series being forecasted:

PARTS LI	Line items of parts shipped, deseasonalized.
PTSLI3AV	Three-month moving average of line items shipped, deseasonalized.
PARTS $	Parts sales, deseasonalized.
PTS$ 3AV	Three-month moving average of parts sales, deseasonalized.
PTS$ LD6	Three-month moving average of parts sales, deseasonalized, leading six months.

Calculate Correlation Matrix

The data for each of the dependent and independent variable series are next processed by the computer, making least squares calculations, yielding correlation coefficients for each paired set of variables. The Daisy program performs this operation in 4.5 minutes for a 20-column by 30-row matrix. A mainframe computer would do the same in a matter of seconds, handling a much larger matrix. Such are the fundamental differences between a micro and its big brother. Those interested in a 16-bit microcomputer—because of the increased speed—may want to make a comparison with this type of an evaluation. The minutes saved can be compared to the additional hardware cost—assuming desirable software is available. The availability of desirable software is proportional to the market density of different computer operating systems.

A portion of the correlation matrix described above is shown in Table 31–3. This tells us that a number of IVs are candidates to be used in a forecasting model for PTS$ 3AV. We also note that PTSLI3AV—line items—is also correlated with several of the series. PARTS $ and PARTS LI, the deseasonalized but unsmoothed data series, do not correlate as well with the IVs as the smoothed series.

This suggests that some irregular components may be interfering with the fit. We can begin to formulate some ideas about the parts sales series by inspecting the correlation matrix. For example, it tends to be a leading series, inversely related to the lagging components of the economy. Note that parts sales tend to reflect consumer attitudes.

Linear Regression Analysis

At this point we can carry out a regression calculation for any of the combinations (for example, parts sales dollars as the DV and LAG930 as the IV). This yields the following:

$$PTS\$ \; 3AV = 2,032,243 - 11,595(LAG930)$$

where

$r = .669$ (the regression coefficient).

r-squared $= .45$ (the coefficient of determination, interpreted to mean that 45 percent of the variance in PTS$ 3AV is explained by the regression equation).

$F = 22.7$

$T = -4.7$

SEE $= 60,848$

(F and T are statistical qualities of the regression equation, and SEE is the standard error of the estimate—an indication of the expected error in a given calculation.)

TABLE 31–3
Correlation Matrix for Parts Sales versus Economic Series

A correlation matrix suggests the fit between dependent and independent variables. Such a matrix displays correlation coefficients for each set of paired variables, only partially illustrated below. Note the improvement in fit of parts sales and line items shipped after the data has been smoothed (compare PARTS $ to PTS$ 3AV and PARTS LI to PTSLI3AV). The names assigned to variables are limited to eight characters by the Daisy program's internal spreadsheet.

```
->CORR
```

CORRELATION COEFFICIENTS

CURRENT NAMES:	DATE	PARTS $	PARTS LI	PTS$ 3AV	PTSLI3AV
1 DATE	1	.549	.412	.649	.697
2 PARTS $	.549	1	.399	.918	.587
3 PARTS LI	.412	.399	1	.415	.426
4 PTS$ 3AV	.649	.918	.415	1	.602
5 LD910	.471	.461	.193	.512	.238
6 COIN920	-.819	-.378	-.309	-.485	-.569
7 LAG930	-.639	-.597	-.225	-.669	-.32
8 MON917	.793	.467	.312	.547	.501
9 PROF916	.066	.125	-.064	.147	-.147
10 INV915	-.221	.086	-.071	.071	-.245
11 WK CLMS5	.324	.087	.091	.115	.234
12 ORDERS 8	-.449	-.113	-.15	-.166	-.355
13 MFGSLS57	-.57	-.178	-.172	-.248	-.393
14 STOCK 19	.516	.475	.17	.529	.19
15 HLPAD 46	-.842	-.499	-.371	-.59	-.638
16 INDPRD47	-.71	-.289	-.243	-.379	-.509
17 FORBES	-.248	.057	-.068	3E-03	-.25
18 BUS WK	-.795	-.41	-.3	-.515	-.561
19 CONS ATT	.486	.504	.234	.544	.298
20 PTSLI3AV	.697	.587	.426	.602	1

Statistical terms and tests which explain the important relationships relative to the forecasting process are listed at the end of the chapter.

We could stop at this point and use the LAG930 series in the forecasting equation to forecast parts sales. However, in order to do so, we would need to predict LAG930 for the future period to be forecasted. This is not too difficult, but the expected accuracy would be poor.

Another alternative would be to try several of the independent variables—those that have low correlation with each other—in a three- or four-variable multiple regression with parts sales. This is not good practice, because we end up having to predict the future values for two or more IVs, such as LAG930 and CONS ATT. This could lead to a high multiple regression coefficient with good qualities but with a high error factor, due to errors in predicting the IVs.

Regressions Based on Lead-Lag Relationships

One of the most desirable alternatives is to find an independent variable that leads the dependent variable by several months. This can be done by calculating a series of correlation matrixes, with PTS$ 3AV leading the IVs by selected periods. A similar and much faster analysis of the same alternative can be done by overlaying plots of the DV and IVs. With the available series it becomes apparent that, with PTS$ 3AV leading by six months, there are some strong fits to several of the IVs. To verify this prospect, correlation matrixes are calculated for lead periods of four, five, and six months. This yields the findings illustrated in Table 31–4 for PTS$ LD6.

And Eureka, we've hit the jackpot! The correlation matrix shows very high correlation coefficients for no less than nine of the IVs. The computer is now used to calculate the regression equations and summary statistics for the logical candidate IVs. A good choice turns out to be ORDERS 8 (new orders for consumer goods and materials in 1972 dollars). The statistic is readily available on a month-by-month basis from *BCD*. The regression equation and summary statistics are as follows:

$$\text{PTS\$ LD6} = 1{,}637{,}537 - 32{,}062 \text{ (ORDERS 8)}$$

Stated in the working format:

$$\text{PTS\$ 3AV} = 1{,}637{,}537 - 32{,}062 \text{ (ORDERS 8, lagged six months)}$$

TABLE 31–4
Correlation Matrix for Parts Sales with Lead Relationship

The computer is instructed to rearrange the data table with PTS$ 3AV in a six-month leading relationship to the other series. The new series, designated PTS$ LD6, is assigned a column in temporary storage unless saved to a new file. The correlation matrix is calculated with the new column added. We find strong correlative relationships of PTS$ LD6 to a number of the economic reference series—a basis for selecting one independent variable for the linear regression relationship. It turns out that ORDERS 8 is the preferred IV.

```
->CORR
```

■■■
                    CORRELATION COEFFICIENTS

CURRENT NAMES:		DATE	PARTS $	PTS$ LD6	PTS$ 3AV
1	DATE	1	.439	.745	.541
2	PARTS $	.439	1	.269	.914
3	PTS$ LD6	.745	.269	1	.338
4	PTS$ 3AV	.541	.914	.338	1
5	LD910	-.654	-.131	-.55	-.119
6	COIN920	-.925	-.459	-.857	-.552
7	LAG930	.091	-.307	-.083	-.392
8	MON917	.154	-.017	-.159	.037
9	PROF916	-.828	-.278	-.489	-.311
10	INV915	-.834	-.321	-.788	-.368
11	WK CLMS5	.819	.32	.798	.375
12	ORDERS 8	-.824	-.253	-.911	-.328
13	MFGSLS57	-.846	-.264	-.873	-.331
14	STOCK 19	-.41	-.021	-.077	5E-03
15	HLPAD 46	-.91	-.478	-.736	-.562
16	INDPRD47	-.933	-.453	-.86	-.543
17	FORBES	-.927	-.422	-.786	-.506
18	BUS WK	-.929	-.493	-.837	-.601
19	CONS ATT	-.315	-.176	-.191	-.173
20	PTSLI3AV	.725	.537	.466	.545

where

$$r = .911$$
$$r\text{-squared} = 82 \text{ percent}$$
$$F = 107.8$$
$$T = -10.4$$
$$\text{SEE} = 35,902$$

To illustrate the regression relationship, the computer plot of PTS$ LD6 versus ORDERS 8 is shown in Figure 31–3, a picture so beautiful as to bring tears of joy to the eyes of any sales director.

FIGURE 31–3
Regression Statistics and Plot of PTS$ LD6 versus
ORDERS 8

The computer has calculated the regression statistics and
plotted the relationship for the linear regression of PTS$ LD6
versus ORDERS 8. The plot illustrates the negative correlation. Closeness of the points to the regression line suggests
the high regression coefficient of .911.

```
->REGR


   DEP VAR -
        COLUMN (NAME OR #)? 3
HOW MANY INDEPENDENT VARIABLES? 1
INDEP VAR #1 -
        COLUMN (NAME OR #)? 12


MULTIPLE R   = .911299499
STD ERR EST = 35902.9408
        F   = 107.768074


  B              STD ERR (B)      T

ORDERS 8
-32062.2393    3088.50832    -10.381141

CONSTANT
1637536.56

->PLOT
```

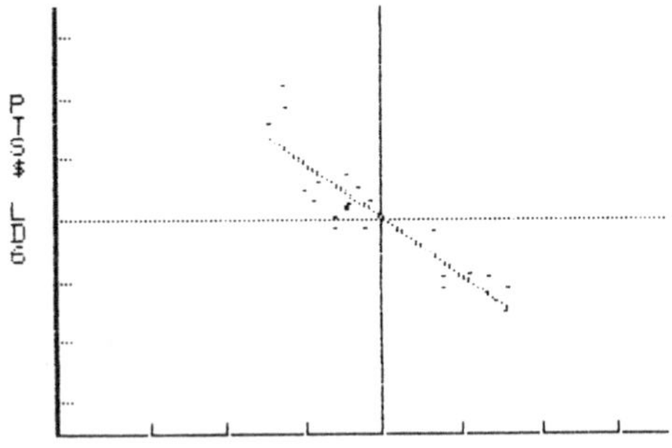

```
ORDERS 8
```

Let's construct a mother–child analogy to illustrate what has just
happened. Assume that a little child named PTS$ LD6 has been placed
in an orphanage. Finally he has been put up for adoption, and a number
of prospective mothers come for interviewing. Of this group of mothers, a number were found to be suitable for adoption of the little boy.
So, a series of tests were given to the boy and the prospective mothers

(call them correlation calculations, if you like), and it was decided that the woman named ORDERS 8 was the best suited. Our story ends as we see PTS$ LD6 and his new mother, ORDERS 8, walking out of the orphanage together. They are so fond of each other that they walk very closely, hands tightly clasped. You see, their love can be expressed by a "love quotient" of .911 (call it a regression coefficient, if you like) because they fit so well together. As you would surmise, we can also look into the future and see the boy and his mother walking very closely together, at least for the next six months. It might have worked just as well if PTS$ LD6 had been adopted by the woman called COIN920, or even the ones called INDPRD47 or BUS WK. Let's hope we've made the best selection in our adoption!

Making the Forecast

One of the confusing things about causal forecasting is to get clear in your mind what is meant by a lead or lag relationship. The confusing thing is trying to conceptualize how ORDERS 8 is going to be used to forecast PTS$ 3AV if it (ORDERS 8) is the *lagging* variable. To explain, ORDERS 8 is used with a six-month lagged relationship in the linear regression equation, meaning that in January 1984, PTS$ 3AV will relate to what ORDERS 8 was in July 1983. Thinking of the little boy and his mother, we all know that little boys like to skip ahead of their mothers. In the analogy the little boy is six "steps" ahead of his mother, but they will travel together over the same walkways, passing the same destinations. Thus, we visualize the leading relationship of PTS$ 6LD to ORDERS 8 and how a lagging variable—ORDERS 8—is used for forecasting.

To actually make the forecast, we will carry out the following steps:

1. Determine values of the IV for the forecast period. This may involve reading values of the IV from a published table if the IV lags the DV; otherwise, values of the IV must be predicted.
2. Plug values of the IV into the linear regression equation to calculate values of the DV for the periods to be forecasted.
3. Multiply the forecasted values by the seasonal index values (previously designated MI) for each period. The products are the final seasonalized forecast values.
4. Test the forecast using the above process, by calculating forecast values for the period when actual forecast values are known, subtracting from actual values to determine the forecast error for each month, then plotting the forecast values, actual values, and error for each period. The actual performance of the

forecasting model is evaluated using this test procedure. Refer to Table 31–5 and Figure 31–4 for illustrations of this process.

Several alternatives are available to calculate the forecast values. Hopefully, your computer program has a regression PLUG command (the Daisy command) to calculate the values. A good alternative is to use a programmable calculator. I use a Sharp EL–512 scientific calculator to perform the calculations. This calculator can also be used to

---

TABLE 31–5
Parts Sales Forecast

1 Month	2 Raw Data	3 Deseas. Index	4 ORDERS 8 Index (Lag 6)a	5 F′cst (Deseas) b	6 F′cst c	7 Error d	8 Month % yr.
81.07	$535426	1.03	33.31	$569552	$586638	$51212	8.6
81.08	474585	0.96	34.50	531398	510142	35557	8.0
81.09	609640	1.04	34.15	542619	564324	-45315	8.7
81.10	489290	0.81	34.92	517932	419525	-69765	6.8
81.11	554878	1.14	35.29	506069	576919	22041	9.5
81.12	516930	0.97	35.16	510237	494930	-22000	8.1
82.01	615187	1.22	34.45	533001	650261	35074	10.2
82.02	647892	1.21	33.44	565383	684114	36222	10.1
82.03	647357	1.02	32.48	596163	608086	-39270	8.5
82.04	635708	0.92	31.00	643615	592126	-43585	7.7
82.05	512663	0.78	30.22	668623	521526	8863	6.5
82.06	539293	0.89	30.50	659646	587085	47792	7.4
82.07	727888	1.03	29.18	701968	723027	-4861	8.6
82.08	692516	0.96	29.45	693311	665578	-26937	8.0
82.09	658802	1.04	30.55	658043	684365	25562	8.7
82.10	501998	0.81	29.30	698120	565477	63479	6.8
82.11	839068	1.14	30.77	650989	742128	-96940	9.5
82.12	670696	0.97	30.29	666379	646387	-24308	8.1
83.01	821355	1.22	30.29	666379	812982	-8373	10.2
83.02	623716	1.21	29.60	688502	833087	209371	10.1
83.03	696839	1.02	29.62	687860	701617	4778	8.5
83.04	665625	0.92	27.91	742686	683272	17646	7.7
83.05	704339	0.78	28.22	732747	571543	-132796	6.5
83.06	753781	0.89	28.25	731785	651289	-102491	7.4
83.07	655105	1.03	31.54	626302	645090	-10014	8.6
83.08	n.a.	0.96	31.52	626942	601865	n.a.	8.0
83.09		1.04	31.84	616683	641350		8.7
83.10		0.81	32.16	606423	491203		6.8
83.11		1.14	34.04	546146	622607		9.5
83.12		0.97	33.26	571155	554020		8.1

a: See Business Conditions Digest. Values are $Billion, lagged 6 months. Use index for 83.01 to forecast 83.07.
b: PTS$ 3AV = 1,637,537 - 32,062 (ORDERS 8, lagged 6 mo.)
c: Column 5 x Column 3.
d: Column 6 - Column 2.

FIGURE 31–4
Actual Parts Sales versus Forecast and Error

These curves illustrate the success or failure of the forecasting effort. If things have worked out properly, the turning points will coincide between the actual and forecast curves, and the error will be minimal throughout the relationship. The forecast results are good, but one must question the cyclical error characteristic and large errors at 83.02, 83.05, and 83.06.

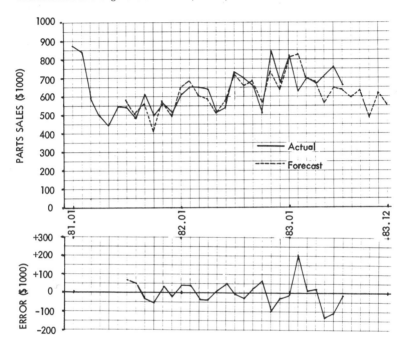

determine parameters of a linear regression equation; thus, a computer is not really necessary, except to calculate the all-important correlation matrixes in a reasonable period of time. A good alternative is to use a calculating spreadsheet program (like Magicalc, Visicalc, and Supercalc) on your computer, setting up a format such as illustrated in Table 31–5. The spreadsheet calculates values for the forecast and error (residuals between the actual and calculated values) using formulas that you enter into the spreadsheet. Notes *a*, *b*, and *c* at the bottom of Table 31–5 suggest the needed formulas.

We now construct Table 31–5 to record the forecast values and some of the working data. It is early August 1983, and our objective is to forecast parts sales—PTS$ 3AV—for the period July 1983 through December 1983. We will also verify the validity of the forecasting model by calculating forecast values for the historical period of January 1982 through June 1983. If we wanted to forecast beyond December 1983, it would be necessary to predict—forecast—values for ORDERS 8, the IV that is going to be used in the calculations.

Next, we go to page 64 of the July 1983 issue of *Business Conditions Digest*. This provides the data for ORDERS 8 for January 1981 through June 1983.

A progammable calculator (like the Sharp EL–512) is then programmed with the forecast equation: PTS$ 3AV = 1,637,537 − 32,062 (ORDERS 8, lagged six months). Alternatively, we could use the computer, with the Daisy program on PLUG. The calculated values for the deseasonalized parts sales are multiplied by the values of MI (see previous for MI, the deseasonalization index), and the error for each period is entered in Table 31–5. These multiple arithmetic functions can be programmed into a computer spreadsheet with instantaneous calculation of results. (Caution: check your keying of data and the logic of the answers.)

Figure 31–4 is next constructed to depict the graphical relationships between actual and forecasted values of parts sales. The important point at this time is to see how bad the forecast error is for the historical period and to observe any irregularities in the results. The following details are noted:

1. The shape and form of the forecast and actual curves tend to exhibit the same characteristics; most important, the turning points are essentially the same throughout the comparison period. This is a nicety that we might dream about for a lifetime and never achieve!

2. The monthly error amounts are generally within a range of plus or minus 10 percent. We can suspect that these variations are due as much to data discrepancies as anything else.

3. The large errors in February, May, and June 1983 suggest the need for an investigation to determine what has happened. We can suspect stocking problems following the economic upturn starting in December 1983. We can also suspect a problem with the deseasonalization index, MI, for January and February. The forecast values for February 1983 look suspicious: what is the problem?

4. With recovery of the economy, the forecast is showing a down trend. We can expect the demand for part sales to follow orders for consumer goods (ORDERS 8), lagged six months. We will want to keep close watch over *BCD* in months to come—to be aware if the IV signals a turning point.

5. Inspection of the errors leads to the observation that the error values are alternatively positive and negative for equal time periods. This phenomena is due to autocorrelation—sometimes called serial correlation—between the forecast and actual values. A test—calculation of Durbin–Watson statistic—should be carried out to evaluate severity of this problem. Compensating procedures may be needed. See the statistical terms and tests for further explanation.

Management Forecasting Adjustments

To this point we have discussed only the process for developing a forecast based on causal relationship to an economic series. The forecasting process is not complete until we have made adjustments that reflect management expectations for the business. Anticipating a good—or bad—year, the forecast figures should be factored by an appropriate percentage to reflect management optimism or pessimism. If, for example, there is to be a merchandising program to increase the sales level of service parts, this adjustment needs to be made for the period affected. Conversely, "will-fitters" might be making inroads, and the forecast must be adjusted downward to reflect this loss of business. Likewise, major additions or drops in the product line, affect of new products, additions due to acquisitions, or new export sales adjustments must be made by management.

The overall process we have described allows a company to make a forecast with a realistic base projection, anticipating expectations for the market economy. Appropriate adjustments due to management expectations are the essential modification to any forecast. These practices are realistic, practical, and lead to sound business forecasting and planning; but, they require periodic attention and adjustments as the economy and business outcome is monitored.

Multiple Linear Regression

We still have not resolved the question as to whether or not we should have used multiple IVs to forecast parts sales. For example, there may be a dependent relationship between parts sales and advertising expense or another of the indicator series. Logically, we would plot advertising expense relative to parts sales, trying to lead relationship of one or two months to see if there is some relationship between the two series. If a relationship is found, we would enter this series in the data, prior to calculating the correlation matrix shown in Table 31–4. In reality, the manufacturer has not been promoting parts sales, so this alternative cannot be considered. However, it is interesting to speculate that consumer attitudes, or another series that does not serially correlate with the previously selected IV, ORDERS 8, might be used.

Before doing this, there is a problem to talk about. When we examine Figure 31–4, we quickly note that there are large error factors in

FIGURE 31–5
Plot of Parts Sales to Lagging Indicator Series

This comparison of sequence plots illustrates the strong inverse relationship between the dependent variable, PTS$ LD6, and the principal independent variable, ORDERS 8. The independent variable, CONS ATT, is under consideration with ORDERS 8 in a multiple regression forecasting model to forecast parts sales.

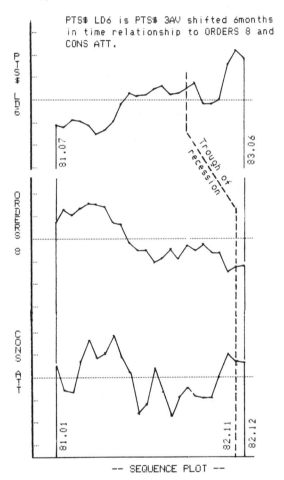

-- SEQUENCE PLOT --

FIGURE 31-6
Multiple Regression Statistics for PTS$ LD6

The computer has calculated the multiple regression statistics for a forecasting model for PTS$ LD6, using ORDERS 8 and CONS ATT as the independent variables. The results show very little improvement over the linear regression model illustrated in Figure 31-3. The three variables are illustrated in sequence plots in Figure 31-5.

```
MULTIPLE R   = .926299562
STD ERR EST = 33628.0167
        F   = 63.4597444

   B            STD ERR (B)     T

ORDERS 8
-34451.5982    3125.47028    -11.022853

CONS ATT
3581.21073     1773.55745     2.019225

CONSTANT
1463896.77


->SUMM

                MULTIPLE R     R-SQUARE
UNADJUSTED     .926299562     .858030878
ADJUSTED       .918972257     .844510009

STD ERROR OF ESTIMATE = 33628.0167
SAMPLE SIZE = 24


ANOVA OF CURRENT REGRESSION:

SS                  DF    MS

REGRESSION--
1.43526079E+11      2     7.17630397E+10

RESIDUALS--
2.37477136E+10     21     1.13084351E+09

TOTAL--
1.67273793E+11     23     7.27277361E+09

F = 63.4597444

->DURB
DURBIN-WATSON STATISTIC ON RESIDUALS:
D = 1.33455733
```

83.02, 83.05, and 83.06. It would be nice to compare orders booked versus orders shipped for these months to see if there was a management error. If so, I would recommend adjusting the monthly data to remove the irregulars, then redo the correlation matrix and forecast. Let us *assume that this has been done* and proceed to construct a demonstration model for multiple regression forecasting.

Let us use consumer attitudes, CONS ATT, on a trial basis for the second independent variable. Figure 31–5 illustrates the sequence plots for PTS$ LD6, ORDERS 8, and CONS ATT. Table 31–4 tells us that there is a correlation of −.176 between PTS$ LD6 and CONS ATT. You should make your own observations about the selection of CONS ATT as an independent variable with a truly dependent relationship to PTS$ LD6. With adjustment of 81.01, 81.05, and 81.06? Smoothing of the CONS ATT data series might be desirable to minimize the large irregular components in the series.

Calculation of the multiple regression coefficients yields the information shown in Figure 31–6. The multiple regression coefficient is .93—a slight improvement over the .91 for the linear regression model—with an *r*-squared of .84 (adjusted value). The multiple regression forecasting equation is as follows:

$$PTS\$ \ 3AV = -34452(ORDERS \ 8, \ lagged \ 6 \ months)$$
$$+3581(CONS \ ATT, \ lagged \ 6 \ months)$$

Personally, I do not see that we would gain anything by using the multiple regression model. Thus, I'd use the previously described linear regression forecasting equation, results shown in Figure 31–4. I would, however, want to clear up the question about irregulars in 81.01, 81.05, and 81.06 before using the results.

A point to be made at this time is that causal forecasting using regression models is not an exact science. It always requires managerial judgment and tough decisions, often wagering your severance pay that you are right.

IN RETROSPECT

The work we have talked about is a description of the causal forecasting method. Those wanting to apply this method should probably have studied statistics and be familiar with the multiple regression techniques in particular. Linear regression procedures are pretty straightforward, absent of many complications associated with multiple regression. To be sure of your work, you must be familiar with the process, particularly to apply the proper statistical tests.

The choice of a microcomputer, minicomputer, or mainframe is going to dictate the software program used. Personally, I would shop for the software and access the computer needed to run it. The current version of Statistics with Daisy (or the new substitute product, Professional Daisy) will interface with Visicalc, Multiplan, and other spreadsheet programs that are structured in the DIF File format. It will download from a mainframe system using an available utility. With its exceptional capabilities—and user friendliness—it should be seriously considered. The Apple IIe or II+ may not have the snob appeal for a big corporate user, but it isn't that bad when you consider that an accessory card allows one to display up to 128 columns (using the Videx Ultraterm card in slot 3) and extends that applications capability to a variety of excellent programs. Those who want a separable keyboard can also make this adaptation to an Apple IIe or II+. At this writing, appropriate integrated software with combined spreadsheet, statistical, and plotting capability for other brands of personal computers are coming available. Minimal requirements for the software are as follows:

— User friendly, preferably usable by a secretarial or clerical person with minimum supervision.
— Spreadsheet capability to array and display data.
— Capable of calculating correlation matrixes.
— Capable of shifting data columns to lead or lag relationships.
— Capable of plotting sequence plots of data.
— Capable of calculating linear and multiple regression equation coefficients.
— Capable of calculating various summary statistics, "F" and "Students-t" statistics, and performing the Durbin-Watson statistical test.
— Capable of calculating forecast results using a "plug" command with the regression equation.
— Capable of plotting the regression line and data points for a linear regression equation.
— Adaptable to calculate seasonal index values, to deseasonalize and reseasonalize data.

The Daisy programs are useful because they have these attributes. I would also recommend companion use of a calculating spreadsheet to array data and make calculations, such as suggested by Table 31–2 and 31–5. I find this approach to be advantageous, using the Magicalc program, operating with a 128-column capability of the Apple II+ with the Videx Ultraterm multimode video display peripheral.

Managers of the parts distribution center have not yet adapted the computer forecasting method but continue to struggle with the traditional approaches. They had not anticipated the year-end upturn, thus the discrepancies suggested by Figure 31–4 were concluded to be management errors rather than forecasting errors. Hindsight suggests that the computer forecasting process would have given them a six-month informational lead in the inventory planning process.

They have benefited from the sharper awareness of seasonality—brought about by the forecasting study. The study also suggested a strong correlation on a day-to-day basis with the economic lead indicators. It would be useful for them to watch the newly introduced *Business Week* lead indicator series—surrogate for the Commerce Department series, Lead910. This information confirms what they have observed happening in the period since the forecast was made.

The present plan is to repeat the computer forecast on a quarterly basis. A *Sales and Marketing Management* magazine article about a competitor has been a stimulus to accept computer forecasting guidance in their planning.[2] At the same time, dynamics of the marketplace have added complexity to the issues. For example, suppliers are under strong pressures to reduce inventories, thus reducing the flexibility in the parts supply chain.

STATISTICAL TERMS AND TESTS

r. Coefficient of regression. Ranges from $+1$ to -1. Indicates positive or negative correlation, suggesting the amount of "fit" between dependent and independent variables.

r-squared. Coefficient of determination. A ratio that is converted to a percentage value, to predict the amount of variance in the dependent variable that is explained by the independent variable(s) in the regression equation.

F-test. A statistical test that indicates the quality of the regression equation in predicting the dependent variable. Values are verified from a table for the *F*-values. Usually, a value greater than 10 indicates that the regression equation is a better estimator than the mean (average) value of the series.

T-test. Usually designated T-Statistic. A statistical test that shows the significance of each independent variable in predicting the dependent variable. Qualifies the coefficient of regression and assists in selecting explanatory variables. Desirable values are determined from a T-table. Usually, a value greater than 2 indicates that the slope of the regression line is other than zero.

SEE. Standard Error of the Estimate. This statistic allows one to estimate error in the forecast calculations, based on known values of

---

[2] "Sharp Forecasting Helps Maytag Clean up," *Sales and Marketing Management,* January 1984, p. 18.

the independent variable(s). As a rule of thumb, think of the SEE as being the average error within one standard deviation (67 percent) of the forecasted values—that there is a 67 percent chance that calculated forecast values will have an error less than the SEE. A desirable procedure is to calculate the forecast errors—called residuals—for the forecasted (fitted) values, compared to actual values, to check the predictive accuracy of a regression equation.

ANOVA Table. The Analysis of Variance Table for a regression is constructed by the computer's statistical software program. The ANOVA Table displays statistics describing the quality of the resultant regression. Of particular importance is yield of a calculated *F*-value. ANOVA Tables can be compared for different independent variables, to aid in selection of the most desirable predictor variable.

Durbin–Watson test. A test performed on a regression relationship to determine if there is a problem due to autocorrelation (serial correlation, when successive values of an independent variable are correlated). Characteristically, time series have this problem, suggesting the absence of an important predictor variable in the regression relationship. The condition also arises due to data smoothing—smoothing introduces the affect of prior and later values. The Durbin–Watson value should be +2 or −2. A value of less than 1.5 or greater than 2.5 suggests the problem. With a low or high D–W, be careful with longer-term forecast projections, particularly if the fit is poor—with lower r-values. A high or low D-W suggests a skewed regression line, thus introducing error as the data deviates from the mean-X and mean-Y values of the respective data series.

REFERENCES

Bails, D. G., and L. C. Peppers. *Business Fluctuations: Forecasting Techniques and Applications.* Englewood Cliffs, N.J.: Prentice-Hall, 1982.

Business Conditions Digest. U.S. Department of Commerce (monthly, subscription).

Heinze, David. *Managerial Statistics.* Cincinnati: South-Western Publishing, 1980.

Interpreting Linear Regression. Morristown, N.J.: General Learning Press, 1954. 250 James Street,

Killion, K. C. *Statistics with Daisy.* Northridge, Calif.: Rainbow Computing, 1983.

Wonnacott, T. H., and R. J. Wonnacott. *Introductory Statistics.* New York: John Wiley & Sons, 1969.

32

SUCCESSFUL PRICING: ESTABLISHING STRATEGY, DETERMINING COSTS

by
Stewart A. Washburn CMC

Consultant to Sales and Marketing Management

THERE ARE TWO KINDS OF FOOLS IN ANY MARKET.
ONE DOESN'T CHARGE ENOUGH. THE OTHER CHARGES
TOO MUCH.

Russian Proverb

INTRODUCTION

Determining what people are willing to pay for something is a very complex business. Under some circumstances, for example, a person will work for a day or more for a hot meal. That's a question of *need*.

In another situation someone else will pay $1.49 for a 12-ounce box of Keebler Town House crackers. That's a matter of *perceived value*. The 12-ounce box of Town House crackers is always displayed full-face on the grocer's shelf. The 16-ounce package only costs $1.29, but all one sees of it is the narrow edge of the box. Even full-face, the heavier box appears smaller.

Still others will pay $7,500 for a Mount Blanc fountain pen. A 19 cent Bic will write just as well. That's a question of *status*. After all, as the girl in the L'Oreale shampoo commercial says, "It costs more. But, I am worth it."

All of these factors—need, perceived value, and the desire for status—are involved in determining what a buyer will pay for something. It is, as we said, a complex business. But that complexity increases when we also have to consider our need to recover our costs and to optimize our earnings.

Simple complexity becomes very complex, indeed. So much so, in fact, that some claim successful pricing to be an art. Others say it is a matter of witchcraft. In fact, not so long ago prices for an entire industry were established by the phases of the moon. This method for establishing prices turned out not to be astrology but a simple code to which the antitrust people took exception. Several high-priced executives, as a result, spent time in the pokey.

Successful pricing decisions do contain a large component of art; or, if not art, then at least sound judgment. Even the most inspired pricing decisions, though, turn out to be not so much intuition as a shrewd weighing of costs against what the market can afford to pay. It was, for example, no accident that Henry Ford's Model T was priced at $500 and just fit America's pocketbook. Here, development began with a careful determination that most people could and would buy a car priced at $500. The car itself was then designed and built to meet this basic requirement. The inspiration here lay in first determining what the market could afford to pay. Other manufacturers designed and built first. Then they calculated the price needed to recover costs and generate a profit.

Establishing prices based upon what the market can afford to pay is just one way. There are others in common use. Recently, for example, the publisher of a major paperback book house described the pricing procedure he followed. Ten or 12 factors were considered in establishing cover prices. These included editorial costs; production costs; sales, marketing, and distribution costs; the sales prices of comparable titles; and so on. Ultimately, though, the cover price is based on a sense of what the traffic would bear.

Others let competition establish their prices. In this situation the assumption seems to be, "If they can sell at that price and make money, so can we." This justification cloaks a lot of assumptions. The principal one seems to be about the competitor's ability to make money at the price they charge. The more prestigious the competitor, the surer people are that the assumption is correct.

Yet, others follow traditional pricing formulas that have come to have the force of gospel—direct costs of labor and materials plus 40 percent; three times the cost of labor plus twice the cost of materials; twice all direct costs—plus many more. The principal weakness with such methods is making sure that all costs are covered. Chances are that they are not.

We'll mention one more common method for establishing prices. Here, a total for overhead and profits is added to the direct costs of production. This *burden* is divided among all products in proportion to the volume each product generates. This is traditional *absorption accounting*. It is neat and tidy; but, as we shall see it makes it difficult to measure the true profitability of the products being sold.

All of this merely illustrates what we all know: that successful pricing is indeed a complex business. Unfortunately, nothing that follows will make it any less complex. However, by taking a view of pricing that may be a bit different from conventional views—indeed, at one point we will literally stand our calculations on their heads—we hope to provide a more realistic perspective on the process and to sort some of the complications into more manageable piles.

MARKETS, PRODUCTS, AND PRICES

What people are willing to pay for something depends in large measure on the role they play in the buying process. When a person buys for his or her own account (that is, buys as a consumer), the buying decision tends to be based on subjective considerations.

In contrast, when a person buys for someone else's account, as is the case with most business or industrial purchasing, the buying decision tends to be based on more or less objective criteria. This is not to say that subjectivity is absent from the industrial marketplace. However, even where it does exist, it is cloaked by the appearance of objectivity.

This is a major difference between consumer and industrial or business markets: the way in which buying decisions are made. There is also another difference. Paradoxically, with consumer products, the primary sale is made to the reseller. In industrial selling the primary sale is made to the user. There is, yet, one more significant difference. New products are rare in consumer markets. Phonographs, radios, TVs, home computers—something that is really different—come along about once every 20 years or so. Consumers, therefore, think they know everything about anything that is offered to them. Maybe that is why they seldom read labels or instruction books.

It is characteristic of both markets that the more people that become involved in a buying decision, the more expressed concern there is with value, often merely apparent value.

In industrial markets, which are continually asked to evaluate new products, most purchases involve at least three people. Further, they are not husband and wife with a limited budget buying a TV set. They are people from separate disciplines making the buying decision. Here, the search for value frequently becomes bizarre as engineering, manufacturing, and purchasing, unused to working together as a team, decide what to buy. These differences have a considerable bearing on successful pricing for these markets.

There are, however, not just two markets here, consumer and industrial. There are at least six that are readily identifiable, and many many more if services are included. However, we'll look briefly at just two consumer markets and four industrial markets and see how they work (see Figure 32–1). The way that markets work and the way that products behave in them dictate the strategy of pricing products for them.

FIGURE 32–1
Six Common Markets

Consumer
  Consumer packaged goods
  Consumer durables

Industrial
  Industrial support consumables
  Industrial process consumables (commodities)
  Industrial make-or-buy consumables
  Industrial capital goods

Consumer Packaged Goods

Here we are talking about food products, soaps, paper goods, soft drinks, health and beauty aids, tobacco products, laundry and cleaning supplies, and similarly packaged merchandise. These are all standard products, and everyone who buys them knows, or thinks they know, what functions they serve and how to use them.

Such products are rarely, if ever, sold by the manufacturer directly to the consumer. The primary sale is made at the executive level to a buyer or buying committee of a department store; a discounter; a specialty store; or a supermarket, drug, or convenience store chain. Purchases are made at this level on the basis of anticipated performance— stock turns and contribution measured in terms of sales per square foot. The manufacturer's claims in this area are supported by test market results, details of performance elsewhere, and the particulars of the advertising and promotional efforts which will support the product and build traffic for the reseller. Costs to the reseller are not as important as considerations of stock turns and contribution. Optimizing the productivity of available space, not cost, is the major concern.

Sales at this level are sweetened by devices which effectively lower the cost of the merchandise but not its invoice price: things like *two-fers,* super pacs, and 1 case extra with every 10. Major advertising allowances are uncommon, although co-op programs are a requirement. The advertising costs of such resellers is typically under 3 percent of sales, and this must support thousands of inventory line items.

Once accepted, a product is assigned shelf and display space and expected to produce. The reseller, in effect, becomes a landlord and the product a concessionaire. If the rent isn't paid—out! It is up to the manufacturer to see that the product produces at least as well as claimed during the sell-in. (See Figure 32–2.)

FIGURE 32–2
Characteristics of the Consumer Packaged Goods Market

Little opportunity for salesmanship at the point of purchase.

Bargaining or price negotiations between buyer and reseller very rare.

Wide price spreads between similar or identical products tolerated at the point of purchase.

Buying decisions based on apparent value.

Movement at the point of purchase responds to advertising not pricing.

Consumer will do without rather than downscale the purchase.

Primary sale is to reseller with cost less important than performance.

With consumer packaged goods, there is little if any opportunity for salesmanship. The buying decision is made on the basis of what the consumer knows about the product. What he or she knows is the combined result of past experience and advertising. What the customer knows may be nothing more than that the stuff comes in a yellow box and fixes headaches. Thereafter, it is a combination of packaging and posted shelf price. At this level purchasing is made on the basis of the appearance of value, not true value itself. For example, there are at least three kinds of acetaminophen on the market: Tylenol, *the hospital's choice;* Datril, *which costs less;* and Panadol, *the European secret.* For doses of equal efficacy, the costs of these products at a local cut-rate drug store compare like this:

	Customer Price	Store Price
Panadol	0.112	0.095
Tylenol	0.063	0.053
Datril	0.053	0.045

The retail price spread is from 0.053 to 0.112, or better than 110 percent for the same quantity and quality of headache relief. This price differ- · ence is supported by advertising for which these manufacturers will spend from a quarter to a third of their sales income. Each brand has its own loyal followers.

Another example is even more illustrative of this kind of consumer buying. For years, cotton percale has been used for the finest bed linen; Wamsutta Supercale, 200 threads to the inch, has been the standard of excellence. (To be sure, pure linen is available, but at two-digit multiples of the cost of percale.) At a recent white sale Wamsutta Supercale, double-bed top sheets were barely moving at $20 each, while the same sheet made by J. P. Stevens and carrying the Ralph Lauren label was moving along nicely at $28.

With consumer packaged goods the price on the package is less critical than the deal with the reseller. It is the price the reseller pays that covers everything, including profits. The consumer's perception of value can be shaped by packaging and advertising. Hence, these are critical elements in the total cost of the product. The price the customer pays is a secondary consideration. Most consumers will go to another store or will do without rather than downscale their purchases.

Consumer Durables

Here we are talking about small appliances like coffee machines, mid-priced appliances like TVs, and high-cost durables like automobiles, homes, and even college educations. With each of these products, the consumer understands or thinks he or she understands both the function it serves as well as how to use it.

Due to general economic conditions and past products of questionable value, the high end of this market is reshaping itself. But even though these three high-end market segments are changing, there remains a sizable market for low- and mid-priced durables—some quite new—that behaves as it always has.

In this market, as in the packaged goods market, the primary sale is to the reseller, although there are a number of firms who sell their own products directly to the consumer: Singer, Radio Shack, Sears, Roebuck, and Curtis Mathes come to mind. Resellers in this market have the same concerns as resellers in the packaged goods market: turnover and productivity. Turnovers of three to four times, productivity of $200 per square foot, and a 40 percent to 50 percent markup are goals.

At the low end of this market are a host of small, no-name appliances made and priced for use as promotional items and traffic builders.

The next tier includes exactly the same kind of appliances but with a difference. These are brand-named goods and receive nationwide advertising, service, and warranty support. These, too, turn up as traffic builders and, because of their name and quality, are very effective. These appliances—coffeemakers, popcorn machines, and toaster-broilers—behave pretty much as consumer packaged goods but with a significant difference or two. The principal movement at the point of purchase results from price promotions. But, since they carry such a narrow markup for the reseller, there is danger that price promotions will erode already narrow margins. Manufacturer's rebates directly to the customer are, therefore, the common promotional device. Further, there are real differences between appliances of the same kind. Different features mean different benefits, making personal salesmanship possible even though the economics of retailing do not permit much of it.

Finally, these low-end items are well within the means of a single purse. One person can make the buying decision which will be based on a combination of price and advertising. (See Figure 32–3.)

FIGURE 32–3
Characteristics of the Consumer Durable Goods Market

The function and purpose to be served by the item is well known to prospective buyers.

Product differences (features and benefits) justify personal salesmanship at the point of purchase.

The market has a good sense of what the item should cost.

Buyers believe they can sort out the features and benefits and reach an enlightened buying decision.

Product movement responds equally to features-benefits advertising and to pricing.

Bargaining and price negotiating are an accepted part of the purchasing process.

The prime sale is to the reseller, not the consumer.

As the price of these durables increases, the purchase becomes less of an impulse and more the result of consultation and deliberation. Buying decisions become a joint activity of two or more people. When it becomes time to buy, the customers will ask questions. This provides one more opportunity for salesmanship, a challenge that is imperfectly met. Resellers substitute price negotiations for salesmanship, causing a serious deterioration of margins.

Withall, this market requires that price differences between makes and models be justified by observable differences between them. Further, buyers in this market have a general idea of what a freezer or TV should cost. For years a large segment of this market consulted the

Sears, Roebuck catalog to find out how much something should cost. This method of establishing value is less common than it once was. These days, the price advertising of discounters establishes what something should cost. This market will accept a modest increase above these preconceptions of price but requires that sizable increases be justified.

Because of the lack of salesmanship for these products, advertising carries a considerable burden. It must justify prices and explain the relationship between features and benefits.

When a product is really new to this market and neither the functions it serves nor how it is to be used is completely understood, the situation becomes a bit different. The home computer is a case in point. Manufacturers contended for market share, and one price cut followed another. Potential buyers did not understand what the machine was for beyond its gaming capabilities, and no one had an idea about how much it should cost. Texas Instruments, Intelevision, Osborne, and, perhaps, Atari were consumed in the process, and others were severely crippled. This situation changed dramatically when IBM introduced its own version of the home computer. The market stabilized on the assmption that, although no one else did, IBM at least knew what the machine was for and how much it should cost. Atari and Apple immediately raised their prices.

The key price in this market is that offered to the reseller. There must be enough of a spread between it and the ticket to allow considerable negotiation with the buyer and still leave a reasonable markup for the reseller.

Industrial Support Consumables

The products included here range from paper clips and paper towels to welding gases and janitorial supplies. The need, purpose, and use for these items is well known to everyone. Orders and reorders are nearly automatic. They may be placed by a purchasing agent but more usually are placed by the users themselves: secretaries, shop supervisors, and maintenance supervisors.

The buying patterns here correspond closely with those for consumer packaged goods. Compared with the cost of other consumables purchased by business, the amount spent for these supplies is low. Price, therefore, is rarely a consideration. Further, since the level of these purchases rises or falls with general business activity, these are not budgeted items. (See Figure 32–4.)

Purchases are usually made from a stocking distributor or supply house on the basis of availability and familiarity with the brand. Orders are not placed until the cupboard is nearly bare. Buyers can be induced

FIGURE 32-4
Characteristics of the Industrial Support Consumables Market

Purchases are unbudgeted with low dollar volume compared to process consumables.

Not a price-sensitive market.

Ordered when needed by the user: secretary, maintenance supervisor, or shop supervisor.

Consumption can be encouraged by special industrial packages which promote waste or pilferage.

Product movement responds more to sales promotion than to price or advertising.

Buying decisions are based on familiarity, availability, and price, in that order.

---

to buy more than they need through special industrial packages which encourage waste or pilferage. Purchases can be guided or stimulated by sales promotional devices—give-aways which range from coffee machines for the office to TVs for the home. The spread between the list or package price and that charged the distributor must be large enough to accommodate specials, markdowns, and give-aways.

Industrial Process Consumables (Commodities)

The products we are talking about here include wire, sheet steel, nuts and bolts, paint, and other material actually consumed in the manufacturing processes. Such material is often of a commodity nature. So long as it meets established specifications (which often include price), its source is a matter of indifference. Purchasing from approved sources is usually automatic, triggered by projected materials requirements. Availability is the first consideration, then price. Since production cannot be shut down for lack of material, it is customary for there to be both a primary and a secondary supplier. (See Figure 32–5.)

FIGURE 32-5
Characteristics of the Industrial Process Consumables (Commodity) Market

Complete indifference as to source so long as specs, which may include price and availability, are met.

Purchasing is automatic from suppliers whose offerings have been approved jointly by engineering, purchasing, and manufacturing.

The market is potentially unstable if a supplier wants to buy volume.

Second sourcing at a higher price is often the preferred position for a supplier to hold.

Success and the higher price go to the supplier who can differentiate his or her product from the rest.

The buying decision takes on a different form with this kind of material. It is primarily a joint decision involving engineering, production, and purchasing.

Selling-in a new product or the product of a new supplier requires demonstrable superiority in quality and availability at or near established prices. Becoming a second source is often the easy way to introduce a superior product at a superior price.

Commodity markets can become quite unstable. A new supplier with a lower price can be very unsettling. Established prices become a football and are badly kicked around as first one supplier then another drops his price to preserve share or volume. This situation can often be prevented through the establishment of industrywide specifications which some suppliers can meet handily and others only with difficulty. Many Military Specs, for example, are there more to stabilize a market than to assure quality.

Often a single supplier can upgrade his product, remove it from commodity considerations, by enhancing the packaging or the product surrounds or by building into it one or more steps of the customer's process. Sheet steel, for example, is often given a first coat of paint, treated to make forming easier, or perforated in special ways. Close familiarity with the customer's personnel and processes are required to accomplish this. Often what the supplier sees as obvious and of no value is of immense value to the customer. The dotted line on the outside of a corrugated box to show how it should be opened to make a display is a case in point. Successful pricing for commodity products depends upon finding ways to make them something else: specialty or proprietary products.

Make-or-Buy Consumables

This class of industrial consumables is made up of items which the purchaser has decided are cheaper to buy than to make: electrical contacts, cabinet hardware, microprocessors, and even ready-to-plug-in major components. Since this is a make-or-buy proposition, initial competition is the customer's in-house capability, or presumed capability.

There is a basic tension here between vendor and buyer. One aims to sell a standard product at a special price, while the other aims to buy a special product at a standard product price. Further, the buyer wants a low price guaranteed for a long time with no volume commitment, while the vendor wants the volume commitment with no guaranty on price. This creates another kind of tension between vendor and buyer.

If the products being sold are indeed standard products for the vendor and if those products are in distribution (that is, on the shelves of independent distributors), there is another kind of problem. Because of the deep discounts afforded to stocking distributors, they are able to undercut factory prices and will do so at the most inconvenient times. Established supply relationships can be upset. Controlling this situation without reducing factory margins is difficult.

Pricing strategy here requires the vendor to expand the product surrounds to include many engineering and marketing services which the buyer cannot afford to provide. They, then, become part of the product and its cost, just as advertising and packaging are with consumer packaged goods. This is another source of tension in the lower-price long-term relationship situation that each strives for. (See Figure 32–6.)

FIGURE 32–6
Characteristics of the Make-or-Buy Consumables Market

Basic conflict 1—Selling a standard product at the price of a special versus buying a special product at the price of a standard.

Basic conflict 2—Long-term supply contract which guarantees price but not volume versus long-term contract which guarantees volume but not price.

Standard products in distribution may upset carefully arranged supply relationship.

The major competition is the customer's presumed in-house capability.

The buying decision is jointly made by engineering, manufacturing, and purchasing.

The major challenge is assuring margin over the life of the supply agreement.

Industrial Capital Goods

Here the reference is to big-ticket items: new plants, a forklift truck, executive jets, a new milling machine. The bigness of the ticket is relative. This market behaves very much like the consumer durable goods market. (See Figure 32–7.)

Other industrial purchases cannot be postponed. Typewriter ribbons are needed; so is rolled steel or cabinet hardware. Production cannot go ahead without them. But the purchase of capital equipment can be postponed indefinitely. And, unless there is some clear economic or competitive advantage to be gained, the buying decision will be put off. When the decision to buy is made, the decision may be swayed as much by emotional factors as by considerations of economic gain.

Selling has to take place at two levels. One level is technical-engineering, at which engineers, manufacturing, purchasing, and the vendor's sales staff hammer out technical recommendations and cost justifications. These contacts must be maintained until the sale is consummated. Selling also takes place at the executive, decision-making

---

FIGURE 32–7
Characteristics of the Industrial Capital Goods Market

Purchases are rarely made on an impulse or emergency basis.

Purchases can be and often are postponed through several budgeting cycles.

The acquisition is usually planned and budgeted according to this process:

    a. Need or benefit/advantage identified.

    b. Potential suppliers identified.

    c. Anticipated benefits and costs quantified.

    d. Budget line item scaled and approved.

    e. RFQs/RFPs issued.

    f. Bids and quotes evaluated.

    g. Expenditure authorized.

    h. Contract or PO negotiated, signed, and issued.

Senior management makes the buying decision.

The decision is subject to "consultative" influences.

The decision may be influenced by status considerations.

---

level. These contacts must also be maintained until the decision is finally made to buy.

There doesn't seem to be a problem with maintaining sales contacts at both levels over three, four, or even five budget cycles. However, vendors in the capital equipment market require enormous staying power. Sustaining a sales effort through several years is not easily accomplished by the under-financed. The particular challenge here is to bring up to date a price quoted several years ago and have it reflect reality. In three to five years much more than labor rates or the cost of materials will have changed. Pricing techniques should accommodate all such changes—even, perhaps, changes in the capital structure of the vendor.

FULL-COST RECOVERY PRICING

When we talk about successful pricing, we simply mean that the prices for all products have been set so that when the sales of each product reach a reasonable target volume, the firm will have recovered all of its costs and made a healthy profit. That's what we mean, and everybody knows what we mean. However, there is a problem: the word *profit*.

When one speaks of profit, the question always comes up, "How much is enough?" So far as profits are concerned, the general notion is that more is better, and a lot more is a lot better. The problem with profit as we understand the word is that it's merely a residue. After all, *profit* is a term meaning what's left over after all the bills have been paid. That's why it is called the bottom line. We need a more positive way of looking at things.

We are going to discuss successful pricing from another point of view. We will speak of earnings and targeted earnings, and we will start with the notion that the earnings of a firm must be large enough to cover all of its costs, including the cost of the capital it uses. ROI (return on investment) will be the measure, not the conventional notions of profit. And the ROI required for success must be a return on all the capital employed. The shortfall in this area will be a measure of the lack of success, and the size of the excess will be the measure of success.

It is a curious fact that although most firms employ two kinds of capital (equity and debt), they are only conscious of the cost of the borrowed funds. They seem to have no notion that there might be or should be a cost associated with equity capital.

A stockbroker's fiction called "earnings per share" is used to price stock and indicate the relative value of equity. Suppliers of borrowed funds take a different view. They want to know what their interest will be. The interest is a measure of their risk.

Suppliers of equity capital have no such measure. Yet, so far as operations are concerned, all dollars are green. The source is unimportant. If a dollar of debt capital fetches a certain interest, the suppliers of equity should expect the same.

It is a curious fact that over the years, the cost of borrowed capital for most industrial firms of normal risk comes close to 1.5 to 2.0 times the prime rate. No matter that prime is a fiction and that most banks lend money to their best customers at well below prime. (When the First National Bank of Atlanta's posted prime was 12.25 percent, Coke was paying 7.25 percent.) Prime, nevertheless, is still a useful measure. This observation on the cost of money is confirmed elsewhere. SBICs are permitted to charge seven points more than they are charged by the Federal Financing Bank, currently 11 percent. They loan out at 19 percent.

By either measure, the cost of borrowed funds is 18 percent to 20 percent. If prudent lenders get this return, why shouldn't it be paid for equity capital? The goal, therefore, should be a 20 percent return on all capital, not just borrowed funds. This is not a frivolous goal. Faqua Industries of Atlanta requires all its operations to generate returns at least equal to the cost of borrowed funds, and it has managed to sustain an annual compounded growth rate of 30 percent. (See Figure 32–8.)

Targeted earnings should produce a return on the total capital employed equal to the highest interest paid any long-term lender. For most firms the targeted ROI is 20 percent, and that is the goal we will use in our discussion of pricing.

There is a danger here. Achievement of a targeted ROI is being proposed as a measuring tool and as the basis for establishing prices. This is a financial goal. The business goal is different. It is to produce

FIGURE 32–8
Operating Statement
Standard Bottom-Line Format

1.	Net sales	$10,000
2.	Cost of goods sold	6,000
3.	Gross margin	4,000
4.	Sales and general expenses	
	Sales	500
	General and administrative	2,000
		2,500
5.	Operating profit	1,500
6.	Cost of borrowed capital	500
7.	Earnings before taxes	1,000
8.	Income tax	500
9.	Earnings after taxes	500
	Capital employed	
	Borrowed	$ 2,500
	Equity	2,500
	Total	5,000

ROI 10 percent

high-quality products which have long market lives, make money, and provide a competitive edge. The goal is a product line made up of Ivory soaps, Campbell's tomato soups, Doublemint gums, and Arm & Hammer baking sodas. The means of measurement, ROI, must not become confused with the goal, which is the successful behavior of products in the marketplace.

Figure 32–8 provides an operating statement in typical bottom-line format. It shows earnings after taxes of $500 for a return on total capital of 10 percent. There is an apparent shortfall here of $500. A 20 percent ROI would require $1,000. However, a complicating factor is at work here. According to the view we are expressing, interest payments become a distribution of profits before taxes. Consequently, an adjustment will be required in the bottom line to account for this. The after-tax or net cost of borrowed capital must be added back to bottom-line earnings. Figure 32–9 shows this.

Real earnings become $750, for a return on total capital of 15 percent. The shortfall is only $250 instead of $500. This is a technical point, perhaps. But at the risk of making our calculations and examples more complicated, we will continue to include it in our illustrations. However, regardless of any pre-tax distribuion of profits, our goal

FIGURE 32–9
Standard Bottom-Line Format (extended)

1.	Net sales	$10,000
2.	Cost of goods sold	6,000
3.	Gross margin	4,000
4.	Sales and general expenses	
	Sales	500
	General and administrative	2,000
		2,500
5.	Operating profit	1,500
6.	Cost of borrowed capital	500
7.	Earnings before taxes	1,000
8.	Income tax	500
9.	Earnings after taxes	500
10.	Net cost of borrowed capital	250
11.	Real earnings	750
	Capital employed	
	Borrowed	2,500
	Equity	2,500
	Total	5,000
	Return on capital employed	15 percent
	Cost of capital (20 percent)	1,000
	Excess (or shortfall)	250

remains a 20 percent rate of return on the capital we employ. Pricing the products we sell is the most significant means we have for achieving these targeted earnings.

Figure 32–10 shows this and compares actual performance with the required performance. An upward price adjustment to increase net sales by $500 seems necessary. This may not always be possible. The same 20 percent ROI goal may have to be achieved by other means: the reduction of costs or of the capital employed.

The leverage points are indicated by an asterisk. For purposes of the present discussion, we will assume that improving prices is the only means we have for improving ROI. Later on, we will discuss the other options: reducing the capital employed and reducing costs.

So, if our goal is to improve earnings by improving the prices of what we sell, we need to know how we fare in this regard. Therefore, as a next step, an analysis of product or product line profitability is required. Under standard, absorption accounting methods, all nondirect costs, generally thought of as overhead and profits, are charged against all products according to a formula. Usually this total charge

FIGURE 32–10
Inverted ROI Format

		Required	Actual
1.	Capital employed*	$ 5,000	$ 5,000
2.	Targeted ROI	20 percent	15 percent
3.	Earnings	1,000	750
4.	Net cost of borrowed capital	250	250
5.	Earnings after taxes	750	500
6.	Income tax	750	500
7.	Earnings before taxes	1,500	1,000
8.	Cost of borrowed capital	500	500
9.	Operating profit	2,000	1,500
10.	Sales and general expenses*	2,500	2,500
11.	Gross margin	4,500	4,000
12.	Cost of goods sold*	6,000	6,000
13.	Net sales*	$10,500	$10,000

* Leverage points.

for overhead and profits is distributed in proportion to the volume generated by each product. This method would be fine were there only one product. It might work well for the WD–40 Company whose only product is WD–40.

Figure 32–11 shows such a standard analysis of the profitability of three products. While it is conceivable that each may have the same

FIGURE 32–11
Product Contribution—Standard Absorption Accounting

		Product			
		A	B	C	Total
1.	Net sales	$3,000	$2,000	$5,000	$10,000
2.	Cost of goods sold	1,800	1,200	3,000	6,000
3.	Gross margin	1,200	800	2,000	4,000
4.	Gross margin as percent of sales	40 percent	40 percent	40 percent	40 percent
5.	Sales expenses, general expenses, and cost of borrowed capital	900	600	1,500	3,000
6.	Earnings before taxes	300	200	500	1,000
7.	Income tax				500
8.	Earnings after taxes				500
	Total capital employed				$ 5,000
ROI					10 percent

percentage of gross margin, it seems unlikely that they will all require proportionately the same amount of management time and resources to move in the marketplace. This commonly used technique of expense and cost allocation forces a sameness on all products. Our goal should be to highlight the differences among them. This method of analysis suggests that an equal effort on all products will make up the shortfall or that a concerted effort behind any one of them may achieve the same results. We know in our bones that this is just not the way it is.

What's required is a more accurate way of comparing the productivity of the three products. This comes through the application of the technique known as *direct costing*. (See Figure 32–12.) Direct costing takes a different view of both costs and assets. It views costs as of three kinds. There are those costs, principally labor and materials, which are charged directly to each product and which will vary up or down directly with the volume of product produced. (Line 4, Figure 32–12.) That's the commonsense, traditional view.

Then, there are other more-or-less fixed costs also associated with each product. If the product didn't exist, the cost wouldn't either. Sales, advertising, and quality control might be typical of such costs for consumer packaged goods. (Packaging that is, boxes, cartons, packing materials, etc., no matter how elaborate, is always a direct cost of manufacturing.) The special marketing and engineering services associated with make-or-buy industrial consumables would also be typical of such costs. These costs remain more or less fixed for a period and then increase or decrease by increments as a salary, for example, is added or another advertising commitment made. (Line 7, Figure 32–12.)

Finally, there are the ongoing costs of simply being in business—expenses like insurance, rent, and headquarters salaries—that would remain fixed for a period if none of the products were sold or even existed. These are the ongoing costs of keeping the doors open. (Line 12, Figure 32–12.) They are not associated with any product and should not be charged against any of them.

Direct costing also takes its own view of assets. It is concerned only with specifically productive assets, those associated with specific products. If the product were canceled, the asset would be liquidated. These are the assets which make money for the firm. (Line 9, Figure 32–12.) Included here among these assets are inventory (raw materials, work in process, and finished goods); special-purpose tooling and equipment; receivables; special distribution and storage equipment; and special sales tools such as display equipment, demonstrators, and testing devices. The other assets are, to a degree, unimportant and include everything else not specifically associated with a single product.

FIGURE 32–12
Product Contribution—Direct Costing

		Product		
	A	*B*	*C*	*Total*
1. Gross sales	$3,300	$2,150	$5,050	$10,500
2. Adjustments*	300	150	50	500
3. Net sales*	3,000	2,000	5,000	10,000
4. Cost of goods sold*	1,800	1,200	3,000	6,000
5. Gross margin	1,200	800	2,000	4,000
6. Gross margin as percent of sales	40 percent	40 percent	40 percent	40 percent
7. Assigned fixed costs*	100	200	700	1,000
8. Contribution	1,100	600	1,300	3,000
9. Assets assigned*				
Inventory	150	100	250	500
Receivables	650	350	250	1,250
Tooling	—	—	250	250
Total assets assigned	800	450	750	2,000
10. Turnover assigned assets	×3.8	×4.4	×6.7	×5
11. Contribution as return on assigned assets	140 percent	132 percent	174 percent	150 percent
12. Unassigned fixed costs*				
Manufacturing				600
Sales and marketing				500
Engineering				150
Administration				250
Total unassigned fixed costs				1,500
13. Operating profit				1,500
14. Cost of borrowed capital				500
15. Earnings before taxes				1,000
16. Income tax				500
17. Earnings after taxes				500
18. Net cost of borrowed capital				250
19. Total earnings				750
Capital employed				$ 5,000
ROI				15 percent

* Leverage points.

According to this view of product profitability, the $2,000 of productive assets of the firm (those associated with the three products) return 150 percent. This enables the firm to cover all other costs and generate an ROI of 15 percent on total capital employed of $5,000. However, the goal is not 15 percent but 20 percent. The question then becomes what should the rate of return be on the $2,000 of productive assets to assure a 20 percent return on total capital.

FIGURE 32–13
Return Required—Assets Employed by Products

		Required	Actual
1.	Capital employed	$5,000	$5,000
2.	Cost of borrowed capital	20 percent	15 percent
3.	Earnings	1,000	750
4.	Net cost of borrowed capital	250	250
5.	Earnings after taxes	750	500
6.	Income tax	750	500
7.	Earnings before taxes	1,500	1,000
8.	Cost of borrowed capital	500	500
9.	Operating profit	2,000	1,500
10.	Unassigned fixed costs	1,500	1,500
11.	Contribution	3,500	3,000
12.	Assets assigned	2,000	2,000
13.	Return on assigned assets	175 percent	150 percent

Figure 32–13 presents this analysis and shows that the productive assets of the firm must generate a return of 175 percent if the overall ROI goal of 20 percent is to be achieved. Product C, with a return of 174 percent, comes close to doing so. But products A and B, with returns of only 140 percent and 132 percent, need attention.

PRICING AND REPRICING

The procedure for repricing an existing product or for pricing a new product begins with a determination of the quantity that can be produced at various levels of capacity. Prudence suggests that a relaxed pace over one shift would be a better measure of capacity than all-out production for two or three shifts.

At least five levels of capacity should be calculated. Our illustration uses 20 percent increments. However, if a great deal of data is available, it may be possible to project productivity at 10 percent increments of capacity. (See Line 1, Figure 32–14, where product B is being

FIGURE 32–14
Pricing Algorithm—Product B

		Capacity (percent)				
		20%	40%	60%	80%	100%
1.	Units	2,000	4,000	6,000	8,000	10,000
2.	Unit cost (direct)	0.60	0.60	0.60	0.60	0.60
3.	Assets assigned					
	Inventory	100	130	170	220	285
	Receivables	350	385	424	466	513
	Tooling	—	—	—	—	—
	Total assets assigned	450	515	594	686	798
4.	Return required	175%	175%	175%	175%	175%
5.	Contribution					
	(Line 4 × Line 3)	788	901	1,040	1,200	1,397
6.	Assigned fixed costs	200	200	200	200	200
7.	Gross margin					
	(Line 5 + Line 6)	988	1,101	1,240	1,400	1,597
8.	Cost of goods sold					
	(Line 2 × Line 1)	1,200	2,400	3,600	4,800	6,000
9.	Net sales					
	(Line 7 + Line 8)	2,188	3,501	4,840	6,200	7,597
10.	Unit price					
	(Line 9/Line 1)	1.09	0.88	0.81	0.78	0.76
11.	Net sales/Cost of goods sold					
	(Line 9/Line 8)	1.82	1.45	1.34	1.29	1.26
12.	Break-even ratio					
	([Line 9 − Line 5]/Line 8)	1.17	1.08	1.05	1.04	1.03

repriced.) Direct costs (labor and materials) are easily established and likely will remain constant across all levels of production.

Determining the assets assigned to a product also requires considerable prudence. Just as capacity is perhaps best underestimated, receivables, inventory, and special tooling might be overestimated (Line 3, Figure 32–14).

The required rate of return, 175 percent, has already been calculated (Figure 32–13), and the rest of the price determinations follow smoothly. Unit prices to assure the 175 percent rate of return at various levels of capacity are easily calculated by dividing net sales by the number of units sold (Line 9/Line 1). However, this analysis will be much more useful if two simple ratios are calculated and a simple graph drawn. This usefulness will soon become apparent.

The first calculation involves determining the price to cost ratio at various levels of productivity for unit prices that give us the targeted

175 percent rate of return. This ratio is readily calculated by dividing net sales by the cost of goods sold (Line 9/Line 8). These values are then plotted on a graph which has percent capacity as the abscissa and price to cost as the ordinate. When these values are plotted, we have the upper curve of Figure 32–15.

FIGURE 32–15

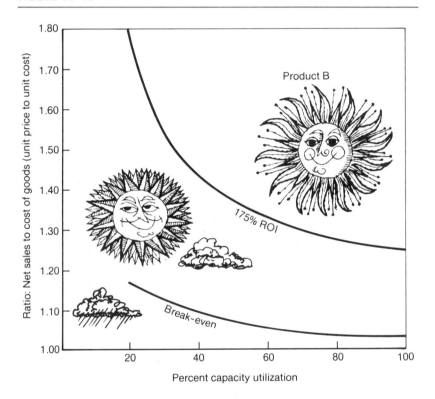

The second calculation involves determining the price to cost ratio at various levels of capacity for break-even prices. Break-even prices cover direct variable and assigned fixed costs but make no contribution beyond that. The calculation is simple: (Line 9 − Line 5)/Line 8. When the value of these ratios are plotted, we get the lower curve of Figure 32–15.

These two curves (the break-even curve and the 175 percent ROI curve) have divided all possible prices for product B into three zones. Prices that would put us into the zone below the break-even curve spell disaster. In spite of this, some use such prices to build volume and market share. Prices that would put us into the zone between the curves will all result in a contribution; the range is from mere break-even to our full targeted 175 percent rate of return. And, of course, above the 175 percent ROI curve it is all milk and honey. The utility of these curves can be demonstrated in several ways. They are, for example, extremely useful in competitive situations. Assume, for example, that a competitor offers a product identical to ours at a $.78 price. A natural concern of ours would be to find out what effect matching that price would have on our earings. All that's required is to divide that price by our own unit cost. The resulting ratio of price to cost (78/60) would be 1.30. This point is located on the ordinate and a line extended from it into the quadrant (product 1, Figure 32–16). It is clear that at this price we would make money at any level of capacity and would be assured of meeting our ROI goal at about 76 percent of capacity.

For another example, assume that a second competitor offered the same product at $.66. Again, all that is required is to calculate the price to cost ratio and plot it on the chart: 66/60 = 1.10 (product 2, Figure

FIGURE 32–16

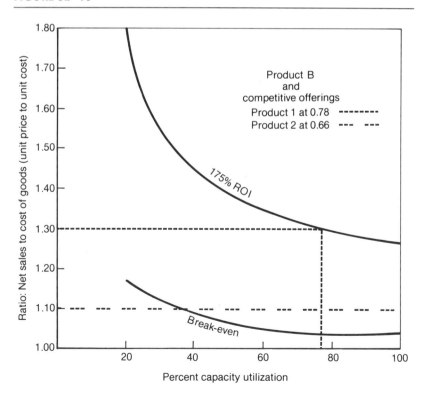

32–16). From this plot we see that we would not hit break-even until nearly 40 percent of capacity had been reached, and that at 100 percent of capacity we would still be quite a way from hitting our ROI goal.

In making this kind of competitive analysis, too many firms become concerned about competitive costs and spend considerable effort in speculation and pettyfogging espionage. Such knowledge is immaterial. What is important is that we know our own costs. In thinking about the recent and sad Texas Instruments home computer fiasco, one is forced to wonder what kind of cost information its marketing people had to work with, and if the quarter of a billion write-off of the whole line would have been necessary if our view of pricing had been held. The Russian proverb with which we opened may apply here.

Fortunately, such competitive situations are a rare thing for most of us. Using these pricing curves as we have (Figure 32–16) is a valuable aid in auditing competitive offerings. However, their greatest utility comes in guiding our own sales efforts, especially in negotiating large-volume sales where guesswork often substitutes for certainty.

Once direct (as opposed to absorption) costing has been adopted, charts like these (Figure 32–15) are readily prepared for all products and easily kept up to date. Marketing and sales can then walk with certainty on the rocks and leave the water walking to competitors.

OCCASIONAL CAUSES OF PRICE AND PROFIT EROSION

Tradition has a large part in the way we do business. Often an entire industry does business in a certain way for no reason other than that is the way it has always been done. Trade practices and long-established policies need frequent examination. Occasionally, they can be the causes of serious price and profit erosion.

One illustration makes this point. A mighty conglomerate got its start making heavy forgings (railroad wheels, axles, and blanks for naval rifles). Its freight terms were FOB, point of origin. As this firm grew it acquired other firms. One was a ladies high-fashion house; another was a manufacturer of electronic devices. The products of both acquisitions were light as feathers and shipped pre-paid via air freight. The added costs were miniscule, and the competitive advantages of this policy were great. However, tradition prevailed. The acquisitions were forced to conform to the policies of the new parent. The customers were suddenly forced to pick up the tab for freight. After some months of confusion, the market forced a reversion to the pre-paid freight policy but not without some loss of position.

There are a number of areas where the possibility of price and profit erosion are large. Figure 32–17 lists a few of them. They all need

---

FIGURE 32–17
Occasional Causes of Price
and Profit Erosion

Terms: 2 percent, 10 days; net 30
Collection procedures
Freight policy
Volume discounts and rebates
Extended terms
Returns and allowances
Warranties
Trade discounts

---

to be investigated. Often they buy us more than they cost. As frequently, though, they are a serious and unnoticed drain. Evaluating them, therefore, requires care and judgment.

The simple terms under which we sell need looking into. Two percent—10 days; net—30 seems harmless enough, even though most customers will claim the discount without earning it. Month to month, these terms may not seem like much, but in a year it adds up—a high cost for trying to collect money 20 days early.

Collection procedures are also a source of profit and price gain or of erosion. If receivables are out 60 to 90 days on average, that, too, is a considerable penalty. Such increased costs should be built into the price structure.

Freight policy is another area requiring a close look. Federal regulations used to require that common carriers be paid in seven days. Perhaps they still do. If freight is pre-paid, that's money out of the shipper's pocket and a considerable burden should the customer be slow in paying. However, if freight is FOB origin, the problem is eliminated. The burden is shifted to the customer. Further, if freight terms are FOB origin, that's where buyer takes title to the merchandise. The cost of insurance also is shifted.

Volume rebates and discounts are a valuable selling aid if the discounts take the form of additional merchandise and not price concessions. For example, 1 case extra with every 10 is, effectively, a 10 percent discount for the buyer. But it is not a 10 percent reduction in the money we receive. If manufacturing costs are 40 percent of the selling price, then the buyer has a 10 percent discount, but it costs us only 4 percent.

Extended terms and dating are traditional in some lines of business and may be valuable sales aids. But they also may be the cause of serious erosion. The value of obtaining advanced bookings in this way must be weighed against the costs of maintaining an expanded inventory.

The policy covering exchanges and returns needs careful scrutiny. If there is a flaw in the system, it will be found. Obsolete merchandise will turn up for credit against current sales. For example, a firm which had added to its product line over the years through both development and acquisition decided to redesign its packaging to give everything a modern, family look. Some packages dated from the late 20s, others from the early 50s. It declared a liberal exchange policy so that all dealers and distributors could have the new packages on their shelves. Some of the merchandise returned was nearly as old as the design of the package that held it and should have been sold years before.

Warranty procedures also need careful evaluation. The volume of claims ought to be compared with the cost of administering them. Often it is cheaper and makes a better impression on the customer to replace without question than to maintain a system of paperwork and supervision.

Finally, discounts to dealers and distributors need to be looked into. Frequently, these discounts are deep enough to permit the reseller to undercut the factory on large orders. This kind of direct, in-house competition plays hob with established supply relationships.

RATIONAL RESPONSES TO COMPETITIVE PRICING SITUATIONS

One characteristic of successful firms is that they maintain an ongoing effort aimed at (1) maintaining or improving the quality of existing products; (2) reducing the costs of producing them; (3) finding new markets for them; (4) improving their distribution; and (5) increasing the effectiveness of the sales and marketing efforts that support them. As just one small example of part of this process, during its long and happy market life Ivory soap has been reformulated at least 70 times (more likely, close to 80 times).

In fact, in most successful companies, the bulk of R&D expenditures are in support of these five activities and are not directed toward the development of new products. These five activities are part and parcel of the continuing responsibilities of manufacturing and sales and marketing. These five activities are all market-centered; and, while improvements are measured against a firm's own past performance, there is always the acceptance and performance of competitive products in the served markets to supply a more objective standard against which to measure improvement. These activities are the obligation of marketing and manufacturing.

At the corporate level there are analogous activities to be pursued. These take the form of calculating various operating ratios, watching them change over time, and comparing them with industry averages available from several sources. The operating ratios take the form of turnover rates or the percentage to sales of each operating line item. Turnover rates and percentages to sales of major operating accounts for our example (the profit and price leverage points) are shown in Figure 32–18.

FIGURE 32–18
Critical Operating Ratios

		Total	Turnover	Percent of Sales
1.	Gross sales	$10,500		
2.	Adjustments*	500	20	5%
3.	Net sales*	10,000	1	100
4.	Cost of goods sold*	6,000	1.6	60
5.	Gross margin	6,000		
6.	Gross margin as percent of sales	40 percent		
7.	Assigned fixed costs*	1,000	10	10
8.	Contribution	3,000		
9.	Assets assigned*			
	Inventory	500		
	Receivables	1,250		
	Tooling	250		
	Total	2,000	5	20
10.	Turnover assigned assets	5×		
11.	Contribution as return on assigned assets	150 percent		
12.	Unassigned fixed costs*			
	Manufacturing	600		
	Sales and marketing	500		
	Engineering	150		
	Administration	250		
	Total	1,500	6.7	15
13.	Operating profit	1,500		
14.	Cost borrowed capital*	500	20	5
15.	Earnings before taxes	1,000		
16.	Income tax	500		
17.	Earnings after taxes	500		
18.	Net cost of borrowed capital	250		
19.	Total earnings	750		
	Capital employed*	5,000	2	50
	ROI			15%

* Leverage points.

Turnover is calculated by dividing the operating line item into net sales. The percentage relationship is calculated by dividing the line item by net sales. The two ratios are, therefore, reciprocals of each other. This makes comparison with third-party figures easy.

Standard operating ratios for various kinds of businesses are available from Dun & Bradstreet. The Robert Morris Associates of Philadelphia, an association of commercial bank lending officers, publishes annual statement studies. The Federal Trade Commission publishes an annual line of business report on 275 separate four-digit SICs. And, many trade associations publish operating ratios based upon information supplied by their members.

Once a year, at least, a firm's own ratios should be compared with those furnished by third-party organizations. Significant differences between the homegrown ratios and the third-party ratios do not necessarily mean a problem. A difference may merely reflect another way of doing business or a different kind of organization—one that is more vertically or horizontally integrated, for example. However, where such differences in operating ratios do exist, an effort should be made to find out why they exist. The results may lead to an improvement in one's own operations or to valuable insights into the way competitors organize and conduct their businesses.

These activities—the comparisons of operating ratios, the five-part ongoing effort of manufacturing and sales and marketing, coupled with the direct-costing techniques for pricing products—should make a firm quite sophisticated about its products and their movement in competitive marketplaces. Firms who carry out these activities need never be spooked by changes in a competitor's prices. Panic reactions can be avoided and competitor's pricing surprises can be met with rational reactions.

The point here is that prices are only one form of competition, only one component in the competitive mix. The appropriate response to a reduction in a competitive price should not be a reflex reduction in one's own price. It will not be, if one has the kind of sophisticated overview we recommend. For example, overcapacity, especially in capital-intensive, continuous process industries, is a frequent cause of price reductions. This was commonly encountered in traditional steel-making and more recently in the conversion of atmospheric nitrogen to process- and fertilizer-grade ammonia. Usually, excess production is dumped overseas so as not to poison the domestic market. However, when such reductions affect the at-home market, the move frequently is a prelude to the liquidation of a facility.

With other products a price reduction may signify a liquidation prior to the dropping of a line. To illustrate: on the same day that full-page newspaper ads were announcing new, low prices for RCA video discs and video disc players, the business pages told why. After nearly a decade of effort and over half a billion dollars in losses, the line was being abandoned. Not all line liquidations are announced so publicly. Often there is just the price reduction. It may indicate an attempt to maintain share with an inferior product or with a product that has been overpriced. Or, it may indicate a need to generate cash by whatever means.

Rarely will a producer reduce prices out of charitable impulses; and, it is just as rare for a manufacturer to poison the market by cutting prices voluntarily. Predatory pricing to cut out or cripple competition is much rarer than is supposed and, even in monopoly situations (AT&T, for example), very hard to establish.

Occasionally, however, a market may discover that the specifications it has established for a product have been set too high. Therefore, there may be situations in which the price reduction signals the replacement of an overengineered product by one that is equally serviceable but less costly. The substitution of idiot lights for meters and gauges would be a simple illustration of this kind of thing.

More frequently, however, the problem is not a drop in a competitor's prices but a necessary increase in one's own prices. A frequent response to this situation is to announce the price increases but to guarantee the old, lower prices for orders received before a specified future date. This is, in a way, the reverse of a dealer loading or dating program; but, it puts a vendor in competition with himself.

A more rational response, if the increase will generate undue resistance, is to offset the increase, to add sufficiently to the product so the increase is not noticed. Since most buying decisions are based upon some combination of quality, availability, and price, any increase in price should be balanced by improvements in one or both of the other two factors.

In the face of rising prices, changes in the product packaging or the product surrounds are common devices for keeping prices within the range which people are used to paying. Ocean Spray Cranberries, for example, appears to be shifting its unrefrigerated, single-strength juices from glass to paper containers. The new containers weigh considerably less than glass and thus have a positive effect on shipping costs. They cost less than glass and thus have a positive effect on packaging costs; and, because the containers are sterile, a step in processing is eliminated. Further, empties are stored in a knocked-down state and free up space for the storage of finished goods. The changeover appears to be proceeding cautiously because the consumer's reaction to buying unrefrigerated juice in paper is not completely known.

Heinz, too, shifted its ketchup from the old-fashioned 12- and 14-ounce bottle to 32- and 48-ounce jugs. In so doing, it cloaked a price increase as well as increased its volume.

The recent recession, by reducing spending power, effectively increased prices for all kinds of products. As a result, many producers changed the way their products were made available. Leasing programs or rental-purchasing plans became common where once there had been none. This permitted many industrial buyers to acquire new capital equipment from operating funds in the face of drastic cuts in capital budgets.

Segmenting an established market is another device for maintaining unit sales volume in the face of raising prices. Hard data is difficult to come by, but it appears likely that the White Letter *tire market* was created as much to cloak an increase as to capture a market opportunity.

Incorporating a product into a system is another device frequently used to hide a price increase and maintain volume. The components of many home and personal computer systems are assembled as frequently to protect prices as to assure system performance.

Occasionally, one encounters firms who try to maintain or reduce prices by increasing their productive capacity. If the product is or is likely to become a staple or standard for the market it serves, and if that market is growing, the increase in productive capacity can be justified. However, buying equipment to support a product often has the effect of forcing prices downward. Emphasis shifts from maintaining profitable sales to keeping capital equipment busy. The move is more readily justified if the new productive capacity can support several products and is not dedicated to just one.

Another device frequently used to control prices in the face of inevitable price increases is to eliminate a middleman in distribution. The idea here is that the net to the user can be maintained and the net-back to the producer can be sweetened by retaining the distributor's markup. The result is often to alienate the distributor, and other products suffer.

CONCLUSIONS

We have discussed a number of aspects of successful pricing. We have shown, for example, that the worth of a product—what people will pay for it—is based upon some combination of need, perceived value, and the desire for status. We have also shown that the way a market behaves determines how products should be priced for that market. In consumer markets the perception of value tends to be based on subjective criteria, while in industrial markets those perceptions tend toward the objective.

Indeed, the more people involved in a buying decision, the stronger the tendencies will be toward objective criteria for defining value. This notwithstanding, however, the markets for industrial support consumables and for industrial capital goods behave very much like consumer markets. In these the buying decision is, for the most part, made by a single individual, and subjective values may become paramount.

We have also demonstrated a method for establishing costs and determining prices which reduced the guesswork in both activities and which also provides a sure way of evaluating price activities in the markets we serve.

We have reviewed a few trade practices which can erode prices. And, finally, we have discussed briefly the requisites for rational responses to competitive price situations as well as a few of those responses.

In all of this, our assumption has been that pricing is not the only form of competition. We hope that we have demonstrated how this is so. However, even if successful pricing is not the only form of competition, it is critical to the longevity of a business. To price successfully we must know both costs and the size of the earnings we require, but we must also know the markets we serve and what drives them.

33

MARKETING THROUGH DISTRIBUTORS

by
Porter Henry

Porter Henry and Company, Inc.

The full-service distributor performs, usually on a local or regional level, various distributive functions for manufacturers who find that channel more economical than direct distribution. A manufacturer in, say, Pittsburgh has customers in Iowa. To sell direct the manufacturer must have a factory sales representative or a manufacturer's representative call on them; must either maintain a local warehouse or go to the expense of shipping small orders direct from the factory; and must extend credit, bill, and collect from headquarters, in addition to providing customer service as needed.

The *distributor* or *wholesaler* (the words are synonymous; usage varies with the industry) purchases the products, carries them in inventory, sells, delivers, extends credit, invoices, collects, and provides varying degrees of customer service. The distributor can perform many of these functions more economically because the costs are shared among the many suppliers the distributor represents. Delivering a gross of product X to factory A costs the manufacturer less because that same truck is delivering the products of many other manufacturers at the same time.

To determine whether to sell direct or through distributors, the manufacturer must do a functional cost analysis which will include a forecast of sales volume and revenue through the alternative channels, as well as the comparative costs.

Some manufacturers find that it is more effective to sell direct in most of the country but let distributors handle the sales in the 11 states west of the Rockies. Others use distributors to sell to certain categories of customers, while the manufacturer goes direct to others—government buyers, for example. A manufacturer may sell some products through distributors and others direct. If a product is new or highly technical, the manufacturer usually must do the initial missionary selling and may then turn the product over to distributors after establishing a market for it.

The percentage of sales handled through distributors, rather than direct, is growing. A study conducted by Arthur Andersen and Company for the National Association of Wholesaler–Distributors revealed that distributor sales are growing faster than gross national product.

ESTABLISHING A DISTRIBUTOR POLICY

If the distributor is expected to invest inventory costs and sales time in a supplier's product, the distributor must know exactly where he or she stands with the manufacturer. The first essential ingredient in marketing successfully through distributors is to establish a written distributor policy.

Among the items covered in the policy should be the following[1]:

Density of Distribution

The distributor is entitled to know how many other distributors will be competing in selling the same products from the same manufacturer. The three basic types of distribution are:

Exclusive. The manufacturer sells the product to only one distributor in the area. This is the usual pattern if the product is highly technical or requires considerable missionary selling. The distributor needs to know that the results of this investment will not go to a competitor.

Selective. Here the manufacturer establishes only a few, carefully qualified distributors. This is the characteristic pattern for specialty products which require some sales effort on the distributor's part.

Open distribution. Here the manufacturer sells the products to any distributor who wishes to handle them. This is the usual pattern for commodity products which require no selling effort.

---

[1] Adapted from a suggested distributor policy developed by the National Industrial Distributors Association and the Southern Industrial Distributors Association.

Inventory

This portion of the policy statement covers such procedures as: (1) Is there a required opening order? (2) Are there any requirements as to minimum inventory carried? and (3) What assistance will the manufacturer provide in maintaining inventory levels?

Terms

How much credit will the manufacturer extend to the distributor? What is the payment policy? An example would be: "2 percent 10, net 30," meaning that the distributor gets a 2 percent discount if he or she pays within 10 days of receiving the invoice, but it must be paid within 30 days. This section should also cover policies regarding freight costs and in-transit insurance.

Pricing and Commissions

There is almost always a price sheet, showing the cost to the distributor for each product in various quantities and, often, a sheet of suggested prices to the end user. This portion of the policy also covers costs and policies on drop shipment—products sold and billed through the distributor but shipped to the user directly from the manufacturer.

Account Coverage

Are all accounts open to the distributor, or does the manufacturer retain the right to deal directly with certain types of accounts, such as government installations, buying offices of major chain outlets, etc.?

Advertising and Promotional Assistance

What will the manufacturer do to help the distributor sell the product? This category includes co-op advertising, participation in local trade shows, user training sessions, participation or sponsorship in distributor open-house promotions, direct mailings to the distributor's customers, camera-ready materials for inclusion in the distributor's catalog, and many similar activities.

Sales and Technical Training

If the product is technical, how will the manufacturer train the distributor's sales force and service people? Will they attend factory schools or will the distributor conduct training sessions on the distributor's premises or at another local facility?

Customer Assistance

What kind of assistance will the manufacturer provide to the distributor's customers? Will factory salespeople call on them to build the user demand for the products? What about warranties, technical service, etc.?

Returned Goods Policies

What is the manufacturer's policy with regard to products returned, either by the distributor or by the end user, whether because of defects or for any other reasons?

Marketing Assistance from the Manufacturer

What is the manufacturer's national advertising program? How will leads be turned over to distributors? (A sticky question when there is more than one distributor in the area.) Will the manufacturer provide prospect lists, sales potential estimates, and other marketing data?

Assistance from the Distributor?

What marketing assistance will the manufacturer expect from the distributor? Names of his or her customers for mailing lists? Sales forecasts? Reports on leads received as a result of the manufacturer's national advertising? A breakdown of sales by customer or by region? (This last one is important if the distributor has branches or otherwise ships into the territory of more than one manufacturer's sales rep. The data may be needed for the manufacturer's sales compensation plan.)

Other Topics

This listing is by no means complete. Other topics which might be covered include product warranties and product liability insurance, samples and sampling policy, packaging, order facilitation (800 numbers, etc.), catalogs, and contract termination.

PUTTING THE POLICY INTO ACTION[2]

Opening a New Distributor

This is a crucial decision: both the supplier and the distributor will be putting effort into the introduction of the new line, which will not pay off over the long run unless the marriage is a happy one.

---

[2] The author is indebted to Edward L. Reid, Jr., Vice President Industrial Distribution, Loctite Corporation, Newington, Connecticut, for many of the suggestions in the balance of this chapter.

The obvious steps in selecting a new distributor are:

1. First, and most important, ask prospective customers in the area which distributor could do the best job of selling and servicing your line.

2. Check the directories of distributors that are available in most industries. You can find, for each distributor in the area where you need coverage, its sales volume, product lines carried, number of outside sales reps, number of inside service people, etc.

3. Select a handful of the most promising candidates. The lines they carry should indicate that they are calling on the markets the supplier wants to reach but should not include strong immediate competitors of the supplier.

4. Check credit ratings—carefully!

5. Talk to some of the sales reps of noncompeting lines who sell through the distributors. This is the best indication of what kind of marketing partners they will become.

In making the sales call to persuade the distributor to take on the line:

1. Don't confine the presentation to the features of the products themselves or even to their benefits to the user. The distributor owner/ manager (or branch manager) is primarily interested in what the product can do for the bottom line. Depending on the strong points of your product, talk gross margin, turnover, net profits (gross margin minus operating costs incurred by this product line), profit per line of billing, and return on inventory investment.

2. Go through the distributor policy statement. In some industries the mere existence of such a statement is a big plus.

The Distributor's Marketing Plan

With established as well as new distributors, market-wise manufacturers sit down once a year with the distributor's key management to discuss the distributor's basic marketing plans for this product line for the coming year.

The session usually starts with a projection of sales, profits, and return on inventory, all calculated to stimulate the distributor's salivary glands. Then comes a discussion of sales coverage: what additional products in the line can be sold to existing users, what prospective new users should be called upon. Decisions are made as to distributor sales meetings the factory rep will conduct, and the scheduling of the factory rep's field work with the distributor's sales force. Then there is the calendar of promotional events in which the distributor and manufacturer will both participate: technical schools for users, open houses, trade shows, mailings, mobile training vans which visit users, and so on.

Sales Calls on Distributors

The frequency of the factory salesperson's regular calls on each distributor depends upon the distributor's volume in that product line, as well as its importance in the distributor's total sales.

It's good policy for the factory rep, once each quarter, to get to the manager or principal to discuss the previous quarter's results (and profits!) and next quarter's plans.

On the regular in-between calls the manufacturer's sales rep will usually be working with the distributor's buyer—to discuss inventory levels, new products, etc.—and with the distributor's sales manager— to discuss sales opportunities, solve problems, and schedule field work with the distributor sales force.

Depending on the industry, the factory rep may also see the advertising and/or sales promotion manager, the counter and telephone personnel, the merchandise manager, and other specialized people.

Distributor Sales Meetings

The opportunity to appear at one of the distributor's regular meetings for its sales force is a great chance for the factory rep to multiply the territory coverage. If the supplier rep does an effective job in these meetings (as well as in the follow-up work in the field), there'll be 10 salespeople making good presentations on the product rather than just 1.

The two biggest mistakes made by many manufacturers' salespeople at distributor sales meetings are (1) they're poorly prepared, and (2) they talk too much about products instead of how to sell the products. In some industries it's not unusual for the factory person simply to read from spec sheets and then ask if there are any questions.

The effective factory sales rep will plan this important appearance very carefully and often will make up some homemade visuals in the form of hand-lettered flipcharts or 35mm slides photographed personally. Meeting aids prepared by the manufacturer are a big help if aimed realistically at the needs of the distributor sales force.

While the distributor salespeople naturally need to know about any changes in the product line, they want to know how to sell it—easily and quickly, since they may have anywhere from 100 to 200 other items in the line.

Who are the prospective buyers? What are the most important

benefits the product offers them? Who is using the product in this area? What objections is the buyer likely to bring up, and what is the best way of handling them? How can the distributor rep use this product to open new accounts or help sell some of the other products in the catalog? Perhaps the manufacturer's rep even makes a demonstration sales presentation on the product.

This is the kind of information that makes the distributor sales meeting a real tool in market penetration.

Field Work with Distributor Sales Personnel

The manufacturer's sales representative will spend some time calling on users alone, to do missionary work on new products and to build user demand on established products. But the rep will also spend a reasonable amount of time making joint calls with distributor sales reps. The factory person kills two birds with one stone on these calls: selling the product to the user and training the distributor person to make better presentations on the product when the factory rep is not there to assist.

In handling field work with the distributor sales force, the manufacturer's rep will usually:

1. Confer with the distributor sales manager to determine how much time to spend with each distributor sales rep, and when. Many distributors schedule factory personnel field days a full year in advance.

2. Spend some time with the top sales reps instead of concentrating solely on building up the weaker ones. To the distributor sales force it's a form of recognition for the factory person to travel with them for a day (assuming the factory rep has established good rapport and is truly helpful).

3. Be sensitive to the wants and needs of each individual distributor sales rep. Loctite Corporation, in Newington, Connecticut, is a maker of industrial adhesives which has an outstanding sales program through industrial distributors and certain specialty distributors. Its vice president for industrial distribution, Ed Reid, makes this point about field work:

> Find out what the individual distributor sales rep wants out of life. If it's money, show him how to sell more of your product and his other products. If it's recognition, send a letter to his boss commenting on an outstanding sale he closed. If it's participation, have him conduct the demonstration on some of the calls.

4. The distributor salesperson and the manufacturer's rep plan their calls for the day. Since the supplier's person is devoting the day to training the rep, they will call primarily on customers and prospects for the manufacturer's products, enabling the distributor sales people to use presentations and demonstrations of various products.

5. Before each call, the two salespeople decide on the role each will play. Perhaps the factory rep makes the presentation on the first few calls, then observes as the distributor rep handles the later calls.

6. In the curbstone conference after each call, the factory person compliments the distributor rep on those parts of the sale that were well handled and, when appropriate, offers tactful suggestions in areas where the presentation might have been more effective.

MARKETING HELP FROM THE DISTRIBUTOR

The distributor can be an important source of marketing information to the supplier—and please, suppliers, *listen* to what your distributors have to say!

Distributor Advisory Councils

Many suppliers select a few outstanding distributors and ask them to serve on advisory councils. These councils meet once or twice a year, usually at a resort spot with time off for sports activities, to talk directly to the manufacturer about market conditions, suggested changes in products or policies, and so on. Their information can be very helpful.

Marketing Information

Other ways in which distributors can provide useful marketing information to their suppliers include:

1. Making forecasts of sales by product and customer category.
2. Providing customer names, addresses, and executives' names for the supplier's mailing lists.
3. Reporting on the number of leads received as a result of the supplier's national advertising and on the results of the leads (number of sales closed, new customers acquired, resulting sales volume).
4. Submiting information on local economic trends, competitors' actions, etc.

FUTURE TRENDS IN DISTRIBUTION

What will distributors and wholesalers be like 10 years from now? The Arthur Andersen study, conducted for the Distribution Research and

Education Foundation for the National Association of Wholesaler-Distributors, makes these predictions:

1. The average size of the distributor will increase as the result of acquisitions and the addition of branches. Wholesalers selling more than $100 million a year have 26.3 percent of the market at present and are expected to capture 44.5 percent by 1990.
2. Distributors will add more services, such as inventory control for their customers, some product fabrication, expanded maintenance and repair service, or more training seminars for customers.
3. Foreign competition is expected to increase from 2 percent in 1970 to 15 percent by 1990.
4. Productivity will increase as a result of computerization, information systems, and mechanization.
5. There will be a growing number of publicly owned companies.
6. The average wholesaler will cover a wider geographic area by opening branches or sales offices in new territories. In many industries there are now major distributing firms that are national in scope.[3]

---

[3] "Future Trends in Wholesale Distribution—The Time of Opportunity," National Association of Wholesaler-Distributors, Washington, D.C.

34

MARKETING THROUGH INDEPENDENT SALES AGENCIES

by
James Gibbons
Manufacturers' Agents National Association

THE MANUFACTURERS' AGENCY TODAY

Depending on who you talk with, you will hear these terms used frequently: *manufacturers' representatives, reps, sales agents, manufacturers' agents,* and *agents.* For our purposes in this chapter, and where they are used in other chapters in this handbook, the terms are interchangeable. However, the Manufacturers' Agents National Association refers to its members as Manufacturers' Agencies. This may seem like hair splitting, but a little history will put the question into perspective and help you understand those entrepreneurs who will go into business for themselves, work for nothing more than a commission, and often build very successful operations.

Years ago most agents were one-person operations. The singular term *agent* was appropriate under these circumstances. However, most of the people in the field now run multiperson operations, and they represent far more than the two or three lines the earlier reps carried into the field. Many of the contemporary multiperson agencies cover rather diverse territories with branch offices, often with resident partners.

Although the term *manufacturer's agency* is preferred by us and by most who are in the business, the word *agent* should not lead you to believe that an agency arrangement exists with manufacturers in the legal sense of the word. Manufacturers' agencies are really commission representatives in the legal sense of the term.

Here are the guidelines that MANA uses to define a manufacturers' agency:

1. An agency will represent two or more principals, and they will sell products on a commission basis. A manufacturer may ask an agency to undertake special projects, such as market research, but these projects will be paid for by the manufacturer by a fee. The agency's main income is derived from commissions.
2. Manufacturers' agencies usually sell related but not competitive products. Agencies sell to distributors or to end users.
3. Agencies are assigned exclusive territories.
4. Most agencies work with their principals on a firm contractual basis. In earlier days most agents took on a line with a handshake. Contracts are important, not to establish honesty, but to protect agencies and manufacturers from events that simply can't be foreseen early on.
5. Agencies seldom have control over the prices of the products they sell, and they rarely take title to the products. There are, however, some agencies that do provide warehousing facilities, and some even act as distributors for their principals. Those who act as distributors buy and store the products and can set prices themselves, unless their agreement with the principal forbids them from doing so.

The field of agency selling has grown and changed greatly in the past few years. Agencies selling technical products are staffed with highly qualified engineers; those selling consumer goods perform very sophisticated training of the retail salespeople who will sell the products to consumers; and many agencies are tightly linked with the new-product development people who work for the manufacturers they represent. In short, the manufacturer's agency of today is, in many cases, a complete marketing department.

For those readers who have not worked with agencies, this may seem like a redundancy, something that should be handled by a salaried staff at the plant. In some cases an internal and salaried staff is advantageous; but, in many cases today, the agency method of selling has a lot more to offer.

These points should put agency selling into perspective before we go on to the mechanics of selecting agencies and working with them.

1. The use of a manufacturers' agency gives the manufacturer a predetermined, fixed sales cost that is tied directly to goods shipped. No sales—no expense!

2. Those running agencies and those selling for them are self-motivated. Because they work on commission, they have the most powerful incentive of all to do well for themselves and for the manufacturers they represent—profit.
3. Manufacturers' agencies provide local management for their principals, no matter where they are located. Experienced, competent agents know the territory, where the business is, and how to get it.
4. By using manufacturers' agencies, a manufacturer can put a trained sales force into the field immediately. The training costs the principal nothing, and there is no downtime.
5. Manufacturers who use agencies have immediate access to a market. Agency salespeople are in place, and they know the territory and the customers.
6. There is no overhead when agencies are used. Fringes, auto expenses, insurance, and other expenses that are usually considered for a salaried salesperson simply don't exist when agencies are used.

Manufacturers' agencies are used by large and small companies alike. They are used by those just starting out and by those who have been in business for many years. Many multiproduct manufacturers go the agency route with some products and use salaried salespeople for other products. The agency method of selling should not be thought of as an alternative to direct selling. It should be evaluated in terms of what it can do for the company. All too frequently manufacturers start with agencies because they have limited funds and like the idea of low overhead. Their goal, however, is to replace the agencies with salaried salespeople just as soon as they can afford it. You can't argue with the zero overhead approach, but it's a serious mistake to think of agencies only as an interim way of selling. Agencies have some very definite advantages, and so does a direct sales force. Let's now look at the choices that have to be made.

How to Determine if Agencies Are the Best Way to Market Your Products

The economic fortunes of the country change from time to time, but there are a number of points you should consider, regardless of the economy. Let's look at the factors that point toward the use of agencies. Then we'll look at some of the points that make direct salespeople more practical.

Opening up New Territories. The time it takes a salaried factory salesperson to open a territory is often much longer than it takes an in-place agency to do it. During the growth stages of any territory, income is usually small, and the territory operates at a loss. Agencies can do the job because they can spread the sales cost.

Reaching Specialized Markets. There are more and more specialized markets appearing every year. Consider the splintering of the solid-state and computer fields, for example. Even in retailing, the number of specialty products and stores has burgeoned. It can be too costly to have salaried people do the job, but agencies that spread their operating costs over several specialty lines can do the job effectively. Agencies tend to specialize to be most effective.

Getting the Most out of Smaller Customers. It can often be too expensive for a salaried salesperson to call on what the factory considers to be marginal accounts. However, agents that can cover several lines in a single call can make these calls economically. By the very nature of the agency business, their salespeople must be more aggressive than the factory salespeople who highlight the large accounts. An agency with compatible lines usually gets much more out of a territory than a factory salesperson who has only his or her employer's product to sell.

New-Product Introduction. For most manufacturers the time factor in the ROI equation is getting smaller and smaller. Because agencies are in place in a territory and know the market and the people to see, they can do the job in a hurry. This problem is especially critical today. In many high-technology fields and very competitive consumer fields it can be just too expensive to run fast enough with a factory sales force to catch up with agencies already in the race.

Marketing a Very Narrow Product Line. There are many small companies in the country with a single product or a very narrow product line. The cost to move these products to market with any system other than agency selling can often be prohibitive.

Technical Credentials. Not too long ago, many agents who sold technical products were not themselves technical-oriented people. They made up for this with good general knowledge and a tremendous amount of enthusiasm and selling skill. Today, there is hardly a sales agency selling technical products that doesn't have professionally trained engineers available for customer contact. However, you should also consider that agency salespeople are generally more aggressive and better qualified in selling techniques than many factory people. As mentioned earlier, agency people are moved by the mightiest motivator of all—profit gained strictly by commission.

Sales Volume Fluctuations. Many industries are seasonal. Others are victims of financial cycles. And others make products that are bought only when other specific events take place. There is no better way to smooth out the curve than to use agencies to do the selling job. Capital equipment manufacturers and those who make clothing share the same problem—wide swings in volume over time. Both of these industries use agencies heavily.

Cost to Employ Direct Salespeople. In 1983, it cost a minimum of $60,000 a year to field even the greenest and most inexperienced salesperson. Considering that agents are productive from the moment the contract is signed, this factor often becomes the deciding element when agencies and factory-employed salespeople are being compared.

These, then, are the major considerations for going the agency sales route. There are, of course, reasons why agencies might not be the best route and factory salespeople might outperform agencies. Let's look at these factors.

When More than Selling Is Required. There are a number of products sold to technology as well as consumer markets that require more of the salesperson than just a strong selling effort. When a manufacturer depends heavily on its field force to develop market intelligence, or to introduce and test market products, the choice of factory salespeople is usually dictated. However, many agency people are quite capable of doing rather sophisticated research for their principals. Remember, though, that for them and you, time is money. When they aren't selling and are doing your research, selling activity has stopped. Most manufacturers who use their agencies to do research work will pay them for their effort. It's fine for the agencies—they are making money for their time; but remember that the agency doing research is not selling your products. If the curves cross economically and practically for you and the agencies, it may be practical.

When More Selling Time Is Required. Manufacturers' agencies are run by entrepreneurs with a keen sense of time. When they have several lines to show to a buyer, they instinctively give the most time to the products that are of most interest to the buyer. This criticism is often leveled at agencies. But when you consider the nature of their business and your own needs, it's often better to forego the use of agencies when your products require more than average selling time. However, there are a number of ways to get more of your agency's time. This topic is discussed regularly in *RepLetter,* the newsletter for sales executives who sell through manufacturers' agencies.

When Customers Prefer to Deal with Factory People. This barrier has all but disappeared. In the past, because agents were more forceful and high-powered (in the eyes of the buyers), some people were not too fond of dealing with them. This distinction is no longer a major problem except with people whose habits were formed early in life and who don't like to change their way of doing things. In general today, those who still prefer to deal with factory people rather than agency salespeople are buying products that require more time on the part of the salesperson. And, as said earlier, when time is critical, the factory person often has the edge over an agency salesperson.

When Territories Require Tight Management. The management style of some companies includes very tight control of all operations, including field sales. When it's felt that tight control is necessary, you will be better off with a direct sales force. It's difficult for agency salespeople to take the time to attend regular meetings, and it is impossible for them to get involved in filing regular call reports without running afoul of the IRS and the independent contractor regulations.

Unfortunately, there are no pat answers. Agencies are the only way to sell for some companies, and they can be a disaster for others. And it's impossible to make the decision in a vacuum: you're going to have to talk with agencies.

At this point, remember that I am still discussing the decision of whether to use agencies or direct salespeople. The question of deciding *which* agency is another set of problems.

Perhaps the best way to get close to a decision is by first establishing the goals of the sales force—whether it will be agencies or factory people—and evaluating each of the goals in terms of how well each group will be able to accomplish them. If you haven't worked with either, or have worked with one and are thinking about making a change, you should seek input from others who have gone the route. The Manufacturers' Agents National Association runs several national seminars every year for manufacturers who use agencies or who are thinking about using agencies. The input and interchange in these sessions can often be very helpful. MANA has also published a number of research papers that should help you with the decision. They are listed at the end of this chapter.

WHERE AND HOW TO LOCATE MANUFACTURERS' AGENCIES

Finding a good agency is a lot like finding a good employee. The search techniques are pretty much the same, and you should make the selection as carefully as you would if you were adding a salaried person to the payroll. Let's look at a few of the more productive ways to locate agencies. Once you know where to look, there is a system for making the selection.

Trade Shows

Local, regional, and national trade shows are excellent places to meet prospective agencies. In fact, the managers of many shows provide facilities for manufacturers and agencies to meet each other. Some shows will post "agent-wanted" and "line-wanted" notices on bulletin boards, and other larger shows provide space where agencies and manufacturers can meet and discuss their needs and requirements. Most manufacturers who are looking for agencies at trade shows will make contact but reserve post-show time to do in-depth interviews. Remember that the main thrust of a trade show is to meet customers and to sell. However, a thriving agency/manufacturer interchange takes place at most shows.

Advertising

You can waste a lot of time advertising in local newspapers for agencies. Your advertising should be placed where it will have the highest visibility and be read by the people you want to meet. *Agency Sales* magazine publishes heavy classified and display advertising each month for agencies looking for lines and for manufacturers seeking agencies. *The Wall Street Journal,* too, publishes classified advertising that can be quite productive. And the major metropolitan newspapers with significant business sections also carry advertising for agencies. For example, the Sunday edition of the *New York Times,* the *Chicago Tribune,* and the *Los Angeles Times* carries agencies-wanted lineage. Be sure to check the directories of any local associations to which you might belong. Many of the local chapters of the Instrument Society of America, for example, publish regular newsletters and annual directories. If your need is for an agency selling the instrument market, this could be an excellent source.

Other Manufacturers

The chances are that you are on speaking terms with executives in a number of other companies in your area. Even if they are not selling the same markets, their agencies might have contacts that could be of benefit to you.

Your Present Agencies

Assuming you are already selling through agencies and are looking to fill a territory, your present agencies can often be in a good position to make recommendations. Agency principals keep in touch with each other, and they often are able to make recommendations to fellow agents as well as to manufacturers looking for agencies. Good agents know other good agents and are loath to recommend poor ones.

Your Advertising Agency and Publication Space Salespeople

Ad agencies that have a marketing orientation are often aware of who the better manufacturer's agencies are in a given territory. Ask them for their advice.

Distributors

If your marketing system is built around distributors, you can often get good leads on agencies by asking distributor executives to recommend the agencies that have been most helpful to them.

There are, as you can see, many ways and places to look. The most important thing to remember at this stage of the search is to be eclectic—not to narrow your search to one channel. Look in every corner. Ask a number of people. Get input from as many sources as you can. You will be better off with a number of sources when you start narrowing the search than you will be if you have only a few avenues open.

HOW TO SELECT THE BEST AGENCY

Finding agencies is just the beginning. Now you have to select—from those that look promising—the one agency that will be best for you. Or, as you will probably find, how to select one from a number of candidates all of whom seem to be able to do the job.

Many manufacturers spend too little time on the recruiting, screening, and interviewing processes. Later, when they discover that the agencies they have appointed are not quite what they expected, a lot of effort is usually needed to straighten out the situation. If this time were spent up front, rather than trying to make the best of a less-than-successful situation, the relationship would be much more productive for all concerned. Before discussing the agency interview and selection techniques, it's important to understand some of the problems that can lead to poor agency relationships:

    1. *Corporate strategy*. If, for example, you're planning to cut your ad budget, and you know that the number of leads will be diminished, be up front about it during the interview. Don't let the agency find out about it after the fact.

2. *Growth potential.* Good agencies can determine the potential of the territory, but be sure that the agency knows your corporate growth plans. If the agency sees a $2 million territory, and you know your production capabilities could only ship $1.5 million into the territory, be up front right away.

3. *Commission system.* The details should be put in writing for the agency to review prior to offering a contract. State the terms clearly, and make sure that the agency understands the language as well as the figures.

Use this checklist to help you conduct productive agency interviews:

1. Outline the characteristics you know will be important for agency success. When you conduct an interview, cover every point. Gut feelings are important, especially when they correlate with known success factors. Look for the right chemistry. You will have plenty of solid facts that will help you make the decision, but the chemistry must be right.

2. If more than one corporate executive is to interview prospective agencies, be sure that each is acquainted with the success characteristics that have been outlined. After the interviews have been completed, each point should be rated by each executive.

3. Don't play psychologist. You may know what motivates you but, unless you have professional training, stick with the facts. The facts that are most likely to predict success are past successes.

4. Don't let your biases get in the way. Don't rule out a candidate just because he or she wears clothes that don't appeal to you, for example.

5. Watch out for the halo effect. That is, don't assume a person rates well on all scores just because he or she impresses you on one point. Those with good verbal skills are usually thought to be skilled in other areas by most people. Be careful.

6. Look for winners. This may seem like a blinding glimpse of the obvious, but many people tend to look for characteristics that will prevent them from making a blunder rather than looking for the top choice.

7. Don't jump to conclusions too soon. If you do, you will find yourself looking for ways to confirm your judgment rather than gathering more information.

8. Don't be pressured into choosing someone. Even if you have only two choices and neither is satisfactory, don't take the lesser of two evils. It's best to cover the territory from the factory until the right agency can be located.

9. Maintain control of the interview. Unstructured interviews work but only in the hands of skilled professionals. Unless you know what you are doing, a rambling, nondirective interview rarely produces enough solid information to make a sound decision. And you will find it difficult to compare the information gathered from several interviews when you begin the final selection process.

10. Watch the person from the agency. If interested, he or she will try to sell you on the agency's services during the interview. This will be your first chance to watch agency selling in action.

These 10 guidelines will help you structure an agency interview and maintain control of it. They will also insure that you get the most out of the process. Now let's look at the nine questions that will help you get the information you need to make a proper selection.

1. Will your lines be compatible with the lines carried by the agency? Obviously, the lines should be related and not competitive. More important, though, the lines should relate to each other in terms of price and quality. A significant difference could foreshadow problems.

2. Will the territory you want covered be included? Seldom does an agency cover exactly the same territory for each principal. Make sure that your prospect covers the geography and the market you want.

3. Is the agency calling on the right people? The agency may be selling the companies you want to reach, but if calls are being made on the purchasing agent and your products are sold to engineers, there may be a problem. However, most agencies selling to specific industries can shift gears to suit the individuals they see.

4. How about service? If your agencies are required to install equipment, perform calibrations, run seminars, or handle jobber training, be sure that you get a chance to see them in action. And be sure that your conditions are spelled out.

5. What about drive? An agency taking on a new line must be prepared to push hard to build the territory as well as supply the sustained effort needed to keep it productive. This could mean future expansions.

6. Is the agency willing to expand? Being highly motivated people, most agents run the show close to the vest. When the time comes, will your prospective agency be willing to add salespeople, take on partners, or do whatever is necessary to accommodate your growing business? Most agencies want to grow, but it's best to determine their plans early in the game.

7. How long has the agency been in business? Longevity is seldom a critical factor. A good agency could be only a year old and be extremely productive, yet a veteran may have always been a marginal producer. Look at time in service only relative to productivity.

8. What facilities are available? This question has probably been responsible for more manufacturers rejecting good agencies than you can imagine. For example, an agency run from a home may be a red flag for some manufacturers. This is just plain poor judgment. Rather than ask the home question, ask whether the agency can provide the services you need, wherever it's located. Many agencies at that critical growth point between two or three people and larger staff find themselves running an office and not motivating others to sell. Look at results not the physical plant and its location.

9. What does the agency think of you? Remember, the agencies you interview are also interviewing you. Whether they have thought about it formally or not, most agency owners are giving prospective principals the once-over with these thoughts in mind: Is the line compatible with the present lines? Does the product fill a hole in the current product mix? How about profitability? And can the product be sold to existing customers? If the agency comes up with positive answers, they will try to sell you.

You must get the answers to these questions. But, while you're probing, you should be planting the answers to the questions the agent will ask—those that are outlined in point 9. Be up front! There's no sense wasting your time and the time of a prospective agency just to fill out an organization chart.

ENTERING INTO AN AGREEMENT WITH AN AGENCY

The manufacturer/agency relationship is a business agreement. If you and your agency want to shake hands, do it after you have both signed a contract that suits the needs of both parties. It's true, there are a lot of lawyers and a lot of law suits, and many people believe that their word alone will assure a friendly and productive relationship. The point is that contracts are important for both parties. You never know what's going to happen 10 years from now, and no handshake can protect people in a court of law. The MANA contracts, a short form, and a complete contract can serve as a practical guide for your attorney to draw up an agreement that meets your needs and the needs of the agencies you will appoint.

Whether you use the MANA contractual guidelines or have your attorney draw up a contract from scratch, here are the points that must be considered:

The Territory to Be Covered. Territory can be described in terms of geography as well as types of customers served. For example, you may use two agencies in the same territory, each selling to different types of buyers. Be sure to look at your territory from this point of view when you are creating your contract.

The Products to Be Sold. A clause on this subject will insure that your agencies don't enter into competitive arrangements, but such clauses also protect the agency in the case of a manufacturer who tries to dominate an agency with overly restrictive covenants.

The Life of the Contract. Contracts all have specified lives, even those that state that they are to run until terminated. Since you and your new agency will be getting the measure of each other in the first few years, longer contracts are seldom appropriate at first. After you both know the arrangement is going to work, you might go to longer contract periods.

Terms of Contract Renewal. Most agency contracts are created to provide for automatic renewal unless either party gives notice. Even though you may go this route, it's usually best to review the contract each time it comes up for renewal. Times change, there may be elements in the contract that are no longer needed, and new clauses may be appropriate.

Termination. Agency termination is always a sticky problem, even with a good contract. However, your contract should state clearly the rights and obligations of both parties under termination. For example, how long will the agency continue to get commissions for products sold while the contract was in force? What, specifically, can constitute action for termination? You should get good counsel when approaching this section.

The Manufacturer/Agency Relationship. Agencies are not employees of the principal; they are independent contractors. There are many activities that manufacturers would like to have from their agencies that can jeopardize the independent contractor status. For example, if an agency is required to file call reports on every customer visit, the IRS usually deems this the activity of an employee, not an independent contractor. It's smart to get these details ironed out in the contract, long before any problems could occur.

Commissions. Commission rates vary from industry to industry, and so does the method of paying them. Some principals pay upon placement of an order, on shipment of an order, and others when they receive payment from their customer. You should look at your own industry standards and discuss the terms openly with the agencies. When a sale is made in one territory and the product is shipped to another, there are often split commissions involved. That is, agencies in both territories are often entitled to share in the commissions. However, it's important to establish in the contract just how these splits are to be made. Sixty percent for sale and 40 percent for shipment? Eighty percent for engineering and specification and 20 percent for shipment? You can see the problems that can arise.

Credit, Default, and Returns. Normally, credit should not be a problem for the agency. The agency doesn't act in the legal sense of an agent, and the manufacturer is responsible for taking the order or not taking the order. But there are times when merchandise is returned, or when the customer folds, for example, when a clause in the contract will prevent misunderstanding and rancor.

Performance. Performance is most often thought of in terms of quotas, but quotas are one of the worst ways to motivate agencies. Set goals but not quotas. Goals can include the opening of so many new accounts or the introduction of a new product. But financial quotas become clubs held over agency owner's heads that just aren't productive.

Nonsales Effort. Salaried sales force can be told to handle a market research chore, and they will do it without question. Their salary goes on whether they are selling or asking questions. But when you ask an agency to handle a market research project for you, you are asking that agency to take time from selling to do work that won't result in income. If your needs include some nonselling activity, be sure that it's specified in the contract and that the method by which the agency will be compensated is stated clearly. It's a cliche, but people who act as their own attorney have a fool for a client. With the MANA (or equivalent) contractual guidelines and a lawyer who understands the law of sales, you should have no difficulty drawing up agreements that will benefit you and your agencies—now and in the future.

GUIDELINES FOR WORKING WITH MANUFACTURERS' AGENCIES

Many companies spend thousands of dollars and considerable time developing personnel manuals, but when it comes to working with independent manufacturers' agencies, they do it by the seat of their pants. The following guidelines were reported in *MANA Special Bulletin* number 405. The contents have been somewhat abbreviated, but the entire bulletin is available from MANA.

Independent Sales Agencies and You

1. Know your own sales and marketing goals.
2. Analyze each territory individually as to your marketing goals.
3. Examine your selling costs.
4. Determine the amount of control that is needed.
5. Decide how fast you must penetrate a market.
6. Decide whether you know your product and market well enough to provide the agencies with leadership and guidance.
7. Know the trade practices affecting your marketing when using agencies.

Planning Your Work with a Professional Sales Agency

1. Thoroughly understand the functions of professional sales agencies, and be certain that the people in your firm who will interact with the agencies know them. Remember, you will be entering into joint ventures with *each* agency in *each* territory.
2. Establish a set of priorities for your agencies. Make a list of things that you want the agencies to do first. Discuss your plans with the agencies, and be sure that both of you agree on priorities.
3. Devise a checklist of professional qualities that you expect the agencies to have. Develop a plan to determine how the prospective agencies will meet your standards and goals. Provide a program that will assure the maintenance of high standards of professionalism for both agencies and principal by stressing cooperation and communication between your employees and the employees of the agencies.

Communication for a Mutually Profitable Relationship

1. Effective communication with your agencies will always be the result of a well-thought-out program.
2. Establish clear-cut executive responsibility for your communications program.
3. Review the program frequently.
4. Consult with your key agencies and establish a council.
5. Look at the message, the emphasis, and the motivation when analyzing your communications.
6. Communicate with your agencies the same as you would if they

were paid employees, but don't expect elaborate reports in return.

7. Create an environment that stimulates good communications in return from your agencies.
8. Make frequent phone calls to your agencies.
9. Evaluate the rapport you have with your agencies in light of the relationship the agencies have with their other principals.
10. Balance your communications with memos, letters, newsletters, and phone calls.
11. Encourage your agencies to complete the communications cycle by making it easy for them to respond to you.
12. Publish a list of your personnel with whom agency people can and should communicate.
13. Review the effectiveness of your communications program with your agencies regularly.
14. Make regular working visits to each territory.

Know What the Agencies Expect from You

1. They want a team relationship, not a one-sided, do-it-my-way attitude.
2. The new agency wants a complete, nonvarnished history of your company; and, they want to be kept up to date on corporate events, even those that may not directly affect them.
3. Even though agencies you engage will have been covering a territory, it helps for you to give them whatever intelligence you have on the territory.
4. Keep the agencies up to date on products, prices, production, and problems.
5. Agents can help in many ways other than just selling. They can help you determine your sales and even corporate goals based on their field experience. They expect to share this information with you—to be part of the team.
6. Be sure that the relationship is open and honest.
7. Agents expect training from you—but not sales training. Agencies have some of the best salespeople in the country working for them. Giving them sales training is not only a waste of your time and money, it does little to strengthen your relationship with them. Rather, they want all the product and application training they can get.
8. They expect sales leads from you that are developed by advertising, direct mail, and trade shows. And, they expect that you will have at least provided a preliminary qualification on the leads. It's far too costly to follow up unqualified leads.

9. Agencies need good, benefit-laden sales literature. Make sure that your catalogs are up to date and aimed at the audience covered by the agencies.
10. Agencies look for prompt responses to their requests. This includes everything from requests for quotes to product samples and refills on their literature supply.
11. Agencies expect their commissions to be paid on time. Whatever your contract calls for, make sure that you live up to the agreement.

HOW TO MOTIVATE MANUFACTURERS' AGENTS

This question is usually asked by manufacturers who feel that they simply aren't getting enough of their agencies' time. To get this time and attention, they usually turn to tried and trite sales contests. However, the best motivation techniques are found in just being a good manager of your agency sales force. Agency people are motivated—highly motivated! But they do need your help and factory backup. In a practical sense motivation is really the application of all of the elements that contribute to success. Put in simplest terms, motivation and good management are really the same thing. To be successful in managing a team of agencies, you must take into account all of the factors that have been identified as positive motivators, and they must be used regularly as part of your total management program, not as bail-out techniques when sales dip. Before getting into some of the specifics, you should understand that the factors identified as contributing most heavily to success in selling through agencies are:

1. Proper agency selection.
2. Effective communications and feedback.
3. Fair compensation and reward.
4. Quality and style of management.
5. Effective product training.

Most systems of motivation try to strike an average to move all members of the group. Some of these systems do work but, because the target is usually relatively low, they are not especially effective. If you want to positively motivate your agencies, *you must know and understand each agent individually.* When you learn how to achieve success with each individual agent, you will be in a position to succeed with the entire team.

The Elements of Practical Agency Motivation

Financial Success. When you recognize that most agency owners are primarily motivated by financial success, you have a strong key to successful motivation. Sales contests don't motivate agencies; good potential for short- and long-term profit does. If you are going to be successful in motivating agencies with financial incentives, make sure that they provide long-term potential. Bonuses help, especially when they come out of the blue. When bonuses are predictable they have the same effect as quotas and are much less of an incentive factor. People tend to shoot for quotas, collect the bonus, and move on to other things. But when a bonus for a job well done is given without an agency expecting it, it has a very positive effect. This doesn't mean that you should rule out any sort of predictable bonus system, but be sure to include a few surprises. It's the surprises that keep the wheels turning.

Recognition. Everybody loves a pat on the back—agents are no exception. The exception is, though, that too many manufacturers have gone the plaque-on-the-wall route for every trivial accomplishment. If you're going to give plaques or other types of displayable awards, make them meaningful. Give them for some real accomplishment. However, you will find that an unexpected phone call or letter complimenting an agent for an especially well-done job will do much more to motivate than all the brass and mahogany you can lay your hands on. Make sure that your awards are given for real accomplishment. Don't fall into the little league trap of giving every player an award, regardless of how well he or she played.

Group Approval. This is important enough to mention apart from the previous section on recognition. Agencies are part of a team, and they do share a sense of belonging. They want to have their accomplishments seen and appreciated by their peers, the other agencies on the team. Make sure that everyone knows of the accolades you bestow on some, and you will have the best effort of all.

Provide a Sense of Belonging. Agency owners are free spirits, entrepreneurs who like to run their own shows but still like to know that they are part of a heads-up team. They like to know that the principals they represent are growing, dynamic, and exciting companies. You don't have to be a horn blower to get this message across; just be realistic about your accomplishments while letting them know that you couldn't have done it without them.

The Opportunity for Expression. Encourage your agencies to send you ideas that they feel will help you. You are bound to get some good ideas, and you will have told your agents that you value their thoughts. One of the best ways to implement this expression is through the use of rep councils.

The Opportunity for New Experiences. Managing an agency network can at times be as boring as being an agent making the same calls on the same stuffy buyers day after day. If you can arrange to provide new and unusual experiences in line with your agent's work, you will have given a good motivational shot in the arm. Giving tough problems to your rep council fits the bill; so does seeking their input on some of your new-product ideas.

The Sense of Personal Power. Make no mistake about it, anyone who has the guts to make it as a manufacturer's agent has a sense of personal power. I don't mean this in the negative sense, but in the positive sense of self-mastery. When agents achieve certain goals, they like to bask in the glow of personal accomplishment. Help them achieve a sense of accomplishment, and you will have highly motivated agents.

A Sense of Dignity and Self-Respect. The image of a salesperson has changed a lot in the past few years. But there are still enough people whose image of a salesperson is derived from the comics to make the job difficult. Consider that most agents today have at least one college degree—many have graduate degrees—and you know that poor Willy Loman has finally been laid to rest. Treat your agency people as professionals, make sure that your employees have the same respect, and you will have a lot to motivate them.

All of these elements should be used together. It's not enough to dip in and work with the elements with which you are most comfortable. In a sense, this is a *system* of motivation.

I have saved one point for last simply because it summarizes the whole system very nicely. As I have stressed, effective motivation depends very heavily on your ability to understand the individual goals of each of your agencies. However, the value of this knowledge hinges on one important factor. It's a factor that applies to motivating not only those individuals working directly within the company but also to those individuals who work independently—your agents. The point is this: *You will be much more successful motivating people if you tailor the job to fit the person, rather than trying to fit the person to the job.* This is why I have stressed understanding each individual agent. It's only when you really understand each agent that you will be able to effectively fit your assignments and tailor your motivational programs. Of course, much of any motivational effort with agents will apply to all of them. However, when you get to the factors that turn on each individual, you are at the heart of a sound motivational program.

HOW TO EVALUATE AGENCY PERFORMANCE

There's no way around the bottom line—sales performance is a prime measure of agency achievement. However, if you let the bottom line be your only guide, the chances are that you will miss a lot and short-change your future efforts. Here are four major areas that *must* be considered when you evaluate agency performance:

Territory Expansion. The 80/20 rule may keep some accountants happy for a time, but when 80 percent of your business comes from 20 percent of your customers, there's bound to be trouble sooner or later. Smart sales managers do urge their agencies to do more business with their present customers, but they also do everything they can to help them develop the territory. The sales managers who pushed their agencies to sell existing customers harder during the past few bad years learned how quickly inventory can pile up on customers' shelves. When this happened, buying seldom slowed down—it came to a jarring halt! However, those sales managers who took the opportunity to work with their agencies in territorial development not only weathered bad times, but they reaped the benefits as the economy returned to strength.

How can you help your agencies develop their territories? First, you can promote more aggressively. Expand your advertising program; take part in more and better trade shows and spend time in the field with your agencies, finding out just what they need to succeed. There are many things that will collectively benefit all of your agencies. Remember, though, that each agency has its own timetable and priorities. Tune in on these elements, and help make them happen.

Agency Staff Development. It's not too difficult for a sales manager to make a swing through the territory, hit the high spots, and bump up sales. But agents who feel that the principal sales managers are helpful all report that the guys who take the time to work with agency salespeople in the field are most productive. Skip sales training, and emphasize product training and competitive knowledge. Hit the road with the field people, and handle the customer problems as an agency/manufacturer team. Discover the needs of customers and the needs of the agency salespeople who are on the firing line.

Sales Lead Qualification. It's no trick to run an ad offering a free catalog and pull a few thousand inquiries. But the real trick is to qualify these leads in a way that makes it practical for your agencies to follow up. Don't judge your success by the number of qualification forms you get back; use the amount of new business that results from the leads that have been qualified before they were sent to the field.

Nonsales Goals. So far, we have talked about things that can be measured directly. However, there are a lot of personal things you can do that will help the bottom line but that can never be measured. For example, have you really made friends with your agencies? You don't have to be buddy-buddy if that isn't your style. But just doing the things one friend does for another is very important. For example, if you read business publications regularly, the chances are that you will spot items that will be of interest. Why not send clips? If you spot an item that might help one of your agencies sell products manufactured by another principal, send it along. Most sales managers spend an inordinate amount of time trying to get the lion's share of their agent's time. Throwing business their way for one of their other lies shows that you are really interested in them, not just in what they can do for you. This will do more to cement relations than just about any motivational management program you could use.

If you evaluate your agencies using these four points and use the tips included in the descriptions of each point, you'll end up with more than a score. You'll end up with an understanding of what agencies are about in general, and what each of your agencies is doing to develop business for you.

SOURCES OF INFORMATION

Considerable help for manufacturers and manufacturer's agencies is available from the Manufacturers' Agents National Association. Services include membership directory, information exchange, *Agency Sales* magazine, *RepLetter*, research bulletins, education, seminars, counseling service, surveys, tax bulletins, sample contracts, insurance, answering service, and much more. For a complete kit of helpful information, contact The Manufacturers' Agents National Association, P.O. Box 3467, Laguna Hills, California, 92654.

Magazines

> *Agency Sales* magazine. P.O. Box 3467, Laguna Hills, California, 92654. (Monthly journal of the Manufacturers' Agents National Association.)
>
> *Sales & Marketing Management.* 633 Third Avenue, New York, New York, 10164. (Published by Bill Communications.)

Newsletters

> *RepLetter.* The newsletter for sales executives who use manufacturer's representatives. (A monthly publication of the Manufactur-

ers' Agents National Association, P.O. Box 3467, Laguna Hills, California, 92654).

Research reports

The Manufacturers' Agents National Association has many reports available at nominal cost for manufacturers who are using or are planning to use agencies. A complete list of these reports is available by writing to MANA. The following special reports are of special interest to manufacturers:

#401. *The Value of Using Manufacturers' Agents.*

#403. *Why Opportunities in Agency Sales Continue to Grow.*

#404. *How to Select and Work with Manufacturers' Agents.*

#405. *Guidelines for Working with Manufacturers' Agents.*

#407. *Ten Advantages of the Agency Method of Marketing.*

#408. *Getting More of Your Agent's Time.*

#409. *Three Types of Agency Marketing.*

#411. *Cost Advantages of Marketing through Manufacturers' Agents.*

#412. *How Agents and Manufacturers Can Get the Most out of Rep Councils.*

#413. *A Peek at Your Agent's Finances.*

#414. *How to Get a $100,000 Salesperson.*

#417. *How to Find Manufacturers' Agents and Agency Salesmen.*

#418. *Is the Independent Sales Agent for You?*

#421. *How to Motivate Manufacturers' Agents.*

Books

Berry, Dick. *Understanding and Motivating the Manufacturers' Agent.* Boston: CBI Publishing, 1981.

Bobrow, Edwin E. *Marketing through Manufacturers' Agents.* Sales Builders, a division of *Sales & Marketing Management,* 1976.

Bobrow, Edwin E., and Larry Wizenberg. *Sales Manager's Handbook.* Homewood.: Dow Jones-Irwin, 1983.

Britt, Stuart Henderson, ed. *Marketing Manager's Handbook.* The Dartnell Corporation, 1978.

Riso, Ovid, ed. *Sales Manager's Handbook.* The Dartnell Corporation 1980.

35

TRADE SHOWS

by
Sonja Muller Haggert

Keystone Filter Division/Met Pro Corporation

INTRODUCTION

The best way to begin any examination of trade show participation is to list or in some way categorize what you intend to achieve at a show. If you expect to do a certain dollar volume in sales, then you would only be interested in buying shows. This would limit the number of shows you attend. It would also make your show decisions easier. However, if you decide to attend trade shows for company recognition and leads, then your choices become much greater. In narrowing down your options you will first want to look at the trade shows in your primary industry.

Another important consideration is to determine at whom you wish to direct most of your trade show participation. If your pattern of distribution has a distributor, dealer, and end user network, you may find directing all your efforts at one has advantages over the others.

Now, list all the shows you are interested in by location. Proceed by determining the cost of attendance at each one that you have selected.

To sum up, look at the pros and cons of trade show participation. How do they fit into your company's short-term and long-term goals?

Trade Show Pros and Cons

Pros

1. Minimizes the cost of sales calls.
2. Allows managers in company more direct exposure to customers.

3. Allows salespeople more contacts.
4. Offers you a chance to look at your industry to see what is changing (i.e., old and new products) and, at the same time, study competitors.
5. Develops or reinforces company image.
6. Allows customer to get a hands-on feel of product primarily when product is too large to move.
7. Generates leads and inquiries.

Cons
1. Requires sales staff to take time away from the field.
2. Can be costly, especially in terms of advertising, promotion, etc.
3. Often only reinforces old customers rather then generating new ones.
4. Booth attendants only have a limited amount of time with prospects.

You would certainly want to add your own observations to this list of pros and cons.

SETTING GOALS

Research Shows in Industry

Now that you have decided to participate in trade shows, set goals that pinpoint what you expect to accomplish at and from these shows. You are probably familiar with the shows directly related to your industry. Now you need to find out which ones are worth your while. You can do this in four ways.

Mailing. Look for promotional pieces in your mail that pertain to trade shows. If you have your secretary discretionally dispose of "unimportant" mail, change this policy for a period of time so you don't miss some trade show information.

Talk to Customers and Reps. Assuming that you are familiar with the shows offered in your particular industry, do some research into other related industries that could open significant new markets. The best way to determine their fit in your areas of marketing is to find out the dates of the shows and walk them. You will meet people who can give you direction or put you in touch with the people to contact to expand your customer base. As for the shows in your industry, never pick them randomly or because you have exhibited before. Too often decisions are made because "we did it last year" or "we have always done it this way.'' Talk to your customers, and get their opinions on which shows they feel are worthwhile.

Don't overlook speaking with potential customers. Any dialogue with a possible customer is certainly worthwhile. It may also lead to the discovery that a certain potential customer has a strong affiliation with a trade group that may be the sponsor of one or more shows. Your participation in the group's show may be an indication of your support for the industry in a particular customer's eyes. That could get you some business.

I have come across this need for a show of company commitment a number of times. The trade show effort is worth participation if the customer can be a big enough factor in terms of sales, or if you feel the industry support is worthwhile.

Attend the Show. Nothing beats walking through a show before making a commitment to participate. It gives you a feel for the interest level of both booth personnel and attendees, the types of exhibits expected (tabletop or more elaborate), and the size and scope of show.

Read Publications. Be on the lookout, in your trade magazines, for special sections that list upcoming events such as trade shows. A great many publications do special features before and after a show. Prior to the show they list attendees and events or seminars planned. After the show they review attendance and get reactions from attendees and exhibitors.

Now that you have information on the various shows available, set up an annual calendar (see Figure 35–1).

Type of Show to Emphasize

To make easier your decision on which shows to attend, look at the two basic categories: (1) selling versus nonselling and (2) regional versus national. Consider participation in a showing of each. However, if your industry's national shows do not go directly to your immediate customers, you might want to emphasize regional shows. Shows centered in a certain area of the country will put you in more of a limelight. The fact that they are smaller allows you to be remembered. Small is hardly bad.

Selling Show. This is probably the most justifiable show of all. If the event is promoted and attendance is good, the orders should be able to justify your expenses. This type of show has some other major advantages. It forces salespeople to spend more time concentrating on attendees because they want to get an order. As a result, there is a

FIGURE 35–1
Calendar of Shows

	Jan	Feb	Mar	Apr	May	June	July	Aug	Sep	Oct	Nov	Dec
Show												
Dates												
Sponsor												
Location												
Expected attendance												
Actual attendance												
Total projected expected												
Yes												
No												
Maybe												

closer bond of communication developed between the company and its customers. You also get instant feedback as to what sells and what does not. This can be extremely valuable for a new product.

Nonselling Show. This type of show looks for justification at a later point in time. The salespeople hand out literature in the hopes of stimulating future interest. This type of show is hard to justify in dollars of sales because even if a lead develops into a customer, there is no pinpointing it as a direct result of a trade show.

National Show. This type of show brings in a large cross-section of people. Because attendance is national, so is the exposure. If you want to introduce yourself to a market for the first time, this may be a good way to do it.

Regional Show. Your participation is noted while you have the opportunity for more personal contact. Before attending you should get some feedback on the show. Some have only one goal in mind, and that is to have fun. The location, especially if it's a resort, should be a tip-off to you. If you feel you can work on the golf course and really make some major contacts—great. However, look for substance, such as planned conference activities mixed in with recreation. If there is a lot of recreation, a large price tag, and not much else scheduled, don't bother.

FIGURE 35–2

Exhibit Type	Advantages	Limitations	Design Flexibility	Exhibit Cost	Field Cost*
Self-contained	Packing case unfolds into exhibit. Easy to set up, dismantle and pack. Few packages to keep track of. Minimum space needed.	Design is restricted by container configuration. Restricted presentation capabilities. Damage to packing case damages exhibit itself.	Low to medium	High	Low
Performance (live talent or demonstration)	Increases interest. Allows detailed answers to inquiries.	Large response at exhibit sometimes reduces ability to identify key buying influences.	High	Low to high	High
Modular	Permits interchangeability of elements. Allows flexibility in arrangement and size.	Many packages to keep track of.	Medium to high	Medium	Medium
Cubic content	Utilizes three dimensions, having properties in the air space over entire area to height of 8′ or more. Practically eliminates competitive booths from view.	High cost.	High	High	High

FIGURE 35–2 *(concluded)*

Exhibit Type	Advantages	Limitations	Design Flexibility	Exhibit Cost	Field Cost*
Rental	Useful during interim periods of promotion and one-shot shows. No storage or expenses between shows. Tailor to application.	Somewhat inflexible. Look-alike exhibit. Limited approach.	Medium to high	Medium	Medium
System	Series of professionally finished parts. Looks customized.	Other advertisers may use same parts.	Low to medium	Low to medium	Medium
Single use	Useful for unique presentations and short campaigns.	Ends in scrap. Limited budgets.	Low to medium	Low to high	Low to high
Tabletop	Ideal for local shows. Easy setup. Simple shipping.	Not applicable for larger, national shows.	Low	Low	Low
Mobile	Flexible in pinpointing markets. High audience reception. Avoids repetitive take-downs and setups.	Continuous traveling costs.	Medium	High	High

* *Field cost* refers to freight, erection, rentals, maintenance, and dismantling.

Overall Goals

Generally speaking, the main purpose for participating in a trade show is to sell more products. You may have these more specific goals in mind also:

1. Introduction of a new product or line of products.
2. Introduction of new services.
3. Increase in the number of new customers.
4. Increase of distribution channels.
5. Reaction to new products.
6. Bringing together sales and other personnel for meetings.
7. Company image.
8. Appointment of new reps.

Type of Exhibit

Be sure to select an exhibit that fits with the type of shows you attend. Regional shows are often tabletop and require either no props or minimal ones at best.

The national shows are a different story. If you do not have the money or personnel to look strong and at your best—do not go. You could fall on your face by not having a professional exhibit at a national show.

Figure 35–2 will give you some idea of the various exhibit styles from which to choose.

One person in the company should be selected to be in charge of all shows. This should be someone in marketing, sales, or advertising. This person will, no doubt, want a committee with which to work. Begin by notifying all the people in your company who will be involved in show planning. Each person should be willing to commit a certain amount of time. This means that the sooner you make a decision on your show schedule, the more cooperation you will get from all concerned. A one-year schedule in advance would be appropriate. Bear in mind the following when making your show selections:

1. Types of people who will attend.
2. Attendance.
3. Competitive shows scheduled for the same timespan.
4. Sponsor of show.
5. Value of workshops or seminars to your firm.
6. Where the show is held. Some shows tend to focus more on recreational diversions. Although many people register, many never show up.
7. Details regarding the show, such as union labor, booth layout and size, and utility costs.

Pre-Show Promotion

A lot can be done to develop interest before the actual event. Consider the following:

1. Encourage your sales force to start talking up your attendance. Give them information on booth number, etc.
2. Mention the show continuously in routine correspondence.
3. Do a special mailing, about two weeks prior to the show, to all of your customers and potential customers. Mention your booth number and/or hospitality suite number.
4. Include your booth number in ads in trade magazines.
5. Take advantage of trade magazine show issues which enable you to list your booth number, booth personnel, and what you will be exhibiting.
6. Develop a press kit to hand out to any media reps that will be walking the show. If well done, this could land you a good story. This kit should contain *solid new* information not old press releases or copies of ads. Include photographs and important fact sheets.

ASSIGNING RESPONSIBILITY

The Worksheet and Schedule

Schedule the shows you plan to attend. You may want to use the worksheet pictured in Figure 35–3.

Send a copy of your proposed schedule to all salespeople. You can revise this to your actual scheduled attendance when necessary.

Some of your salespeople may decide to attend at the last minute. The more contact with your salespeople, the better.

Booth Personnel

Above all else, the people who work your booth should be enthusiastic and anxious to talk to the attendees. We have all seen too many people spending their time in a booth reading newspapers and talking to their associates. Perhaps the best way to avoid this is to convey to the person in charge of shows that this is unacceptable behavior. That person, in turn, is responsible for providing the example to other booth personnel. Weariness and other nonshow-related activities will always occur, especially if the show is poorly attended or about to end. The extent of it should be minimized and indicated as unacceptable.

FIGURE 35–3
Trade Show Worksheet and Schedule

Dates of Shows (Chronologically)	Show and Sponsor	Location	Booth Number	Expected Attendance	Cost Booth Space	Total Budget	Key Deadlines								
							Select Builder	Reserve and Pay for Booth	Conduct Pre-Show Promotions	Conduct Other Pre-Show Planning	Pack and Ship Exhibit	Set up and Manage Show Operation	Dismantle—Ship Exhibit and Equipment	Evaluate Show	Follow-up Leads

Here are some other guidelines for booth personnel.

1. Make sure specific times are scheduled for booth personnel and other workers. Make sure they realize their commitment. Otherwise, you may have too many people at the booth at 10:00 A.M. and none at 4:00 P.M.
2. Select people who are especially knowledgeable about your company. These people represent your company as a whole.
3. Encourage all who attend the show to use the time to learn as much as possible about your competitors.
4. Give editors of publications information that could lead to good press release coverage.
5. There are two schools of thought on literature at a show. Some say you should give out all the literature you can, in the belief that at the end of the day people will go over what they have collected. I subscribe to the belief that you should hand out a minimal amount of literature but get all the names and addresses and pertinent information about potential customers. Then, mail your catalog to these leads at their place of business. At that point they will be back in their work environment and ready to concentrate on looking at suppliers. (The latter philosophy really applies more to a national nonbuying show. At a buying show, people study literature to make decisions at the show itself.)

Setup and Teardown

An important consideration in budgeting and planning for use of trade show personnel is how setup and teardown are to be accomplished.

Most regional shows, especially smaller tabletop shows, expect that you will bring in your own people to set up and tear down. However, national shows, especially in large cities, have a pool of union labor which in most cases must perform all these functions. In 1982, these labor rates ranged from $6.50 per hour to $15 for laborers and from $15 per hour to $18 for electricians.

COMMUNICATING GOALS TO THE SALES FORCE

In determining who to send to a trade show, consider your objective. If you are there to get leads and sell, send your best salespeople. They will recognize customers and potential customers and will do you the most good. If you want to introduce a new technically oriented product or explain the technical aspects of your present product, send the scientists, engineers, etc. If your goal is company image, send some of the upper echelon who can talk about the company's stock position in the marketplace, etc. However, always include some salespeople.

FIGURE 35–4
Post-Show Evaluation

Name of show _____

Dates _____

Location _____

Criteria	Analysis				Comments
		Good	*Average*	*Poor*	
1. Total Show					
A. Attendance		☐	☐	☐	_____
B. Cooperation of show management		☐	☐	☐	_____
C. Adequate utilities		☐	☐	☐	_____
D. Number of visitors to booth		☐	☐	☐	_____
E. Cost per visitor		☐	☐	☐	_____
F. Percent of show attendees visiting your booth		☐	☐	☐	_____
G. Adequate publicity by show management		☐	☐	☐	_____
2. Your booth					
A. Sales orders	$ _____				
B. Number of valid inquiries	_____ Units				

C. Cost of your booth $ _____

D. Number of visitors to booth _____

E. Cost per visitor $ _____ /visitor

F. Percent of show attendees visiting your booth _____ %

	Good	Average	Poor	Comments
G. Content	☐	☐	☐	_____
H. Use of space	☐	☐	☐	_____
I. Image	☐	☐	☐	_____
J. New and improved products displayed	☐	☐	☐	_____
K. Competent staff	☐	☐	☐	_____
L. Location	☐	☐	☐	_____
M. Sales appeal	☐	☐	☐	_____
N. Interest created	☐	☐	☐	_____
O. General booth design	☐	☐	☐	_____
P. Audience involvement	☐	☐	☐	_____
Q. Adequate demonstrations	☐	☐	☐	_____
R. Adequate handouts	☐	☐	☐	_____

Many companies hire entertainers or have girls in skimpy clothing in their booths. Most advertising professionals will tell you that they create a lot of interest and people will certainly stop in your booth—but will they remember what product you were selling?

Hospitality Suites

This is an optional extra your company may wish to provide at the show. Only do so if you can afford the added expense.

Begin by establishing a theme. The unusual, done in a clever way, can attract a lot of attention. A company I am familiar with recently used an ice cream parlor theme. Rather than serve drinks, the company invited people to make their own sundaes. It was a great success.

Be sure reservations for your hospitality suite are confirmed by the hotel so no mixup in time, room, etc. can occur. Be sure the room is easily accessible and can accommodate all of your guests and some extras.

Sales Meetings

Shows are a great opportunity to get salespeople together. Use the time before or after the show to meet with your salespeople. You can cover new sales tools, changes you have made in packaging or design, and a multitude of other news.

The biggest advantage of sales meetings like these is that they are a minor expense. Most of the participants are there anyway.

MEASURING RESULTS

The best way to begin an evaluation of the show you have attended is to make a point of recording impressions every day that you are there. Then, put these impressions into a general report that you can look at when you are deciding if you want to attend that show again.

Your indicator of a successful show, however, is in terms of sales and/or leads. The most concise way to put all the information together is by using a standard evaluation form. The form shown in Figure 35–4 may prove helpful.

Trade shows are a vital link to people and products in your industry. When used to their best advantage, they can provide a company with a valuable marketing tool.

BIBLIOGRAPHY

Chase, Cochrane, and Kenneth L. Barasch. *Marketing Problem Solver*. Edited by Edmund Van Deusen. Radnor, Pa.: Chilton, 1977.

36

THE SALES PLAN

by
Porter Henry

Porter Henry and Company, Inc.

The sales plan is a road map by which the sales manager or vice president of sales specifies goals, the strategies and tactics for achieving them, and benchmarks for measuring progress along the way. The advantages of having this type of plan are many:

1. Definition of objectives—by territory, product line, or market segment—enables the manager to practice a form of management by objectives, whether or not it is formalized in that way. Every segment of the sales effort knows what is expected of it.
2. Goal definition enables the manager to do a better job of formulating the strategies for reaching those goals.
3. The existence of a detailed plan facilitates coordination with other departments. For example, sales contests can be tied in with advertising campaigns; the sales promotion department gets adequate advance warning about materials needed for distributor or district sales meetings.
4. Perhaps most important, the manager is able to identify quickly areas where performance is falling behind expectations, can take corrective action before it is too late, or can spot instances where sales are above expectation and exploit these opportunities.

In view of such obvious benefits, it is surprising how little attention is paid to sales plans in literature on marketing. For example, a booklet on market planning published by an illustrious nonprofit business research organization includes the marketing plans of 27 well-known corporations. All these plans cover financial returns, product life cycles, market research, and other familiar components of market planning—but not one of them so much as mentions the existence of a sales plan!

Throughout this chapter we'll discuss the sales plan for an imaginary manufacturer. The same principles apply to a wholesaler or retailer.

The plan usually projects the coming year in detail, with a brief statement of goals for the next three or five years. These future targets must be considered because, based on future plans, a product might get more or less effort than its current status would indicate.

RELATIONSHIP WITH MARKETING PLAN

The sales plan is really a subdivision of the corporate marketing plan. The latter establishes goals and strategies for the entire corporation; the sales plan specifies exactly what the sales force intends to do as its share in meeting the corporate objectives.

The sales department feeds information into the formulation of the overall corporate plan and receives output from the corporate plan in the form of targets assigned to the sales force.

Input from the Sales Department

No matter how sophisticated the company's advertising agency and market research department, the sales force can contribute realistic, grassroots data to be used by the market planners. Field sales personnel are asked to provide information like this:

1. Forecasts of the coming year's sales, by product and by customer category.
2. Information about economic and business trends in each territory.
3. Knowledge about users' reactions to the company's products or services, advertising, merchandising, credit policies, etc.
4. Suggestions for new products, modifications of old ones, new distribution channels, new advertising themes, etc.

Most companies find that the sales forecasts made by the field are reasonably accurate in total, although the individual sales rep may be a consistent underforecaster or overforecaster. Some companies track the accuracy of each individual's predictions so that, after a few years' experience, they'll know that John Doe's forecasts are usually 15 percent too high and Jane Roe's 10 percent too low.

VOLUME AND PROFIT OBJECTIVES

A frequent complaint of top management is that the sales department thinks primarily about sales volume and not sufficiently about profits. A sales plan targeted toward profit objectives is the cure for this.

For the sales force as a whole and for each element in it (such as each district, region, the national accounts department, or the military sales department), the plan sets forth goals as to:

1. Dollar sales volume.
2. Gross margin (dollar sales minus cost of the products).
3. Contribution to corporate net profit (gross margin minus selling costs).

The total sales objectives of the U.S. Widgets Company might look like this:

	Objective
Total sales volume	$100,000,000
Less cost of products	70,000,000
Gross margin	30,000,000
Less direct selling costs	10,000,000
Contribution to corporate overhead and profit	$ 20,000,000

To illustrate the difference between concentrating on volume and on profit, let's say that the company has three products: Specialty, with a 50 percent margin (figured as a percentage of sales); Soso, with a 30 percent margin; and Commodity, with a 10 percent margin.

Next year's sales forecast by product is as follows:

Product	Sales ($000)	Margin (Percent)	Gross Profit ($000)
Specialty	$ 30,000	50%	$15,000
Soso	40,000	30	12,000
Commodity	30,000	10	3,000
Totals	$100,000		$30,000

Which is the real goal—the $100 million in sales or the $30 million in gross profits? A manager too devoted to mere volume might boost volume by selling a higher percentage of Commodity, which is easy to sell. The results might be:

Product	Sales	Margin	Profit
Specialty	$ 10,000	50%	$ 5,000
Soso	30,000	30	9,000
Commodity	60,000	10	6,000
Totals	$100,000		$20,000

Yes, this manager hit the sales goal—but profits are only two thirds of what they should be.

Now, look at a manager who actually missed the total sales goal by concentrating on Specialty.

Product	Sales	Margin	Profit
Specialty	$50,000	50%	$25,000
Soso	30,000	30	9,000
Commodity	10,000	10	1,000
Totals	$90,000		$35,000

This manager is 10 percent below the sales goal, but weep not for him or her—profits are 16.6 percent above targets. Which type of manager will be a hero to the CEO?

SUBDIVIDING THE GOALS

The sales and target figures are further broken down by market segment and by divisions of the sales department. Market segmentation, for example, might include class A, B, and C direct customers, wholesalers or distributors, government purchases, national accounts, etc. Sales force segments would include geographic divisions like territories, districts, and regions, as well as any specialized sales departments like national accounts, hospital sales, export, and so on.

Goals for each section of the sales department are shown in a two-dimensional matrix to indicate sales and gross profits (GP) targets both by product and by market, like this:

Sales Targets for District X *(all figures in $000)*

	Specialty		Soso		Commodity		Totals	
	Sls	GP	Sls	GP	Sls	GP	Sls	GP
Direct								
A customers	400	200	200	60	300	30	900	290
B customers	100	50	100	30	100	10	300	90
C customers	50	25	50	15	100	10	200	50
Military	—	—	100	30	300	30	400	60
Export	50	25	150	45	—	—	200	70
Totals	600	300	600	180	800	80	2,000	560

These annual goals are broken down into monthly targets, seasonally corrected if possible. As soon as possible after the end of each month, sales results are sent to sales reps and field managers so corrective action can be taken where results are below target.

Any additional breakdowns which may be helpful to the field can usually be provided by the company's computer. For example, in addition to the coming year's goals as shown in the table above, another table might show last year's figures in each category and the percentage increase forecast. The product/customer combinations for which the highest percentage increases are planned will usually require the greatest amount of sales efforts.

THE SALES FORCE INVENTORY

The planner's next step is to take a look at the sales force to determine future requirements and schedule the steps for meeting them. The sales force inventory looks something like this:

	Number at Present	Probable Losses, Next 3 Years	Total Needed in 3 Years	To Be Developed	
				This Year	Next Year
Sales reps	40	6	45	6	5
Promotable	2				
District					
managers	4	1	4		1

U.S. Widgets Company now has 40 sales reps and four district managers. The sales manager estimates that 12 reps will be lost in the next three years, based on a historic turnover rate of about 5 percent. This includes one rep to be promoted to district manager.

At the end of three years, therefore, there will be only 34 of the current reps, and 45 will be needed. Eleven new reps must be found. The manager decides to recruit six this year and five the following year.

One manager is scheduled to retire, so one of the two promotable reps will be trained to step into that position.

THE BUDGET

This is the one part of the sales plan almost every sales manager has: a forecast of expenses for the coming year. In addition to the usual budget items such as salaries, bonuses, branch office costs, automobile purchases, travel and entertainment, etc., the budget must allow for the costs of sales contests, training sessions, participating in trade shows, and the travel and programs for district and national sales meetings.

COMMUNICATIONS

The sales plan may include a review of upward and downward communications, including:

Communications to Customers. For example, newsletters, product information, etc. (Promotional mailings are usually handled by the advertising or sales promotion departments.)

Communications to the Sales Force.

1. From headquarters: summaries of sales results, newsletters, etc. Perhaps the most important element in headquarters-to-field communications is the speedy circulation of actual sales compared with targets.
2. From regional or district headquarters.

Communications from the Sales Force.

1. Call reports and customer information.
2. Territory market forecasts and marketing plans.
3. Customer applications, problems, and suggestions.
4. Competitive activity.

Preparation of the annual sales plan provides an opportunity for reviewing the paperwork burden imposed upon the sales force in order to see if any reports can be eliminated, simplified, or combined.

SALES COMPENSATION PLAN

This is also a good time to see if any changes should be made in the compensation plan. Assuming the sales force is compensated with some form of commission or salary-plus-incentive plan, does the plan motivate the sales force to attain the profit goals?

In U.S. Widgets Company, for example, sales of Specialty are much more profitable than those of Commodity. If sales reps are compensated on the basis of total sales volume, and if Commodity is easier to sell, they will be motivated to devote an unprofitable amount of sales effort on it.

TRAINING PLANS

The complete sales plan will include a schedule of the times, places, and primary content of training programs for new salespeople, experienced salespeople, middle-line managers, distributors, dealers, and customers.

SCHEDULING

Part of the sales plan is a calendar showing the dates of scheduled events as well as dates on which preparation should start to allow enough lead time. The calendar is best visualized if it is a Gantt chart with horizontal bars indicating preparatory time and occurrence time for such events as:

1. New-product or new-promotion introductions.
2. Sales contests.
3. National sales meetings.
4. District and regional sales meetings.
5. Training sessions for the sales force, distributors or wholesalers, dealers, and customers.

An example of such a chart for hypothetical U.S. Widgets Company is shown in Figure 36–1.

It will be seen that the current sales contest will end in March. The contest runs during the winter months, with monthly sprints to maintain motivation. Awards will be given at the district meetings, scheduled for April. Since this company provides audiovisual aids to help the district managers run better meetings, planning for these meetings is scheduled for February and March.

A new product is to be launched in September, coinciding with the national sales meeting. The sales department's role in the product launch, as well as the national sales meeting, will be planned in July and August.

FIGURE 36–1

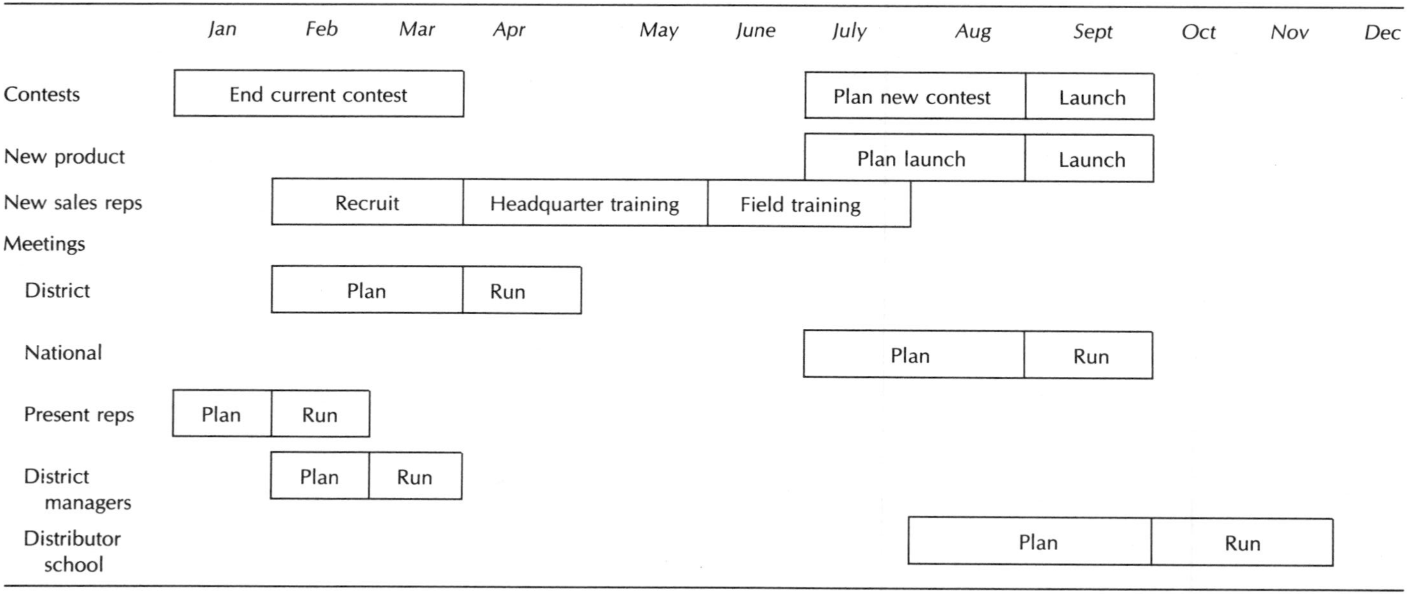
Jan
Feb
Mar
Apr
May
June
July
Aug
Sept
Oct
Nov
Dec
Contests
End current contest
Plan new contest
Launch
New product
Plan launch
Launch
New sales reps
Recruit
Headquarter training
Field training
Meetings
District
Plan
Run
National
Plan
Run
Present reps
Plan
Run
District managers
Plan
Run
Distributor school
Plan
Run

Tied in with the new product will be a new sales contest, planned during the summer and launched at the national sales meeting.

New sales reps will be recruited, primarily by the district managers, in February and March, given their initial headquarters training in April and May, and field training in June or July. They will have one month's actual sales experience before the national sales meeting.

Refresher and advanced training for present reps will be planned in January and presented in February—five-day sessions for two regions at a time, thus limiting the groups to about 20 reps each.

Training for district managers, in the form of a four-day session on various managerial techniques, will be planned in February and conducted in March.

Distributor schools will be conducted in a number of cities in October, shortly after the launching of the new product. These schools will be somewhat technical in nature. The training needed by distributors to handle inquiries about the new product will be handled by the sales reps.

37

SELECTING AN ADVERTISING AGENCY

by
Jack H. Shapiro

The Penn Management Group, Inc.

SELECTING AN ADVERTISING AGENCY

Properly implementing the process of selecting an advertising agency and the ultimate selection of the right agency are critical elements in a company's marketing program. The execution of a creative strategy which results in increased revenues, in improved market share, and in helping to achieve maximum profitability starts with deciding to begin the search for an agency, if it is determined that the support of an agency is necessary. The approach to selecting an agency must be based on recognizing its future role in carrying out aspects of the marketing plan, and perhaps even in developing that plan. Choosing an agency must be done with great care.

The trade press and the business pages of daily newspapers report on the constant movement of accounts from one agency to another. In some instances, such as an agency for some reason acquiring the responsibility for a competitive product, movement is a must. However, in other situations it is for less than sound reasons—perhaps emotional, for example. The act of moving an account is inefficient, slowing or possibly even halting marketing momentum, and it is expensive in money and particularly, in time. Devoting considerable effort to making a wise first choice is the superior method.

Two essential points must be kept in mind as the selection program proceeds. The first is that the interviewing of possible agencies must be handled as if it were new employees who were being hired. The same standards and the same criteria (such as talent, competence, reliability, dependability, integrity, and financial responsibility) must be applied not only to the candidate agencies themselves but, also, to those within the agencies who would be handling the account—those with whom company personnel would be working.

Second, after the choice is made, both the integration of the agency into the company's marketing function and operations and the overall company–agency relationship must be managed, in a way not dissimilar to that in which departments within the company are managed. The fact that the agency is external cannot allow abdication of the management responsibility, nor denial of the point that the agency is fulfilling a charge which, were it not for the highly specialized and yet diverse creativity required, would belong inherently on the company marketing department's organization chart. Unless that responsibility is exercised, the agency will not be able to assume its role as an integral part of the company's marketing apparatus.

DECIDING THAT AN AGENCY IS REQUIRED

This should be based on the marketing intensity of the field or business in which the company is involved, the company's own advertising and marketing capability relative to that intensity, and the financial means and budget level to support the extent of advertising agency services desired. Not all businesses require, or are able to support financially, an advertising agency relationship; and not all businesses need all of the services that an agency can provide, even when it is determined that an agency is necessary.

Firms operating in highly competitive areas of the consumer marketplace, sometimes in cases in which product differences are not that apparent, must use advertising agency creativity to position their products against a host of similar goods. In developing and executing approaches designed to position profitably the item or items in the product spectrum, these firms also would utilize the full range of aid and expertise that an agency could offer. These companies almost always maintain their own substantial advertising departments and marketing groups, but the need for objectivity, for help in planning, preparing, and implementing campaigns, is so significant that employing an agency or agencies is standard practice.

Other businesses might feel little need for advertising or marketing help. The position of the product or products is, by its nature, well defined, it has little competition, and the company can well accomplish what is demanded to survive in the marketplace on its own. These firms might never utilize ad agencies or might, from time to time, use only a minimum of what might be the full-service shop's capabilities, such as research or media or pure creative support (the latter based on the company's own marketing plan and its already developed positioning and creative strategies).

DETERMINING WHAT IS EXPECTED FROM THE AGENCY

This cannot be achieved by a simple formula. The agency's job description must be developed in the same way that an executive's or department's work definition is established. One has to list in detail each of the aspects of the advertising and marketing function which the company requires to be performed. The responsible party has to choose those areas in which help could be efficiently utilized for improved results, relative to the company's standards and the market's demands. For example, the need might be based on technical knowledge beyond the company's ability, such as in broadcast creative, production, or media, or perhaps in research. With the growth of cable, allocation of budget itself has possibly become more complex than that with which the firm is able to cope; or, the company might be interested in undertaking a direct marketing program and wants help in deciding if and how it should.

DECIDING WHOM TO INTERVIEW

This should be based on a large amount of research and investigation. The number of agencies with whom one finally meets is arbitrary, of course, but attempting to develop a list of a dozen names to be researched and investigated would be advisable. Through checking and studying, this list might be culled to six agencies for initial interviewing. These six might then be cut to three for the extensive and in-depth interviews and discussions preliminary to making the final determination.

It should be recognized that in larger firms where there might be political considerations, one might have to interview more than six. There is an excitement, even a glamour to advertising; and upper management might want to, or have to, ask that a certain agency be included in the process.

Normally, the company's advertising director is responsible for the process, certainly for handling the logistics of scheduling and other essentials. Assuming that the ad director reports to a vice president of marketing, these two (or the latter alone) would make the determination as to which agency is chosen. Upper management might be involved in the final process and should approve the selection; but, the responsibility for performance is the marketing vice president's, and that person should have the final say.

The preliminary list of 12 agencies should be developed from contacts, research, and creative and financial reputation. Marketing executives or others with whom one is acquainted can be a source of names; another source is media representatives with whom the various agencies work. Articles in trade publications, such as *Advertising Age,* can be used as a reference. At various times throughout the year, *Advertising Age* publishes listings—based on differing criteria—which could be of aid. *The Agency Red Book, The Standard Directory of Advertising Agencies,* also provides helpful information about a virtual multitude of agencies. The American Association of Advertising Agencies' membership roster can be particularly valuable, both as a list of names of agencies who might be candidates and as a checking resource. The AAAA, in accepting members, determines that they meet certain financial qualifications, operate ethically, and are experienced, able, and capable of reasonable performance.

To determine which agencies to interview, review both business and creative reputation, analyze financial stability and credit rating, and check again client lists for both quality of clients and potential adaptability to the types of goods marketed by the company. At this point, checking might or might not include calls to agency clients. Certainly, once interviewing itself begins, conversations with current and past agency clients are a necessity in narrowing the choice.

Some advertisers, in the process of developing a list of agencies to interview, prepare and forward questionnaires to the group of possible agencies. These forms, they feel, are useful as a means of preliminary screening. There are strong pro and con opinions regarding the use of questionnaires; among them the thought that both proper completion and later analysis take considerable time, without giving a full and even accurate picture of an agency's capabilities. Also, it is felt that the written pieces do not compare, as a communications vehicle, with even the simplest interview. However, some might prefer to put together a relevant list of questions to be used as a checklist during the actual interviewing process.

Obviously, agency size and physical location are considerations that enter into the decision whether or not to include an agency on the roster of interviewees. Ease of travel and communication is an absolute. Size compatability is important because a small agency might not be physically and otherwise capable of handling the needs of a large firm.

THE INITIAL INTERVIEWING PROCESS

This is intended to bring the list of candidates from six down to three. The number of people visiting the agencies at this point is small, perhaps the vice president of marketing and the advertising director by themselves, or possibly with an additional person. The meetings are general, providing both parties with a chance to gain a sense of the other and to decide whether or not each wishes to extend the interviewing process.

The various agency presentations are simple, encompassing a review of the agency's credentials, its depth and breadth of experience, its capabilities, and its approach to past work. Visiting the agencies' offices allows the advertiser to determine whether or not the working environment would be acceptable. Also, the potential client can gain an impression of agency employees, the way they work, their own feelings about their agency and its efforts, and their attitude toward their clients. In total, the advertiser has the opportunity to sense if there would be a creative responsiveness, and to judge whether or not working with the agency would be comfortable—whether or not there would be an intellectual compatability.

The potential client provides a description of the company, in broad terms, at each of these meetings. Information is provided regarding its conceptual foundation, goals and objectives, operations, marketing programs, basic financial data, eccentricities of the business and the company's problems and opportunities.

It is essential from this series of initial interviews that the advertiser achieve some understanding of each agency's thought processes relative to the development of its creative work. The core questions in the project of selecting an advertising agency are those which focus on the products the agencies have produced and, more important, the reasons for and results of their actions.

INTERVIEWING THE FINALISTS

This is better accomplished in a two-step procedure. Once the number of candidates is reduced to the finalists, two rounds of meetings should be held. Both series should be at the agencies' offices because maximum exposure to the agency environments and staffs is important in making the final selection.

The first set of meetings should involve the representatives of the advertiser who participated in the initial interviewing and possibly others who might be involved in the decision. Each of the finalists should make a more formal presentation, reviewing in greater depth and breadth its capabilities. Discussion probably would again include history of the agency, its client list, the longevity of each client and account turnover, the scope of services, and the background and experience of agency people in general—all in greater depth than at the initial meeting.

The concentration should be on the agency's advertising philosophies—the way in which it handles accounts and would anticipate handling work for the advertiser. Extensive questioning is required at this point, so that from this meeting the potential client will emerge with an accurate feeling for the way the agency thinks, how it approaches a situation, and how a creative campaign is conceived, nurtured, and implemented. The agency people should present work done for their clients, describing in detail the complete process of concept development and execution, and reporting the effectiveness of those efforts.

The advertiser's specific needs must be reviewed in depth, as well as the range of additional items that might be required with the growth both of the client's business and of the agency relationship. It is important to both parties that the agency's capabilities be well-suited to the client's assignments.

Other subjects must be pursued at this meeting. Fee structure, extra payments, contractual arrangements such as the obligation of each party to the other, and contract timing and length are some. Also important are the specifics regarding the agency people who would be supervising and performing work on the account and those who would represent the client. It is impossible, of course, for the client to conduct formal interviews of those who would be doing the advertising; but, at this juncture, one must have a clear perception of their backgrounds, experience, and capacity to comprehend the marketing objectives and to perform well in effectuating their portion of the strategic approach.

At the conclusion of this first round of interviews, the participating advertiser representatives should meet and determine their preliminary choice among the three, ranking the other two. The second series of meetings should then be scheduled. This final group of interviews must result in a firm decision. All three agencies might be screened again, or the meetings might be with only the top two. Attending for the advertiser should be not only those who must make the decision but those members of upper management who must approve it.

The agenda for these last sessions is the same, essentially, as that for the first series. All discussions must be in depth. Agency subjects should include its credentials, business and creative reputation, structure, scope of services, client list and longevity, background and experience of organization, creative work and the reasoning behind it (and the results), the account team's capabilities, and the way the agency and the team feel about the potential account. The advertiser should again review the company's situation, needs, and the way in which the working relationship would be handled. A summary of the contract and fee basis should be provided.

Following this final set of meetings, the decision must be made and approved by those responsible. The review of the finalists should take place as quickly after the last presentation as possible, so that recalled details and reactions supplement notes.

Some advertisers favor assigning a speculative presentation requirement to candidate agencies. This would be an actual creative project. The rationale for this is that the potential client can make judgments regarding agencies more satisfactorily when the work being judged is theirs than when it is work for others. Some agencies prefer this method since they find it difficult to express the logic and reasoning behind their creative concepts. Many agencies, however, refuse to undertake speculative efforts. They are time-consuming, disrupt the efficient flow of regular agency work, and are expensive to the agency and to the advertiser who agrees to pay a fee for the assignment.

The speculative presentation technique should be discouraged. No agency, in a short period of time, can gain an understanding of a client's business sufficiently enough to develop and execute even the simplest, soundly based creative strategy or tactical approach. Thus, one short-term effort cannot illustrate an agency's true competence, or lack of it; and the selection decision is subject to being based on emotional response to a single piece or group of advertising.

EVALUATING THE AGENCIES AS A BASIS FOR THE DECISION

Obviously, this is the bottom line of the entire process. The decision, although in a sense founded on intangibles and certainly on criteria that are difficult to quantify, must be based on a precise set of specifications, some of which were reviewed previously. The agency finally selected should have impeccable credentials and a reputation for business, financial, and creative integrity. It should have a history of growth and of client longevity and satisfaction.

The people of the agency should be those with whom the advertiser could feel comfortable. They would have to have withstood extensive interviewing and personal scrutiny—as if they were candidates for direct employment—for the agency selected should be felt to be, in truth, an extension of the company's marketing department. In essence, the people of the agency and those of the advertiser must be intellectually compatible.

The agency, of course, must exhibit creative strength and be strong in creative ability, talent, responsiveness, and creative lasting power. It must understand that creativity is not an end in itself but merely a means to a productive end, a business goal, a financial objective. The selection project must show that the agency thoroughly grasps that advertising is an element in the marketing process and that creative implementation must be based on a marketing plan that builds a creative strategy on a positioning strategy, which in turn is founded on an overall market or situation analysis. This is a requirement regardless of the advertiser's size or of the size of the agency.

If the agency is a tiny creative house, too small to have a marketing function per se, it still must understand that whatever work it does must be marketing-based. In this case the advertiser's marketing people must direct and support the agency's efforts, the two together doing what a larger agency might be able to accomplish unilaterally. If both the agency and the advertiser are large, the agency itself should have a strong marketing and research capability, able to prepare or at least to contribute to the marketing plan, as the client desires. In short, whatever its size, the agency must show that it is capable of integrating the marketing requirements of its clients into its creative thinking and advertising execution.

An analysis of the agency's past and current work—and the strategic and tactical reasoning underlying that work—should indicate an ability to adapt continually to contemporary lifestyles and to change approach as demographics, attitudes, styles, and fashions change. The agency's work must show a comprehension of relevant trends, both short-term and longer-term. In its interpretation of those trends the agency must be upbeat and innovative.

Except in limited situations, the agency must be technically and creatively competent in multimedia assignments, particularly with the growth of electronic media and of more sophisticated target marketing approaches. Also, the agency must be able to work with the client to make the advertising budget totally productive. It must have the ability to stay within budget guidelines in its own work, as well.

INTEGRATING AGENCY ACTIVITIES WITH COMPANY GOALS

This requires, first, a completely open relationship and, second, that the overall company–agency relationship be managed similarly to the way company departments are managed. The agency must be privy to company sales breakdowns, the marketing plan, strategic and tactical moves, product changes, competitive developments, and the myriad other continual happenings that will reflect on the way it plans advertising programs and presents the company in advertising. Management must show in its attitude and actions that it considers the agency trustworthy, capable, and competent. In the overall relationship and in daily dealings, there must be continual give and take, constructive criticism, and approval. Both parties must feel that the agency is respected and that it has management's confidence.

Finally, once the two parties have a smooth working arrangement, there must be periodic (probably annual) performance reviews, detailed objective discussions evaluating agency activities from a broad perspective, and goal setting for future work. The process of agency selection is time-consuming, expensive, and disruptive to the business; it is successful only through a major effort. Once the careful choice is made, it must be carefully managed, nurtured, and sustained.

38

INDUSTRIAL MARKETING PLANNING: A CASE HISTORY

by
Boris M. Krantz

Krantz Associates, Inc.

This is a true example of market planning transacted during the mid- to late-1970s in the United States. The situations depicted actually occurred, although all specific references to individuals and companies are fictitious. At the end of this presentation, editorial comments will be added to cite not only the critical points of the case's evolution but also the practical steps in the strategic planning process.

BACKGROUND

Specialty Steel, Inc. is a division of Specialty Steel International. Historically a large, billion-dollar sales company, SSI has sales offices or operating plants throughout the world. SSI's products are basic steel alloys manufactured into several common product forms (e.g., tube and pipe, wire, and precision strip). To achieve a measure of product differentiation from other worldwide steel producers, Specialty designed excellence and quality into its products. They sold alloys of higher-value stainless steels and nickel and supported them by a well-equipped, well-staffed research and development center in the home location.

In the late 60s, Specialty Steel invested in its first marketing facility in the United States and upgraded its marketing effort there. This plant provided domestic technical support to the marketplace, offering minimal finishing capabilities for raw material imported from the mother plant.

577

Specialty's management upgraded its sales force with eight sales-people. For a direct knowledge of the U.S. market, several salespeople were hired from the principal domestic competition. As members of the new team often replaced foreign personnel, the marketing reflected their influence and changed radically. Externally influencing Specialty's rapid growth was the construction of nuclear power plants: they created a major market for Specialty Steel's alloy products. By the mid-70s, Specialty Steel had not only made its presence felt in several markets but had also achieved several significant goals:

— Their products were recognized as high-quality.
— Their market share gained significantly, i.e., to approximately 8 percent.
— Their senior management at the home location was confident about the American venture.

Based upon this information, the request was made and authoriza-tion received for the U.S. managers to analyze the feasibility of addi-tional investment into new products. Board approval was granted, and, by the late 70s, the plant was constructed. Because of the tonnage required to achieve profitable plant operation, sales would have to increase significantly.

The U.S. senior managers then went through a period of taking stock—the first rule of good market planning. The questions to be answered were: "Where have I been?" "Where am I going?" "How do I get there?" The answers had to accurately define past, present, and future status of the business. During this process, other factors of concern developed:

— Despite the positives, Specialty's business had stagnated. Over-all sales had remained static, in the $5-to-$7 million range.
— Because of the necessity and inefficiency of importing all raw materials from the mother plant, the previous year's profits were marginal.
— Specialty's sister U.S. division had an alternate model of distri-bution strategy. These groups had focused their marketing ef-forts toward industrial distributors, and they consequently de-veloped a far broader market penetration and higher average selling prices. In marked contrast to the Specialty Steel group, their sales volume had increased significantly.

NEW MANAGEMENT

With these observations made, management began a complete review of its strategy and goals. A redefined, ambitious product program re-sulted. The first decision was to hire a new general manager. According to the study, it was felt current management lacked the industrial stature and management sophistication to carry out senior management's goals.

Also, they considered the new plant projected for completion in late 82 with optimism based on the past 10 years' market penetration. The U.S. management set new marketing goals:

1. Achieve 20 percent market share within three years in all products.
2. Change marketing strategy from focus upon direct, end user sales to focus upon local industrial distributors.
3. Create an image of a corporation committed to product excellence as a domestic, prime supplier.

With the aid of an executive search firm, Specialty Steel's management rapidly identified candidates with the key criteria of extensive industry experience and knowledge of industrial distribution. Soon, Dan was hired as general manager.

After routine introductions and review of the business's history, Dan analyzed the issues:

— What is the first priority(ies)?
— Is the organization structure right for the task?
— How can volume be increased by a factor of three?

He decided to avoid immediately resolving these and to hit the road. Dan thought the situation was just too pat. Success, growth, and profits were too easily forecast in what he knew, from years of experience, to be a very competitive and price-sensitive market. He felt that only after firsthand observation of his inherited team could he make the assessments necessary to develop direction and plans.

THE FIRST DECISIONS

By traveling, observing, and learning, Dan became aware of the markets in which Specialty was successful. Foremost was Specialty's great reliance upon specification-intensive customers (e.g., nuclear and the U.S. military). Both customers not only required extreme technical detail in product manufacture but also participated in a blind-bid auction staged by the purchasing utility, government agency, etc. The result was a poor combination of high manufacturing cost, high volume, and low-price business.

Other external events were affecting the U.S. nuclear energy industry. Record inflation in construction costs, interest rates, political confusion, and the inaction caused by the environmental lobbies virtually stopped U.S. nuclear construction. The oil embargo of 1973–74, the subsequent economic inflation, and the accident at Three Mile

Island aroused public concern over nuclear energy's safety and future. A pall was cast upon the domestic U.S. nuclear program specifically, with uncertain consequences for the industry generally.

Specialty Steel's marketing program had to redirect its focus from the nuclear market to obvious targets of opportunity, i.e., those inevitably crowded by their competitors. Consistent with this observation, there was nearly total neglect by Specialty of the local distributor, a principal market channel. The previous management established distributors in an unconventionally casual manner. Agreements were verbal and minimally defined, and single exclusive companies were primed in ill-defined local marketplaces. The result of these strategies was a 2 : 1 ratio of end user/distributor sales.

From previous experience Dan knew 60 to 70 percent of national sales were sold by distributors—the reverse of Specialty's actual ongoing experience! Therefore, during these initial travel and get-acquainted trips, Dan was prepared to question management and the sales force.

— Why should Specialty Steel have different market channels than their major competitors?
— Were there unique factors (e.g., products or markets served) dictating a reversal of the general market trend?

Along with the questions relating to the distributor marketing channel, Dan also had questions regarding Specialty's ability to market its products under the private label of others. He discovered little had really been done. To reduce travel, field salespeople were responsible for potential accounts in their individual territories. This type of account was Dan's first introduction to even more practical and more immediate problems: pricing, terms, and conditions of the sales practiced by Specialty.

New problems meant new questions focusing on this channel:

— Were there other opportunities?
— How should this sales program be organized?
— What were the potential and costs?

The answers were immediately apparent to Dan. His boss, who, of course, had been part of the senior management team that set up or at least supported the initial program, recognized these areas of concern. He also recognized some real problems.

THE FIRST MARKETING DECISIONS

With the initial realities setting in, Dan found time and other pressures demanding the outline of a formal marketing plan. Analyses were prepared defining the principal characteristics of Specialty's competitors, in particular their strengths and weaknesses. It revealed common characteristics of individual companies, marketing strategies, people, resources, and market shares. Of vital importance was the market study's indication that the estimated market size, formulated years earlier to justify the investment in the new domestic U.S. plant, was as much as 60 percent higher than the actual market size. Therefore, the new plant was doomed to an excess capacity as far in the future as could be forecast.

Reviewing the competition, more similarities than differences were found. These included intensive local marketing coverage by distributors, local distributors handling two or three brand names simultaneously, retrenchment in services, and a capable staff able to handle sophisticated customers. To Dan, this review implied Specialty's market opportunity was in providing the services being dropped by their competitors.

EXAMINING THE MARKETING PROGRAM

The major forces in the market sold through distributors, and Dan was convinced many enjoyed far higher market shares than Specialty, despite its rapid growth. The first reaction from the in-house skeptics focused upon the competitors' longevity in the market; therefore, they got all the business. While this was a valid comment, among the conclusions this generated was, "Therefore, a new market entrant cannot succeed!" Less emotional and prejudicial analysis of Specialty's incoming order patterns indicated that few small, unit-size orders were received. The dominant experience was for few, large orders, typical of a direct, large target account sales program.

A closer look at the distributors' functioning supported this argument. If the most likely customer of a distributor is small, the normal order the distributor receives will be equivalently small. Then, Dan ordered an informal survey of distributors and users to test the theory.

The answers supported his tenet: distributors tend not to inventory and to purchase "to order." While this didn't make Dan's management happy, thinking through the implications of the service costs, nevertheless it solidified the distributor tilt evolving at Specialty Steel's small-products division. Distributors handled approximately 50 percent of the products in Specialty's markets. Currently focusing on large target users took Specialty *out of* one half of the total available market. When Dan and his supervisor reviewed the final data, they realized their 8 percent share represented almost 16 percent of the market *in which they really competed!*

They decided to commit the marketing program to distributors. The first step was to write a policy suitable for both current and potential distributors. From prior experience Dan understood this market channel's characteristics quite well. Distributors were owned and operated by private individuals, often families, and were effective in reaching local markets. Common knowledge identified the reasons for this marketing strength to be close friendships, clubs, etc. This answer, although having some merit, is nevertheless too simple. In actuality, the sales achieved were based upon one strategic strength—service.

Prior to joining Specialty Dan participated in a major national survey to determine distributors' and users' market attitudes and their opinions about each other. The single unifying theme was the need for service. Dan, therefore, had little need to challenge this information since Specialty's business offered no real difference except in product detail.

DEVELOPING THE PLAN

Local management approved Dan's developing a guideline to implement the company's goals. Dan prepared the following outline.

— Marketing emphasis placed upon distributors, and a written policy developed.
— Image and strategy of SSI promoted through a major communications effort.
— Sales force instructed on the historical perspective of the new policy and trained in distributors' management. A new sales incentive program readied for the next fiscal year.
— New organization plan created with the corporate human resources managers.

The president of Specialty once told Dan the following corporate goal: *Achieve rapid growth, but have the organization in place to handle it immediately, thereby preventing default on the newly developing distributor network!!*

Dan felt that, once the policy guidelines were in place, this corporate goal would become the cornerstone of Specialty's marketing plan and program.

THE DISTRIBUTOR POLICY

The first priority was a professional document presenting this policy to distributor owners/managers. Dan recognized that owners, having several million dollars in fixed business assets, dealt formally in manufacturer relationships. Suppliers who did otherwise were considered secondary and unimportant. Therefore, to build Specialty's image and enhance its position as a strong, serious company, packaging the policy appropriately was vital.

The next consideration was policy specifics: i.e., what would be the hard contents of the policy package? Basically, the needs of the distributor had to be defined and matched with benefits. To accomplish this, a series of meetings with current and potential distributors was set in motion. Several issues dominated distributors' attitudes:

— Direct selling.
— Selecting distributors and multiple representation.
— Revising prices.
— Changing ownership.

Related issues, where the distributors and Specialty had reciprocity of responsibilities, were prominently listed. The distributor became cognizant of its responsibilities to SSI, and SSI's attention was drawn to its responsibilities to the distributor. (A summary of these issues is found in Tables 38–1 and 38–2, together with editorial comments.) In the basic policy document Specialty deliberately forced a statement of mutual interests—an unconventional business strategy at that time.

Along with these responsibilities, Specialty reiterated unequivocaly two *critical aspects* of its new policy. First, Specialty retained the

---

TABLE 38–1
Responsibility of Specialty Steel to Its Distributors

1. To maintain a policy. (Many distributors rarely have written guidelines for their suppliers' program.)

2. To field a competent sales force capable of training and assisting in the sales of Specialty's products. (The most critical problem for many distributors.)

3. To maintain an efficient organization, facility, and people providing complete service. (The fundamental purpose of the distributor was service. Formally establishing this principle, Specialty could justifiably deny requests from small, marginal-facility companies.)

TABLE 38–2
Responsibility of Distributor to Specialty Steel

1. To set target sales goals regularly; at the minimum, annually. (This became a critical procedure which created the image and commitment Specialty sought.)

2. To maintain an inventory consistent with sales. (Dan's market survey indicated that distributors didn't inventory; this specific listing clearly presented Specialty's expectation.)

3. To maintain an efficient organization, facility, and people providing complete service. (The fundamental purpose of the distributor was service. Formally establishing this principle, Specialty could justifiably deny requests from small, marginal-facility companies.)

sole right to determine representation and number in each local market; selection would be based *solely on its opinion* of adequate market share and penetration. Having lost sales in the local market because exclusive distributors failed to represent Specialty, it would no longer grant exclusives. Second, Specialty reaffirmed its commitment to sell through its selected distributors. Distributors welcomed this written pledge. However, Specialty clearly stated its prerogative to sell directly in circumstances where the distributor could not support the business (e.g., due to technical or pricing demands).

Stating these policies in writing achieved two critical consequences. Specialty could retain, within the guidelines of its new distributor program, ongoing, direct, low-priced accounts. It could also make a commitment to distributors to market through them, not in competition with them.

THE COMMUNICATIONS PROGRAM

With a policy developed with which Specialty's sales team could approach the market, Dan's attention then turned to publicity. From previous involvement with distributors and the internal staff, Dan concluded:

The marketplace recognized Specialty as a prime, high-quality manufacturer only within segments that its previous marketing policy had penetrated. The planning research for what became the distributor program indicated that Specialty was unknown not only within the distributor community but also within the broad-based, end user market segment. Marketing communications had to be designed to reach the general marketplace.

Reviewing the available media, Dan decided to select a variety: i.e., trade magazines, industry exhibitions, direct mailings to distributor owner/managers, participation in the major distributor trade associations, and extensive person-to-person visits by Specialty's executives, as required. In this manner the general marketplace and the key distributors would receive company messages.

An industrial advertising agency having specific qualifications was selected to implement this communication program. This group became integrated into the management team and applied their creativity and experience in high-technology and industrial products in the planning of alternate strategies. Dan demanded this specialized background in an agency to minimize his and his staff's time in getting the agency representatives up to speed.

Initially, intensive time and effort were spent with the agency principals, first explaining the program, then planning the theme of the first year's advertising. The strategy was the amplification of the corporate goals in print (i.e., commitment, product quality and reliability, and distributor marketing). A new logo featuring the name *Specialty* was displayed in bold, repetitive fashion on all advertising, product literature, business cards, product packaging, etc.

Frequent magazine advertising and use of other aforementioned communication tools rapidly achieved the desired recognition and image building. Specialty was soon perceived as a market leader by both customers and distributors, an observation frequently made by all segments of the market, including competitors.

ORGANIZATION STRUCTURE

The new distributor marketing policy, begun with the first advertisements published, focused attention on the organizational structure already in place. The reporting plan was simple. As general manager, Dan had the sales and customer service departments reporting to him. Analyzing the functioning of this simple line structure, he recognized several areas requiring supervision. First, with the implementation of the advertising and distributor program, a marketing section, separate and distinct from field sales, was necessary. Second, the customer service department needed strengthening to handle the anticipated volume. (Recall management's mandate to have the ability to handle the business *before* it occurred!) Third, he recognized the potential sales magnitude if a determined effort in developing private label sales was made. But Dan believed this was the province of the home office, not the public sales force. Finally, he felt the customer service receiving customers' orders should load the plant through a planned, finished goods inventory. These criteria set, the following middle-management positions were created:

Marketing manager
> Responsible for all definition and evaluation of new products, packaging, advertising and public relations, literature pricing terms and conditions, liaison with in-house research and development department, and special assignments.

National sales manager
> Supervision of field sales force, trade show representation, customer visits, distributor selection and development.

Manager—Customer service
> Supervision of home office and branch warehouse order entry, budgeting, inventory planning, coordination of raw materials (their procurement from both home plant and domestic U.S. suppliers).

Manager—Private label sales
> Solicitation of private label sales opportunities and sales of U.S.-manufactured products to Specialty's international subsidiaries.

A small group of key managers was created through a combination of internal promotion and transfer, as well as recruiting from the outside. Each manager had well-defined responsibilities for his or her specified areas. Objectives were set according to MBO principles (measurable, defined, quantitative, etc.). Based upon achievement of the goals and objective, compensation bonuses were established.

AN ANALYSIS OF SPECIALTY STEEL, INC.

When a company plans and carries out successfully a marketing strategy, other businesses can benefit from asking the most basic question: *Why?* The answers can help anyone improve their firm's performance; the simple steps Dan followed are adaptable to any business.

Fully Understand the Current Situation

Before a new manager begins making changes, he or she should gather all the facts.

Environment. Always learn the general environment in which the business will function. For example, in this industry some of the important market-controlling factors by the mid-70s were the initial growth and then collapse in nuclear plant construction, the worldwide energy crisis, and inflation. The American market's approach by a foreign company was another important consideration. Often, foreign organizations assume that the U.S. market is a larger replica of their domestic one and manage it similarly.

Competitors. It is important to understand:

1. Who are the competitors?
2. With which segments of your market do they compete?
3. What are their successful and unsuccessful approaches to the market?
4. What is their growth potential?

Products. Products must be scrutinized carefully.

1. Which ones are profitable?
2. Does the market indicate a need for products compatible with the current line, and can they be added easily?
3. What is the best distribution channel for each product?

Customers. The customer must be studied as carefully as the product.

1. Who has traditionally bought similar products? At SSI, for example, Dan had valuable information about competitors from his prior experience plus salespeople who had worked for these companies. He also knew from the marketplace that other vendors sold through networks of local distributors.
2. What specifically are these customers' needs?
3. Can you fill these needs well?
4. Who is currently serving your target customers?
5. Are the buyers satisfied? If not, what can your company do better?

Company. Know the company capabilities in plant, production, people, and image. Determine the major strengths and the major weaknesses.

Long-Term Goals

Once management understands the present status and environment of the company, long-term goals should be set: where does the company want to go?

Specialty Steel's new general manager planned to:

— Achieve a 20 percent market share.
— Set up a distributor network.

Before finalizing goals, managers should consider all alternatives, then narrow the possibilities down to the realistic ones.

Market Research

Market research will answer exactly how realistic the long-term goals are.

Dan had four sources of market information:

1. A previous market study in which he had been involved.
2. His personal experience in the industry.
3. A company staff, particularly the salespeople, who were in the field and had firsthand knowledge.
4. A survey of the distributors to whom he hoped to sell.

The market information Dan had was a collection of facts—some irrefutable and undeniably accurate, while others were soft impressions that strongly reflected the person who gathered the data. He interpreted the facts, planned a strategy, and implemented the ideas. Management is never relieved of ultimate decision-making responsibility. Good data increases the chance of formulating a workable strategy;

however, strategies must be carefully chosen and implemented to achieve the desired results.

Design a Detailed Market Plan

Once the long-term goals are set, short-term objectives and quantifiable goals should be defined. Success is best measured against formally stated objectives and goals.

For example, Dan planned on SSI achieving a 20 percent market share. His short-term goal for the next six months would have been to increase the market share by 1 percent. How? Dan planned to sign distributors and prepared a program that would have satisfied both SSI and the target customers.

The key to a successful marketing plan is thinking through all the details. Successful managers should know:

— What the specific goal and all the tasks involve.
— Who will implement the work toward that goal.
— When the goal will be reached.

One of Dan's strongest management assets was understanding the importance of the team required to make his ideas into reality. No manager can perform all duties himself. He or she must trust the team and be comfortable that they will follow through. This trust frees the general manager to concentrate on the overall picture and not get bogged down in each detail of operations.

It is realistic to turn to outside support services. Dan and his managers needed their own energies in the field. Dan selected an advertising agency that could support his marketing program with a minimum of time-consuming introduction to industrial products. Communications successfully reinforced Dan's marketing emphasis.

All managers can work through these four general steps (as Dan did) to get a marketing program in operation. However, Dan's job is not done! He had to manage the program he began. Managers must constantly reevaluate their goals and the work still to be done. As a goal is almost reached, the next steps can be set and implementation can begin. Management is a continuing activity.

39

NONPROFIT MARKETING: A CASE HISTORY

by
Francine Moskowitz

U.S. Medical Enterprises, Inc.

When the federal government enacted legislation to begin cutting back on Medicare and Medicaid and changed the regulations covering payment for hospital services, a whole range of forces was set in motion that immediately began transforming the very nature of how hospitals do business.

In the past, hospitals have largely been motivated by internal forces and have concentrated on providing the services that doctors wanted to offer, that administrators felt would be convenient or profitable, and that hospital facilities were equipped to support. Any marketing efforts were directed at physicians, as the hospital's indirect conduits to patients.

In the new, relatively de-regulated health care system, hospitals are turning much more often to consumer marketing techniques as a new method of maximizing their revenue and insuring their survival.

BACKGROUND

Hospitals depend on third-party payments which are made on behalf of patients by government agencies and/or insurance companies. Private payers largely followed the government's lead. Before the cutbacks, most payments were retrospective, or made after the hospital services had already been rendered. Hospitals were virtually guaranteed payment for any and all services a doctor deemed appropriate for a patient according to a "reasonable and customary cost" formula.

Under this system, efforts to contain costs and control fees charged by hospitals were more symbolic than effectual. As a result, hospital administrators grew "fat and lazy," uninterested in the problems and possibilities of marketing because they were quite successful without making any special effort.

The new emphasis on cost reduction in the health care field, however, changed the rules of the game. Health care payers—insurance companies, government agencies, and large-scale employers—began to want to know more about where their dollars were going and how they were being used. They wanted clear controls on the costs of particular illnesses and courses of treatment. They insisted on paying only for the most important or most commonly needed services and began refusing to pay for optional, unnecessary, or precautionary hospital services. In addition they began demanding that such services as laboratory tests required prior to surgery take place on an outpatient basis in order to reduce the time and expense of hospitalization.

A major change was the influx of for-profit hospitals and large chains, which brought the first sophisticated marketing expertise to the health care field. These hospitals practice a brand of health care which tends to skim the most profitable patients from the area and leaves the relatively unsophisticated, not-for-profit sector to deal with the problems of patients who are under cost-based reimbursement programs.

One of the biggest changes was the shift to a complex system of prospective payments, or contracts which specified in advance what a hospital would be paid for treating patients with particular diagnoses. Illnesses were categorized into diagnosis-related groups (DRGs), and hospitals had to bear the economic risk of treating patients admitted with certain diagnoses. Under the new system a hospital would be paid only a certain amount for treating each patient in a specific DRG, no matter what treatment was actually provided, what tests were ordered, what ancillary services were needed, or what complications arose.

The result was to choke off the steady stream of income on which hospitals had come to depend. Hospitals had to find ways to replace this income or face the possibilities of cutbacks. In special cases certain hospitals simply went out of business or stopped providing certain types of health care which they felt were no longer economically viable. But the vast majority of hospitals tried to provide the same comprehensive range of care. To do this, they had to seek new sources of income.

THE RISE OF HOSPITAL MARKETING

In order to compensate for the increased financial risk of treating most patients and for the new ceiling and restrictions on third-party revenues, hospital administrators began turning for help to marketing consultants. They hoped these specialists could help them find ways to increase the number of patients coming from more favorable payer groups, particularly employed persons with private insurance.

Other reasons marketing suddenly became imperative for traditional hospitals included the growth of HMOs and other alternative systems of health care that locked in their patients. Such systems offered consumers lower out-of-pocket costs but less flexibility and freedom of choice: there was only one doctor, one hospital, one clinic to which such a patient could go. Hospitals had no such commitment from their patient bases. Most patient populations feel such a commitment only to their doctors, and the good doctors were being wooed away from nonprofit hospitals to competing, for-profit hospitals. The large chains promised these doctors considerable financial benefits if they would admit their more desirable, better-insured patients to their facilities. In a fast turnaround the nonprofit hospitals were seeing the number of uncommitted families from whom they could expect to draw patients dwindle year by year. In reaction to the expansion of HMOs and other locked-in systems of care, nonprofit hospitals and their physicians had to become partners in marketing directly to consumers. They had to create a desire for patients to retain their freedom of choice in health care.

Finally, hospital administrators turned to marketing in order to combat the general influence of insurance companies, HMOs, and government agencies. Together, these groups are working to restructure the package of incentives and disincentives facing consumers of health care. Their effort was to have patients and their families shoulder a larger share of the cost of providing care in an effort to reduce the overall demand for hospital services. The plan worked, at least to some extent. In marketing parlance demand for health care services began to develop elasticity, becoming more and more contingent on price. The immediate effect was to reduce the number of elective procedures being performed in hospitals, thereby reducing hospital income. One of the big thrusts of hospital marketing efforts is to reverse this trend, to increase the demand for inpatient services, and to make hospitals the provider of choice for more and more elective health care services.

It should be noted that in recent years many nonprofit hospitals have become involved in sophisticated networking arrangements providing them the flexibility to develop and market their own alternative delivery systems to compete with the large chains and the locked-in systems. At the same time, these not-for-profit hospitals have been positioning themselves to become contracting hospitals of these locked-in systems, actually providing the health care that these systems are selling. The advantage of such arrangements is that they allow the not-for-profit hospitals to retain their market share of those "cream" patients while their networks grow and develop competitive strategies.

BACKGROUND TO THE MARKETING CASE STUDY[1]

Almost every hospital presents some unique challenges and opportunities for the marketing specialist. This case study of a nonprofit hospital is not intended to describe all the factors of importance nor all the techniques of value to people interested in hospital marketing. However, it does serve to illustrate the importance of marketing to nonprofit institutions, and it shows how a well-conceived and well-implemented marketing plan can dramatically improve a hospital's market position.

The not-for-profit hospital in this case study—we'll call it Conestoga Community Hospital (not its real name)—is a 150-bed facility in a suburban town outside of a major city. Built in the early 1970s, the hospital is surrounded by an affluent community and has traditionally maintained an 80 percent occupancy rate—what most hospital administrators would consider good but not great. Although there are several other hospitals serving the same community, Conestoga Community Hospital has been able to retain a 40 percent market share over the past several years without making any special marketing efforts.

However, the rapid changes in the health care system, described at the beginning of this chapter, made for disruptions in the market position of this hospital. The competing hospitals in the area saw the possibilities of adopting a more aggressive marketing stance. The hospital saw its number of empty beds tending to increase. Certain key people in management ranks began to worry that Conestoga Community Hospital might have a harder time than ever holding onto its market share and might even lose some of that share. The threat was not unique to this hospital, of course. Other hospitals serving the community were facing the same changes, the same problems, the same uncertainties.

It was quickly realized that those who adapted best to the new payment systems would fare much better than hospitals which refused to make changes. Faced with a choice of doing nothing and losing market share or fighting with new strategies and tactics to maintain or even increase it, Conestoga Community Hospital decided to experiment with new approaches to marketing.

The administrator of this hospital—we'll call him Mr. Gray—is in his mid-30s. Because of his relative youth he is less afraid of making changes and experimenting with new strategies than his counterparts in

[1] The author would like to thank Carolynn Schore, president, Innovative Health Associates, Los Angeles, California, for the data used in this case study.

other hospitals. Unlike some older administrators who had grown totally dependent on the regulated system of health care that had prevailed for so many years, Gray was not overly intimidated by the tremendous shifts in the payment systems on which hospitals have always depended. His main goal was not merely to maintain his hospital's economic viability but to look ahead and to prepare Conestoga Community Hospital to compete more effectively in the future. Gray wanted to identify coming changes and to position his hospital to meet those changes head on.

Some of the key questions that Gray and his staff posed were of a fundamental nature, the answers to which could conceivably change every aspect of the hospital's operations and marketing strategy. Some of these soul-searching questions included:

- What services are we going to provide during the next five years? Are we going to emphasize primary care, secondary care, or tertiary care?
- How will we reconcile the need to be more self-supporting (and profitable) with the need to provide adequate health care facilities, staff, and services for the community, regardless of ability to pay?
- What level of community growth are we going to plan for? How are we going to adapt the hospital to the changing needs of the community we serve?
- Who will be our target population? What types of services will they demand from us? What pricing levels can these people support?
- What services are going to be most profitable, and least profitable, for us during the next 5 to 10 years?

This last question is in many ways the most interesting because it reflects the new awareness in the health care field that a single small, community hospital can no longer be all things to all people. Nor can it provide certain services and specialties just because the doctors like them. It represents the beginning of a new and more sophisticated consideration by hospital administrators of the competition presented by other nearby hospitals, and of marketing strategies based on the relative strengths and weaknesses of a particular institution.

To prepare Conestoga Community Hospital for the future, Administrator Gray obtained board approval to hire a marketing consultant. He began by ordering a series of market studies and analyses so he and his staff would have solid evidence on which to base their judgments and decisions. These initial studies were simple demographic profiles drawn from established sources such as the census and the files of local planning agencies.

One of the most significant facts uncovered in this first market analysis was the existence of subtle demographic shifts in the hospital's surrounding community. Generally, the town was a planned community with a variety of housing developments, shopping centers, and office and light industrial complexes. People tended to move to the area because of jobs and business opportunities. For these reasons the town had been able to plan its growth, and for years it had been able to fulfill the details of these plans. For example, the town had an established growth rate averaging about 10 percent per year. Recently, however, and for the first time, the rate had dipped below established projections and plans. Part of the shortfall in population growth could be attributed to the general economic recession prevailing during the early 80s. Since the economy was stagnant, few new jobs were available, few new businesses were developing, and the number of families who could afford the new, relatively high-priced housing in the community was more limited than usual. But key people at the highest levels of management in the hospital feared that other, more long-term factors might also be at work, threatening the viability of the hospital.

Another interesting fact turned up in this first study of the hospital's market was that too many doctors were available. The same trend had been noted in other American towns and by now it is an accepted fact of life in the health profession. Eventually, the oversupply of doctors will have far-reaching effects. For example, physicians will probably lose some of their power to command high fees. In addition, they will probably have to begin competing for their patients in a variety of new ways. One immediate change caused by the oversupply of doctors had a direct bearing on Gray's ability to market the services of Conestoga Community Hospital: physicians were asking for more guarantees from the hospitals with which they affiliated and were more nervous than ever about cooperating with any hospital activity that might put the hospital in competition with them for patients.

Using the picture of the community provided by this preliminary study, Gray and his consultants discussed a variety of options and possibilities for more effectively marketing the hospital, its resources, and its services. Eventually, they came up with several feasible possibilities.

To determine which ones made the most sense, they decided to carry out a more comprehensive study of the community and to reposition the hospital in the light of what this study turned up.

TWO-PRONGED STUDY OF THE MARKET

The study was designed to take a very specific look at the purchasers of hospital care—the people living in the hospital's service area. It used a two-pronged approach. First, there would be a detailed analysis of the area's demographics and health care habits. On the basis of these findings, the hospital would try to select a target population for their future marketing efforts. Second, there would be a very detailed direct-mail survey focused on this newly selected target group.

In the first part of the study, researchers used indicators of purchasing power culled from census information such as average family incomes, average family size, employment information, and age. Additionally, they looked at morbidity—illness rates and the kinds of illness experienced—and mortality to help determine the present and future demand for hospital care from different segments of the community. As a cross-check, projected demands for hospital care were compared with actual hospital statistics to determine how well local hospitals were meeting the community's needs for care.

The survey turned up some interesting facts. For example, there was a high birthrate in the community but a low hospital maternity utilization. It seemed that women were selecting hospitals outside the community, most likely in the nearby urban center, as better places than the local hospitals in which to have their babies.

The survey found the following community demographic profile:

Age distribution	
Under 17	29%
18–34	28
35–54	23
55–64	10
Over 65	10
Household size	
One person	15%
2 people	35
3–5 people	45
6 or more people	5
Income distribution	
$20,000–$39,000	29%
$40,000–$59,000	29
$60,000 or more	20
Types of health insurance	
Private	72%
HMO or similar	2
Medicare	17

The survey turned up a lot more information. Generally, the picture developed into that of an upscale, family-oriented community full of highly trained professionals in the prime of their careers, and most of them were very well insured by the very types of private insurance companies that provide the most lucrative third-party payments to hospitals. This is the ideal community for a growth-oriented hospital willing to take a step forward into sophisticated marketing strategies.

When this first part of the study was completed, Gray and his staff analyzed the figures and decided to take as their target populations both affluent working families and the elderly. The demographic study proved there were good numbers of these people in the hospital's service area and that they commanded or were eligible for sufficient resources to pay for their hospital stays.

THE FOLLOW-UP SURVEY

The second part of the study would now focus on these two groups. The study was accomplished by mailing survey forms to specific Zip codes within the hospital's service area. The Zip codes chosen were those which the most current census data showed to contain the highest concentrations of the hospital's two new target populations.

This direct-mail survey did not carry the Conestoga Community Hospital name. Instead, it mentioned only the name of the market research firm and was written to give the impression the survey was equally concerned with all hospitals in the community. This was done to avoid polluting the data with skewed or prejudiced information.

To make the study more cost-effective and to increase the accuracy of the data it developed, Gray and his consultants considered it very important to maximize the response rate from the survey mailings. This all-important response rate can fall to as low as 1 percent or less in some direct mailings. If that happened in this case, the return would not constitute a statistically significant sample of the community and, consequently, any inferences drawn from it would have limited or no value to the hospital. To encourage as many people as possible to respond, the survey's cover letter included a space where respondents could check off or list their favorite charity. The letter explained that a donation of 50 cents would be made to the specified charity on receipt of the completed survey form. The technique worked, and the survey generated an impressive response rate in excess of 11 percent. This was more than enough to provide a valid sample susceptible to statistical analysis.

The survey itself covered a wide range of issues and topics of importance to the Conestoga Community Hospital. Briefly, these included such questions as:

How do you obtain your information about hospitals? Suggested answers included such possibilities as reading newspapers, seeing advertisements, talking to friends, listening to doctors, and personal experience as a patient or as a visitor.

What criteria do you use to choose a hospital? Suggested answers included only the items which Gray and his staff felt their hospital could reasonably capitalize on in their subsequent marketing efforts, such as doctor's suggestion, hospital reputation, cost of care, and location. The survey asked people to think about this and respond both for emergency care and for regular care, such as having a a baby.

How would you rate or rank the hospitals in this community? The survey listed all six community hospitals by name, including Conestoga Community Hospital. The idea was to have people reveal their perceptions of each of the hospitals, with particular emphasis on such factors as overall quality, medical staff, nursing staff, and the general appearance of its facilities.

Have you used any of these hospitals? What was your level of satisfaction? Would you use it again? The effort here was to determine how well the various hospitals in the community, and particularly Conestoga Community Hospital, were satisfying their patients. Hospitals with a good record of satisfaction would present stiffer competition. Gray and his staff felt it would be better to identify them early and perhaps modify future marketing plans to position their own hospital more advantageously against the others.

What hospital services do you think would be beneficial for this community? The survey listed some new services that Conestoga Community Hospital was considering and asked: "Do you think this would benefit the community?" and "Would you use any of these?"

The survey form concluded with an extensive set of demographic inquiries designed to help survey analysts correlate the answers with the actual demographic patterns of the community. This demographic information was important to help determine how much weight to give the responses. For example, if people with family incomes under $20,000 tended to ask for more emergency room services, the hospital might feel this was a dominant community need. But comparative analysis would show this group to be a very small part of the community, and therefore the request should not carry an inordinate amount of weight. Similarly, if those with large families felt that expanded maternity and neonatal services would be useful, the hospital might ordinarily decide to expand these services. But comparative analysis would show that only 5 percent of the family units in the community have more than four children, and so the opinion is not as significant as it might seem.

On the other hand, if affluent, young married couples ask for expanded maternity services, the hospital would give this request increased weight because of the high probability that such people would use any such services that became available.

The findings of the survey were quite enlightening.

Sources of Information

The survey showed that two thirds of the people in the community obtain their information on hospitals from friends and relatives, while doctors are the primary source of information for just over half the population. This was a surprise, since most hospital administrators tend to look at their doctors as the main source of information on where to obtain quality health care. In addition, nearly half the survey respondents said they got an important part of their information on hospitals from having been patients. An equal number relied on their experiences while visiting family and friends while they were hospital inpatients to form their opinions of the various hospitals in the community. These findings demonstrated to Gray and his staff that Conestoga Community Hospital had a good many opportunities to sell itself to the community by reaching out to everyone who entered as a visitor or as a patient.

Selection Criteria

Ninety-five percent of those responding to the survey claimed nursing care as the most important factor in their choices regarding which hospital to use. Ninety-two percent cited a hospital's general reputation. The advice of the attending physician was much lower down in the ratings than anyone would have guessed. The physical location of the hospital turned out to rank the lowest of all. This pattern helped explain why so many local mothers were having their babies in distant hospitals. Apparently, they were willing to travel several dozen miles in order to check into a hospital with better nursing care or a better general reputation.

Hospital Rankings

Conestoga Community Hospital received the highest ratings of all the hospitals in the community. This was not entirely unexpected by Administrator Gray. But, the reasoning behind the choice was something of a surprise. Survey respondents said they preferred Conestoga Community mainly because it was close by. In fact, when compared with the other hospitals in the community, Conestoga Community did not rate as high on any of the other criteria listed. These results shocked both hospital administrators and medical staff! They thought their hospital to be highly respected for its quality care. Instead, it turned out to be liked for its location more than anything else. This was dangerous as well as shocking because the survey also revealed the information that people in the community consider a hospital's location to be the least important basis for choosing one institution over another. It doesn't take much marketing sophistication to see that such a combination of factors made Conestoga Community Hospital vulnerable to any serious marketing efforts that might be mounted by competing hospitals in the community.

Satisfaction

Gray and his team were even more dismayed when they noticed people claiming they would not be likely to use Conestoga Community Hospital a second time. The survey showed people in the community were more likely, in fact, to look favorably on returning to any other hospital in the community. This was correctly considered to be a serious problem.

For marketing purposes people who have already used your facilities or services are usually considered the best prospects for future business. Although hospitals are somewhat different from companies selling soft drinks or plumbing supplies, there is every reason to believe that loyalty and satisfaction could influence people's choice of hospitals in non-emergency situations. Unfortunately, the survey clearly showed that Conestoga Community Hospital was not doing a good job of generating patient loyalty or insuring repeat business. Gray and his staff realized that if previous patients were not satisfied with the hospital, the long-range trend would almost certainly be to lose market share.

NEW PROGRAMS TO MARKET THE HOSPITAL

On the basis of information developed in this study, Conestoga Community Hospital began to make some significant changes in its operations and to seriously expand the scope of its marketing efforts.

The primary result of the market study was to confirm the need for special programs for senior citizens and for general programs of health screening. In reaction to this information, Gray and his staff have created a broad-ranging program of health screening services for cancer, Alzheimer's disease, hypertension, diabetes, Tay-Sachs disease, and more. The services are available through local employers, free to their employees. Several times a year, the hospital also provides open screenings free of charge to all residents of the community.

For senior citizens the hospital has developed a core of its own services and networking relationships with other community agencies that provide them with a comprehensive web of services. These include adult day-care programs, senior companion programs, homemaker services, home health care services, and low-cost "meals on wheels." All of these are accessible to the hospital's community through the expanded transportation services provided by the hospital, including vans with wheelchair lifts, minibuses, and station wagons. Transportation is seen as a critical element of the overall marketing effort because it makes health care services more accessible to a segment of the population that are high users of health care. The hospital hired several full-time drivers and trained many of their existing staff to drive these vehicles and obtain the required licenses. During off-peak hours the same vehicles and drivers provide social transportation, transportation for shopping, and also access to special functions at many of the local service clubs (a good way to make friends in the community for the hospital). In a variety of aggressive marketing moves and in cooperation with other community hospitals, Gray has established his hospital as a leader in providing extended psychosocial services and hospital-sponsored independent or supported living centers. As the community ages and the demographics demand the development of intermediate and skilled nursing facilities, Conestoga Community Hospital is positioned to grow in both these areas.

The hospital decided to work hard with their medical staff leaders to head off any of the medical staff's perceptions that the hospital was competing with them in providing its new services, and to engender more feelings of commitment and loyalty, which normally translates into more patients and more admissions. Gray hired a specialist in physician relations and charged her with developing the best methods to accomplish these important purposes.

All of these programs were suggested by results of the market survey, and probably none would have come to fruition without the support of that research and the pressure to provide new sources of income. But a hospital is more than a business. It survives on community support and a positive perception, as well. For this reason Gray has committed hospital resources to the effort to improve the standing of the hospital in the minds of community residents.

The market survey demonstrated that most people rely on their own experiences for information about a hospital and that their own perception of a hospital's reputation and qualifications is much more important in making a selection than anyone had previously suspected. Gray decided to capitalize on these findings by supporting new programs designed to bring people in from the community to see the hospital.

To make this happen, Gray expanded the public relations department and allocated a larger budget for community relations. The goal was to create a more positive image of the hospital in the minds of community residents. To this end, the hospital worked up a series of community service days. This included free screenings for particular illnesses, free blood pressure and respiratory evaluations, and cardio-pulmonary resuscitation classes that were both well attended and well publicized in the local newspapers and on TV. The public relations staff also produces an attractive, monthly newsletter that is mailed to every household in the community. The newsletter covers events of importance at the hospital, new equipment and programs, and general health information.

The hospital's education department developed community-oriented training programs for babysitters, new parents, and people coping with the placement of an elderly relative in a nursing home. The hospital also made its meeting rooms available to community organizations.

Along the same lines, the hospital set up programs to advise visitors about the hospital's special services and to make visiting patients a more pleasant experience.

The idea is simple: visitors present an ideal opportunity for the hospital to put its best foot forward. These experiences strongly shape public opinion about the overall quality and care of a hospital. Accordingly, Gray had his staff develop new brochures describing the hospital and helping make visitors feel more welcome. They also prepared new flyers which advised visitors about what they can do to make patients more comfortable and which outlined hospital rules for visitors in a new, more patient-oriented tone.

The admissions procedure was seen as another opportunity to make a good impression on community residents. Patients and their families are resentful of any delay or any unnecessary paperwork in completing the admissions procedure. This is typically a time of great emotional stress and worry. Unfeeling clerks who are sticklers for details may be doing their jobs, but they create a terribly negative impression of their hospital in the minds of the patient's entire family. But it does not have to be this way.

Gray's staff redesigned the hospital's admissions process to make it easier, faster, and simpler for patients and their families. They created a new admissions packet of information and advice designed to generate a warmer, friendlier feeling. The packet contains information on all the hospital's services, food-service facilities, and volunteer resources, as well as its routines and common practices. As many pre-admits as possible are done through the physician's offices, so these patients have no paperwork at all when they arrive at the hospital. To cut through any conflicts or resolve any difficulties before they become unnecessarily large, the brochures and information packets contain all the hospital's many special phone numbers. Patients or their families can more easily locate the right person to call to obtain help with any problems that might come up. In addition to resolving problems before they become too large, such materials help to encourage positive feelings about the facility. This is part of the new effort to build patient and visitor loyalty to the hospital.

The survey had also revealed that nursing care was the most important criteria people used in selecting a hospital. It was therefore decided to emphasize nursing in all hospital advertising and communications. For example, the hospital now includes an illustration or a photo of a nurse on nearly every piece of printed material. In addition, hospital descriptive literature emphasizes the professionalism and dedication of the nursing staff at Conestoga Community Hospital.

Generally, the content of all brochures, advertisements, and other informative pieces was reviewed and revised to reflect the new marketing philosophy of the hospital. Specific pieces were rewritten to accomplish specific parts of the overall marketing strategy.

For example, one of the hospital's main problems was that community residents perceived it as the local hospital suitable for simple problems or for emergencies. In their minds more distant facilities were better places to go for quality care. To fight this perception, Conestoga Community Hospital began discussing its other strong points in all of its literature. Quality of care, concern for patients, a strong nursing staff, new medical equipment and facilities, and other features that people equate with a high-quality hospital were linked to the hospital's name. In particular, a new brochure was prepared and distributed to all patients, all visitors, and placed in the offices of cooperating physicians. The main message of this piece became: "We're a local hospital, and we provide the highest quality of care you can get."

Perhaps the most important change was a comprehensive *Patient Satisfaction Program* that Gray and his staff installed in order to improve the hospital's rating on this all-important scale. The program involved a number of important elements.

Grievance Procedures

Patients who are unhappy about anything during the hospital stay can air their grievances to the patient representative on the hospital payroll. The patient rep visits every patient as soon as possible after admission and lets them know she is available to help them. She doesn't just wait for complaints to develop. This person is charged with doing whatever she can to help satisfy any patients' complaints, consistent with good health care. She makes no effort just to mollify them or convince them not to complain again. Instead, she deals with hospital staff and the physician to seek meaningful changes that will eliminate the problem or improve the patient's satisfaction.

For example, a patient may be unhappy with the hospital's food service. If so, the patient advocate makes a strong effort to have the food-service staff provide an improved diet. Another patient may feel uncomfortable with the person sharing their hospital room—this is quite common, in fact, since many patients do not like to be in a room with someone who is sicker than they are. In such a case the patient advocate works with the floor nurses and the physicians to try to arrange for a room transfer.

Obviously, not all grievances can be settled to the patient's satisfaction. But the program does away with a lot of the small complaints, the nagging annoyances, and the feeling that the hospital does not care. The result of the program has been a steady improvement in the hospital's satisfaction rating from patients and visitors alike.

Post-Discharge Questionnaire

Under the new marketing program all patients receive a short questionnaire about a week after they are discharged from the hospital. If the hospital sends the questionnaire home in the discharge packet, it may be lost or discarded. If the questionnaire is delayed three weeks or a month, the patient and family have time to solidify any negative feelings they harbor about the hospital. A week is just enough time for the hospital experience to be fresh in their minds but long enough for the questionnaire to be a pleasant surprise and a signal that the hospital really cares.

The form asks patients and their families what they liked and disliked about their stay in the hospital, about its food, its staff, its services, and its overall quality of care. Each questionnaire is scrutinized for weak points in the hospital's image and services, and all questionnaires are periodically analyzed as a group to spot trends and patterns of dissatisfaction. The administrator responds in writing to every returned questionnaire, acknowledge his appreciation for the patient's help and addressing any issues or complaints that were raised.

The main emphasis of the patient satisfaction program is to deal with complaints quickly and cheerfully, regardless of how little merit they may contain. The goal is that no patient will leave the hospital unhappy.

Other, more subtle changes were made to improve the hospital's image and to help market its facilities and services.

The administrators began considering every staffperson's personality and outlook. Although no one was terminated or hired solely because of this factor, over the long run the hospital has begun to favor happy, supportive people in positions of patient contact.

To improve patient contact procedures, the hospital put its entire staff through patient satisfaction training. Specific lectures and workshops covered how to work with patients, what special needs might be expected from patients, what responses to give to difficult situations, and where to turn in the hospital for help in resolving any difficulties. These programs were brought to the hospital environment by consultants and experts with retailing backgrounds. Once the obvious differences are accounted for, it becomes clear that both stores and hospitals require the ability to deal skillfully and positively with customers as an important part of the organization's long-term success.

Another interesting approach to building a more satisfied patient base was an internal program aimed at the nursing staff. The campaign was designed to show these people, primarily women, that they were well appreciated by hospital administrators and that their efforts were crucial in making patients satisfied as well as healthy again.

An incentive/recognition program was also instituted at the hospital, designed to acknowledge and reward those employees who went out of their way to make patients comfortable and welcome. The incentives include such simple benefits are preferred parking spaces for a week or a month, photos of the employee in the cafeteria and in the hospital newsletter, simple plaques, a handshake from the administrator, a special luncheon once a year, and, in special cases, additional vacation days or bonuses.

RESULTS

Although it is far too early to determine the long-range results of all these new programs and strategic marketing efforts, it is clear that Conestoga Community Hospital has turned the corner. The patient questionnaires reflect a continuing improvement in the perception of the hospital and the satisfaction of its patients and their families. The hospital staff shows a much higher morale than in past years.

Perhaps most important, the number of empty beds in the hospital have stopped their steady increase, at least partly due to the hospital's efforts to market directly to physicians. There are early signs, in fact, that the patient census is actually beginning to increase and that the hospital is reaching out to a larger segment of the market than it had previously. More babies are being born there, which leads to more business for their primary care physicians and in turn leads to more business for the hospital in years to come.

The new services for senior citizens have brought the hospital a high profile in the community and won for it a tremendous amount of publicity and goodwill, in addition to significant opportunities for patient admissions.

In the last few months, the Board of Trustees and the administrator have become more confident that the hospital will penetrate deeper into these new market segments and that the patient census will increase significantly beyond 80 percent, securing the hospital's future survival and prosperity.

BIOGRAPHIES

Howard "Hap" Berrian

Howard "Hap" Berrian is president of the management consulting firm of Berrian Associates, Inc. His business experience includes management consultant, vice president of marketing, general sales manager, and director of management development. Mr. Berrian has been an instructor in these areas for the American Management Associations, Presidents Association, Sales and Marketing Executives International, and the graduate school of sales management and marketing, Syracuse University, as a faculty associate.

Dick Berry

Mr. Berry is the author of over 100 articles and monographs on marketing, service management, and general management topics. A former engineering and marketing executive with 20 years industrial experience, Mr. Berry joined the Management Institute in 1969, with responsibility for executive programs in marketing. Since joining the university, he has attained his full professorship and received the Chancellor's annual distinguished service award for his work in advancing the profession of service management.

Ardis Burst

Ardis Burst is president of Burst-Lazarus Associates, Inc., Scarsdale, New York. She specializes in applying the principles of packaged goods marketing to new areas, including nonprofit organizations. She was formerly in product management in the Maxwell House division of General Foods. She holds an MBA with distinction from Harvard Business School.

Lloyd B. Chaisson, Jr.

Lloyd B. Chaisson, Jr. holds an A.B. from Dartmouth and an M.P.P.M. from the Yale School of Management. A management consultant with McKinsey & Company, he has been associated with the U.S. Environmental Protection Agency and the National League of Cities. He has also served as director of energy programs for the Academy for State and Local Government.

Dorothy E. Demmy

Dorothy E. Demmy is a writer/counselor specializing in marketing plans, presentations, and all-media communications. Before starting her own consulting firm in 1968—primarily for Whirlpool Corporation and U.S. Steel—she spent 26 years in AAAA advertising agencies, from copywriter to marketing vice president on a long list of national brands. Mrs. Demmy holds an M.B.A. in marketing.

Edward Epstein

Since 1971, Edward Epstein has been president of Edward Epstein & Associates, Inc., a national marketing research firm located in Nassau County, New York. Prior to that, he held executive marketing and research positions at leading manufacturers and ad agencies. He has an MBA from Columbia and has taught at NYU. Mr. Epstein has been a speaker, moderator, and program chairperson for various industry conferences and seminars.

Kenneth B. Erdman

Kenneth B. Erdman, a consultant in sales promotion, has been active in every aspect of sales promotion for more than 25 years. He has won two CLIO awards (advertising's highest honor), a Direct Marketing Association award, and numerous other awards from local advertising and promotion groups. Ken regularly writes and lectures on sales promotion topics.

John C. Faulkner CMC

Mr. Faulkner, an independent consultant practicing in Darien, Connecticut, has concentrated on marketing and strategic planning during his 30 years as a professional management consultant. In New York, he is an officer/director of the Harvard Business School Club and the New York chapter of the Institute of Management Consultants.

Steve Feinstein

Steve Feinstein was vice president/general manager, retail division, of Forest City Enterprises, and he is credited with putting them into the home center business. He has also been affiliated with Evans Products Company as executive vice president of their retail group, consisting of Grossman's and Moore's. He has been operating his own chain of home centers in the St. Louis area under the name of B&B Home Supply since 1978. He is a director of the Better Business Bureau and has written articles for various retail publications. Mr. Feinstein is a director of the Home Center Institute, a member of the Steering Committee of the Home Center Leadership Council, a keynote speaker at the National Home Center Show, and a panelist and speaker at numerous retail and marketing conferences.

Edward B. Flanagan

Edward B. Flanagan is president of the Sales Executives Club of New York, a nonprofit organization with over 2,500 members—the largest group of its kind in the nation. The club is dedicated to bringing a strong sense of professionalism to the sales, marketing, and management fields, while serving the needs of its members through luncheon programs, seminars, and related business-focused activities. Its platform is one of the most sought after in the nation.

Victor Gelb

Mr. Gelb is president of Victor Gelb, Inc. and chairman of Capital American Financial Corporation. In addition, he is director of Cardinal Federal Savings & Loan, Cook-United, and Pioneer Standard Electronics. For many years Mr. Gelb has been active in community affairs, currently serving as national vice president of United Jewish Appeal and vice president of United Way Services of Cleveland. From 1969–1978 he was president and chief executive officer of Woodhill-Permatex.

James J. Gibbons

James J. Gibbons, an outstanding exponent of the professional relationship between manufacturer's agents and their principals, was named chief executive officer of Manufacturers' Agents National Association (MANA) in 1970. In his capacity as president of MANA, each year Gibbons conducts eight regional seminars on working together for mutual profit for manufacturers and manufacturers' agents. Additionally, he has spoken to many groups throughout the U.S., and authored hundreds of articles published in marketing and trade magazines.

Sol Goldin

Sol Goldin, of Marketing Affiliates Corp., is a nationally known authority on consumer durables marketing. Since retirement from Whirlpool Corporation, as director of retail marketing, he has consulted with Whirlpool, Toro, Quasar, RCA, and others in distribution planning, new-product programming, and retailing research and development. His experience covers all levels of distribution, including 17 years with Sears, Roebuck.

Sonja M. Haggert

Sonja Muller Haggert is consumer products manager of the Keystone Filter Division of MET PRO Corporation. She is a member of the National Association of Female Executives.

Porter Henry

Born in Webster Groves, Missouri, in 1911, Porter Henry holds an A.B. from Washington University. He has worked as a reporter and feature writer on the St. Louis *Post-Dispatch* and the New York *Daily News*. During World War II, Henry trained bomber gunners for the Eighth Air Force in England.

In 1945 Mr. Henry established Porter Henry & Co., Inc., one of the nation's leading trainers of salesmen and sales managers. He retired in 1974 to travel, loaf, and contribute to books like this one.

Thomas C. Jones CMC

Thomas C. Jones, President of the management consulting firm, Tom Jones and Company, Inc., has had extensive experience as a marketing executive and management consultant in large and small organizations, including the Ingersoll–Rand Company and the Singer Company. He is a former officer and director of The Society of Professional Management Consultants and is a Certified Management Consultant. An author and lecturer, his publications include "COSMOS: An Application of Management Science Techniques to Marketing Decision Making," a chapter in *Computer Innovations in Marketing*, published by the American Management Association, and practical, timely monographs for his clients.

Boris M. Krantz

Mr. Krantz has intensive experience with new-product marketing and management with both Airco and Sandvik. In 1980, he formed his present company and has since provided planning, market research, public relations, and advertising services to a wide variety of domestic and international clients. In addition, his company provides sales and management training designed specifically for industrial salespeople. He also writes a regular column ("Professional Management") for *The Welding Distributor* magazine, the first series of which *(Sales Fundamentals)* has just been published by TWD.

Robert F. LaRue

From 1968 Mr. LaRue has operated LaRue Marketing Consultants, Inc. Earlier, he has headed marketing services organizations. Twice he has gone inside companies—once as vice president of marketing services/director of corporate communications and another time as president. Mr. LaRue's activities have always involved marketing communications and marketing research. He has undertaken assignments for a wide variety of products and services, lately emphasizing projects related to alternative channels of distribution, including franchising. He has increasingly served companies in the fields of lawn and garden, home improvement, and restaurant.

James Lazarus

James Lazarus is a principal of Burst-Lazarus Associates, Inc., in Scarsdale, New York. As a marketing consultant, he works primarily with moderately sized companies that market consumer-oriented goods and services. Previously, he worked in marketing at Fieldcrest Mills. He is a graduate of Harvard Business School (M.B.A.) and Dartmouth College (B.A.).

Robert L. McLaughlin

Robert L. McLaughlin is president of Micrometrics, Inc., Cheshire, Connecticut. He is a graduate of Notre Dame and Syracuse Universities. He has been marketing research manager for General Electric's electronics communications department and director of corporate commercial research for Scovill Manufacturing Company. He is a member of McGraw-Hill's economic panel; and recently he received the Abrahamson Award of the National Association of Business Economists. In addition to his many publications on forecasting, since 1969 he has been the publisher of *Turning Points,* a monthly forecasting newsletter.

Belden Menkus

Since 1953 Mr. Menkus has been helping management improve information-handling techniques. From 1953 to 1968 he occupied progressively more responsible staff positions with various organizations. Since 1968 he has been a full-time consultant to management. He writes and lectures extensively on various aspects of business management.

Francine Moskowitz

Ms. Moskowitz has been a leader in the health care field for 15 years as a clinician, administrator, and corporate executive. She has worked with a wide variety of health care institutions on both the East and West coasts, including urban teaching hospitals, diversified multihospital systems, and alternative delivery systems. She has been involved in the development of some of the most innovative health care delivery and financing projects in the nation, including PPOs, HMOs, and integrated health care and housing facilities for the elderly. She now concentrates on health care program development, strategic planning, and marketing of alternative delivery and financing systems.

John A. Murray

Mr. Murray is director of marketing for Geocel Corporation, a manufacturer of consumer and construction caulks and sealants. He was formerly a vice president of international marketing for Miles Laboratories. He is a graduate of Harvard University with an AB and MBA.

Ronald N. Paul

Ronald N. Paul is co-founder and president of Technomic Consultants, a Chicago area-based international marketing, strategy, and research organization. Mr. Paul has been a consultant for 20 years and has worked closely with more than 75 *Fortune* 500 companies. Mr. Paul has an engineering degree and an MBA from Northwestern University.

Steven E. Permut, Ph.D.

Dr. Permut is Associate Professor of Marketing at the Yale University School of Management, and principal of Marketing Sciences, Inc. He is founding editor of the Praeger Series in Public and Nonprofit Sector Marketing, and coeditor of *Government Marketing: Theory and Practice*. He serves on the editorial boards of the *Journal of Marketing, Journal of Consumer Marketing, Journal of Public Policy & Marketing*, and *Journal of Business Forecasting*, among others.

J. Leonard Schatz

Mr. Schatz is president of J. L. Schatz Research, Inc. This firm provides marketing research and consulting services to retailers, real estate developers, and syndicators. Previously he was director of research for several large chain retailers, including Stop & Shop and Zayre. He taught marketing at Northeastern University and is past president of the Boston chapter of the American Marketing Association.

Elinor Selame

Elinor Selame is the president of Selame Design, one of the country's foremost marketing and design consulting firms. Ms. Selame is a nationally recognized authority on corporate, retail, and product identity. She is listed in the *International Who's Who of Women, Who's Who of American Women*, and *Who's Who in the East*. She serves on the board of directors of the Package Designers Council, the Marketing Advisory Council of Babson College, is on the Board of Trustees of The Artists

Foundation, and is a member of the International Platform Society and the National Speakers Association. Ms. Selame is co-author of *Developing A Corporate Identity: How to Stand out in the Crowd,* considered by many to be the standard reference on the subject of corporate and retail identity; and *Packaging Power, Corporate Identity and Product Recognition,* a reference on planning a package design program for management.

Dennis W. Shafer

Dennis W. Shafer, group vice president, Wagner Spray Tech Corporation, Minneapolis, Minnesota, has been involved with strategic planning, marketing management, and new product development in both international and domestic markets for more than 15 years.

Jack H. Shapiro

Mr. Shapiro is president of The Penn Management Group, Inc., a consulting firm specializing in consumer products marketing and retailing. A Harvard M.B.A., he has been a marketing vice president, a general merchandise manager, an executive vice president, and twice president, all of large retail companies.

Harvey Stein

Mr. Stein has spent the past 20 years in sales and marketing and in the management of national companies. His background and experience encompass broad areas, including program and product development as well as packaging and product design.

Charles W. Stryker, Ph.D.

As the executive vice president of Trinet, Inc., Dr. Stryker has been involved with market planning and analysis for many industrial clients. He has worked with over 30 of the *Fortune* 500 companies as well as other large and medium-sized businesses. He has a Ph.D. in operations research from New York University. He has been a frequent author and speaker on the topic of industrial marketing productivity.

Gregory D. Upah, Ph.D.

Dr. Upah is vice president, director of market analysis and planning at Wunderman, Ricotta & Kline, part of the Young & Rubicam Direct Marketing Group. He has worked on strategy and creative development research for a variety of clients including AT&T, Gillette, Nynex, Manufacturers Hanover, and Warner-Lambert. Prior to joining Young & Rubicam he was an assistant professor of marketing at VPI. He holds a Ph.D. in business administration from the University of Illinois.

Robert C. Vereen

Mr. Vereen is senior vice president of DIY Retailing (formerly Hardware Retailing) and for the National Retail Hardware Association in Indianapolis. He is an experienced distribution analyst and observer, having spent 33 years in the hardware/home center business, including three and a half years as managing director of a wholesale merchandising group. He has become, as well, well versed in international hardlines distribution, and he travels extensively overseas.

Stewart A. Washburn CMC

Mr. Washburn is recognized internationally as an authority on the management of the sales and marketing functions, and his work on these subjects is widely published. He is a Certified Management Consultant, a founding member of the Institute of Management Consultants, a member of the commercial panel of the American Arbitration Association, and practice development editor of the *Journal of Management Consulting*. He is listed in *Who's Who in Finance and Industry*. Mr. Washburn's clients include a number of *Fortune* 500 firms and a host of smaller companies and associations.

Rochelle Wilensky

Rochelle (Shelley) Wilensky is research director at J. Walter Thompson. She was previously vice president of marketing research and information, and vice president of industry marketing at American Express Company, payment systems division. She has held prior research positions at Bristol-Meyers Co., Kenyon & Eckhardt, BBDO, and Needham, Harper & Steers. She received her M.A. from the New School for Social Research. Shelley is the former secretary of the American Marketing Association,

New York chapter, and is now a director of AMA–New York. She is also a member of Financial Women's Association.

Robert F. Young

Mr. Young is Associate Professor of Management at Northeastern University in Boston. He received his B.A. in economics from Washington and Jefferson College, and both his M.B.A. and D.B.A. from Harvard Business School. His research interests include the implementation of marketing strategy and the marketing of consumer services. These have resulted in a recent book on cooperative advertising and an article in *Harvard Business Review*. Mr. Young has a total of nine years industrial experience as sales manager and marketing manager in the appliance, furniture, and consumer electronics industries. He continues to consult in these areas.

INDEX